Advanced Pulse Laser Machining Technology

Advanced Pulse Laser Machining Technology

Editors

Jörg Krüger
Jörn Bonse

MDPI • Basel • Beijing • Wuhan • Barcelona • Belgrade • Manchester • Tokyo • Cluj • Tianjin

Editors

Jörg Krüger
Bundesanstalt für Materialforschung und
-prüfung (BAM)
Germany

Jörn Bonse
Bundesanstalt für Materialforschung und
-prüfung (BAM)
Germany

Editorial Office
MDPI
St. Alban-Anlage 66
4052 Basel, Switzerland

This is a reprint of articles from the Special Issue published online in the open access journal *Materials* (ISSN 1996-1944) (available at: https://www.mdpi.com/journal/materials/special_issues/pulse_laser_machining).

For citation purposes, cite each article independently as indicated on the article page online and as indicated below:

LastName, A.A.; LastName, B.B.; LastName, C.C. Article Title. *Journal Name* **Year**, *Volume Number*, Page Range.

ISBN 978-3-0365-6632-0 (Hbk)
ISBN 978-3-0365-6633-7 (PDF)

Contents

About the Editors

Jörg Krüger

Jörg Krüger (Dr.) received a diploma degree in Physics from the Friedrich Schiller University Jena (Germany) and a doctoral degree with distinction from the Brandenburg University of Technology Cottbus (Germany). In 1991, he joined the Bundesanstalt für Materialforschung und -prüfung (BAM) in Berlin (Germany). Currently, he is deputy head of BAM's division "Interfacial Processes and Corrosion". He has coauthored about 130 refereed journal publications and more than 70 proceedings papers and book chapters. He has served as a guest editor for Special Issues in three scientific journals. His research interests include short and ultrashort pulse laser material processing, laser applications for the preservation of the cultural heritage, and laser safety issues including secondary hazards.

Jörn Bonse

Jörn Bonse (Dr.) is a tenured scientist at the German Federal Institute for Materials Research and Testing (BAM) in Berlin, Germany. His research interests include the fundamentals and applications of laser–matter interaction, especially with respect to ultrashort laser pulses, laser-induced periodic nanostructures, time-resolved optical techniques, laser processes in photovoltaics, surface functionalization, and laser safety. He received a doctoral degree in Physics from the Technical University of Berlin (Germany) in 2001 and a diploma degree in Physics from the University of Hannover (Germany) in 1996. Dr. Bonse has occupied various research positions at institutions such as the Max Born Institute for Nonlinear Optics and Short Pulse Spectroscopy (MBI) in Berlin, the Spanish Research Council (CSIC) in Madrid, and the Laser Zentrum Hannover (LZH) in Hannover. He was appointed as a senior laser application specialist at Newport's Spectra-Physics Lasers Division in Stahnsdorf, Germany. In 1999, he was a recipient of an award for applied research, presented by the federal German state Thuringia, for the development of high-power fiber lasers. He received an OSA Outstanding Reviewer Award from the Optical Society of America in 2013. Between 2014 and 2017, he served as an Associate Editor for the journal *Optics Express* of the Optical Society of America. Since 2020, he is a member of the Editorial Board of the journal *Advanced Optical Technologies*. He has authored more than 160 refereed journal publications and 2 patents related to his research activities.

materials

Editorial

Special Issue "Advanced Pulse Laser Machining Technology"

Jörg Krüger * and Jörn Bonse *

Bundesanstalt für Materialforschung und -prüfung (BAM), Unter den Eichen 87, D-12205 Berlin, Germany
* Correspondence: joerg.krueger@bam.de (J.K.); joern.bonse@bam.de (J.B.)

"Advanced Pulse Laser Machining Technology" is a rapidly growing field that can be tailored to special industrial and scientific applications. This is significantly driven by the availability of high-repetition-rate laser sources and novel beam delivery concepts. In recent publications, Saraceno et al. [1], Schille and Löschner [2], and Weber and Graf [3] presented graphs of the development of ultrashort-pulse laser technology over the past few decades (see the synthesis of data from [2,3] provided in Figure 1). Obviously, the average power of ultrafast lasers follows a type of Moore's law, leading to the doubling of the average power of these lasers every two years [4]. Additionally, the average power attained by the lasers in research laboratories precedes the average power of standard industrial lasers by about ten years [3], visualized here as the horizontal separation between the two lines in Figure 1. The impressive progress in laser technology currently culminates in the availability of a fiber-laser-based average power of 10.4 kW at a 1.4 μm wavelength, 254 fs pulse duration, and 80 MHz repetition rate [5]. Currently, the industrial standard is ultrashort-pulse lasers emitting average powers of the order of 100 W.

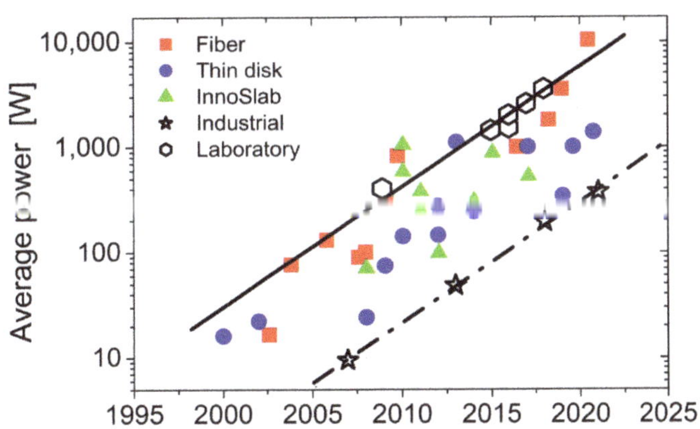

Figure 1. Progress in ultrafast laser technology featuring an exponential increase in the average output power over the past 20 years. The plot is a synthesis of data, indicating the related laser technology (fiber, thin disk, and InnoSlab) as fully colored data points [2], as well as their realization in laboratories or as commercial industrial products as open black data points [3]. The black lines guide the eye.

Citation: Krüger, J.; Bonse, J. Special Issue "Advanced Pulse Laser Machining Technology". *Materials* **2023**, *16*, 819. https://doi.org/10.3390/ma16020819

Received: 11 January 2023
Accepted: 13 January 2023
Published: 14 January 2023

For industrial use, the high output power of ultrafast lasers must be directed to the workpieces to be machined by appropriate beam guidance and deflection systems [6]. For many materials such as metals and semiconductors, moderate laser fluences (i.e., laser pulse energies) are sufficient to process the workpiece with high precision and efficiency [7–9]. Therefore, high laser pulse repetition rates up to the above-mentioned MHz level can be utilized to significantly reduce the processing times. This requires extremely fast beam deflection systems, possibly coupled with optics for multibeam processing. In a recent study, an area processing rate up to 3.8 m^2/min was demonstrated with a single-pass raster on steel sheets with a scanning speed of the laser beam of 950 m/s [10]. The key element of the experimental setup was a polygon scanner [11] in connection with a MHz laser system.

The Special Issue addresses not only the advantages of modern laser processing using short and ultrashort laser pulses, but also limitations caused by unwanted secondary hazards such as X-ray emissions. This phenomenon is not completely new and was described for laser machining applications using ultrashort laser pulses with repetition rates of the order of 1 kHz two decades ago [12–14]. However, the use of high pulse repetition rates in the multi-100 kHz range and burst pulses has recently exacerbated the problem [15–21]. Therefore, it is a pleasant fact that five publications in this Special Issue discuss this problem area in detail and, thus, make an important contribution to the field of combined laser and radiation protection for improving work safety aspects [22–26].

The use of laser pulse bursts enables new process regimes for metals and allows for an increase in the structuring rates and surface quality of machined samples. Results of both experimental and numerical investigations in this context are reviewed by Förster et al. [27]. The machining strategies using pulse bursts with intraburst repetition frequencies in the MHz up to GHz regime must consider an increased risk of secondary X-ray emissions with this mode of operation [21,25,26].

This Special Issue bundles together 1 review paper [27], 1 perspective article [28], and 14 original research articles [22–26,29–37], all focusing on the latest achievements in areas of surface and volume laser material processing, including laser-induced forward transfer and laser printing technologies [28], spatial and temporal beam shaping [29–32], Bessel-beam structuring of high-aspect-ratio void channels inside glass [34], direct laser interference patterning [35], pulse burst machining [27], waveguide writing [36], fs-pulse laser-induced amorphization and recrystallization of single-crystalline silicon [37], and a comparison of different beam shuttering technologies [33]—an aspect that is often neglected, but most practically relevant.

Author Contributions: Conceptualization, J.K. and J.B.; methodology, J.K. and J.B.; software, not applicable; validation, J.K. and J.B.; formal analysis, J.K. and J.B.; investigation, not applicable; resources, not applicable; data curation, not applicable; writing—original draft preparation, J.K. and J.B.; writing—review and editing, J.K. and J.B.; visualization, J.B.; supervision, J.K. and J.B.; project administration, J.K. and J.B.; funding acquisition, not applicable. All authors have read and agreed to the published version of the manuscript.

Funding: This Editorial received no external funding.

Institutional Review Board Statement: Not applicable.

Informed Consent Statement: Not applicable.

Data Availability Statement: Not applicable.

Acknowledgments: Administrative and technical support of Anson Geng and the editorial staff of *Materials* is to be acknowledged here.

Conflicts of Interest: The authors declare no conflict of interest.

References

1. Saraceno, J.C.; Sutter, D.; Metzger, T.; Ahmed, M.A. The amazing progress of high-power ultrafast thin-disk lasers. *J. Eur. Opt. Soc. Rapid publ.* **2019**, *15*, 15. [CrossRef]
2. Schille, J.; Löschner, U. Ultrashort pulse lasers in high-rate laser micro processing—Quo vadis? *Adv. Opt. Technol.* **2021**, *10*, 233–237. [CrossRef]
3. Weber, R.; Graf, T. The challenges of productive materials processing with ultrafast lasers. *Adv. Opt. Technol.* **2021**, *10*, 239–245. [CrossRef]
4. Han, M.; Smith, D.; Ng, S.H.; Anand, V.; Katkus, T.; Juodkazis, S. Ultra-short-pulse lasers—Materials—Applications. *Eng. Proc.* **2021**, *11*, 44.

5. Müller, M.; Aleshire, C.; Klenke, A.; Haddad, E.; Légaré, F.; Tünnermann, A.; Limpert, J. 10.4 kW coherently combined ultrafast fiber laser. *Opt. Lett.* **2020**, *45*, 3083–3086. [CrossRef] [PubMed]
6. Račiukaitis, G. Ultra-short pulse lasers for microfabrication: A review. *IEEE J. Sel. Top. Quantum Electron.* **2021**, *27*, 1100112. [CrossRef]
7. Kautek, W.; Krüger, J. Femtosecond pulse laser ablation of metallic, semiconducting, ceramic, and biological materials. *Proc. SPIE* **1994**, *2207*, 600–611.
8. Račiukaitis, G.; Brikas, M.; Gecys, P.; Voisiat, B.; Gedvilas, M. Use of high repetition rate and high power lasers in microfabrication: How to keep the efficiency high? *J. Laser Micro Nanoeng.* **2009**, *4*, 186–191. [CrossRef]
9. Neuenschwander, B.; Jäggi, B.; Schmid, M.; Hennig, G. Surface structuring with ultra-short laser pulses: Basics, limitations and needs for high throughput. *Phys. Procedia* **2014**, *56*, 1047–1058. [CrossRef]
10. Schille, J.; Schneider, L.; Mauersberger, S.; Szokup, S.; Höhn, S.; Pötschke, J.; Reiß, F.; Leidich, E.; Löschner, U. High-rate laser surface texturing for advanced tribological functionality. *Lubricants* **2020**, *8*, 33. [CrossRef]
11. De Loor, R. Polygon scanner system for ultra short pulsed laser micro-machining applications. *Phys. Procedia* **2013**, *41*, 544–551. [CrossRef]
12. Thogersen, J.; Borowiec, A.; Haugen, H.K.; McNeill, F.E.; Stronach, I.M. X-ray emission from femtosecond laser micromachining. *Appl. Phys. A* **2001**, *73*, 361–363. [CrossRef]
13. Bunte, J.; Barcikowski, S.; Püster, T.; Burmester, T.; Brose, M.; Ludwig, T. Secondary hazards: Particle and X-ray emission. *Topics Appl. Phys.* **2004**, *96*, 309–321.
14. Prieto-Pena, J.; Gómez, F.; González-Castaño, D.M.; Flores-Arias, M.T.; Arines, J.; Bao-Varela, C.; Cambronero-López, F.; Martínez Maqueira, A. X-ray emission from femtosecond laser micromachining. *J. Radiol. Prot.* **2018**, *38*, 716–730. [CrossRef]
15. Legall, H.; Schwanke, C.; Pentzien, S.; Dittmar, G.; Bonse, J.; Krüger, J. X-ray emission as a potential hazard during ultrashort pulse laser material processing. *Appl. Phys. A* **2018**, *124*, 407. [CrossRef]
16. Behrens, R.; Pullner, B.; Reginatto, M. X-ray emission from materials processing lasers. *Radiat. Prot. Dosim.* **2019**, *183*, 361–374. [CrossRef]
17. Weber, R.; Giedl-Wagner, R.; Förster, D.J.; Pauli, A.; Graf, T.; Balmer, J.E. Expected X-ray dose rates resulting from industrial ultrafast laser applications. *Appl. Phys. A* **2019**, *125*, 635. [CrossRef]
18. Legall, H.; Schwanke, C.; Bonse, J.; Krüger, J. X-ray radiation protection aspects during ultrashort laser processing. *J. Laser Appl.* **2020**, *32*, 022004. [CrossRef]
19. Freitag, C.; Giedl-Wagner, R. X-ray protection in an industrial production environment. *PhotonicsViews* **2020**, *17*, 37–41. [CrossRef]
20. Legall, H.; Bonse, J.; Krüger, J. Review of X-ray exposure and safety issues arising from ultra-short pulse laser material pro-cessing. *J. Radiol. Prot.* **2021**, *41*, R28–R42. [CrossRef]
21. Metzner, D.; Olbrich, M.; Lickschat, P.; Horn, A.; Weißmantel, S. X-ray generation by laser ablation using MHz to GHz pulse bursts. *J. Laser Appl.* **2021**, *33*, 032014. [CrossRef]
22. Mosel, P.; Sankar, P.; Düsing, J.F.; Dittmar, G.; Püster, T.; Jäschke, P.; Vahlbruch, J.-W.; Morgner, U.; Kovacev, M. X-ray dose rate and spectral measurements during ultrafast laser machining using a calibrated (high-sensitivity) novel X-ray detector. *Materials* **2021**, *14*, 4397. [CrossRef]
23. Schille, J.; Kraft, S.; [illegible] in materials processing. *Materials* **2021**, *14*, 4537. [CrossRef]
24. Stolzenberg, U.; Schmitt Rahner, M.; Pullner, B.; Legall, H.; Bonse, J.; Kluge, M.; Ortner, A.; Hoppe, B.; Krüger, J. X-ray emission hazards from ultrashort pulsed laser material processing in an industrial setting. *Materials* **2021**, *14*, 7163. [CrossRef]
25. Schille, J.; Kraft, S.; Kattan, D.; Löschner, U. Enhanced X-ray emissions arising from high pulse repetition frequency ultrashort pulse laser materials processing. *Materials* **2022**, *15*, 2748. [CrossRef] [PubMed]
26. Böttcher, K.; Schmitt Rahner, M.; Stolzenberg, U.; Kraft, S.; Bonse, J.; Feist, C.; Albrecht, D.; Pullner, B.; Krüger, J. Worst-case X-ray photon energies in ultrashort pulse laser processing. *Materials* **2022**, *15*, 8996. [CrossRef]
27. Förster, D.J.; Jäggi, B.; Michalowski, A.; Neuenschwander, B. Review on experimental and theoretical investigations of ultra-short pulsed laser ablation of metals with burst pulses. *Materials* **2021**, *14*, 3331. [CrossRef]
28. Florian, C.; Serra, P. Printing via laser-induced forward transfer and the future of digital manufacturing. *Materials* **2023**, *16*, 698. [CrossRef]
29. Hauschwitz, P.; Stoklasa, B.; Kuchařík, J.; Turčičová, H.; Písařík, M.; Brajer, J.; Rostohar, D.; Mocek, T.; Duda, M.; Lucianetti, A. Micromachining of invar with 784 Beams using 1.3 ps laser source at 515 nm. *Materials* **2020**, *13*, 2962. [CrossRef]
30. Wenisch, C.; Engel, S.; Gräf, S.; Müller, F.A. Dual laser beam processing of semiconducting thin films by excited state absorption. *Materials* **2021**, *14*, 1256. [CrossRef] [PubMed]
31. Zhou, T.; Kraft, S.; Perrie, W.; Schille, J.; Löschner, U.; Edwardson, S.; Dearden, G. Backward flux re-deposition patterns during multi-spot laser ablation of stainless steel with picosecond and femtosecond pulses in air. *Materials* **2021**, *14*, 2243. [CrossRef] [PubMed]
32. Schlutow, H.; Fuchs, U.; Müller, F.A.; Gräf, S. Squared focal intensity distributions for applications in laser material processing. *Materials* **2021**, *14*, 4981. [CrossRef] [PubMed]
33. Aboud, D.G.K.; Wood, M.J.; Zeppetelli, G.; Joy, N.; Kietzig, A.-M. A practical comparison of beam shuttering technologies for pulsed laser micromachining applications. *Materials* **2022**, *15*, 897. [CrossRef] [PubMed]

34. Vetter, C.; Giust, R.; Furfaro, L.; Billet, C.; Froehly, L.; Courvoisier, F. High aspect ratio structuring of glass with ultrafast Bessel beams. *Materials* **2021**, *14*, 6749. [CrossRef]
35. El-Khoury, M.; Voisiat, B.; Kunze, T.; Lasagni, A.F. Prediction of optimum process parameters fabricated by direct laser interference patterning based on central composite design. *Materials* **2020**, *13*, 4101. [CrossRef]
36. Macias-Montero, M.; Moreno-Zárate, P.; Muñoz, F.; Sotillo, B.; Garcia-Pardo, M.; Serna, R.; Fernandez, P.; Solis, J. Competition effects during femtosecond laser induced element redistribution in Ba- and La-migration based laser written waveguides. *Materials* **2021**, *14*, 3185. [CrossRef]
37. Florian, C.; Fischer, D.; Freiberg, K.; Duwe, M.; Sahre, M.; Schneider, S.; Hertwig, A.; Krüger, J.; Rettenmayr, M.; Beck, U.; et al. Single femtosecond laser-pulse-induced superficial amorphization and re-crystallization of silicon. *Materials* **2021**, *14*, 1651. [CrossRef]

materials

MDPI

Review

Review on Experimental and Theoretical Investigations of Ultra-Short Pulsed Laser Ablation of Metals with Burst Pulses

Daniel J. Förster [1,2,*], Beat Jäggi [3], Andreas Michalowski [4] and Beat Neuenschwander [5,*]

1 Institut für Strahlwerkzeuge, University of Stuttgart, Pfaffenwaldring 43, 70569 Stuttgart, Germany
2 LightPulse LASER PRECISION, Pfaffenwaldring 43, 70569 Stuttgart, Germany
3 LASEA Switzerland SA, Rue du Soleil 11, 2504 Bienne, Switzerland; bjaeggi@lasea.com
4 Robert Bosch GmbH, Renningen, 70465 Stuttgart, Germany; andreas.michalowski@de.bosch.com
5 Institute for Applied Laser, Photonics and Surface Technologies ALPS, Bern University of Applied Sciences, Pestalozzistrasse 20, 3400 Burgdorf, Switzerland
* Correspondence: daniel.foerster@ifsw.uni-stuttgart.de (D.J.F.); beat.neuenschwander@bfh.ch (B.N.)

Abstract: Laser processing with ultra-short double pulses has gained attraction since the beginning of the 2000s. In the last decade, pulse bursts consisting of multiple pulses with a delay of several 10 ns and less found their way into the area of micromachining of metals, opening up completely new process regimes and allowing an increase in the structuring rates and surface quality of machined samples. Several physical effects such as shielding or re-deposition of material have led to a new understanding of the related machining strategies and processing regimes. Results of both experimental and numerical investigations are placed into context for different time scales during laser processing. This review is dedicated to the fundamental physical phenomena taking place during burst processing and their respective effects on machining results of metals in the ultra-short pulse regime for delays ranging from several 100 fs to several microseconds. Furthermore, technical applications based on these effects are reviewed.

Keywords: laser ablation; ultra-short pulses; double pulses; burst processing; MHz bursts; GHz bursts

Citation: Förster, D.J.; Jäggi, B.; Michalowski, A.; Neuenschwander, B. Review on Experimental and Theoretical Investigations of Ultra-Short Pulsed Laser Ablation of Metals with Burst Pulses. *Materials* **2021**, *14*, 3331. https://doi.org/10.3390/ma14123331

Academic Editors: Jörg Krüger and Jörn Bonse

Received: 30 April 2021
Accepted: 9 June 2021
Published: 16 June 2021

1. Introduction

To enable increased throughput, the development of ultra-short pulsed lasers for materials processing has always aimed for higher laser powers. In recent years, ultrafast lasers with average output powers exceeding 1 kW [1–5] and even 10 kW [6] have been demonstrated. Industrially available lasers currently already provide pulse energies of up to some 100 µJ, whereas laser systems in academia provide several mJ. Thus, the available energy per pulse is often much higher than the energy actually needed for single pulse ablation. In order to attain the highest possible ablated volume for a given amount of energy, the energy can be distributed among pulses within a pulse package, a so-called pulse burst consisting of a minimum of two pulses and up to several hundred or thousand pulses [7–24]. Each of these burst packages then carries a sufficiently high amount of energy that can be used for laser machining, while the total energy of all pulses together is close to the maximum available pulse energy of the laser. In recent years, ultra-short pulsed laser ablation with burst pulses for micromachining has been intensively investigated both experimentally and numerically.

The aim of this article was to provide a comprehensive review of the physics of ultra-short pulsed laser ablation of metals with burst pulses and the applications based on the physical processes involved. In the next subsection, processing strategies and definitions used in this article are introduced. In the second section, the physics of ablation using ultra-short burst pulses of metals is discussed, summarizing the physics involved during single pulse laser ablation in the first place, followed by the pulse-to-pulse interactions of two subsequent ultra-short laser pulses. Afterwards, special attention is paid to machining with triple pulses, followed by two sections dedicated to the physics involved when processing with multiple pulses with intra-burst repetition rates of MHz and GHz. In Section 3, several MHz and GHz burst processing applications are summarized and reviewed, ranging from punching and drilling processes via line scribing, milling, and surface structuring to several special applications. The article closes with conclusions and an outlook.

Processing Strategies and Definitions

In material processing, different strategies can be applied depending on the application. Using a stationary beam, the so-called punching process is realized. In this process, a certain number of consecutive laser pulses N is focused on the same spot and each pulse ablates a thin layer of material. Using a Gaussian beam with a $1/e^2$-radius of w, this results in a parabolic dimple, as shown in Figure 1a. If the applied number of pulses and the fluence are high enough, the material can be drilled through. This drilling strategy is called percussion drilling and represents only one of the possible drilling strategies used in ultra-short pulse laser machining [25].

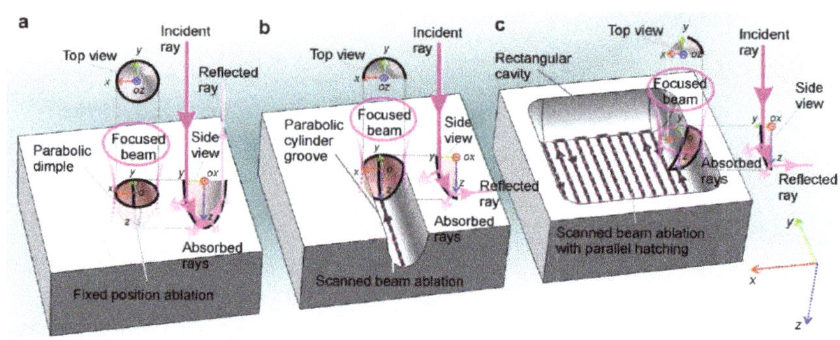

Figure 1. Schematic illustration of the processes and machining results: (**a**) dimple with the shape of a paraboloid ablated by multiple laser pulses with a stationary beam, resulting out of the punching process; (**b**) groove with the shape of a parabolic cylinder ablated by a scanned laser beam (line scan), representing the scribing process; (**c**) rectangular-shaped cavity ablated by a scanned laser beam and parallel line hatching (bidirectional meandering scan) resulting out of laser milling. The 3D Cartesian coordinate system x (red arrow), y (green arrow), and z (blue arrow) holds for all sketches (**a–c**). The center positions of the focused Gaussian beams are indicated by o. The multiple reflections of incident rays from the interior walls are given as side views (yz planes). Incident and multiple reflected rays are also given as side views (yz planes). The interaction area (cf. xy and yz planes) of laser and material decreases from (**a–c**). Reproduced under the terms of a Creative Commons Attribution 4.0 International License, (https://creativecommons.org/licenses/by/4.0/ (accessed on 31 May 2021)) [26]. Copyright 2018, the authors, published by Springer Nature.

In contrast to using a stationary beam, scribing can be realized if the laser beam is moved along one lateral direction. This results on the workpiece in a parabolic-shaped groove if a Gaussian beam is used (cf. Figure 1b). The linear movement of the beam can be realized using a linear stage or a galvanometric scanner for example. In the scribing process, consecutive pulses overlap each other. The overlap o_{line} can be calculated using the moving speed of the axis v_{scan}, the radius w, and the used pulse repetition rate of the laser f_{rep} by

$$o_{line} = 1 - \frac{v_{scan}}{f_{rep} \cdot 2 \cdot w} \tag{1}$$

If a deeper groove is demanded, the laser beam is moved several times along the same line path. These repetitions are the number of machined layers or overscans N_L. If the ratio between material thickness, laser parameters, and repetitions is chosen correctly, the material can even be cut through using this line scribing technique. The third ablation process, called milling (cf. Figure 1c), is realized by machining several parallel lines with a defined line spacing. This line spacing is called the hatch distance d_h. In the milling process, in addition to the overlap of two consecutive pulses along the scan direction, there is also an overlapping in the perpendicular direction to the machined lines o_{cross}:

$$o_{cross} = 1 - \frac{d_h}{2 \cdot w} \quad (2)$$

In milling applications, the laser spot must be moved in two lateral directions. The straight-forward approach is to use a galvanometric scanner to perform this movement [26]. Additionally, solutions using a rotational axis in combination with different technologies such as linear stages [27], galvanometric scanners [28], or acousto-optic deflectors (AODs) [29] are used to allow such 2D movement. In the z-direction, the material is removed layer by layer, resulting in a so-called 2.5D process [27]. Using this strategy, 3D structures can be engraved by changing the processing region from layer to layer, as shown in Figure 2a. In addition, the direction of the hatch pattern (direction of the parallel lines) can be rotated from layer to layer by the hatch angle to avoid scanning the same lines multiple times, which could lead to line irregularities. If a central unprocessed square in the middle of a process region is enlarged linearly layer by layer (making the scanned area per layer smaller), the result is a square pyramid as a subtractively generated geometry (cf. Figure 2b).

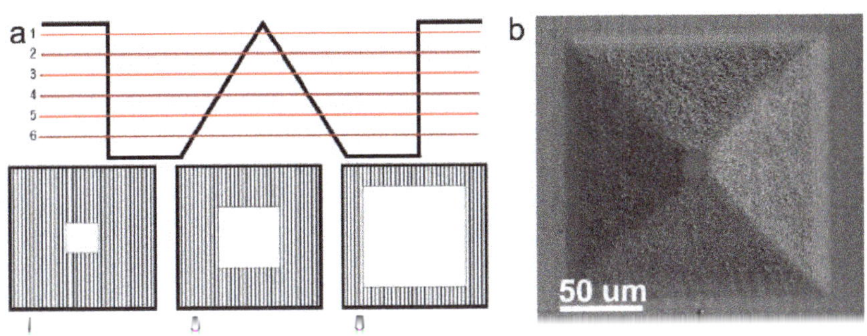

Figure 2. 2.5D processing; (**a**) slicing of the 3D structure and three corresponding 2D slices with the hatch pattern (no rotation of the hatch pattern from layer to layer); (**b**) SEM image of a 3D structure machined in copper. Reprinted from [27], copyright 2013, with permission from Elsevier.

The described processing strategies have been used principally with single pulses, which are emitted at a given repetition rate from the used laser system. In burst processing, the single pulse is replaced by a pulse package including several pulses with a temporal distance much shorter than the pulse repetition rate (intra-burst delay t_B, cf. Figure 3). This package of pulses is called a burst. Depending on the intra-burst delay time, it can be distinguished between MHz bursts (with an intra-burst delay of tens of ns) and GHz bursts (with an intra-burst delay of hundreds of ps). The temporal distance between the burst packages is called the inter-burst delay and corresponds to the pulse repetition rate in single pulse operation. During scribing and milling, it can be assumed that for such time delays the burst package is applied within the area of one sole spot, i.e., it acts similarly to a stationary beam.

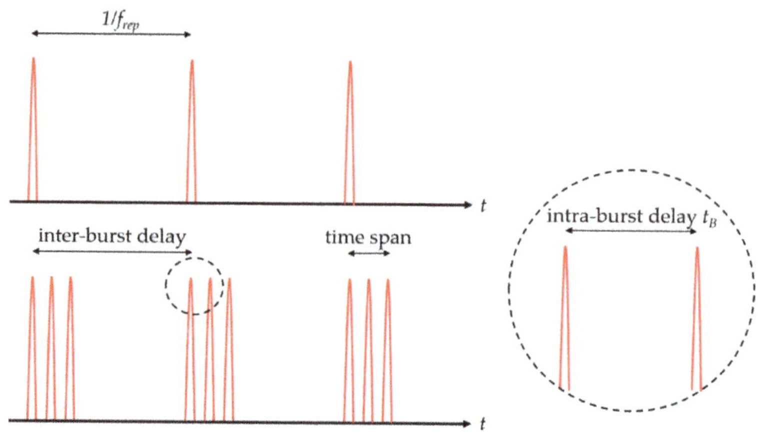

Figure 3. Upper row: single pulse operation with a defined repetition rate *frep*; lower row: burst operation with display of the two delay times inter-burst delay and intra-burst delay t_B as well as the time span.

2. Physics of Ultra-Short Burst Pulse Ablation of Metals

The focus of this article lies on metal processing. For laser processing of different materials such as semiconductors [30–32], dielectrics [30,31,33–35], or ceramics [31,36], the reader may refer to the corresponding articles. In the following, the physical mechanisms of laser–material interactions relevant in the machining of metals are discussed. First, the mechanisms during and after the processing of metals with single ultra-short laser pulses (for repetitive processing, this corresponds to inter-pulse delays of tens of microseconds or repetition rates below 100 kHz) is discussed and summarized in Section 2.1. Although several articles exist on this topic and deal especially with the micromachining of different metals in this regime [30,31,37–40], a summary of the essential effects regarding processing in a single pulse operation is given for completion and as a basis for the following sections. After introducing and summarizing the involved physical mechanisms for single pulse laser ablation of metals, the pulse-to-pulse interactions of two subsequent pulses are introduced in Section 2.2. The focus in that section lies on interactions between two pulses with inter-pulse delays of several 100 fs to several 10 ns, since the experimental and theoretical findings differ fundamentally from metal processing in single pulse operation. In Section 2.3, the physical mechanisms and state-of-the art findings for triple pulse processing with intra-burst delays in the range of tens of ns are discussed. Finally, in Sections 2.4 and 2.5, machining with bursts containing multiple pulses with intra-burst repetition rates of MHz and GHz are summarized.

2.1. Single Pulse Laser Ablation

When light irradiates a metal surface, photons interact with free electrons and energy is transferred to the electronic system via inverse Bremsstrahlung. Subsequently, the electronic system transfers energy to the lattice (ions) and excites vibrations of the ionic system, leading to a heating of the metal surface resulting in an increase of temperature. For laser pulses with pulse durations strongly exceeding the electron–phonon coupling time, the excitation of the electronic and ionic system can be considered to happen in thermal equilibrium. Hence, conventional heat conduction and physical mechanisms such as melting and evaporation take place. During ultra-short pulsed processing, short heating times allow physical states of matter to cross borders in the phase diagram (e.g., the solid–liquid line) within picoseconds and induce high pressures (tens of GPa and more) within tens of picoseconds within thin surface layers [41–46]. For a deeper understanding, details of the involved physical mechanisms can be found in several references including theoretical and numerical modeling [37,41–46]. The most important measure to distinguish between the ultra-short pulse regime and classical thermal heating in equilibrium is the electron–phonon coupling time $\tau_{el-phon}$, which is a characteristic time for heating the ionic lattice. In first approximation, this value is a constant, but, in principle, it depends on the deposited energy, and the time of relaxation can be multiples of that characteristic time [23]. It can be estimated by $\tau_{el-phon} = C_P/\gamma$, with C_P being the heat capacity of the ionic system and γ being the electron-phonon coupling constant [37]. Both values are material-dependent. For metals and their alloys, the electron–phonon coupling time lies in the range of several 100 fs to more than 100 ps (e.g., pure gold even has a coupling time of around 115 ps). Exemplary values are given in Table 1. For alloys, the electron–phonon coupling times can differ from the original elements forming the alloy, e.g., for AISI 304 stainless steel, an electron–phonon coupling time of 0.5 ps was reported [47], whereas it amounts to 1.3 ps for pure iron.

Table 1. Electron–phonon coupling times for various metals at room temperature.

Material	Ag	Al	Au	Cu	Fe	Mb	Ni	Pt	Ti	W
$\tau_{el\text{-}phon}$ in ps	84.3 [1]	4.5 [1]	115.5 [1]	57.5 [2]	1.3 [3]	2.2 [4]	1.1 [4]	2.2 [5]	1.9 [5]	12.1 [5]

[1] calc. from C_i [48], g [49]; [2] [50]; [3] calc. from C_l [48], γ [51]; [4] calc. from C_l [48], γ [52]; [5] calc. from C_l [48], γ [53].

Another crucial quantity for the description of different regimes of laser processing with ultra-short pulses is the laser fluence ϕ. It is defined as the energy per irradiated area, and for a Gaussian beam the peak fluence ϕ_0 equals

$$\phi_0 = 2 \cdot \phi_{av} = 2 \cdot \frac{E_P}{\pi \cdot w^2} \tag{3}$$

E_P corresponds to the pulse energy of the incoming laser pulse, w to the laser spot radius ($1/e^2$), and ϕ_{av} is the average fluence. The fluence can be increased by increasing the laser pulse energy or decreasing the irradiated area (spot size). If the fluence is increased above the ablation threshold ϕ_{th}, material is removed from the surface (ablation). With increasing fluence, the ultra-short pulsed laser interaction with metals can be characterized by the following physical processes [41–46,54]:

- heating of the metal surface;
- melting of the metal surface;
- spallation of surface layers (rupture of material when the fluence is above the ablation threshold);
- phase explosion (explosive boiling of the surface with the generation of vapor and plasma).

A microscopic view of the occurring processes for ablation of aluminum is given in Figure 4 [46]. When a laser pulse hits the target with a fluence below the ablation threshold, the material is heated and melting of the surface may also take place. Furthermore, two sorts of pressure waves propagate into the material from the surface. A shockwave (SW) leading to a compression of material (higher density, darker orange color) is followed by a rarefaction wave (RW), leading to a dilution of material (lower density, lighter orange color). When the fluence is increased above the ablation threshold, the intensity of both pressure waves is increased and, as a result of the lower density of the rarefaction wave, a fragmentation of surface layers takes place (spallation regime). The travel velocity of such dense layers evolving from the surface for metals lies in the range of several 100 m/s [45,46,54–57]. If the fluence is increased above values of approximately 10 times the ablation threshold, not only spallation takes place but the upper surface layers (in this representation on the left) disintegrate and show a transition into the gaseous phase. Particles and clusters in the gaseous phase then travel principally with the speed of sound (of the initial bulk material), which lies in the range of several km/s [45,46,54–57].

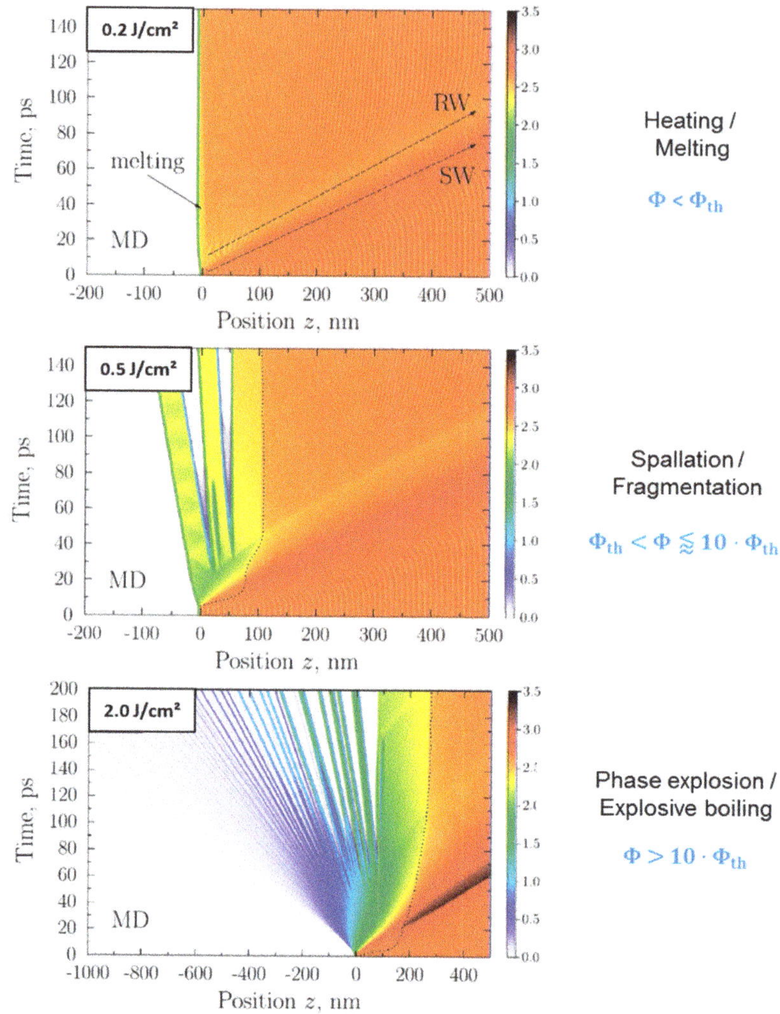

Figure 4. Results from molecular dynamics (MD) simulations for single pulse irradiation of aluminum. The *x*-axis corresponds to spatial coordinates with z = 0 nm being the initial surface of the material. The *y*-axis corresponds to the simulation time with t = 5 ps being the maximum of the laser pulse. The color of the heat maps corresponds to the density of aluminum. With increasing fluence (from **top** to **bottom**), the material passes different regimes, ranging from melting of the surface (no ablation) to phase explosion with an excessive development of gaseous and ionized matter. In the spallation regime (**center**), ablation is characterized by a fragmentation of the material, leading to high surface qualities and well-defined ablation depths during laser processing. Adapted from [46], copyright 2015, with permission from Elsevier.

Although not displayed here, atoms in the gaseous phase also become ionized for higher fluences, and some regions reach temperatures of several 1000 K or more [45,46,54–57]. If successive pulses have inter-pulse delays of several tens of microseconds or more (corresponding to repetition rates of f_{rep} = 100 kHz or less), a subsequent pulse does not significantly interact with the ablation plume of its preceding pulse [58]. For laser material processing, the different ablation regimes result in differently efficient micromachining processes. One quantity for the description of an efficient ablation process is the energy specific volume $\Delta V/\Delta E$. For Gaussian laser beams it holds [14]:

$$\frac{\Delta V}{\Delta E} = \frac{1}{2} \cdot \frac{\delta}{\phi_o} \cdot \ln^2\left(\frac{\phi_0}{\phi_{th}}\right) \quad (4)$$

where δ corresponds to the effective penetration depth of energy, ϕ_0 is the incident peak fluence, and ϕ_{th} is the ablation threshold. Experimental data and, for the sake of clarity, only one fit function (brass, 400 fs, cyan curve) is given in Figure 5. The values were obtained in laser milling experiments by ablating cavities (cf. Figure 1c), measuring the ablated volume, and relating it to the incident total laser energy. The values follow the trend of Formula (4), having a maximum that can be extracted from the data. The corresponding values of δ, ϕ_{th}, and the fluence $\phi_{0,opt}$ where the maximum value was achieved and the maximum energy specific volume $\Delta V/\Delta E_{max}$ (maximum values in Figure 5) as well as the experimental conditions such as wavelength and pulse duration are summarized in Table 2.

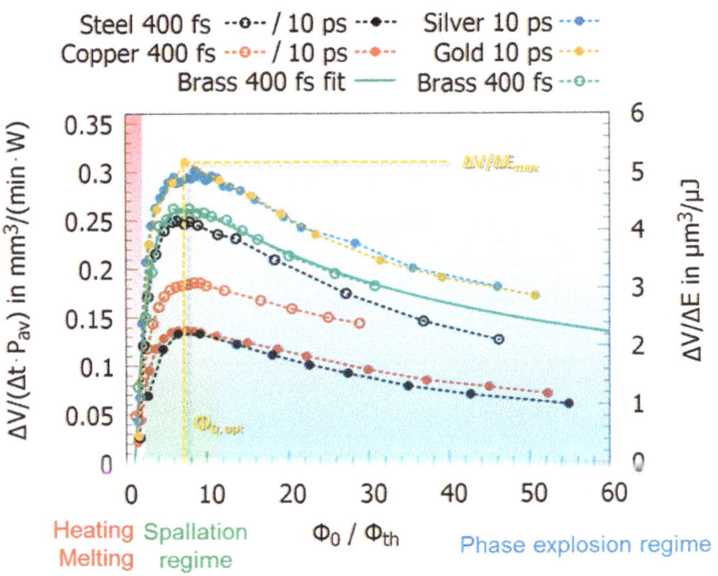

Figure 5. Energy specific volume for single pulse laser ablation of different metals processed in the near infrared. The fluence along the x-axis is normalized to the ablation threshold since different metals have different ablation thresholds. The corresponding values are given in Table 2. Original data taken from [59,60].

Table 2. Material parameters corresponding to the plots in Figure 5. Some of the fit parameters were calculated from original data.

Quantity		Brass [1]	Copper [1]	Copper [2]	Gold [2]	Silver [2]	Steel [1]	Steel [2]
λ	nm	1030	1030	1064	1064	1064	1030	1064
τ	ps	0.4	0.4	10	10	10	0.4	10
δ (fit)	nm	62.3	55.7	29.1	64.8	67.2	13.9	4.5
ϕ_{th}(fit)	J/cm^2	0.39	0.49	0.35	0.35	0.36	0.09	0.06
$\Delta V/\Delta E_{max}$	mm^3/W/min	0.26	0.19	0.14	0.30	0.30	0.25	0.13
$\Delta V/\Delta E_{max}$	µm^3/µJ	4.3	3.1	2.3	5.0	5.0	4.2	2.2
$\phi_{0,opt}$	J/cm^2	2.7	4.5	2.2	2.4	2.7	0.5	0.5

[1] [60], [2] [59].

For single pulse operation, this formula resembles well the experimental findings. The different metals show different maximum energy specific volumes and ablation thresholds, but the general trend is the same. Principally, such curves are found for metals when processed with pulses with a pulse duration between a few 100 fs and several ns [60,61].

Independent of the metals investigated, the ablation process when using ultra-short pulses is most efficient in the spallation regime, since the greatest amount of deposited energy is used for ablation. For lower fluences, only heating of the material takes place, whereas for much higher fluences the amount of energy being used for heating and ionization increases [62].

Beside the ablated volume per energy, the ablated volume per time (a measure for the productivity) is a very important parameter for micromachining processes such as milling or drilling. It increases for higher fluences, while the ablation process itself becomes less energetically efficient ($\Delta V/\Delta E$ decreases). At the same time, low fluences close to the ablation threshold (or several times the ablation threshold) correlate with low surface roughness and less spatter occurrence [14,63,64]. For industrial micromachining processes, it is often important to maintain a smooth surface while keeping the ablated volume per time high. Since the available laser pulse energy and average power of industrial laser systems have been significantly increasing within the last decade, the available energy per pulse is often much higher than the energy needed for ablation. Among other strategies such as defocusing of the processing beam to lower the fluence while keeping the productivity at a high level [18,65], the concept of laser burst pulses was introduced, allowing the principle use of the totally available laser energy by splitting it into several pulses with lower energy each [66,67]. The resulting limitations of this concept will be further discussed in the following sections.

Beside the ablated volume per energy and time, the residual energy is another important quantity influencing micromachining processes, mainly in terms of surface quality, e.g., surface roughness. If a sufficiently high amount of energy is coupled into the machined sample as heat, the surface structure and physical mechanism of material removal may change. For example, a temporary molten surface can lead to higher roughness and spatter production, decreasing the surface quality. During ablation with an ultra-short pulse, a certain amount of energy remains as heat in the bulk material. Depending on the irradiated metal and the used fluence, the amount of residual energy per pulse lies between 10% and 50% [16,17,68–76]. If high repetition rates are used, the heat accumulates and can affect the surface quality, the drilling time, and the amount of occurring melt [14,73,77–84]. Additionally, the amount of residual energy can increase when the geometry is changed, e.g., in hole drilling [68,70,72,74], or when surface structures like laser-induced periodic surface structures (LIPSS) or bumps evolve [69,84].

2.2. Double Pulses: Pulse-to-Pulse Interaction

The first investigations of laser treatment of metals with ultra-short double pulses go back to around the turn of the 21st century, when investigations about the enhancement of spectroscopic signals—today also often known as laser-induced breakdown spectroscopy (LIBS)—with ultra-short double pulses were performed [7,85–87]. While it was shown that signal enhancement was possible, the depths of the ablation craters formed showed a special behavior, i.e., the crater depths could only be as deep as using a single pulse or even less deep, which is not intuitive in the first place, since twice as much energy was used to create these craters. As will be summarized in the following, both effect signal enhancement from the irradiated plume as well as the development of less deep craters are mutually dependent. Many experimental [7,8,14,16,19,57–59,66,88–114] and numerical [9,10,12,54,93,115–119] studies have been performed since the first observations about metal ablation with ultra-short double pulses were published. The following paragraphs summarize the findings to provide an overview of the effects involved in ultra-short double pulse laser ablation.

When a double pulse with short inter-pulse delay times in the range of the electron–phonon coupling time is used, the ablated volume of such a double pulse equals the volume ablated by a single pulse with doubled pulse energy. With increasing inter-pulse delay, several physical effects can occur. For delays in the range of 10 ps to a few 100 ps, rarefaction wave interference takes place. As shown in Figure 4 (center), the ablation process of single ultra-short pulses is characterized by the occurrence of a shock wave and a following rarefaction wave. The intensity of the rarefaction wave is a critical parameter of a successful ablation event. If a rarefaction wave is too weak, no ablation occurs (cf. Figure 4 (top)). For double pulse ablation, weakening of such rarefaction waves is an important process. Exemplarily, calculated density and pressure distributions for different regimes of double pulse laser ablation are given in Figure 6 [10]. For the pressure distributions given in Figure 6, red regions denote regions with compressive pressures, whereas blue regions denote regions of tension. Figure 6a shows the result of double pulse irradiation with an inter-pulse delay of $\Delta t = 0$ ps (corresponding to a single pulse of double pulse energy). An intense shockwave is followed by an intense rarefaction wave. From the regions of highest tension (blue), ablation is initiated. If the inter-pulse delay is increased to around $\Delta t = 20$ ps, the first shockwave is weaker, since this wave is only initiated by the first pulse. The following rarefaction wave is less pronounced because the second pulse increases the pressure and, hence, lowers tension. As a result, less material is removed and the ablation depth is decreased (cf. Figure 6b). This effect of "rarefaction interference" is the reason for a lowering of the ablation depth for metals if the pulses are separated by several tens of picoseconds (blue region in Figure 7) [10,120]. If the inter-pulse delay is increased to $\Delta t = 50$ ps, the second pulse interacts with material that has already left the initial metal surface and no physical connection for the exchange of pressure remains. Instead, the second pulse is shielded by the ablation cloud induced by the first pulse [9,10,54,57,118–120]. The ablation cloud evolving from the surface after the first pulse is heated and partially disintegrates, leading to an extreme increase in temperature and plasma formation.

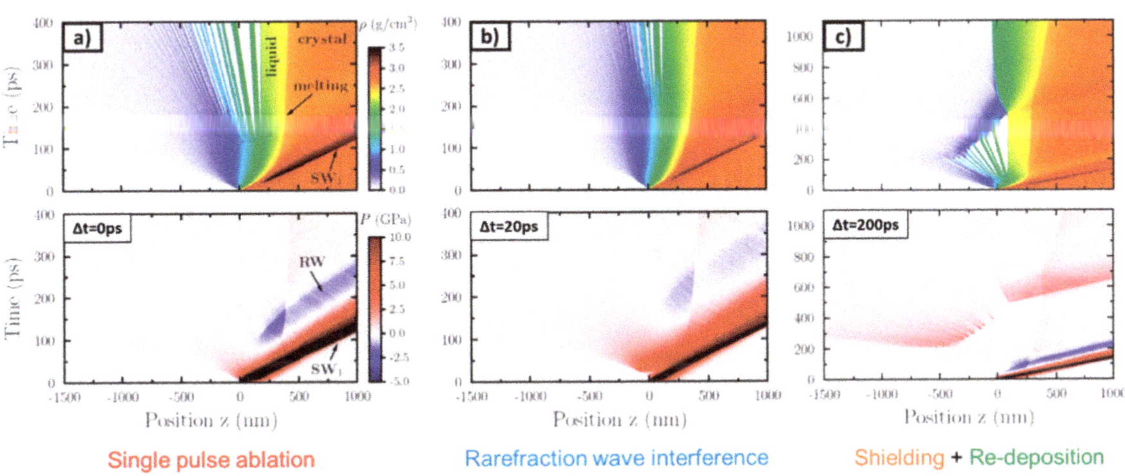

Figure 6. (**a**–**c**) Results from MD simulations showing the density (**top**) and pressure (**bottom**) distributions in space and time for different inter-pulse delays of double pulses. Material: aluminum, pulse duration 100 fs, wavelength 800 nm. Adapted with permission from Ref. [10]. Copyright (2015) by the American Physical Society.

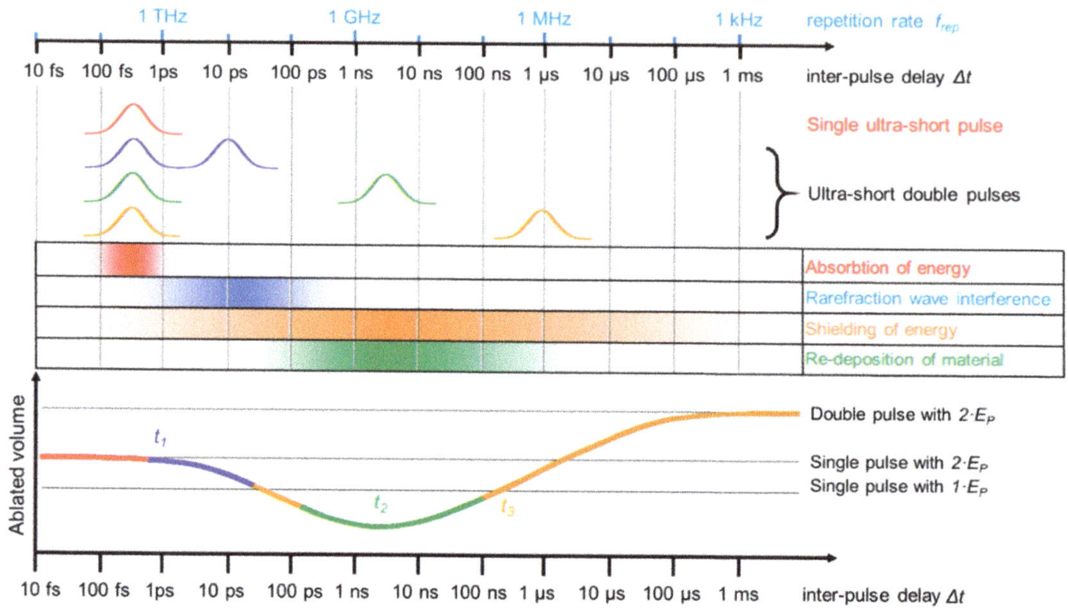

Figure 7. Interaction mechanisms of metals and ultra-short single and double pulses for different inter-pulse delays.

The latter is an important effect beneficial for LIBS measurements and allows a better characterization of material due to an increased plasma temperature and, hence, a more pronounced spectrum (cf. Section 3.5.2). Depending on the fluence, not only the second pulse is shielded (and is not contributing to further material removal) but a re-deposition of the material ablated by the first pulse can take place (cf. Figure 6c). As a result, the ablated volume of a double pulse can be lower than the volume ablated only by the first pulse (valley of death) [57,75,95,103,109,111,121–123]. This effect is material- and fluence-dependent. For example, the valley of death for stainless steel ranges between 100 and 200 ps at a fluence of 0.5 J/cm^2 [75] and shows a minimum at around 50 ps for 5 J/cm^2 [121]. Copper shows a valley of death for inter-pulse delays between 100 ps and 2 ns at fluences of 0.69 J/cm^2 [57] and 5 J/cm^2 [121]. Aluminum shows a valley of death between 100 and 300 ps for an incident fluence of 5 J/cm^2 [121]. Titanium and platinum show valleys of death between 100 and 500 ps for incident fluences close to the ablation threshold [123]. For steel, a broader study with different time delays and fluences was also performed, and it was reported that the highest suppression of ablation takes place for steel at around a 1 ns time delay. The highest suppression ratio was close to 10, so only 10% of the volume ablated by a single pulse was finally removed using a double pulse (parameters: wavelength 1028 nm, fluence approx. 2.3 J/cm^2) [103]. If the inter-pulse delay is increased to several tens of nanoseconds, the shielding and re-deposition becomes less pronounced, since the ablation cloud formed after the first pulse dilutes with increasing time delay. For inter-pulse delays of $\Delta t > 10$ µs, no significant interaction of the second pulse and the plume induced by the first pulse occurs anymore [58]. The discussed principal physical effects are summarized in Figure 7. Of course, the exact time delays, fluences, and pulse durations when these effects occur are material-dependent. The most significant differences between the materials are the time delay t_1, when the decrease of volume starts (blue region in Figure 7), the time delay t_2, when the minimum of ablated volume is reached, and the time delay t_3, when the re-deposition is not taking place anymore and the volume ablated by a single pulse is reached again (transition from the green to the yellow region in Figure 7).

For short delay times in the range of the electron–phonon coupling time (red color), the volume ablated by a double pulse equals the volume ablated by a single pulse with doubled pulse energy and the ablation process the same as for a single pulse, cf. Figures 4 and 6a. For delays in the range of 10 ps to a few 100 ps, rarefaction wave interference takes place, cf. Figure 6b. For inter-pulse delays between a few 100 ps and several 100 ns, a shielding of the second pulse by the ablated material of the first pulse takes place. For inter-pulse delays of a few nanoseconds, re-deposition of material ablated by the first pulse is another effect that can occur, cf. Figure 6c. The shielding effect diminishes for longer inter-pulse delays of several tens of nanoseconds due to the dilution of the plume initially induced by the first pulse. For delays of several tens of microseconds and longer, the second pulse does not interact with the plume, and the volume ablated by a double pulse is twice the volume ablated by a single pulse.

Although it is still the subject of current research, it seems that theses characteristic delay times are dependent on the electron–phonon coupling time. If the second pulse is reaching the target before the transfer of energy between the electronic and ionic system is finished, the material mainly reacts similar to an irradiation with a single pulse of double energy. For example, steel has a much shorter electron–phonon coupling time than copper (approx. 50 times lower), and the decrease in ablated volume starts from shorter time delays ($t_1 \approx 1$ ps for steel, $t_1 \approx 10$ ps for copper) [75,103]. For all metals investigated in the literature and as discussed before, t_2 lies between time delays of several 100 ps and several nanoseconds. For steel and copper, the difference is significant, e.g., for the fluences: 0.5 J/cm^2 for steel and 0.69 J/cm^2 for copper in the infrared, and t_2 for steel amounts to ~200 ps, whereas for copper t_2 amounts to ~2 ns [75]. Additionally, the delay time t_3, when the volume ablated by the double pulse again is the same as for a single pulse, differs for both metals in this fluence regime. For steel, t_3 amounts to approximately 1–3 ns [75,103,122], whereas for copper $t_3 > 10$ ns [75,122]. For aluminum, it was also reported that $t_3 > 10$ ns [122].

2.3. Triple Pulses with Intra-Burst Delays in the Range of Tens of Nanoseconds

As described in the previous section, the characteristic delay times t_1, t_2, and t_3 strongly depend on the material, especially on the electron–phonon coupling time, which also has a dominating influence onto the removal rates when a third pulse is added to the double pulse. If t_1 and t_2 are short compared to the intra-burst delay and t_3 shows a value in the range of this delay, the energy specific volume obtained for a triple pulse only slightly differs from the one of single pulses, e.g., steel 1.4301 (AISI 304) shows such short delay times and was intensively investigated. Different reported maximum energy specific volumes for single, double, and triple pulses are summarized in Figure 8a [14,19,23,24,102,107]. For pulses with a pulse duration of 10 ps, an intra-burst delay of 12 ns, and wavelengths of 1064 nm and 532 nm, the maximum energy specific volume slightly decreased for a triple pulse compared to a single pulse [14,102,107]. An almost identical behavior was observed for a 2 ps pulse duration but with higher ablated volumes due to the usage of shorter pulses [19]. Similar results with even higher energy specific volumes have been reported for 300 fs and 350 fs pulse duration in the near infrared (NIR) [23,60]. In contrast to the rest of the literature, in [24], a significant drop by a factor of two of the maximum energy specific volume for steel (from about 0.4 $mm^3/min/W$ for single pulses down to less than 0.2 $mm^3/min/W$, Figure 8a, blue empty squares) for a triple pulse burst was reported for a 210 fs pulse duration for a wavelength of 1030 nm. Here, in contrast to most other reported experiments by different authors, the fluence was varied by defocusing. This leads to different spot sizes at the fluences where the maximum energy specific volume was detected for the three situations. It was found for single pulse operation that there is a dependence of the threshold fluence, the energy penetration depth, and the maximum energy specific volume for steel 1.4301 (AISI 304) and copper when using different spot sizes [124]. This could serve as a possible explanation for the atypical behavior reported in [24] in contrast to all other studies in this field. The influence of the spot size on laser milling in general, but especially for bursts, still needs to be clarified by further studies.

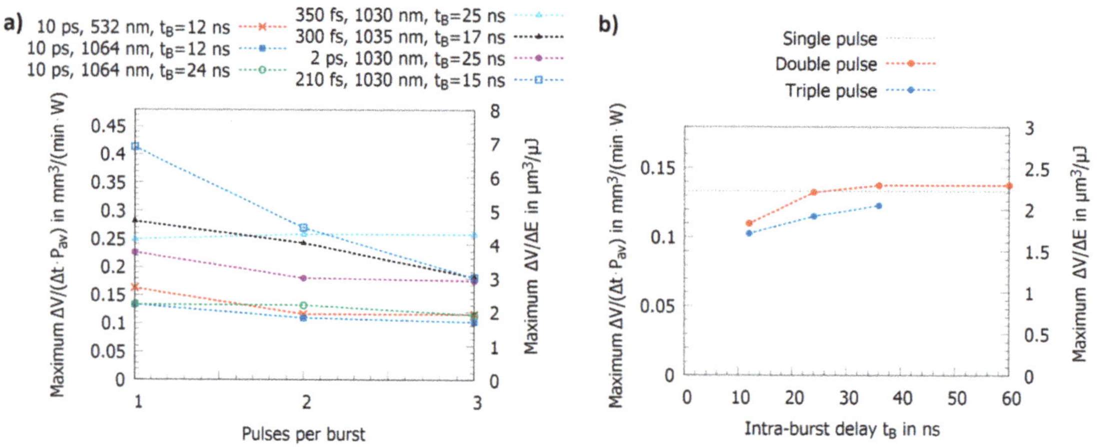

Figure 8. Maximum measured energy specific volumes for single, double, and triple pulses for steel 1.4301 (AISI 304) for (**a**) different pulse durations, wavelengths, and intra-burst delays and (**b**) as a function of the intra-burst delay for double and triple burst pulses with a 10 ps pulse duration and a 1064 nm wavelength. Data taken from [14,19,23,24,102,107].

Figure 8b shows the maximum energy specific volume for steel 1.4301 (AISI 304) using pulses with a pulse duration of 10 ps at a wavelength of 1064 nm and an intra-burst delay increasing from 12 ns to 36 ns for triple pulses and 60 ns for double pulses [14]. For the shortest intra-burst delay of 12 ns, the maximum volumes are smaller than the value for single pulse operation. For double pulses with an intra-burst delay of 24 ns and more, the same maximum value as for single pulse operation is reached (deviations are in the range of the measurement error). For triple pulses, the maximum energy specific volume also increases with increasing intra-burst delay but does not yet reach the value of single pulse operation with a 36 ns pulse delay.

The situation completely changes for copper (having longer delay times t_1, t_2, and t_3) as shown in Figure 9a,b. For double pulses, the aforementioned valley of death with a reduction in the maximum energy specific volume to less than 50% of the value for single pulses due to shielding effects is observed [14,24,59,60,102]. On the other hand, for triple pulse processing, the value strongly increases again and may even exceed the value for single pulses [14,24,59,60,102]. As can be seen in Figure 9a, the maximum energy specific volumes are functions of the pulse duration (an increase for shorter pulse durations is observed) and wavelength (for copper, green radiation is beneficial and results in higher maximum energy specific volumes, which is mainly due to higher absorptance [16]). For triple pulses, in the first place, it seems that after the described re-deposition effect (cf. Section 2.2) induced by the second pulse, the third pulse should simply contribute again to the ablated volume. However, assuming only a complete shielding and no re-deposition of the second pulse (no contribution to the ablated volume) and a full contribution of the third pulse to the ablated volume, the maximum energy specific volume should not exceed two-thirds of the value of single pulses. This is not the case. Indeed, for triple pulse processing, the maximum energy specific volume is the same or even higher than for single pulse processing.

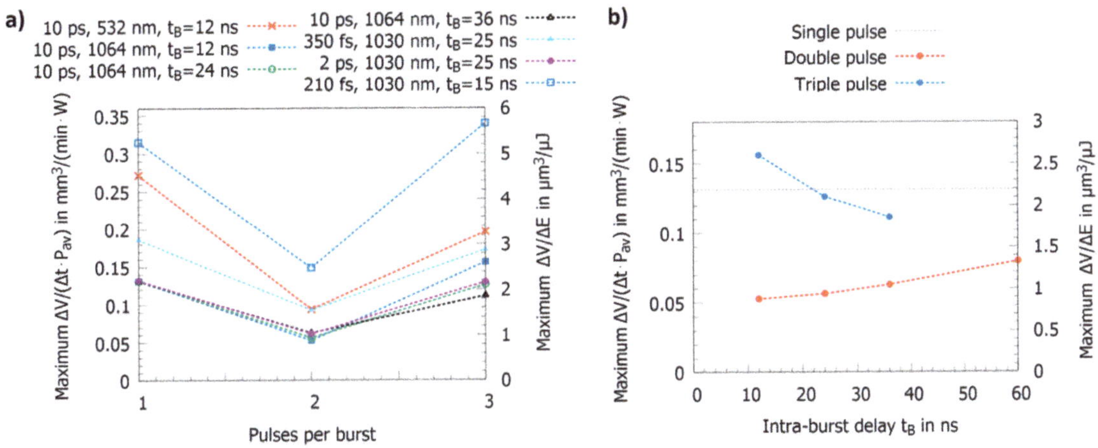

Figure 9. Maximum measured energy specific volumes for single, double, and triple pulses for (**a**) different pulse durations, wavelengths, and intra-burst delays for copper and (**b**) as a function of the intra-burst delay for double and triple burst pulses on copper with 10 ps pulse duration and 1064 nm wavelength. Data taken from [14,19,23,24,102,107].

The contribution of the second pulse was further investigated in [102,125], where the energy of the second pulse was varied compared to the first and third pulse, i.e., the relative energies were chosen to be $(1, \eta, 1)$. The pulses had a pulse duration of 10 ps, a wavelength of 1064 nm, and an intra-burst delay of 12 ns. For the situation (1, 0.25, 1), the energy specific volume does not differ from the one of a double pulse with an intra-burst delay of 24 ns. When the energy of the second pulse is then raised to (1, 0.5, 1), the maximum energy specific volume is almost doubled and even exceeds that for single pulses for the (1, 0.75, 1) and (1, 1, 1) situations. This shows that a minimum energy for the second pulse is demanded to start its clearing effect and that it saturates at a maximum energy. However, the high maximum energy specific volume for a triple pulse cannot be explained only by this effect.

Therefore, it was stated that additional effects influence the ablation process in case of triple burst pulses on copper to allow an enhanced ablation. In [16,17], results from calorimetric measurements with 10 ps pulse duration were obtained from two different calorimeter set-ups. For copper, it is shown that the residual energy coefficient, resembling the part of the applied laser energy remaining and heating up in the material only slightly varies between single, double, and triple pulses processing. For both measurement setups, the residual energy coefficient was measured to be slightly higher (an increase in the range of 2%) for the double pulse, but the difference was in the order of the measurement error. However, the absorptance of the machined surface changes significantly when using lasers in the NIR. The corresponding absorptance increased from 1.5% of the initial surface (high reflectivity) to 15.7%, 17.9%, and 26.8% for single, double, and triple pulses, respectively. This increase was obtained from the first machined layer and rests almost unchanged when the number of layers was increased to 48. For a triple pulse, the first pulse in the burst sequence could be absorbed much more strongly compared to single pulses, since 26.8% of incident energy was absorbed instead of 15.7% [16]. This could explain the further increase in the maximum energy specific volume for triple pulses on copper. This assumption is further supported by the results obtained for a wavelength of 532 nm, where the absorptance of the machined surface again increases from 35.7% for single pulses to 49.5% and 58.5% for double and triple pulses, respectively. This increase was lower than for 1064 nm, which is in accordance with the smaller increase in the energy specific volume for 532 nm and the triple pulse burst shown in Figure 9a. Hence, the absorptance seems to play a crucial role, and, due to significantly increased absorptance after the second pulse, the energy specific volume of copper might be increased to or even above the value of the single pulse operation. It should be kept in mind that these absorptances were measured on a cold surface ca. 10 mm out of the focal plane and therefore with a spot diameter between 400 μm and 700 μm, whereas, during machining, the surface is hot, and the spot diameter is in the range of 25 μm to 40 μm. Furthermore, the absorptance of a surface can also vary during irradiation with an ultra-short pulse, as shown in [126]. How this behavior affects burst pulse processing is unknown today and still a subject to further investigation.

In Figure 9b, the maximum energy specific volumes for double and triple pulses for pulses with a pulse duration of 10 ps at a wavelength of 1064 nm are shown as a function of the intra-burst delay t_B [17]. Due to the longer delay times t_1, t_2, and t_3 of copper, the values seem to increase for intra-burst delays exceeding 60 ns in contrast to steel, where the single pulse value is already obtained for an intra-burst delay of 24 ns, as illustrated in Figure 8b. However, in contrast to steel, the maximum energy specific volume decreases for triple pulses when the intra-burst delay is increasing (cf. Figure 9b). This is a surprising behavior as the shielding effect of the second pulse is definitively reduced. A possible explanation is that since less material is redeposited, more material remains above the workpiece in a less dense ablation cloud, leading then to a shielding of the third pulse. However, this is only a hypothesis and further investigations are needed to clarify the physical processes involved during triple pulse ablation.

Figure 10a shows the maximum energy specific volumes for brass [60], aluminum [23,107], silver [59], gold [59], and molybdenum [23]. Except for molybdenum, a strong shielding effect for the double pulse burst followed by a significant increase in the maximum energy specific volume for the triple burst pulse is observed. Following Formula (4), the energy specific volume for a Gaussian beam shows a maximum value at the optimum peak fluence $\phi_{0,opt} = e^2 \cdot \phi_{th}$ [61]. Introducing this optimum peak fluence into the expression for the energy specific volume (Formula (4)) leads to the ablated volume per pulse at the optimum fluence, which does not depend on the threshold fluence but directly scales with the energy penetration depth δ [65,127], i.e., the higher the energy penetration depth, the higher the volume ablated per pulse. The value of δ can be obtained by a least square fit of the formula to the data for single pulses reported in [14,23,59,60,107,128] following Formula (4). A larger ablated volume should lead to a stronger shielding effect for double pulses and therefore the ratio

$$\left(\frac{\Delta V}{\Delta E}\right)_{max,double\ pulse} / \left(\frac{\Delta V}{\Delta E}\right)_{max,single\ pulse} \tag{5}$$

should drop for higher energy penetration depths. This is confirmed in Figure 10b where this ratio is plotted as a function of the energy penetration depth δ. The circles denote situations where a clear shielding for the double burst pulse followed by a significant increase of the energy specific volume for the triple burst pulse is observed, whereas for the triangles, the maximum energy specific volumes for the three situations only slightly differ. The figure indicates a trend of ratios near 1 for short energy penetration depths in the range of 10 nm towards values below 0.5 for energy penetration depths of 40 nm and higher. Hence, the removed volume per single pulse could also be a factor describing the ablation behavior for double and triple pulses. Again, further investigations are needed to gain a clearer picture and to be able to distinguish between the influence of parameters such as the spot size, the intra-burst delay, and the energy penetration depth.

2.4. Multi-Pulse Bursts with Intra-Burst Repetition Rates in the MHz Range

The results for multi-pulse bursts for copper, brass, and aluminum are summarized in Figure 11a [19,23,24,60]. Copper, brass, and aluminum show an alternating behavior of the maximum energy specific volumes with high values for odd numbers of pulses in the burst and low values for even numbers of pulses. This can be explained as follows: the second pulse is fully or partially shielded but its energy clears the ablation cloud such that the third pulse can be absorbed by the surface. The third pulse again generates an ablation cloud, and the fourth pulse is therefore shielded again. The fourth pulse again clears the plume of the third pulse so that the fifth pulse can again contribute to the ablation process etc. For copper and a 210 fs pulse duration [24], aluminum and a 300 fs pulse duration [23], and brass and a 350 fs pulse duration [60], this oscillation seems to be damped.

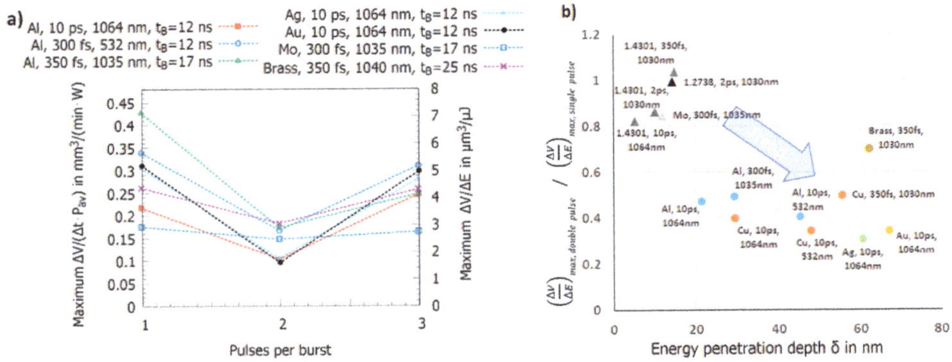

Figure 10. Maximum energy specific volumes for single, double, and triple pulses for (**a**) brass, aluminum, silver, gold, and molybdenum and (**b**) the ratio of the maximum energy specific volume of a double burst pulse and single pulses as a function of the corresponding energy penetration depth for different metals. The triangles denote metals where the energy specific volume of a double and triple pulse burst does not show a shielding effect for the double pulse burst followed by an increase in the energy specific volume for the third pulse within a triple pulse. Data taken from [19,23,24,60,128,129].

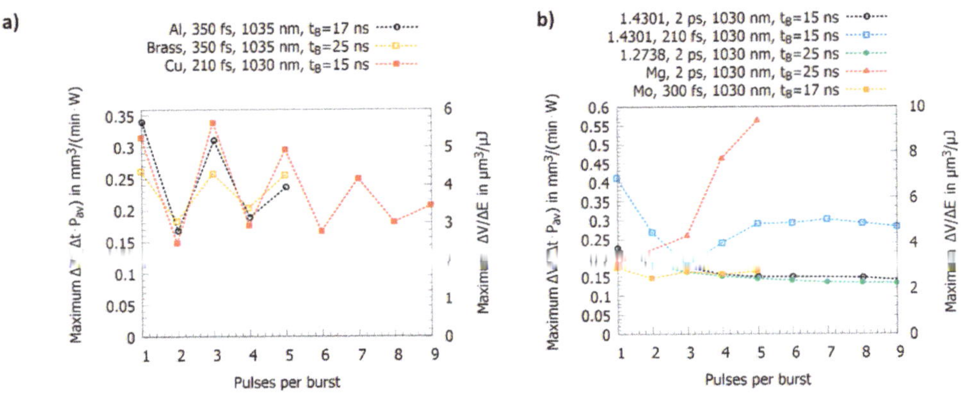

Figure 11. Maximum energy specific volumes as a function of the number of pulses per burst for (**a**) copper, brass, and aluminum as well as for (**b**) stainless steel, molybdenum, and magnesium alloy. Data extracted from [19,23,24,60,128,129].

In contrast to this oscillating behavior, this alternating behavior is not observed for steel 1.4301 (AISI 304) [19,24], steel 1.2738 [130], molybdenum [23], and magnesium (cf. Figure 11b). For steel and molybdenum, the maximum energy specific volume shows a tendency to slightly lower values when the number of pulses per burst is increased. Steel 1.4301 (AISI 304) machined with 210 fs pulses [24] shows an atypical behavior up to 4 pulses per burst, but these results were obtained by defocusing to vary the peak fluence. Hence, different effects cannot be distinguished, as has been explained before. For magnesium alloy [129], the threshold fluence and the energy penetration depth amounts to 0.06 J/cm^2 and 6.5 nm, respectively. Therefore, a similar behavior as for steel 1.4301 (AISI 304) could be expected, but, as can be seen, the maximum energy specific volume increases by about a factor of three when the number of pulses per burst is raised from one to five. This is in contrast to the other metals and is similar to the behavior of silicon [17], where the maximum energy specific volume also increases with the number of pulses per burst. For silicon, this increase of energy specific volume is mainly due to changes in absorptance due to multi-photon absorption and stable liquid surface layers (having a higher absorptance) during processing [17].

Recently, the behavior of stainless steel was investigated for pulses at a wavelength of 1030 nm and with pulse durations of 270 fs, 1 ps, and 10 ps for single pulses for up to 9 pulses per burst with an intra-burst delay of 15.4 ns. The results show that the energy specific volumes for peak fluences of 0.5 J/cm^2, 1.5 J/cm^2, and 2.5 J/cm^2 mainly depend on the pulse duration, but follow identical trends when the number of pulses per burst is increased. Depending on the pulse duration and the peak fluence, regimes where a melt film is formed leading to smooth surfaces can be identified [131]. Similar smoothing effects were already reported for steel 1.4301 (AISI 304) in [14,60] and for cobalt and titanium alloys in [78,132]. Neither for copper nor for brass could a smoothing effect be observed, and the surfaces only start to oxidize when they are machined with pulse bursts [14,60].

In contrast to double pulses, the theory behind triple pulse ablation still shows an ambiguous picture. To allow for a better understanding of the physical mechanisms taking place during processing with triple pulses, further investigations with varying intra-burst delays need to be performed.

2.5. Multi-Pulse Bursts with Intra-Burst Repetition Rates in the GHz Range

In 2016, a new type of laser emitting ultra-short burst pulses with intra-burst repetition rates in the GHz range, and, hence, with intra-burst delays of several nanoseconds and down to a few 100 ps, gained attraction for material processing due to a report showing that the efficiency of the ablation process was significantly improved for a variety of materials [15]. However, the reported physical mechanism influencing the ablation process, the "ablation cooling effect," appears highly questionable and has been partially disproven for metal processing. Since it can be mainly attributed to heat accumulation [133–135], the publication was the starting point for materials processing with a completely new class of laser systems emitting pulse bursts with intra-burst delays of several 100 ps or at intra-burst repetition rates of several GHz, which have since then been built and studied by various research groups. In general, it can be concluded that drilling processes are always more efficient than milling processes in this processing regime [135,136], which was explained by different melt flows in those two regimes [133]. Furthermore, the increase in energy specific volume is highly dependent on the time span of the used burst train and increases with longer time spans [22,136–139]. Moreover, the used inter-burst delay plays a crucial role. For short time delays (corresponding to higher repetition rates) between the burst trains, heat accumulation is also more pronounced and contributes to an increase in energy specific volume [112].

It has been reported by several groups that both the ablated volume per time $\Delta V/\Delta t$ and the energy specific volume $\Delta V/\Delta E$ can be increased by several factors when processing material with ultra-short burst pulses with intra-burst repetition rates in the GHz regime compared to single pulse operation. For the milling of copper, it was reported that the maximum energy specific volume $\Delta V/\Delta E_{max}$ can increase by a factor of three [135], whereas for steel it can increase by a factor of two when using GHz burst pulses instead of single pulses [112,135,137]. For the drilling of copper, it was reported that the maximum energy specific volume $\Delta V/\Delta E_{max}$ can increase by a factor of 3.5; for steel, it can increase by a factor of 4.6; and, for aluminum, it can increase by a factor of 5.8 when using GHz burst pulses instead of single pulses [136]. All these effects diminish and are less pronounced when during experimental design the spot diameters on the samples investigated are also changed for optimization [24].

To be able to account for different study designs, a comprehensive overview of data from different authors is given in Figure 12 (top) for laser milling using GHz laser sources. When using double pulses, the previously discussed shielding effect is dominant, and the maximum achievable energy specific volume drops by a factor of five for intra-burst delays in the range of several 100 ps. Furthermore, with the increasing number of burst pulses the decrease in maximum achievable energy specific volume drops even further and is suppressed by approximately 93% for steel when using 5 to 25 pulses in a pulse burst [23,24]. From around 30 pulses per burst the energy specific volume increases again, and, for several hundred or thousands of pulses per burst, it even increases above the value for single pulse ablation for both copper and steel. For a small number of pulses within a burst, a region of higher density in the interaction zone of the laser and the target develops, and the shielding effect is even more pronounced [134]. For a moderate number of pulses (several tens to hundred pulses), the ablation process is dominated by heat accumulation, allowing material to be removed in a gaseous state even for pulses with a fluence far below the ablation threshold (which is the case because the totally available laser pulse energy is principally split between many pulses within the burst) [133–135,140]. For a high numbers of pulses (several hundred to many thousand pulses) within a burst, the ablation process can be compared to ablation with pulses of nanosecond duration, resulting in higher energy specific volumes as well as a lowering of the surface quality due to melt expulsion, which indeed is the case for GHz laser ablation [64,135,136]. This simple but fair comparison is given in Figure 12 (bottom), where the maximum achievable energy specific volumes as a function of the time span of burst packages are compared to the energy specific volumes of ns and µs laser processes. It can be seen that the maximum energy specific volumes of GHz laser processes fully follow the ones of ns and µs lasers in the same time domain. This is not only the case for steel but also for copper (not displayed here). Therefore, it can be concluded that GHz processing is comparable to ns laser processing for pulses of the same time span for metals. Of course, more detailed studies need to be performed to gain a full view on this topic. Finally, it can be seen from the reviewed and summarized studies that the surface roughness shows a minimum for a low number of burst pulses (corresponding to short burst time spans), which can be significantly lower compared to single pulses [21,23,24,64,124,135,141–144]. For longer time spans and a higher number of pulses, heat accumulation highly dominates laser processing, leading to higher energy specific volumes as well as significantly higher roughness, which is also the case for longer pulses in the ns and µs regime due to the emerging occurrence of melting.

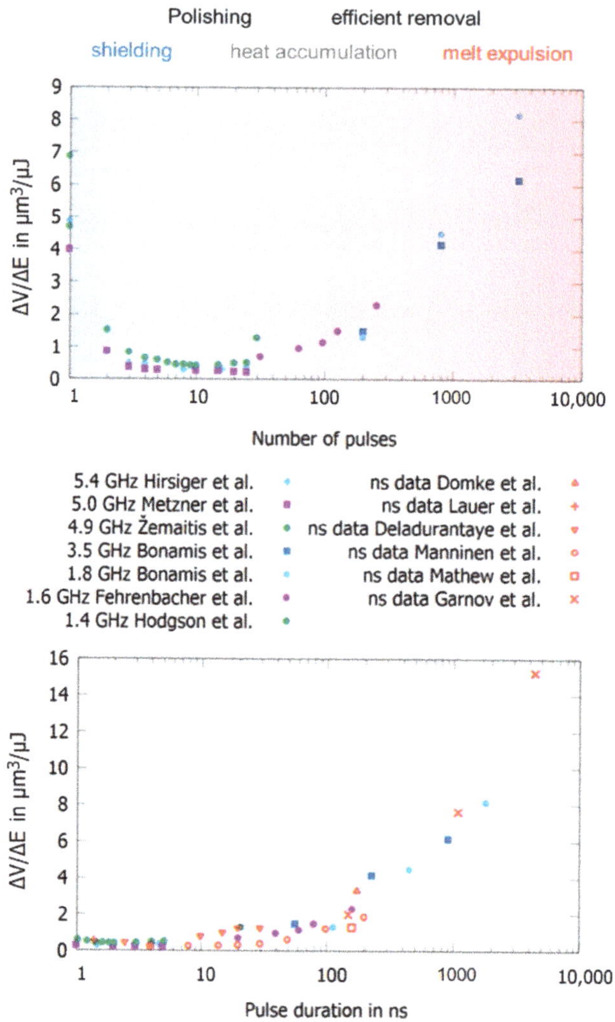

Figure 12. Maximum achievable energy specific volumes as a function of applied laser pulses within GHz bursts (**top**) and maximum energy specific volumes as a function of the duration of GHz bursts and durations of ns and µs pulses (**bottom**). Data from laser milling of stainless steel, data extracted from [21,23,24,64,98,124,135,141–147].

Beside materials processing with ultra-short burst pulses with intra-burst repetition rates in the MHz and GHz range, processing with THz intra-burst repetition rates (corresponding to delay times between subsequent pulses of several ps) is also a subject of investigation [20,148–152]. However, in this regime, matter reacts to excitation with subsequent pulses similar like to excitation with longer pulses in the same time domain. Beside a dependence of the incubation effect (a weakening of material) on the burst spacing [149,153], the material answer is similar when using multiple subsequent ultra-short pulses over a certain time span and when using a single pulse with a pulse duration of the same time span, e.g., a pulse burst with 10 pulses that are applied over a time span of 10 ps shows similar effects to a pulse with a 10 ps pulse duration. Hence, a differentiation of physical effects on these time scales is challenging. From the material processing point of view, the use of burst pulses with THz intra-burst repetition rates is less important but has found its way into the generation of particle beams and X-rays (cf. Section 3.5.3).

3. Applications Using Burst Pulses

In the following subsections, applications involving pulse burst processing of metals are summarized and discussed. The focus mainly lies on micromachining applications, while applications from other fields making use of pulse bursts are also summarized in the last subsection.

3.1. Punching and Drilling

Drilling with ultra-short pulsed laser radiation has been a widely used production technique for making precise holes in various materials for a long time. A large number of laser pulses and a sufficiently high pulse energy is typically required to produce blind and through holes with high aspect ratios of 1:10 or more. The reason lies in the nature of the drilling process, where, in general, the irradiated area increases with drilling depth and pulse number, and, hence, the fluence within the bore holes decreases over time [74,154,155]. Principally, this requirement contradicts the splitting of pulse energy during burst processing to allow for an improvement in laser drilling processes in terms of drilling time and, hence, efficiency. The same holds for an increase in the pulse repetition rate, since shielding effects can be even more pronounced due to lateral confinement of the ablation cloud. Laser drilling involves interaction of the radiation with ablation products from previous laser pulses. Shorter time spans between successive laser pulses intensify this effect [57,61].

There have been comparatively few studies on the influence of bursts in laser drilling with ultra-short pulses. A particularly early investigation into percussion drilling with MHz bursts of aluminum showed advantages in terms of drilling time [156]. However, these advantages must be seen in the context of the repetition rates in the kHz range that were common at the time. The main advantage was therefore the higher number of pulses per time achieved by the burst, resulting in more ablated volume per time.

Interactions of burst pulses with the ablation products within bore holes were investigated diagnostically, whereas drilling glass was investigated by time-resolved imaging [157]. As the investigated material was not a metal, the observed effects are presumably very similar. Although there appeared to exist shielding effects of radiation within the bore hole, the holes obtained showed a more uniform geometry with smoother walls. Similar observations were made when drilling silicon [158], where processing with MHz burst resulted in fewer unwanted side channels and overall higher reproducibility of the hole shape. This is highly due to re-deposited material, leading to smoother surfaces.

In [159], the drilling of copper and aluminum was studied with double pulses, varying the inter-pulse delay from −90 ps to 90 ps. Here, the observed reduction in drilling speed in the case of using double pulses was attributed to shielding as well. This is clearly in contrast to the conclusions provided in [15], where much higher removal rates were reported for machining copper and silicon with GHz bursts. In [133], an attempt was made to reproduce these advantages, but significant melting was observed; so, as discussed before, GHz processing seems to have similarities with the use of nanosecond pulse durations. It was shown that the maximum energy specific volumes achievable when using a burst with 200 pulses at an intra-burst repetition rate of 1.76 GHz are almost identical when processing with a laser at a pulse duration of 100 ns for percussion drilling of copper, aluminum, and stainless steel [64,135].

A study about laser drilling of invar with ultra-short MHz and GHz bursts has shown an ambiguous picture. Depending on the sample thickness and intra-burst delay, slightly shorter drilling durations or even longer drilling durations were reported compared to drilling without bursts [137].

Most studies on laser drilling with ultra-short burst pulses show a rather minor influence on the drilling speed but an increased melt formation. With regard to the question of how far the special properties of bursts can be used to advantage in laser drilling, there is still a considerable need for research.

3.2. Scribing and Cutting

In several works, line scribing using bursts have been performed [22,133,135,151,160] with similar results. The removal rate using bursts is smaller, and the burr formation is increased compared to single pulses. These effects were confirmed by the simulations of Matsumota et al. [133]. Using a 10-pulse burst with an intra-burst delay of 16.7 ns (corresponding to an intra-burst repetition rate of 60 MHz) led to a decrease in the ablation depth of about 40% compared to single pulse operation using the same average power in the case of stainless steel [22]. The authors have attributed this decrease to plasma shielding, as the small ablation geometry (machining of deep trenches) does not allow a fast dissolution of the plasma between two pulses. In [160], a decrease in the removal rate for stainless steel (>15%) and copper (>5%) using bursts with an intra-burst delay of 1 ns (corresponding to an intra-burst repetition rate of 1 GHz) and different energy distributions was reported. Using a similar intra-burst delay of 1.13 ns (corresponding to an intra-burst repetition rate of 0.88 GHz), it was reported by Bonamis et al. that in certain conditions (high fluence and a pulse overlap higher than 70%) the grooves were refilled by molten material [135]. The same effect was also observed in line scribing using single pulse operation at a comparably high pulse repetition rate of 4.1 MHz [161]. Simulations confirm this phenomenon for GHz bursts [133]. It has also been shown that using a pulse burst consisting of 160 pulses with an intra-burst delay of 1.16 ns (corresponding to a frequency of 864 MHz) leads to a larger burr compared to single pulses [133].

Principally, no advantages in using ultra-short pulse bursts for line scribing has been reported in the literature so far. Further research is also needed to clarify the influence of pulse bursts in the field of precision cutting.

3.3. Surface Structures

3.3.1. Polishing/Smoothing

In ultra-short pulsed laser machining of some metals like steel and titanium, it is well known that in certain conditions bumpy surfaces can appear [29,162]. In most applications, these bumps usually need to be avoided.

As it was found by Bauer et al., those surfaces are created if the surface temperature is higher than about 600 °C before the next laser pulse impinges on the surface in case of stainless steel 1.4301 (AISI 304) [73]. Heat accumulation is the limiting factor for the productivity of laser processes where a good surface quality is required. Alternatively, heat accumulation can also be used as an advantage. Lickschat et al. [105] and Herrmann et al. [163] have shown a smoothing of cavities using pulse bursts. Nyenhuis et al. [142] and Michalowski et al. [143] have made the same observations and have further developed a smoothing process for stainless steel 1.4301 (AISI 304). Using GHz bursts with an intra-burst delay of 625 ps (corresponding to an intra-burst repetition rate of 1.6 GHz) and a fluence for each individual pulse below the threshold fluence, the heat input into the material can be utilized to create a small melt film that smoothens the bumpy surface (cf. Figure 13).

It has been found that high fluences lead to pores in the solidified melt films. Therefore, it is favorable to use more pulses in the burst, i.e., a burst of longer time span at lower fluences of the burst pulses. In comparison to a MHz burst (intra-burst delay of 12.5 ns), the smoothing using GHz bursts is much more energy efficient as the total fluence of the burst needed is about 2/3 smaller using such GHz bursts [142]. The low fluences used in the GHz burst processing lead to a very thin melt film which can also be used for polishing of microstructures without damaging them [142,143]. Using this kind of polishing process can lead to a surface roughness of S_a =0.13 µm and S_z = 3.4 µm [164]. Using an intra-burst delay of 200 ps (corresponding to a repetition rate of 5 GHz) Metzner et al. have shown a smoothing on stainless steel surfaces [21]. The bumpy surface created during single pulse engraving was smoothed using GHz bursts. The more layers with GHz bursts are applied to the surface, the smoother the surface gets. No bumps are present on the surface anymore after 20 overscans (scan levels), as can be seen in Figure 14. After 20 overscans, a surface roughness of $S_a = 0.1 \pm 0.05$ μm and $S_z = 1.3 \pm 0.3$ μm was measured.

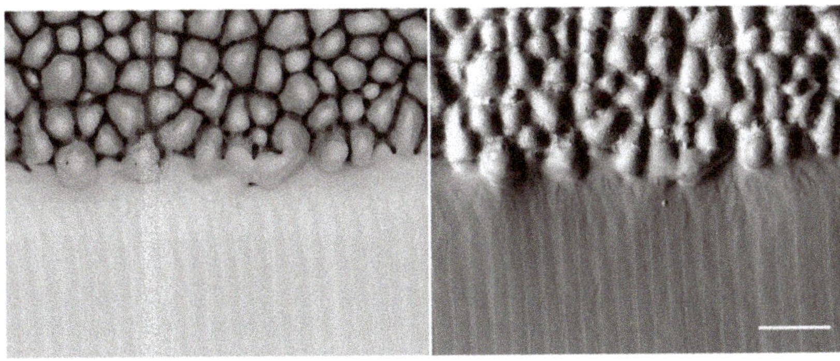

Figure 13. SEM images of a bumpy surface on 1.4301 (AISI 304) steel, where the lower part is polished using GHz bursts. The right-hand image shows the topological view. The length of the scale bar represents 40 μm. Reprinted from [142].

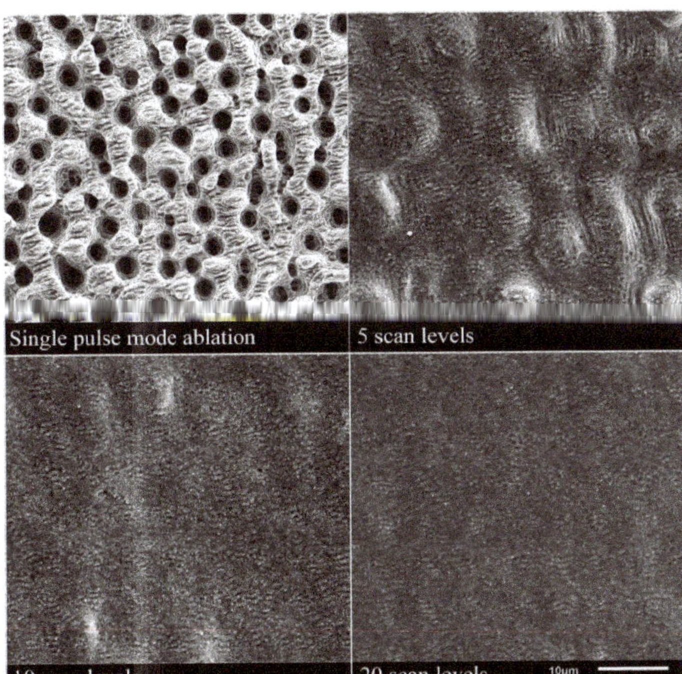

Figure 14. SEM images of surface structures on stainless steel. Top left: Surface structure, ablated in single pulse operation, a scan speed of 1.2 m/s, a pulse duration of 270 fs and 20 overscans (scan levels). The other SEM images visualize the structure after the surface treatment in the GHz burst mode with four pulses per burst, a pulse duration of 270 fs and a variation of the overscans (scan levels) between 5 and 20. Reprinted from [21], Copyright 2020, with permission from Elsevier.

To be able to use the maximum available pulse energy provided by a laser system, engraving processes can be done using MHz bursts instead of single pulse operation, followed by a GHz-polishing step. For such multi-step strategies, surface roughness values of $S_a = 0.15 \pm 0.02$ µm and $S_z = 1.1 \pm 0.1$ µm have been measured. Again, after 20 overscans, the surface was found to be smoothed [21]. The advantage of processes combining MHz and GHz bursts is the higher productivity, i.e., smaller cycle time during engraving processes.

In contrast, Brenner et al. used MHz bursts with an intra-burst delay t_B of 12.5 ns (corresponding to a repetition rate of 80 MHz) at a base repetition rate f_{rep} of 2 MHz (inter-burst delay of 500 ns) instead of GHz bursts to polish the surface of conducted hot-working steel (1.2738) [130]. The achieved surface roughness amounted to $S_a = 0.21$ µm and $S_z = 3.65$ µm. Osbild et al. analyzed the polishing process using MHz bursts in more detail [128]. It was found that using a low number of repetitions in the polishing process is favorable to achieve a melt pool depth of only 1 to 3 µm. By doing so, the roughness can be reduced also on small and fine structures.

On a CoCrMo alloy, 3 to 5-pulse bursts with an intra-burst delay of 12.5 ns (corresponding to a repetition rate of 80 MHz) may lead to a much smoother surface compared to single pulse operation [78]. The surface roughness for single pulses increases with the structure depth, i.e., with increasing number of overscans, ranging from 300 nm for 10 overscans to 2.7 µm for 399 overscans. Using pulse bursts the smoothing effect can be maintained regardless of the structure depth. In another study, Metzner et al. used bursts with up to 8 pulses and an intra-burst delay of 12.5 ns (corresponding to a repetition rate of 80 MHz) and a repetition rate of 100 kHz (inter-burst delay of 10 µs) to reduce the surface roughness on cobalt and titanium alloys below $S_a = 100$ nm [132]. Depending on the material and the used fluence of an individual pulse in the burst, different numbers of pulses in the burst (in general 6–8 pulses) need to be applied. Using a higher number of pulses in the burst also helps to avoid the formation of nanoscopic cavities on the surface as shown in Figure 15 for cobalt alloy. The same also can be observed for titanium [132].

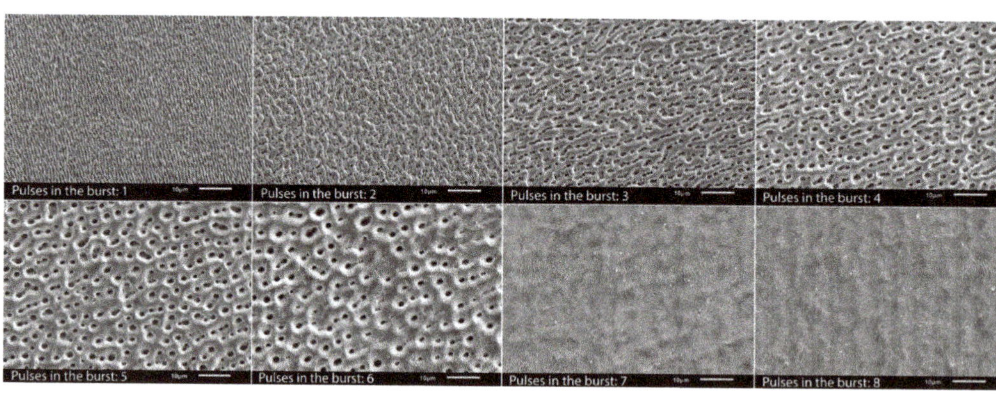

Figure 15. SEM images of the irradiated cobalt alloy surface as a function of the number of pulses in the burst at a fluence of 0.5 J/cm^2 per pulse.

Recently, Sassmannshausen et al. introduced the possibility of surface smoothing by continuous surface melting using a laser emitting ultra-short pulses at a pulse repetition rate of 49 MHz (corresponding to an inter-pulse delay of 20.4 ns). This extreme case on one hand represents classical repetitive processing at a constant repetition rate, while on the other hand it can be interpreted as a very long burst pulse in the MHz regime. This continuous processing shows the capability of long, finely tuned burst pulses. It was shown that the surface roughness could be lowered by this polishing process to around 80 nm. While also an oxidation of the surface was introduced, this value belongs to the smallest ever achieved by laser surface processing [165].

In a comprehensive study, Metzner et al. compared the smoothing effects using a MHz burst, a GHz burst, and a biburst (a combination of MHz and GHz bursts) on stainless steel [131]. It was found that the smoothing process shows a higher stability and reproducibility when using GHz bursts compared to MHz bursts. A surface roughness of $S_a < 200$ nm was measured for processing with the GHz burst in optimal conditions. It should be mentioned that not only metals but also polymers can be polished applying pulse bursts with an intra-burst delay of 400 ps (corresponding to an intra-burst repetition rate of 2.5 GHz) [166].

3.3.2. Coloring

Laser coloring was intensively investigated for ns pulse processing where oxide layers are formed [167–170]. Alternatively, ultra-short pulsed lasers can be used. This is mainly realized by the following approaches: utilizing laser-induced periodic surface structures (LIPSS) as diffraction gratings to produce angle-sensitive colors [171,172] and creating tempering colors by heating up the surface [173], which results in angle-independent colors. Another way is to create micro- and nanostructures on the surface to obtain a certain color on the surface [171,174]. The coloring strategy using nanostructures was further developed by Guay et al. [175]. Plasmonic colors are excited from metallic nanoparticles and nanostructures, which are re-deposited after the laser irradiation leads to angle-independent colors on silver surfaces (cf. Figure 16).

Figure 16. Photograph of a colored silver coin (height approx. 1 cm); detailed view on the right-hand side. Reproduced under the terms of a Creative Commons Attribution 4.0 International License (https://creativecommons.org/licenses/by/4.0/ (accessed on 31 May 2021)) [175]. Copyright 2017, the authors, published by Springer Nature.

It was shown that by using pulse bursts with an intra-burst delay of 12.8 ns (corresponding to an intra-burst repetition rate of 82 MHz), higher quality colors can be generated on silver compared to a single pulse operation. The authors quantified the colors using a Chroma meter (CR-241, Konica Minolta) in the CIELCH color space. The Chroma is a parameter used to measure the colorfulness of an object. The Chroma is increased by about 50% over the full color range when processing with burst pulses compared to colors produced with single pulses [176]. The increase in Chroma using bursts can be explained by the simultaneous creation of LIPSS onto which the nanoparticles are re-deposited, compared to single pulses where no LIPSS are formed (cf. Figure 17c). The increase in the surface area created by the LIPSS and the field enhancement in these crevices would cause higher absorption, explaining the more vibrant colors unique to the burst process. In addition, a larger color palette can be created using pulse bursts. By using the FlexBurst^{TM} technology of the laser manufacturer Lumentum (formerly Time-Bandwidth Products, Zurich, Switzerland) [177], it is possible to fade out some pulses in the burst, i.e., adapting the intra-burst delay in steps of 12.8 ns and also adapting the pulse energy of every individual pulse within the burst. This modification of the bursts leads to a further increase in Chroma (Figure 17a) and a larger color palette (Figure 17b) [178]. The developed strategy was applied on the metals: gold, silver, copper, and aluminum.

3.3.3. Laser-Induced Periodic Surface Structures (LIPSS)

Laser-induced periodic surface structures, often also called ripples, can be applied on almost every material surface using polarized light. Usually, linearly polarized light is used to create such structures. Applications for LIPSS can be found in various fields. The surfaces appearing in nature (colored surfaces, anti-reflection surfaces, hydrophobic surfaces, wet and dry adhesion, and friction reduction) can be imitated [179] or the melt flow resistance in injection molding of polypropylene can be reduced [180]. LIPSS can be replicated as well on plastic parts [181,182]. The phenomena behind the creation of ripples is discussed in several publications [183–186]. In the last years, multiple investigations using pulse bursts have been performed with different polarizations of the pulses in double pulses [187], different wavelengths in double pulses [188], and with variations in the energy distribution [189,190]. In addition, the number of pulses in the burst has been varied by up to 32 pulses [191].

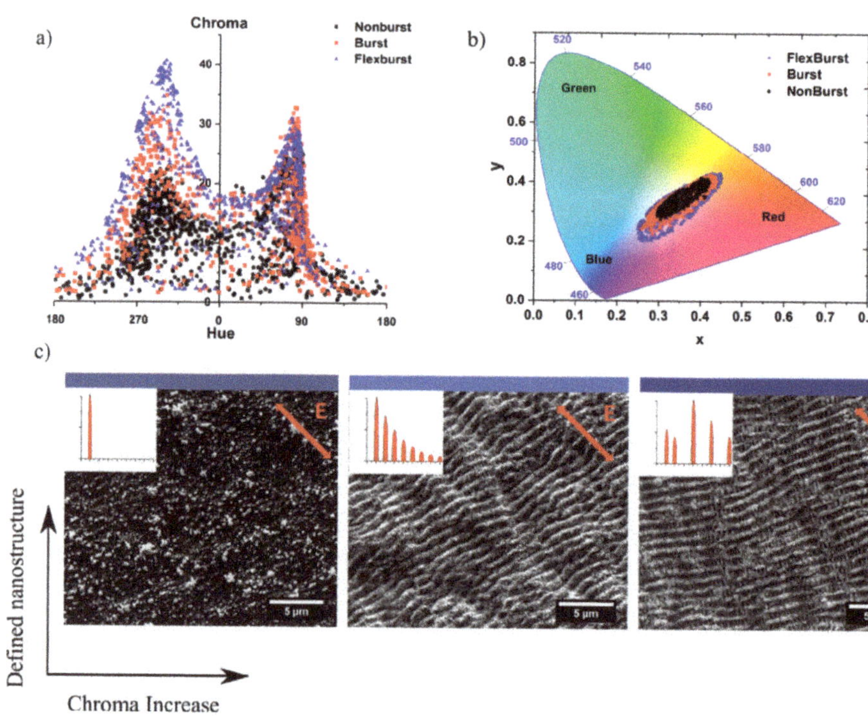

Figure 17. Colors and corresponding topographies on a silver surface. (**a**) Graph of Chroma versus hue comparing colors obtained after single pulse operation (•), burst (■), and flexburst (▲) coloring. (**b**) CIE *xy* chromaticity diagram comparing single pulse operation (•), burst (■), and flexburst (▲) coloring. (**c**) SEM images of blue surfaces produced using single pulse operation (**left**), burst (**middle**), and flexburst (**right**) coloring. The hue was more or less the same for all squares ($H \approx 295°$), whereas the Chroma values equalled 22.3, 31.2, and 39.44. Nanostructures can be observed on the surfaces for burst and flexburst processing. The relative energy distribution of the burst pulses and the orientation of the electric field are given as insets. Reprinted from [178], Copyright Wiley-VCH GmbH. Reproduced with permission.

Combining two time-delayed ultra-short pulses with different polarization states can generate different structure types than conventional LIPSS, which are formed parallel to the polarization direction for linear polarization [187]. Figure 18 shows the variations of the surface structures produced by double pulses with delays of up to 10 ps (corresponding to an intra-burst repetition rate of 100 GHz) and either cross-polarized (XP) or counter-rotating circular-polarized (CP) pulses.

Increasing the number of pulses in the burst from 2 to 32 pulses while maintaining the intra-burst delay of 1.5 ps (corresponding to a repetition rate of 666 GHz) and linear polarization leads to an increase in the spatial period of the low spatial frequency LIPSS on stainless steel, while the depth of the LIPSS remains almost constant [191]. It should be mentioned that the spatial period of multiple pulses is always larger than for single pulse operation. Increasing the intra-burst delay from 1.5 ps to 24 ps using double pulses also leads to an increase in the spatial frequency, while the depth of the structures decreases drastically. This decrease is attributed to shielding effects taking place for delays larger than about 6 ps [191].

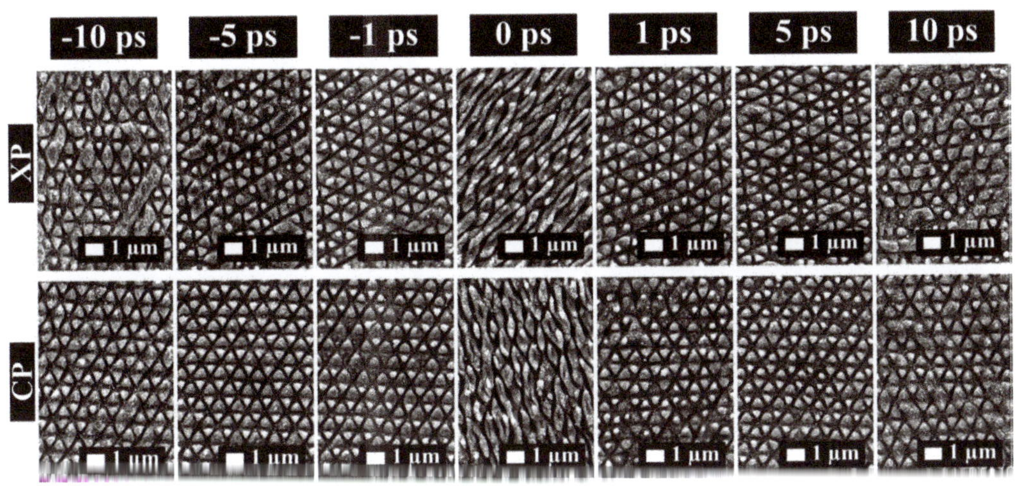

Figure 18. SEM images of the surface structures on stainless steel irradiated with two different polarization configurations: cross-polarized double pulses (XP) and counter-rotating circular-polarized pulses (CP). The rest of the process parameters were fixed: 10 pulses per spot, hatch distance of 1 μm, and a fluence of 0.1 J/cm^2. The delay of the two pulses was varied as indicated on top of the images. Reprinted from [187], copyright 2019, with permission from Elsevier.

Using cross-polarized light instead of the parallel polarization for all pulses in the burst will lead to similar structures, as shown in Figure 18 [192]. Comparing the wettability of triangular structures produced with a four-pulse burst at an intra-burst delay of 1.5 ps (corresponding to an intra-burst repetition rate of 666 GHz) with normal LIPSS created with a 16-pulse burst and an identical intra-burst delay shows only a difference in the evolution of the water contact angle over time, known as the aging effect, for the two different surface structures. The final water contact angle, which is reached after about eight weeks, was principally the same. It can be concluded that not only does the surface structures have an influence on the wettability but also the surface chemistry [192].

Another approach is to combine two cross-polarized pulses with different fluences. The LIPSS' orientation on a titanium substrate can be influenced by the fluence of the delayed pulse and is in good agreement with the direction obtained by the vector sum of the laser fields. For example, using two pulses with polarizations perpendicular to each other with the same pulse energy, the LIPSS are formed at an angle of 45 degrees, while when one pulse has half the energy of the other pulse, LIPSS are formed at an angle of

24.5 degrees [190]. A similar setup but with equal polarization states for both pulses and a fixed intra-burst delay of 160 fs (corresponding to a repetition rate of 6.25 THz) was used by Hashida et al. [189]. The fluence of the first pulse was always below the threshold fluence, whereas the fluence of the delayed pulse was above the threshold fluence. It was shown that the laser fluence of the first pulse plays an important role for the spacing of the LIPSS. The higher the fluence of the first pulse, the larger the spacing becomes. Comparing the grating spacing produced with double pulses with the one produced with single pulses with the same total energy shows no difference [189]. Larger intra-burst delays of 20 ns (corresponding to a repetition rate of 50 MHz) have been used by Wang et al. [193] together with a higher number of pulses. Depending on the used fluence of an individual pulse in the burst, either low spatial frequency LIPSS (LSFL) or high spatial frequency LIPSS (HSFL) are formed on the surface. For a fixed total fluence of the burst of 0.25 J/cm^2, the formation of HSFL is enhanced by using three or four pulses in the burst, as the fluence of each pulse in the burst becomes smaller. Increasing the total fluence will lead to microgrooves, nanoholes, and melt formations in the central region of the machined grooves, sometimes referred to as "micro-hills" [194].

The use of double pulses with different wavelength (800 nm and 400 nm), fluences, and intra-burst delays and the use of cross-polarization states was investigated by Hashida et al. [188]. It was found that the fundamental pulse (800 nm) is responsible for the LIPSS creation and its orientation, while the second harmonic pulse will optimize the uniformity of the LIPSS if intra-burst delays of 0 to 2 ps are used. For delayed pulses (first pulse with 400 nm and the second pulse with 800 nm), the period and the direction of the ripples can be changed [188].

Experiments investigating the influence of double pulses onto the LIPSS formation have also been performed on semiconductors and glasses but are not further discussed in this article [195,196].

3.4. Milling

The basic benefit of the burst mode for milling applications is illustrated by the following consideration: milling applications are generally realized with galvanometric scanners offering maximum marking speeds of a few tens of m/s [197]. The pulse to pulse distance, i.e., the pitch, is defined by the repetition rate of the laser and the marking speed of the scanner. Thus, the maximum scanner speed limits the applicable laser repetition rate if a certain minimum value of the pitch has to be kept. Therefore, often pulse energies and peak fluences far above the optimum value are used to take advantage of the full average power of the used laser system. At this high fluence, the energy specific volume is significantly lower than its maximum value, as illustrated in Figure 19a, for single pulses having a peak fluence of 8 times the optimum value. Dividing this energy into n sub-pulses, i.e., into an n-pulse burst, reduces the fluence of these sub-pulses and shifts the energy specific volume for each pulse within the burst nearer to its optimum value (cf. Figure 19a). Additionally, following Figure 5, the ablation process is moved from the phase explosion into the spallation regime and an improved surface quality can be expected. It has to be noted that the heat accumulation is only slightly affected. Calculations for steel 1.4301 (AISI 304) [14] following the analytical model presented in [73] reveal that the temperatures just before the next burst sequence impinges on the surface do not differ between a four-pulse burst and single pulses with four times higher pulse energy (cf. Figure 19b).

The machining of stainless steel in single pulse operation is only possible in the low fluence regime, as the hole and spike formation limit the surface quality and therefore the productivity at higher fluences [14,198]. Using MHz bursts, the fluence of an individual pulse in the burst can be above the optimal fluence, as the bursts help to avoid this hole formation and therefore are more beneficial [60]. As shown in Section 2.3., machining using a triple pulse on copper can be more efficient than using single pulse operation. A milling result using this strategy is shown in Figure 20.

It should be mentioned here that, to optimize the productivity in ultra-short pulsed laser milling, not only the ablation process itself must be optimized but also the scan strategy. It has been shown that by using optimized scan speeds, the time for machining a certain geometry, e.g., a line, can be optimized in the case of galvanometer scanners [197]. The given values of the energy specific volume are for 100% laser-on time, which is not true for galvanometer-based scanning using the sky-writing mode, which is used to obtain the best machining quality, i.e., no over-engraving near the edges [199]. The optimization of the energy specific volume alone makes no sense if the duty cycle of the scanner is near zero in the final application.

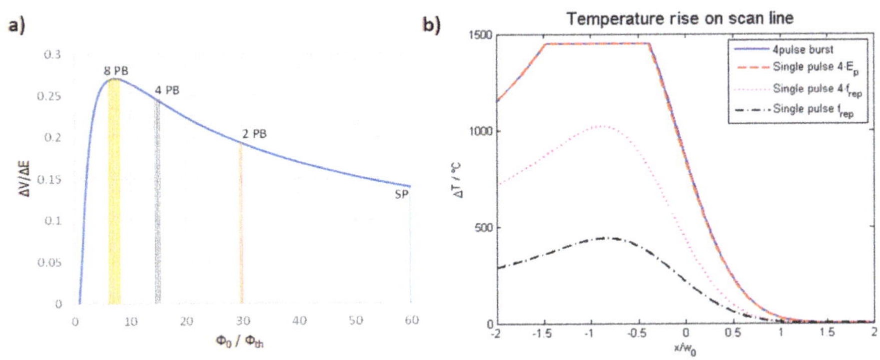

Figure 19. (**a**) Normalized energy specific volume as a function of the normalized peak fluence and the corresponding energy specific volumes for a total fluence of 60 times the threshold fluence for single pulses, double pulses, and bursts consisting of 4 and 8 pulses. (**b**) Temperature rise on the scan line just before the next burst sequence impinges on the surface for a 4-pulse burst on steel 1.4301 (AISI 304) with 12 W average power, 500 kHz repetition rate, and a pitch of 8 µm. The temperature rise is plotted for a burst with 4 pulses (blue line), single pulses with 4 times higher pulse energy (red dashed line), single pulses with 4 times higher repetition rate of 2 MHz (magenta dotted line), and single pulses having the same energy at a repetition rate of 500 kHz (black dash-dotted line). The plateau denotes the region where melting happens. The distance x is given in units of the spot radius w, and, as the previous pulse has struck the surface at $x = -0.5 \cdot w$, the maximum temperatures appears around this region. (**b**) was reprinted from [14].

The former considerations are based on the assumption that only the peak fluence of the single pulses in a burst defines the energy specific volume and that the latter does not depend on the number of pulses per burst. This is definitively not the case, as, e.g., shown in [14,130] for stainless steel and as discussed in Sections 2.3 and 2.4, as the number of pulses as well as the intra-burst delay affect the energy specific volume. Further, to compare situations with equal average power single pulse operation, a repetition rate f_{rep} should be compared with a n-pulse burst with a repetition rate of f_{rep}/n. In Figure 21, based on the results for stainless steel 1.4301 (AISI 304) machined with 10 ps pulse duration at a wavelength of 1064 nm and a spot radius of 15.5 µm [14], the energy specific volumes as well as the removal rates are shown for bursts consisting of eight, four, two, and one pulses at corresponding repetition rates of 200 kHz, 402 kHz, 804 kHz, and 1610 kHz, respectively. Up to an average power of about 7.5 W, the energy specific volume for single pulses at a repetition rate of 1610 kHz exceeds that of the burst with eight pulses, and the corresponding removal rates are higher for single pulses. For higher average powers, the situation changes, and bursts with eight pulses become more efficient, while the removal rate exceeds that of all other presented situations. These effects could eventually be caused by the smoothing effect and the reduction in the surface structures as shown in Figures 13–15.

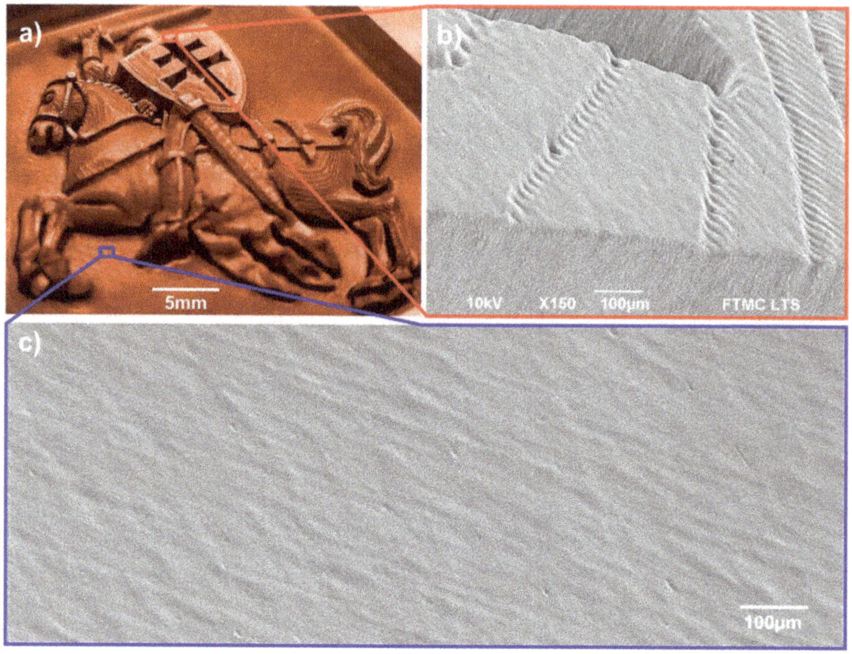

Figure 20. Example of efficient laser milling. (**a**) Optical image of the coat of arms of Lithuania milled in a copper plate. (**b**) SEM image of laser-milled surface illustrating layer-by-layer removal. (**c**) SEM image of the bottom surface of the laser-milled cavity. Laser parameters—triple pulse, laser wavelength of 1030 nm, burst repetition rate 300 kHz, intra-burst repetition rate of 64.5 MHz, and beam scanning speed of 1 m/s. Reproduced under the terms of a Creative Commons Attribution 4.0 International License, (https://creativecommons.org/licenses/by/4.0/ (accessed on 31 May 2021)) [18]. Copyright 2019, the authors, published by Springer Nature.

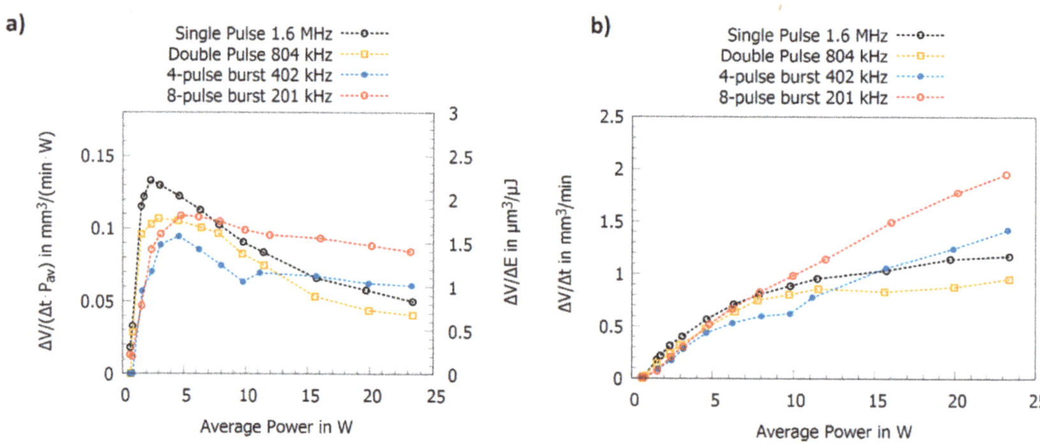

Figure 21. (**a**) Energy specific volumes and (**b**) removal rates for steel 1.4301 (AISI 304) machined with pulses of 10 ps pulse duration with a wavelength of 1064 nm and a spot radius of 15.5 μm. To guarantee identical peak fluence of the individual pulses, the laser repetition rate was 1610 kHz for single pulses, 804 kHz for the double pulse burst, 402 kHz for the burst with four pulses, and 200 kHz for the burst with eight pulses. Data extracted from [14].

The situation may change when higher repetition rates are used for single pulses, e.g., by using polygon line scanners, which can now achieve marking speeds of several 100 m/s [200,201]. However, the scale-up process is limited either by heat accumulation, especially for steel, and/or shielding effects discussed in the double pulse section, as shown in [202].

Therefore, for concrete applications, an optimization of processing strategies with respect to the number of pulses per burst, the laser repetition rate, the spot size, and the machining quality is demanded to find the best-suited parameters. Dual process strategies using different parameter sets, e.g., one for roughing with high energies and high removal rates followed by one with pulse bursts, either in the MHz or even the GHz regime used for finishing/polishing are very promising. For example, a dual process strategy of alternating GHz bursts and conventional processing was presented to achieve a good surface quality of machined pockets while decreasing the processing time by a factor of two, as illustrated in Figure 22.

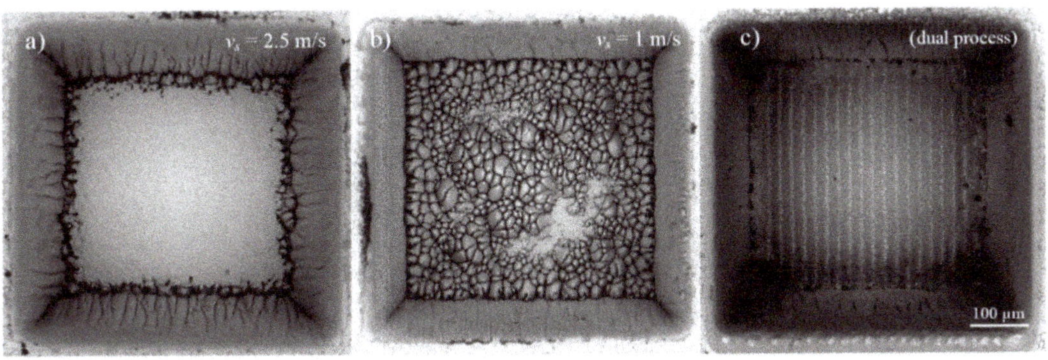

Figure 22. SEM images of milled squares with a scan speed of (**a**) 2.5 m/s and (**b**) 1 m/s at a conventional process and 1 m/s for (**c**) using the dual process strategy. The surface roughness of the inner ground was $S_a = 0.23$ µm and $S_z = 4.1$ µm for (**a**), but was not measurable because of high occurrence of bumps for (**b**); and $S_a = 0.13$ µm and $S_z = 3.4$ µm for (**c**). Although the scanning speed equaled that of (**b**), the edge and surface quality was the best and just the line spacing during polishing limited the relatively high S_z value. Reproduced from ref. [illegible] with permission from Japan Laser Processing Society.

Brenner et al. [203] demonstrated another interesting application by combining ablation processing in burst mode followed by a cleaning and an additional polishing process for large-format 3D mold tools. Another new approach of combining MHz and GHz bursts, the bi-burst mode, was recently presented in [24,131], but, in milling applications for copper and steel, this mode did not reveal higher removal rates compared to single pulses. In the field of laser burst processing, a comparison of literature data regarding roughness and energy specific volumes for different metals is a challenging task due to different study designs. For a comprehensive comparison of data for at least the metals of copper and stainless steel, the reader may refer to [24].

To conclude, the combination of different processes taking benefit of the advantages of each milling process to obtain optimum quality and machining time when using MHz and GHz bursts is a widely open field and still demands further research.

3.5. Further Applications

Besides the micromachining of metals in the industrial environment, pulse bursts are also used in several other fields. As a completion, these topics are briefly introduced in the following subsections.

3.5.1. Laser-Ablative Space Propulsion

Another possible application of ultra-short laser pulses is the propulsion of either space vessels or space debris. When irradiating material and inducing ablation, the sample experiences a small force in the range of nN or even μN. The ablated material serves as propellant material. This force can be used as thrust to either stabilize and correct the orbits of space vessels, such as satellites, or to decelerate space debris in order to clean the earth's orbit [204–210]. Recently, it was shown that using ultra-short double pulses can give added value to this specific application. When using double pulses, material is pushed back to the initial surface. It was shown that, on the one hand, the measured thrust increases by a factor of two when using a double pulse instead of a single pulse of the same total energy (or using the same average power for processing) [114]. On the other hand, since the material is pushed back and can be used as propellant again, the thrust per ablated mass increases by a factor of three, leading to a more efficient propulsion and propellant conservation at the same time [114].

3.5.2. Laser-Induced Breakdown Spectroscopy

Since ablated material is able to shield subsequent laser pulses, a specific technique allowing the characterization of matter, laser-induced breakdown spectroscopy, can profit from the atomization of the shielding matter due to the emittance of characteristic spectra. LIBS relies on spectra emitted from the vapour and plasma created after a laser pulse hits a material surface. Either the occurrence or the intensity of specific characteristic emission lines as well as the ratios of such lines is investigated to gain information about the material. This characterization technique principally goes back to the early years of the laser in the 1960s after the first demonstration of Q-Switch lasers, and, until the end of the 20th century, it was basically performed using lasers with nanosecond pulse durations [211–213]. In 1998, the first LIBS measurements were reported using ultra-short pulsed lasers [214], and it was found that the ablation process itself and the atom excitation is more reproducible for fs than for ns pulses [215]. Hence, less energy is needed for excitation, which is crucial for the characterization of specific samples in order to keep the destruction of those limited, e.g., when examining paintings [216–218] or explosives [219–221]. Additionally, the sensitivity is higher when using fs lasers [215]. Several summarizing papers can be found in the literature regarding the single pulse fs-LIBS technique [222–224]. Signal enhancement of the observed spectra can be obtained when using double pulses or multiple burst pulses [7,91,223,225,226], since the atomistic and plasma excitation and resulting temperatures are much higher compared to single pulses, as has been discussed before. While material processing scientists may suffer from ablation suppression when using double pulses, spectroscopists look forward to the enhanced excitation of matter due to the atomization of the shielding material.

3.5.3. Generation of Particle Beams and X-rays

Ultra-short laser pulses can also be used for the generation of beams consisting of particles such as protons, electrons, and heavy ions as well as X-rays [227–237] due to the excitation of matter and the generation of high-energy plasmas. The range of radiation that can be generated is already extensive, but the range of applications is even wider and includes medical applications in radiology and radiotherapy [227,238–240]. Moreover, characterization of matter can be performed using a variety of investigation methods based on particle beams [233,235,236]. Several aspects, such as generated intensity, quality and purity of the spectra, as well as well-defined energies of the created radiation, are important for such applications and rely highly on the correct excitation of matter.

Double pulses (sometimes referred to as pre-pulses in this specific field of particle science) allow a specific manipulation of the excitation states of warm matter. The pulse delays lie in the range of the pulse duration (several 10 to 100 fs) and up to several ps and allow the energy and spectrum of highly charged silver ions [241], the energy and spectrum of created protons [231,242], and the spectrum of created X-rays to be tuned [243].

4. Conclusions

Metal processing using ultra-short burst pulses has been an emerging field in laser processing in the past decade and is still a subject for further investigation. In this review article, the physical mechanisms involved during laser burst processing were summarized. Several aspects such as the shielding of radiation, the re-deposition of material, enhanced absorptance, and heat accumulation have to be considered when designing ablation processes as the intra-burst delay is shortened and the number of pulses within bursts is increased. Although the occurring phenomena are widely understood for double pulses, the involved phenomena being able to explain the measured removal rates and energy specific volumes for triple and multi-pulse burst ablation for different metals are not understood to a large extent. Therefore, research in this field is still needed.

Re-deposition of material can be utilized for surface polishing when using burst pulses in the MHz regime for processing. It allows a smoothing of material surfaces with a low number of burst pulses due to re-deposition of material in the liquid state. For higher pulse numbers within a burst, heat accumulation enhances this effect and can lead to stable melt layers on the surface during processing. If the intra-burst repetition rate is increased to several GHz or more, heat accumulation effects can be utilized to smooth the surface (for lower pulse energies) and to enhance ablation (for higher pulse energies) in the sense that it becomes as effective as ns laser processing. The increase in ablated volume per energy and per time is accompanied by a higher surface roughness, which fits the effects known from ns laser ablation.

The occurring physical mechanisms allow a variety of innovative applications, including surface smoothing, plasmonic coloring of surfaces, and, in general, an optimum distribution of energy in order to completely utilize the average power of ultra-short pulsed lasers. The future belongs to laser systems that allow a variety of burst pulse combinations with intra-burst repetition rates in the MHz and the GHz regimes, allowing a realization of combined processes on the machined workpiece.

Author Contributions: Conceptualization, D.J.F.; writing—original draft preparation, D.J.F., B.J., A.M. and B.N.; writing—review and editing, D.J.F., B.J., A.M. and B.N.; visualization, D.J.F. All authors have read and agreed to the published version of the manuscript.

Funding: This research received no external funding.

Institutional Review Board Statement: Not applicable.

Informed Consent Statement: Not applicable.

Data Availability Statement: No new data were created or analyzed in this study. Data sharing is not applicable to this article.

Acknowledgments: The authors thank Hizniye Isabella Boga for proofreading of the manuscript.

Conflicts of Interest: The authors declare no conflict of interest.

References

1. Negel, J.-P.; Voss, A.; Ahmed, M.A.; Bauer, D.; Sutter, D.; Killi, A.; Graf, T. 11 kW average output power from a thin-disk multipass amplifier for ultrashort laser pulses. *Opt. Lett.* **2013**, *38*, 5442–5445. [CrossRef] [PubMed]
2. Negel, J.-P.; Loescher, A.; Bauer, D.; Sutter, D.; Killi, A.; Ahmed, M.A.; Graf, T. Second Generation Thin-Disk Multipass Amplifier Delivering Picosecond Pulses with 2 kW of Average Output Power. In *Advanced Solid State Lasers, Proceedings of the Lasers Congress 2016 (ASSL, LSC, LAC), Boston, MA, USA, 30 October–3 November 2016*; The Optical Society of America: Washington, DC, USA, 2016; p. ATu4A.5.
3. Nubbemeyer, T.; Kaumanns, M.; Ueffing, M.; Gorjan, M.; Alismail, A.; Fattahi, H.; Brons, J.; Pronin, O.; Barros, H.G.; Major, Z.; et al. 1 kW, 200 mJ picosecond thin-disk laser system. *Opt. Lett.* **2017**, *42*, 1381–1384. [CrossRef] [PubMed]
4. Gaida, C.; Gebhardt, M.; Heuermann, T.; Stutzki, F.; Jauregui, C.; Limpert, J. Ultrafast thulium fiber laser system emitting more than 1 kW of average power. *Opt. Lett.* **2018**, *43*, 5853–5856. [CrossRef]

5. Schnitzler, C.; Mans, T.G.; Dolkemeyer, J.; Dittmann, P. High Power, High Energy, and High Flexibility: Powerful Ultrafast Lasers Based on InnoSlab Technology. In *High-Power Laser Materials Processing: Applications, Diagnostics, and Systems VIII, Proceedings of the SPIE LASE, 2019, San Francisco, CA, USA, 2–7 February 2019*; International Society for Optics and Photonics: Bellingham, WA, USA, 2019; p. 1091103.
6. Müller, M.; Aleshire, C.; Klenke, A.; Haddad, E.; Légaré, F.; Tünnermann, A.; Limpert, J. 104 kW coherently combined ultrafast fiber laser. *Opt. Lett.* **2020**, *45*, 3083–3086. [CrossRef] [PubMed]
7. Semerok, A.; Dutouquet, C. Ultrashort double pulse laser ablation of metals. *Thin Solid Films* **2004**, *453*, 501–505. [CrossRef]
8. Donnelly, T.; Lunney, J.G.; Amoruso, S.; Bruzzese, R.; Wang, X.; Ni, X. Double pulse ultrafast laser ablation of nickel in vacuum. *J. Appl. Phys.* **2009**, *106*, 013304. [CrossRef]
9. Povarnitsyn, M.E.; Itina, T.E.; Khishchenko, K.V.; Levashov, P.R. Suppression of Ablation in Femtosecond Double-Pulse Experiments. *Phys. Rev. Lett.* **2009**, *103*, 195002. [CrossRef] [PubMed]
10. Povarnitsyn, M.E.; Fokin, V.B.; Levashov, P.R.; Itina, T.E. Molecular dynamics simulation of subpicosecond double-pulse laser ablation of metals. *Phys. Rev. B* **2015**, *92*, 174104. [CrossRef]
11. Hartmann, C.; Gillner, A.; Aydin, U.; Noll, R.; Fehr, T.; Gehlen, C.; Poprawe, R. Investigation on laser micro ablation of metals using ns-multi-pulses. *J. Physics Conf. Ser.* **2007**, *59*, 440–444. [CrossRef]
12. Hu, W.; Shin, Y.C.; King, G. Modeling of multi-burst mode pico-second laser ablation for improved material removal rate. *Appl. Phys. A* **2009**, *98*, 407–415. [CrossRef]
13. Hernandez-Rueda, J.; Siegel, J.; Galvan-Sosa, M.; De La Cruz, A.R.; Solis, J. Surface structuring of fused silica with asymmetric femtosecond laser pulse bursts. *J. Opt. Soc. Am. B* **2013**, *30*, 1352–1356. [CrossRef]
14. Neuenschwander, B.; Kramer, T.; Lauer, B.; Jaeggi, B. Burst Mode with Ps- and Fs-Pulses: Influence on the Removal Rate, Surface Quality, and Heat Accumulation. In *Laser Applications in Microelectronic and Optoelectronic Manufacturing (LAMOM) XX, Proceedings of the SPIE LASE, San Francisco, CA, USA, 9–12 February 2015*; SPIE: Bellingham, WA, USA, 2015; Volume 9350, p. 93500U.
15. Kerse, C.; Kalaycıoglu, H.; Elahi, P.; Cetin, B.; Kesim, D.K.; Akcaalan, O.; Yavas, S.; Asik, M.D.; Oktem, B.; Hoogland, H.; et al. Ablation-cooled material removal with ultrafast bursts of pulses. *Nature* **2016**, *537*, 84–88. [CrossRef] [PubMed]
16. Jäggi, B.; Förster, D.J.; Weber, R.; Neuenschwander, B. Residual heat during laser ablation of metals with bursts of ultra-short pulses. *Adv. Opt. Technol.* **2018**, *7*, 175–182. [CrossRef]
17. Neuenschwander, B.; Jaeggi, B.; Foerster, D.J.; Kramer, T.; Remund, S. Influence of the burst mode onto the specific removal rate for metals and semiconductors. *J. Laser Appl.* **2019**, *31*, 022203. [CrossRef]
18. Zemaitis, A.; Gecys, P.; Barkauskas, M.; Raciukaitis, G.; Gedvilas, M. Highly-efficient laser ablation of copper by bursts of ultrashort tuneable (fs–ps) pulses. *Sci. Rep.* **2019**, *9*, 1–8. [CrossRef]
19. Bornschlegel, B.; Finger, J. In-Situ Analysis of Ultrashort Pulsed Laser Ablation with Pulse Bursts. *JLMN* **2019**, *14*, 88–94.
20. Gaudiuso, C.; Kämmer, H.; Dreisow, F.; Ancona, A.; Tünnermann, A.; Nolte, S. Ablation of Silicon with Bursts of Femtosecond Laser Pulses. In *Frontiers in Ultrafast Optics: Biomedical, Scientific, and Industrial Applications XVI, Proceedings of the SPIE LASE, San Francisco, CA, USA, 13–18 February 2016*; Heisterkamp, A., Herman, P.R., Meunier, M., Nolte, S., Eds.; SPIE: Bellingham, WA, USA, 2016; p. 974017.
21. Metzner, D.; Lickschat, P.; Weißmantel, S. High-quality surface treatment using GHz burst mode with tunable ultrashort pulses. *Appl. Surf. Sci.* **2020**, *531*, 147270. [CrossRef]
22. Hodgson, N.; Allegre, H.; Starodoumov, A.; Bettencourt, S. Femtosecond Laser Ablation in Burst Mode as a Function of Pulse Fluence and Intra-Burst Repetition Rate. *JLMN* **2020**, *15*. [CrossRef]
23. Hodgson, N.; Steinkopff, A.; Heming, S.; Allegre, H.; Haloui, H.; Lee, T.S.; Laha, M.; van Nunen, J. Ultrafast Laser Machining: Process Optimization and Applications. In *Laser Applications in Microelectronic and Optoelectronic Manufacturing (LAMOM) XXVI, Proceedings of the SPIE LASE, San Francisco, CA, USA, 6–12 March 2021*; SPIE: Bellingham, WA, USA, 2021; Volume 11673, p. 1167308.
24. Žemaitis, A.; Gaidys, M.; Gečys, P.; Barkauskas, M.; Gedvilas, M. Femtosecond laser ablation by bibursts in the MHz and GHz pulse repetition rates. *Opt. Express* **2021**, *29*, 7641–7653. [CrossRef]
25. Führa, B.; Russ, S.; Hammers-Weber, P.; Diego-Vallejo, D.; Kahmann, M.; Andreev, A.; Hesse, T. High precision drilling with ultra-short laser pulses. In Proceedings of the Lasers in Manufacturing Conference 2017, Munich, Germany, 26–29 June 2017.
26. Žemaitis, A.; Gaidys, M.; Brikas, M.; Gečys, P.; Raciukaitis, G.; Gedvilas, M. Advanced laser scanning for highly-efficient ablation and ultrafast surface structuring: Experiment and model. *Sci. Rep.* **2018**, *8*, 17376. [CrossRef]
27. Jaeggi, B.; Neuenschwander, B.; Meier, T.; Zimmermann, M.; Hennig, G. High Precision Surface Structuring with Ultra-Short Laser Pulses and Synchronized Mechanical Axes. *Phys. Procedia* **2013**, *41*, 319–326. [CrossRef]
28. Kramer, T.; Remund, S.; Gafner, M.; Zwygart, D.; Neuenschwander, B.; Holtz, R.; Witte, R.; Dury, N. Novel strategy for ultrafast pulsed laser micromachining of rotational symmetric metallic parts. *Procedia CIRP* **2018**, *74*, 611–617. [CrossRef]
29. Bruening, S.; Hennig, G.; Eifel, S.; Gillner, A. Ultrafast Scan Techniques for 3D-µm Structuring of Metal Surfaces with high repetitive ps-laser pulses. *Phys. Procedia* **2011**, *12*, 105–115. [CrossRef]
30. Liu, X.; Du, D.; Mourou, G. Laser ablation and micromachining with ultrashort laser pulses. *IEEE J. Quantum Electron.* **1997**, *33*, 1706–1716. [CrossRef]
31. Shirk, M.D.; Molian, P.A. A review of ultrashort pulsed laser ablation of materials. *J. Laser Appl.* **1998**, *10*, 18–28. [CrossRef]

32. Sundaram, S.K.; Mazur, E. Inducing and probing non-thermal transitions in semiconductors using femtosecond laser pulses. *Nat. Mater.* **2002**, *1*, 217–224. [CrossRef]
33. Perry, M.D.; Stuart, B.C.; Banks, P.S.; Feit, M.D.; Yanovsky, V.; Rubenchik, A.M. Ultrashort-pulse laser machining of electric materials. *J. Appl. Phys.* **1999**, *85*, 6803–6810. [CrossRef]
34. Krüger, J.; Kautek, W. Ultrashort Pulse Laser Interaction with Dielectrics and Polymers. In *Advances in Polymer Science*; Springer Science and Business Media: New York, NY, USA, 2012; Volume 168, pp. 247–290.
35. Bulgakova, N.M.; Zhukov, V.P.; Collins, A.R.; Rostohar, D.; Derrien, T.J.-Y.; Mocek, T. How to optimize ultrashort pulse laser interaction with glass surfaces in cutting regimes? *Appl. Surf. Sci.* **2015**, *336*, 364–374. [CrossRef]
36. Samant, A.N.; Dahotre, N.B. Laser machining of structural ceramics—A review. *J. Eur. Ceram. Soc.* **2009**, *29*, 969–993. [CrossRef]
37. Chichkov, B.N.; Momma, C.; Nolte, S.; von Alvensleben, F.; Tünnermann, A. Femtosecond, picosecond and nanosecond laser ablation of solids. *Appl. Phys. A* **1996**, *63*, 109–115. [CrossRef]
38. Cheng, J.; Liu, C.; Shang, S.; Liu, D.; Perrie, W.; Dearden, G.; Watkins, K. A review of ultrafast laser materials micromachining. *Opt. Laser Technol.* **2013**, *46*, 88–102. [CrossRef]
39. Mishra, S.; Yadava, V. Laser Beam MicroMachining (LBMM)—A review. *Opt. Lasers Eng.* **2015**, *73*, 89–122. [CrossRef]
40. Lei, S.; Zhao, X.; Yu, X.; Hu, A.; Vukelic, S.; Jun, M.B.G.; Joe, H.-E.; Yao, Y.L.; Shin, Y.C. Ultrafast Laser Applications in Man-ufacturing Processes: A State-of-the-Art Review. J. *Manuf. Sci. Eng.* **2020**, *142*, 031005. [CrossRef]
41. Momma, C.; Nolte, S.; Chichkov, B.; Tunnermann, A.; Von Alvensleben, F. Precise Laser Ablation with Ultra-Short Pulses. In Proceedings of the European Meeting on Lasers and Electro-Optics CLEOE-96, Hamburg, Germany, 8–13 September 1996.
42. Zhigilei, L. Dynamics of the plume formation and parameters of the ejected clusters in short-pulse laser ablation. *Appl. Phys. A* **2003**, *76*, 339–350. [CrossRef]
43. Ivanov, D.S.; Zhigilei, L. Combined atomistic-continuum modeling of short-pulse laser melting and disintegration of metal films. *Phys. Rev. B* **2003**, *68*, 064114. [CrossRef]
44. Povarnitsyn, M.E.; Andreev, N.E.; Apfelbaum, E.M.; Itina, T.E.; Khishchenko, K.; Kostenko, O.F.; Levashov, P.R.; Veysman, M.E. A wide-range model for simulation of pump-probe experiments with metals. *Appl. Surf. Sci.* **2012**, *258*, 9480–9483. [CrossRef]
45. Wu, C.; He, M. Microscopic mechanisms of laser spallation and ablation of metal targets from large-scale molecular dynamics simulations. *Appl. Phys. A* **2014**, *114*, 11–32. [CrossRef]
46. Povarnitsyn, M.E.; Fokin, V.B.; Levashov, P.R. Microscopic and macroscopic modeling of femtosecond laser ablation of metals. *Appl. Surf. Sci.* **2015**, *357*, 1150–1156. [CrossRef]
47. Breitling, D.; Ruf, A.; Dausinger, F. Fundamental Aspects in Machining of Metals with Short and Ultrashort Laser Pulses. In *Photon Processing in Microelectronics and Photonics III—Fundamental Aspects in Machining of Metals with Short and Ultrashort Laser Pulses, Proceedings of the SPIE Lasers and Applications in Science and Engineering, San Jose, CA, USA, 25 January 2004*; SPIE: Bellingham, WA, USA, 2004; p. 49.
48. Lide, D.R. *CRC Handbook of Chemistry and Physics*; CRC Press: Boca Raton, FL, USA, 2004.
49. Wright, O.B. Ultrafast nonequilibrium stress generation in gold and silver. *Phys. Rev. B* **1994**, *49*, 9985–9988. [CrossRef]
50. Hüttner, B.; Rohr, G. On the theory of ps and sub-ps laser pulse interaction with metals I. Surface temperature. *Appl. Surf. Sci.* **1996**, *103*, 269–274. [CrossRef]
51. Nedialkov, N.N.; Imamova, S.E.; Atanasov, P.A. Ablation of metals by ultrashort laser pulses. *J. Phys. D Appl. Phys.* **2004**, *37*, 638–643. [CrossRef]
52. Wellershoff, S.-S.; Hohlfeld, J.; Güdde, J.; Matthias, E. The role of electron–phonon coupling in femtosecond laser damage of metals. *Appl. Phys. A* **1999**, *69*, S99–S107.
53. Lin, Z.; Zhigilei, L.; Celli, V. Electron-phonon coupling and electron heat capacity of metals under conditions of strong electron-phonon nonequilibrium. *Phys. Rev. B* **2008**, *77*, 075133. [CrossRef]
54. Foumani, A.A.; Förster, D.J.; Ghorbanfekr-Kalashami, H.; Weber, R.; Graf, T.; Niknam, A.R. Atomistic simulation of ultra-short pulsed laser ablation of metals with single and double pulses: An investigation of the re-deposition phenomenon. *Appl. Surf. Sci.* **2021**, *537*, 147775. [CrossRef]
55. Amoruso, S.; Bruzzese, R.; Pagano, C.; Wang, X. Features of plasma plume evolution and material removal efficiency during femtosecond laser ablation of nickel in high vacuum. *Appl. Phys. A* **2007**, *89*, 1017–1024. [CrossRef]
56. Düsing, J.F.; Hwang, D.J.; Grigoropoulos, C.; Ostendorf, A.; Kling, R. Optical emission imaging and spectroscopy during femtosecond laser ablation of thin metal films on flexible polymer substrates. In Proceedings of the International Congress on Applications of Lasers & Electro-Optics, Orlando, FL, USA, 2–5 November 2009; p. 888.
57. Förster, D.J.; Faas, S.; Gröninger, S.; Bauer, F.; Michalowski, A.; Weber, R.; Graf, T. Shielding effects and re-deposition of material during processing of metals with bursts of ultra-short laser pulses. *Appl. Surf. Sci.* **2018**, *440*, 926–931. [CrossRef]
58. König, J.; Nolte, S.; Tünnermann, A. Plasma evolution during metal ablation with ultrashort laser pulses. *Opt. Express* **2005**, *13*, 10597. [CrossRef]
59. Neuenschwander, B.; Jaeggi, B.; Schmid, M.; Hennig, G. Surface Structuring with Ultra-short Laser Pulses: Basics, Limitations and Needs for High Throughput. *Phys. Procedia* **2014**, *56*, 1047–1058. [CrossRef]
60. Kramer, T.; Zhang, Y.; Remund, S.; Jaeggi, B.; Michalowski, A.; Grad, L.; Neuenschwander, B. Increasing the Specific Removal Rate for Ultra Short Pulsed Laser-Micromachining by Using Pulse Bursts. *JLMN* **2017**, *12*, 107–114. [CrossRef]

61. Jaeggi, B.; Cangueiro, L.; Bruneel, D.; de Campos, J.A.R.; Hairaye, C.; Neuenschwander, B. Micromachining using pulse bursts: Influence of the pulse duration and the number of pulses in the burst on the specific removal rate. In *Laser Applications in Microelectronic and Optoelectronic Manufacturing (LAMOM) XXIII*; International Society for Optics and Photonics: Bellingham, WA, USA, 2018; Volume 10519, p. 1051905.
62. Neuenschwander, B.; Jaeggi, B.; Schmid, M.; Rouffiange, V.; Martin, P.-E. Optimization of the Volume Ablation Rate for Metals at Different Laser Pulse-Durations from ps to fs. In Proceedings of the SPIE LASE, San Francisco, CA, USA, 15 February 2012; p. 824307.
63. Schille, J.; Schneider, L.; Loeschner, U. Process optimization in high-average-power ultrashort pulse laser microfabrication: How laser process parameters influence efficiency, throughput and quality. *Appl. Phys. A* **2015**, *120*, 847–855. [CrossRef]
64. Domke, M.; Matylitsky, V.; Stroj, S. Surface ablation efficiency and quality of fs lasers in single-pulse mode, fs lasers in burst mode, and ns lasers. *Appl. Surf. Sci.* **2020**, *505*, 144594. [CrossRef]
65. Raciukaitis, G.; Brikas, M.; Gecys, P.; Voisat, B.; Gedvilas, M. Use of High Repetition Rate and High Power Lasers in Microfabrication: How to Keep the Efficiency High? *JLMN* **2009**, *4*, 186–191. [CrossRef]
66. Gillner, A.; Hartmann, C.; Dohrn, A. High Quality Micro Machining with Tailored Short and Ultra Short Laser Pulses. In *Proceedings of the Pacific International Conference on Applications of Lasers and Optics*; Laser Institute of America: Orlando, FL, USA, 2008; Volume 2008, p. 685.
67. Knappe, R.; Haloui, H.; Seifert, A.; Weis, A.; Nebel, A. Scaling ablation rates for picosecond lasers using burst micromachining. In *Laser-Based Micro- and Nanopackaging and Assembly IV, Proceedings of the SPIE LASE, San Francisco, CA, USA, 23–28 January 2010*; SPIE: Bellingham, WA, USA, 2010; Volume 7585, p. 75850H.
68. Vorobyev, A.Y.; Guo, C. Direct observation of enhanced residual thermal energy coupling to solids in femtosecond laser ablation. *Appl. Phys. Lett.* **2005**, *86*, 011916. [CrossRef]
69. Vorobyev, A.Y.; Guo, C. Enhanced absorptance of gold following multipulse femtosecond laser ablation. *Phys. Rev. B* **2005**, *72*, 195422. [CrossRef]
70. Vorobyev, A.Y.; Guo, C. Enhanced energy coupling in femtosecond laser-metal interactions at high intensities. *Opt. Express* **2006**, *14*, 13113–13119. [CrossRef]
71. Vorobyev, A.; Kuzmichev, V.; Kokody, N.; Kohns, P.; Dai, J.; Guo, C. Residual thermal effects in Al following single ns- and fs-laser pulse ablation. *Appl. Phys. A* **2005**, *82*, 357–362. [CrossRef]
72. Vorobyev, A.Y.; Guo, C. Thermal response and optical absorptance of metals under femtosecond laser irradiation. *Nat. Sci.* **2011**, *03*, 488–495. [CrossRef]
73. Bauer, F.; Michalowski, A.; Kiedrowski, T.; Nolte, S. Heat accumulation in ultra-short pulsed scanning laser ablation of metals. *Opt. Express* **2015**, *23*, 1035–1043. [CrossRef]
74. Förster, D.J.; Weber, R.; Graf, T. Residual heat during ultrashort laser drilling of metals. In Proceedings of the LPM2017—The 18th International Symposium on Laser Precision Microfabrication, Toyama, Japan, 5–8 June 2017.
75. Bauer, F. Grundlegende Untersuchungen zum Abtragen von Stahl mit Ultrakurzen Laserpulsen. Ph.D. Thesis, Friedrich-Schiller-Universität Jena, Jena, Germany, 2018.
76. Bornschlegel, B.; Koller, J.; Finger, J. In-Situ Analysis of Heat Accumulation during Ultrashort Pulsed Laser Ablation. *JLMN* **2020**, *15*, 56–62.
77. Wu, B.; Deng, L.; Liu, P.; Zhang, F.; Duan, J.; Zeng, X. Effects of picosecond laser repetition rate on ablation of Cr12MoV cold work mold steel. *Appl. Surf. Sci.* **2017**, *409*, 403–412. [CrossRef]
78. Metzner, D.; Lickschat, P.; Weißmantel, S. Influence of heat accumulation during laser micromachining of CoCrMo alloy with ultrashort pulses in burst mode. *Appl. Phys. A* **2020**, *126*, 84. [CrossRef]
79. Martan, J.; Prokešová, L.; Moskal, D.; de Faria, B.F.; Honner, M.; Lang, V. Heat accumulation temperature measurement in ultrashort pulse laser micromachining. *Int. J. Heat Mass Transf.* **2021**, *168*, 120866. [CrossRef]
80. Weber, R.; Graf, T.; Berger, P.; Onuseit, V.; Wiedenmann, M.; Freitag, C.; Feuer, A. Heat accumulation during pulsed laser materials processing. *Opt. Express* **2014**, *22*, 11312–11324. [CrossRef]
81. Weber, R.; Graf, T.; Freitag, C.; Feuer, A.; Kononenko, T.; Konov, V.I. Processing constraints resulting from heat accumulation during pulsed and repetitive laser materials processing. *Opt. Express* **2017**, *25*, 3966–3979. [CrossRef]
82. Di Niso, F.; Gaudiuso, C.; Sibillano, T.; Mezzapesa, F.P.; Ancona, A.; Lugarà, P.M. Role of heat accumulation on the incubation effect in multi-shot laser ablation of stainless steel at high repetition rates. *Opt. Express* **2014**, *22*, 12200–12210. [CrossRef] [PubMed]
83. Raciukaitis, G.; Brikas, M.; Gecys, P.; Gedvilas, M. Accumulation Effects in Laser Ablation of Metals with High-Repetition-Rate Lasers. In *High-Power Laser Ablation VII, Proceedings of the SPIE LASE, San Francisco, CA, USA, 23–28 January 2008*; SPIE: Bellingham, WA, USA, 2008.
84. Faas, S.; Bielke, U.; Weber, R.; Graf, T. Prediction of the surface structures resulting from heat accumulation during processing with picosecond laser pulses at the average power of 420 W. *Appl. Phys. A* **2018**, *124*, 612. [CrossRef]
85. St-Onge, L.; Sabsabi, M.; Cielo, P. Analysis of solids using laser-induced plasma spectroscopy in double-pulse mode. *Spectrochim. Acta Part B At. Spectrosc.* **1998**, *53*, 407–415. [CrossRef]
86. Mao, S.; Mao, X.; Greif, R.; Russo, R.E. Influence of preformed shock wave on the development of picosecond laser ablation plasma. *J. Appl. Phys.* **2001**, *89*, 4096–4098. [CrossRef]

87. Corsi, M.; Cristoforetti, G.; Giuffrida, M.; Hidalgo, M.; Legnaioli, S.; Palleschi, V.; Salvetti, A.; Tognoni, E.; Vallebona, C. Three-dimensional analysis of laser induced plasmas in single and double pulse configuration. *Spectrochim. Acta Part B At. Spectrosc.* **2004**, *59*, 723–735. [CrossRef]
88. Scuderi, D.; Albert, O.; Moreau, D.; Pronko, P.P.; Etchepare, J. Interaction of a laser-produced plume with a second time delayed femtosecond pulse. *Appl. Phys. Lett.* **2005**, *86*, 071502. [CrossRef]
89. Hanada, Y.; Sugioka, K.; Miyamoto, I.; Midorikawa, K. Double-pulse irradiation by laser-induced plasma-assisted ablation (LIPAA) and mechanisms study. *Appl. Surf. Sci.* **2005**, *248*, 276–280. [CrossRef]
90. Le Harzic, R.; Breitling, D.; Sommer, S.; Föhl, C.; König, K.; Dausinger, F.; Audouard, E. Processing of metals by double pulses with short laser pulses. *Appl. Phys. A* **2005**, *81*, 1121–1125. [CrossRef]
91. Babushok, V.; DeLucia, F.; Gottfried, J.; Munson, C.; Miziolek, A. Double pulse laser ablation and plasma: Laser induced breakdown spectroscopy signal enhancement. *Spectrochim. Acta Part B At. Spectrosc.* **2006**, *61*, 999–1014. [CrossRef]
92. Suttmann, O.; Wojakowski, B.; Klug, U.; Kling, R.; Ostendorf, A. Picosecond double-pulse ablation in silicon and aluminium with variable delay. *J. Laser Appl.* **2008**, *42*. [CrossRef]
93. Bogaerts, A.; Chen, Z.; Autrique, D. Double pulse laser ablation and laser induced breakdown spectroscopy: A modeling investigation. *Spectrochim. Acta Part B At. Spectrosc.* **2008**, *63*, 746–754. [CrossRef]
94. Singha, S.; Hu, Z.; Gordon, R.J. Ablation and plasma emission produced by dual femtosecond laser pulses. *J. Appl. Phys.* **2008**, *104*, 113520. [CrossRef]
95. Noel, S.; Hermann, J. Reducing nanoparticles in metal ablation plumes produced by two delayed short laser pulses. *Appl. Phys. Lett.* **2009**, *94*, 53120. [CrossRef]
96. Wojakowski, B.; Suttmann, O.; Klug, U.; Kling, R. Micromachining with Picosecond Double Pulses on Silicon and Aluminium. In *Laser-Based Micro- and Nanopackaging and Assembly III, Proceedings of the SPIE LASE: Lasers and Applications in Science and Engineering, San Jose, CA, USA, 24 January 2009*; SPIE: Bellingham, WA, USA, 2009; p. 72020O.
97. Roberts, D.; du Plessis, A.; Botha, L. Femtosecond laser ablation of silver foil with single and double pulses. *Appl. Surf. Sci.* **2010**, *256*, 1784–1792. [CrossRef]
98. Deladurantaye, P.; Cournoyer, A.; Drolet, M.; Desbiens, L.; Lemieux, D.; Briand, M.; Taillon, Y. Material Micromachining Using Bursts of High Repetition Rate Picosecond Pulses from a Fiber Laser Source. In *Fiber Lasers VIII: Technology, Systems, and Applications, Proceedings of the SPIE LASE San Francisco, CA, USA, 22–27 January 2011*; SPIE: Bellingham, WA, USA, 2011; Volume 7914, p. 791404.
99. Axente, E.; Mihailescu, I.N.; Itina, T.; Hermann, J. Probing electron-phonon coupling in metals via observations of ablation plumes produced by two delayed short laser pulses. *Appl. Phys. Lett.* **2011**, *99*, 081502. [CrossRef]
100. Sailer, M.; Bauer, F.; Kleiner, J.; Kaiser, M. Scaling of ablation rates. Ablation efficiency and quality aspects of "Burstmode"—Micromachining of metals. In Proceedings of the Lasers in Manufacturing Conference, Munich, Germany, 22–25 June 2015; p. 8.
101. Hänel, N.; Stolze, M.; Herrmann, T.R.W.; Lhuillier, J.A. Fundamental Investigations of ps-Laser Burst-Mode on Common Metals for an Enhanced Ablation Process. In *Laser-Based Micro- and Nanoprocessing IX, Proceedings of the SPIE LASE San Francisco, CA, USA, 7–12 February 2015*; SPIE: Bellingham, WA, USA, 2015; Volume 9351, p. 93510E.
102. Kramer, T.; Neuenschwander, B.; Jäggi, B.; Remund, S.; Hunziker, U.; Zürcher, J. Influence of Pulse Bursts on the Specific Removal Rate for Ultra-fast Pulsed Laser Micromachining of Copper. *Phys. Procedia* **2016**, *83*, 123–134. [CrossRef]
103. Schille, J.; Schneider, L.; Kraft, S.; Hartwig, L.; Loeschner, U. Experimental study on double-pulse laser ablation of steel upon multiple parallel-polarized ultrashort-pulse irradiations. *Appl. Phys. A* **2016**, *122*, 644. [CrossRef]
104. Finger, J. Puls-zu-Puls-Wechselwirkungen beim Ultrakurzpuls-Laserabtrag mit hohen Repetitionsraten. Ph.D. Thesis, RWTH Aachen, Aachen, Germany, 2017.
105. Lickschat, P.; Demba, A.; Weissmantel, S. Ablation of steel using picosecond laser pulses in burst mode. *Appl. Phys. A* **2017**, *123*, 137. [CrossRef]
106. Mayerhofer, R. Ultrashort-pulsed laser material processing with high repetition rate burst pulses. In *Laser Applications in Microelectronic and Optoelectronic Manufacturing (LAMOM) XXII, Proceedings of the SPIE LASE, 2017, San Francisco, CA, USA, 28 January–2 February 2017*; SPIE: Bellingham, WA, USA, 2017; p. 100910.
107. Jaeggi, B.; Remund, S.; Zhang, Y.; Kramer, T.; Neuenschwander, B. Optimizing the Specific Removal Rate with the Burst Mode Under Varying Conditions. *JLMN* **2017**, *12*, 107–114.
108. Rosenfeld, A.; Höhm, S.; Krüger, J.; Bonse, J. Dynamics of Ultrashort Double-Pulse Laser Ablation of Solid Surfaces. In *Encyclopedia of Interfacial Chemistry*; Elsevier: Amsterdam, The Netherlands, 2018; pp. 338–347.
109. Hashida, M.; Masuno, S.; Furukawa, Y.; Kusaba, M.; Inoue, S.; Sakabe, S.; Sakagami, H.; Tsukamoto, M. Suppression of ablation by double-pulse femtosecond laser irradiation. In *Frontiers in Ultrafast Optics: Biomedical, Scientific, and Industrial Applications XVIII, Proceedings of the SPIE LASE, San Francisco, CA, USA, 27 January–1 February 2018*; SPIE: Bellingham, WA, USA, 2018; p. 105220.
110. Zhang, K.; Zhang, J.; Jiang, L.; Li, X.; Liu, Y.; Li, B.; Lu, Y. Ablation enhancement of metal in ultrashort double-pulse experiments. *Appl. Phys. Lett.* **2018**, *112*, 261906. [CrossRef]
111. Takenaka, K.; Tsukamoto, M.; Hashida, M.; Masuno, S.; Sakagami, H.; Kusaba, M.; Sakabe, S.; Inoue, S.; Furukawa, Y.; Asai, S. Ablation suppression of a titanium surface interacting with a two-color double-pulse femtosecond laser beam. *Appl. Surf. Sci.* **2019**, *478*, 882–886. [CrossRef]

112. Bruening, S.; Du, K.; Gillner, A. Micro processing with ultrafast bursts of pulses. *Procedia CIRP* **2020**, *94*, 856–862. [CrossRef]
113. Lin, Z.; Ji, L.; Hong, M. Enhancement of femtosecond laser-induced surface ablation via temporal overlapping double-pulse irradiation. *Photon Res.* **2020**, *8*, 271. [CrossRef]
114. Förster, D.J.; Faas, S.; Weber, R.; Graf, T. Thrust enhancement and propellant conservation for laser propulsion using ultra-short double pulses. *Appl. Surf. Sci.* **2020**, *510*, 145391. [CrossRef]
115. Cheng, C.-W.; Chen, J.-K. Drilling of Copper Using a Dual-Pulse Femtosecond Laser. *Technologies* **2016**, *4*, 7. [CrossRef]
116. Förster, G.D.; Lewis, L.J. Numerical study of double-pulse laser ablation of Al. *Phys. Rev. B* **2018**, *97*, 224301. [CrossRef]
117. Roth, J.; Krauß, A.; Lotze, J.; Trebin, H.-R. Simulation of laser ablation in aluminum: The effectivity of double pulses. *Appl. Phys. A* **2014**, *117*, 2207–2216. [CrossRef]
118. Povarnitsyn, M.E.; Itina, T.E.; Levashov, P.R.; Khishchenko, K. Simulation of ultrashort double-pulse laser ablation. *Appl. Surf. Sci.* **2011**, *257*, 5168–5171. [CrossRef]
119. Kudryashov, S.I.; Samokhvalov, A.A.; Golubev, Y.D.; Ivanov, D.S.; Garcia, M.E.; Veiko, V.P.; Rethfeld, B.; Mikhailovskii, V.Y. Dynamic all-optical control in ultrashort double-pulse laser ablation. *Appl. Surf. Sci.* **2021**, *537*, 147940. [CrossRef]
120. Spellauge, M.; Winter, J.; Rapp, S.; McDonnell, C.; Sotier, F.; Schmidt, M.; Huber, H.P. Influence of stress confinement, particle shielding and re-deposition on the ultrashort pulse laser ablation of metals revealed by ultrafast time-resolved experiments. *Appl. Surf. Sci.* **2021**, *545*, 148930. [CrossRef]
121. Ackerl, N. Laser Surface Functionalization from Fundamentals to Application. Ph.D. Thesis, ETH Zurich, Zurich, Switzerland, 2020.
122. Börner, P. Ultra-Short Pulsed Laser Ablation of Diamond. Ph.D. Thesis, ETH Zurich, Zurich, Switzerland, 2019.
123. Furukawa, Y.; Inoue, S.; Hashida, M. Temporal change in laser penetration length of titanium and platinum for double-pulse ablation measured by a novel ablation method. *J. Laser Appl.* **2021**, *33*, 012023. [CrossRef]
124. Lauer, B.; Jaeggi, B.; Zhang, Y.; Neuenschwander, B. Measurement of the maximum specific removal rate: Unexpected influence of the experimental method and the spot size. In Proceedings of the International Congress on Applications of Lasers & Electro-Optics, Atlanta, GA, USA, 18–22 October 2015; Laser Institute of America: Orlando, FL, USA, 2015; Volume 2015, p. 146.
125. Kramer, T.; Remund, S.; Jäggi, B.; Schmid, M.; Neuenschwander, B. Ablation dynamics—From absorption to heat accumulation/ultra-fast laser matter interaction. *Adv. Opt. Technol.* **2018**, *7*, 129–144. [CrossRef]
126. Winter, J.; Rapp, S.; Schmidt, M.; Huber, H.P. Ultrafast laser processing of copper: A comparative study of experimental and simulated transient optical properties. *Appl. Surf. Sci.* **2017**, *417*, 2–15. [CrossRef]
127. Neuenschwander, B.; Bucher, G.F.; Nussbaum, C.; Joss, B.; Muralt, M.; Hunziker, U.W.; Schuetz, P. Processing of metals and dielectric materials with ps-laser pulses: Results, strategies, limitations and needs. In *Laser Applications in Microelectronic and Optoelectronic Manufacturing XV, Proceedings of the SPIE LASE, San Francisco, CA, USA, 12 March 2010*; 75840R-SPIE; SPIE: Bellingham, WA, USA, 2010.
128. Osbild, M.; Brenner, A.; Röther, L.; Finger, J. Ultrashort pulse laser micro polishing of steel—Investigation of the melt pool depth. *Procedia CIRP* **2020**, *94*, 936–941. [CrossRef]
129. Remund, S.; Kramer, T.; Neuenschwander, B.; Jäggi, B. Method for Producing an Implant, and Implant Produced by Said Method. U.S. Patent WO/2020/038925, 27 February 2020.
130. Brenner, A.; Röther, L.; Osbild, M.; Finger, J. Laser Polishing Using Ultrashort Pulse Laser. In *Laser-Based Micro- and Nanoprocessing XIV, Proceedings of the SPIE LASE, San Francisco, CA, USA, 1–6 February 2020*; SPIE: Bellingham, WA, USA, 2020; Volume 11268, p. 112680.
131. Metzner, D.; Lickschat, P.; Weißmantel, S. Optimization of the ablation process using ultrashort pulsed laser radiation in different burst modes. *J. Laser Appl.* **2021**, *33*, 012057. [CrossRef]
132. Metzner, D.; Lickschat, P.; Weißmantel, S. Surface treatment on cobalt and titanium alloys using picosecond laser pulses in burst mode. *Appl. Phys. A* **2021**, *127*, 1–9. [CrossRef]
133. Matsumoto, H.; Lin, Z.; Kleinert, J. Ultrafast Laser Ablation of Copper with ~GHz Bursts. In *Laser Applications in Microelectronic and Optoelectronic Manufacturing (LAMOM) XXIII (International Society for Optics and Photonics, Proceedings of the SPIE LASE, San Francisco, CA, USA, 29–31 January 2018*; SPIE: Bellingham, WA, USA, 2018; Volume 10519, p. 1051902.
134. Povarnitsyn, M.E.; Levashov, P.R.; Knyazev, D.V. Simulation of ultrafast bursts of subpicosecond pulses: In pursuit of efficiency. *Appl. Phys. Lett.* **2018**, *112*, 051603. [CrossRef]
135. Bonamis, G.; Audouard, E.; Hoenninger, C.; Lopez, J.; Mishchik, K.; Mottay, E.; Manek-Hönninger, I. Systematic study of laser ablation with GHz bursts of femtosecond pulses. *Opt. Express* **2020**, *28*, 27702. [CrossRef]
136. Bonamis, G.; Mishchick, K.; Audouard, E.; Hönninger, C.; Mottay, E.; Lopez, J.; Manek-Hönninger, I. High efficiency femtosecond laser ablation with gigahertz level bursts. *J. Laser Appl.* **2019**, *31*, 022205. [CrossRef]
137. Butkus, S.; Jukna, V.; Paipulas, D.; Barkauskas, M.; Sirutkaitis, V. Micromachining of Invar Foils with GHz, MHz and kHz Femtosecond Burst Modes. *Micromachines* **2020**, *11*, 733. [CrossRef] [PubMed]
138. Hendow, S.T.; Takahashi, H.; Yamaguchi, M.; Xu, J. Enhanced Ablation Using GHz-Pulsed fs Laser. In *Laser-Based Micro- and Nanoprocessing XIV, Proceedings of the SPIE LASE, San Francisco, CA, USA, 1–6 February 2020*; SPIE: Bellingham, WA, USA, 2020; Volume 11268, p. 1126809.

139. Hirsiger, T.; Gafner, M.; Remund, S.M.; Chaja, M.W.; Urniezius, A.; Butkus, S.; Neuenschwander, B. Machining Metals and Silicon with GHz Bursts: Surprising Tremendous Reduction of the Specific Removal Rate for Surface Texturing Applications. In *Laser Applications in Microelectronic and Optoelectronic Manufacturing (LAMOM) XXV, Proceedings of the SPIE LASE, San Francisco, CA, USA, 1–6 February 2020*; SPIE: Bellingham, WA, USA, 2020; Volume 11267, p. 112670T.
140. Cheng, C.-W.; Chen, J.-K. Ultrafast laser ablation of copper by GHz bursts. *Appl. Phys. A* **2020**, *126*, 1–7. [CrossRef]
141. Fehrenbacher, A.; Sailer, M.; Fuehra, B.; Jansen, F.; Tan, C.; Baumbach, S.; Flaig, R.; Eberhardt, C.; Ruebling, S.; Quentin, U.; et al. New generation TruMicro Series 2000: Micromachining Versatility by GHz-burst, Higher Average Power, Flexible Pulse on Demand and Integrated Hollow-Core Fiber Interface. In *Laser-Based Micro- and Nanoprocessing XV, Proceedings of the SPIE LASE, San Francisco, CA, USA, 6–11 March 2021*; SPIE: Bellingham, WA, USA, 2021; Volume 11674, p. 116740U.
142. Nyenhuis, F.; Michalowski, A.; L'Huillier, J.A. Surface Treatment with GHz-Bursts. In *Laser-Based Micro- and Nanoprocessing XIV, Proceedings of the SPIE LASE, San Francisco, CA, USA, 1–6 February 2020*; SPIE: Bellingham, WA, USA, 2020; Volume 11268, p. 112680B.
143. Michalowski, A.; Nyenhuis, F.; Kunz, G. Smooth Surfaces by Pulsed Laser Processing with Bursts. *Photonics Views* **2020**, *17*, 42–45. [CrossRef]
144. Obata, K.; Caballero-Lucas, F.; Sugioka, K. Material Processing at GHz Burst Mode by Femtosecond Laser Ablation. *JLMN* **2021**, *16*, 5.
145. Manninen, M.; Hirvimäki, M.; Poutiainen, I.; Salminen, A. Effect of Pulse Length on Engraving Efficiency in Nanosecond Pulsed Laser Engraving of Stainless Steel. *Met. Mater. Trans. A* **2015**, *46*, 2129–2136. [CrossRef]
146. Mathew, M.M.; Bathe, R.N.; Padmanabham, G.; Padmanaban, R.; Thirumalini, S. A study on the micromachining of molybdenum using nanosecond and femtosecond lasers. *Int. J. Adv. Manuf. Technol.* **2017**, *104*, 3239–3249. [CrossRef]
147. Garnov, S.; Konov, V.; Kononenko, T.; Pashinin, V.; Sinyavsky, M. Microsecond laser material processing at 1.06 μm. *Laser Phys.* **2004**, *14*, 910–915.
148. Mur, J.; Petkovšek, R. Precision and resolution in laser direct microstructuring with bursts of picosecond pulses. *Appl. Phys. A* **2018**, *124*, 62. [CrossRef]
149. Gaudiuso, C.; Giannuzzi, G.; Volpe, A.; Lugarà, P.M.; Choquet, I.; Ancona, A. Incubation during laser ablation with bursts of femtosecond pulses with picosecond delays. *Opt. Express* **2018**, *26*, 3801–3813. [CrossRef] [PubMed]
150. Rong, Y.; Ji, P.; He, M.; Zhang, Y.; Tang, Y. Multiscale Investigation of Femtosecond Laser Pulses Processing Aluminum in Burst Mode. *Nanoscale Microscale Thermophys. Eng.* **2018**, *22*, 324–347. [CrossRef]
151. Mur, J.; Petkovšek, R. Near-THz bursts of pulses—Governing surface ablation mechanisms for laser material processing. *Appl. Surf. Sci.* **2019**, *478*, 355–360. [CrossRef]
152. Wang, A.; Das, A.; Grojo, D. Ultrafast Laser Writing Deep inside Silicon with THz-Repetition-Rate Trains of Pulses. *Research* **2020**, *2020*, 1–11. [CrossRef]
153. Ancona, A.; Gaudiuso, C.; Giannuzzi, G.; Choquet, I.; Lugarà, P.M. Incubation Effect In Burst Mode Fs-Laser Ablation Of Stainless Steel Samples. In *Laser-Based Micro- and Nanoprocessing XII, Proceedings of the SPIE LASE, San Francisco, CA, USA, 27 January–1 February 2020*; SPIE: Bellingham, WA, USA, 2018; Volume 10520, p. 105200A.
154. Förster, D.J.; Weber, R.; Holder, D.; Graf, T. Estimation of the depth limit for percussion drilling with picosecond laser pulses. *Opt. Express* **2018**, *26*, 11546–11552. [CrossRef]
155. Holder, D.; Weber, R.; Graf, T.; Onuseit, V.; Brinkmeier, D.; Förster, D.J.; Feuer, A. Analytical model for the depth progress of percussion drilling with ultrashort laser pulses. *Appl. Phys. A* **2021**, *127*, 1–8. [CrossRef]
156. Lapczyna, M.; Chen, K.; Herman, P.; Tan, H.; Marjoribanks, R. Ultra high repetition rate (133 MHz) laser ablation of aluminum with 1.2-ps pulses. *Appl. Phys. A* **1999**, *69*, S883–S886. [CrossRef]
157. Esser, D.; Rezaei, S.; Li, J.; Herman, P.R.; Gottmann, J. Time dynamics of burst-train filamentation assisted femtosecond laser machining in glasses. *Opt. Express* **2011**, *19*, 25632–25642. [CrossRef]
158. Kammer, H.; Dreisow, F.; Tünnermann, A. Analysis of the Hole Shape Evolution in fs-Pulse Percussion Drilling with Bursts. In *Frontiers in Ultrafast Optics: Biomedical, Scientific, and Industrial Applications XVI, Proceedings of the SPIE LASE, San Francisco, CA, USA, 13–18 February 2016*; SPIE: Bellingham, WA, USA, 2016; Volume 9740, p. 974012.
159. Wang, Q.; Luo, S.; Chen, Z.; Qi, H.; Deng, J.; Hu, Z. Drilling of aluminum and copper films with femtosecond double-pulse laser. *Opt. Laser Technol.* **2016**, *80*, 116–124. [CrossRef]
160. Balachninaitė, O.; Tamulienė, V.; Eičas, L.; Vaičaitis, V. Laser micromachining of steel and copper using femtosecond laser pulses in GHz burst mode. *Results Phys.* **2021**, *22*, 103847. [CrossRef]
161. Schille, J.; Loeschner, U.; Ebert, R.; Scully, P.; Goddard, N.; Exner, H. Laser micro processing using a high repetition rate femto second laser. *J. Laser Appl.* **2010**, 1491–1499. [CrossRef]
162. Tsukamoto, M.; Kayahara, T.; Nakano, H.; Hashida, M.; Katto, M.; Fujita, M.; Tanaka, M.; Abe, N. Microstructures formation on titanium plate by femtosecond laser ablation. *J. Physics Conf. Ser.* **2007**, *59*, 666–669. [CrossRef]
163. Herrmann, T.; Harth, F.; Henrich, B.; L'Huillier, J.; Hajri, M. How to Improve Efficiency in USP Laser Micromachining. *Laser Tech. J.* **2016**, *13*, 16–19. [CrossRef]
164. Nyenhuis, F.; Michalowski, A.; L'Huillier, J. Dual Process Strategy to Increase the Usable Power for Laser-Milling. *JLMN* **2020**. [CrossRef]

165. Sassmannshausen, A.; Brenner, A.; Finger, J. Ultrashort pulse laser polishing by continuous surface melting. *J. Mater. Process. Technol.* **2021**, *293*, 117058. [CrossRef]
166. Kažukauskas, E.; Butkus, S.; Tokarski, P.; Jukna, V.; Barkauskas, M.; Sirutkaitis, V. Micromachining of Transparent Biocompatible Polymers Applied in Medicine Using Bursts of Femtosecond Laser Pulses. *Micromachines* **2020**, *11*, 1093. [CrossRef] [PubMed]
167. Antończak, A.J.; Stępak, B.; Kozioł, P.E.; Abramski, K.M. The influence of process parameters on the laser-induced coloring of titanium. *Appl. Phys. A* **2013**, *115*, 1003–1013. [CrossRef]
168. Veiko, V.; Odintsova, G.; Ageev, E.; Karlagina, Y.; Loginov, A.; Skuratova, A.; Gorbunova, E. Controlled oxide films formation by nanosecond laser pulses for color marking. *Opt. Express* **2014**, *22*, 24342–24347. [CrossRef]
169. Lecka, K.M.; Wojcik, M.R.; Antonczak, A.J. Laser-Induced Color Marking of Titanium: A Modeling Study of the Interference Effect and the Impact of Protective Coating. *Math. Probl. Eng.* **2017**, *2017*, 1–11. [CrossRef]
170. Liu, H.; Lin, W.; Hong, M. Surface coloring by laser irradiation of solid substrates. *APL Photon.* **2019**, *4*, 051101. [CrossRef]
171. Vorobyev, A.Y.; Guo, C. Colorizing metals with femtosecond laser pulses. *Appl. Phys. Lett.* **2008**, *92*, 041914. [CrossRef]
172. Dusser, B.; Sagan, S.; Soder, H.; Faure, N.; Colombier, J.-P.; Jourlin, M.; Audouard, E. Controlled nanostructrures formation by ultra fast laser pulses for color marking. *Opt. Express* **2010**, *18*, 2913–2924. [CrossRef]
173. Ackerl, N.; Gugger, P.; Warhanek, M.; Gysel, J.; Wegener, K. Ultra-Short Pulsed Laser Marking and Coloration of Metals with Segmented Pixel Parameter Transformation. *JLMN* **2020**, *15*. [CrossRef]
174. Vorobyev, A.Y.; Guo, C. Direct femtosecond laser surface nano/microstructuring and its applications: Direct femtosecond laser surface nano/microstructuring and its applications. *Laser Photonics Rev.* **2013**, *7*, 385–407. [CrossRef]
175. Guay, J.-M.; Lesina, A.C.; Cote, G.; Charron, M.; Poitras, D.; Ramunno, L.; Berini, P.; Weck, A. Laser-induced plasmonic colours on metals. *Nat. Commun.* **2017**, *8*, 16095. [CrossRef]
176. Berini, P.; Guay, J.-M.; Lesina, A.C.; Walia, J.; Ramunno, L.; Weck, A.; Krupin, O.; Warren, M. Plasmonic Colours on Bulk Metals: Laser Coloring of Large Areas Exhibiting High Topography. In *Frontiers in Ultrafast Optics: Biomedical, Scientific, and Industrial Applications XVIII, Proceedings of the SPIE LASE, San Francisco, CA, USA, 27 January–1 February 2018*; SPIE: Bellingham, WA, USA, 2018; Volume 10522, p. 105220G.
177. Lumentum. *FlexBurstTM—Picosecond Micromachining Lasers Offer "Burst Mode" with Full User Control of Intra-Burst Pulse Energy Distribution*; Lumentum: San Jose, CA, USA, 2016.
178. Guay, J.-M.; Lesina, A.C.; Baxter, J.; Killaire, G.; Ramunno, L.; Berini, P.; Weck, A. Topography Tuning for Plasmonic Color Enhancement via Picosecond Laser Bursts. *Adv. Opt. Mater.* **2018**, *6*, 1800189. [CrossRef]
179. Stratakis, E.; Bonse, J.; Heitz, J.; Siegel, J.; Tsibidis, G.; Skoulas, E.; Papadopoulos, A.; Mimidis, A.; Joel, A.-C.; Comanns, P.; et al. Laser engineering of biomimetic surfaces. *Mater. Sci. Eng. R Rep.* **2020**, *141*, 100562. [CrossRef]
180. Masato, D.; Sorgato, M.; Batal, A.; Dimov, S.; Lucchetta, G. Thin-wall injection molding of polypropylene using molds with different laser-induced periodic surface structures. *Polym. Eng. Sci.* **2019**, *59*, 1889–1896. [CrossRef]
181. Florian, C.; Kirner, S.V.; Krüger, J.; Bonse, J. Surface functionalization by laser-induced periodic surface structures. *J. Laser Appl.* **2020**, *32*, 022063. [CrossRef]
182. Piccolo, L.; Sorgato, M.; Batal, A.; Dimov, S.; Lucchetta, G.; Masato, D. Functionalization of Plastic Parts by Replication of Variable Pitch Laser-Induced Periodic Surface Structures. *Micromachines* **2020**, *11*, 429. [CrossRef] [PubMed]
183. Bonse, J.; Höhm, S.; Kirner, S.V.; Rosenfeld, A.; Krüger, J. Laser-Induced Periodic Surface Structures—A Scientific Evergreen. *IEEE J. Sel. Top. Quantum Electron.* **2017**, *23*, 9000615. [CrossRef]
184. Bonse, J.; Graf, S. Maxwell Meets Marangoni—A Review of Theories on Laser-Induced Periodic Surface Structures. *Laser Photonics Rev.* **2020**, *14*, 2000215. [CrossRef]
185. Bonse, J. Quo Vadis LIPSS? Recent and Future Trends on Laser-Induced Periodic Surface Structures. *Nanomaterials* **2020**, *10*, 1950. [CrossRef]
186. Bonse, J.; Kirner, S.V.; Krüger, J. Laser-Induced Periodic Surface Structures (LIPSS). In *Handbook of Laser Micro- and Nano-Engineering*; Sugioka, K., Ed.; Springer International Publishing: New York, NY, USA, 2021; pp. 1–59.
187. Fraggelakis, F.; Mincuzzi, G.; Lopez, J.; Manek-Hönninger, I.; Kling, R. Controlling 2D laser nano structuring over large area with double femtosecond pulses—ScienceDirect. *Appl. Surf. Sci.* **2019**, *470*, 677–686. [CrossRef]
188. Hashida, M.; Furukawa, Y.; Inoue, S.; Sakabe, S.; Masuno, S.; Kusaba, M.; Sakagami, H.; Tsukamoto, M. Uniform LIPSS on titanium irradiated by two-color double-pulse beam of femtosecond laser. *J. Laser Appl.* **2020**, *32*, 022054. [CrossRef]
189. Hashida, M. Periodic Grating Structures on Metal Self-organized by Double-pulse Irradiation. *J. Laser Micro Nanoeng.* **2014**, *9*, 234–237. [CrossRef]
190. Hashida, M.; Nishii, T.; Miyasaka, Y.; Sakagami, H.; Shimizu, M.; Inoue, S.; Sakabe, S. Orientation of periodic grating structures controlled by double-pulse irradiation. *Appl. Phys. A* **2016**, *122*, 1–5. [CrossRef]
191. Giannuzzi, G.; Gaudiuso, C.; Di Franco, C.; Scamarcio, G.; Lugarà, P.M.; Ancona, A. Large area laser-induced periodic surface structures on steel by bursts of femtosecond pulses with picosecond delays. *Opt. Lasers Eng.* **2019**, *114*, 15–21. [CrossRef]
192. Giannuzzi, G.; Gaudiuso, C.; Cinquino, M.; Di Mundo, R.; Mirenghi, L.; Di Franco, C.; Scamarcio, G.; Lugarà, P.M.; Ancona, A. 1-D and 2-D Surface Structuring of Steel by Bursts of Femtosecond Laser Pulses. In *Laser-Based Micro- and Nanoprocessing XIII, Proceedings of the SPIE LASE, San Francisco, CA, USA, 4 February 2019*; SPIE: Bellingham, WA, USA, 2019; Volume 10906, p. 109060O.

193. Wang, X.; Li, C.; Ma, C.; Feng, J.; Hong, W.; Zhang, Z. Formation of laser induced periodic structures on stainless steel using multi-burst picosecond pulses. *Opt. Express* **2018**, *26*, 6325–6330. [CrossRef]
194. Fraggelakis, F.; Giannuzzi, G.; Gaudiuso, C.; Manek-Hönninger, I.; Mincuzzi, G.; Ancona, A.; Kling, R. Double- and Multi-Femtosecond Pulses Produced by Birefringent Crystals for the Generation of 2D Laser-Induced Structures on a Stainless Steel Surface. *Materials* **2019**, *12*, 1257. [CrossRef]
195. Höhm, S.; Rosenfeld, A.; Krüger, J.; Bonse, J. Area dependence of femtosecond laser-induced periodic surface structures for varying band gap materials after double pulse excitation. *Appl. Surf. Sci.* **2013**, *278*, 7–12. [CrossRef]
196. Höhm, S.; Herzlieb, M.; Rosenfeld, A.; Krüger, J.; Bonse, J. Femtosecond laser-induced periodic surface structures on silicon upon polarization controlled two-color double-pulse irradiation. *Opt. Express* **2015**, *23*, 61–71. [CrossRef]
197. Jaeggi, B.; Neuenschwander, B.; Zimmermann, M.; Zecherle, M.; Boeckler, E.W. Time-Optimized Laser Micro Machining by Using a New High Dynamic and High Precision Galvo Scanner. In *Laser Applications in Microelectronic and Optoelectronic Manufacturing (LAMOM) XXI, Proceedings of the SPIE LASE, San Francisco, CA, USA, 13–18 February 2016*; SPIE: Bellingham, WA, USA, 2016; Volume 9735, p. 973513.
198. Häfner, T.; Heberle, J.; Holder, D.; Schmidt, M. Adjustment of surface energy on steel surfaces due to CLP generation by picosecond laser processing. In Proceedings of the Lasers in Manufacturing Conference, Munich, Germany, 22–25 June 2015; pp. 1–10.
199. Jaeggi, B.; Neuenschwander, B.; Hunziker, U.; Zuercher, J.; Meier, T.; Zimmermann, M.; Selbmann, K.H.; Hennig, G. Ultra-High-Precision Surface Structuring by Synchronizing a Galvo Scanner with an Ultra-Short-Pulsed Laser System in MOPA Arrangement. In *Laser Applications in Microelectronic and Optoelectronic Manufacturing (LAMOM) XVII, Proceedings of the SPIE LASE, San Francisco, CA, USA, 21–26 January 2012*; 82430K; SPIE: Bellingham, WA, USA, 2012.
200. Loeschner, U.; Schille, J.; Streek, A.; Knebel, T.; Hartwig, L.; Hillmann, R.; Endisch, C. High-rate laser microprocessing using a polygon scanner system. *J. Laser Appl.* **2015**, *27*, S29303. [CrossRef]
201. Schille, J.; Schneider, L.; Mauersberger, S.; Szokup, S.; Höhn, S.; Pötschke, J.; Reiß, F.; Leidich, E.; Löschner, U. High-Rate Laser Surface Texturing for Advanced Tribological Functionality. *Lubricants* **2020**, *8*, 33. [CrossRef]
202. Jaeggi, B.; Remund, S.; Streubel, R.; Goekce, B.; Barcikowski, S.; Neuenschwander, B. Laser Micromachining of Metals with Ultra-Short Pulses: Factors Limiting the Scale-Up Process. *JLMN* **2017**, *12*, 267–273.
203. Brenner, A.; Zecherle, M.; Verpoort, S.; Schuster, K.; Schnitzler, C.; Kogel-Hollacher, M.; Reisacher, M.; Nohn, B. Efficient production of design textures on large-format 3D mold tools. *J. Laser Appl.* **2020**, *32*, 012018. [CrossRef]
204. Phipps, C.; Luke, J. Diode Laser-Driven Microthrusters: A New Departure for Micropropulsion. *AIAA J.* **2002**, *40*, 310–318. [CrossRef]
205. Phipps, C.; Birkan, M.; Bohn, W.; Eckel, H.-A.; Horisawa, H.; Lippert, T.; Michaelis, M.; Rezunkov, Y.; Sasoh, A.; Schall, W.; et al. Review: Laser-Ablation Propulsion. *J. Propuls. Power* **2010**, *26*, 609–637. [CrossRef]
206. Phipps, C.R.; Baker, K.L.; Libby, S.; Liedahl, D.A.; Olivier, S.S.; Pleasance, L.D.; Rubenchik, A.; Trebes, J.E.; George, E.V.; Marcovici, B.; et al. Removing orbital debris with lasers. *Adv. Space Res.* **2012**, *49*, 1283–1300. [CrossRef]
207. Scharring, S.; Lorbeer, R.A.; Karg, S.; Pastuschka, L.; Förster, D.J.; Eckel, H.A. The MICROLAS Concept: Precise Thrust Generation in the Micronewton Range by Laser Ablation. In *Technology for Small Satellite Research: Payloads and Subsystem Technologies Small Satellite Applications, Missions, and In-Orbit Experiences*; International Academy of Astronautics: Stockholm, Sweden, 2018; pp. 27–34.
208. Phipps, C.R. Laser Ablation Propulsion and Its Applications in Space. In *Superconductivity*; Springer Science and Business Media: New York, NY, USA, 2018; Volume 274, pp. 217–246.
209. Levchenko, I.; Bazaka, K.; Mazouffre, S.; Xu, S. Prospects and physical mechanisms for photonic space propulsion. *Nat. Photon.* **2018**, *12*, 649–657. [CrossRef]
210. Lorbeer, R.-A.; Zwilich, M.; Zabic, M.; Scharring, S.; Eisert, L.; Wilken, J.; Schumacher, D.; Roth, M.; Eckel, H.-A. Experimental verification of high energy laser-generated impulse for remote laser control of space debris. *Sci. Rep.* **2018**, *8*, 1–9. [CrossRef]
211. Cremers, D.A.; Knight, A.K. Laser-Induced Breakdown Spectroscopy. In *Encyclopedia of Analytical Chemistry*; Meyers, R.A., Ed.; John Wiley & Sons: Hoboken, NJ, USA, 2000; p. a5110t.
212. Song, K.; Lee, Y.-I.; Sneddon, J. Recent developments in instrumentation for laser induced breakdown spectroscopy. *Appl. Spectrosc. Rev.* **2002**, *37*, 89–117. [CrossRef]
213. Miziolek, A.W.; Palleschi, V.; Schechter, I. *Laser-Induced Breakdown Spectroscopy (LIBS): Fundamentals and Applications*; Cambridge University Press: Cambridge, MA, USA, 2006.
214. Kim, B.-M.; Feit, M.; Rubenchik, A.; Mammini, B.; Da Silva, L. Optical feedback signal for ultrashort laser pulse ablation of tissue. *Appl. Surf. Sci.* **1998**, *127-129*, 857–862. [CrossRef]
215. Margetic, V.; Pakulev, A.; Stockhaus, A.; Bolshov, M.; Niemax, K.; Hergenröder, R. A comparison of nanosecond and femtosecond laser-induced plasma spectroscopy of brass samples. *Spectrochim. Acta Part B At. Spectrosc.* **2000**, *55*, 1771–1785. [CrossRef]
216. Burgio, L.; Melessanaki, K.; Doulgeridis, M.; Clark, R.; Anglos, D. Pigment identification in paintings employing laser induced breakdown spectroscopy and Raman microscopy. *Spectrochim. Acta Part B At. Spectrosc.* **2001**, *56*, 905–913. [CrossRef]
217. Serifaki, K.; Boke, H.; Yalcin, S.; Ipekoglu, B. Characterization of materials used in the execution of historic oil paintings by XRD, SEM-EDS, TGA and LIBS analysis. *Mater. Charact.* **2009**, *60*, 303–311. [CrossRef]

218. Borba, F.D.S.L.; Cortez, J.; Asfora, V.K.; Pasquini, C.; Pimentel, M.F.; Pessis, A.-M.; Khoury, H.J. Multivariate treatment of LIBS data of prehistoric paintings. *J. Braz. Chem. Soc.* **2012**, *23*, 958–965. [CrossRef]
219. Dikmelik, Y.; McEnnis, C.; Spicer, J.B. Femtosecond and nanosecond laser-induced breakdown spectroscopy of trinitrotoluene. *Opt. Express* **2008**, *16*, 5332–5337. [CrossRef] [PubMed]
220. Gottfried, J.L.; De Lucia, F.C.; Munson, C.A.; Miziolek, A.W. Laser-induced breakdown spectroscopy for detection of explosives residues: A review of recent advances, challenges, and future prospects. *Anal. Bioanal. Chem.* **2009**, *395*, 283–300. [CrossRef]
221. Shaik, A.K.; Epuru, N.R.; Syed, H.; Byram, C.; Soma, V.R. Femtosecond laser induced breakdown spectroscopy based standoff detection of explosives and discrimination using principal component analysis. *Opt. Express* **2018**, *26*, 8069–8083. [CrossRef]
222. Gurevich, E.L.; Hergenröder, R. Femtosecond Laser-Induced Breakdown Spectroscopy: Physics, Applications, and Perspectives. *Appl. Spectrosc.* **2007**, *61*, A233–A242. [CrossRef]
223. Malvezzi, A.M. Laser–Matter Interaction in LIBS Experiments. In *Laser-Induced Breakdown Spectroscopy*; Musazzi, S., Perini, U., Eds.; Springer Series in Optical Sciences; Springer: Berlin/Heidelberg, Germany, 2014; Volume 182, pp. 3–29.
224. Labutin, T.A.; Lednev, V.N.; Ilyin, A.A.; Popov, A. Femtosecond laser-induced breakdown spectroscopy. *J. Anal. At. Spectrom.* **2015**, *31*, 90–118. [CrossRef]
225. Piñon, V.; Fotakis, C.; Nicolas, G.; Anglos, D. Double pulse laser-induced breakdown spectroscopy with femtosecond laser pulses. *Spectrochim. Acta Part B At. Spectrosc.* **2008**, *63*, 1006–1010. [CrossRef]
226. Lu, Y.; Zorba, V.; Mao, X.; Zheng, R.; Russo, R.E. UV fs–ns double-pulse laser induced breakdown spectroscopy for high spatial resolution chemical analysis. *J. Anal. At. Spectrom.* **2013**, *28*, 743–748. [CrossRef]
227. Bulanov, S.V.; Khoroshkov, V.S. Feasibility of using laser ion accelerators in proton therapy. *Plasma Phys. Rep.* **2002**, *28*, 453–456. [CrossRef]
228. Ditmire, T.; Donnelly, T.; Rubenchik, A.M.; Falcone, R.W.; Perry, M.D. Interaction of intense laser pulses with atomic clusters. *Phys. Rev. A* **1996**, *53*, 3379–3402. [CrossRef] [PubMed]
229. Malka, V.; Fritzler, S. Electron and proton beams produced by ultra short laser pulses in the relativistic regime. *Laser Part. Beams* **2004**, *22*, 399–405. [CrossRef]
230. Neely, D.; Foster, P.; Robinson, A.; Lindau, F.; Lundh, O.; Persson, A.; Wahlström, C.-G.; McKenna, P. Enhanced proton beams from ultrathin targets driven by high contrast laser pulses. *Appl. Phys. Lett.* **2006**, *89*, 021502. [CrossRef]
231. Andreev, A.; Sonobe, R.; Kawata, S.; Miyazaki, S.; Sakai, K.; Miyauchi, K.; Kikuchi, T.; Platonov, K.; Nemoto, K. Effect of a laser prepulse on fast ion generation in the interaction of ultra-short intense laser pulses with a limited-mass foil target. *Plasma Phys. Control. Fusion* **2006**, *48*, 1605–1619. [CrossRef]
232. Passoni, M.; Bertagna, L.; Zani, A. Target normal sheath acceleration: Theory, comparison with experiments and future perspectives. *New J. Phys.* **2010**, *12*, 045012. [CrossRef]
233. Daido, H.; Nishiuchi, M.; Pirozhkov, A. Review of laser-driven ion sources and their applications. *Rep. Prog. Phys.* **2012**, *75*, 056401. [CrossRef]
234. Fourmaux, S.; Buffechoux, S.; Albertazzi, B.; Capelli, D.; Levy, A.; Gnedyuk, S.; Lecherbourg, L.; Lassonde, P.; Payeur, S.; Antici, P.; et al. Investigation of laser-driven proton acceleration using ultra-short, ultra-intense laser pulses. *Phys. Plasmas* **2013**, *20*, 013110. [CrossRef]
235. Barberio, M.; Veltri, S.; Scisciò, M.; Antici, P. Laser-Accelerated Proton Beams as Diagnostics for Cultural Heritage. *Sci. Rep.* **2017**, *7*, 40415. [CrossRef] [PubMed]
236. Barberio, M.; Scisciò, M.; Vallières, S.; Cardelli, F.; Chen, S.N.; Famulari, G.; Gangolf, T.; Revet, G.; Schiavi, A.; Senzacqua, M.; et al. Laser-accelerated particle beams for stress testing of materials. *Nat. Commun.* **2018**, *9*, 372. [CrossRef] [PubMed]
237. Torrisi, L.; Cutroneo, M.; Torrisi, A.; Silipigni, L.; Costa, G.; Rosinski, M.; Badziak, J.; Wołowski, J.; Zaraś-Szydłowska, A.; Parys, P. Protons accelerated in the target normal sheath acceleration regime by a femtosecond laser. *Phys. Rev. Accel. Beams* **2019**, *22*, 021302. [CrossRef]
238. Bulanov, S.; Esirkepov, T.; Khoroshkov, V.; Kuznetsov, A.; Pegoraro, F. Oncological hadrontherapy with laser ion accelerators. *Phys. Lett. A* **2002**, *299*, 240–247. [CrossRef]
239. Malka, V.; Faure, J.; Gauduel, Y.A. Ultra-short electron beams based spatio-temporal radiation biology and radiotherapy. *Mutat. Res. Mutat. Res.* **2010**, *704*, 142–151. [CrossRef]
240. Schardt, D.; Elsaesser, T.; Schulz-Ertner, D. Heavy-ion tumor therapy: Physical and radiobiological benefits. *Rev. Mod. Phys.* **2010**, *82*, 383–425. [CrossRef]
241. Döppner, T.; Fennel, T.; Diederich, T.; Tiggesbäumker, J.; Meiwes-Broer, K.H. Controlling the Coulomb Explosion of Silver Clusters by Femtosecond Dual-Pulse Laser Excitation. *Phys. Rev. Lett.* **2005**, *94*, 013401. [CrossRef]
242. Markey, K.; McKenna, P.; Brenner, C.M.; Carroll, D.C.; Günther, M.M.; Harres, K.; Kar, S.; Lancaster, K.; Nürnberg, F.; Quinn, M.N.; et al. Spectral Enhancement in the Double Pulse Regime of Laser Proton Acceleration. *Phys. Rev. Lett.* **2010**, *105*, 195008. [CrossRef] [PubMed]
243. Uryupina, D.S.; Ivanov, K.A.; Brantov, A.; Savel'Ev, A.B.; Bychenkov, V.Y.; Povarnitsyn, M.E.; Volkov, R.V.; Tikhonchuk, V.T. Femtosecond laser-plasma interaction with prepulse-generated liquid metal microjets. *Phys. Plasmas* **2012**, *19*, 13104. [CrossRef]

materials MDPI

Perspective

Printing via Laser-Induced Forward Transfer and the Future of Digital Manufacturing

Camilo Florian [1,2,*] and Pere Serra [3]

1 Princeton Institute for the Research and Technology of Materials (PRISM), Princeton University, 70 Prospect Av, Princeton, NJ 08540, USA
2 Instituto de Óptica Daza de Valdés, Consejo Superior de Investigaciones Científicas (IO-CSIC), Calle Serrano 122, 28006 Madrid, Spain
3 Departament de Fisica Aplicada, Universitat de Barcelona, Martí i Franqués 1, 08028 Barcelona, Spain
* Correspondence: camilo.florian@csic.es

Abstract: In the last decades, digital manufacturing has constituted the headline of what is starting to be known as the 'fourth industrial revolution', where the fabrication processes comprise a hybrid of technologies that blur the lines between fundamental sciences, engineering, and even medicine as never seen before. One of the reasons why this mixture is inevitable has to do with the fact that we live in an era that incorporates technology in every single aspect of our daily lives. In the industry, this has translated into fabrication versatility, as follows: design changes on a final product are just one click away, fabrication chains have evolved towards continuous roll-to roll processes, and, most importantly, the overall costs and fabrication speeds are matching and overcoming most of the traditional fabrication methods. Laser-induced forward transfer (LIFT) stands out as a versatile set of fabrication techniques, being the closest approach to an all-in-one additive manufacturing method compatible with virtually any material. In this technique, laser radiation is used to propel the material of interest and deposit it at user-defined locations with high spatial resolution. By selecting the proper laser parameters and considering the interaction of the laser light with the material, it is possible to transfer this technique from robust inorganic materials to fragile biological samples. In this work, we first present a brief introduction on the current developments of the LIFT technique by surveying recent scientific review publications. Then, we provide a general research overview by making an account of the publication and citation numbers of scientific papers on the LIFT technique considering the last three decades. At the same time, we highlight the geographical distribution and main research institutions that contribute to this scientific output. Finally, we present the patent status and commercial forecasts to outline future trends for LIFT in different scientific fields.

Keywords: laser printing; laser-induced forward transfer (LIFT); digital manufacturing; additive manufacturing; printing of materials

Citation: Florian, C.; Serra, P. Printing via Laser-Induced Forward Transfer and the Future of Digital Manufacturing. *Materials* **2023**, *16*, 698. https://doi.org/10.3390/ma16020698

Academic Editor: Jun Liu

Received: 16 November 2022
Revised: 19 December 2022
Accepted: 3 January 2023
Published: 11 January 2023

1. Introduction

Digital manufacturing comprises fabrication approaches and techniques to create functional structures and devices where the design, modification, and final optimization can be performed digitally. The biggest advantage over conventional fabrication is the possibility to work without masks, master samples, or molds, allowing design correction in parallel with fabrication. In general, these techniques constantly try to solve key open challenges, such as low overall fabrication costs, industrial scalability, and compatibility with current techniques, wide material compatibility, and high spatial resolution and reproducibility. Researchers and engineers pursue the creation of an all-in-one technique that tackles these challenges but, unfortunately, this is an elusive task, since in most of the cases, there are limitations in at least one of these fronts. For example, despite the fact that there are numerous fabrication techniques with good performances in laboratory conditions, one of the biggest problems still comes when these fabrication techniques are required to perform in real industrial workspaces, where scalability and mass production at the lowest costs and highest speeds mark clear quests for developers.

In the present paper, we center our attention on a specific laser printing technique commonly known as laser-induced forward transfer (LIFT). In laser printing via LIFT, irradiation from a laser source is focused on a donor substrate that contains the material of interest. The interaction of the radiation with the donor material results in the propulsion of a tiny amount of material towards an acceptor substrate conveniently positioned, giving a place for the formation of a printed voxel. Through the sequential printing of voxels, it is possible to generate practically any layout. Originally, the technique was mostly suitable for pulsed laser sources using mainly solids as donor material, which limited its scope but, nowadays, the increasingly wider availability of reliable and affordable laser sources (either pulsed or CW, with different wavelengths), combined with the adequate material preparation (solid, paste, or liquid form), it is possible to create devices for the microelectronics industry, as well as miniaturized tests for microbiology, and it has lately shown potential for tissue engineering applications, among many others. Importantly, this paper does not intend to be the ultimate review of the technique (for that, we will direct the reader to corresponding review papers), and neither is it an open discussion on the most recent advances. We start the introduction by surveying review papers on the current developments and sky edge applications that implement this printing technique, such as the ones in references [1–3]. From there, the principle of operation for the transfer of materials disposed in solid, paste, and liquid films for diverse applications is discussed. With this information in hand, we then provide a general assessment on the past, present, and future of the LIFT technique considering published patents and patent applications where the LIFT is the central technique. Finally, by analyzing commercial data from the broader picture of additive manufacturing, we present commercial forecasts and possible trends for the LIFT technique in exploitable scientific areas, such as electronics, biology, and medicine, to name a few.

2. A Brief Overview of the Laser-Induced Forward Transfer (LIFT) Technique

In the printing of materials via laser-induced forward transfer (LIFT), the material of interest is generally disposed as a thin film onto a transparent substrate called the "donor substrate". A laser beam is then focused at the interface between the thin film and the holding transparent substrate, producing a micro-explosion that propels the material forward. When another "receptor substrate" is positioned at a convenient distance from the donor, the propelled material is safely deposited at specific user-defined positions. Traditionally, a pulsed laser is used, and each pulse produces a printed voxel of material, the volume of which volume can be as low as a few femtoliters [4]. Recent developments have implemented approaches that allow the printing of materials with two or more laser pulses [5,6], and even continuous wave (CW) laser sources [7]. The resulting pixel geometry and amount of transferred material depend on parameters regarding the initial conditions of the donor material (thickness, viscosity, optical properties), the use of an additional sacrificial absorbing layer (commonly known as a dynamic release layer or 'DRL'), the physical and chemical properties of the receptor substrate (wetting, oxidation, temperature), and the laser conditions (fluence, intensity distribution, wavelength, pulse duration). Figure 1 contains a sketch that displays the general configuration and main elements in a traditional configuration to transfer materials via LIFT.

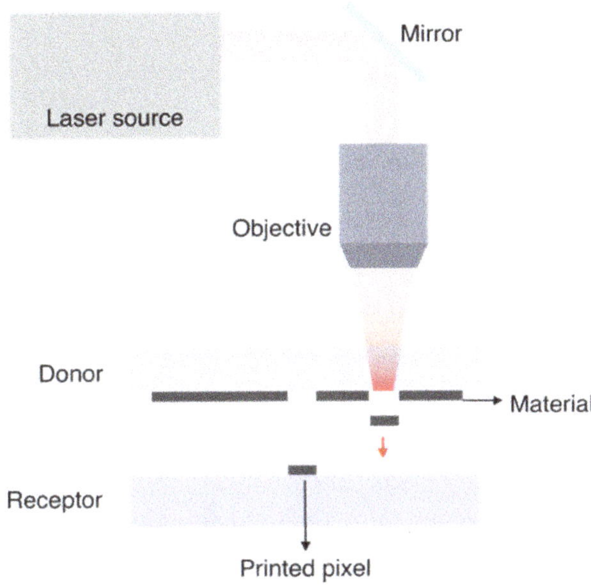

Figure 1. Sketch (not to scale) that includes the main elements of an experimental setup to print materials via LIFT.

In order to provide a classification scheme for all the LIFT variants, we can use as a sorting parameter the disposition of the material to be transferred, being (i) materials in a solid state, (ii) pastes, (iii) or simply liquids. In the following, we will briefly discuss the principles of operation for each case and provide relevant examples for each case.

2.1. LIFT from Solids

In this group of applications for the LIFT technique, the starting base material in the donor film corresponds to a solid layer that usually absorbs the incoming radiation and is expelled towards the receptor substrate [1]. Two general scenarios could be drawn depending on how the material is modified by the laser radiation; in the first one, the solid material is locally melted, and it is the liquid phase that is propelled forward [8]. The solidification occurs generally on the receptor substrate in the form of isolated hemispherical droplets, as displayed in Figure 2A. A second case takes place when the material to be transferred should not undergo any material phase change. This particular approach is suitable for extremely sensitive materials where the crystalline structures should be conserved after the transfer, or the material is highly sensitive to thermal changes induced by the laser irradiation. In this case, the use of an intermediate sacrificial layer is implemented. This layer will absorb most of the incoming radiation, producing the localized explosion that will propel the material of interest towards the receptor substrate [9]. The transfer dynamics in this case is more complex, since it involves the participation of an additional material that will react differently to the laser radiation, as displayed in Figure 2B.

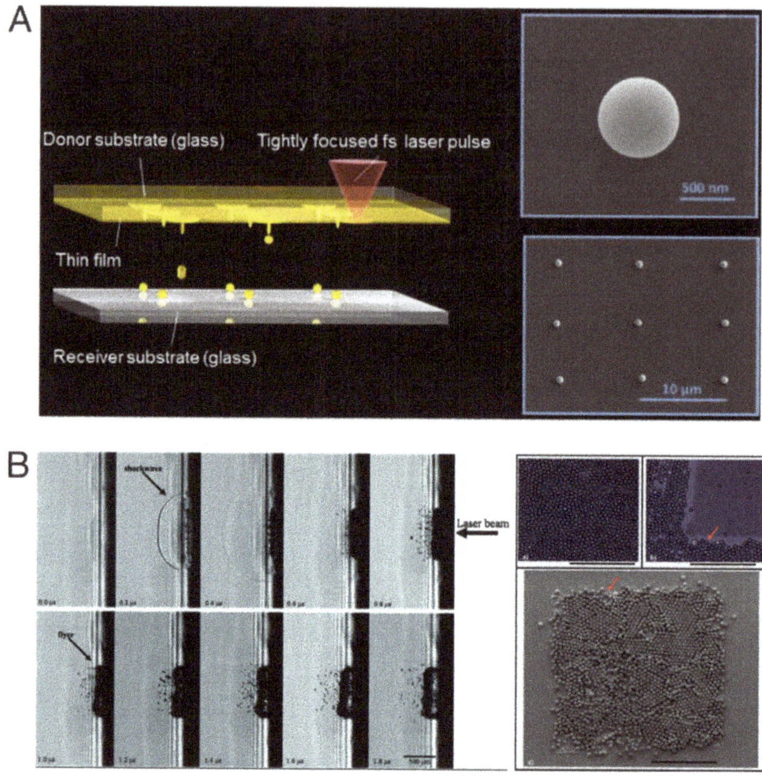

Figure 2. Printing of materials starting from a solid donor film following two different scenarios. (**A**) Melted material, where the final output corresponds to individual spherical particles. Reprinted under creative commons permission (CC BY-NC-ND 4.0) from [8], copyright 2018, De Gruyter. (**B**) In this transfer, the use of a sacrificial layer allowed the printing of an array of microspheres that followed the square shape distribution of the incident laser beam. Reprinted with permission from [9], with the permission of AIP Publishing (Copyright 2010).

2.2. *LIFT from Pastes*

In this particular case of the LIFT technique, also known as laser decal transfer (LDT), the donor material is a highly viscous paste. Due to the nature of both material and processing conditions, the paste is not subjected to deformation due to surface tension effects. Typically, the transferred material shape has the same geometry as the laser intensity distribution, which allows the transfer of voxels of material with complex shapes when a regular LIFT setup is combined with digital micromirrors, spatial light modulators, or phase masks to define a particular intensity distribution profile. In the example shown in Figure 3 [10], the donor material corresponds to a silver nanoparticle suspension with a viscosity of 100 Pa.s. Congruent transfers occur when the right viscosity is achieved. The laser radiation impinges the donor film from the top and the interaction is produced at the interface between the transparent holder substrate and the paste film. In the figure, each image corresponds to a frame of a video acquired with a high-speed camera at the times indicated in the insets. The whole transfer process corresponds to a single event. When a receiving substrate is placed close by, the resulting deposition corresponds to a flat cylinder in the form of a wafer, the thickness of which is similar to the one of the donor films.

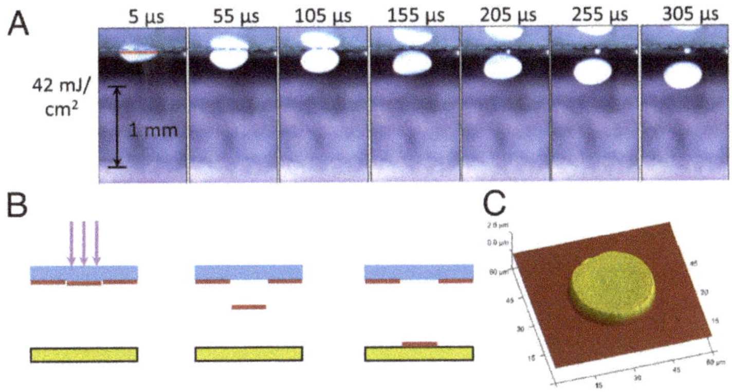

Figure 3. (**A**) Snapshots of a high-speed video of the transfer via LIFT of a high viscosity silver paste. In the top figure, a single laser pulse with a circular shape comes from the top, pushing downwards a 'coin-like' voxel that flies towards the receptor substrate without breaking. The schematics is included in (**B**), and a topography acquired via AFM of the final printed material is shown in (**C**). The figure has been reprinted from [10], with the permission of AIP Publishing (Copyright 2013).

2.3. *LIFT from Liquids*

A plethora of variants exist when the material to be printed is disposed as a liquid film in the donor substrate [1,3]. The transfer dynamics are similar to the previous examples; however, there are additional parameters to consider, particularly regarding the energy absorption in the liquid and the rheological conditions of the material. In general, once the laser is absorbed by the liquid or the intermediate absorbing layer, a bubble is produced, followed by the formation of a jet that travels at high speed towards the receptor substrate conveniently placed in the vicinity of the donor substrate. The liquid jet gently feeds what will finally turn into a printed pixel in the shape of a hemispherical droplet, the dimensions of which depend on the amount of transferred material and the surface energy of the liquid on the surface of the receptor substrate. Figure 4 shows examples of LIFT of liquids with no use of an intermediate layer (Figure 4A [11]), with a metallic absorbing layer (Figure 4B [12]), and with the use of an absorbing polymer layer (Figure 4C [13]). More detailed examples can be found in the most recent review articles on the technique [1,3].

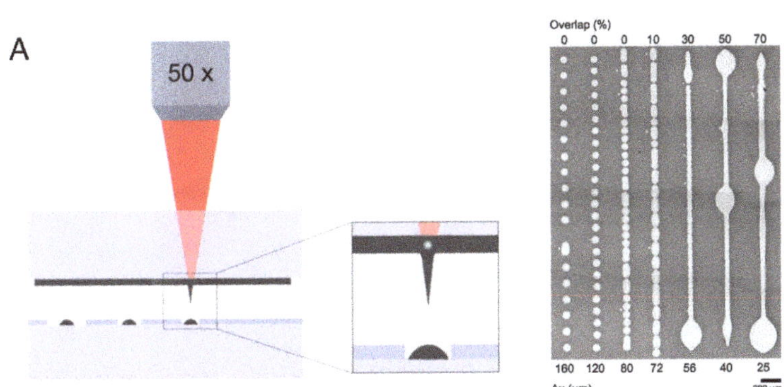

Figure 4. *Cont.*

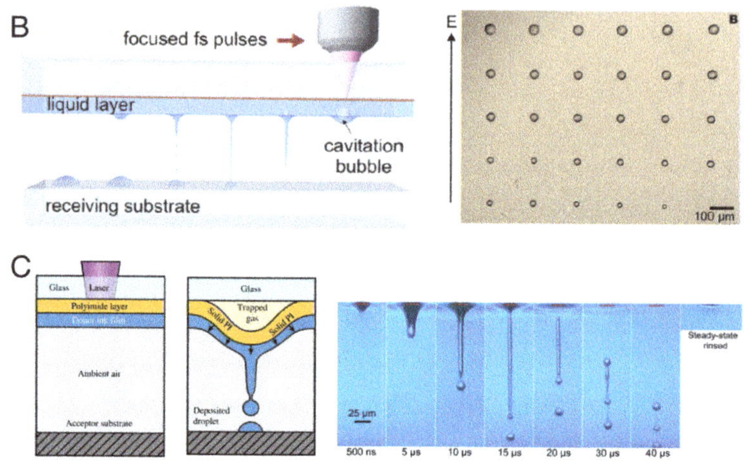

Figure 4. (**A**) No sacrificial layer (the liquid absorbs the laser radiation). Reprinted from [11], copyright (2016), with permission from Elsevier. (**B**) Metallic intermediate layer. Reprinted from [12], copyright (2017), with permission from Elsevier. (**C**) Blister-actuated LIFT based on the use of a polymer absorbing layer. Reprinted/adapted from Ref. [13] (Copyright 2018) with permission from Wiley Books.

3. LIFT Scientific Literature

The first report on the idea of using a laser beam to propel materials towards a receptor substrate was published by Levene et al. in 1970 [14]. In that experiment, the donor substrate was a polyethylene typewriter ribbon covered with black ink. Material deposition was reported to be feasible for both forward (such as in Figure 1) and backward configuration (originally called 'reverse transfer', where the material is ejected in the opposite direction to the laser beam), producing continuous printed lines of ink. It was not until 1986 that Bohandy et al. [15] coined the term LIFT (laser-induced forward transfer) in what became one of the most cited papers on the field. Since then, numerous reports have been published, accounting for 661 peer-reviewed papers, as can be seen in the plot of Figure 5, with an increasing number of citations according to the ISI Web of Science database.

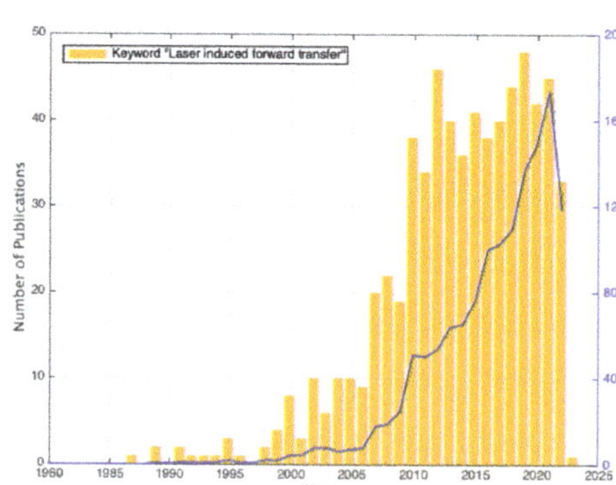

Figure 5. Number of published peer-reviewed articles (grand total of 661) and total number of citations per year. Data obtained via the ISI Web of Science, by sorting the keyword "laser induced forward transfer" as of 11 November 2022.

It has to be noted that, in most cases, when talking about transferring materials via LIFT, the material to be deposited is virtually the same as that disposed in the donor substrate. In the cases where the material is significatively altered compared to the donor material, we have only included studies called reactive LIFT (r-LIFT), in which the material changes its chemical composition mainly due to the action of traveling through a reactive atmosphere or by producing certain structural change due to the laser radiation [16]. It is not the case for the papers regarding matrix-assisted pulsed laser evaporation (MAPLE), which also follows the printing principle of LIFT, but that are not included in the data of Figure 5. The MAPLE technique has grown significantly and independently, generating a full string of numerous papers that deserve their own study; for this reason, they are out of scope in the present paper.

Among the publications included in Figure 5, the top five journals where the research was published were Applied Surface Science (13%), Proceedings of SPIE (9%), Applied Physics A (7%), Applied Physics Letters (3.6%), and the Journal of Laser Micro Nanoengineering (3.2%). An extended list is included in Table 1. Using the classification proposed by the ISI Web of Science, the fields which these publications fall into include applied physics, materials science, optics, physical chemistry, and condensed matter.

Table 1. Journal names and number of papers published on LIFT, according to the ISI Web of Science, by sorting the keyword "laser induced forward transfer" as of 11 November 2022.

Publication Name	Number of Papers	Percentage (%)
Applied Surface Science	84	12.7
Proceedings of the Society of Photo Optical Instrumentation Engineers SPIE	59	8.9
Applied Physics A Materials Science Processing	48	7.2
Applied Physics Letters	24	3.6
Journal of Laser Micro Nanoengineering	21	3.1
Optics Express	14	2.1
Journal of Applied Physics	11	1.6
Conference on Lasers and Electro Optics	9	1.3
Journal of [illegible]	9	1.3
Nanomaterials	9	1.3

We have plotted the same data of Figure 5 in a map displayed in Figure 6. The number of publications is sorted by the country where the corresponding author institution was reported. From here, we can see how the most productive region overall is Europe, with notable contributions from North America and Asia. An interactive tool is included as a Supplementary Material.

Table 2 contains a list with the names of the main funding agencies that made possible most of the contributions of the researchers on the field in these countries, including the number of papers produced and its percentage with respect to the total number of publications (661). This information is also available at the ISI Web of Science database.

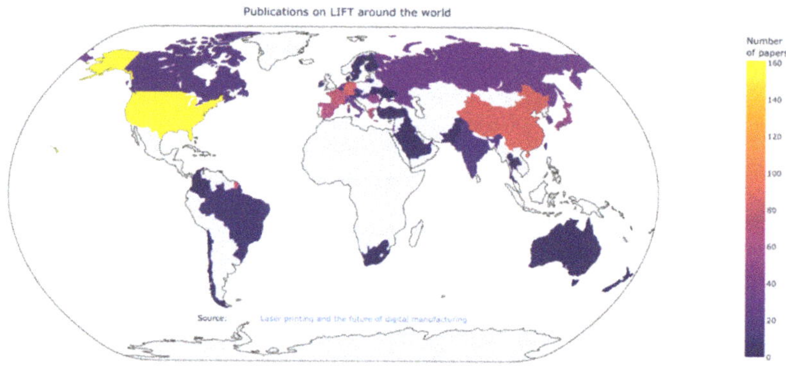

Figure 6. Geographical distribution of the total amount of publications per country on LIFT around the world. Data obtained via the ISI Web of Science by sorting the keyword "laser induced forward transfer" as of 8 June 2022. An interactive resource is available as a Supplementary Material.

Table 2. Main international funding agencies that support the research reflected in the published papers on LIFT, according to the ISI Web of Science, by sorting the keyword "laser induced forward transfer" as of 11 November 2022.

Institution	Country	Number of Papers	Percentage (%)
European Commission	European countries	99	14.9
National Natural Science Foundation of China	China	34	5.1
National Science Foundation	United States	25	3.7
German Research Foundation	Germany	24	3.6
Office of Naval Research	United States	23	3.4
Engineering Physical Sciences Research Council	United Kingdom	21	3.1
UK Research Innovation	United Kingdom	21	3.1
French National Research Agency	France	19	2.8
Spanish Government	Spain	19	2.8
Swiss National Science Foundation	Switzerland	13	1.9

4. Industrial Perspectives

4.1. Patent Applications Landscape

Relevant technological throughputs are often published as patents in order to grant intellectual property rights to the authors. It is important to note that patent applications and the process for their publication follows a procedure that is dramatically different from the one of scientific publications, and technical language is often used in combination with economic and legal terms, in order to provide a solid legal ground for protecting the technology as much as possible. For this reason, we focus our attention on patents that contain the keywords "laser induced forward transfer" from two public patent office databases, considering that the majority of publications on LIFT are located in these two regions according to Figure 6. These patent office databases are the European Patent Office (EPO) and the United States Patent and Trademark Office (USPTO). Based on this premise, we select patents publications that are publicly accessible and published with an assigned patent publication number, regardless of the acceptance or licensing status. In the following data we, therefore, jointly present patents with patent applications. We find 321 patents reported in the EPO and 303 in the USPTO, that, regardless of the publication country, are reported in these databases. Due to the large number of items, the specific lists are included as a Supplementary Material. The following plot in Figure 7 shows the number of patents and patent publications over time, considering the early publication date for the EPO results and the publication date for the USPTO results.

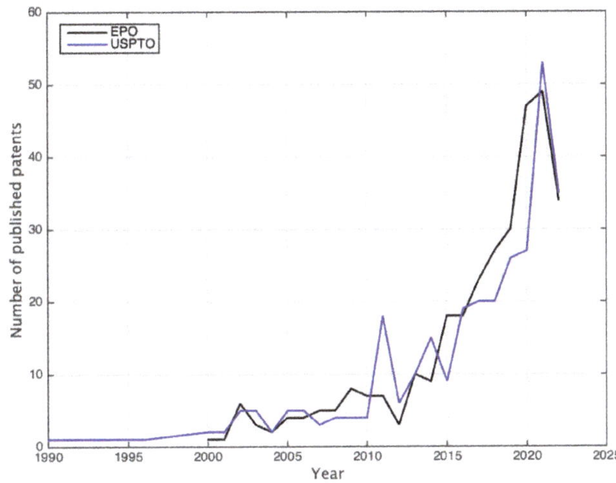

Figure 7. Number of published patent applications reported in the European Patent Office (EPO) and the United States Patent and Trademark Office (USPTO) per year. Data obtained on the respective databases, by sorting the keyword "laser induced forward transfer" as a whole string on 11 November 2022.

4.2. Commercial Forecast and Future Trends

From the current report on "The worldwide market for lasers: market review and forecast 2020" [17] from the European Photonics Industry Consortium (EPIC), that includes projections from 2020 to 2025 on different industries where laser processing of materials is at the center, we can extract an overview for future projections from the economical point of view.

We identify three main areas of revenue where laser printing can find a niche for development into industrial applications, including all the available commercial applications. As a disclosure note, these are just a limited selection of the biggest commercial areas. These areas are additive manufacturing, laser-based paper printing, and medicine. In the case of additive manufacturing, the reported total gross revenue for all applications accounted for 75.3M US dollars in 2022. It is projected a growth of 13.1% over the current decade. The second area of laser-based paper printing accounted for a revenue of around 48.5M US dollars for the year 2022; however, in this case, it is forecast that laser-based technology revenue in this commercial area will decrease over 4% over the current decade, mainly due to a shift toward a paper-less work culture that will mean a decrease in sales of printers in general. Finally, for the area of medicine, the revenue accounted for about 1500M US dollar in 2022, with an average growth estimation of about 7.4% over the current decade. For the LIFT technique, these figures are encouraging, particularly since the characteristic properties of the technique are suitable for the printing of complex materials in all the mentioned areas, as we will discuss in the following.

In the area of additive manufacturing, the selective deposition of materials to fabricate three-dimensional structures has been commercially exploited thanks to important developments in techniques and machines for the printing of polymers, metals, and ceramic-based materials. Commercial 3D printers are one successful example that has been booming in the last decade, and allows us to produce easily accessible methods for functional devices without the need for expensive lab equipment. In these printers, the material of interest is generally deposited in a layer-by-layer fashion, and it is subsequently melted at user-defined locations due to the interaction with an energetic laser beam [18–20]. At the end, several two-dimensional stacked layers lead to the fabrication of three-dimensional solid structures. The fundamental operation of these 3D printers has been applied for the additive deposition of diverse materials, allowing the fabrication of glass and polymer lab-on-a-chip devices with micrometer resolutions [21,22], as well as the construction of resin boats [23] and metallic rocket fuel tanks [24] of exceptional quality. The same principles for printing are used with the LIFT technique. There are numerous publications where the printing of solids, pastes, and liquid containing conductive materials have been used for the fabrication of conductive paths [25–27], light-emitting diodes [28], solar cells [29], and materials used for microsensors [30]. An important advantage over other printing techniques, such as ink-jet printing, relies on the fact that these systems are able to work with a wider viscosity range of inks with nanoparticle suspensions, which opens a wider variety of printable materials suitable for electronic applications, especially in the case of high-viscosity pastes made from particles with particle sizes in the microscale [1].

In the area of laser-based paper printing, there is one example of a commercial initiative that used the LIFT technique for graphical design paper printing on large areas. The machine was named Lasersonic, and it was capable of printing inks on paper at rates of 1.3 m^2/min, with resolutions of 600 dpi [31]. In this application, the ink used was disposed as a thin liquid film, the thickness of which was regulated by cylinders that provided a virtually unlimited ink supply, allowing for printing the ink at such high speeds in a roll-to-roll setup, demonstrating compatibility with current industrial fabrication techniques. The same principle can be applied for the commercial printing of flexible substrates, largely used in electronic devices, such as sensors [32], displays [33], electronic components [34], and solar cells [35], to name a few. In addition, it has been recently demonstrated that the printing of conductive inks via LIFT on paper can also be used for the fabrication of low-cost electronic devices [32].

In the area of medicine, the LIFT technique is of particular interest in the development of tissue printing for the fabrication of organs and organelles [36–40]. A success commercial example is the company Poietis, whose 4D Bioprinting technique incorporates a LIFT device into a commercial bioprinting machine for single-cell transfer. The advantages of the LIFT technique regarding positioning and controlled volume deposition, in combination with an in situ optical microscope, allows this machine to track over time the growth of individual cells and extracellular matrices. The company founders have different publications on the characterization of the technique towards its usage in bioprinting [41], as well as different patents where the LIFT technique is the core approach for the transfer of different biological materials. Although there are open challenges to be overcome, such as open questions regarding donor film drying (in the case of liquid donor films), cell aggregation, and potential metal toxicity, among others [38], there are advances on the field where the LIFT technique has been shown as useful for the transfer of biological materials [36–39]. It is also interesting to point out that by sorting out the strings "laser induced forward transfer" with "organ" and "organelle" in the EPO patent database, just in the last decade, 45 + 12 patents have been filed, which constitutes 17.7% of all of the patents data shown in Figure 7 for the EPO results. This demonstrates the exploitation potential for future technologies and a crescent interest not only from researchers, but also from companies in the medical and biological areas.

Supplementary Materials: The following supporting information can be downloaded at: https://www.mdpi.com/article/10.3390/ma16020698/s1.

Author Contributions: C.F. wrote the original draft. C.F. and P.S. edited the manuscript. All authors contributed to the scientific discussion and revision of the article. All authors have read and agreed to the published version of the manuscript.

Funding: C.F. acknowledges the support from the European Commission through the Marie Curie Individual Fellowship—Global grant No. 844977, while P.S. acknowledges the support from project PID2020-112669GB-I00 funded by MCIN/AEI/10.13039/501100011033.

Institutional Review Board Statement: Not applicable.

Informed Consent Statement: Not applicable.

Data Availability Statement: The data presented in this paper is available upon request to the corresponding author.

Acknowledgments: Special thanks to Antonio Castello from EPIC for helpful discussions.

Conflicts of Interest: The authors declare no conflict of interest.

References

1. Serra, P.; Piqué, A. Laser-Induced Forward Transfer: Fundamentals and Applications. *Adv. Mater. Technol.* **2019**, *4*, 1800099. [CrossRef]
2. Morales, M.; Munoz-Martin, D.; Marquez, A.; Lauzurica, S.; Molpeceres, C. Laser-Induced Forward Transfer Techniques and Applications. In *Advances in Laser Materials Processing: Technology, Research and Applications*; Elsevier: Amsterdam, The Netherlands, 2017; pp. 339–379. ISBN 9780081012529.
3. Fernández-Pradas, J.M.; Serra, P. Laser-Induced Forward Transfer: A Method for Printing Functional Inks. *Crystals* **2020**, *10*, 651. [CrossRef]
4. Zenou, M.; Sa'ar, A.; Kotler, Z. Laser Jetting of Femto-Liter Metal Droplets for High Resolution 3D Printed Structures. *Sci. Rep.* **2015**, *5*, 17265. [CrossRef] [PubMed]
5. Li, Q.; Alloncle, A.P.; Grojo, D.; Delaporte, P. Generating Liquid Nanojets from Copper by Dual Laser Irradiation for Ultra-High Resolution Printing. *Opt. Express* **2017**, *25*, 24164. [CrossRef] [PubMed]
6. Nakata, Y.; Tsubakimoto, K.; Miyanaga, N.; Narazaki, A.; Shoji, T.; Tsuboi, Y. Laser-Induced Transfer of Noble Metal Nanodots with Femtosecond Laser-Interference Processing. *Nanomaterials* **2021**, *11*, 305. [CrossRef] [PubMed]
7. Sopeña, P.; González-Torres, S.; Fernández-Pradas, J.M.; Serra, P. Spraying Dynamics in Continuous Wave Laser Printing of Conductive Inks. *Sci. Rep.* **2018**, *8*, 7999. [CrossRef]
8. Li, Q.; Grojo, D.; Alloncle, A.P.; Chichkov, B.; Delaporte, P. Digital Laser Micro-and Nanoprinting. *Nanophotonics* **2018**, *8*, 27–44. [CrossRef]
9. Palla-Papavlu, A.; Dinca, V.; Paraico, I.; Moldovan, A.; Shaw-Stewart, J.; Schneider, C.W.; Kovacs, E.; Lippert, T.; Dinescu, M. Microfabrication of Polystyrene Microbead Arrays by Laser Induced Forward Transfer. *J. Appl. Phys.* **2010**, *108*, 033111. [CrossRef]
10. Mathews, S.A.; Auyeung, R.C.Y.; Kim, H.; Charipar, N.A.; Piqué, A. High-Speed Video Study of Laser-Induced Forward Transfer of Silver Nano-Suspensions. *J. Appl. Phys.* **2013**, *114*, 064910. [CrossRef]
11. Florian, C.; Caballero-Lucas, F.; Fernández-Pradas, J.M.; Ogier, S.; Winchester, L.; Karnakis, D.; Geremia, R.; Artigas, R.; Serra, P. Printing of Silver Conductive Lines through Laser-Induced Forward Transfer. *Appl. Surf. Sci.* **2016**, *374*, 265–270. [CrossRef]
12. Florian, C.; Piazza, S.; Diaspro, A.; Serra, P.; Duocastella, M. Direct Laser Printing of Tailored Polymeric Microlenses. *ACS Appl. Mater. Interfaces* **2016**, *8*, 17028–17032. [CrossRef] [PubMed]
13. [illegible] Induced Forward Transfer (BA-LIFT). In *Laser Printing of Functional Materials*; Wiley-VCH Verlag GmbH & Co. KGaA: Weinheim, Germany, 2018; pp. 91–121.
14. Levene, M.L.; Scott, R.D.; Siryj, B.W. *Electro-Optics Handbook (RCA Defense Electronic Products)*; RCA Aerospace Systems Division: Burlington, MA, USA, 1968; Volume 1.
15. Bohandy, J.; Kim, B.F.; Adrian, F.J. Metal Deposition from a Supported Metal Film Using an Excimer Laser. *J. Appl. Phys.* **1986**, *60*, 1538. [CrossRef]
16. Piqué, A. The Matrix-Assisted Pulsed Laser Evaporation (MAPLE) Process: Origins and Future Directions. *Appl. Phys. A Mater. Sci. Process.* **2011**, *105*, 517–528. [CrossRef]
17. *The Worldwide Market for Lasers and Five-Year Forecast (2019–2025)*; Strategies Unlimited: Mountain View, CA, USA, 2020.
18. Duda, T.; Raghavan, L.V. 3D Metal Printing Technology. *IFAC-PapersOnLine* **2016**, *49*, 103–110. [CrossRef]
19. Yuk, H.; Lu, B.; Lin, S.; Qu, K.; Xu, J.; Luo, J.; Zhao, X. 3D Printing of Conducting Polymers. *Nat. Commun.* **2020**, *11*, 1604. [CrossRef]
20. Melzer, J.E.; McLeod, E. 3D Nanophotonic Device Fabrication Using Discrete Components. *Nanophotonics* **2020**, *9*, 1373–1390. [CrossRef]
21. Sanchez Noriega, J.L.; Chartrand, N.A.; Valdoz, J.C.; Cribbs, C.G.; Jacobs, D.A.; Poulson, D.; Viglione, M.S.; Woolley, A.T.; van Ry, P.M.; Christensen, K.A.; et al. Spatially and Optically Tailored 3D Printing for Highly Miniaturized and Integrated Microfluidics. *Nat. Commun.* **2021**, *12*, 5509. [CrossRef] [PubMed]
22. Mahmood, M.A.; Popescu, A.C. 3D Printing at Micro-Level: Laser-Induced Forward Transfer and Two-Photon Polymerization. *Polymers* **2021**, *13*, 2034. [CrossRef]
23. The University of Maine. Available online: https://umaine.edu/news/blog/2019/10/10/umaine-composites-center-receives-three-guinness-world-records-related-to-largest-3d-printer/ (accessed on 2 November 2022).
24. Relativity Space, Inc. Relativity Space. Available online: https://www.relativityspace.com (accessed on 2 November 2022).
25. Fernández-Pradas, J.M.; Sopeña, P.; González-Torres, S.; Arrese, J.; Cirera, A.; Serra, P. Laser-Induced Forward Transfer for Printed Electronics Applications. *Appl. Phys. A Mater. Sci. Process.* **2018**, *124*, 214. [CrossRef]

26. Zenou, M.; Kotler, Z. Printing of Metallic 3D Micro-Objects by Laser Induced Forward Transfer. *Opt. Express* **2016**, *24*, 1431. [CrossRef]
27. Makrygianni, M.; Zacharatos, F.; Andritsos, K.; Theodorakos, I.; Reppas, D.; Oikonomidis, N.; Spandonidis, C.; Zergioti, I. Eco-Friendly Lead-Free Solder Paste Printing via Laser-Induced Forward Transfer for the Assembly of Ultra-Fine Pitch Electronic Components. *Materials* **2021**, *14*, 3353. [CrossRef]
28. Shaw-Stewart, J.R.H.; Mattle, T.; Lippert, T.K.; Nagel, M.; Nüesch, F.A.; Wokaun, A. The Fabrication of Small Molecule Organic Light-Emitting Diode Pixels by Laser-Induced Forward Transfer. *J. Appl. Phys.* **2013**, *113*, 043104. [CrossRef]
29. Pozov, S.M.; Andritsos, K.; Theodorakos, I.; Georgiou, E.; Ioakeimidis, A.; Kabla, A.; Melamed, S.; de La Vega, F.; Zergioti, I.; Choulis, S.A. Indium Tin Oxide-Free Inverted Organic Photovoltaics Using Laser-Induced Forward Transfer Silver Nanoparticle Embedded Metal Grids. *ACS Appl. Electron. Mater.* **2022**, *4*, 2689–2698. [CrossRef] [PubMed]
30. Dinca, V.; Fardel, R.; Shaw-Stewart, J.; di Pietrantonio, F.; Cannatà, D.; Benetti, M.; Verona, E.; Palla-Papavlu, A.; Dinescu, M.; Lippert, T. Laser-Induced Forward Transfer: An Approach to Single-Step Polymer Microsensor Fabrication. *Sens. Lett.* **2010**, *8*, 436–440. [CrossRef]
31. Hennig, G.; Baldermann, T.; Nussbaum, C.; Rossier, M.; Brockelt, A.; Schuler, L.; Hochstein, G. Lasersonic® LIFT Process for Large Area Digital Printing. *J. Laser Micro Nanoeng.* **2012**, *7*, 299–305. [CrossRef]
32. Sopeña, P.; Arrese, J.; González-Torres, S.; Fernández-Pradas, J.M.; Cirera, A.; Serra, P. Low-Cost Fabrication of Printed Electronics Devices through Continuous Wave Laser-Induced Forward Transfer. *ACS Appl. Mater. Interfaces* **2017**, *9*, 29412–29417. [CrossRef]
33. Li, R.Z.; Yang, M.; Guo, L.; Qu, K.; Jian, T.; Yu, Y.; Yan, J. Laser-Induced Forward Transferred Optical Scattering Nanosilica for Transparent Displays. *Nanomaterials* **2022**, *12*, 3674. [CrossRef]
34. Weidling, A.M.; Turkani, V.S.; Akhavan, V.; Schroder, K.A.; Swisher, S.L. Large-Area Photonic Lift-off Process for Flexible Thin-Film Transistors. *NPJ Flex. Electron.* **2022**, *6*, 14. [CrossRef]
35. Chen, Y.; Munoz-Martin, D.; Morales, M.; Molpeceres, C.; Sánchez-Cortezon, E.; Murillo-Gutierrez, J. Laser Induced Forward Transfer of High Viscosity Silver Paste for New Metallization Methods in Photovoltaic and Flexible Electronics Industry. *Phys. Procedia* **2016**, *83*, 204–210. [CrossRef]
36. Murphy, S.V.; Atala, A. 3D Bioprinting of Tissues and Organs. *Nat. Biotechnol.* **2014**, *32*, 773–785. [CrossRef] [PubMed]
37. Guillotin, B.; Souquet, A.; Catros, S.; Duocastella, M.; Pippenger, B.; Bellance, S.; Bareille, R.; Rémy, M.; Bordenave, L.; Amédée, J.; et al. Laser Assisted Bioprinting of Engineered Tissue with High Cell Density and Microscale Organization. *Biomaterials* **2010**, *31*, 7250–7256. [CrossRef] [PubMed]
38. Antoshin, A.A.; Churbanov, S.N.; Minaev, N.V.; Zhang, D.; Zhang, Y.; Shpichka, A.I.; Timashev, P.S. LIFT-Bioprinting, Is It Worth It? *Bioprinting* **2019**, *15*, e00052. [CrossRef]
39. Devillard, R.; Pagès, E.; Correa, M.M.; Kériquel, V.; Rémy, M.; Kalisky, J.Ô.; Ali, M.; Guillotin, B.; Guillemot, F. Cell Patterning by Laser-Assisted Bioprinting. In *Methods in Cell Biology*; Academic Press Inc.: Cambridge, MA, USA, 2014; Volume 119, pp. 159–174.
40. Kryou, C.; Leva, V.; Chatzipetrou, M.; Zergioti, I. Bioprinting for Liver Transplantation. *Bioengineering* **2019**, *6*, 95. [CrossRef]
41. Ali, M.; Pages, E.; Ducom, A.; Fontaine, A.; Guillemot, F. Controlling Laser-Induced Jet Formation for Bioprinting Mesenchymal Stem Cells with High Viability and High Resolution. *Biofabrication* **2014**, *6*, 045001. [CrossRef] [PubMed]

materials

MDPI

Article

Worst-Case X-ray Photon Energies in Ultrashort Pulse Laser Processing

Katrin Böttcher [1,*], Mayka Schmitt Rahner [2], Ulf Stolzenberg [2], Sebastian Kraft [1], Jörn Bonse [1], Carsten Feist [2], Daniel Albrecht [2], Björn Pullner [2] and Jörg Krüger [1]

[1] Bundesanstalt für Materialforschung und -prüfung (BAM), Unter den Eichen 87, 12205 Berlin, Germany
[2] Physikalisch-Technische Bundesanstalt (PTB), Bundesallee 100, 38116 Braunschweig, Germany
* Correspondence: katrin.boettcher@bam.de

Abstract: Ultrashort pulse laser processing can result in the secondary generation of unwanted X-rays if a critical laser irradiance of about 10^{13} W cm^{-2} is exceeded. Spectral X-ray emissions were investigated during the processing of tungsten and steel using three complementary spectrometers (based on CdTe and silicon drift detectors) simultaneously for the identification of a worst-case spectral scenario. Therefore, maximum X-ray photon energies were determined, and corresponding dose equivalent rates were calculated. An ultrashort pulse laser workstation with a pulse duration of 274 fs, a center wavelength of 1030 nm, pulse repetition rates between 50 kHz and 200 kHz, and a Gaussian laser beam focused to a spot diameter of 33 µm was employed in a single pulse and burst laser operation mode. Different combinations of laser pulse energy and repetition rate were utilized, keeping the average laser power constant close to the maximum power of 20 W. Peak irradiances I_0 ranging from 7.3×10^{13} W cm^{-2} up to 3.0×10^{14} W cm^{-2} were used. The X-ray dose equivalent rate increases for lower repetition rates and higher pulse energy if a constant average power is used. Laser processing with burst mode significantly increases the dose rates and the X-ray photon energies. A maximum X-ray photon energy of about 40 keV was observed for burst mode processing of tungsten with a repetition rate of 50 kHz and a peak irradiance of 3×10^{14} W cm^{-2}.

Keywords: ultrashort pulsed laser; X-ray emission; X-ray spectrum; X-ray energies; X-ray dose rate; radiation protection

Citation: Böttcher, K.; Schmitt Rahner, M.; Stolzenberg, U.; Kraft, S.; Bonse, J.; Feist, C.; Albrecht, D.; Pullner, B.; Krüger, J. Worst-Case X-ray Photon Energies in Ultrashort Pulse Laser Processing. *Materials* **2022**, *15*, 8996. https://doi.org/10.3390/ma15248996

Academic Editor: Chih-Wei Luo

Received: 11 November 2022
Accepted: 14 December 2022
Published: 16 December 2022

1. Introduction

Already since the 1980s, it has been established that X-rays can be emitted from laser-induced plasmas. Early investigations were performed in vacuum [1]. In the early 2000s, the first investigations during ultrashort pulse laser materials processing of copper with a repetition rate of 1 kHz in air were conducted. Thogersen et al. [2] measured a maximum dose rate of X-rays of approximately 10 mSv h^{-1} at a distance of 13 cm and Bunte et al. [3] determined a maximum dose rate of approximately 50 mSv h^{-1} at a distance of 10 cm, whereby the specifically measured radiological operational quantity was not explicitly specified in both studies. For steel and tungsten processed at higher repetition rates of 400 kHz, Legall et al. [4] found in 2018 even higher dose equivalent rates $\dot{H}'(0.07)$ of 163 mSv h^{-1} at a distance of 42 cm exceeding typical radiation protection safety limits, which revealed a potential safety risk for the operating staff of the ultrashort pulse laser (USPL) machine.

Several investigations were performed to analyze the X-ray emission for different laser and process parameters during ultrashort pulse laser machining of various technical materials [5–17]. Recently, possibly harmful X-ray emission was observed already at laser irradiances below 10^{13} W cm^{-2} [18,19]. Especially the burst modes of laser machines were identified as a configuration that can lead to very high dose rates in the ultrashort laser pulse processing of metals [20,21]. During burst mode processing, pulse trains (bursts) with up to 100 sub-pulses per burst and intra-burst pulse repetition rates in the MHz to GHz range are typically generated by current commercial laser systems [22,23]. When using burst mode settings, the pulse energy from a single laser pulse is divided into a predefined number of sub-pulses with corresponding (lower) sub-pulse energies.

Besides the dose equivalent rates, the spectral flux of the emitted X-ray photons is of special interest as the transmission of X-rays through a radiation protection housing strongly depends on its spectral distribution.

This study aims to identify an X-ray photon spectrum showing the maximum X-ray energies that can be generated during ultrashort pulse laser material processing of steel and tungsten in air, the so-called "worst-case spectrum". For that, the X-ray spectra were measured during the machining process for different laser and process parameters. The corresponding dose equivalent rates were calculated from the spectra.

2. Materials and Methods

2.1. Ultrashort Pulse Laser System

The investigation was performed with an ultrashort pulse laser machine emitting an average power of 20 W at a center wavelength of 1030 nm (GL.evo, GFH GmbH, Deggendorf, Germany), equipped with a Pharos-Laser (PH2-20W, Light Conversion, Vilnius, Lithuania). The laser pulse duration of 274 fs was kept constant. The laser beam was focused on the workpiece featuring an $1/e^2$-spot diameter of 33 μm. This value was taken from a configuration file provided by the manufacturer of the laser machine. It was operated here in an industrial setting that regularly does not involve an individual beam diameter evaluation for each laser process. The detailed processing parameters are listed in Table 1. Different combinations of laser pulse energy and repetition rate were chosen, whereby the laser pulse energy was varied between 91 μJ and 371 μJ and the pulse repetition rate between 50 kHz and 200 kHz. For each combination of laser pulse energy and repetition rate, single pulse and burst mode experiments were performed.

For the burst mode investigations, the single pulse (with 100% energy) is split into two sub-pulses showing equal energy of 50% of the total single pulse energy. The two sub-pulses have a temporal separation of 200 ps here.

Laser peak irradiances I_0 in a range of 7.3×10^{13} W cm^{-2} to 3.0×10^{14} W cm^{-2} were calculated under the assumption of a temporal and spatial Gaussian distribution of the laser pulse and an angle of incidence of 0°

$$I_0 = 8\sqrt{\frac{4\ln 2}{\pi}}\frac{Q}{\tau_H \cdot \pi \cdot d^2}, \tag{1}$$

where Q is the pulse energy, τ_H is the pulse duration and d is the laser beam spot diameter ($1/e^2$) [24].

The calculation of the irradiance for the burst mode in Table 1 considers the total energy of the burst (which equals the single pulse energy). Three different repetition rates (50 kHz, 100 kHz, and 200 kHz) and pulse energies (371 μJ, 184 μJ, and 91 μJ) were selected, resulting in an average power of 18.2 W to 18.6 W close to the maximum average power of the laser of 20 W. The experiments were performed with flat 5 mm thick plates of tungsten (99.97% purity) and steel alloy (St37) targets. The target surfaces were prepared by parallel surface grinding achieving an average roughness of 1.6 μm to 4 μm. With a laser beam scanning configuration, 1.5×1.5 cm^2 squares were treated. The laser processing time was 250 s for each square.

Table 1. Experimental processing parameters.

Experiment No.	Repetition Rate	Laser Pulse Energy	Average Power	Burst Mode	Peak Irradiance	Material
	in kHz	in µJ	in W		in W cm^{-2}	
1	50	371	18.6	No	3.0×10^{14}	tungsten
2	100	184	18.4	No	1.5×10^{14}	tungsten
3	200	91	18.2	No	7.3×10^{13}	tungsten
4	50	371	18.6	Yes	3.0×10^{14}	tungsten
5	100	184	18.4	Yes	1.5×10^{14}	tungsten
6	200	91	18.2	Yes	7.3×10^{13}	tungsten
7	50	371	18.6	No	3.0×10^{14}	steel
8	100	184	18.4	No	1.5×10^{14}	steel
9	50	371	18.6	Yes	3.0×10^{14}	steel
10	100	184	18.4	Yes	1.5×10^{14}	steel

2.2. Spectral X-ray Emission

The measurement of the spectral X-ray emission in the context of ultrashort pulse laser processing is challenging due to non-matching energy detection ranges of different spectrometers, electromagnetic compatibility (EMC) requirements, possible pile-up effects, and potential X-ray screening through the environment. Up to now, X-ray energies between approximately 2 keV and 30 keV were reported during ultrashort pulse laser processing in air [4]. However, detectors based on different sensor materials measure reliably in different X-ray energy ranges. Typical silicon drift detectors (SDDs) are only applicable for photon energies up to approximately 15 keV as the quantum efficiency of 500 µm thick silicon rapidly drops for larger energies (see for example Figure 1 in [25]). Strüder et al. reported a quantum efficiency that was always above 85% for photon energies between 500 eV and 11 keV for a 450 µm thick SDD [26]. However, as most of the X-ray spectra measured during laser material interactions cover a rather low photon energy range, measurements with an SDD can still provide valuable insights. As an alternative, CdTe detectors exhibit a much larger energy detection range than SDDs. For the X-123 spectrometer (Amptek Inc., Bedford, MA, USA) with a sensor thickness of 1000 µm for example, the manufacturer specifies an optimum energy range from 5 keV to 100 keV. The manufacturer data give a minimum intrinsic efficiency of 98% for photon energies between 10 keV and 50 keV.

For CdTe spectrometers, previous measurements indicate that the spectra can be influenced by noise and electronical issues caused by electromagnetic fields emitted from the plasma [14]. Unwanted electronic events may happen because of the laser-target interactions that create strong electromagnetic pulses potentially inducing electronic noise in the data acquisition system [27]. Additionally, the spectra for both detector types can be affected by pile-up [4].

For the reliable measurement of X-ray spectra and to compensate for some disadvantages of the individual spectrometer types, a comparative study using three spectrometers simultaneously was conducted in this work. The spectrometers were placed 60 cm to 70 cm away from the laser interaction point within the housing of the industrial ultrashort pulse laser machining system. The experimental setup with the arrangement of the detectors can be seen in Figure 1a,b showing a photograph of the machining process with the optics, the target (with the bright optical plasma emission) and the exhaust system. The measurements were performed in ambient air.

For the measurements of the higher X-ray photon energies (> 13 keV), two CdTe-based spectrometers (Amptek X-123) were used. The first X-123 spectrometer had a sensor size of $3 \times 3 \times 1$ mm^3 (X123_S09) and the second had a sensor size of $5 \times 5 \times 1$ mm^3 (X123_S25). Both X-123 spectrometers were equipped with a 100 µm Beryllium window. For the lower energy range (< 13 keV), an SDD-based spectrometer (PNDetector with the designation "XRS-30-128-100-BeP Complete" with module type SDD-30-128-BeP) with a sensor area of

30 mm^2, a thickness of 450 ± 20 μm and a beryllium window with a thickness of 8 μm was used. This spectrometer is referred to as "PN" in the following.

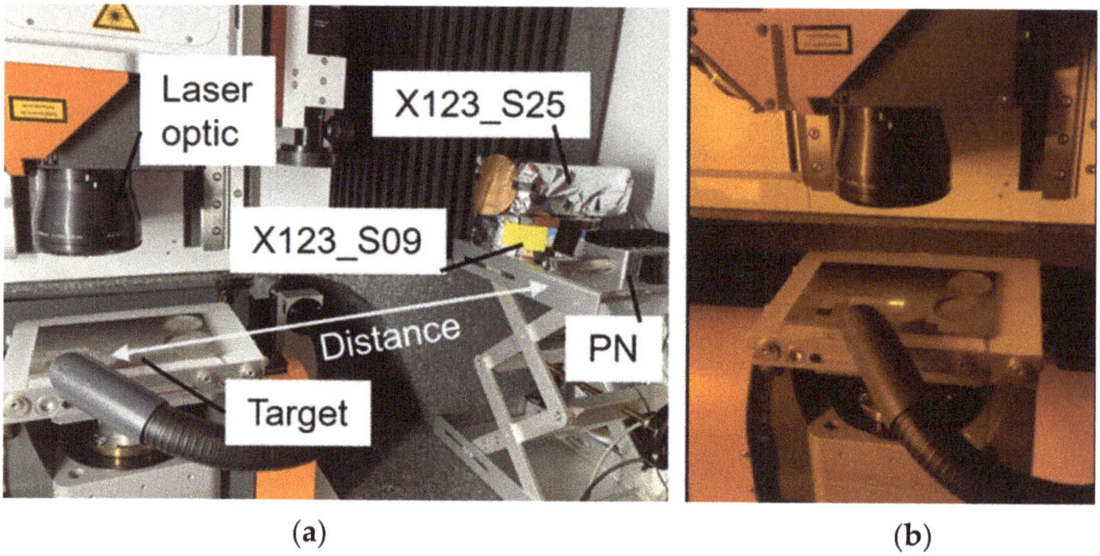

Figure 1. Experimental setup, (**a**) Arrangement of the spectrometers, (**b**) Image during laser processing.

The X-ray emission investigations showed EMC issues for both CdTe spectrometers (X-123). The SDD (PN) was not affected. To reduce the influence due to the EMC issues, the X-123 spectrometers were encased in special housings. The X123_S09 was placed in a tinplate box and the X123_S25 in an aluminum box. To further suppress electronic noise, aluminum foils were put in front of the measurement window. The thickness of the aluminum foils (different thicknesses for X123_S09 and X123_S25) was calculated from absorption measurements using an X-ray tube with and without aluminum foils (see Section 3.1). To evaluate the influence of pile-up effects on the measured spectra, the measurements were performed with and without a 50 μm thick copper foil (see Section 3.1).

The placement of the spectrometers with respect to the X-ray emission source and its spatial homogeneity was controlled with a radiographic imaging plate placed at a distance of 60 cm from the laser-induced emission source about 10 cm in front of the three spectrometers. A 2-D Radiography Scanner CR 35 NDT Plus system (DÜRR, Stuttgart, Germany) was used. Figure 2a shows the grayscale image of the X-ray field recorded by the 2-D radiography plate along with the positions of the detectors that are marked by green, red, and blue circles, respectively. To compare the X-ray intensities arriving at the three spectrometers, the recorded data contained in the blue and yellow boxes were then binned vertically and then plotted as a function of the horizontal position in Figure 2b as blue and yellow curves. The additional green, red, and blue vertical lines mark the individual positions of the three spectrometers, while the corresponding horizontal lines indicate the average grayscale level as a measure of the local X-ray intensity incident to the detector. The spectrometer that received more intensity of laser-generated X-ray intensity (a higher average grayscale value) was the X123_S09. The X123_S25 and the PN received in comparison to X123_S09 about 14.5% and 24% less X-ray intensity during the measurements.

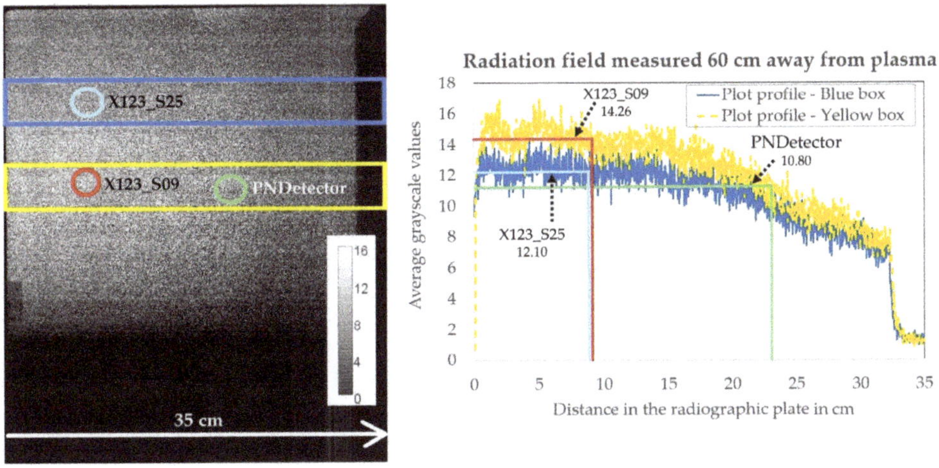

(a) (b)

Figure 2. Grayscale image captured with the radiographic imaging plate (**a**) placed 10 cm in front of the three spectrometers used in this study. The blue and yellow rectangles are the areas used to calculate the X-ray intensity profile shown in the plot (**b**). The continuous decrease in grayscale value with an increased distance on the x-axis revealed that the PN spectrometer (PNDetector) received less X-ray intensity in comparison to the two X-123 spectrometers. Additionally, X123_S25 received about 14.5% less radiation than the X123_S09 spectrometer.

3. Results

3.1. Spectrometer Characterization

The spectrometers were characterized by background measurements (Figure 3a) and measurements of an X-ray tube (Figure 3b–d). For a comparison between the different spectrometer properties, the same (known) spectrum of an X-ray tube (Amptek Mini-X Gold (Au) X-ray tube) operated at a current of 10 mA and a voltage of 20 kV was measured by all three devices.

Every data point in the measured pulse height spectrum $X(E)$ is corrected with the spectral sensitivity of the sensor $S(E)$ and normalized to the area and time with the sensor area A and measuring time interval t and yields the photon flux $\Phi_0(E)$:

$$\Phi_0(E) = \frac{X(E)}{A\, t\, S(E)} \tag{2}$$

Typically, in order to determine the photon flux from the pulse height spectrum, an unfolding procedure is required which depends on the inverse response matrix of the detector. Here, due to the low energies and negligible influences due to scattering because of the very low energies, the detector response was estimated by employing only the sensitivity of the detector. Afterward, the spectral photon flux $\Phi_E(E)$ was calculated by the normalization of Φ_0 with the energy channel's width ΔE

$$\Phi_E(E) = \frac{\Phi_0(E)}{\Delta E} \tag{3}$$

To have a comparative situation like during the measurement of the X-ray emission from the laser generated plasma, the X-ray tube was positioned inside the USPL machine on the position, where the laser-induced plasma generation would take place. The X-ray tube measurements were performed when the USPL machine was turned off.

Furthermore, the background signal for all detectors was measured during the USPL machine was running, but no laser material processing took place (Figure 3a). This way, it was proven, whether the detection was disturbed by any influence from the USPL machine such as electronic issues, for example, but without the additional influence from the transient plasma generation during the laser processing.

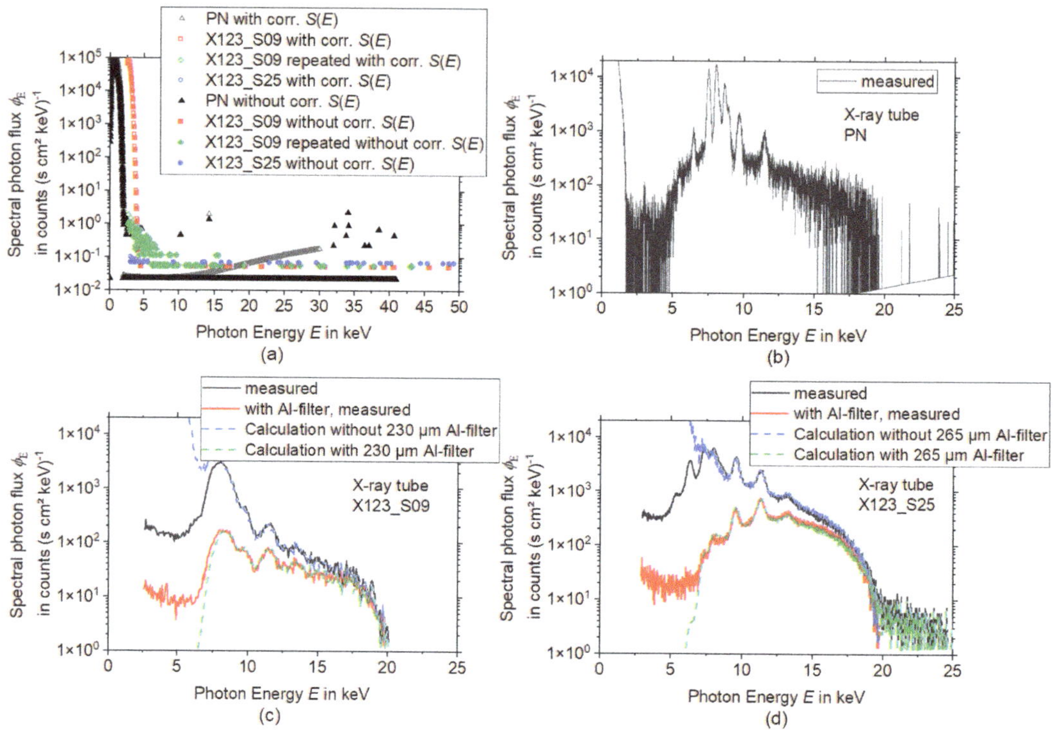

Figure 3. Characterization of the spectrometers without laser material processing, (**a**) Background measured inside the running USPL machine without laser processing (with and without correction of the spectral sensitivity of the sensor $S(E)$), (**b**) X-ray tube spectrum measurement with the PN spectrometer, (**c**) X-ray tube spectra measured with X123_S09 with and without Al-filter (solid lines) along with two calculated spectra (dashed curves), (**d**) X-ray tube spectra measured with X123_S25 with and without Al-filter (solid lines) along with two calculated spectra (dashed curves). Note the logarithmic scaling of the ordinate axes.

From Figure 3a,b one can see that the PN spectrometer has always a high-intensity count range in the low-energy region up to around 2 keV. This noise signal happens due to the high sensitivity of the silicon detector material. This signal also occurred during the background measurement and is independent of the X-ray tube, see Figure 3a.

The PN spectrometer shows the highest spectral resolution of the characteristic peaks from the spectra shown in Figure 3b and the X123_S25 has a higher resolution than the X123_S09, which can be due to the larger sensor size and the higher number of channels of the X123_S25.

For the PN spectrometer signal (Figure 3a) only background noise in the very low count range within the energy region from 2 keV to about 40 keV can be seen. For both Amptek X-123 spectrometers, for energies above 5 keV to 8 keV only background noise with a spectral photon flux $\Phi_E < 0.1$ counts (s cm^2 keV)$^{-1}$ occurs. For the X123_S09 a region with somewhat higher spectral photon flux is found below 8 keV. Repeated measurements showed that this is not a stable signal, and it was not observed during the measurement of the X-ray tube, revealing that the signal is caused by EMC or other electrical issues.

Since all spectral detectors show no significant or stable background within the interesting energy region above 5 keV, a subtraction of the background was not performed. To calculate the influence of the Al foils, which are highly recommended to be used in front of the detector window of an Amptek X-123 spectrometer to avoid EMC issues and spectral artifacts due to pile-up, measurements of the X-ray tube spectrum were performed with and without the aluminum foil. Then the expected spectrum after the transition of aluminum filters with different thicknesses was calculated and the filter thickness was determined with a least-squares-fit. The results can be found in Figure 3c,d.

The spectral calculation is based on linear absorption according to Beer's law. Hereby, the measured X-ray flux without filters is reduced by *i*-filters with their attenuation coefficient from the NIST database [28] μ_i and thickness d_i.

$$\Phi(E) = \Phi_0(E)\, e^{-\sum_i \mu_i d_i} \tag{4}$$

The procedure was repeated in reverse with the measured spectrum with aluminum foils to calculate the spectrum without foils. For the X123_S09 an aluminum thickness of 230 µm (Figure 3c) and for the X123_S25 (Figure 3d) an aluminum thickness of 265 µm was determined. For energies higher than 7 keV the calculation and the measurements are in good agreement. The deviations for energies lower than 7 keV are due to absorption in the beryllium window in front of the CdTe sensor volume and electronic noise for the low photon energies.

3.2. Spectroscopy during Ultrashort Pulse Laser Processing

To evaluate the influence of pile-up effects or EMC on the spectra, the measurements were performed during the laser processing with and without a 50 µm thick copper foil. From the measurements without copper foil, the spectra after the transmission through the copper foil were calculated. This way, a comparison between the measurements with copper foil and the calculations could be performed. Deviations indicate that the spectra measured without copper foil are still influenced either by pile-up (in high-energy regions) or by electronic noise induced in the acquisition system of the spectrometers due to low-frequency electromagnetic fields emitted from the laser-induced plasma.

The results for the spectral measurements during the laser processing of tungsten are presented in Figures 4 and 5, while the results during the laser processing of steel are shown in Figures 6 and 7 for all three detectors. Except for experiments no. 1, 3, and 7 (see Table 1) the measurements without copper foil were performed twice for each set of processing parameters and each detector. In the case of two available measurements, the mean value was used for the evaluation. For experiments no. 3 and 7 a single measurement was utilized for the spectrometers X123_S25 and the PN. For experiment no. 1 a single measurement was used for the spectrometers X123_S09 and the PN.

For the PN spectrometer all results, i.e., the comparison of the measurements with copper foil and the corresponding calculations, show a good agreement for X-ray photon energies < 11 keV. However, deviations occur for the measurements with a burst mode for energies > 11 keV, which indicates that pile-up plays a role during the processing with burst mode.

Both X-123 detectors reveal broad spectral peaks with very high intensities for X-ray energies below approximately 9 keV. For the X123_S09, one measurement (100 kHz burst mode, steel) even shows this signal for a photon energy up to 15 keV. It is assumed that these broad peaks are due to EMC issues.

Additionally, also for the X-123 detectors, pile-up can be observed during the laser processing measurements with burst mode. This effect is minimized when the measurement is performed with copper foil. For further evaluation, it follows that the PN spectrometer delivers accurate data (without pile-up) for photon energies < 11 keV. On the other hand, for measurements without burst mode the X-123 spectrometers deliver valid data for photon energies > 13 keV. For energies between 11 and 13 keV, the PN spectrometer data are only valid for processing parameters without burst mode.

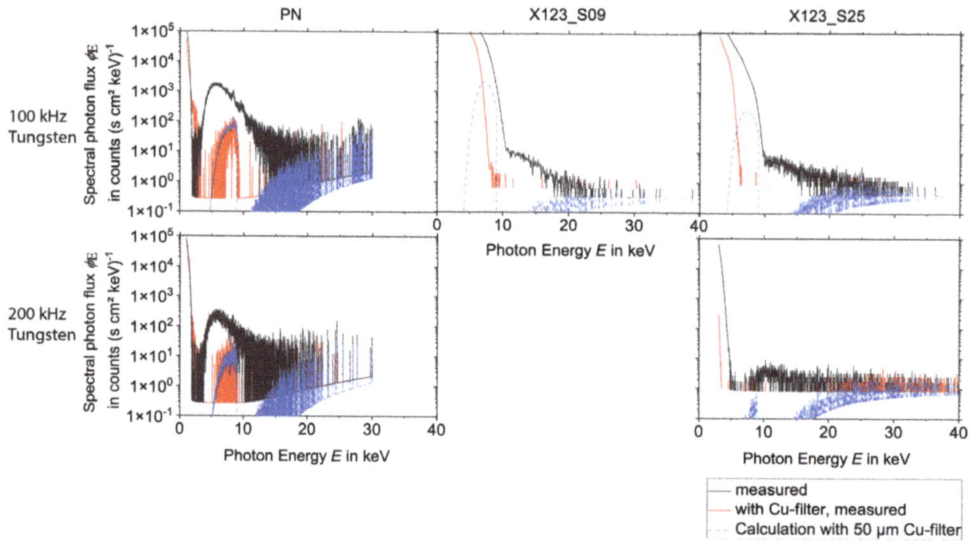

Figure 4. X-ray spectra measured during the laser processing of tungsten without burst mode for the three spectrometers PN, X123_S09, and X123_S25, the measurement with and without Cu-filter was compared with the calculation with copper filter of 50 µm thickness. Note the logarithmic scaling of the ordinate axes.

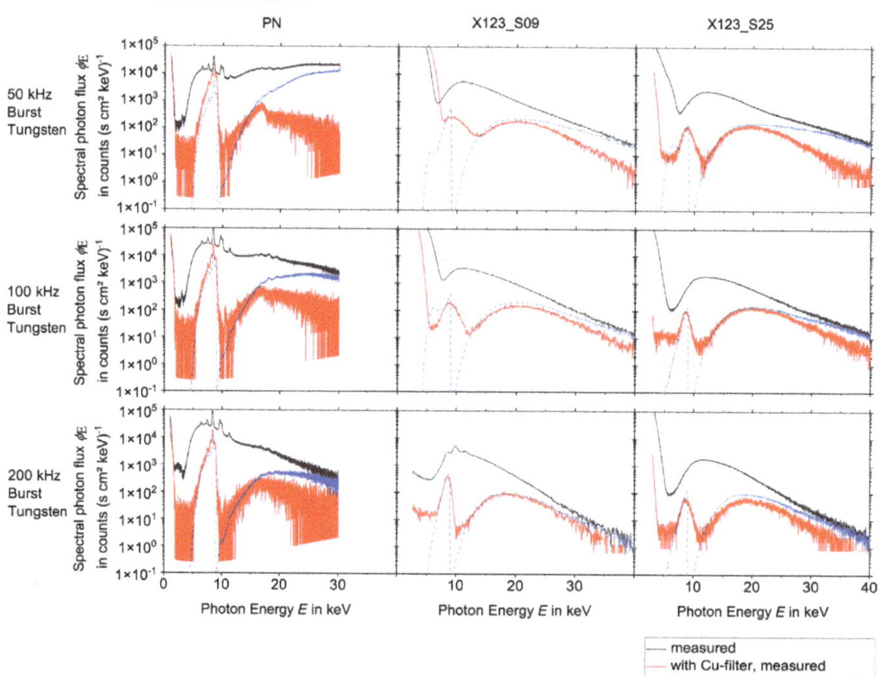

Figure 5. X-ray spectra measured during the laser processing of tungsten with burst mode for the three spectrometers PN, X123_S09, and X123_S25, the measurement with and without Cu-filter was compared with the calculation with copper filter of 50 µm thickness. Note the logarithmic scaling of the ordinate axes.

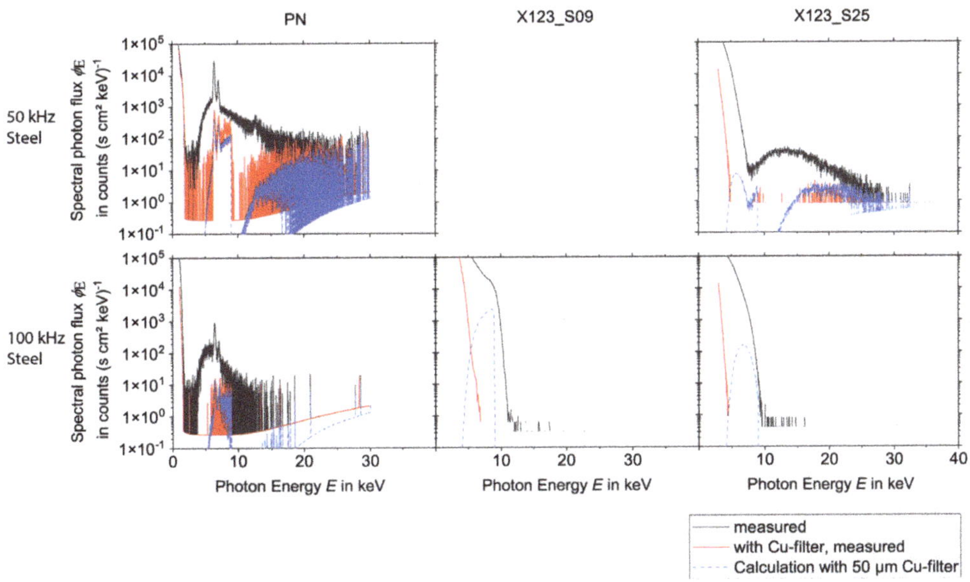

Figure 6. X-ray spectra measured during the laser processing of steel without burst mode for the three spectrometers PN, X123_S09, and X123_S25, the measurement with and without Cu-filter was compared with the calculation with copper filter of 50 µm thickness. Note the logarithmic scaling of the ordinate axes.

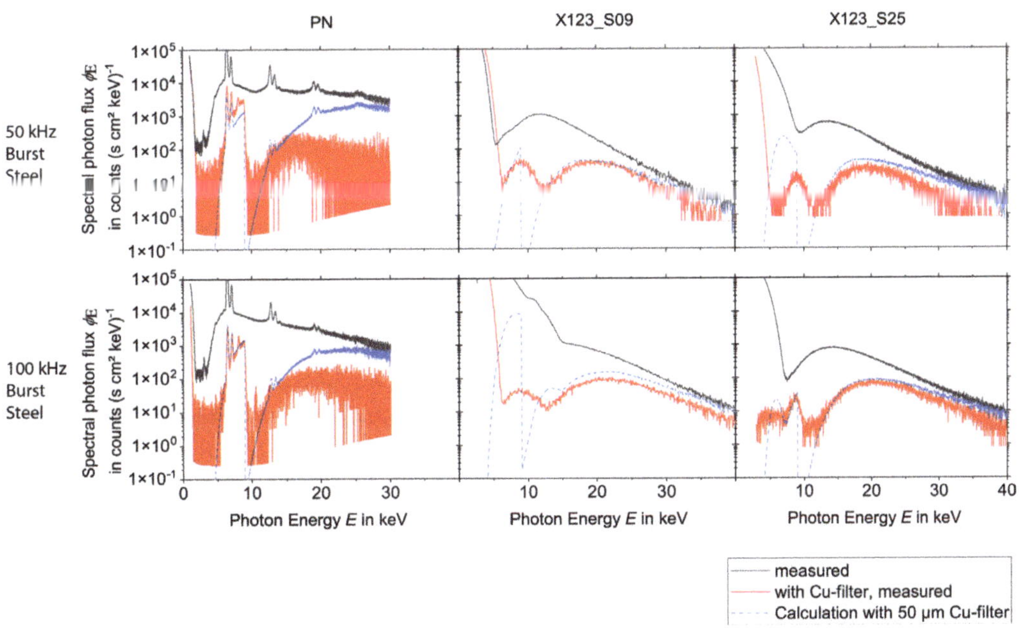

Figure 7. X-ray spectra measured during the processing of steel with burst mode for the three spectrometers PN, X123_S09, and X123_S25, the measurement with and without Cu-filter was compared with the calculation with copper filter of 50 µm thickness. Note the logarithmic scaling of the ordinate axes.

As the measurements with burst mode are affected by pile up, the spectra with a copper filter were used. Then the effect of the copper filter was removed by employing Equation (4) and calculating the spectrum without the effects of the copper filter from them.

Due to these findings on the validity of the data in different energy regions, combined spectra with the data from the different detectors were composed for each set of laser processing parameters according to Table 1. The combined spectra for the processing of tungsten can be found in Figure 8, while the spectra for the processing of steel are depicted in Figure 9.

The data from the PN spectrometer were used for photon energies from 2 keV to 13 keV and the data from the X-123 were utilized for energies > 13 keV. As already mentioned, the PN spectrometer data show a slightly increased photon flux for photon energies between 11 and 13 keV upon processing in the burst mode and these data are probably influenced by pile-up effects. This influence is eliminated by a fitting routine which will be explained later in this chapter. For laser processing without burst mode, i.e., in the normal single pulse mode, the X-123 measurements with aluminum foil were used, whereby the spectra before the transmission of the aluminum foil were calculated by using Equation (4). For burst mode laser irradiation, the X-123 measurements with copper and aluminum foil were selected and the influence of the copper and the aluminum filter was considered also by employing Equation (4).

Taking into account the different energy binning and the different sensor sizes for the calculation of the spectral photon flux, the data of the two X-123 spectrometers are in good agreement. For laser processing parameters without burst mode (i.e., in single pulse mode), an almost continuous transition from the PN spectra to the X-123 spectra can be observed. The PN spectra for laser processing parameters with burst mode have an overall significantly higher photon flux than the spectra from the X-123 detectors. The origin of this deviation is unclear. For an estimation of the uncertainty of the spectra, the curves of the X123_S09 were fitted with a Boltzmann function within the photon energy region of 13–30 keV and extrapolated to the energy region between 11 and 13 keV. In the next step, the PN spectra were scaled down in global amplitude until continuous spectra were achieved together with the extrapolation from the Boltzmann fit and the X-123 spectra. As explained before for the burst mode laser processing, the energy region between 2 and 13 keV is associated with some uncertainty. This uncertainty can be quantified by using two combined spectra. On the one hand, the downscaled PN spectrum together with the Boltzmann extrapolation and the X-123 spectrum as a combined spectrum describes the minimum overall flux. The unchanged PN spectrum together with the X-123 spectrum in a combined spectrum characterizes the maximum overall flux.

The comparison of the spectra recorded with and without the laser burst mode reveals a significant increase in the photon flux for the burst mode processing. A detailed analysis of the estimated dose rates from the spectra will be presented later in Section 3.3. An increase in the spectral photon flux can be observed for lower laser repetition rates. This increase can be found for both the processing with and without burst mode. As expected from previous publications, e.g., [4] the spectral photon flux emitted during the processing of tungsten is higher when compared to the processing of steel. This is mainly due to the higher atomic number Z of tungsten ($Z = 74$) compared to iron ($Z = 26$) [4]. The maximum energies are limited to about 40 keV. The maximum energy of 40 keV was observed during the laser processing of tungsten and steel with the burst mode with 50 and 100 kHz laser pulse repetition rates. For the processing of tungsten with a higher repetition rate (200 kHz), the maximum X-ray energy is approximately 35 keV. For the laser processing without burst mode, i.e., for single pulse mode, a signal for energies up to 40 keV was measured in the case of the 50 kHz repetition rate. However, with a spectral photon flux of around one count $(\mathrm{s\ cm^2\ keV})^{-1}$ the signal is very low. Compared to the burst mode, for the processing without burst mode, the spectral photon flux significantly decreases already for lower energies and reaches the minimum spectral photon flux of about one count $(\mathrm{s\ cm^2\ keV})^{-1}$

for energies between 20 and 30 keV. As a general trend, the maximum X-ray photon energy tends to increase with higher laser pulse energies.

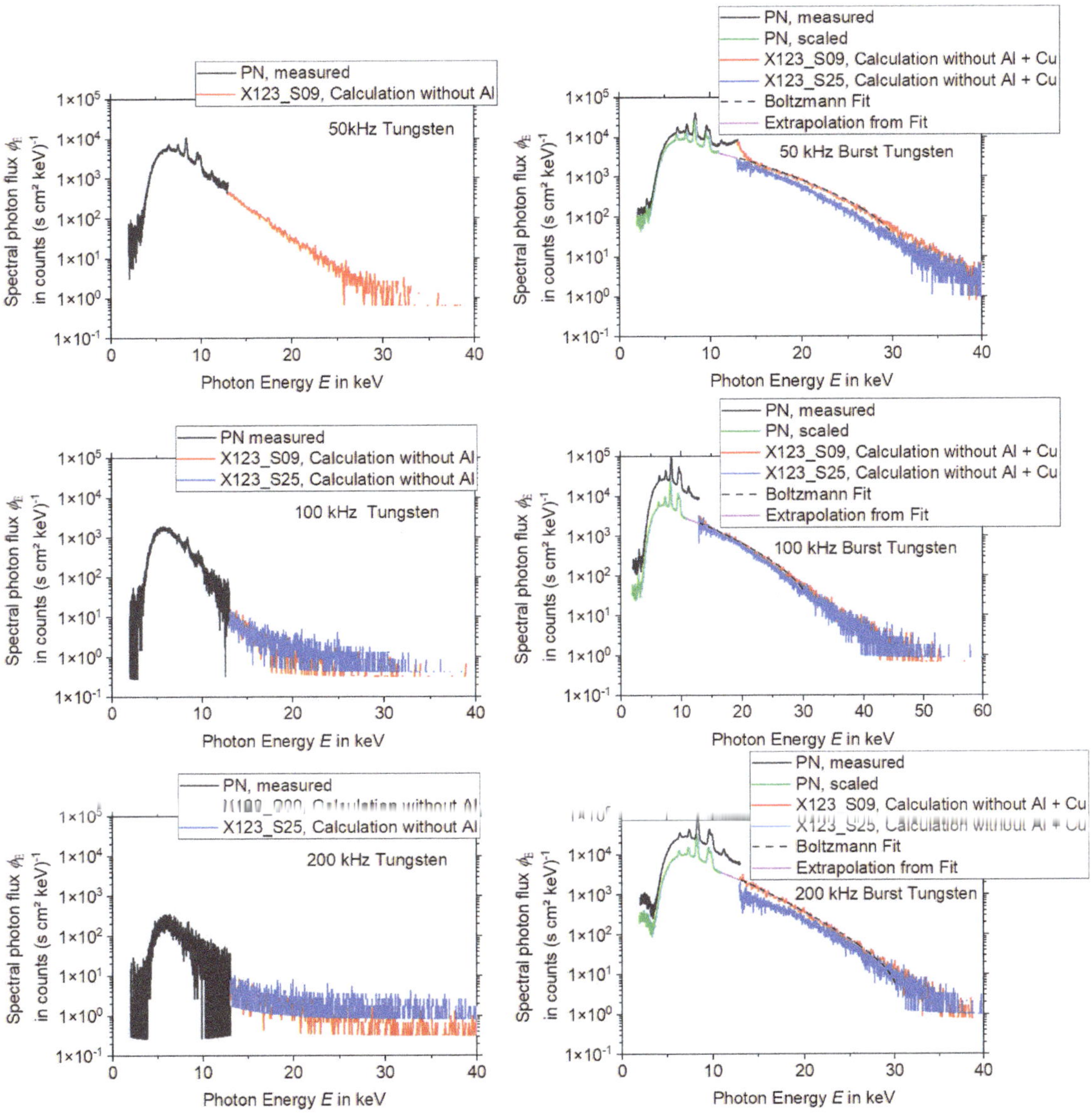

Figure 8. X-ray spectra during the processing of tungsten. Detector type, filter materials, and evaluation constraints are indicated through labels for the different curves. Note the logarithmic scaling of the ordinate axes.

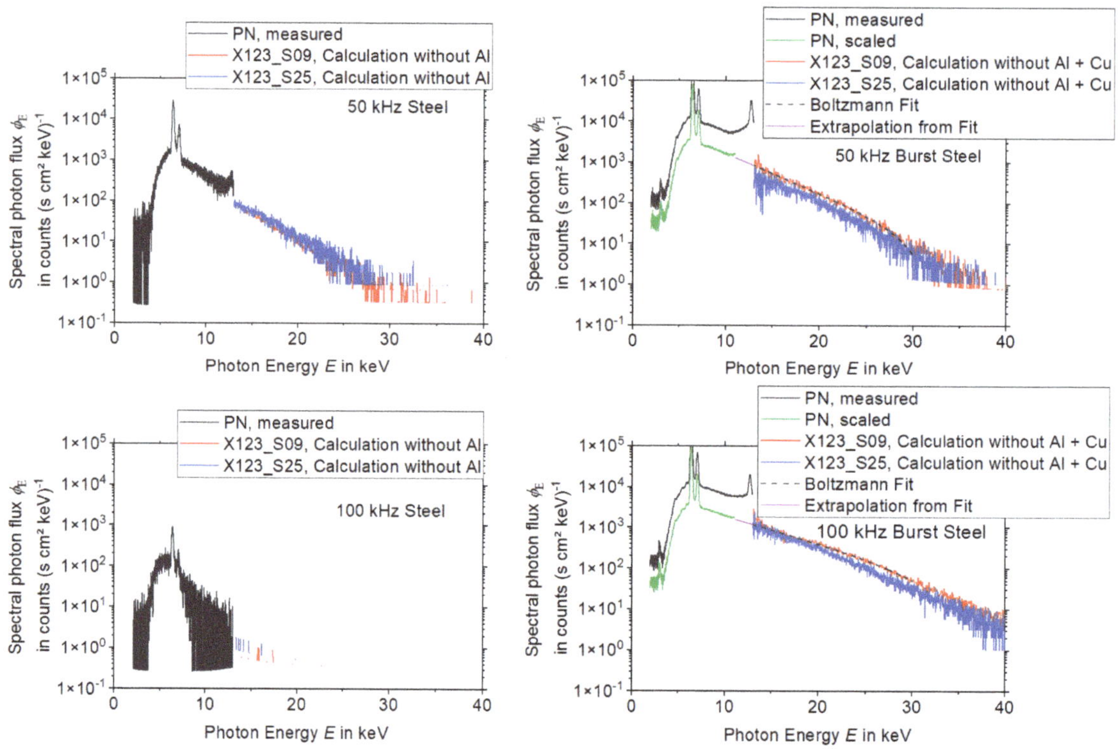

Figure 9. X-ray spectra during the processing of steel. Detector type, filter materials, and evaluation constraints are indicated through labels for the different curves. Note the logarithmic scaling of the ordinate axes.

Altogether, the "worst-case" processing scenario of this study is represented by the laser processing of tungsten at a repetition rate of 50 kHz and in burst mode.

3.3. Dose Rate Estimations

The X-ray dose rates ($\dot{H}'(0.07)$, $\dot{H}'(3)$, and $\dot{H}^*(10)$) were calculated from the measured spectra at a distance of 60 cm.

The ambient dose equivalent rate corresponds to the dose equivalent per time at different depths of penetration in the ICRU sphere [28]. Due to the energy-dependent absorption properties of ICRU tissue, three depths of penetration d_p were used. The ambient dose equivalent rates can be calculated from the spectral photon flux $\Phi(E)$ along with the tissue properties via

$$\dot{H}(d_p) = \int_{E=0}^{E=\infty} \Phi(E) \frac{E_{\text{Photon}}}{\Delta E} \frac{e^{-\mu_{en}^t(E)\, d_p}\, \mu_t(E)}{\rho^t} dE, \tag{5}$$

where E is the photon energy, E_{Photon} is the channel energy, ΔE is the bin size from the channel (energy channel's width) and the tissue properties are the X-ray photon energy-dependent energy absorption coefficient $\mu_{en}^t(E)$ of Tissue (Soft ICRU-44) and its density ρ^t. [9]. The data for the attenuation coefficients and density of standard tissue were taken from the NIST database [28]. Equation (5) is a good approximation for low-energy spectra, where the scattering of the X-ray photons can be neglected. Another method to determine the ambient dose equivalent rates would be to employ conversion coefficients from ICRU report 57 [29], for example, used in [30] to determine the spectral ambient dose equivalent rate from the spectral photon fluence and then integrate overall available photon energies. Here, both methods have been compared and due to the low energy of the spectra, no significant deviation has been observed.

The results of the dose equivalent rate calculations for the three quantities $\dot{H}'(0.07)$, $\dot{H}'(3)$, $\dot{H}^*(10)$ are presented in Figure 10. The dose equivalent rates were calculated for the different parts of the combined spectra shown in Figures 8 and 9. Due to the already discussed large uncertainty for the burst mode processing within the photon energy region between 0 and 13 keV, the dose equivalent rates were calculated for the downscaled PN spectra and the Boltzmann extrapolation as well as for the measured PN spectra. This way, a possible maximum and minimum was estimated for the dose equivalent rates. Furthermore, the dose equivalent rate calculations for the different energy regions of the spectra illustrate how the different quantities $\dot{H}'(0.07)$, $\dot{H}'(3)$ and $\dot{H}^*(10)$ are affected by different energy regions of the laser-generated X-ray spectra. Due to the higher penetration depth of X-rays with higher photon energies, the ambient dose equivalent rate $\dot{H}^*(10)$ depends more on the higher energy region, while the directional dose equivalent rate $\dot{H}'(0.07)$ depends more on the lower energy region of the spectrum. Therefore, the high uncertainty of the energy region between 0 and 13 keV, which is represented by the data from the PN spectrometer, result in larger differences between the maximum and minimum dose rates and, therewith, in high uncertainties for the quantity $\dot{H}'(0.07)$. Compared to that, the uncertainty for the ambient dose equivalent rate $\dot{H}^*(10)$ is smaller. From the "worst-case" spectrum (repetition rate of 50 kHz, burst irradiation mode, tungsten), which was defined due to the highest observed energies, a value of $\dot{H}'(0.07)$ between 2.8 and 4.2 mSv h^{-1}, a value of $\dot{H}'(3)$ between 0.3 and 0.5 mSv h^{-1} and a value of $\dot{H}^*(10)$ between 0.07 and 0.08 mSv h^{-1} were estimated. An even higher maximum dose rate $\dot{H}'(0.07)$ of 7.8 mSv h^{-1} was estimated for the laser processing of tungsten with a repetition rate of 200 kHz in burst mode. However, for these parameters, the deviation between the minimum and maximum dose equivalent rate is significantly larger and, therefore, associated with high uncertainty. If the mean value is calculated from the maximum and minimum dose rate and the uncertainty is calculated by the standard deviation, the maximum dose rate $\dot{H}'(0.07)$ found in this study is 5.3 ± 3.5 mSv h^{-1} at an operator distance of 60 cm.

The values of $\dot{H}'(3)$ and $\dot{H}^*(10)$ are significantly lower, which is due to the lower spectral photon flux within the region of higher energies. Looking at the increase in the dose equivalent rates due to the applied burst irradiation mode compared to the same processing without burst mode, one can see that from $\dot{H}'(0.07)$ to $\dot{H}'(3)$ and to $\dot{H}^*(10)$ the enhancement of the dose equivalent rate increases: for the defined "worst-case" spectrum (repetition rate = 50 kHz, burst mode, tungsten) the value of $\dot{H}'(0.07)$ is increased by a factor of approximately 2, $\dot{H}'(3)$ by a factor of approximately 4 and $\dot{H}^*(10)$ by a factor of approximately 9 when burst mode is applied. This behavior illustrates, that the burst mode laser processing results in a higher spectral photon flux for higher energies and in higher maximum energies. The highest enhancement due to burst mode application could be observed for a laser repetition rate of 200 kHz (tungsten) and a repetition rate of 100 kHz (steel). $\dot{H}'(0.07)$ was increased by a factor of approximately 60 for these parameters. Although the absolute dose equivalent rates were rather low for these parameters when processing single pulse mode, remarkably high dose rates were measured during the burst mode laser processing.

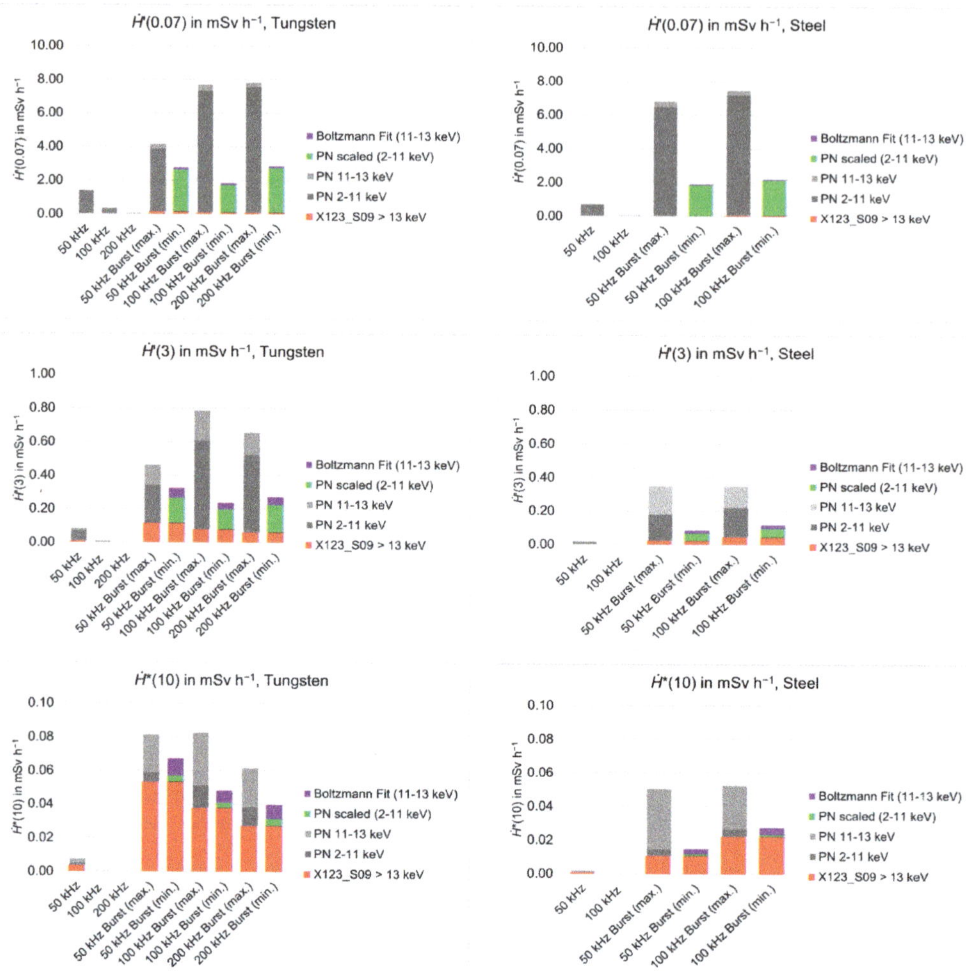

Figure 10. Dose equivalent rate estimations for the quantities $\dot{H}'(0.07)$, $\dot{H}'(3)$, and $\dot{H}^*(10)$, as calculated from the spectra presented in Figures 8 and 9. The results for laser processing of tungsten are summarized in the left column, while the results for laser processing of steel are given in the right column.

4. Discussion

Within the presented investigation of the X-ray emission during USPL processing, different difficulties during the measurements of X-ray spectra within an USPL machine were encountered. The main problems are associated with pile-up effects, electromagnetic incompatibility, a photon energy-dependent reduced sensitivity of the detector materials and other electronic issues. Minimization of the disturbing influences was achieved by the complementary use of different detector types (CdTe sensor in combination with an SDD) and the application of shielding and reduction in pile-up by using aluminum and copper foils as filters, whereby an evaluation routine that eliminates the absorption effects due to the foils from the measured spectra had to be applied. The radiation protection operational quantities $\dot{H}'(0.07)$, $\dot{H}'(3)$, and $\dot{H}^*(10)$ were calculated from the spectra.

Different combinations for the laser pulse energy (varied between 91 μJ and 371 μJ) and repetition rate (varied between 50 kHz and 200 kHz) were selected for the investigations, whereby the average laser power was kept nearly constant. It was shown that the average laser power cannot be used as the main parameter for an estimation of the dose equivalent rates. The measured dose equivalent rates significantly depend on the combination of the laser pulse repetition rate and the selected pulse energy. Parameter combinations with high laser pulse energy and low repetition rate show significantly higher dose rates than combinations with a high repetition rate and low laser pulse energy although they have almost equivalent average laser power, especially in the case of single pulse operation. Additionally, the burst mode laser operation significantly increases the dose rates although the average laser power remains the same when the burst mode is applied.

The increase in dose equivalent rate during burst mode processing was already described in the literature. A possible explanation for the significant increase in the X-ray dose rate is the interaction between ultrafast laser radiation and the formed ablation cloud or a high-density plasma [20,21].

Metzner et al. [20] investigated the dependence of the number of pulses per burst and the total fluence on the resulting X-ray dose rate by ablating stainless steel (X100CrMoV-8-1-1) with ultrafast laser pulses emitting a wavelength of 1030 nm and a pulse duration of 0.24 ps in the MHz-(MBM), GHz-(GBM), and the BiBurst (BBM) mode in comparison with conventional ultrafast laser radiation in the single-pulse mode (SPM). Compared to the SPM, producing a maximum dose equivalent rate $\dot{H}'(0.07)$ of approximately 7×10^3 μSv h^{-1}, an increase in the X-ray dose rate by more than a factor of 30 was found in the BBM with two and three sub-pulses in the MHz- and two sub-pulses in the GHz-bursts. For these parameters a dose rate of $\dot{H}'(0.07) = 2.5 \times 10^5$ μSv h^{-1} was determined. This is within the range between a factor of 2 and 60 which was determined within this study for the increase in the dose equivalent rate $\dot{H}'(0.07)$ due to burst mode application. Additionally, the absolute values of $\dot{H}'(0.07)$ are comparable with the results presented here for steel and burst mode taking into account the detector distance of 10 cm in [20] and 60 cm in this work.

Schille et al. [21] observed a significant increase in the dose equivalent rate of the emitted X-rays accompanied by pronounced characteristic X-ray emissions for laser bursts irradiating at a 1.0 MHz burst repetition frequency and corresponding lower peak intensity of the intra-burst pulses. The analysis was performed during the processing of technical-grade AISI 301 stainless steel targets. The maximum X-ray emissions were measured to $\dot{H}'(0.07) = 32.8 \pm 3.6$ mSv h^{-1} (3rd scan) with the two-pulse burst mode. For burst and bi-burst pulses, the second intra-burst pulse was found to significantly enhance the X-ray emission potentially induced by the laser pulse and plasma interaction. The measured X-ray spectra showed an energy region between 0 and 15 keV, which were measured with a SiLi-based detector. This is significantly lower than the maximum energy of 40 keV, which was observed in this study for burst mode processing of tungsten at a repetition rate of 50 kHz and a laser pulse energy of 371 μJ. Until now, maximum X-ray energies up to 30 keV were reported by Legall et al. [4] during USPL processing of tungsten in single-pulse mode. Additionally, higher dose equivalent rates of $\dot{H}'(0.07) = 163$ mSv h^{-1} for the processing of tungsten with a repetition rate of 400 kHz and a peak irradiance of 2.6×10^{14} W cm^{-2} were reported in a distance of 42 cm. The maximum X-ray photon energy must be considered if a safety housing is configured for a USPL machine. Legall et al. [12] calculated the equivalent thickness of different shielding materials for X-ray protection up to photon energies of 60 keV in units of iron. Since the here observed maximum energy of 40 keV is lower, these recommendations should still be valid here. The knowledge about the spectral flux of the emitted X-ray photons can also support the work on new testing concepts for USPL machines. Since the actual testing concept, which is based on the "worst-case" processing scenario, is connected with many difficulties [14] a new testing concept that is based on an alternative X-ray source is highly demanded.

To summarize, a "worst-case" spectrum with X-ray photon energies up to 40 keV was found in this study for the machining of tungsten at a repetition rate of 50 kHz and in burst operation mode. Additionally, equivalent dose rates $\dot{H}'(0.07)$ of the order of 200 mSv h^{-1} were calculated for the processing of tungsten with 200 kHz repetition rate, burst mode and a peak irradiance of 7.3×10^{13} W cm^{-2} if a distance between the laser interaction point and detector of 10 cm is assumed without consideration of the absorption in air.

It should be noted here that if the "worst-case" spectrum from USP laser machining is known, it can be simulated by an X-ray tube as a model system for mimicking the USP laser machine. This may lead to a simplified testing concept for USP laser machines in the future, which does not depend on the unstable USP laser-generated plasma as an X-ray source during the testing of the safety housing and is compatible with current standard testing procedures.

5. Conclusions

Ultrashort pulse laser processing of tungsten and steel was investigated with respect to the generation of undesired secondary X-rays. Spectral X-ray measurements were performed with complementary CdTe- and SDD-based spectrometers. The radiation protection operational quantities $\dot{H}'(0.07)$, $\dot{H}'(3)$, $\dot{H}^*(10)$ were calculated from the measured X-ray spectra. Regarding the laser processing strategy, the dose equivalent rate of the X-rays increases for lower repetition rates and higher pulse energy if a constant average power is used. The average laser power of ultrashort pulse laser processing alone does not qualify as a suitable parameter for the prediction of X-ray dose rates. Processing with pulse burst mode significantly increases the dose rates and the X-ray photon energies. A maximum dose rate $\dot{H}'(0.07)$ of 5.3 ± 3.5 mSv h^{-1} at a distance of 60 cm was found for the laser processing of tungsten with a repetition rate of 200 kHz in burst mode and a peak irradiance of 7.3×10^{13} W cm^{-2}. A maximum X-ray photon energy of about 40 keV was observed for burst mode processing of tungsten with a repetition rate of 50 kHz and a peak irradiance of 3×10^{14} W cm^{-2}.

Author Contributions: Conceptualization, K.B., M.S.R., U.S., B.P. and J.K.; methodology, K.B., M.S.R., U.S., B.P. and J.K.; software, S.K.; validation, K.B., M.S.R., U.S., S.K., J.B. and J.K.; formal analysis, K.B. and S.K.; investigation, K.B., M.S.R., U.S., C.F., D.A. and B.P.; resources, K.B., C.F., D.A. and B.P.; data curation, K.B. and U.S.; writing—original draft preparation, K.B.; writing—review and editing, K.B., M.S.R., U.S., S.K., J.B., C.F., D.A., B.P. and J.K.; visualization, K.B. and M.S.R.; project administration, B.P. and J.K.; funding acquisition, B.P. and J.K. All authors have read and agreed to the published version of the manuscript.

Funding: This research was funded by the German Federal Office for Radiation Protection (BfS), grant number 3620S22373.

Institutional Review Board Statement: Not applicable.

Informed Consent Statement: Not applicable.

Data Availability Statement: The data presented in this study are available on request from the corresponding author.

Conflicts of Interest: The authors declare no conflict of interest.

References

1. Kühlke, D.; Herpers, U.; Von der Linde, D. Soft X-ray emission from subpicosecond laser-produced plasmas. *Appl. Phys. Lett.* **1987**, *50*, 1785–1787. [CrossRef]
2. Thogersen, J.; Borowiec, A.; Haugen, H.K.; McNeill, F.E.; Stronach, I.M. X-ray emission from femtosecond laser micromachining. *Appl. Phys. A* **2001**, *73*, 361–363. [CrossRef]
3. Bunte, J.; Barcikowski, S.; Puester, T.; Burmester, T.; Brose, M.; Ludwig, T. Secondary hazards: Particle and X-ray emission. In *Femtosecond Technology for Technical and Medical Applications*; Dausinger, F., Lubatschowski, H., Lichtner, F., Eds.; Springer: Berlin/Heidelberg, Germany, 2004; pp. 309–321.
4. Legall, H.; Schwanke, C.; Pentzien, S.; Dittmar, G.; Bonse, J.; Krüger, J. X-ray emission as a potential hazard during ultrashort pulse laser material processing. *Appl. Phys. A* **2018**, *124*, 407. [CrossRef]

5. Behrens, R.; Pullner, B.; Reginatto, M. X-Ray Emission from Materials Processing Lasers. *Radiat. Prot. Dosim.* **2019**, *183*, 361–374. [CrossRef]
6. Legall, H.; Schwanke, C.; Bonse, J.; Krüger, J. The influence of processing parameters on X-ray emission during ultra-short pulse laser machining. *Appl. Phys. A* **2019**, *125*, 570. [CrossRef]
7. Legall, H.; Schwanke, C.; Bonse, J.; Krüger, J. X-ray emission during ultrashort pulse laser processing. In *Frontiers in Ultrafast Optics: Biomedical, Scientific, and Industrial Applications XIX, Proceedings of the SPIE LASE, San Francisco, CA, USA, 2–5 February 2019*; SPIE: Bellingham, WA, USA, 2019; Volume 10908, p. 1090802.
8. Weber, R.; Graf, T. X-ray emission during materials processing with ultrashort laser pulses—A serious problem? *Procedia CIRP* **2022**, *111*, 844–849. [CrossRef]
9. Weber, R.; Giedl-Wagner, R.; Förster, D.J.; Pauli, A.; Graf, T.; Balmer, J.E. Expected X-ray dose rates resulting from industrial ultrafast laser applications. *Appl. Phys. A* **2019**, *125*, 635. [CrossRef]
10. Legall, H.; Schwanke, C.; Bonse, J.; Krüger, J. X-ray radiation protection aspects during ultrashort laser processing. *J. Laser Appl.* **2020**, *32*, 022004. [CrossRef]
11. Freitag, C.; Giedl-Wagner, R. X-Ray Protection in an Industrial Production Environment: Industrial implementation of the requirements of the German Radiation Protection Act. *PhotonicsViews* **2020**, *17*, 37–41. [CrossRef]
12. Legall, H.; Bonse, J.; Krüger, J. Review of X-ray exposure and safety issues arising from ultra-short pulse laser material processing. *J. Radiol. Prot.* **2021**, *41*, R28–R42. [CrossRef]
13. Mosel, P.; Sankar, P.; Düsing, J.F.; Dittmar, G.; Püster, T.; Jaschke, P.; Vahlbruch, J.W.; Morgner, U.; Kovacev, M. X-ray Dose Rate and Spectral Measurements during Ultrafast Laser Machining Using a Calibrated (High-Sensitivity) Novel X-ray Detector. *Materials* **2021**, *14*, 4397. [CrossRef] [PubMed]
14. Stolzenberg, U.; Schmitt Rahner, M.; Pullner, B.; Legall, H.; Bonse, J.; Kluge, M.; Ortner, A.; Hoppe, B.; Krüger, J. X-ray Emission Hazards from Ultrashort Pulsed Laser Material Processing in an Industrial Setting. *Materials* **2021**, *14*, 7163. [CrossRef] [PubMed]
15. Rücker, J.; Fricke, A.; Kahle, M. Unwanted X-ray emission during ultra-short pulse laser material processing and the influence of processing parameters. *Procedia CIRP* **2022**, *111*, 850–854. [CrossRef]
16. Barkauskas, V.; Plukis, A. Prediction of the irradiation doses from ultrashort laser-solid interactions using different temperature scalings at moderate laser intensities. *J. Radiol. Prot.* **2022**, *42*, 011501. [CrossRef]
17. Holland, J.; Weber, R.; Sailer, M.; Graf, T. Influence of Pulse Duration on X-ray Emission during Industrial Ultrafast Laser Processing. *Materials* **2022**, *15*, 2257. [CrossRef] [PubMed]
18. Schille, J.; Kraft, S.; Kattan, D.; Löschner, U. Enhanced X-ray Emissions Arising from High Pulse Repetition Frequency Ultrashort Pulse Laser Materials Processing. *Materials* **2022**, *15*, 2748. [CrossRef] [PubMed]
19. Mosel, P.; Sankar, P.; Appi, E.; Jusko, C.; Zuber, D.; Kleinert, S.; Düsing, J.; Mapa, J.; Dittmar, G.; Püster, T. Potential hazards and mitigation of X-ray radiation generated by laser-induced plasma from research-grade laser systems. *Opt. Express* **2022**, *30*, 37038–37050. [CrossRef] [PubMed]
20. Metzner, D.; Olbrich, M.; Lickschat, P.; Horn, A.; Weißmantel, S. X-ray generation by laser ablation using MHz to GHz pulse bursts. *J. Laser Appl.* **2021**, *33*, 032014. [CrossRef]
21. Schille, J.; Kraft, S.; Pflug, T.; Scholz, C.; Clair, M.; Horn, A.; Loeschner, U. Study on X-ray Emission Using Ultrashort Pulsed Lasers in Materials Processing. *Materials* **2021**, *14*, 4537. [CrossRef]
22. Elahi, P.; Kalaycioğlu, H.; Akçaalan, Ö.; Şenel, Ç.; Ilday, F.Ö. Burst-mode thulium all-fiber laser delivering femtosecond pulses at a 1 GHz intra-burst repetition rate. *Opt. Lett.* **2017**, *42*, 3808–3811. [CrossRef]
23. Bonamis, G.; Mishchick, K.; Audouard, E.; Hönninger, C.; Mottay, E.; Lopez, J.; Manek-Hönninger, I. High efficiency femtosecond laser ablation with gigahertz level bursts. *J. Laser Appl.* **2019**, *31*, 022205. [CrossRef]
24. Shchatsinin, I. Free Clusters and Free Molecules in Strong, Shaped Laser Fields. Ph.D. Thesis, Free University, Berlin, Germany, 3 June 2009.
25. Becker, J.; Tate, M.W.; Shanks, K.S.; Philipp, H.T.; Weiss, J.T.; Purohit, P.; Chamberlain, D.; Ruff, J.P.C.; Gruner, S.M. Characterization of CdTe sensors with Schottky contacts coupled to charge-integrating pixel array detectors for X-ray science. *J. Instrum.* **2016**, *11*, P12013. [CrossRef]
26. Strüder, L.; Niculae, A.; Holl, P.; Soltau, H. Development of the Silicon Drift Detector for Electron Microscopy Applications. *MTO* **2020**, *28*, 46–53. [CrossRef]
27. Cimmino, A.; Horváth, D.; Olšovcová, V.; Stránský, V.; Truneček, R.; Tsinganis, A.; Versaci, R. Radiation Protection at ELI Beamlines: A Unique Laser Driven Accelerator Facility. In Proceedings of the 40th International Conference on High Energy physics—PoS(ICHEP2020), Prague, Czech Republic, 28 July–6 August 2020.
28. Hubbell, J.H.; Seltzer, S.M. *NIST Standard Reference Database 126*; National Institute of Standards and Technology (NIST): Gaithersburg, MD, USA, 1996.
29. International Commission on Radiation Units and Measurements (ICRU). *Conversion Coefficients for Use in Radiological Protection against External Radiation*; ICRU Report 57; International Commission on Radiation Units and Measurements (ICRU): Bethesda, MD, USA, 1998.
30. Ankerhold, U.; Behrens, R.; Ambrosi, P. X Ray Spectrometry of Low Energy Photons for Determining Conversion Coefficients from Air Kerma, K_a, to Personal Dose Equivalent, $H_p(10)$, for Radiation Qualities of the ISO Narrow Spectrum Series. *Radiat. Prot. Dosim.* **1999**, *81*, 247–258. [CrossRef]

materials

MDPI

Article

Enhanced X-ray Emissions Arising from High Pulse Repetition Frequency Ultrashort Pulse Laser Materials Processing

Jörg Schille [1,*], Sebastian Kraft [1], Dany Kattan [2] and Udo Löschner [1]

[1] Laserinstitut Hochschule Mittweida, University of Applied Sciences Mittweida, Technikumplatz 17, 09648 Mittweida, Germany; kraft@hs-mittweida.de (S.K.); loeschne@hs-mittweida.de (U.L.)
[2] Institut für Laser-und Plasmaphysik, Heinrich-Heine-Universität Düsseldorf, Universitätsstraße 1, 40225 Düsseldorf, Germany; dany.kattan@hhu.de
* Correspondence: schille@hs-mittweida.de

Abstract: The ongoing trend in the development of powerful ultrashort pulse lasers has attracted increasing attention for this technology to be applied in large-scale surface engineering and modern microfabrication. However, the emission of undesired X-ray photon radiation was recently reported even for industrially relevant laser irradiation regimes, causing serious health risks for laser operators. In the meantime, more than twenty influencing factors have been identified with substantial effects on X-ray photon emission released by ultrashort pulse laser processes. The presented study on enhanced X-ray emission arising from high pulse repetition frequency ultrashort pulse laser processing provides new insights into the interrelation of the highest-contributing parameters. It is verified by the example of AISI 304 substrates that X-ray photon emission can considerably exceed the legal dose rate limit when ultrashort laser pulses with peak intensities below 1×10^{13} W/cm^2 irradiate at a 0.5 MHz pulse repetition frequency. The peak intensity threshold value for X-ray emissions decreases with larger laser spot sizes and longer pulse durations. Another key finding of this study is that the suction flow conditions in the laser processing area can affect the released X-ray emission dose rate. The presented results support the development of effective X-ray protection strategies for safe and risk-free ultrashort pulse laser operation in industrial and academic research applications.

Keywords: X-ray; ultrashort pulse; laser; plasma; dose rate; Bremsstrahlung; resonance absorption

Citation: Schille, J.; Kraft, S.; Kattan, D.; Löschner, U. Enhanced X-ray Emissions Arising from High Pulse Repetition Frequency Ultrashort Pulse Laser Materials Processing. *Materials* 2022, *15*, 2748. https://doi.org/10.3390/ma15082748

Academic Editor: Beat Neuenschwander

Received: 15 February 2022
Accepted: 6 April 2022
Published: 8 April 2022

1. Introduction

Ultrashort pulse lasers (USPLs) have become established as a versatile tool for high-efficiency and high-precision micromachining, which is a result of their excellent laser beam performances. Moreover, the ongoing trend toward higher laser powers enables high throughputs and short processing times in modern microfabrication, and, thus, the USPL will shortly move forward from the laboratory state to industrial production. However, the emission of X-ray photon radiation constitutes a secondary laser beam hazard from USPLs in materials processing that can cause serious health risks for laser operators. The undesired X-ray photons can potentially arise when high-intense laser beams interact with solid surfaces, producing hot, dense plasma including very hot electrons of several keV. Since earlier studies in the 1970s, three main processes are known for X-ray radiation fields generated by ultrafast laser-excited electrons: (i) the Bremsstrahlung continuum arising from free-free transitions of accelerated free electrons, (ii) the recombination continuum from free-bound electron transitions, and, finally, (iii) characteristic line emissions originating from bound-bound transitions of the inner-shell electrons of ionized atoms. The energy distribution of the Bremsstrahlung X-ray photons follows a Maxwell–Boltzmann distribution where the released X-ray emission dose rate can be approximated by integration over the entire spectral X-ray photon flux. The X-ray emission dose released by a single laser pulse ranges typically from only a few pico Sievert (pSv) to several nano Sievert (nSv), and the potential risk for laser operators is fairly low. The X-ray emission dose rates and associated hazards and risks can considerably increase when employing high-average-power USPLs in materials processing. This is the result of the amazing progress in the development of modern USPL systems towards kilowatt average power that is delivered by ultrashort pulses at high pulse repetition frequencies (PRF) ranging between ten to hundreds of megahertz (MHz) [1]. In this case, millions of ultrashort pulses interact with the substrate surface in a short time, and the X-ray photons released by each single pulse accumulate to high X-ray dose levels, reaching up to 1 Sv/h [2,3]. In fact, such high X-ray emissions exceed innumerably the limit values for the general population and occupationally exposed persons in a calendar year, which are specified in the German Radiation Protection Act, and can cause serious health damage to the exposed parts of the human body.

So far, the onset of X-ray photon emissions has been detected for peak intensities above 10^{13} W/cm^2, which can be delivered, for example, by ultrashort pulses of 1 ps pulse duration and a 10 J/cm^2 fluence. This fluence is about ten times beyond the optimum fluence for the energy-efficient laser processing of metals [4–6] and can be achieved by tightly focusing the laser beam of µJ level optical pulse energy to spot sizes in the range of ten micrometers in the focal plane. In a recent article, the emission of harmful X-ray photon dose rates was demonstrated for much lower fluence or, rather, intensity, which was even below the legal peak intensity limit [7]. This was achieved under specific processing circumstances when MHz PRF pulses were irradiated at a small geometrical pulse distance.

A critical review of the actual literature in this field identified more than 20 factors affecting the X-ray photon emissions arising from ultrashort laser pulses irradiating solid surfaces (see Table 1). These factors also influence each other and can be subdivided into three different categories: (i) laser-sided, (ii) process-sided, and (iii) material-sided parameters of influence. First of all, on the laser side, the peak intensity of the laser pulse can be suggested as the most likely parameter, as doubling the peak intensity increases the released X-ray photon emissions about ten times. Therefore, when considering pulses of similar peak intensities, higher X-ray emission dose rates are detected for longer pulses and higher pulse energies. Another universal expectation from the results presented so far is that the X-ray emissions scale up almost linearly with increasing average laser powers. Furthermore, the PRF was figured out in a recent study on substantially affecting the released X-ray photon flux [7]. This was, in particular, the case when MHz PRF pulses irradiated with high spatial pulse overlapped at submicrometer spatial distances between the individual pulses within a laser-processed line. For the resulting strong increase in X-ray photon emissions, efficient plasma resonance absorption of the irradiating laser beam was suggested as the enhancing effect. The hypothesis is supported by the fact that MHz PRF pulses with very short time delay can interact with the still-remaining plasma plume induced by the preceding pulses [8]. So far, resonance absorption in the laser-produced plasma has been reported only for high-intense laser pulses where both the laser beam polarization and the angle of incidence have considerable influence on the total absorption of the incident laser beam [9–11]. Accordingly, it is validated in the presented article that, even for low-intense pulses, X-ray emissions can increase to high levels when the polarization of the MHz PRF laser beam is aligned parallel to the beam moving direction. This provides evidence that plasma resonance absorption might also be effective in low-intense and high PRF ultrashort pulse laser regimes. In addition, the suction flow speed in the processing zone is introduced as another influencing factor on X-ray emission dose rate. It is shown that reproducible X-ray emissions can only be detected in the case of controlled and stable suction flow conditions. A third key finding of this presented study is that X-ray photon emissions can be detected at low peak intensities up to five times below the legal peak intensity limit for approval-free laser operation in Germany. This can occur under certain processing conditions, e.g., when high PRF pulses of picosecond pulse durations irradiate at a small intra-line distance, the polarization of the laser beam is aligned parallel to the laser beam moving direction, and the suction flow speed is comparably low.

Table 1. A summary of the influencing factors affecting X-ray photon emissions arising from ultra-short pulse laser materials processing.

	Parameter	Impact on X-ray Emission	References
Laser-sided parameters	Peak intensity	- Doubling the peak intensity increases the X-ray dose rate by around ten times	[3,12–14]
	Pulse energy	- With higher pulse energies, higher X-ray dose rates tend to be expected, - The released X-ray emission increases non-linearly with higher energies, the effective peak intensity has a stronger effect on X-ray emission	[15,16]
	Average laser power	- The released X-ray emission scales approximately linearly with higher average laser powers, pay attention to the non-linear effects with higher pulse energies, - Strongly increased X-ray dose rates for high-PRF laser processes or in burst mode laser processing, in particular when high-PRF pulses irradiate at small geometrical (micro meter) pulse distances	[3,7,16,17]
	Pulse repetition frequency	- X-ray dose rate increases approximately linearly with higher PRF resulting from the accumulation of X-ray emissions respectively released by the individual pulses. - Caution concerning strong increased X-ray emissions for MHz PRF or burst mode laser processing which results from strong laser pulse with plasma interactions	[3,7,16]
	Focus spot diameter	- Doubling the focus spot size at constant peak intensities yields 2.5 times higher X-ray dose rates - The spectral distribution and amplitude shifts towards higher X-ray photon energies with increasing focus spot area	[18]
	Wavelength	- Tendency of lower X-ray dose rates for ultrashort pulses of shorter wavelength	[14]
	Polarisation	- Laser radiation polarized parallel to the scan direction increases the dose rate	[11,16,19]
	Pulse duration	- Tendency of higher X-ray dose rates for ultrashort pulses of longer pulse duration	[15,16,20]
Process-sided parameters	Processing regime	- Absorption of the released X-ray emission at the walls of the laser engraved or laser drilled structures reduces the X-ray emission during the ongoing processing - Caution: X-ray dose rate increases as a result of strong laser pulse with plasma/ablation plume interaction, i.e., during stationary laser machining, with deflected beams at high pulse overlap, in laser turning	[7,11,16]
	Scanning direction	- Stronger X-ray emission opposite to the scan direction	[13]
	Intra-line pulse distance	- Pulse irradiations at small geometrical distances cause high surface roughness, in turn lowering the released X-ray dose rate (see surface roughness) - Pulses of small geometrical pulse distances (micro meter) irradiating at MHz PRF amplify the X-ray dose rate by feedback coupling of the pulses with the previously generated laser ablation/plasma plume	[7,11,16]
	Hatch distance	- Larger hatch distances result in higher X-ray dose rates	[11]
	Scan number	- Tendency for lower X-ray dose rates with increasing number of scan crossings	[7]
	Focus position	- Highest X-ray dose rate arises in the focal plane at the position of highest peak intensity - For high-average power laser beams, thermal shift of the optical elements in the beam path can have an effect on the position of highest peak intensity	[2]
	Cross jet	- A larger volume flow rate of the cross jet induces higher X-ray emissions	[16]
	Fume extraction	- A larger distance between sample and suction nozzle decreases the flow rate in turn increasing the X-ray dose rate	[16]
	Angle of incidence	- Oblique laser beams with increased angle of incident with respect to the plasma flank enhance resonance absorption that tends to cause higher X-ray emissions	[7,16,21]
Material-sided parameters	Material	- Higher X-ray dose rates occur with elements with a higher atomic number - Highest X-ray dose rate was determined on tungsten, the X-ray dose rate is comparably high on steel and stainless steel materials	[2,12,14]
	Suface roughness	- A higher surface roughness leads to lower X-ray dose rates due to the shielding of the X-rays on microscopic substructures, similar to the shielding effect of boreholes or trenches	[11,16]
	Dimension	- Large-area laser processing under similar irradiation conditions and corresponding X-ray dose rates releases a larger X-ray emission dose	

2. Experimental Section

Two types of USPL systems were utilized in this study: a UFFL 100 (Active Fiber Systems GmbH, Jena, Germany) and an FX 200 (Edgewave GmbH, Würselen, Germany). This provided a wide range of complementary laser beam parameter settings, i.e., 87 W maximum average laser power, up to 50 MHz PRF, and pulse durations from 340 fs $\leq \tau_H \leq$ 10 ps ($sech^2$ pulse shape). Near-infrared laser beams of 1030 nm wavelength were passed through individual beam expanders and were individually expanded and aligned through an f-theta focusing objective of 167 mm focal length. This resulted in a similar laser spot radius w_0 in the focal plane, as determined by $w_{0/UFFL} = w_{0/FX200}$ = 15.0 µm (1/e^2-method), for the beam caustic measurements (Micro Spot Monitor, Primes GmbH, Pfungstadt, Germany). In addition, a galvanometer scan system (intelliScan 30, Scanlab GmbH, Puchheim, Germany) was assembled in the beam path for raster-scanning the laser beams in a line pattern across the studied stainless steel (AISI 304) substrate surfaces. The intra-line pulse distance d_X, representing the geometrical distance of the impinging laser pulses within a scanned line, was varied as function of scan speed v_S and PRF f_P according to the following relationship: $v_S = d_X \times f_P$. The distance between the scanned lines in the line pattern was set by the hatch distance d_Y. The polarization state of the linearly polarized laser beams was adjusted by a half-wave retarder plate aligned either parallel ($\vec{E} \parallel \vec{v}_{scan}$) or perpendicular $\left(\vec{E} \perp \vec{v}_{scan}\right)$ to the laser beam scan direction. In terms of safety precautions, all the experiments carried out in this study were performed inside a laser safety enclosure to protect the operators from direct and scattered laser beams, X-ray radiation, and other secondary harmful effects originating during high PRF ultrashort pulse laser processing.

The maximum pulse energy used in this study was Q_P = 36 µJ. The pulse energy was calculated from the measured average laser power divided by the PRF, taking into account the optical losses in the beam path. The peak power of a laser pulse P_0 was calculated as the pulse energy divided by the pulse duration. Following Equation (1), the peak intensity of the laser pulses I_0 was given by the pulse peak power divided by the focus spot area A_f, considering a pulse-shape-dependent numerical factor of f_S = 0.88 for the $sech^2$ ultrashort pulses:

$$I_0 = f_S \frac{P_0}{A_f} = f_S \frac{2\, Q_P}{\tau_H\, \pi\, w_0^2} \tag{1}$$

Accordingly, the maximum peak intensity of the ultrashort pulses was $I_{0/UFFL}$ = 2.7×10^{13} W/cm^2 and $I_{0/FX}$ = 1.5×10^{13} W/cm^2 for the UFFL 100 and FX 200 lasers, respectively. Notably, these peak intensity values were only slightly above an intensity of 1×10^{13} W/cm^2, where the X-ray emission dose rate can exceed 1 µSv/h [3,7,12]. In fact, according to the German Radiation Protection Regulations, both the values 1×10^{13} W/cm^2 and 1 µSv/h at a 100 mm distance from the accessible area represent the legal limits for approval-free laser operations [22].

The X-ray emissions arising from the laser beam with AISI 304 substrate interaction were analyzed using two different detectors: a survey meter OD-02 (STEP Sensortechnik und Elektronik Pockau GmbH, Pockau-Lengefeld, Germany) measuring the directional X-ray emission dose $H'(0.07)$ and a SILIX lambda detector (Ingenieurbüro Prof. Dr.-Ing. Günter Dittmar, Aalen, Germany) for monitoring the X-ray emission spectra and X-ray emission dose rate $\dot{H}'(0.07)$ in the soft X-ray photon energy range between 2 and 20 keV. In each experiment, the detectors were aligned parallel to the laser beam scan direction towards the center of the laser-processed area. The dimensions of the raster-scanned processing field were 20 × 20 mm^2. The distance between the detectors and the scanning field center point was 200 mm, and the detection angle was 35°. A unidirectional scan regime was applied with a "laser-ON" cycle, with the laser beam moving away from the X-ray detector receiving maximum X-ray emission dose levels [13]. The laser ON/OFF duty cycle was determined to be 46% in oscilloscope measurements; thus, the monitored values were corrected by a factor of 2.17 to discuss process-typical X-ray emissions in the following sections. The background X-ray radiation in the laboratory was determined below 0.1 μSv/h, which was negligibly small compared to the detected laser-generated X-ray dose levels. Furthermore, it should be mentioned that in each case the X-ray emissions were captured from the first scan crossing of the laser beam over the substrates and were obtained after every six seconds. Respectively, the presented X-ray emission dose values represent mean values averaged from at least ten individual X-ray measurements. The standard deviation of the measured values is indicated in the diagrams.

3. Results

3.1. X-ray Emission as a Function of Intra-Line Pulse Distance

First, the X-ray emission dose per pulse $H'(0.07)_{PP}$ was investigated as a function of the intra-line pulse distance and PRF. Therefore, ultrashort pulses with a peak intensity of $I_0 = 1.5 \times 10^{13}$ W/cm^2 were irradiated at $f_P = 0.5$ MHz and 1.6 MHz. The intra-line pulse distance was varied in the range of 0.15 μm < d_X < 2.0 μm by increasing the scan speed from 75 mm/s to 3200 mm/s, depending on the respective PRF, while the hatch distance was kept constant at $d_Y = 20$ μm. The X-ray emission dose per pulse, as shown in Figure 1, was derived from the averaged SILIX detector readings captured in individual test series on four different days. At $f_P = 0.5$ MHz, the highest X-ray emission dose per pulse of $H'(0.07)_{PP} = 1$ pSv was detected at 0.2 μm. For the larger intra-line pulse distances, there was a clear tendency towards lower X-ray emissions. Therefore, at $d_X = 2$ μm (representing the widest studied distance) the X-ray emission dose per pulse reduced up to two orders of magnitude to $H'(0.07)_{PP} = 0.02$ pSv, which emphasized the great effect of intra-line pulse distance on laser-induced X-ray emissions.

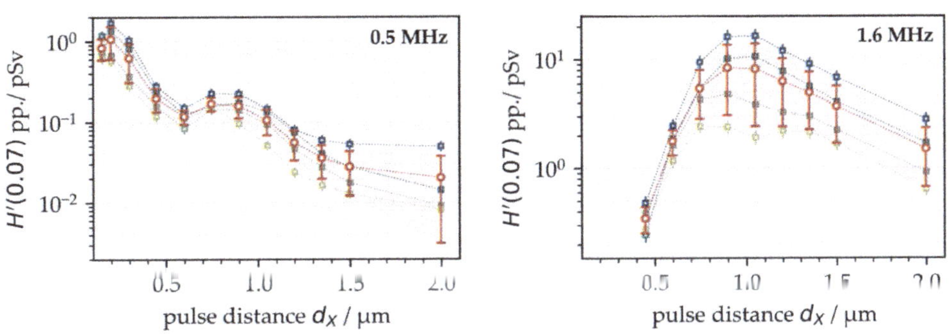

Figure 1. X-ray emission dose per pulse as a function of the intra-line pulse distance at 0.5 MHz (**left**) and 1.6 MHz (**right**) PRF obtained on 4 different days. The mean values are highlighted by the red symbols (circles).

At higher PRFs (for example, 1.6 MHz in Figure 1 (right)), the highest X-ray emissions were found in the range of $d_X = 1$ μm, steadily decreasing with larger intra-line pulse distances. The highest X-ray emission dose per pulse was assessed at an $H'(0.07)_{PP} = 16.0$ pSv maximum with about 8.5 pSv average value. In comparison to low PRF pulses, this was more than a ten-fold increase referring to the maximum value and almost a hundred times higher than the X-ray emission dose arising at $d_X = 1$ μm and 0.5 MHz PRF. This strong increase in the X-ray emissions observed for the high PRF pulses provided evidence of stronger laser beam interaction with plasma during processing, thus, further enhancing X-ray photon generation, which will be discussed more in detail in the following subchapters. However, a significant drop in the X-ray emission dose rate per pulse occurred when 1.6 MHz pulses irradiated at small intra-line pulse distances (d_X < 1 μm), which was in contrast to the X-ray emission characteristics observed at 0.5 MHz. Therefore, a potential explanation can be found in the increased roughness of the high-PRF-processed surfaces, which could behave similar to the X-ray shielding recently observed on kerf walls and boreholes [3,11]. In the particular case of high PRF pulses irradiating at small intra-line pulse distances, self-organizing microscopic surface structures emerged at the substrate surfaces [23]. These rough and protruded surface features potentially screened the laser-induced X-ray photon flux, which in turn caused the lower monitored X-ray emission doses at small intra-line pulse distances seen in Figure 1 (right). In order to validate the proposed influencing effect of surface roughness on X-ray emission, X-ray photon fluxes arising from the laser processing of four different laser-pretextured substrates were analyzed, Figure 2.

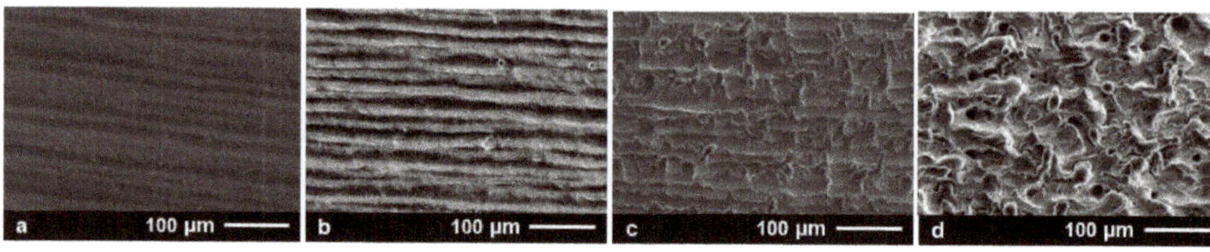

Figure 2. Laser surface textures produced on AISI 304 by raster-scanning of the laser beam across the substrates at 3.0 μm (**a**), 1.5 μm (**b**), 0.9 μm (**c**), and 0.6 μm (**d**) intra-line pulse distance.

For surface pretexturing, a laser beam of $I_{0/FX}$ = 1.5 × 10^{13} W/cm^2 and f_P = 1.6 MHz was raster-scanned across the AISI 304 substrates at a d_Y = 20 μm hatch distance. The intra-line pulse distances were varied between d_X = 3.0 μm (Figure 2a), 1.5 μm (Figure 2b), 0.9 μm (Figure 2c), and 0.6 μm (Figure 2d). In this way, specific surface roughness conditions were provided for the next impinging pulses similar to the ones discussed above in Figure 1. In the X-ray measurements, the laser processing conditions were as follows: $I_{0/FX}$ = 1.5 × 10^{13} W/cm^2, f_P = 1.6 MHz, d_X = 0.9 μm, and d_Y = 20 μm.

The highest X-ray emission dose per pulse of $H'(0.07)_{PP}$ = 9.1 pSv was captured for the smooth surface, which was laser-pretextured with d_X = 3.0 μm and S_a = 0.49 μm corresponding area roughness, Figure 3. For the d_X = 1.5 μm laser-pretextured surface and resulting S_a = 0.94 μm, the X-ray emission dose per pulse was marginally lower in the range of $H'(0.07)_{PP}$ = 8.2 pSv. These X-ray emission doses were almost equal to the ones measured for the nontextured basic material of similar surface roughness, S_a = 0.44 μm. For the rougher surfaces featured with area roughness measures of S_a = 1.8 μm and 6.8 μm resulting from laser pretexturing at smaller intra-line pulse distances of d_X = 0.9 μm and 0.6 μm, respectively, the detected X-ray emission doses per pulse amounted to $H'(0.07)_{PP}$ = 5.4 pSv and 0.9 pSv, respectively. Remarkably, these dose values were even below the X-ray emissions arising from laser processing of the nontextured steel surface at d_X = 0.6 μm in Figure 1 (right), which was proof for the screening of laser-induced X-ray photons by rough surface features.

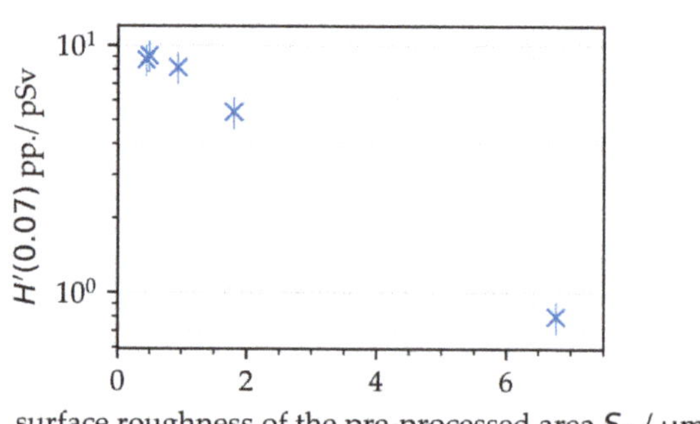

Figure 3. X-ray emission dose per pulse as a function of the area roughness of specifically laser pre-textured AISI 304 substrate surfaces.

However, a closer look at Figure 1 shows a large variance of the X-ray emission dose levels, diverging up to a factor of ten for the measurements carried out on four consecutive days. An influencing effect of the laser beam or, rather, the ambient air conditions on the X-ray emission dose can largely be ruled out, as the laser beam parameters were carefully controlled during the study. Moreover, the experiments were performed in an air-conditioned laboratory room (temperature: 22.5 ± 0.5 °C; humidity: 44% ± 2%) in order to provide constant processing conditions.

3.2. Influencing Effect of Dust and Fume Extraction on X-ray Emission

After a detailed inspection of the experimental conditions, both the position of the fume extraction element (FEE) related to the processing area, as well as the suction flow speed v_{fs}, were identified as potentially influencing factors for the monitored different X-ray emission dose levels. For a more precise investigation of this effect, the distance of the FEE from the processing area d_{eff} was varied during the measurements of X-ray photon emission arising from laser surface processing with pulses of $I_{0/FX} = 1.5 \times 10^{13}$ W/cm^2, $f_P = 1.6$ MHz, and $d_X = 0.75$ µm. As another control parameter, the suction flow speed was monitored at the center position of the laser-processed field using a resistance anemometer. The measurements showed a continuous reduction in the suction flow speed with increasing distance of the FFE from the processing area, Figure 4. At about a 190 mm distance, the suction flow turned from laminar to turbulent, which was indicated by the larger deviation of the measured suction flow speed. From this position, no further reduction in the suction flow speed was detected with larger distances because the cross jet air flow protecting the focusing objective was more predominant within the processing area.

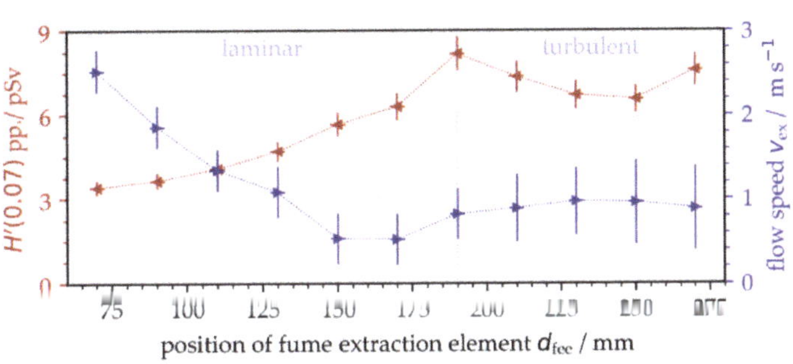

Figure 4. X-ray emission dose per pulse as a function of suction flow speed that was varied by increasing the distance of the fume extraction element from the laser processing area.

The results obtained in this set of experiments validated a strong impact of the surrounding air flow on X-ray photon emission for the first time. In the laminar flow regime, the X-ray emission dose increased almost linearly with lower suction flow speed, while the maximum X-ray photon flux was measured in the turbulent flow regime. Hence, the experiments of Figure 1 were repeated under controlled suction flow conditions. As a result, the X-ray emissions arising from laser processing under stable suction flow speeds ($v_{fs} = 0.9$ m/s ± 0.3 m/s) showed a considerably reduced standard deviation ranging within the measurement accuracy of the SILIX detector. This was proven for both $f_P = 0.5$ MHz and 1.6 MHz repetitive pulses studied on two different days, Figure 5.

In Figure 5, the critical intra-line pulse distances $d_{X,crit}$ are indicated. These values represent the geometrical pulse distances within a raster-scanned line where the maximum X-ray emission doses were detected. For the low PRF pulses, Figure 5 (left), the highest X-ray emission was achieved at $d_{X,crit} = 0.15$ µm, which was similar to the intra-line distance shown in Figure 1 for the highest X-ray dose level. For high PRF pulses, in contrast, the highest X-ray emission dose was recorded at $d_{X,crit} = 0.75$ µm, Figure 5 (right). This intra-line distance was achieved under stable suction flow conditions and was a little smaller than those for uncontrolled laser processing conditions, further underlining the influence of suction flow or, rather, the prevailing dust and fume concentration surrounding the laser processing area on X-ray photon emission.

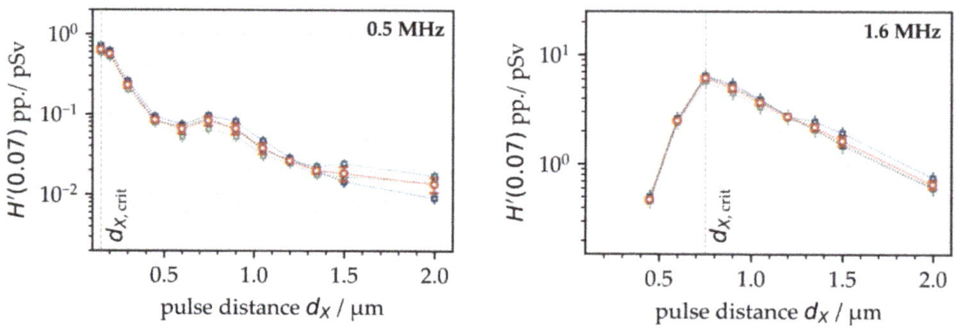

Figure 5. X-ray emission dose per pulse as a function of the intra-line pulse distance at 0.5 MHz (**left**) and 1.6 MHz (**right**) PRF obtained on 2 different days under controlled suction flow conditions. The suction flow speed was kept constant at 0.9 m/s ± 0.3 m/s. The mean values are highlighted by the red symbols (circles). The critical intra-line pulse distances $d_{X,\mathrm{crit}}$ are indicated.

3.3. *X-ray Emission as a Function of PRF and Polarization State*

A detailed analysis of the results obtained showed that the critical intra-line pulse distance for the maximum X-ray emission dose was strongly affected by the specifically applied PRF. For example, the critical intra-line distance was $d_{X,\mathrm{crit}}$ = 0.2 µm at f_P = 0.5 MHz, enlarging to $d_{X,\mathrm{crit}}$ = 0.9 µm at f_P = 1.4 MHz and above, Figure 6. Therefore, a potential explanation can be found in the complex interaction of the laser beam with the plasma plume induced by preceding pulses in a pulse train. Moreover, in the particular case of low-intense ultrashort pulses irradiating at MHz PRF, plasma resonance absorption might be the dominant absorption mechanism for the laser beam, which was already evidenced in a previous work [7]. This, in turn, implies optimum plasma characteristics in terms of the degree of ionization, plasma carrier density, dimension and flank angle of the critical plasma density layer, etc., for the most efficient coupling of impinging optical pulse energies with the laser-induced plasma plume. In fact, plasma plume formation and expansion are highly dynamic processes [8]. Therefore, it became evident for the dynamically changing plasma plume that both timing (defined by PRF) and position (defined by intra-line pulse distance) of the next impinging laser pulse had a great effect on optimum laser beam coupling resulting maximum X-ray photon emission. The general trend of increasing X-ray emission dose and enlarging critical intra-line pulse distance with higher PRFs can be seen in Figure 6 for two different suction flow speeds: v_{fs} = 0.9 m/s and 2.8 m/s. In addition to the X-ray emission dose per pulse, for a better comparison to the literature data, the measured values are also presented in the form of X-ray emission dose rate per irradiated laser power. The higher X-ray dose values and the larger critical intra-line pulse distances were found for the lower suction flow speed, which is in line with the data presented above in Figure 4. In this context, it is worth mentioning that the highest X-ray emission doses can be seen in Figure 6 with about same value of 0.8 mSv/h/W for PRFs ranging between 1.0 MHz and 1.8 MHz. This broad range of MHz PRF for the highest X-ray emissions seems to be contrary to previous results (e.g., Figure 5 (right) shows a distinct maximum at 1.6 MHz). The X-ray emission doses of Figure 6, however, represent maximum values that were achieved at different intra-line pulse distances.

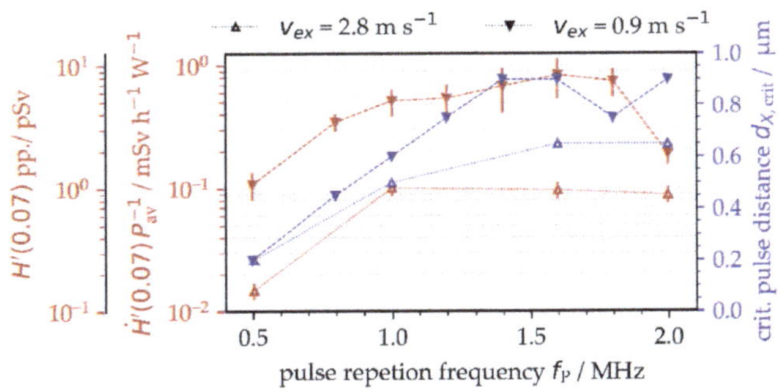

Figure 6. X-ray emission doses per pulse and X-ray emission dose rates related to the applied average laser power as a function of PRF detected at different suction flow speeds. The critical intra-line pulse distances for maximum X-ray emissions are presented.

In addition to PRF and intra-line pulse distance, the polarization state of the laser beam was another enhancing effect of ultrashort pulse laser-induced X-ray emissions, Figure 7. This applies in particular to MHz pulses and linear polarization aligned parallel to the beam scanning direction. When comparing with the perpendicularly polarized laser beam, a maximum four-fold increase in X-ray emission was figured out for the f_{P} = 1.0 MHz repetitive pulses irradiating at a $d_{\text{X,crit}}$ = 0.5 µm critical intra-line pulse distance, Figure 7 (left, middle). At the higher PRF of 1.6 MHz, the X-ray emission of the parallel-polarized laser beam was about twice the X-ray dose obtained with perpendicular polarization, Figure 7 (left, bottom). A difference by the factor of two between the X-ray emission dose levels was also observed for the 0.5 MHz pulses irradiated either parallel or perpendicularly polarized with respect to the laser beam scanning direction, Figure 7 (left, top). The maximum X-ray emission dose levels of Figure 7, ranging up to $H'(0.07)_{\text{PP,max}}$ = 1 pSv, were almost one order of magnitude below the values presented above in Figure 5 of $H'(0.07)_{\text{PP,max}}$ = 10 pSv. This is mainly due to the fact that different suction flow speeds were applied (v_{fs} = 0.9 m/s in Figure 5 vs. 2.8 m/s in Figure 7), which further confirms the strong impact of suction flow speed on X-ray photon emission already shown above in Figure 6. From these results, it can be postulated that the suction flow speed manipulated the shape of the plasma plume, which, in turn, affected the efficient coupling of the following laser pulses into the plasma under resonant absorption conditions. The proposed influencing effect of laser beam polarization on X-ray emission can also be assessed from the X-ray emission spectra provided in Figure 7 (right) showing higher X-ray photon yields and wider X-ray spectra that were further enlarged to higher X-ray photon energies for the parallel-polarized laser beam.

Nevertheless, the strong dependence of X-ray emission spectra and dose rate on laser beam polarization is a further indication of plasma resonance absorption as an effective absorption mechanism when MHz PRF pulses interact with well-formed plasma states. This is validated by the fact that the polarization of laser beams has already been proven as an influencing factor for resonance absorption in high-intense laser-produced plasma. The originality of our study, however, is the evidenced resonance absorption of following pulses (irradiating with short time delays at MHz PRF) on the well-formed plasma plume induced by the preceding pulses in a pulse train. This was also confirmed by the monitored X-ray photon spectra and corresponding X-ray dose rates increasing disproportionately from $\dot{H}'(0.07)$ = 2.7 mSv/h to 9.0 mSv/h at 1.0 MHz or, rather, $\dot{H}'(0.07)$ = 7.0 mSv/h to 21.0 mSv/h at f_{P} = 1.6 MHz when using a parallel- instead of a perpendicular-polarized laser beam.

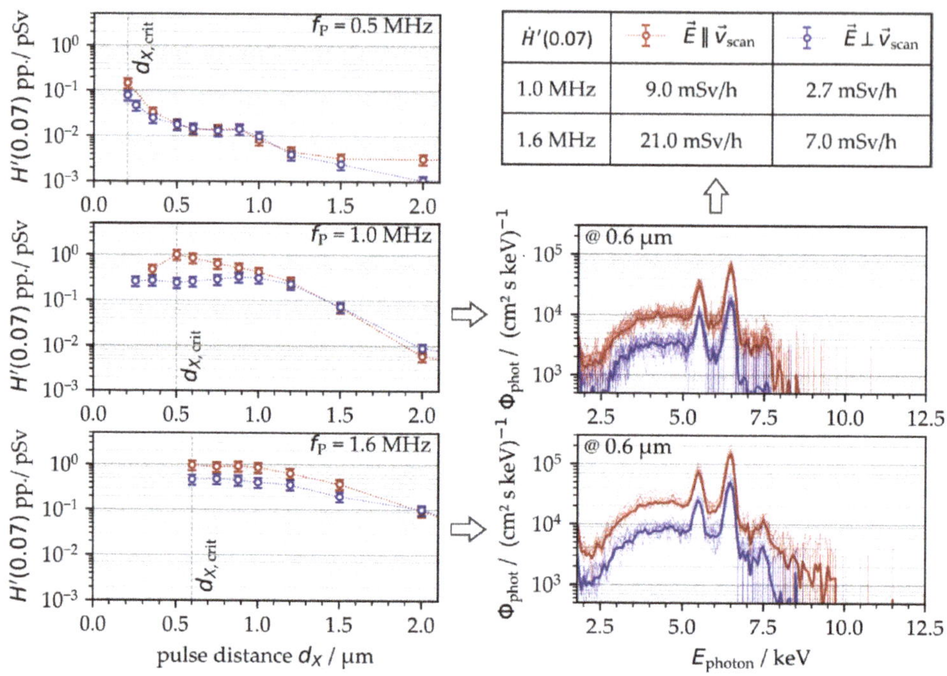

Figure 7. (**Left**): X-ray emission dose per pulse as a function of pulse distance, PRF, and polarization direction at a 2.8 m/s ± 0.4 m/s suction flow speed; (**right**): corresponding X-ray photon spectra monitored for 1.0 MHz or 1.6 MHz PRF, 0.6 intra-line pulse distance, 0.9 m/s ± 0.3 m/s suction flow speed, and either parallel (red) or perpendicular (blue) laser beam polarization.

3.4. *Influence of the Peak Intensity on X-ray Emission*

In this study, maximum X-ray emission dose rates up to $\dot{H}'(0.07)$ = 35 mSv/h were produced with pulses of comparably low peak intensity somewhat above 10^{13} W/cm^2. As a rough estimate, the doubling of the peak intensity could induce 10 times higher X-ray emission dose rates, which implied that peak intensity is a significantly influencing variable of X-ray photon emission. Following Equation (1), the peak intensity denotes the maximum optical power related to the laser spot area and can be varied either by the pulse energy, the pulse duration, or the spot size of the irradiating laser beam. For a better understanding of the specific effect of these individual parameters on X-ray emission and further to identify a threshold value for the start of X-ray photon generation, the peak intensity was gradually reduced by (i) increasing the pulse duration between 330 fs $\leq \tau_H \leq$ 10 ps, (ii) reducing the pulse energy by lowering the average laser power to a constant f_P = 0.5 MHz, and (iii) increasing the laser spot area by placing the substrate surface out of the focal plane (defocusing). In the case of defocusing, the effective laser spot radius $w_{86}(z)$ of the laser beam depended on the distance of the substrate surface from the focal plane, hereinafter referenced as defocusing distance z. In order to define the peak intensity of the ultrashort pulses specifically applied in the defocused substrate position, according to Equation (1), the effective laser spot radius was calculated following Equation (2) by taking into account the Rayleigh length of z_R = 0.6 µm and the focus spot radius of $w_{0.86}$ = 15.0 µm

$$w_{86}(z) = w_{0.86}\sqrt{1 + \frac{z^2}{z_R^2}} \tag{2}$$

In Figure 8 (left), the pulse energy showed the greatest effect on the released dose rate when comparing the X-ray emissions from pulses of varying peak intensities. This was validated by the steepest curve growth (blue, squares) in the $\dot{H}'(0.07)$ vs. I_0 log-log plot. At a fixed peak intensity, the pulses of longer pulse duration induced higher X-ray emission dose levels (green, circles). The results also confirm that pulse duration affected the threshold intensity value, where X-ray photons were detected for the first time. For example, the intensity threshold was figured from $I_{0/\mathrm{UFFL}} = 1.3 \times 10^{13}$ W/cm^2 for 340 fs pulses. In contrast, with the longer 10 ps pulses, the X-ray photon emission started at $I_{0/\mathrm{UFFL}} = 2.3 \times 10^{12}$ W/cm^2. This was about four times below the legal peak intensity limit for approval-free laser operation in Germany. Moreover, the corresponding $\dot{H}'(0.07) = 10$ μSv/h for the applied low-intense 30 W average power laser beam exceeded considerably the permitted 1 μSv/h maximum X-ray emission dose rate.

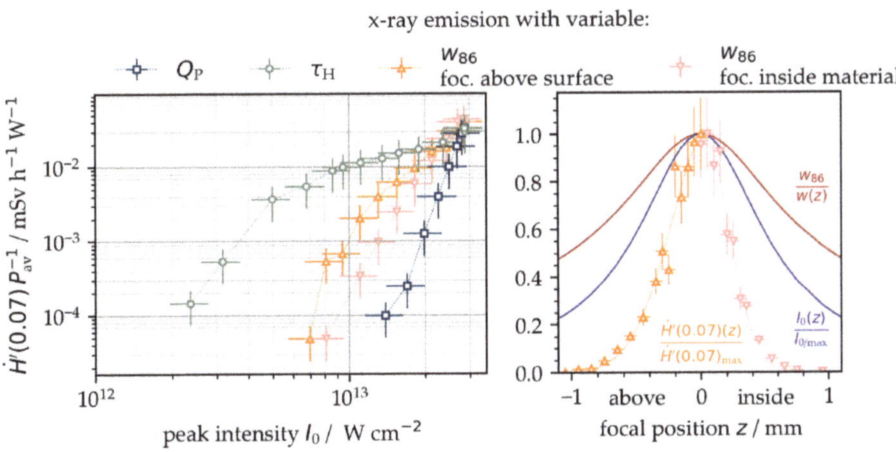

Figure 8. (**Left**): X-ray emission dose rate as function of pulse energy, pulse duration, and laser spot size; (**Right**): effect of laser beam defocusing on laser spot radius, peak intensity, and X-ray emission dose rate obtained at 0.5 MHz PRF, 1.0 μm intra-line pulse distance, and 2.8 m/s ± 0.4 m/s suction flow speed.

The spot size of the laser beam at the substrate surface was varied by defocusing. For larger spot sizes with focus positions above instead of inside the laser beam, the substrate surface showed up to three times higher X-ray emission dose rates. A potential explanation, therefore, can be found with the heel effect by screening X-ray photons generated inside the craters on the rough and protruded surface features. As a matter of fact, in the case of placing the focus position inside the material, the outer areas of the laser beam were cut off by the original surface, reducing the effective peak intensity of the laser beam travelling to the deeper areas being processed. The main effects of laser beam defocusing on X-ray emissions are indicated in Figure 8 (right), showing larger laser spot radii, lower peak intensity, and decreasing X-ray emissions for the greater distances of the laser focus plane from the substrate surface.

4. Summary and Main Conclusions

The emission of undesired X-ray photon radiation in ultrashort pulse laser materials processing poses a secondary laser beam hazard and can cause serious health risks for laser operators. The generation of harmful X-ray dose levels is affected by a wide range of laser parameters and processing conditions. In total, more than 20 influencing factors on the laser-, process- and material-sides have been identified as considerably affecting the X-ray emission dose, while the individual parameters also can have a direct influence on each other. In this article, in addition to peak intensity as the most likely variable, the PRF, intra-line pulse distance, polarization direction, and suction flow speed were shown as other contributing parameters enhancing laser-induced X-ray emissions. Based on the results obtained in the presented study, the following key findings were concluded:

1. X-ray emission dose levels could increase up to ten-fold when ultrashort laser pulses irradiate at MHz PRF and submicrometer intra-line pulse distances;
2. A critical intra-line distance depending on PRF existed for maximum X-ray emissions;
3. Higher X-ray emissions could be released from smoother surfaces;
4. The suction flow conditions in the laser processing area affected X-ray photon emissions, where higher suction flow speeds induced lower X-ray dose levels;
5. A laser beam parallel-polarized to the beam moving direction induced higher X-ray emissions, which further confirmed plasma resonance absorption as an efficient laser beam absorption mechanism in a low-intense ultrashort pulse laser regime;
6. Harmful X-ray emission dose rates exceeding the legal limit of 1 μSv/h could be generated with peak intensities below 1×10^{13} W/cm, and, finally;
7. The peak intensity threshold value for X-ray emissions decreased with larger laser spot sizes and longer pulse durations.

These summarizing statements provide new insights into the fundamental mechanisms for X-ray photon emissions arising from USPLs applied in materials processing. Essentially, the detailed understanding of the interrelation between the main contributing parameters is particularly helpful for the development of effective X-ray protection strategies for safe and risk-free operation of powerful USPLs in industrial and academic research applications. Furthermore, the presented X-ray emission dose rates monitored in industrial-relevant USPL processes can provide a basis for the correct selection and dimensioning of X-ray radiation shielding enclosures.

Author Contributions: Conceptualization, J.S., S.K. and U.L.; methodology, J.S., S.K., D.K. and U.L.; investigation, S.K, D.K. and J.S.; writing—original draft preparation, J.S. and S.K.; writing—review and editing, J.S., S.K., D.K. and U.L.; funding acquisition, U.L. and J.S. All authors have read and agreed to the published version of the manuscript.

Funding: The authors thank the European Social Fund of Germany (ESF) for funding from the EilaSax project (no. 100339506) and the German Federal Ministry of Education and Research (BMBF) for financial support from the project FH-Europa 2020: MACH-XLT (No. 13FH009EX0).

Institutional Review Board Statement: Not applicable.

Informed Consent Statement: Not applicable.

Data Availability Statement: Not applicable.

Conflicts of Interest: The authors declare no conflict of interest.

References

1. Schille, J.; Löschner, U. Ultrashort pulse lasers in high-rate laser micro processing—Quo vadis? *Adv. Opt. Technol.* **2021**, *10*, 233–237. [CrossRef]
2. Mosel, P.; Sankar, P.; Düsing, J.F.; Dittmar, G.; Püster, T.; Jäschke, P.; Vahlbruch, J.-W.; Morgner, U.; Kovacev, M. X-ray Dose Rate and Spectral Measurements during Ultrafast Laser Machining Using a Calibrated (High-Sensitivity) Novel X-ray Detector. *Materials* **2021**, *14*, 4397. [CrossRef] [PubMed]
3. Weber, R.; Giedl-Wagner, R.; Förster, D.J.; Pauli, A.; Graf, T.; Balmer, J.E. Expected X-ray dose rates resulting from industrial ultrafast laser applications. *Appl. Phys. A* **2019**, *125*, 635.
4. Raciukaitis, G.; Brikas, M.; Gečys, P.; Voisiat, B.; Gedvilas, M. Use of high repetition rate and high power lasers in microfabrication: How to keep the efficiency high? *J. Laser Micro Nanoeng.* **2008**, *4*, 186–191. [CrossRef]
5. Neuenschwander, B.; Bucher, G.F.; Nussbaum, C.; Joss, B.; Muralt, M.; Hunziker, U.W.; Schuetz, P. Processing of metals and dielectric materials with ps laser pulses: Results, strategies, limitations and needs. In Proceedings of the Laser Applications in Microelectronic and Optoelectronic Manufacturing XV, San Francisco, CA, USA, 23–28 January 2010.
6. Schille, J.; Schneider, L.; Löschner, U. Process optimization in high-average-power ultrashort pulse laser microfabrication: How laser process parameters influence efficiency, throughput and quality. *Appl. Phys. A* **2015**, *120*, 847–855. [CrossRef]

7. Schille, J.; Kraft, S.; Pflug, T.; Scholz, C.; Clair, M.; Horn, A.; Löschner, U. Study on X-ray Emission Using Ultrashort Pulsed Lasers in Material Processing. *Materials* **2021**, *14*, 4537. [CrossRef] [PubMed]
8. Kraft, S.; Schille, J.; Mauersberger, S.; Schneider, L.; Löschner, U. Pump-probe imaging for process control and optimization in high-speed laser micro machining. In Proceedings of the Laser-based Micro-and Nanoprocessing XIV, San Francisco, CA, USA, 1–6 February 2020.
9. Ballmer, J.E.; Donaldson, T.P. Resonance Absorption of 1.06-µm Laser Radiation in Laser-Generated Plasma. *Phys. Rev. Lett.* **1977**, *39*, 17. [CrossRef]
10. Teubner, U.; Bergmann, J.; van Wonterghem, B.; Schaefer, F.P.; Sauerbrey, R. Angle-dependent x-ray emission and resonance absorption in a laser-produced plasma generated by a high intensity ultrashort pulse. *Phys. Rev. Lett.* **1993**, *70*, 794. [CrossRef] [PubMed]
11. Legall, H.; Schwanke, C.; Bonse, J.; Krüger, J. The influence of processing parameters on X-ray emission during ultra-short pulse laser machining. *Appl. Phys. A* **2019**, *125*, 570.
12. Legall, H.; Schwanke, C.; Pentzien, S.; Dittmar, G.; Bonse, J.; Krüger, J. X-ray emission as a potential hazard during ultrashort pulse laser material processing. *Appl. Phys. A* **2018**, *124*, 407. [CrossRef]
13. Freitag, C.; Giedl-Wagner, R. X-Ray Protection in an Industrial Production Environment. *Photonics Views* **2019**, *17*, 37. [CrossRef]
14. Legall, H.; Bonse, J.; Krüger, J. Review of x-ray exposure and safety issues arising from ultra-short pulse laser material processing. *J. Radiol. Prot.* **2021**, *41*, R28. [CrossRef] [PubMed]
15. Chichkov, B.N.; Momma, C.; Tünnermann, A.; Meyer, S.; Menzel, T.; Wellegehausen, B. Hard-x-ray radiation from short-pulse laser-produced plasmas. *Appl. Phys. Lett.* **1996**, *68*, 2804. [CrossRef]
16. Kattan, D. Untersuchung der Röntgenemissionen durch laserinduzierte Plasmen in der Materialbear-beitung mit Ultrakurzpulslasern an Luft (written in German). Master's Thesis, Heinrich Heine University, Düsseldorf, Germany, 18 August 2021.
17. Metzner, D.; Olbrich, M.; Lickschat, P.; Horn, A.; Weißmantel, S. X-ray generation by laser ablation using MHz to GHz pulse bursts. *J. Laser Appl.* **2021**, *33*, 032014. [CrossRef]
18. Dittmar, G. Arbeitsblatt 2: Zunahme der laserinduzierten ionisierenden Strahlung (LIS) bei größer werdender Fokusfläche trotz gleicher Bestrahlungsstärke. Available online: https://www.researchgate.net/publication/339537884_Arbeitsblatt_2_Zunahme_der_laserinduzierten_ionisierenden_Strahlung_LIS_bei_grosser_werdender_Fokusflache_trotz_gleicher_Bestrahlungsstarke?channel=doi&linkId=5e57f406299bf1bdb8408aa0&showFulltext=true (accessed on 1 February 2022).
19. Sauerbrey, R.; Fure, J.; Le Blanc, S.P. Reflectivity of laser-produced plasmas generated by a high intensity ultrashort pulse. *Phys. Plasmas* **1994**, *1*, 5. [CrossRef]
20. Holland, J.; Weber, R.; Sailer, M.; Graf, T. Influence of Pulse Duration on X-ray Emission during Industrial Ultrafast Laser Processing. *Materials* **2022**, *15*, 2257. [CrossRef] [PubMed]
21. Cerchez, M.; Jung, R.; Osterholz, J.; Toncian, T.; Willi, O.; Mulser, P.; Ruhl, H. Absorption of ultrashort laser pulses in strongly overdense targets. *Phys. Rev. Lett.* **2008**, *100*, 245001. [CrossRef] [PubMed]
22. German Federal Office for Radiation Protection. Limit Values in Radiation Protection. Available online: https://www.bfs.de/EN/topics/ion/radiation-protection/limit-values/limit-values_node.html (accessed on 1 February 2022).
23. Schille, J.; Schneider, L.; Mauersberger, S.; Szokup, S.; Höhn, S.; Pötschke, J.; Reiss, F.; Leidich, E.; Löschner, U. High-Rate Laser Surface Texturing for Advanced Tribological Functionality. *Lubricants* **2020**, *8*, 33. [CrossRef]

materials

MDPI

Article

X-ray Emission Hazards from Ultrashort Pulsed Laser Material Processing in an Industrial Setting

Ulf Stolzenberg [1,*], Mayka Schmitt Rahner [1], Björn Pullner [1], Herbert Legall [2], Jörn Bonse [2], Michael Kluge [3], Andreas Ortner [3], Bernd Hoppe [3] and Jörg Krüger [2]

1 Physikalisch-Technische Bundesanstalt (PTB), Department of Radiation Protection Dosimetry, Bundesallee 100, 38116 Braunschweig, Germany; mayka.schmitt-rahner@ptb.de (M.S.R.); bjoern.pullner@ptb.de (B.P.)

2 Bundesanstalt für Materialforschung und -prüfung (BAM), Materials Chemistry Department, Unter den Eichen 87, 12205 Berlin, Germany; kontakt-legall@t-online.de (H.L.); joern.bonse@bam.de (J.B.); joerg.krueger@bam.de (J.K.)

3 SCHOTT AG, Hattenbergstrasse 10, 55122 Mainz, Germany; michael.kluge@schott.com (M.K.); andreas.ortner@schott.com (A.O.); bernd.hoppe@schott.com (B.H.)

* Correspondence: ulf.stolzenberg@ptb.de

Abstract: Interactions between ultrashort laser pulses with intensities larger than 10^{13} W/cm^2 and solids during material processing can lead to the emission of X-rays with photon energies above 5 keV, causing radiation hazards to operators. A framework for inspecting X-ray emission hazards during laser material processing has yet to be developed. One requirement for conducting radiation protection inspections is using a reference scenario, i.e., laser settings and process parameters that will lead to an almost constant and high level of X-ray emissions. To study the feasibility of setting up a reference scenario in practice, ambient dose rates and photon energies were measured using traceable measurement equipment in an industrial setting at SCHOTT AG. Ultrashort pulsed (USP) lasers with a maximum average power of 220 W provided the opportunity to measure X-ray emissions at laser peak intensities of up to 3.3×10^{15} W/cm^2 at pulse durations of ~1 ps. The results indicate that increasing the laser peak intensity is insufficient to generate high dose rates. The investigations were affected by various constraints which prevented measuring high ambient dose rates. In this work, a list of issues which may be encountered when performing measurements at USP-laser machines in industrial settings is identified.

Keywords: X-ray emission hazards; ultrashort pulsed laser; radiation protection; industrial applications; protection housing; ambient dose rate; X-ray spectrum

Citation: Stolzenberg, U.; Schmitt Rahner, M.; Pullner, B.; Legall, H.; Bonse, J.; Kluge, M.; Ortner, A.; Hoppe, B.; Krüger, J. X-ray Emission Hazards from Ultrashort Pulsed Laser Material Processing in an Industrial Setting. *Materials* **2021**, *14*, 7163. https://doi.org/10.3390/ma14237163

Academic Editor: Andres Sotelo

Received: 29 October 2021
Accepted: 22 November 2021
Published: 24 November 2021

Publisher's Note: MDPI stays neutral with regard to jurisdictional claims in published maps and institutional affiliations.

1. Introduction

The use of ultrashort laser pulses in air for material processing has many advantages such as the lateral and vertical precision of the surface contours down to the nanometer range and the high reproducibility of the laser-generated structures [1]. Due to the progressive development in the laser sector, average powers in the kW range with pulse repetition rates exceeding the MHz level are currently available [2]. Machining with high-intensity laser pulses can be accompanied by the generation of a near-surface electron plasma due to absorption and ionization of the material, a subsequent plasma heating by the laser pulse, and finally an interaction of "hot" plasma electrons with the processed material, leading to continuous and characteristic X-ray emissions.

The fact that ultrashort sub-ps pulsed laser material interaction can lead to X-ray radiation has been well established since the late 1980s [3–8]. Twenty years ago, X-ray emission was reported as an unwanted secondary effect during femtosecond laser micromachining of copper in air using kHz repetition rates [9,10]. The authors registered X-ray dose rates requiring radiation protection measures. The amount of this X-ray radiation is determined by the laser parameters (pulse duration, peak intensity, pulse energy, wavelength, and polarization), the workpiece (atomic number and surface preparation), and the laser process management (scanning or stationary regime, laser turning, etc.). The use of laser peak intensities above 10^{13} W/cm^2 in combination with laser pulse repetition rates in the few 100 kHz range can already lead to X-ray dose rates clearly exceeding the permitted limits for members of the public. Tungsten and steel in particular show significant X-ray emission [11–19]. In [11], it was demonstrated that other materials such as aluminum and glass show significantly lower X-ray emissions. The measured dose rate for an aluminum target was approximately two orders of magnitude lower than the dose rate of steel and tungsten. For a fixed intensity, an increase in the measured dose rate with a raising atomic number Z was observed as a general trend. Under typical ultrashort pulse laser machining conditions in the intensity range of 10^{13} to 10^{15} W/cm^2, collision-less resonance absorption appears to be the driving X-ray generation mechanism [17].

It has been shown very recently, experimentally, that significantly higher X-ray dose rates can be generated during USP-laser machining when using a laser burst mode instead of the single-pulse mode utilizing the same total laser intensity. The increase in X-ray yield was attributed to the interaction between the ultrafast laser radiation and an ablation cloud or high-density plasma [19,20]. This special regime was not investigated within the framework of this paper.

Due to the possible emission of ionizing radiation during material processing with a USP-laser machine, radiation monitoring and protection measures for staff working on such machines must be implemented. One such measure is dosimetry measurements outside of the protective housing or structural radiation protection features during the authorization process for operation of USP-laser machines. To ensure conservativity during the radiation protection inspection, the material processing scenario with maximum radiation exposure and the highest photon energies of laser-induced X-ray radiation would typically have to be employed. However, due to the large number of relevant laser and processing parameters, determining and setting up a worst-case scenario is time-consuming and impractical during regular safety inspections. Nevertheless, for consistent and reproducible inspection results, a reference condition must be defined. In the case of USP-laser machines, this is especially important as laser–plasma interactions and the subsequent energy spectra and intensities of the X-ray emission strongly depend on various operational parameters such as laser parameters, the manufacturing process and its geometry, and the previously mentioned laser-irradiated material.

The possible reference scenario used here is based on the laser surface processing of a metal sample such as steel or tungsten. For the measurements, a bidirectional configuration is used. During this process, grooves with a certain length (e.g., 15 mm) are machined into the target material. After finishing one groove, the material is moved by one focus diameter in the direction perpendicular to the groove, and another groove is manufactured in the opposite direction. This process is repeated until a surface scan area of, for example, 15×15 mm^2 has been covered. This includes the ablation of a single "process layer". To increase the duration of the laser processing, either the size of a single layer can be increased or multiple layers can be vertically stacked. However, as demonstrated in [13] processing multiple ablated layers can lead to changed X-ray emission characteristics due to the modified surface topography after the machining of each layer. Such a reference material processing scenario has the advantage that the direction of the radiation field is well known. Due to intrinsic absorption in the target material, the highest dose rates of the laser-induced radiation are measured in the opposite direction to the movement of the laser, i.e., parallel to the laser ablated grooves [11,13,14].

A reference scenario employed during radiation protection inspections should be conservative with respect to the ambient dose rate of the X-ray emission and the maximum photon energy of the X-ray spectrum. This ensures that, during a radiation protection evaluation of the protection housing of the USP-laser machine, the transmission of the ionizing radiation is not underestimated. According to the literature [11], one of the most important parameters for generating laser-induced X-ray radiation with large ambient dose rates is the laser peak intensity. Increasing the laser peak intensity via the laser pulse energy will lead to an increase in the ambient dose rate of the emitted laser-induced X-ray radiation. It has also been shown in previous studies that the emitted dose rate strongly depends on the specific material of the workpiece [11,14]. The highest dose rates have been observed when employing either steel or tungsten as targets. Therefore, it can be assumed that, during radiation protection inspections on a USP-laser machine, the best approach would be to use either one of these two materials and to employ the maximum available laser pulse energy at a given laser pulse duration.

Another important prerequisite of the reference scenario is a temporally stable X-ray emission with an almost constant dose rate level during the radiation protection inspection. Additionally, the geometry of the entire radiation field should be well known and have a large area of homogeneous X-ray emission. Both requirements ensure reliable radiation protection measurements over the whole area of the protection housing.

The requirements for evaluating radiation protection inspection approaches at USP-laser machines under realistic industrial settings were met at the company SCHOTT AG. A USP-laser of 1 ps pulse duration, a wavelength of 1030 nm, and an average power of 220 W embedded in an aluminum protection housing was available for the measurements. The theoretically achievable peak intensity of 3.3×10^{15} W/cm^2 is comparatively high and normally used for the processing of transparent glasses making use of nonlinear absorption mechanisms. So far, only Schille et al. have employed higher laser peak intensities of up to 5.2×10^{16} W/cm^2 in a recent study [19]. The aluminum protection housing at the USP-laser machine at SCHOTT AG was an interesting test subject as the protective effect is expected to be much smaller than for steel enclosures. Lastly, some interesting safety features, as explained later, are present in the machine.

Next, the experimental setup, some issues encountered during the measurements, and the results for the measurements in an industrial setting at SCHOTT AG with two different experimental setups are summarized. In particular, constraints imposed on the placement of the X-ray measurement equipment due to safety features inside the protection housing had a large impact on the measurements. Because of these issues and despite experience with the generation of laser-induced X-ray radiation, the dose rates measured at SCHOTT AG are lower than those obtained during measurements at similar laser peak intensities of other groups.

2. Materials and Methods

2.1. USP-Laser Machine

The measurements were performed in a walk-in microSHAPE™ machine (3D-Micromac, Chemnitz, Germany), which has an XHE 200 W (Amphos, Aachen, Germany) laser system. A photo of the interior of the system is shown in Figure 1.

The laser was used with fixed optics (no laser scanner was employed) that focused the laser beam, using standard processing laser parameters, onto the workpiece, creating a spot diameter of about 10 µm. The focus diameter was calculated by the control system of the USP-laser machine from manufacturer information of the laser beam diameter and the different focal lengths of lenses in the focusing optics system. Since the movement of the laser spot and the optics (x- and z-direction) on the workpiece had to be carried out in relation to the sample holder station (y-direction) by translating the sample, the feed speed rate had to be set considerably low at 100 mm/s. The sample holder has a Y-stage assembly and provides a focal plane with a working area of up to 0.5 m^2 (see Figure 1a).

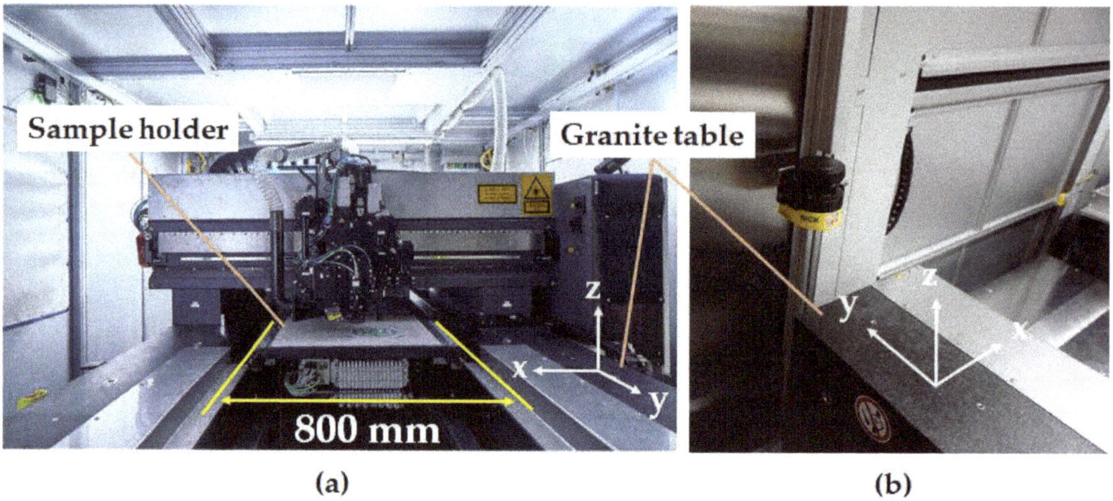

Figure 1. (**a**) Interior of the microSHAPE^{TM} USP laser system at SCHOTT AG. The system is accessible and equipped with several safety systems that are intended to prevent staff from entering the machine during laser operation. One of these safety systems is the Sick laser scanner device (**b**) installed in the wall in front of the operating machine system. The monitored area covers the region between 10 cm and 30 cm above the granite table.

The industrial USP-laser machine used in this work was designed as a walk-in configuration; therefore, it has several safety mechanisms implemented to prevent the trespassing of people during laser operation. Figure 1b shows a laser safety scanner from Sick (Düsseldorf, Germany) [21] placed at the entrance of the microSHAPE^{TM} USP-laser machine. This device uses the time-of-flight principle (ToF) to monitor the room for objects and people and was particularly relevant for setting up the position of the X-ray measuring devices for this study.

2.2. Sample Workpiece and Processing Parameters

As described above, a surface process on a tungsten plate was employed as a reference scenario. The machined areas were 15×15 mm^2 squares (Figure 2a), processed with laser beam scanning in a bidirectional sequence (Figure 2b) n times on the tungsten plate (Figure 2c) without readjusting the distance between optics and sample surface during measurements. The laser pulse duration was 1 ps. Three different configurations of laser pulse energy and repetition rate were measured. These configurations are summarized together with the calculated peak intensity and laser spot distance (in y-direction) in Table 1. For comparison, the parameters of measurements taken with two other experimental setups using an HR50 laser (Coherent, Santa Clara, CA, USA) and a GL.evo (GFH GmbH, Deggendorf, Germany) are also included in Table 1. The offset between two adjacent lines corresponded to one focus diameter (in x-direction). With these settings, two adjacent processing points were approximately 0.250 µm to 2 µm apart along a line. Due to the large overlap between two adjacent machining spots, deep holes were created on the material surface, and a large amount of material was overall removed per laser scan.

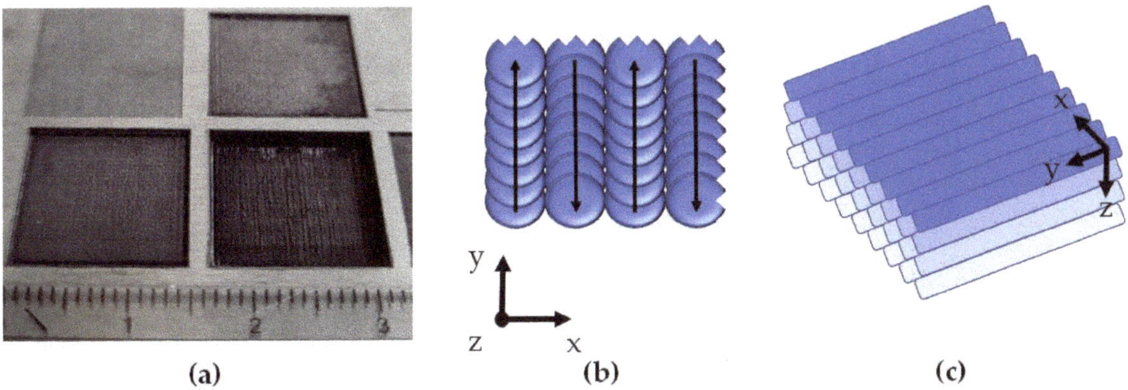

Figure 2. (**a**) The 15 × 15 mm^2 scan areas after USP-laser processing with the microSHAPE^{TM} machine at peak intensities of 1 × 10^{15} W/cm^2 and above (see Table 1). The visibly different depths of the processed areas are caused by different numbers of processing steps and variations of the laser pulse energy. The square in the top left corner was processed at PTB with a much smaller peak intensity of 3.0 × 10^{14} W/cm^2. (**b**) Schematic of the 2D bidirectional laser spot movement with respect to the coordinate system as given in Figure 1. In (**c**), multiple processing layers in the *z*-direction are indicated.

Table 1. Summary of laser processing parameters and corresponding measured dose rates for different USP-laser machines and their respective studied configurations. Pulse durations were 1 ps and 0.274 ps, and laser focus spot diameters were 12 μm and 33 μm (both manufacturer information) for the setups operated at SCHOTT AG and at PTB, respectively. The wavelengths of all lasers listed here were approximately 1 μm. The maximum ambient dose rate measurements at SCHOTT AG were conducted at a distance of 475 mm from the laser processing location. The maximum ambient dose rate at the GL.evo machine of approximately 2.1 mSv/h was measured at a distance of 160 mm during a laser turning process. The uncertainties listed for the dose rate values were calculated via error propagation of the calibration factor of the dosemeter.

USP-Laser Machine		Repetition Rate (kHz)	Pulse Energy (μJ)	Distance of Laser Spots (μm)	Peak Intensity (W/cm^2)	Max. dH*(10)/dt (μSv/h)
Model	**Operator**					
3D-Micromac microSHAPE^{TM}	SCHOTT AG	400 200 50	550 550 1980	0.25 0.5 2	9.1 × 10^{14} 9.1 × 10^{14} 3.3 × 10^{15}	128 ± 8 24 ± 2 0.90 ± 0.06
Second setup, Coherent HR50 laser	SCHOTT AG	200	175	5	1.0 × 10^{13}	Natural background radiation
GFH GmbH GL.evo	PTB	50	371	10	3.0 × 10^{14}	Up to 2.1 × 10^3

In the first processes, to carefully test how the material behaves and not to damage the optics, only a fraction of the power was used. The processing areas produced by the microSHAPE^{TM} USP-laser machine were visibly deeper than those of the GL.evo USP-laser-machine (Figure 2a, top left) due to the high average laser output power of 220 W of microSHAPE^{TM} USP-laser machine, the large available peak intensities, and the large overlap between adjacent laser spots at a scan velocity of 100 mm/s. The GL.evo machine located at PTB uses a laser with a much smaller average power and peak intensity. For example, during one measurement with the microSHAPE^{TM} USP-laser machine, the overall removed material thickness of tungsten was approximately 500 μm (Figure 2a, bottom right) after four processing layer repetitions (z-direction in Figure 2c) in comparison to only a few μm after an equal number of repetitions at the GL.evo machine.

Since the removal rate in the reference scenario was much larger than those routinely applied by SCHOTT AG for glass processes using this machine, the exhaust system had to be temporarily reinforced during the measurements by bringing the suction opening closer to the processing position. This was realized with the help of an additional vacuum pipe and the adjustment of the machine's suction system to bring it as close as possible to the plasma region. Nevertheless, after each processing step (with two to four ablation layer repetitions), the lens of the laser focusing optics had to be cleaned to prevent smoke traces that could reduce the focusing quality and laser energy delivered to the target. In Figure 3, one can see the experimental setup in detail. To be able to estimate the radiation direction and the size of the X-ray radiation field, a radiographic imaging plate from a computer radiography scanner was attached to the interior of the USP-laser system near to the processing point, as shown in Figure 3b.

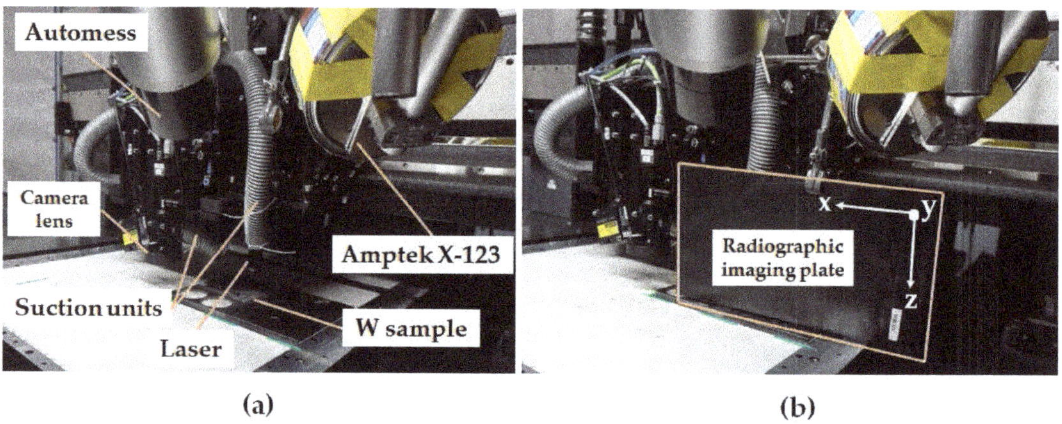

Figure 3. (**a**) Experimental setup and positioning of the measuring devices in the interior of the USP-laser machine. The Amptek X-123 spectrometer was placed in a tinplate box with an opening in front of the window and additionally covered with seven layers of 13 µm thick aluminum foil for shielding to prevent electromagnetic compatibility influences. (**b**) Placement of the radiographic imaging plate to detect the direction and homogeneity of the X-rays emission during USP-laser processing.

2.3. Placement of the Measurement Equipment

As mentioned in Section 2.1, the existence of a coupled safety scanner monitoring system in the investigated microSHAPE^{TM} USP-laser machine made the placement of the measuring instruments challenging. The area monitored by the laser safety scanner encompassed a region with a height of about 10 cm to 30 cm above the granite table and reaching close to the laser head in y-direction of the machine (see Figure 1b). Thus, if any object is detected by the monitoring laser scanner in this region (from now on called the "safety monitored area"), either the USP-laser itself would not start, or it would immediately be switched off as an emergency case during operation. Due to these restrictions, the standard constructions of PTB, which normally include the usage of laboratory tripods or mobile lifting bases, could not be applied here. Instead, an aluminum beam was fixed to the top of the USP-laser machine creating a gantry to hold the X-ray spectrometer and the dosemeter in a way to avoid the safety monitored area of the Sick laser safety scanner. Furthermore, because of the safety monitored area and the shielding by optical components, both devices could only be set up in approximately 45° to 60° angles to the direction of the movement of the laser relative to the sample workpiece, as shown in Figure 3. The distance between the dosemeter and the focus point of the USP-laser was 475 mm, while the distance between the spectrometer and the focus point was 385 mm.

2.4. Instrumentation

Table 2 gives an overview of the instruments used in this study to quantify laser-induced X-ray emissions while operating the USP-laser machines.

Table 2. Overview and description of the measurement instruments. The optimal energy range of the Automess 6150 dosemeter lies above 20 keV. However, it is calibrated in an ISO radiation quality N-15 reference field at PTB.

Instrument	Dosemeter	Spectrometer	Radiography Scanner
Model	Automess 6150AD-b/E	Amptek X-123 CdTe	DÜRR CR 35 NDT
Optimal energy range	20 keV to 7 MeV	8 keV to 70 keV	Not specified
Measured property	Ambient dose rate $dH^*(10)/dt$	X-ray pulse height spectrum	X-ray intensity

For measuring the ambient dose rate during USP-laser processing, the dose rate meter 6150AD-b/E from Automess—Automation and Messtechnik GmbH (Ladenburg, Germany) [22] was used. The dosemeters employed were calibrated in reference X-ray fields at PTB. As the lowest point for the energy calibration, a radiation quality of the narrow ISO X-ray series N-15 [23] with a mean energy of approximately 12.4 keV was used [24].

For measuring the laser-induced X-ray energy spectrum using the tungsten plate as a workpiece, an X-123 CdTe spectrometer from Amptek Inc. (Bedford, MA, USA) [25] was employed. It was placed in a tinplate box and additionally covered with seven layers of 13 µm thick aluminum foil to assure electromagnetic compatibility (EMC) and prevent interference through unwanted electrical or electromagnetic effects in the readout electronics. The transmission as a function of photon energy for 90 µm of aluminum is shown later. The Amptek X-123 detector is based on a CdTe crystal with a thickness of 1 mm used as an X-ray detector [26]. The interaction probability (intrinsic efficiency) as a function of the photon energy for different Amptek detector systems is depicted in Figure 4. The dashed violet curve corresponds to the device used for the measurements at SCHOTT AG. As can be seen, it encompasses the energy region of interest for radiation protection on USP-laser machines up to 70 keV. For low energies, the efficiency is limited by a 100 µm Beryllium window, which is not included in Figure 4, and the additional 90 µm of aluminum in front of the device. Due to absorption in the window material and the aluminum, a slightly decreased efficiency of the detector can be expected for energies lower than 8 keV.

For monitoring the homogeneity and the location of higher concentrations of emitted X-rays during USP-laser machining, a 2D Radiography Scanner CR 35 NDT Plus system from DÜRR (Stuttgart, Germany) [27] was used. As shown in Figure 3b, the radiographic plate could be placed adjacent to the tungsten sample, around 10 cm away from the laser-induced plasma and just outside the safety monitored area.

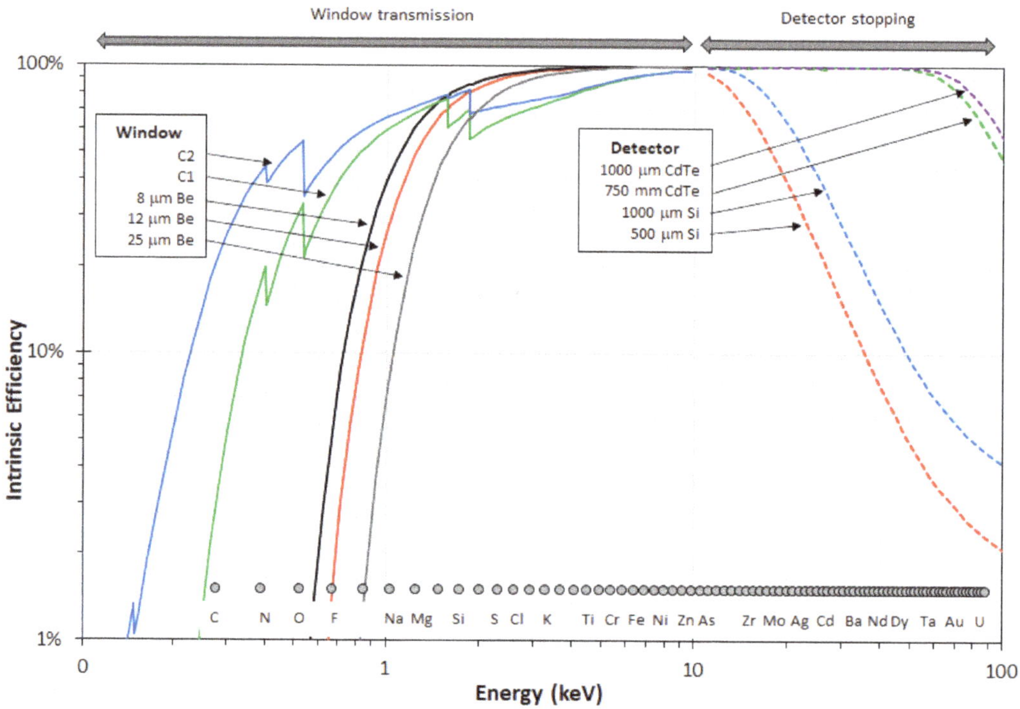

Figure 4. Comparison of the intrinsic efficiency of the X-123 detectors from Amptek. At low energies, the Be window limits sensitivity, and the 1 mm thick CdTe crystal (dashed violet curve) has a good efficiency up to 70 keV. © Amptek Inc 2021. Reprinted with permission.

3. Results

3.1. Monitoring the Generation of X-ray Emissions

The recorded grayscale image of the radiography image plate is depicted in Figure 5a. The area of each pixel of the grayscale image is approximately 200 × 200 μm². As the radiographic imaging plate was located very close to the source of the laser-induced X-ray emission (see Figure 3b), the grayscale image pixels had to be corrected for different distances from the plasma (see Figure 5b).

The shortest distance from the plasma was 10 cm, and the position of this point of shortest distance on the imaging plate is marked with a red dot on the lower left side of the grayscale image in Figure 5b. As the grayscale values are proportional to the local intensity of the X-ray emission and the intensity of a point source decreases with the square of the distance from the source, the distance-corrected grayscale values can be calculated as follows:

$$G(r_0) = G(r)\, r^2/r_0^2, \tag{1}$$

where $G(r_0)$ is the corrected grayscale value at the reference distance r_0 (in this case, the shortest distance of 10 cm), and $G(r)$ is the measured grayscale value at a distance r. The distance r of each grayscale value can be calculated from the row and column position (u, v) on the imaging plate, r_0 and the row and column values (u_0, v_0) of the reference distance on the grayscale image (in this case (u_0, v_0) = (371, 1021)), and the pixel pitch p.

$$r^2 = r_0^2 + p^2\,(u - u_0)^2 + p^2\,(v - v_0)^2. \tag{2}$$

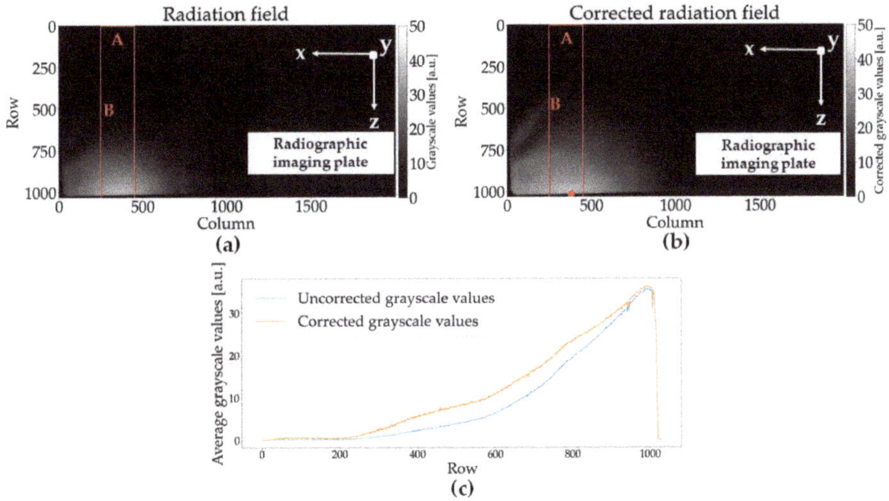

Figure 5. (**a**) Uncorrected and (**b**) distance-corrected grayscale image captured with the radiographic imaging plate. Both images show that a large part of the X-ray radiation is emitted very flat and almost exclusively parallel to the sample plate in the *y*-direction. The edge of the imaging plate can be seen very well as a sudden drop in the grayscale values in the lower and left part of the image. The red rectangles in (**a**,**b**) show the area of the pixels used for the profile curve plotted in (**c**). The red dot in (**b**) marks the position of the shortest distance to the plasma used for the calculation of the distance correction. (**c**) Cross-section of the grayscale values along the rows of the corrected (orange curve) and uncorrected (blue curve) grayscale images. The continuous decrease in grayscale value with a decreasing row number in the profiles indicates that a large part of the laser-induced X-rays is emitted in a very flat angle close to the horizontal plane.

Further corrections due to additional absorption in air for larger distances from the plasma and a possible angle dependency of the radiographic imaging plate have not been applied. The area with the highest X-ray emissions, characterized by bright gray pixels, is located close to the lower edge of the imaging plate. Accordingly, the X-ray radiation is emitted in a very flat angle to the horizontal plane. In addition, as expected, the emission also appears to be largely parallel to the line of movement of the USP-laser (*y*-direction). The edge of the radiographic imaging plate is located in the lower and left part of the grayscale image. The different areas of the radiation field can also be seen in the comparison between the distance-corrected and uncorrected *z*-profile (the image pixels employed to generate the profile are indicated by the red rectangle in Figure 5a,b) of the grayscale values depicted in Figure 5c. From the measurements performed with the radiography imaging plate, one can conclude that the placement of the dosemeter and the spectrometer devices was not optimal regarding the maximum emission of the X-ray radiation, i.e., they were not directly installed in the maximum region but at the edge of the radiation field. However, as discussed in Section 2.3, this was the best arrangement possible for this USP-laser machine.

3.2. Obtained Energy Spectra and Dose Rates

Figure 6 depicts pulse height spectra from laser-induced X-ray emissions with and without a 50 µm thick copper filter in addition to the default aluminum filter with an overall thickness of approximately 90 µm. The spectra were measured with a laser pulse energy of 550 µJ, a pulse duration of 1 ps, and a repetition rate of 400 kHz. The mean X-ray photon energy values obtained during the USP-laser processing with and without a 50 µm thick copper foil were approximately 8.1 keV and 8.9 keV, respectively.

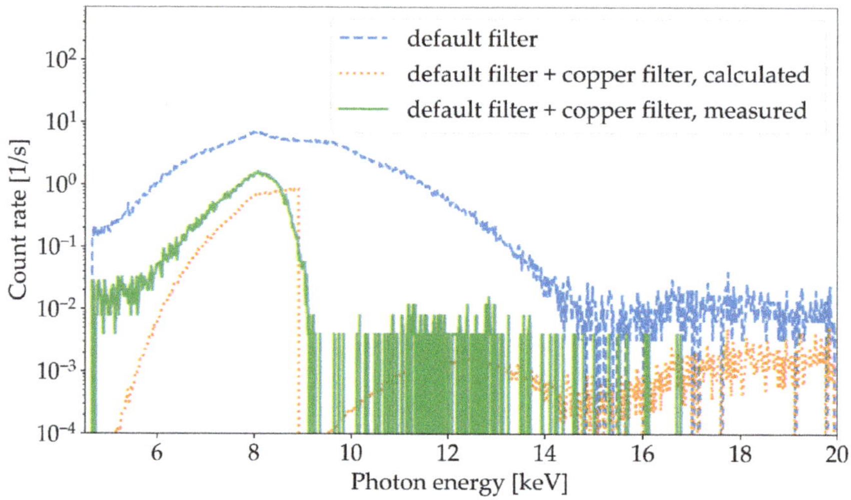

Figure 6. Pulse height spectra measured with the Amptek X-123 CdTe spectrometer during tungsten flat surface processing using a laser pulse energy of 550 μJ, a repetition rate of 400 kHz, a pulse duration of 1 ps, and a focus diameter of 10 μm. Shown are the measured spectra without any additional copper filter (blue curve) and with a copper filter (green curve), as well as the calculated spectrum based on the convolution of the spectrum without copper filter with the transmission function of 50 μm copper (orange curve).

Moreover, for comparison, the expected spectrum after transition of a 50 μm thick copper filter was calculated. This calculated spectrum (orange curve in Figure 6) is based on the measured spectrum without a copper filter (blue curve) multiplied by a transmission function $T(E, d)$ in each energy channel. The function $T(E, d)$ describes the exponential attenuation of photons traversing a material [28] and is given by

$$T\,(E, d) = \mathrm{e}^{-(\mu\,(E)/\rho)\,\times\,\rho d}, \tag{3}$$

where d and ρ are the thickness and density of the material (in this case 50 μm of copper foil), respectively, and $\mu(E)/\rho$ is the energy-dependent mass attenuation coefficient of the material. For the calculation, the list of mass attenuation coefficients from the National Institute of Standards and Technology was used [28]. These tabulated values were logarithmically interpolated to obtain a corresponding value of the mass attenuation coefficient for each energy channel of the Amptek X-123 spectrometer. The $T(E, d)$ for 50 μm of copper and 90 μm of aluminum as a function of the photon energy, together with the curve for no attenuation, i.e., $T(E, d) = 1$, is depicted in Figure 7.

As seen in Figure 6, the pulse height spectrum determined using the transmission function agrees very well with the pulse height spectrum measured with a 50 μm thick copper filter. The sharp drop in the spectrum at around 9 keV, which is caused by the absorption edge of the K-shell of copper, is clearly visible. The deviation for higher energies exceeding 15 keV is most likely caused by background noise and the pileup effect. This is also supported by the fact that the pulse height spectrum with an additional copper filter has no entries in this energy range. The pileup effect arises if multiple X-ray photons hit the single photon detector in the timeframe of the processing time and are registered as one single photon with correspondingly higher energy; this can be minimized by positioning the spectrometers at a large distance to the X-ray radiation source. As verified by the good agreement between the calculated and measured curves in Figure 6, further X-ray emission spectra were measured without the copper filter in front of the spectrometer window.

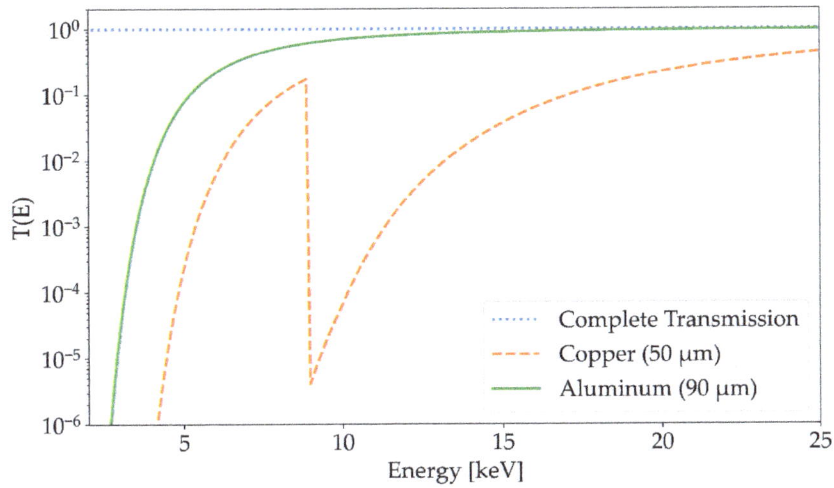

Figure 7. Transmission function $T(E, d)$ (see Equation (1)) for 50 μm of copper (orange dotted curve) and 90 μm of aluminum (solid green curve) as a function of the energy. For the calculation, the list of mass attenuation coefficients from the National Institute of Standards and Technology was used. The values were logarithmically interpolated to get a value for each energy channel of the X-123 spectrometer. The rapid decrease at approximately 9 keV is caused by the sudden increase in the attenuation coefficient of copper due to the Cu-K edge.

Figure 8 shows the comparison of the X-ray emission spectra for a fixed average laser power but two different combinations of pulse energy and repetition rate configured in the microSHAPE^{TM} USP-laser machine. The first measurement (orange curve) took place at a laser repetition rate of 50 kHz and a laser pulse energy of 1980 μJ, while the second measurement (blue curve) was carried out at a laser repetition rate of 200 kHz and a laser pulse energy of 550 μJ. The respective laser peak intensities of the laser pulses were 3.3×10^{15} W/cm^2 and 0.9×10^{15} W/cm^2. To be able to compare the measurements as plotted in Figure 8, the number of photons (counts) per channel with an energy bandwidth of 20 eV was divided by the accumulation time in seconds of each experiment.

An increase in the laser pulse energy and the associated increase in the peak intensity of the laser pulses led to a shift of the spectrum to higher X-ray photon energies, as shown by the two combined spectral measurements in Figure 8. Accordingly, the average power of the laser, which was nearly identical for both configurations, cannot be employed as a simple scaling parameter for the emitted X-ray radiation as the photon energy spectrum is affected by the variation of the repetition rate and the pulse energy. The increase in counts in the low-energy region (between 5 keV and 7 keV) was most likely a consequence of an insufficient shielding of the CdTe detector and may have been caused by the pulsed intense electromagnetic laser plasma field. However, X-ray emissions at such low energies (here below 8 keV) would play only a minor role in relation to the hazard potential in enclosed USP-laser systems, because a large part of the photons would be absorbed in the ambient air and when passing through the protective housing and, thus, would not reach the operating personnel working on the machine.

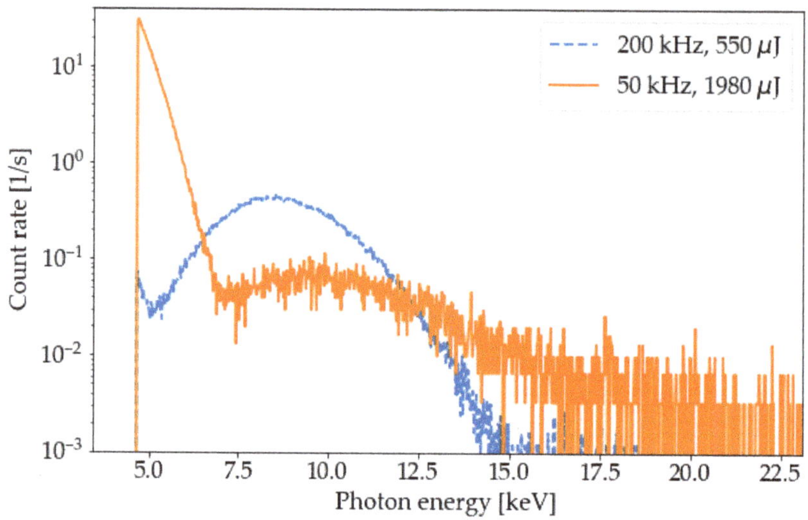

Figure 8. Pulse height spectra measured for the combination of two different USP-laser pulse energies and laser repetition rates: 550 μJ and 200 kHz (blue curve), 1980 μJ and 50 kHz (orange curve). The number of photons per channel with an energy bandwidth of 20 eV was divided by the total USP-laser processing time, to make the two spectra comparable. The increase in irradiance due to the higher pulse energy causes an energetic shift of the maxima of the spectra to higher photon energies. The increase of count rate in the low-energy region (between 5 keV and 7 keV) for the 50 kHz process is most likely caused by electronic noise due to an insufficient shielding of the CdTe detector. Overall, the recorded number of X-ray photons per second is very low, which was also confirmed in separate dose rate measurements with the Automess 6150AD-b/E dosemeter (see Table 1).

Overall, the accumulated X-ray photon energy in the spectra was very low. This was also confirmed by the complementary dose rate measurements with the calibrated Automess 6150 dosemeter. The maximum measured ambient dose rates for the three different configurations at the microSHAPE^{TM} USP-laser system are listed in Table 1. During the surface process with a pulse energy of 1980 μJ, an ambient dose equivalent rate $dH^*(10)/dt$ of around 1 μSv/h was measured. These X-ray emission dose rates are much lower compared to the mSv/h reported recently in the literature for the same laser pulse duration and a lower laser pulse energy [11,12,18,19].

Further measurements were likewise carried out with the tungsten plate and a borosilicate glass sample, using a second experimental setup with a Coherent HR50 USP laser (Santa Clara, CA, USA). The Coherent HR50 laser has an average power of 35 W, a repetition rate of 200 kHz, and an emission wavelength of 1064 nm. For the radiation protection experiments, a pulse energy of 175 μJ and a laser pulse duration of 10 ps were applied; the focus diameter was approximately 20 μm, resulting in a peak intensity of approximately 1.0×10^{13} W/cm^2. Thus, the peak intensity of the laser is significantly lower than that of the microSHAPE^{TM} USP-laser system with an output power of 220 W, reaching up to 3.3×10^{15} W/cm^2.

The second setup with the Coherent laser was selected for further measurements because of the distinctive features of the 2 mm steel protection housing. It has an opening station comprising two doors with windows made of PMMA polymer covered by a thin aluminum layer (see Figure 9). Additionally, in a small slit region where the two doors join when closed, rubber material without any additional steel or aluminum layers is located. In this region, transmission of X-ray radiation is much less suppressed when compared to the surrounding steel protection housing.

Figure 9. Photograph of the protection housing doors of the second experimental setup. The laser used in the system is a Coherent HR50 USP-laser with an average power of 35 W. The housing is made of 2 mm thick steel, and the windows are made of PMMA covered with a thin sheet of aluminum. Between the two doors there is a narrow area where, in the closed position, only rubber material lips join without any additional steel or aluminum layers.

On one hand, those are weak points in the protection housing that must be considered with regard to the transmission of X-rays. On the other hand, during the measurements with tungsten and glass targets, no deviation from the natural background radiation could be observed with the Automess 6150 dosemeter at a distance of 190 mm from the focus point of the laser. Measurements with the radiographic imaging plates and the X-123 CdTe spectrometer also showed no signal from laser-induced X-ray emissions.

4. Discussion

During measurements at the second experimental setup with a Coherent HR 50 laser, tungsten and borosilicate glass target material, and a peak intensity of approximately 10^{13} W/cm^2, no emission of X-ray radiation could be observed with either the Automess 6150 dosemeter, the X-123 spectrometer or radiographic imaging plates at a distance of approximately 19 cm from the plasma. This is not unexpected as the generation of X-rays with energies large enough to traverse short distances of air is expected to be very inefficient for laser peak intensities of 10^{13} W/cm^2 [11].

With the microSHAPE^{TM} USP-laser machine employing a tungsten workpiece, the measured dose rates are much smaller than expected for a laser-induced plasma generated at peak intensities of 3.3×10^{15} W/cm^2 with tungsten as a target material. In the literature, typically, dose rates in the range of mSv/h are measured for such high peak intensities [18,19]. As can be seen from Table 1, the measured dose rate decreased with increasing pulse energy, which is unexpected. There are several possible explanations for these results.

First, the measurement equipment was installed in a nonoptimal position. As explained earlier, the main reason for this was a safety system, which monitored the interior of the USP-laser machine and prevented the installation of objects in a large area directly in front of the laser head and the focus point on the workpiece. As can be seen from the distance-corrected grayscale image (Figure 5b), the radiation field of the laser-induced X-rays is located near the horizontal plane and in the direction of the y-axis parallel to the lines. Due to the space limitations, the dosemeter and spectrometer had to be installed at a large angle of approximately 45° from the horizontal plane and approximately 45° to 60° to the processing grooves in the y-direction. Consequently, the radiometric measurement equipment was located at the fringes of the radiation field, where the X-ray dose rate is expected to be much lower than in the maximum of the field.

Additionally, the large rate of material removal caused large amounts of debris in the air near the workpiece and focusing optics. The exhaust system was not powerful enough to remove all remnants of the laser ablated material. Thus, some residual material was deposited on the focusing optics, degrading the quality of the laser spot and accordingly decreasing the energy deposited in the workpiece. Additional thermal effects which affect the focusing qualities of lenses of the focusing optics may also have had an impact. This degrading effect is most likely even worse when increasing the pulse energy and, therefore, increasing the amount of material removed per laser pulse. This would at least partially explain the low dose rate measurements at a pulse energy of 1980 µJ when compared to the measurements at 550 µJ.

Moreover, the scanning speed of the laser spot on the workpiece was comparably low with 100 mm/s. Other experiments in the literature used a much higher scanning speed ranging from 400 mm/s [19] to 1000 mm/s [11] to prevent large overlap of adjacent laser spots and, thus, the formation of very deep ablated groove structures. For the measurements at SCHOTT AG, the combination of a large laser pulse energy of 550 µJ and 1980 µJ and the slow movement speed of the laser spot led to the formation of very deep ablated groove structures. During the laser material processing, the plasmas at the bottom of these structures were deep within the material; therefore, most of the emitted low-energy X-ray photons were absorbed by the surrounding material. This effect is especially important here because of the placement of the measurement equipment due to safety restrictions. As can be seen from Figure 8, the difference between the high energy tails of the spectrum with pulse energies of 550 µJ and 1980 µJ is in the range of only a few keV. Accordingly, on one hand, increasing the pulse energy will only have a minor effect on the transmission of X-ray photons through the workpiece material, i.e., tungsten. On the other hand, increasing the pulse energy will lead to deeper groove structures and will, therefore, increase the amount of material that has to be traversed by the X-ray photons to reach the measurement equipment, resulting in an increased rate of absorption. This effect might explain the measurement of a lower dose rate at a higher pulse energy.

The acquired X-ray spectra from the highest investigated USP-laser pulse (1980 µJ) showed energies of up to 25 keV, which is consistent with other measurements at lower and similar peak intensities [11,14]. The measured spectra were tested by applying an additional copper filter with a thickness of 50 µm. In a comparison between the measured spectrum with the copper filter and the expected spectrum calculated from the spectrum and the transition function of 50 µm copper, a good agreement could be observed. Additionally, spectra of two different combinations of laser pulse energy and repetition rate were compared. As expected, a higher pulse energy and, consequently, a higher peak intensity led to a spectrum with higher maximum photon energies [14,29,30]. These measurements with nearly identical average laser powers but different pulse energies and repetition rates confirm that the average laser power cannot be employed as a simple scaling factor for the expected photon energy of laser-induced radiation.

The distribution of the distance corrected radiation field depicted in Figure 5b shows a clear maximum in the direction parallel to the laser movement along the processed lines in the material (y-direction). This result is in good agreement with previous measurements [11,13,14]. However, as can be seen from Figure 5c, the distribution of the X-ray emission has a maximum very close to the horizontal plane. In previous measurements, the maximum of the radiation field for the processing of tungsten was found to be at a larger angle of approximately 30° [11]. Two possible explanations for this deviation are presented here. First, this unexpected angular distribution of the radiation field might be caused by differences in laser peak intensity and, consequently, the large amount of residual material in the air near the plasma. This might, in turn, affect the angular characteristics of the plasma emission, due to absorption of the low energy X-rays in the material cloud. Another possibility is that, because of the very deep groove structures and the large overlap between adjacent laser spots, the plasma is located on the side wall of the groove and not at the bottom of the groove parallel to the surface of the target material. This would lead to a different alignment of the plasma density gradient, which significantly affects the emission characteristic of laser-induced X-rays.

As demonstrated, a fast, reliable, and reproducible investigation of the protection housing of the machine or structural radiation protection features may not be feasible using laser-induced X-rays. Consequently, other inspection concepts for future radiation protection tests of USP-laser machines must be considered. One alternative concept could be based on using a stable and continuous X-ray source such as an X-ray tube as a substitute for the laser-induced radiation. Requirements for this approach would be that the X-ray tube has a similar energy spectrum to the laser-induced X-ray emission. By varying the high voltage and current of the X-ray tube, the ambient dose rate and energy spectrum of the radiation can be determined, for which the transition radiation through the protection housing falls below legal dose rate limits. Such a mimicking of the laser-induced X-ray generation by conventional X-ray technology and already well-established inspection procedures appears feasible and would significantly facilitate the legal approval process of USP-laser processing machines by the local authorities.

5. Conclusions

The results and issues while performing dosimetric and spectrometric measurements of laser-induced X-ray emissions in a realistic industrial working environment clearly demonstrate that setting up a typical USP-laser machine for radiation protection inspections under reference conditions with worst-case X-ray emissions is very complicated and time-consuming. Optimizing the laser processing parameters, such as pulse energy and focus diameter with respect to the emission of [illegible] X-ray radiation may lead to damage in the focusing optics or in other crucial components of the machine. Installed safety systems may prevent the person responsible for the radiation protection inspection from measuring under optimal conditions. Redeposition of ablated material on the optics of the laser processing system can additionally affect the measurements if the exhaust system is not powerful enough to remove unusually large amounts of ablated material produced during processing scenarios with high pulse energies and repetition rates.

All the adaptations and difficulties found during the measurement make it clear that, despite extensive experience with the generation of X-rays on USP-laser systems, it is not trivial to find a machining process on a third-party machine which can be employed as a reference scenario with high emissions of X-rays (or even the worst-case scenario). However, considering the numerous developments of USP-laser machines in industrial applications during the last few years and the number of USP-laser machines already in industrial use, the development of a reliable and reproducible radiation protection inspection of USP-laser machines is urgently required.

An alternative inspection concept for USP-laser machines could be based on using a stable and continuous X-ray source such as an X-ray tube as a substitute for the laser-induced radiation during the investigation of the machine housing.

Author Contributions: Conceptualization, U.S., B.P. and J.K.; methodology, U.S., M.S.R., B.P., H.L., J.B. and J.K.; validation, U.S., M.S.R., B.P., H.L., J.B. and J.K.; investigation, U.S., B.P., H.L., J.K., M.K., A.O. and B.H.; resources, M.K., A.O. and B.H.; writing—original draft preparation, U.S. and M.S.R.; writing—review and editing, U.S., M.S.R., B.P., H.L., J.B., J.K., M.K., A.O. and B.H.; visualization, U.S. and M.S.R.; project administration, J.K. and B.P.; funding acquisition, J.K. and B.P. All authors have read and agreed to the published version of the manuscript.

Funding: This research was funded by the German Federal Office for Radiation Protection (BfS), grant number 3619S22370.

Institutional Review Board Statement: Not applicable.

Informed Consent Statement: Not applicable.

Data Availability Statement: The data presented in this study are available on request from the corresponding author.

Conflicts of Interest: The authors declare no conflict of interest.

References

1. Bäuerle, D.W. *Laser Processing and Chemistry*, 4th ed.; Springer: Berlin/Heidelberg, Germany, 2011.
2. Saraceno, J.C.; Sutter, D.; Metzger, T.; Ahmed, M.A. The amazing progress of high-power ultrafast thin-disk lasers. *J. Eur. Opt. Soc.* **2019**, *15*, 15. [CrossRef]
3. Kühlke, D.; Herpers, U.; Von Der Linde, D. Soft X-ray emission from subpicosecond laser-produced plasmas. *Appl. Phys. Lett.* **1987**, *50*, 1785–1787. [CrossRef]
4. Stearns, D.G.; Landen, O.L.; Campbell, E.M.; Scofield, J.H. Generation of ultrashort X-ray pulses. *Phys. Rev. A* **1988**, *37*, 1684–1690. [CrossRef] [PubMed]
5. Harris, S.E.; Kmetec, J.D. Mixed-Species Targets for Femtosecond-Time-Scale X-ray Generation. *Phys. Rev. Lett.* **1988**, *61*, 62–65. [CrossRef] [PubMed]
6. Zigler, A.; Burkhalter, P.G.; Nagel, D.J.; Boyer, K.; Luk, T.S.; McPherson, A.; Solem, J.C.; Rhodes, C.K. High intensity genera-tion of 9–13 Å X-rays from BaF_2 targets. *Appl. Phys. Lett.* **1991**, *59*, 777–778. [CrossRef]
7. Murnane, M.M.; Kapteyn, H.C.; Rosen, M.D.; Falcone, R.W. Ultrafast X-ray Pulses from Laser-Produced Plasmas. *Science* **1991**, *251*, 531–536. [CrossRef]
8. Giulietti, G.; Gizzi, L.A. X-ray emission from laser-produced plasmas. *Riv. Nuovo Cim.* **1998**, *21*, 1–93. [CrossRef]
9. Thogersen, J.; Borowiec, A.; Haugen, H.K.; McNeill, F.E.; Stronach, I.M. X-ray emission from femtosecond laser micromachining. *Appl. Phys. A* **2001**, *73*, 361–363. [CrossRef]
10. Bunte, J.; Barcikowski, S.; Puester, T.; Burmester, T.; Brose, M.; Ludwig, T. Secondary Hazards: Particle and X-ray Emission. *Topics. Appl. Phys.* **2004**, *96*, 309–321. [CrossRef]
11. Legall, H.; Schwanke, C.; Pentzien, S.; Dittmar, G.; Bonse, J.; Krüger, J. X-ray emission as a potential hazard during ultrashort pulse laser material processing. *Appl. Phys. A* **2018**, *124*, 407. [CrossRef]
12. Behrens, R.; Pullner, B.; Reginatto, M. X-ray emission from materials processing lasers. *Radiat. Prot. Dosim.* **2019**, *183*, 361–374. [CrossRef]
13. Legall, H.; Schwanke, C.; Bonse, J.; Krüger, J. The influence of processing parameters on X-ray emission during ultra-short pulse laser machining. *Appl. Phys. A* **2019**, *125*, 570. [CrossRef]
14. Weber, R.; Giedl-Wagner, R.; Förster, D.J.; Pauli, A.; Graf, T.; Balmer, J.E. Expected X-ray dose rates resulting from industrial ultrafast laser applications. *Appl. Phys. A* **2019**, *125*, 635. [CrossRef]
15. Legall, H.; Schwanke, C.; Bonse, J.; Krüger, J. X-ray radiation protection aspects during ultrashort laser processing. *J. Laser Appl.* **2020**, *32*, 022004. [CrossRef]
16. Freitag, C.; Giedl-Wagner, R. X-ray Protection in an Industrial Production Environment. *PhotonicsViews* **2020**, *17*, 37–41. [CrossRef]
17. Legall, H.; Bonse, J.; Krüger, J. Review of X-ray exposure and safety issues arising from ultra-short pulse laser material pro-cessing. *J. Radiol. Prot.* **2021**, *41*, R28–R42. [CrossRef]
18. Mosel, P.; Sankar, P.; Düsing, J.F.; Dittmar, G.; Püster, T.; Jäschke, P.; Vahlbruch, J.-W.; Morgner, U.; Kovacev, M. X-ray Dose Rate and Spectral Measurements during Ultrafast Laser Machining Using a Calibrated (High-Sensitivity) Novel X-ray Detec-tor. *Materials* **2021**, *14*, 4397. [CrossRef] [PubMed]
19. Schille, J.; Kraft, S.; Pflug, T.; Scholz, C.; Clair, M.; Horn, A.; Loeschner, U. Study on X-ray Emission Using Ultrashort Pulsed Lasers in Materials Processing. *Materials* **2021**, *14*, 4537. [CrossRef] [PubMed]
20. Metzner, D.; Olbrich, M.; Lickschat, P.; Horn, A.; Weißmantel, S. X-ray generation by laser ablation using MHz to GHz pulse bursts. *J. Laser Appl.* **2021**, *33*, 032014. [CrossRef]
21. Sick Sensor Intelligence. Available online: https://www.sick.com/de/de/optoelektronische-schutzeinrichtungen/sicherheits-laserscanner/s300-mini-standard/c/g214851 (accessed on 10 September 2021).

22. Automess 6150AD. Available online: https://www.automess.de/produkte/produktfamilie-6150ad/szintillatorsonde (accessed on 15 August 2021).
23. International Organization for Standardization. X and gamma reference radiation for calibrating dosemeters and doserate meters and for determining their response as a function of photon energy—Part 1: Radiation characteristics and production methods. In *International ISO 4037-1*; International Organization for Standardization: Geneva, Switzerland, 2019.
24. Ankerhold, U.; Berens, R.; Ambrosi, P. X ray Spectrometry of Low Energy Photons for Determining Conversion Coefficients from Air Kerma, K_a, to Personal Dose Equivalent, $H_p(10)$, for Radiation Qualities of the ISO Narrow Spectrum Series. *Radiat. Prot. Dosim.* **1999**, *81*, 247–258. [CrossRef]
25. X-123 CdTe Complete X-ray & Gamma Ray Spectrometer. Available online: https://www.amptek.com/internal-products/x-123-cdte-complete-X-ray-gamma-ray-spectrometer-with-cdte-detector (accessed on 27 October 2021).
26. Redus, R.; Huber, A.; Pantazis, J.; Pantazis, T.; Sperry, D. Design and performance of the X-123 compact X-ray and gamma-ray spectroscopy system. In Proceedings of the IEEE Nuclear Science Symposium, IEEE Xplore, Piscataway Township, NJ, USA, 29 October–1 November 2006; Volume 6, pp. 1–40.
27. DÜRR NDT 2D-Scanner CR 35 NDT. Available online: https://www.duerr-ndt.de/produkte/computer-radiographie/cr-35-ndt.html (accessed on 28 October 2021).
28. Hubbell, J.H.; Seltzer, S.M. Tables of X-ray Mass Attenuation Coefficients and Mass Energy-Absorption Coefficients from 1 keV to 20 MeV for Elements Z = 1 to 92 and 48 Additional Substances of Dosimetric Interest (version 1.4, 2004). Available online: http://physics.nist.gov/xaamdi (accessed on 29 September 2021).
29. Eliezer, S. *The Interaction of High-Power Lasers with Plasmas*, 2nd ed.; Institute of Physics: Bristol, UK, 2002.
30. Salzman, D. Theory of energy deposition by suprathermal electrons in laser-irradiated targets. *Phys. Rev. E* **2002**, *65*, 056409. [CrossRef] [PubMed]

materials

MDPI

Article

Study on X-ray Emission Using Ultrashort Pulsed Lasers in Materials Processing

Joerg Schille [1,*], Sebastian Kraft [1], Theo Pflug [1], Christian Scholz [2], Maurice Clair [2], Alexander Horn [1] and Udo Loeschner [1]

1 Laserinstitut Hochschule Mittweida, University of Applied Sciences Mittweida, Technikumplatz 17, 09648 Mittweida, Germany; kraft@hs-mittweida.de (S.K.); pflug@hs-mittweida.de (T.P.); horn4@hs-mittweida.de (A.H.); loeschne@hs-mittweida.de (U.L.)

2 3D-Micromac AG, Technologie-Campus 8, 09126 Chemnitz, Germany; scholz@3d-micromac.com (C.S.); clair@3d-micromac.com (M.C.)

* Correspondence: schille@hs-mittweida.de

Abstract: The interaction of ultrashort pulsed laser radiation with intensities of 10^{13} W cm^{-2} and above with materials often results in an unexpected high X-ray photon flux. It has been shown so far, on the one hand, that X-ray photon emissions increase proportionally with higher laser power and the accumulated X-ray dose rates can cause serious health risks for the laser operators. On the other hand, there is clear evidence that little variations of the operational conditions can considerably affect the spectral X-ray photon flux and X-ray emissions dose. In order to enhance the knowledge in this field, four ultrashort pulse laser systems for providing different complementary beam characteristics were employed in this study on laser-induced X-ray emissions, including peak intensities between 8×10^{12} W·cm^{-2} < I_0 < 5.2×10^{16} W·cm^{-2}, up to 72.2 W average laser power as well as burst/bi-burst processing mode. By the example of AISI 304 stainless steel, it was verified that X-ray emission dose rates as high as $\dot{H}'(0.07) > 45$ mSv h^{-1} can be produced when low-intensity ultrashort pulses irradiate at a small 1 µm intra-line pulse distance during laser beam scanning and megahertz pulse repetition frequencies. For burst and bi-burst pulses, the second intra-burst pulse was found to significantly enhance the X-ray emission potentially induced by laser pulse and plasma interaction.

Keywords: laser; ultrashort pulse; plasma; X-ray; dose rate; Bremsstrahlung; resonance absorption; burst; bi-burst

Citation: Schille, J.; Kraft, S.; Pflug, T.; Scholz, C.; Clair, M.; Horn, A.; Loeschner, U. Study on X-ray Emission Using Ultrashort Pulsed Lasers in Materials Processing. *Materials* **2021**, *14*, 4537. https://doi.org/10.3390/ma14164537

Academic Editors: Jörg Krüger and Jörn Bonse

Received: 8 July 2021
Accepted: 10 August 2021
Published: 12 August 2021

1. Introduction

Ultrashort pulse lasers feature excellent performances for high-efficient and precision machining that also has attracted increasing attention for innovations in micro fabrication and surface engineering. Moreover, the recent power scaling of femtosecond (fs) and picosecond (ps) lasers reaching multi-kW class level [1,2] will pave the way of the ultrashort pulse laser technology from the laboratory into industrial production. Actually, in typical material processing scenarios, ultrashort laser pulses of micro to milli joules optical energy and hundreds of femtoseconds to picoseconds pulse durations are employed, for example, in laser micro drilling [3,4], laser engraving [5,6], or laser surface texturing and modifications [7,8]. By tightly focusing the laser radiation, high peak intensities in the range from 10^{13} to 10^{16} W·cm^{-2} can be reached on the material surface. However, when using laser pulses of such high intensity in material ablation, high-intense electron plasmas will be produced, itself emitting X-ray photons at a several keV level. The X-ray photons result from Bremsstrahlung and characteristic line emissions when accelerated electrons lose their kinetic energy by scattering, acceleration and recombination with other charged particles, in free–free, free–bound, and bound–bound processes.

However, recent works have shown that the X-ray photon emission increases proportionally with higher average laser power, and actual X-ray emission dose rates can cause serious health risks for the laser operators [9–14]. In particular, this is the case when high-pulse repetition frequency lasers will be used in materials ablation as the X-ray emission per pulse can accumulate to harmful X-ray photon dose over time. On the one hand, it is verified that X-ray photon emission increases with peak intensity, pulse repetition rate, and average laser power. On the other hand, there is clear evidence that little variations of the operational conditions can have a considerable effect on the X-ray emission, causing unexpected high dose levels. This is much more relevant, as a great number of parameters (more than 20) have been experimentally validated as influencing factors on X-ray emission dose level, including laser beam characteristics, processing conditions, and the irradiated material, further mutually affecting each other. Moreover, the specific effect of each parameter and their variations is not sufficiently investigated and understood so far, making it difficult for the reliable assessment of the X-ray emission and safety precautions in the operational area.

In the following, the significant impact of the pulse repetition frequency and the intra-line pulse distance during laser beam scanning on the spectral X-ray photon flux and the X-ray emission dose is discussed by comparing low-intensity and high-intensity ultrashort pulses irradiating AISI 304 stainless steel. It will be shown that an unexpected high level of X-ray emission dose rate of tens of mSv$\cdot$h^{-1} could be produced when low-intensity pulses irradiate at 1.6 MHz pulse repetition frequency (PRF). This resulted potentially from plasma resonance absorption as an efficient mechanism for optical energy transfer, also yielding high X-ray emissions in the burst- and bi-burst pulse regime.

2. Materials and Methodology

All experiments were performed in a laser safety enclosure to protect the experimental operators from potential risks and hazards arising from the powerful laser beams and X-ray emissions. A schematic view of the laser machining setup used in this study is presented in Figure 1.

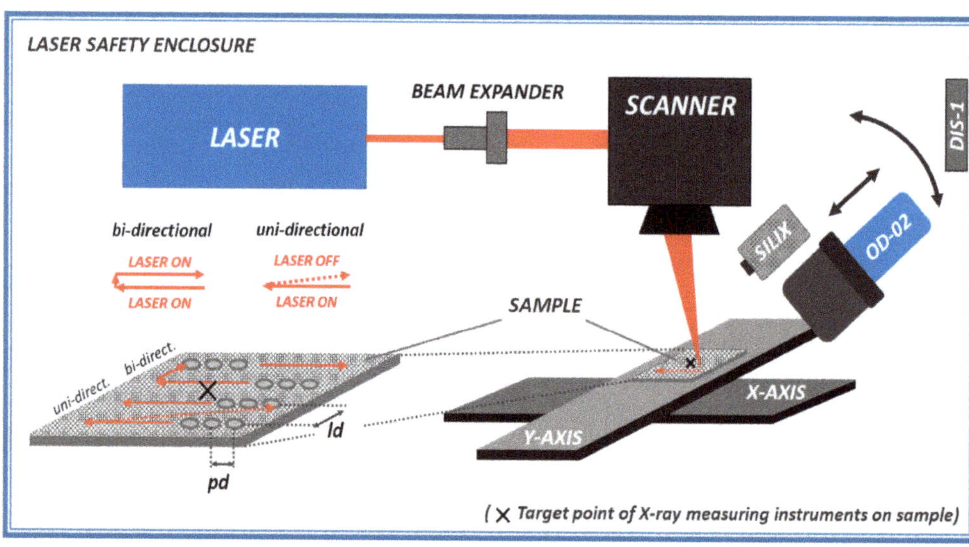

Figure 1. Schematic view of the laser safety enclosure including laser machining setup.

First of all, the efficacy of the enclosure material was verified by initial testing in order to ensure reasonable assurance of the enclosure against the laser-induced X-ray emissions. In addition, three electronic Direct Ion Storage memory cells (DIS-1, Mirion Technologies (Canberra) GmbH, Ruesselsheim, Germany) were applied as safety precautions. Two of the X-ray badge detectors were placed at the inner and outer sides of the laser safety enclosure.

A third one was worn by the operator throughout the experiments. The actual received X-ray dose values were read out at the beginning and the end of each working day from the badges. It should be mentioned here that no increase of the X-ray dose could be detected, whether from the badges placed at the enclosure outside nor the one worn by the operator, confirming the safe working conditions at all time.

In total, four different laser systems were employed in this study for providing a wide range of complementary laser beam characteristics; see Table 1. The studied parameter settings include up to 5.2×10^{16} W·cm^{-2} peak intensity, pulse repetition frequencies in the range between 1 and 2 MHz, maximum 72.2 W average laser power, as well as laser burst and bi-burst processing mode. The energy of the irradiating pulses Q_P was defined by the ratio of the average laser power P_{av} and the pulse repetition frequency f_P described by:

$$Q_P = \frac{P_{av}}{f_P}. \tag{1}$$

Table 1. Summary of the laser systems and studied laser parameter settings.

Laser System / Parameter	Symbol Unit	Astrella Coherent Inc.	FX 200 Edgewave GmbH	UFFL 100 AFS GmbH	Carbide Light Conversion
wavelength	λ in nm	800	1030	1030	1030
pulse duration	τ_H in fs	40	600	340	200
focus spot diameter	$d_{0,86}$ in µm	13.5 **	30.0 ***	30.0 ***	49.7 **
pulse rep. frequency intra-burst frequency bi-burst frequency	f_P in MHz f_{IB} in MHz f_{BB} in GHz	0.001	0.2–2.0	0.51	0.4, 1.0 66.7 2.3
max. average power *	P_{av} in W	1.6	72.2	18.7	33
max. pulse energy *	Q_P in µJ	1600	36.1	37	82.5
max. peak power *	P_0 in W	4×10^{10}	5.6×10^7	9.6×10^8	3.6×10^8
max. intensity *	I_0 in W cm^{-2}	5.2×10^{16}	1.6×10^{13}	2.7×10^{13}	3.8×10^{13}

* on target, ** LIU-plot method, *** MSM measurement.

The focus spot diameters d_{86} (86.5% power enclosure method) presented in Table 1 have been determined by analyzing the laser beam caustic (MSM Micro Spot Monitor, Primes GmbH, Pfungstadt, Germany) or rather from the established semi-log plot method of squared ablation crater diameter versus peak fluence [15].

The X-ray emission induced by the ultrashort pulsed laser irradiations was studied on technical-grade AISI 304 stainless steel metal sheets. The chemical composition of the alloying elements is presented in Table 2. The dimensions of the laser processed substrates were $50 \times 50 \times 2$ mm^3 in width, length, and sample thickness. In each test, the substrates were placed on a sample holder in the focal plane with the help of an XYZ stage assembly. Two different machining strategies were applied depending on the prevailing machinery conditions and setups of the individual laser systems: (i) relative movements between the laser beam and substrate by accelerating the sample in XY directions; and (ii) scanning the laser radiation across the substrate surface via a galvanometer scan system (intelliScan 30, Scanlab GmbH, Puchheim, Germany). As illustrated in Figure 1, the geometrical distance of the irradiating pulses along and between the laser processed lines is defined by the intra-line pulse distance *pd* (as a function of laser beam moving speed and pulse repetition frequency) and the hatch distance *ld*, respectively. The laser pulse peak power P_0 provided in Table 1 for the investigated laser beams was calculated according to

$$P_0 = \frac{Q_P}{c \cdot \tau_H} \tag{2}$$

where the pulse energy Q_P is divided by the measured pulse duration τ_H and by taking into account the correction factor c considering the temporal pulse shape of the respective irradiating pulses, either being Gaussian or sech^2. Following

$$I_0 = \frac{2 \cdot P_0}{\pi \cdot w_{0.86}{}^2}, \tag{3}$$

the peak intensity I_0 was calculated from the peak power and the focus spot radius $w_{0.86}$.

Table 2. Chemical composition of the AISI 304 stainless steel alloying elements.

Element	C	Si	Mn	P	S	Cr	Ni	N
Element Mass Fraction in %	0.07	1.0	2.0	0.045	0.03	17.5–19.5	8.0–10.5	0.1

Two different detector systems were used for the X-ray photon emission measurements: a survey meter OD-02 (STEP Sensortechnik und Elektronik Pockau GmbH, Pockau-Lengefeld, Germany) measuring the directional X-ray emission dose $H'(0.07)$ and the X-ray emission dose rate equivalent $\dot{H}'(0.07) = dH'(0.07)/dt$ in the soft-radiation region above 6 keV. Additionally, a SILIX lambda detector (Ingenieurbüro Prof. Dr.-Ing. Guenter Dittmar, Aalen, Germany) monitored the X-ray emission spectra and X-ray emission dose rate in the photon energy range between 2 and 20 keV. The X-ray detectors were aligned to the center of the samples, which is indicated in Figure 1 by the target point (X). The detector's view was along the X-axis equivalent to the laser processing direction. The nominal detector distance D and the detection angle α were varied with reference to the target point and the horizontal plane. Thereby, the nominal detector distance represented a mean measure because the detector target points were set in the center of the laser processed area. Hence, in the detector's view direction (X-axis), the closest point and most distant point from the sensitive detector surface were at the start and end of a laser scanned line, and likewise the greatest distance in the Y-direction was at the edges of the laser processed fields.

Laser beam scanning was applied either in uni-directional or bi-directional mode depending on the specifics of the studied laser setups in terms of laser beam control and synchronization. In uni-directional processing, the laser beam departs from the X-ray detector, thus receiving maximum X-ray dose levels [13]. The "laser-on" duty cycle was 46% in uni-directional processing controlled by oscilloscope measurements throughout the study. As a consequence, the monitored X-ray emissions represented less than half of the process-relevant emission dose and were corrected (by a factor of 2.17) in order to compare and discuss the process-typical dose rates in the following. In bi-directional mode, by contrast, the laser beam was switched on during all the processing. Hence, the monitored X-ray emissions represent average readings from the bi-directional laser material processing. This is due to the fact that higher X-ray emissions have been reported for a laser beam running away instead of moving toward the sensitive detector surface [13].

3. Results and Discussions

3.1. Effect of the Detection Angle and Detector Distance on X-ray Dose

At first, the dependencies of detector's angle and distance on the monitored X-ray emission dose rate were studied. This was in order to identify the optimum measuring conditions for the assessment of X-ray emissions in the accomplished study. On the one hand, this was encouraged, as the authors´ literature review revealed a dependence between the X-ray emission dose and the detection angle [9]. So far, a maximum X-ray dose rate level was reported at a 30° detection angle, as investigated in the range between 10° and 40°. On the other hand, the correct detector–substrate distance is of relevance because, firstly, the X-ray photons are absorbed in air, and secondly, to ensure that the active detector area is homogeneously exposed by the laser-induced X-ray emissions. Both have a great impact on the detector readings.

The X-ray emissions recorded by the survey meter OD-02 and the SILIX X-ray monitor at a 35° detector angle and different distances from the substrate can be seen in Figure 2a at similar dose values. A fitting curve (dashed line) is included in the plot, showing the recorded X-ray emission dose rate inversely proportional to the square of the distance D of the detector from the substrate target point. However, at the larger distances, the experimental data differ to a greater extent from the inverse square-root relationship resulting from X-ray beam absorption in air. This is pointed out in Figure 2a by the modified fitting curve (solid line) emphasizing good agreement for experimental and computed data when the attenuation coefficient μ is considered in the photon flux Φ_{phot}, calculations

$$\Phi_{phot}(D, \lambda) \propto D^{-2} e^{-\mu(\lambda) D}. \quad (4)$$

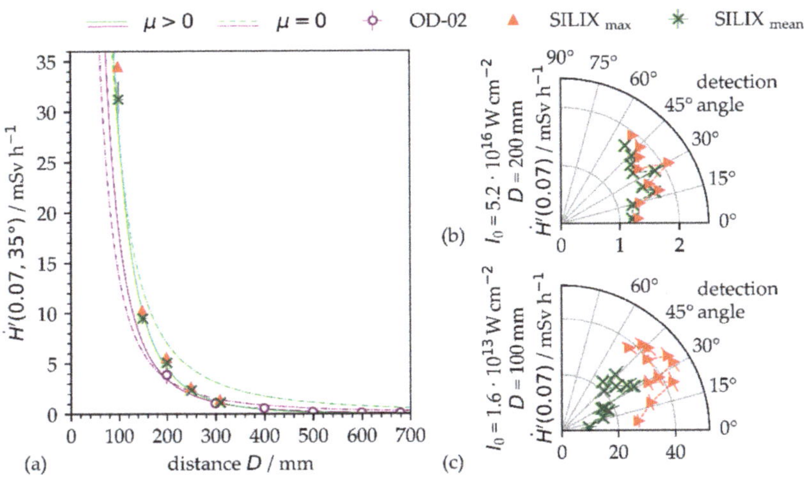

Figure 2. (**a**) OD-02 and SILIX readings of X-ray emission dose rate on AISI 304 as a function of detector distance D; the fitting curves are representative for vacuum (dashed line) and air (solid line) ambient conditions at $I_0 = 1.6 \times 10^{13}$ W·cm^{-2} and 35° detection angle. (**b**) X-ray emission dose rate as a function of detection angle for pulses of $I_0 = 5.2 \times 10^{16}$ W·cm^{-2} at 200 mm SILIX detector distance. (**c**) X-ray emission dose rate as a function of detector angle for pulses of $I_0 = 1.6 \times 10^{13}$ W·cm^{-2} at 100 mm SILIX detector distance.

Thereby, the attenuation coefficient depends strongly on the photon energy and varies in air between 0.94 cm^{-1} $\leq \mu \leq 6.36 \times 10^2$ cm^{-1} for the X-ray photons between 2 keV $\leq E_{phot} \leq$ 20 keV [10]. The attenuation coefficients derived from the fitting curves presented in Figure 2a amount to $\mu = 0.05 \pm 0.02$ cm^{-1} (SILIX) or $\mu = 0.03 \pm 0.02$ cm^{-1} (OD-02), which is about two orders of magnitude lower than the literature data. However, this discrepancy is not clarified yet; the steadily changing distance of the actual laser processing zone to the detector resulting from laser beam scanning, the X-ray dose rate as an integral measure from the X-ray photon spectrum, and measurement uncertainties for X-ray emissions all had a great impact on the experimental data.

In addition, a significant effect of the detector angle on the X-ray emission dose rate has been found by varying the angular orientation of the SILIX detector in the range between 7.0° < α < 51.0° with respect to the specified target point. Most likely independent from the peak intensity, whether $I_0 = 5.2 \times 10^{16}$ W·cm^{-2} (Figure 2b) or $I_0 = 1.6 \times 10^{13}$ W·cm^{-2} (Figure 2c), the maximum X-ray emission dose rate was detected at about 30°. It is noteworthy that a considerably higher X-ray emission dose rate was measured for the pulses of lower intensity, 43 mSv·h^{-1} vs. 2.1 mSv·h^{-1}, potentially resulting from the higher average laser power, 72.2 W vs. 1.6 W, and shorter distance of the detector from the target point, 100 mm vs. 200 mm.

3.2. Spectral X-ray Emission

The spectral X-ray photon flux was analyzed by placing the SILIX X-ray monitor at a fixed 35° detection angle and 100 mm distance from the target point at the substrates. Two representative X-ray photon emission spectra in Figure 3 verify a broad continuous Bremsstrahlung emission in the photon energy range below 10 keV. The detected characteristic line emissions can be related to the main AISI 304 alloying elements. Therefore, as a reference, the principal $K_{\alpha 1\text{-}3}$ and $K_{\beta 1\text{-}5}$ shell interband emissions are included in Figure 3, such as for iron (Fe), chromium (Cr), and nickel (Ni), as provided by the NIST database [16]. By comparing the individual characteristic lines, the photon energy peaks of the alloying elements are slightly offset from the principal X-ray transition energies ($\Delta E_{ph} < 0.09$ keV) to higher photon energy levels being within the measurement accuracy of the SILIX X-ray monitor.

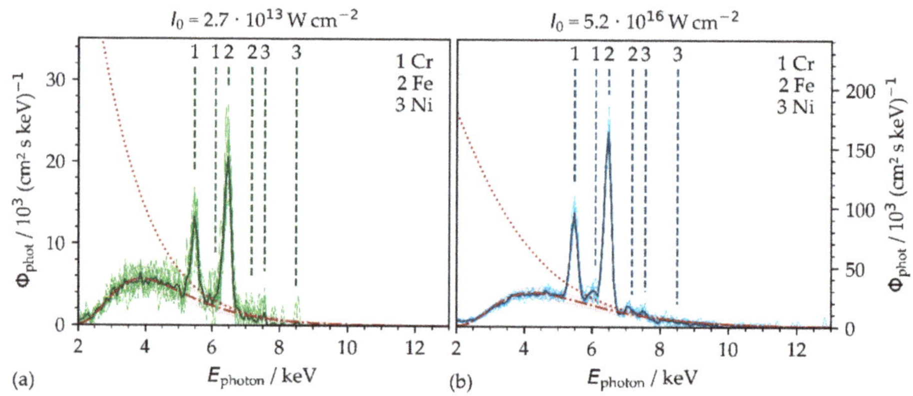

Figure 3. X-ray photon flux Φ_{phot} at a 35° detection angle and 100 mm distance for low peak intensity (**a**) $I_0 = 2.7 \times 10^{13}$ W·cm^{-2} and high peak intensity (**b**) $I_0 = 5.2 \times 10^{16}$ W·cm^{-2}. The characteristic X-ray emission lines of the correlating AISI 304 alloying elements are included. The recorded spectral X-ray photon distribution follows a Maxwell–Boltzmann distribution computed for vacuum (dotted line, non-attenuated) and ambient air (dashed line including 3 σ confidence interval, 100 mm distance) conditions.

The monitored Bremsstrahlung spectra represent qualitatively the energy distribution of the X-ray photon flux at 100 mm distance and can be approximated by a Maxwell–Boltzmann distribution [9,12] according to

$$f_{Maxwell}(E)dE = \sqrt{\frac{4E}{\pi (k_B T_e)^3}}\, e^{-\frac{E}{k_B T_e}}\, dE \tag{5}$$

where k_B represents the Boltzmann constant, T_e is the electron temperature, and E is the energy of the emitted X-ray photons.

The recorded Bremsstrahlung continuum can be seen in good correlation with the computed X-ray emissions when considering the transmission of the X-rays through air at ambient pressure and 100 mm distance in the Maxwell–Boltzmann modeling procedure (Figure 3, dashed line). In addition, the non-attenuated spectrum computed for vacuum surrounding conditions is presented (dotted line). The best fit between the empirically observed and theoretically modeled X-ray photon distribution (in air) was obtained by the electron temperature of either 1.18 ± 0.1 keV (Figure 3a) for the low-intensity or 1.56 ± 0.1 keV (Figure 3b) for the high-intensity pulses. These electron temperatures are in good agreement with the temperatures reported elsewhere for hot electrons and respective laser peak intensities ranging between 0.82 and 1.76 keV [9,15,17].

The averaged X-ray emission dose rate of the above given spectra was measured to $\dot{H}'(0.07) = 1.1 \pm 0.2$ mSv·h^{-1} with the low peak intensity pulses ($I_0 = 2.7 \times 10^{13}$ W·cm^{-2}), as shown in Figure 3a, and $\dot{H}'(0.07) = 11.4 \pm 2.3$ mSv·h^{-1} with the high peak intensity pulses ($I_0 = 5.2 \times 10^{16}$ W·cm^{-2}); see Figure 3b. However, for the high peak intensity pulses, the X-ray emission rate was about one order of magnitude higher in spite of the considerably lower applied average laser power (22.4 W vs. 1.6 W) and PRFs (506 kHz vs. 1 kHz). This finding proves the great impact of the laser peak power and intensity on the X-ray emission and will be discussed more in detail in the following section.

3.3. X-ray Emission in the Low-Intensity and High-Intensity Pulse Regime

The effect of the peak intensity on the X-ray emission was investigated by recording the X-ray photon spectra at 100 mm distance and 35° detection angle of the SILIX monitor from the reference target point at the substrates. The peak intensity of the impinging laser pulses was varied in the range between 8×10^{12} W·cm^{-2} < I_0 < 1.6×10^{13} W·cm^{-2} and 0.3×10^{16} W·cm^{-2} < I_0 < 5.2×10^{16} W·cm^{-2} that also refers to the low-intensity and high-intensity pulse regime in the following.

A closer view to the X-ray emission spectra in Figure 4 reveals a notably higher extent of Bremsstrahlung emissions for pulses of lower peak intensity, while the greater proportional amount of characteristic X-ray emissions can be seen for pulses of higher intensity. The corresponding X-ray emission dose rates were measured of $\dot{H}'(0.07) = 38.9 \pm 4.6$ mSv·h^{-1} for pulses of 1.6×10^{13} W·cm^{-2} and $\dot{H}'(0.07) = 11.4 \pm 2.3$ mSv·h^{-1} for 5.2×10^{16} W·cm^{-2} peak intensity. This was achieved by irradiating a laser beam of 72.2 W and 1.6 MHz (low-intensity regime) or rather 1.6 W and 1 kHz average laser power and pulse repetition frequency (high-intensity regime), respectively.

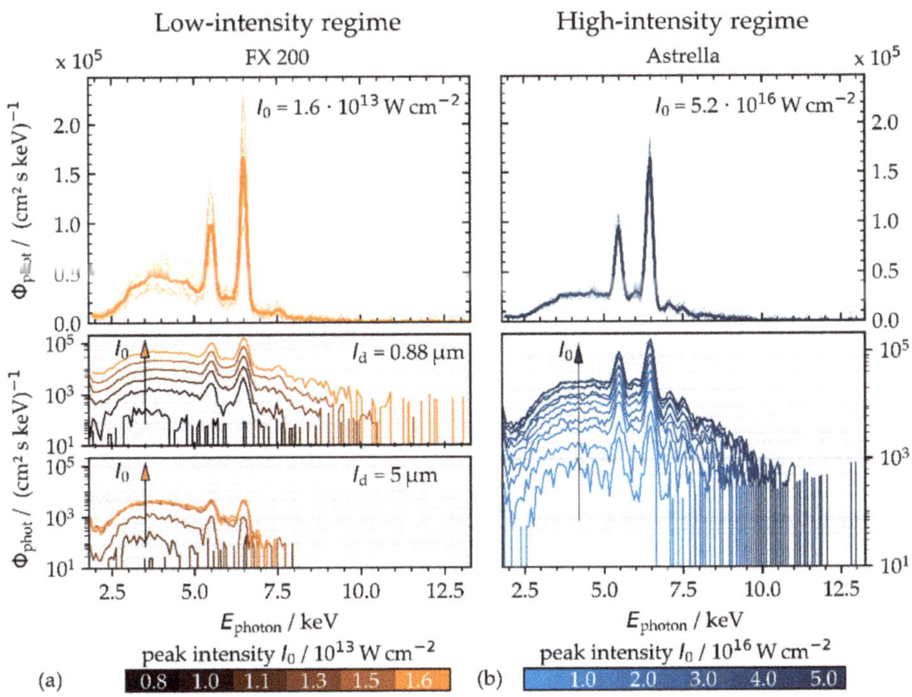

Figure 4. X-ray photon flux Φ_{phot} detected on AISI 304 in the low-intensity (**a**) and high-intensity pulse regime (**b**). The X-ray emission spectra were recorded by using the SILIX X-ray monitor at 35° detection angle and 100 mm distance. In the low-intensity regime, the intra-line pulse distance was varied from 0.88 μm (left, center) to 5 μm (left, bottom). Increasing peak intensity is indicated by the arrow.

The differences of the X-ray photon spectra can be attributed to the different mechanisms of laser plasma interaction and electron plasma heating that largely depend on the irradiating conditions. So, pulses of lower intensity ($I_0 < 10^{14}$ W·cm^{-2}) will be primarily absorbed in the underdense corona region of the plasma by inverse Bremsstrahlung absorption processes [18]. The excited electrons will be accelerated in the Coulomb field that resulted in the emission of the Bremsstrahlung continuum. This free–free generation of Bremsstrahlung X-ray photons is inefficent and yields only a low proportion of X-ray photons per laser pulse. Certainly, a great amount of low-intensity pulses can induce X-rays at a high dose level, as can be seen in Figure 4a (top) by the example of low-intensity pulses ($I_0 = 1.6 \times 10^{13}$ W·cm^{-2}) irradiated at 1.6 MHz pulse repetition frequency.

By contrast, resonance absorption is suggested as the dominant mechanism for pulses of high peak intensity, $I_0 > 10^{15}$ W·cm^{-2}. This collision-less process is most efficient for parallel polarized laser beams irradiating at a large incident angle. The laser energy will be transferred to the electron plasma in the region of the critical plasma density, where the electron plasma frequency is equal to the laser frequency [19]. The highly excited plasma electrons interact with the bound electrons of the target atoms by collisional impact ionization, leaving vacant energy levels. Nevertheless, resonance absorption might also be effective when pulses of lower peak intensity irradiate at megahertz PRF and small spatial pulse distance. This can be supposed from the X-ray emission spectra presented in Figure 4a (center and bottom) recorded for pulses of the same intensity (1.6×10^{13} W·cm^{-2}) and PRF (1.6 MHz) but different intra-line pulse distances varied by the laser beam moving speed. As characteristic X-ray emission lines are clearly distinguishable in the spectra recorded at an 0.88 μm intra-line pulse distance, the Bremsstrahlung continuum is dominant at the larger 5 μm intra-line pulse distance.

In addition, there is a trend toward higher X-ray photon flux when pulses of higher peak intensity irradiate, as clearly observable in Figure 4 for the low-intensity (left) and the high-intensity (right) pulse regime. On the one hand, the displayed spectra indicate no significant dependence of the characteristic X-ray emissions from the iron and chromium alloy elements from the peak intensity. On the other hand, the spectral width of the Bremsstrahlung continuum enlarged to higher X-ray photon energy with pulses of higher peak intensity, such as 10.0 keV or rather 12.0 keV in maximum for the low-intensity ($I_0 = 1.6 \times 10^{13}$ W·cm^{-2}) or high-intensity ($I_0 = 5.2 \times 10^{16}$ W·cm^{-2}) pulse regime. Here, too, the effect of the intra-line pulse distance on the X-ray photon emission spectrum can be recognized in Figure 4a, showing 11.0 keV maximum X-ray photon energy at 0.88 μm, while the maximum of about 7.5 keV can be seen for the 5.0 μm intra-line pulse distance.

The emitted X-ray dose per pulse (Figure 5, green data points) was derived by dividing the monitored X-ray emission dose rate by the number of impinging pulses. In addition, as another evaluation measure, the X-ray emission efficiency represents the X-ray dose per pulse in relation to the applied pulse energy; see Figure 5 (blue data points). In the low-intensity pulse regime, the X-ray dose per pulse increases exponentially with higher peak intensity, and in the studied range, a maximal value of 6.7 pSv/pulse was measured at $I_0 = 1.6 \times 10^{13}$ W·cm^{-2} and $f_P = 1.6$ MHz; see Figure 5a. This is in contrast to the high-intensity regime, as shown in Figure 5b, where the X-ray dose per pulse increases linearly with increasing peak intensity. Here, the determined maximum value of the X-ray dose per pulse of 3.2 nSv/pulse is almost three orders of magnitude larger than for low-intensity pulses. In terms of X-ray emission efficiency, Figure 5a indicates an exponential dependence for the low-intensity regime to 150 fSv·μJ^{-1} maximum, while saturation is given in Figure 5b of about 2.2 pSv·μJ^{-1}.

For pulses of low peak intensity irradiated at megahertz PRF, a remarkable dependence of the X-ray emission efficiency on the spatial pulse distance could be identified. The X-ray dose per pulse is at a considerably lower level with a 5.0 μm intra-line pulse distance under otherwise similar processing conditions; see Figure 5a (imprint). This might be due to the fact that the interaction of the following pulse(s) with the still prevailing laser ablation particle/plasma plume changed dramatically depending on the lateral pulse distance. The underlying physical effects are not clear yet; however, plasma resonance absorption was introduced above as a potential mechanism for the transfer of optical energy to the plasma even when pulses of low peak intensity irradiate at high PRF. This is supported by the fact that the angle of incidence between the incoming laser beam and the critical plasma density layer is continually changing with time. Hence, the actual plasma density profile (affected by the time delay between the pulses determined by the pulse repetition frequency) and the lateral offset of the next impinging pulse determine the optimum conditions for laser beam coupling and energy transfer to the plasma with a consequence of maximum X-ray photon emission. This hypothesis will be tested in the ongoing study.

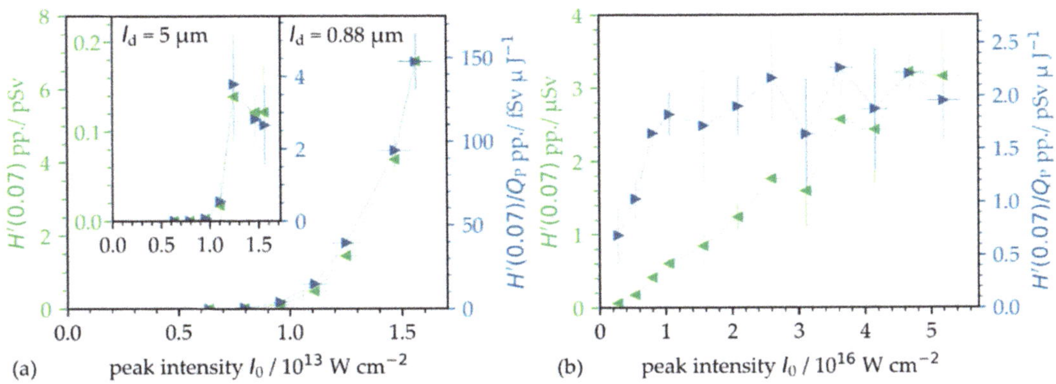

Figure 5. X-ray dose per pulse (green data points) and the X-ray emission efficiency (blue data points) on AISI 304 in the (**a**) low-intensity and (**b**) high-intensity regime. The given data were derived from the X-ray emission dose monitored by the SILIX detector at a 35° detection angle and 100 mm distance. The dotted lines guide the eye.

For the presented data, it should be mentioned that scaling of the X-ray dose per pulse or X-ray emission efficiency with the irradiated pulse number and pulse intensity can underestimate the actual emitted X-ray dose. This is due to the fact that laser plasma and X-ray emission influencing effects are not adequately considered in the proposed assessments [12]. For example, this includes the temporal pulse distance, geometrical pulse distance, angle of incidence as well as surface inhomogeneity, and roughness effects that steadily change with ongoing laser processing and scan numbers, and all of them mutually reinforce each other. To underline this, a more detailed view on the particular effect of the geometrical and temporal distance between the irradiating pulses on X-ray emission is provided in the following sections.

3.4. Effect of Intra-Line Pulse Distance on X-ray Emission in the Low-Intensity Pulse Regime

A remarkable influence of the intra-line distance between the impinging ultrashort laser pulses on X-ray emission has already been reported for tungsten studied with PRFs in the range between 50 kHz < PRF < 400 kHz [10]. Pronounced X-ray emission maxima and minima have been detected where the amplitude of the X-ray doses varied by a factor up to two depending on the spatial distance of the next impinging pulse. These previous findings are supported by the results of our study as a greater effect of the intra-line pulse distance on X-ray emission was measured for AISI 304 irradiated with low-intensity pulses of $I_0 = 1.6 \times 10^{13}$ W·cm^{-2} at 1.6 MHz PRF (Figure 6a). The intra-line pulse distance was varied between 0.5 µm $\leq pd \leq$ 6.5 µm by adjusting the laser beam moving speed from 0.8 to 10.4 m·s^{-1}.

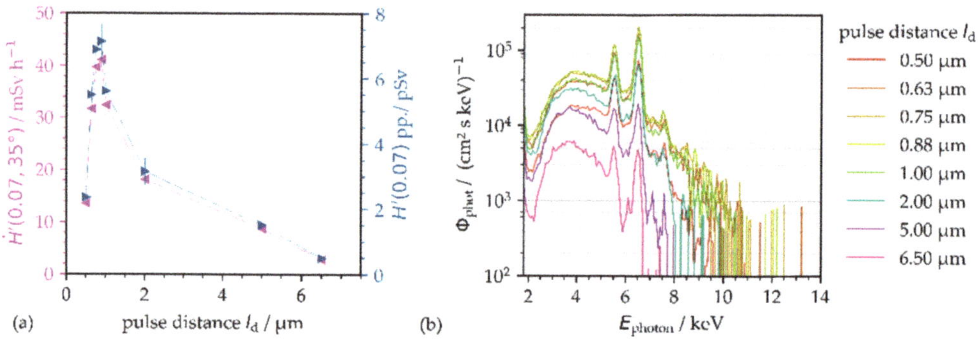

Figure 6. X-ray emissions on AISI 304 at 100 mm distance and 35° detection angle as induced by low-intensity pulse irradiations at $I_0 = 1.6 \times 10^{13}$ W·cm^{-2}, f_P = 1.6 MHz PRF, and P_{av} = 72.2 W average laser power. (**a**) X-ray emission dose rate and (**b**) X-ray photon spectra as a function of intra-line pulse distance. The dotted lines in (**a**) guide the eye.

The highest X-ray emission dose rate was measured of $\dot{H}'(0.07) = 44.9$ mSv·h^{-1} at 0.88 µm intra-line pulse distance. At smaller or larger intra-line pulse distances, the maximum X-ray emission dose reduced significantly to $\dot{H}'(0.07) = 18.3$ mSv·h^{-1} at 0.5 µm or rather $\dot{H}'(0.07) = 3.8$ mSv·h^{-1} at 6.5 µm, respectively.

For tungsten, it is reported in the literature that the X-ray emission maxima and minima resulted from multi-beam reflections at the sidewalls of the ablated grooves [10], which (influenced by the intra-line pulse distance) originated with different micro groove wall angles. Here, in our study on AISI 304, a substantial effect of the surface topography on the X-ray emission dose can largely be ruled out. This is because the pronounced X-ray emission maximum at 0.88 µm intra-line pulse distance could also be confirmed for different surface topographies (not presented here), such as those produced with the intra-line pulse distances specifically addressed in Figure 6a. A more likely explanation for the observed great X-ray emission at small intra-line pulse distance is a strong interaction of the next irradiating pulses with the still existent laser ablated plasma/nanoparticle plume. As a matter of fact, an evident laser plasma/nanoparticle ablation plume has been verified in pump-probe shadowgraph analyses for the times 0.5–1.0 µs after pulse irradiation [20]. These time intervals correlate very well to the time domain of 1.6 MHz repetitive pulses presented in Figure 6.

This can be linked to the effect of the intra-line pulse distance on X-ray emission, as the geometrical spacing defines the angle of incidence for the next impinging laser pulse in relation to the flank of the apparent laser ablation plume; see Figure 7.

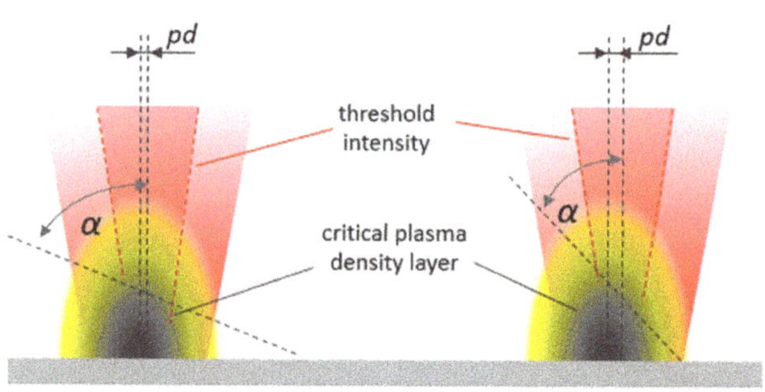

Figure 7. Schematic view on the effect of the intra-line pulse distance *pd* on the angle of incident of the laser beam α with respect to the flank of the critical plasma density layer.

Nevertheless, the laser ablation plume is on a much larger dimension than the very little intra-line pulse distance of only a few micro meters, showing the greatest impact on X-ray emission in Figure 6. Therefore, on the one hand, a reasonable explanation might be that an efficient laser pulse with plasma interaction takes place close to the solid density state [21]. On the other hand, up to 80% absorption levels were reported for p-polarized laser beams under striking incidence at steep plasma density profiles by collision-less resonance absorption mechanisms [21]. Highly excited plasma states and steep plasma density gradients emerge in regions of intense laser excitation at the highest laser peak intensity being in the narrow center of the Gaussian laser beam. So, it is obvious that the effective cross-section area of the high-intensity center part of the laser beam with the critical plasma layer is considerably smaller than the interaction area of the laser beam with the induced plasma/nanoparticle plume. Hence, a variation of a few micrometers of the intra-line pulse distance changes the position of the next irradiating pulse on the flank of the critical plasma layer. In fact, it has been demonstrated so far that plasma resonance absorption is very sensitive to the specific conditions of the resonant field near the critical density surface [22]. From this, it becomes clear that the distance of the next following pulse from the critical plasma density layer could significantly affect the incident angle of the laser beam relative to the critical plasma layer flank, in turn, with a high impact on the laser plasma resonance absorption and thus optical energy transfer.

However, additional collision-less absorption processes have been identified so far for intense laser pulses interacting with overdense plasma; for example, sheath inverse Bremsstrahlung [23], non-linear mechanisms [24] or anharmonic resonance effects [25]. These absorbing processes depend strongly on the angle of incident and the polarization of the incident laser beam and cannot be ruled out to have an effect on the X-ray photon emissions detected in this study.

The higher level of X-ray emission at the smaller intra-line pulse distances is also confirmed by the X-ray emission spectra presented in Figure 6b. It can be seen that X-ray emission is dominated by the Bremsstrahlung continuum at the larger intra-line pulse distance between 2 μm < pd < 6.5 μm, while characteristic X-ray emission and increased X-ray photon flux is obvious for the smaller intra-line pulse distance ranging between 0.5 μm < pd < 1.0 μm.

The highest X-ray photon yield and most prominent characteristic line emission were measured for pulses of 0.75 μm and 0.88 μm intra-line pulse distance corresponding to the position of highest X-ray dose rate in Figure 6b. In addition, the spectral width of the monitored X-ray photon fields enlarged to higher energy with pulses of smaller intra-line pulse distance. In fact, 8.0 keV maximum photon energy was detected at a 5 μm intra-line pulse distance compared to 11.0 keV at 0.88 μm, respectively. These enlarged X-ray spectra indicate even for the low-intensity pulses irradiated at small intra-line pulse distance a higher degree of plasma ionization and, therefore, a more-efficient coupling of the irradiating low-intensity ultrashort pulses. This is supported by the fact that the enlarged X-ray photon spectra of Figure 6b could be observed similar to the ones shown above in Figure 4 for higher electron temperatures induced by high-intensity pulse irradiations. As a consequence, regarding dependency on the applied intra-line pulse distance, a change of the underlying coupling mechanisms can be supposed for the low-intense pulse regime, thus from inverse Bremsstrahlung absorption at a larger intra-line pulse distance to high-efficient optical energy transfer by plasma resonance absorption for the smaller ones. However, the underlying physical principles for the strong impact of the intra-line pulse distance causing up to 12-fold enhanced X-ray emissions even in case of low-intensity ultrashort pulses could not be clarified so far. Even though the interaction of the next following laser pulse(s) with the still apparent laser ablated nanoparticle plume at 1.6 MHz time scale could be a potential effect for the observed higher X-ray emissions. This was not considered yet, but evidence therefore can be found in the literature reporting on enhanced X-ray emissions from nanoparticles irradiated by ultrashort laser pulses [26,27].

3.5. Effect of the Temporal Pulse Distance on X-ray Emission in the Low-Intensity Pulse Regime

It becomes obvious that the temporal delay between the pulses will also affect X-ray emission when considering plasma resonance absorption as the dominant optical transfer mechanism for low-intensity pulses [28]. As already stated above, this is due to the fact that the actual shape of both the laser ablation plume and the critical plasma density layer is continuously changing with time. From this, it can be supposed that the impinging ultrashort pulses will meet different conditions in the interaction cross-section, depending on the inter-pulse delay defined by the PRF. Hence, the operating plasma density and actual flank angle are directly affected by the PRF, in turn, having an immediate impact on the optical energy transfer and further on X-ray photon yield.

With increasing PRF, which corresponds to shorter temporal inter-pulse delays, the X-ray photon emission increases to maximum level, as can be seen in Figure 8 for pulses of $I_0 = 1.6 \times 10^{13}$ W·cm^{-2} irradiated at PRFs in the range of 1.6 MHz. A further increase of the applied PRF to 2 MHz caused a prompt drop of the X-ray photon yield. Here, too, a considerable impact of the intra-line pulse distance is recognizable when comparing the maximum X-ray dose rates presented in Figure 8a,c. At a 5.0 µm intra-line pulse distance, the maximum X-ray dose rate was measured of $\dot{H}'(0.07) = 4.6$ mSv·h^{-1}, while 8-fold higher X-ray emissions of $\dot{H}'(0.07) = 37.7$ mSv·h^{-1} were detected at 0.88 µm, respectively. In addition, a significant difference of the X-ray emission characteristic can be seen in the corresponding X-ray photon spectra pointed out in Figure 8b,d. The X-ray photon spectra recorded at 5.0 µm intra-line pulse distance are characterized by broad continuous Bremsstrahlung emission in the photon energy range below 8 keV; see Figure 8b. At 0.88 µm in Figure 8d, by contrast, the X-ray photon spectra enlarged to 12 keV photon energy featured by dominant peaks of the characteristic X-ray emission lines. These results confirm the aforementioned change of the energy transfer mechanisms in the low-intense pulse regime from inverse Bremsstrahlung absorption to plasma resonance absorption. Thus, a strong influence of the actual conditions of the laser ablated plasma/nanoparticle plume on the effective laser beam absorption mechanism is suggested, which depends on both the temporal and spatial inter-pulse distance.

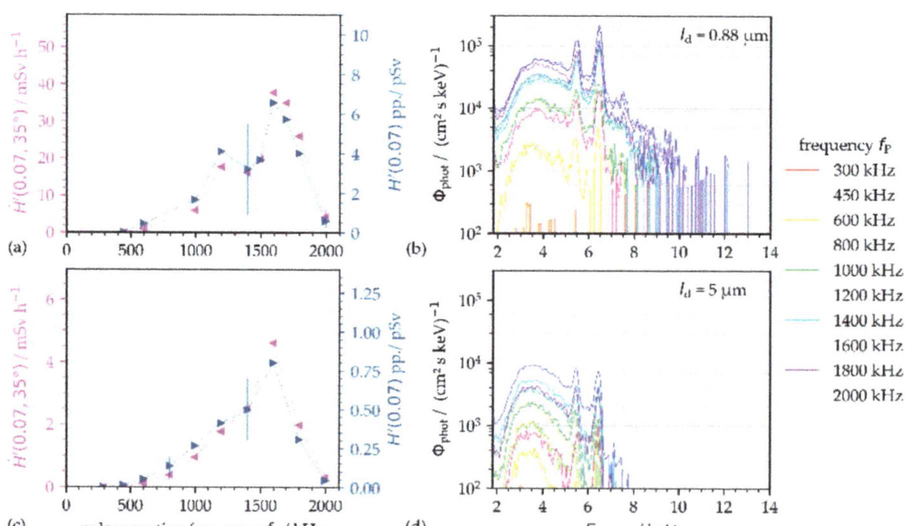

Figure 8. Effect of the pulse repetition frequency on X-ray emissions in the low-intensity pulse regime. Two intra-line pulse distances, (**a**,**b**) 0.88 µm and (**c**,**d**) 5.0 µm, were studied at 100 mm distance and 35° detection angle between the AISI 304 substrate and SILIX monitor. The dotted lines in (**a**,**c**) guide the eye.

3.6. X-ray Emissions in the Burst and Burst-in-Burst Laser Pulse Regime

Laser pulse train processing in the burst and burst-in-burst (bi-burst) regime offers more flexibility to adjust and tailor optical energy deposition into the material. This is mainly due to the fact that the optical energy of a single irradiation event (burst) is divided by the number of individual pulses within the laser burst, while in the bi-burst regime, the individual pulses were further separated in sub-pulses. In the burst regime applied here, the time delay between the individual pulses within the burst was 15 ns and between the burst sub-pulses in the bi-burst regime was 440 ps, respectively. Two burst repetition frequencies were studied: PFR_B = 400 kHz and 1 MHz in bi-directional processing.

Initial studies on the burst mode in laser material processing showed a considerable drop of the material removal rate for each second irradiating pulse, especially when the next-following pulse was delayed to the previous one in the ten-nanosecond time domain [29]. Therefore, a reasonable explanation is the interaction of the second, fourth, sixth (and so on) intra-burst pulse with the ablation plasma/nanoparticle plume induced by the preceding pulse(s). Corresponding to the differences in material removal, a variance can also be observed for the X-ray emissions in the burst-mode regime monitored at a 35° detection angle and 100 mm distance between the substrate and SILIX detector; see Figure 9. For reference, the spectral X-ray photon flux and X-ray emission dose rate for 200 fs pulses of $I_0 = 3.8 \times 10^{13}$ W·cm^{-2} applied in the single pulse (1-pulse burst) regime is presented in Figure 9a. At 400 kHz PRF, the full available power P_{av} = 33.0 W of the burst-mode laser was irradiated by repeated crossing (bi-directional, up to 5 scans) the substrate at 0.4 m·s^{-1} laser beam moving speed and a corresponding 1 µm intra-line pulse distance. The given X-ray emission spectra with a maximum of 12.5 keV photon energy are featured by distinct characteristic X-ray emission lines, and the Bremsstrahlung photon yield is relatively low. For the first scan crossing, the X-ray emission dose rate was measured to $\dot{H}'(0.07) = 0.6 \pm 0.2$ mSv·h^{-1}. This yields about 15 µSv·h^{-1}·W^{-1} and is in the range of the dose rate levels presented above in Figure 8c for pulses at similar PRF (450 kHz) but longer pulse duration (600 fs instead of 200 fs). With ongoing processing, initially, the X-ray emission dose rate increased significantly in the second scan to $\dot{H}'(0.07) = 10.8 \pm 2.0$ mSv·h^{-1} maximum. While in the further course of scanning, the X-ray emission reduced steadily to lower levels measured in the fifth scan of $\dot{H}'(0.07) = 1.4 \pm 0.3$ mSv·h^{-1}.

For two individual pulses in the laser burst (two-pulse burst in Figure 9b), a considerably higher amount of Bremsstrahlung emission was detected. This is potentially arising from the highly excited electron field induced by strong laser pulse with plasma interaction in the time domain of 15 ns, resulting in almost four-fold higher X-ray emissions than in the single pulse regime. It is noteworthy that such a high level of X-ray emission occurred with intra-burst pulses of half of the intensity of the single pulses (one-pulse burst, Figure 9a), because the impinging optical energy of the irradiation event is divided by the number of individual pulses in the two-pulse burst. By comparing these X-ray emissions with dose rates from pulses of similar intensity and PRF in Figure 8c, a major growth from 12.5 µSv·h^{-1}·W^{-1} for single pulses to 1120 µSv·h^{-1}·W^{-1} in the two-pulse burst regime can be recognized. These results confirm the strong plasma plume interaction in the laser burst regime with further evidence on plasma resonance absorption as the dominant energy transfer mechanism for pulses irradiating with very short time delay.

For a three-pulse burst, as shown in Figure 9c, the X-ray emission dose and Bremsstrahlung continuum originated somewhat in between single pulses and two-pulse burst irradiations. In this irradiation regime, the intensity of the individual intra-burst pulses reduced to one-third from the single pulses. With a higher number of pulses in a burst, the X-ray dose rates were found in the range of single pulses or below. This is exemplified in Figure 9d for laser bursts consisting of four intra-pulses. Accordingly, the intensity of the individual pulses reduced by a factor of four, which might be the reason for the Bremsstrahlung dominated X-ray emission spectra of low photon energy ranging between 2 and 7.5 keV.

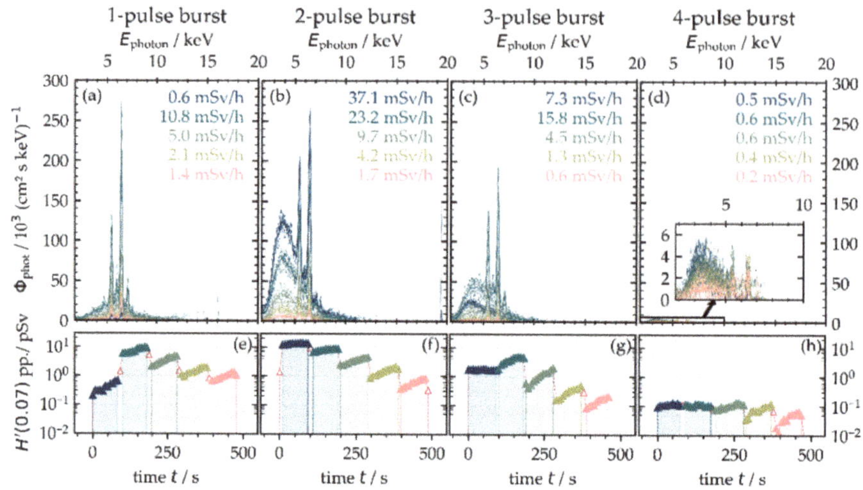

Figure 9. X-ray emission in the laser burst processing regime at a 400 kHz burst repetition frequency monitored at 100 mm distance, 35° detection angle, and five individual scans across the substrate. The intra-burst pulse number was varied between 1 (**a**) and 4 (**d**). The spectral X-ray photon flux and X-ray emission dose rate (**a–d**) as well as the X-ray dose per pulse (**e–h**) are presented for increasing number of scan crossings.

For single-pulse processing at PRF = 1.0 MHz and P_{av} = 33.0 W average laser power, no X-ray emission could be detected, which might be due to the fact that the respective peak intensity $I_0 = 1.6 \times 10^{13}$ W·cm^{-2} of the impinging pulses was too close to the threshold for X-ray photons generation on AISI 304. The observation is a bit in contrast to Figure 5, where the emission of X-ray photons can be seen for intensities even below of $I_0 = 1.0 \times 10^{13}$ W·cm^{-2}. However, this was achieved with pulses of 600 fs duration, while the pulse duration of the burst-mode laser presented here was 200 fs, which will also affect X-ray photon emission and equivalent dose rates.

However, a significant enhancement of the X-ray emission dose rate accompanied by pronounced characteristic X-ray emissions were detected for laser bursts irradiating at a 1.0 MHz burst repetition frequency and corresponding lower peak intensity of the intra-burst pulses. The maximum X-ray emissions were measured to $\dot{H}'(0.07) = 32.8 \pm 3.6$ mSv·h^{-1} (3rd scan) with the two-pulse burst and $\dot{H}'(0.07) = 14.1 \pm 1.6$ mSv·h^{-1} (2nd scan) with the three-pulse burst; see Figure 10a,b. AISI 304 processing with a higher number of intra-burst pulses yields much lower X-ray emissions, and the dominant Bremsstrahlung continuum shifted to X-ray photon energies below 7.5 keV, as can be seen in Figure 10d for the six-pulse bursts.

Another separation of the pulses in the bi-burst regime showed no further X-ray emission enhancement in the studied parameter range. For example, the X-ray emission dose rate was in the range between 0.6 mSv·h^{-1} < $\dot{H}'(0.07)$ < 0.8 mSv·h^{-1} for a two-sub-pulse bi-burst of 440 ps inter-pulse delay at 400 kHz PRF_B and 33.0 W average laser power, as shown in Figure 11a. By irradiating two sub-pulses in a two-pulse burst processing scenario, such as shown in Figure 11b, the X-ray emission dose rate increased significantly to $\dot{H}'(0.07) = 30.0 \pm 1.2$ mSv·h^{-1} maximum level, even when the peak intensity of the operating sub-pulses reduced to a quarter of the original single pulses below $I_0 = 1.0 \times 10^{13}$ W·cm^{-2}. However, with a higher number of pulses within the burst and bi-burst pulse train, the X-ray emission reduced to a lower value, which is mainly attributed to the corresponding lower peak intensity of the sub-pulses limited by the maximum energy of a laser burst; see Figure 11c,d.

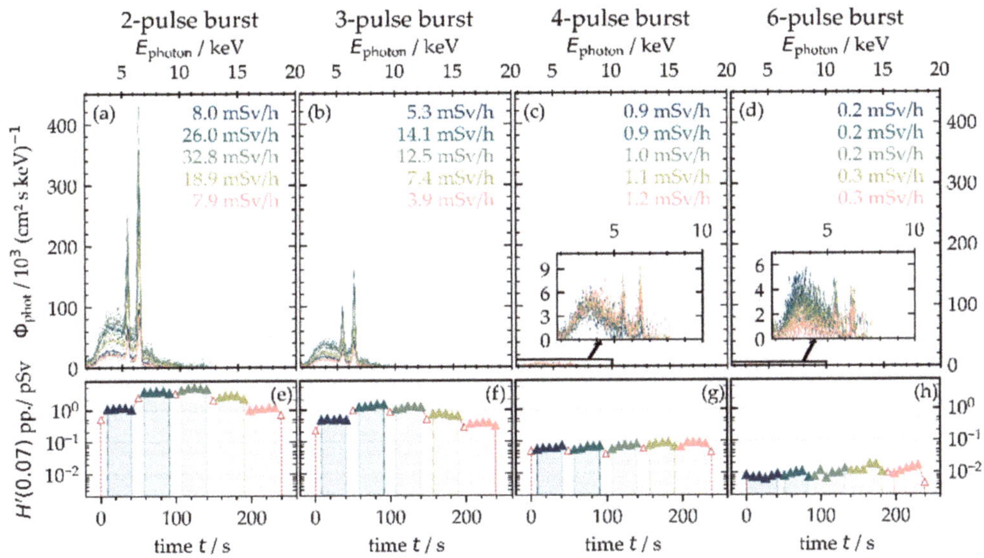

Figure 10. X-ray emission in the laser burst processing regime at 1.0 MHz burst repetition frequency monitored at 100 mm distance, 35° detection angle, and five individual scans across the substrate. The intra-burst pulse number was varied between 2 (**a**) and 6 (**d**). The spectral X-ray photon flux and X-ray emission dose rate (**a**–**d**) as well as the X-ray dose per pulse (**e**–**h**) are presented for an increasing number of scan crossings.

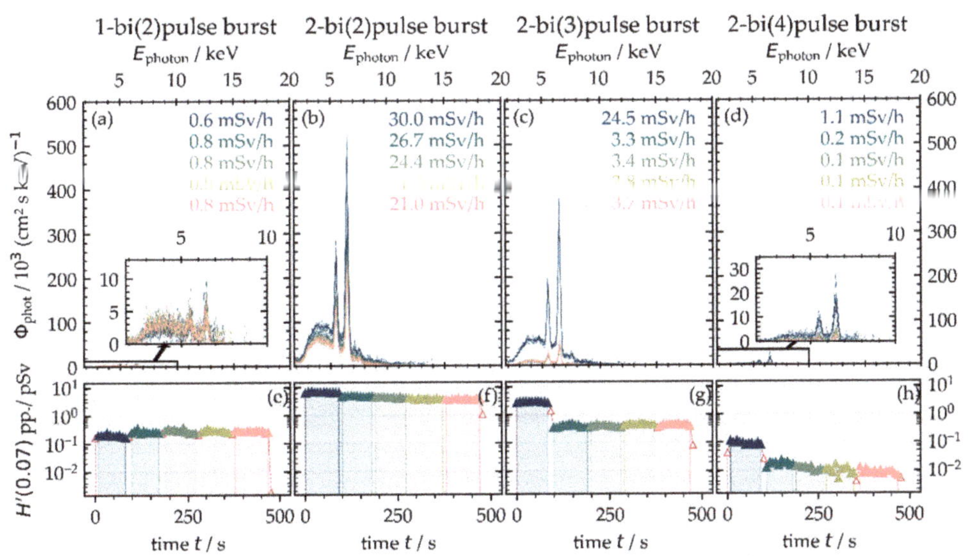

Figure 11. X-ray emissions in the laser bi-burst processing regime with notable X-ray dose rates at 400 kHz burst repetition frequency at 100 mm distance, 35° detection angle, and five individual scans across the substrate. The graphs display the high influence of the second MHz-burst pulse (two-pulse burst) with GHz bi-bursts (2–4 (**b**–**d**)) in contrast to the GHz bi-burst (**a**). The peak intensity of the sub-pulses was I_0 = 1.9/0.95/0.63/0.48 × 10^{13} W·cm^{-2} The spectral X-ray photon flux and X-ray emission dose rate (**a**–**d**) as well as the X-ray dose per pulse (**e**–**h**) are presented for increasing number of scan crossings.

However, these initial results obtained in the burst and bi-burst processing regime emphasize the great influence of laser pulse with plasma interaction for X-ray photon generation. In particular, the second intra-burst pulse is of great importance, causing strong enhancement of the X-ray emission dose rate. This will be proved in the ongoing study even for the case of ultrashort pulses in GHz-pulse trains at hundreds of Watts average laser power.

4. Summary and Main Conclusions

The presented study on laser-induced X-ray emissions on technical-grade AISI 304 stainless steel provides an overview on the laser processing under different conditions and parameter variations affecting the spectral X-ray photon flux and X-ray emission dose rate. In total, four different ultrashort pulse laser systems were applied providing complementary laser beam characteristics, including pulse peak intensities between 8×10^{12} W·cm^{-2} < I_0 < 5.2×10^{16} W·cm^{-2}, 2.0 MHz maximum PRF, up to 72.2 W average laser power as well as burst and bi-burst processing mode. The findings of this study confirm the general trend toward higher X-ray photon emission for pulses of higher peak intensity. Thereby, the monitored X-ray photon emissions are in good agreement with data reported previously by other groups; see Figure 12. The presented efficient X-ray emission dose rates were calculated from the X-ray emission dose rates monitored at 100 mm distance and 35° detection angle divided by the applied average laser power.

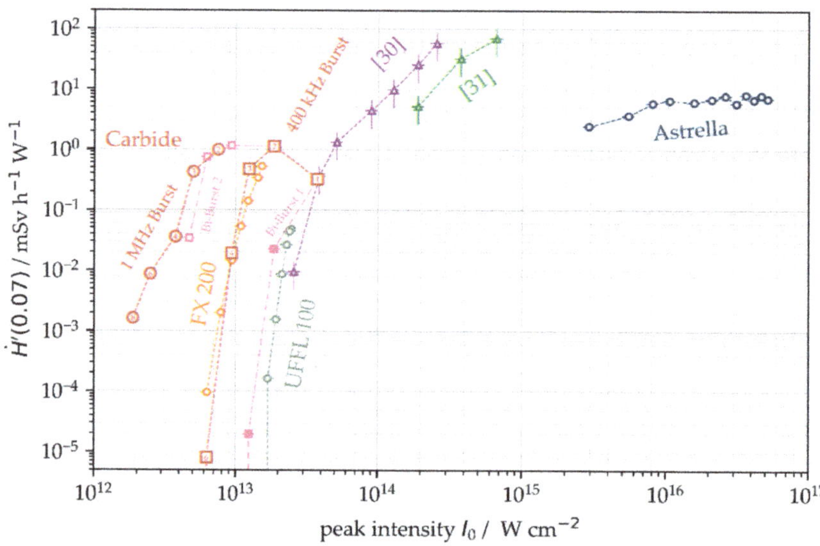

Figure 12. Summary of efficient X-ray emission dose rates as a function of peak intensity for different process regimes and laser systems. FX 200 (f_P = 1.6 MHz, *ld* = 0.88 µm); UFFL 100 (f_P = 506 kHz, *ld* = 0.88 µm); Astrella (f_P = 1 kHz, *ld* = 20 µm); [30] provided data recalculated for 100 mm detector distance, [31] provided data recalculated for 100 mm detector distance.

However, an unexpected high level of X-ray photon emission dominated by broad Bremsstrahlung emission could be detected for low-intensity pulses irradiation under specific processing conditions. For example, a maximum X-ray emission dose rate $\dot{H}'(0.07)$ = 41.3 ± 2.8 mSv·h^{-1} and 0.4 mSv·h^{-1}·W^{-1} corresponding to an effective X-ray emission dose were detected for pulses of I_0 = 1.6×10^{13} W·cm^{-2} irradiated at 1.6 MHz PRF, 0.88 µm intra-line pulse distance, and 65 W average laser power. Therefore, a strong interaction of the next laser pulse(s) with the still apparent nanoparticle/plasma plume induced by preceding laser pulse ablations is suggested. As a consequence, plasma resonance absorption and effective electron plasma heating dominates the optical energy transfer, yielding broad Bremsstrahlung emission from the highly excited electron field. As a result, a considerable amount of X-ray photon emission could be detected even for low-intensity pulses at peak intensities considerably below the threshold value known so far. In summary, the following main conclusions can be stated on the basis of the presented results:

1. X-ray photon emission per pulse increases exponentially with peak intensity in the low-intense pulse regime ($I_0 < 1.6 \times 10^{13}$ W·cm^{-2}) and is on linear growth with high-intensity pulses ($I_0 > 10^{16}$ W·cm^{-2});
2. Unexpected high X-ray emission dose rates ($\dot{H}'(0.07) > 45$ mSv·h^{-1}) are achieved when low-intensity pulses irradiate at a small intra-line pulse distance and megahertz pulse repetition frequency (1.6 × 10^{13} W·cm^{-2}, 1.6 MHz, 0.88 μm intra-line pulse distance);
3. Resonance plasma absorption and strong electron plasma heating are suggested as underlying process for highly excited electron fields yielding broad Bremsstrahlung spectra up to 12.5 keV X-ray photon energies and pronounced characteristic X-ray emission lines;
4. Within burst and bi-burst pulse trains, in particular, the second intra-burst pulses enhance significantly the X-ray emission dose rate that is potentially induced by strong laser pulse with plasma interaction.

With regard to kW-class ultrashort pulses lasers in materials processing, this unwanted X-ray emission can accumulate to harmful X-ray dose levels. In order to enhance the knowledge in this field, our actual research work is focused on high-average power lasers as well as megahertz PRF and burst-mode laser beams in order to understand and determine the dependencies of the characteristic laser beam properties on X-ray emission. Another future challenge is to develop and provide effective X-ray protection strategies, which is a mandatory prerequisite to pave the way for ultrashort pulse lasers as a powerful tool in modern micro fabrication.

Author Contributions: Conceptualization, J.S., U.L. and A.H.; methodology, J.S., S.K., U.L. and A.H.; investigation, S.K, J.S., T.P., M.C. and C.S.; writing—original draft preparation, J.S. and S.K.; writing—review and editing, J.S., S.K., T.P., A.H. and U.L.; funding acquisition, U.L., A.H. and J.S. All authors have read and agreed to the published version of the manuscript.

Funding: The authors thank the European Social Fund for Germany (ESF) for funding the project EilaSax (no. 100339506), the German Federal Ministry of Education and Research (BMBF) for financial support in the project FH-Europa 2020: MACH-XLT (no. 13FH009EX0) and the German Research Foundation (DFG) by the contract no. INST 522/14-1 FUGG.

Institutional Review Board Statement: Not applicable.

Informed Consent Statement: Not applicable.

Data Availability Statement: Data sharing is not applicable to this article.

Acknowledgments: The authors are grateful to Guenter Dittmar for valuable discussions and also acknowledge technical support provided by the SILIX lambda item to loan (Ingenieurbüro Guenter Dittmar, Aalen, Germany) that was used in this study to monitor the X-ray emission spectra and X-ray emission dose rates.

Conflicts of Interest: The authors declare no conflict of interest.

References

1. Roecker, C.; Loescher, A.; Delaigue, M.; Hoenninger, C.; Mottay, E.; Graf, T.; Abdou Ahmed, M. Flexible Sub-1 ps Ultrafast Laser Exceeding 1 kW of Output Power for High-Throughput Surface Structuring. In *Advanced Solid State Lasers*; Optical Society of America: San Diego, CA, USA, 2019; p. AM4A.2.
2. Mueller, M.; Aleshire, C.; Klenke, A.; Haddad, E.; Légaré, F.; Tuennermann, A.; Limpert, J. 10.4 kW coherently combined ultrafast fiber laser. *Opt. Lett.* **2020**, *45*, 3083–3086. [CrossRef] [PubMed]
3. Kamlage, G.; Bauer, T.; Ostendorf, A.; Chichkov, B.N. Deep drilling of metals by femtosecond laser pulses. *Appl. Phys. A* **2003**, *77*, 307–310. [CrossRef]

4. Gruner, A.; Schille, J.; Loeschner, U. Experimental Study on Micro Hole Drilling Using Ultrashort Pulse Laser Radiation. *Phys. Procedia* **2016**, *83*, 157–166. [CrossRef]
5. Mauersberger, S.; Schille, J.; Kujawa, K.; Schneider, L.; Million, C.; Hartung, K.; Oehlert, K.; Loeschner, U. High-precision surface profiling using multi-hundred watts ultrashort pulse lasers and ultrafast polygon-mirror based scanner. *J. Laser Micro Nanoeng.* **2020**, *15*, 1–9.
6. Gafner, M.; Kramer, T.; Remund, S.M.; Holtz, R.; Neuenschwander, B. Ultrafast pulsed laser high precision micromachining of rotational symmetric parts. *J. Laser Appl.* **2021**, *33*, 012053. [CrossRef]
7. Mueller, F.A.; Kunz, C.; Graef, S. Bio-Inspired Functional Surfaces Based on Laser-Induced Periodic Surface Structures. *Materials* **2016**, *9*, 476. [CrossRef] [PubMed]
8. Schille, J.; Schneider, L.; Mauersberger, S.; Szokup, S.; Hoehn, S.; Poetschke, J.; Reiss, F.; Leidich, E.; Loeschner, U. High-Rate Laser Surface Texturing for Advanced Tribological Functionality. *Lubricants* **2020**, *8*, 33. [CrossRef]
9. Legall, H.; Schwanke, C.; Pentzien, S.; Dittmar, G.; Bonse, J.; Krueger, J. X-ray emission as a potential hazard during ultrashort pulse laser material processing. *Appl. Phys. A* **2018**, *124*, 407. [CrossRef]
10. Legall, H.; Schwanke, C.; Bonse, J.; Krueger, J. The influence of processing parameters on X-ray emission during ultra-short pulse laser machining. *Appl. Phys. A* **2019**, *125*, 570. [CrossRef]
11. Behrens, R.; Pullner, B.; Reginatto, M. X-ray emissions from materials processing lasers. *Radiat. Prot. Dosim.* **2019**, *183*, 361–374. [CrossRef]
12. Weber, R.; Giedl-Wagner, R.; Foerster, D.J.; Pauli, A.; Graf, T.; Balmer, J.E. Expected X-ray dose rates resulting from industrial ultrafast laser applications. *Appl. Phys. A* **2019**, *125*, 635. [CrossRef]
13. Freitag, C.; Giedl-Wagner, R. X-ray Protection in an Industrial Production Environment. *Photonics Views* **2020**, *17*, 37–41. [CrossRef]
14. Legall, H.; Bonse, J.; Krueger, J. Review of X-ray exposure and safety issues arising from ultra-short pulse laser material processing. *J. Radiol. Prot.* **2021**, *41*, R28. [CrossRef]
15. Liu, J.M. Simple technique for measurements of pulsed Gaussian-beam spot sizes. *Opt. Lett.* **1982**, *7*, 196. [CrossRef]
16. X-ray Mass Attenuation Coefficients, NIST STANDARD Reference Database 126. Available online: https://dx.doi.org/10.18434/T4D01F (accessed on 5 March 2021).
17. Gibbon, P.; Foerster, E. Short-pulse laser—Plasma interactions. *Plasma Phys. Control. Fusion* **1996**, *38*, 769–793. [CrossRef]
18. Schumacher, D. Investigation of Laser Driven Hohlraum Radiation and Energy Loss of Heavy Ions in Indirectly Heated Plasma. Ph.D. Thesis, Technische Universitaet Darmstadt, Darmstadt, Germany, 6 February 2012.
19. Sheng, Z.M.; Weng, S.M.; Yu, L.L.; Wang, W.M.; Cui, Y.Q.; Chen, M.; Zhang, J. Absorption of ultrashort intense lasers in laser-solid interactions. *Chin. Phys. B* **2015**, *24*, 015201. [CrossRef]
20. Kraft, S.; Schille, J.; Mauersberger, S.; Schneider, L.; Loeschner, U. Pump-probe imaging for process control and optimization in high-speed laser micro machining. In *Laser-Based Micro-and Nanoprocessing XIV*; International Society for Optics and Photonics: Washington, WA, USA, 2020; Volume 11268, p. 112681H.
21. Cerchez, M.; Jung, R.; Osterholz, J.; Toncian, T.; Mulser, W.P.; Ruhl, H. Absorption of Ultrashort Laser Pulses in Strongly Overdense Targets. *Phys. Rev. Lett.* **2008**, *100*, 24500. [CrossRef] [PubMed]
22. Dragila, R. Resonance absorption in inhomogeneous plasma with randomly rippled critical surface. *Phys. Fluids* **1983**, *26*, 1682–1687. [CrossRef]
23. Catto, P.J.; Moore, R.M. Sheath inverse bremsstrahlung in laser produced plasmas. *Phys. Fluids* **1977**, *20*, 704. [CrossRef]
24. Chen, L.M.; Forget, P.; Fourmaux, S.; Kieffer, J.C.; Krol, A.; Chamberlain, C.C.; Hou, B.X.; Nees, J.; Mourou, G. Study of hard X-ray emission from intense femtosecond:sapphire laser–solid target interactions. *Phys. Plasma* **2004**, *11*, 4439–4445. [CrossRef]
25. Mulser, P.; Bauer, D. Anharmonic resonance in intense laser-matter interaction: Key to collisionless absorption. *AIP Conf. Proc.* **2010**, *1308*, 63–65.
26. Mondal, S.; Chakraborty, I.; Ahmad, S.; Carvalho, D.; Singh, P.; Lad, A.D.; Narayanan, V.; Ayyub, P.; Ravindra, G.K.; Zheng, J.; et al. Highly enhanced hard X-ray emission from oriented metal nanorod arrays excited by intense femtosecond laser pulses. *Phys. Rev. B* **2011**, *83*, 035408. [CrossRef]
27. Sankar, P.; Thomas, J.; Shashikala, H.D.; Philip, R. Enhanced bremsstrahlung X-ray emission from Ag nanoparticles irradiated by ultrashort laser pulses. *Opt. Mater.* **2019**, *92*, 30–35. [CrossRef]
28. Horn, A.; Kaiser, C.; Ritschel, R.; Mans, T.; Russbüldt, P.; Hoffmann, H.D.; Poprawe, R. Si-Kα radiation generated by the interaction of femtosecond laser radiation with silicon. *J. Phys. Conf. Ser.* **2007**, *59*, 159–163. [CrossRef]
29. Jaeggi, B.; Cangueiro, L.; Bruneel, D.; de Ramos Campos, J.A.; Hairaye, C.; Neuenschwander, B. Micromachining using pulse bursts: Influence of the pulse duration and the number of pulses in the burst on the specific removal rate. In *Laser Applications in Microelectronic and Optoelectronic Manufacturing (LAMOM) XXIII*; International Society for Optics and Photonics: Washington, WA, USA, 2018; Volume 10519, p. 1051905.
30. Legall, H.; Bundesanstalt für Materialforschung und -prüfung (BAM), Berlin, Germany. Personal communication, 8 December 2020.
31. Giedl-Wagner, R.; GFH GmbH, Deggendorf, Germany. Personal communication, 17 June 2021.

materials

MDPI

Article

X-ray Dose Rate and Spectral Measurements during Ultrafast Laser Machining Using a Calibrated (High-Sensitivity) Novel X-ray Detector

Philip Mosel [1,*], Pranitha Sankar [1], Jan Friedrich Düsing [2], Günter Dittmar [3], Thomas Püster [2], Peter Jäschke [2], Jan-Willem Vahlbruch [4], Uwe Morgner [1] and Milutin Kovacev [1]

1 Institute of Quantum Optics, Leibniz Universität Hanover, 30167 Hannover, Germany; sankar@iqo.uni-hannover.de (P.S.); morgner@iqo.uni-hannover.de (U.M.); kovacev@iqo.uni-hannover.de (M.K.)
2 Laser Zentrum Hannover e. V., 30419 Hannover, Germany; j.duesing@lzh.de (J.F.D.); t.puester@lzh.de (T.P.); p.jaeschke@lzh.de (P.J.)
3 Steinbeis Transfer Center Technology Consultancy and Development, 73433 Aalen, Germany; dittmar-transfer@t-online.de
4 Institute of Radioecology and Radiation Protection, 30419 Hannover, Germany; vahlbruch@irs.uni-hannover.de
* Correspondence: ph.mosel@iqo.uni-hannover.de; Tel.: +49-511-762-8954

Abstract: Ultrashort pulse laser machining is subject to increase the processing speeds by scaling average power and pulse repetition rate, accompanied with higher dose rates of X-ray emission generated during laser–matter interaction. In particular, the X-ray energy range below 10 keV is rarely studied in a quantitative approach. We present measurements with a novel calibrated X-ray detector in the detection range of 2–20 keV and show the dependence of X-ray radiation dose rates and the spectral emissions for different laser parameters from frequently used metals, alloys, and ceramics for ultrafast laser machining. Our investigations include the dose rate dependence on various laser parameters available in ultrafast laser laboratories as well as on industrial laser systems. The measured X-ray dose rates for high repetition rate lasers with different materials definitely exceed the legal limitations in the absence of radiation shielding.

Keywords: X-ray emission; micromachining; dose rate; X-ray spectrum; ultrafast laser

Citation: Mosel, P.; Sankar, P.; Düsing, J.F.; Dittmar, G.; Püster, T.; Jäschke, P.; Vahlbruch, J.-W.; Morgner, U.; Kovacev, M. X-ray Dose Rate and Spectral Measurements during Ultrafast Laser Machining Using a Calibrated (High-Sensitivity) Novel X-ray Detector. *Materials* **2021**, *14*, 4397. https://doi.org/10.3390/ma14164397

Academic Editors: Jörg Krüger and Andrea P. Reverberi

Received: 7 July 2021
Accepted: 2 August 2021
Published: 5 August 2021

1. Introduction

Since the late 1960s, laser has evolved from a laboratory curiosity to a sophisticated industrial tool. Today, the peak-intensity of high-power laser systems can be used in a controlled way to serve as a machining tool for many metallurgical applications, e.g., welding, cutting, drilling, and surface hardening [1]. The main advantage of laser machining is that it generates a higher quality product with minimal deformations or damage at a faster rate, which is a critical manufacturing need [2].

Recently, it has been demonstrated that ultrashort laser machining can be accompanied with an X-ray radiation at high repetition rates, if the peak intensity exceeds 10^{13} W/cm^2 [3–6]. Industrial laser sources used for materials processing typically have pulse durations in the range of pico- to femtoseconds. With these pulse durations, it is straight-forward to generate the above-mentioned intensity. With such high laser intensity, the electron temperatures in the produced plasma approach several keV, resulting in bremsstrahlung emissions in the keV X-ray regime [7]. The laser energy transferred to a plasma electron, depends on the mechanism dominating the laser plasma interaction. If the kinetic energy of the plasma electrons becomes high enough, characteristic X-ray radiation can also be generated.

In recent publications, it has been shown that during ultrafast laser machining at high repetition rates of several 100 kHz, the amount of emitted X-ray radiation can exceed the regulatory exposure limits for members of the public [8]. Low X-ray doses per pulse can accumulate through high repetition rates and exceed radiation protection limits. Therefore, a detailed study of the influence of laser and the material parameters used for measuring the X-ray dose rate is crucial to assess appropriate safety measures. Legall et al. [9] measured the spectral X-ray emission and dose rates ($\dot{H}'(0.07)$) for different target materials using an ultrashort-pulse laser up to maximum peak intensity 2.6×10^{14} W/cm^2. They showed that the unwanted emission of X-ray radiation during ultrashort pulse laser processing of materials in air is commonly observed. These results were confirmed by Behrens et al. (2019) under similar experimental conditions [10]. Also, an analytical model was recently presented by Weber et al. (2019) to estimate the expected X-ray dose when laser machining with ultrashort-pulse lasers under industrial conditions up to an intensity 7×10^{14} W/cm^2 [4].

On the other hand, no work has been published for the X-ray emission during industrial machining, in the moderate intensity regime of 10^{14}–10^{16} W/cm^2 with high repetition rate lasers. One of the reasons is that until now there are no commonly available spectrometer with an immediate readout for measuring dose rates with high sensitivity. X-ray emission ranging from a few eV to about 10 keV occurs when processing most of the materials such as stainless steel, copper, various alloys, and ceramics [10]. This X-ray radiation can cause skin cancer hence, this emission range requires more attention. In this paper, we investigate the X-ray emission from different alloys, metals, and ceramics with two high repetition rate lasers. We use a novel calibrated X-ray detector for the measurements which provides a high sensitivity over 2–20 keV range. Experimental methods employed for the determination of the dose rates and the spectral analysis of the different alloys, metals and ceramics is presented. We also compare the dosimeter OD-02 with the novel spectrodosimeter Silix lambda (engineering office Prof. Dr.-Ing. Günter Dittmar) under identical experimental conditions.

2. Materials and Methods

2.1. Optical Setup

The experiments are performed using two different laser systems with parameters noted in Table 1. The laser beam is focused onto the sample by means of a plano-convex lens/f-theta scanning objective with a focal length of 60 mm. The angle of incidence of the laser beam is perpendicular to the sample plane. The laser intensity varies from 10^{13}–10^{16} W/cm^2. The average power of the pulse is simultaneously measured at one arm from a beam splitter.

Table 1. Laser parameters used during micromachining.

Laser Parameter	KMLabs Dragon	Coherent Monaco
Wavelength	800 nm	1035 nm
Rep. rate	1 kHz	755 kHz
Pulse energy	1 mJ	72 µJ
Avg. power	1 W	54 W
Pulse duration	35 fs	350 fs
Focus diameter ($1/e^2$)	12 ± 2 µm	22 ± 2 µm
Rayleigh length	0.2 mm	0.4 mm
Scanning speed	1.3 mm/s	1000 mm/s
Pulse overlap	10.7 µm	20.7 µm
Polarization	Linear	Linear
Beam profile	Gaussian	Gaussian
Angle of incidence	Perpendicular	Perpendicular
Scanning pattern	20 Spirals	20 Spirals
Scanning time	49 s	49 s

For our measurements we use different metals like titanium, molybdenum, iron, copper, nickel, zinc, and tungsten. In addition, we process ceramics like ZrO_2, Si_3N_4, and Al_2O_3. Moreover, brass, stainless steel, NiCuZn, and NiCrFe alloys have been exposed to intense laser radiation. The percentage composition of alloys can be found in Table 2. The sample is positioned using a motorized three axis stage which is used for ultrafast machining in laboratories for the 1 kHz system and a scanner for the 755 kHz system (Figure 1). To exclude polarization dependence, a spiral with a line spacing of 30 μm is written. The minimum inner diameter is 1 mm. The laser turned-on time is 2.45 s per spiral and turned off for 4 ms during going back to start position. The outer diameter was chosen depending on the repetition rate so that the total duration of the writing process is about 49 s. The distance between pulse to pulse is 1.3 μm for both lasers.

Table 2. List of alloys and its percentage of compositions used for the micromachining.

CuZn	Cu 58%	Zn 39%	Pb 3%
NiCuZn	Cu 47–64%	Ni 10–25%	Zn 15–42%
NiCrFe	Ni 72–76%	Cr 18–21%	Fe 5%
Steel 1.4310	Fe 70–77%	Cr 16–19%	Ni 6–9.5%

Two different detectors are used for the local dose rate ($\dot{H}'(0.07)$) measurements. A calibrated compact portable ion chamber dosimeter (STEP OD-02, PTW Freiburg, Freiburg im Breisgau, Germany) is used for skin dose measurements $\dot{H}'(0.07)$ at a distance of 150 mm from the processing point at an angle of 45° with respect to the laser line. At the same time, we use a calibrated spectrodosimeter Silix lambda, with the same measurement distance and angle, to obtain the X-ray spectral and dose rate information. The detailed description of this calibrated X-ray detector is given in the next section.

Figure 2 depicts the typical appearance of the material surface after processing of 20 spirals with the 755 kHz laser system with an irradiation of 4.2 ± 10^{14} W/cm^2. It should be noted that during this experiment the laser parameters are not optimized for surface quality. Due to high pulse overlap and high average power heat the surface shows formation of resolidified material, indicating that heat accumulation occurred during the laser process. No predominant directional structures are observed in any sample.

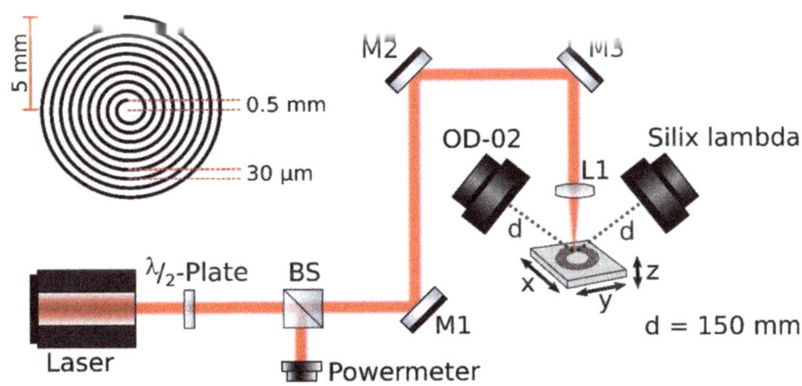

Figure 1. The schematic experimental setup is shown here. M1, M2, M3—Dielectric mirrors; L1—Plano-convex lens (f = 60 mm); BS—beam splitter. The schematic image of the spiral patterning on the material formed during the laser micromachining is shown in the left top. A power meter is used to verify the laser power used for the laser processing.

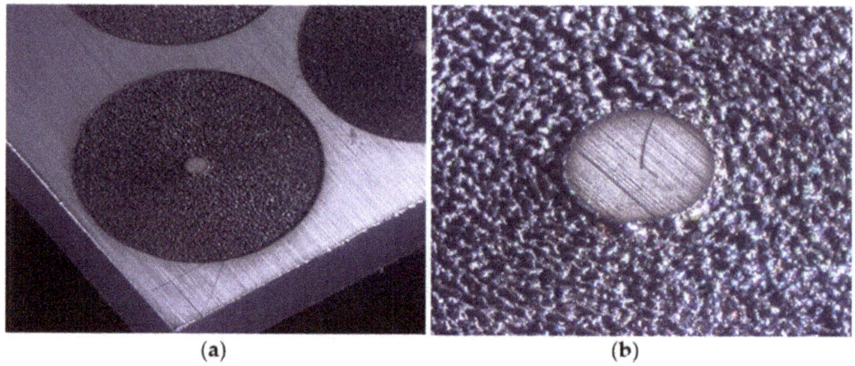

Figure 2. Shown is (**a**) the spiral after laser processing by the Coherent Monaco laser at 4.2×10^{14} W/cm^2, (**b**) a detailed view from the structure.

2.2. Silix Lambda X-ray Spectrodosimeter

The Silix spectrodosimeter is especially developed by the engineering office Prof. Dr.-Ing. Günter Dittmar for measuring X-ray radiation during material processing with ultrashort pulse lasers and to evaluate the X-ray emission with a spectral resolution of 0.08 keV. The Silix spectrodosimeter is calibrated on a reference radiation source of the Physikalisch-Technische Bundesanstalt (PTB) in Braunschweig, Germany using comparative measurements with standardized X-ray spectra.

The working principle of this spectroradiometer is based on the photoelectric effect to detect X-rays. The sensor is a silicon image chip with up to 8 million pixels. The pulsed X-ray radiation generates electrical charge carriers in the silicon chip, which are evaluated by a fast microcontroller. When an image pixel is hit by an X-ray photon, a small current is generated. The greater the energy of the X-ray photon, the greater the photocurrent. Special signal processing separates the photocurrent from interference currents. A new feature is the patented self-monitoring of the device in order to guarantee the proper functioning of the Silix X-ray detector. The equivalent dose rates relevant for radiation protection are calculated internally in the device:

- Directional dose equivalent rate for the skin $\dot{H}'(0.07)$.
- Directional dose equivalent rate for the eyes $\dot{H}'(3)$.
- Ambient dose equivalent rate $\dot{H}^*(10)$.

The energy spectrum of the photon irradiance is recorded in 235 channels ranging from 2–20 keV. It is stored and displayed as a curve with a unit of photons (keV cm^2 s). For measurement at very low irradiances (small dose rate), any number of individual spectra can be averaged. In this way, at photon energies between 2–10 keV—the most important range for laser-induced ionising radiation—dose rates as low as about 0.1 µSv/h can be displayed. In the range of up to 45°, the angular dependence of the measurement signal deviates less than 5% from the cosine function. The measuring sensor has an area of 0.1 cm^2 and thus enables homogeneous irradiation even at a very short distance of about 2 cm to the point of impact of the laser beam. With these features, the Silix lambda X-ray monitor can also be used in safety-critical monitoring tasks for laser processing applications.

3. Results and Discussion

The mechanism generating X-rays during ultrafast laser interaction with materials has been described elsewhere [3,4,8]. Under experimental conditions, high-kinetic-energy electrons would directly collide against electrons in atoms inner shell orbitals, resulting in the emission of characteristic lines for e.g., k-α, k-β line emissions along with a bremsstrahlung mechanism. The X-ray photon flux generated from the laser produced plasma strongly depends on the number of laser photons absorbed. This X-ray photon flux depends on two factors: the initial interaction of material with the laser and subsequent plasma electron heating [11]. Thus, X-ray generation is strongly dependent on laser and material parameters.

Here, we investigate the X-ray emission during ultrashort pulse laser machining of materials which are commonly used in scientific laboratories and laser-based fabrication industries. The intensity is varied in the experiment by rotating a half wave plate in the optical beam path. The results of these experiments are presented in the following sections.

3.1. Dose Rates

The maximum X-ray local dose rates measured for the Monaco (Coherent Inc., Santa Clara, CA, USA) and Dragon (KMLabs, Boulder, CO, USA) lasers in mSv/h as a function of the laser peak intensity using the OD-02 is shown in Figure 3. For the dose rate measurements, three ceramics (Al_2O_3, Si_3N_4, ZrO_2), four alloys (brass, steel, nickel brass, NiCrFe) and three metals (titanium, molybdenum, and tungsten) are used with the two laser systems.

In the case of the Coherent Monaco laser system, the dose rate increases with the laser intensity for all materials. Thus, the dose rate reaches 1 Sv/h at the maximum laser intensity.

This corresponds to a maximum X-ray dose per laser pulse of about 0.37 nSv. At an intensity of 4.2×10^{14} W/cm^2, Iron and Molybdenum show the highest dose rate for metals. Among alloys, the highest dose rate is observed in NiCrFe and among ceramics in Si_3N_4. We notice a power dependence for the dose rate with the laser peak intensity $\dot{H}'(0.07) \propto I^5$.

The maximum dose rate for the KMLabs Dragon 1 kHz system is of 0.3 mSv/h which is significantly lower in comparison with the Coherent Monaco laser. This is about 22% of the dose per laser pulse (0.08 nSv) compared to the 755 kHz system. Despite the higher pulse energy of the KMLabs Dragon laser, we obtained a 4.6 × higher dose rate from the Coherent Monaco. Several parameters—such as central wavelength, pulse duration, spot size, and multi-pulse effects—contribute to this difference in X-ray dose rate. In particular, the bigger focal diameter of the Coherent Monaco laser leads to a 3.4 × larger illuminated area on the surface, while the longer wavelength allows for higher accelerations of the electrons in the plasma and thus contributes to the increase in dose rate. These two parameters could be primarily responsible for such difference in the dose rate measured [12]. Laser absorption to the material has a direct dependence over the wavelength of the laser. If the wavelength is low, the conversion efficiencies of laser photons to the plasma is reduced and it effectively reduces the X-ray dose rates [13]. The material properties have an influence on the conversion efficiency and thus on the resulting dose rate. Additionally, the high repetition rate of the Coherent Monaco laser system may contribute to the higher dose per pulse compared to the 1 kHz system. At high repetition rates heat accumulation in the material can reduce ablation thresholds [14] and increase material removal rates [15]. On the other hand, König et al. [16] have observed that hot material ejected by laser ablation of metals can be present up to several microseconds after the laser pulse. In [16] it is concluded that the material plume possibly consists of metal vapor and droplets which may lead to shielding effects at a repetition rate of some hundreds of kHz and beyond. Thus, it is likely that in our experiments with the 755 kHz laser system particle shielding is present and plasma shielding cannot be completely ruled out. Coupling a considerable amount of laser energy into a particle cloud or plasma of previous ablation events may contribute to an even stronger X-ray emission compared to low repetition rate laser ablation. When processing materials with the KMLabs Dragon laser, Copper has the highest dose rate for metals compared to the Coherent Monaco laser, while NiCrFe has the highest dose rate for alloys.

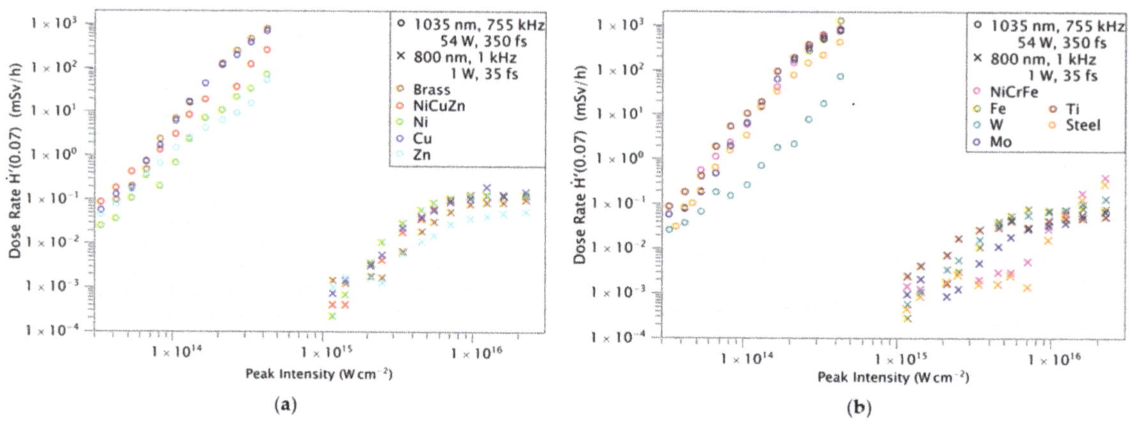

Figure 3. Measured dose rates $\dot{H}'(0.07)$ in dependence on the different target material and the incident laser peak intensity listed as: (**a**) Brass, and NiCuZn alloy and its composition metals Ni, Cu, and Zn are investigated using the ionization chamber dosimeter OD-02 at a distance of 150 mm from the interaction zone in air. The laser intensity was varied between 5×10^{13} and 5×10^{16} W/cm^2 by tuning the laser pulse energy for two different lasers. (**b**) NiCrFe and stainless steel alloys and its composition metals as well as W, Mo, and Ti are plotted in the same experimental conditions.

To understand the physical process of X-ray generation in laser materials processing, the fundamental mechanisms that result in X-ray generation during laser-plasma interaction must be studied. Two different mechanisms are needed to be considered for the generation of X-rays in the intensity range of 10^{12}–10^{16} W/cm^2, namely collisional absorption and collisional less absorption [17–19]. The plasma is heated via 'collisional' absorption (inverse bremsstrahlung), in which electrons disperse the kinetic energy absorbed from the laser radiation field through collisions with other electrons and ions in the plasma. Through this mechanism, hot electrons are generated and these electrons decelerate in the vicinity of ions and produce bremsstrahlung X-rays. These hot electrons produced in the plasma scale with intensity via inverse bremsstrahlung, and this ultimately results in higher X-ray emission and dose rates which is given by, $T_h \propto (I\lambda^2)^\alpha$ with T_h hot electron temperature, I, λ intensity and wavelength of the laser, respectively [20].

It is commonly accepted, that at intensities below 10^{13} W/cm^2 collisional absorption dominates the laser plasma interaction [17–19]. In this regime, the X-ray dose rate is power dependent on the intensity. However, for an intensity regime above 10^{15} W/cm^2, a mechanism where the laser electric field resonantly excites plasma waves, close to the surface of the over-dense plasma region, takes place. Here the laser field cannot propagate which is commonly referred to as 'collision-less' absorption regime and hence the dependency of the dose rate is weaker and almost saturates at a plateau. At this point the intensity depends on the dose rate as $(I\lambda^2)^{1/3}$ which confirms that resonance absorption dominates in this intensity regime.

When we compare the parameters of the used laser systems such as the wavelength, pulse duration, pulse energy and repetition rate, we observe a strong influence on the X-ray dose rate. At high laser pulse repetition rates in the hundreds of kHz range, the accumulated number of pulses over a time is very high. Hence, the heat accumulation on the target is increasing. This will support the plasma generation to produce more hot electrons and can explain the increase of X-ray doses at higher repetition rate.

In addition, the conversion efficiency of X-ray generation should be considered to estimate the dose rates, which is defined as the ratio of the energy emitted as X-rays to the energy of the incident laser pulse. This conversion efficiency depends critically on the target geometry in which the laser–plasma interaction takes place, material absorption coefficient, thermal conductivity and laser parameters—e.g., the laser pulse duration, wavelength, and intensity [11].

When we compare the X-ray emission from alloys with the emission from its composition metals, the dose rates of alloys can be increased or suppressed according to the dose rates of its composite metals. Take brass as an example, its dose rate scales similar to its composition metal of copper. On the contrary, the NiCuZn dose rate is suppressed due to its nickel composition. Similarly, in the case of the NiCrFe alloy, the dose rate follows that of iron and chromium rather than scaling with the Nickel dose rates. Therefore, the alloy dose rate is not completely relying on the dose rates of its metal compositions. However, these first observations are still preliminary and further work is needed in order to fully understand the dependencies on the materials.

The measured X-ray dose rates shown in Figure 2 exceed the skin dose of 20 mSv per year already at an exposure time of 80 s [21]. The maximum dose rate $\dot{H}'(0.07)$ measured at the highest intensity is 899 mSv/h and 0.40 mSv/h for Coherent Monaco and KMLabs Dragon lasers, respectively. So, it is recommended to take necessary measures to ensure personal safety during the micromachining process. Also, we should find the working distance from the interaction zone with an acceptable dose rates and proper shielding for a safe working environment. The permissible occupational radiation exposure should be monitored before each experiment.

3.2. Spectra

This section presents the X-ray spectral distribution for all used materials at the maximum intensity of the KMLabs Dragon and Coherent Monaco laser systems. The Silix lambda spectrodosimeter is used for the spectral measurement and the X-ray detection range is spanned over 2–20 keV. The spectral photon sensitivity of the spectrodosimeter is corrected and calibrated for all 235 channels. In Figures 4 and 5, the spectra are averaged for 6 s and normalized to their maximum values. The X-ray photon counts are higher for the Coherent Monaco laser which is a high repetition rate laser.

The spectral distribution of the plasma emission consists of characteristic lines as well as bremsstrahlung continuum according to the materials interaction with the laser radiation. Here the bremsstrahlung emission is a continuum emission observed below the 5 keV X-ray energy regime. In this intensity regime, the multiphoton ionization (MPI) generates free electrons which become 'hot' electrons with high kinetic energy by resonance absorption of photons from the laser pulse. When these hot electrons decelerate, bremsstrahlung emission of X-rays occurs. Increase in X-ray flux can therefore be achieved by increasing the number of hot electrons which are the primary cause for bremsstrahlung [22]. In such a way the bremsstrahlung emission increases with intensity. For the high repetition rate laser, both bremsstrahlung and characteristic line emission are equally probable.

As like the dose rates discussion, the spectral emission of Brass follows similar as its composition of copper but when we see spectral emission of NiCuZn follows the spectral distribution of nickel composition. In addition, the bremsstrahlung emission is also enhanced in the NiCuZn compared to the brass, but it follows the spectral emission of nickel. The spectral emission of NiCrFe follows the chromium and nickel spectral emission not the iron spectral distribution.

For the 755 kHz laser, a broader bremsstrahlung emission is observed in comparison to the 1 kHz laser. Depending on the material, either bremsstrahlung emission or line emission is more dominant. For example, comparing molybdenum with titanium, the dose rate of titanium consists mainly of the characteristic line emission at k-$\alpha \cong 4.512$ keV, while the dose rate of molybdenum consists mainly of bremsstrahlung. The characteristic line of molybdenum would be at 17.48 keV.

In the case of ceramics, the X-ray emission of Si_3N_4 is significantly higher compared to other materials shown in Figure 6. It may be due to the nitrides mixed to the silicon. Hence more investigation is necessary to understand the X-ray emission and dose rates on the alloys and ceramics.

X-ray dose attenuation using a shielding material depends on the spectral distribution of the incident X-ray radiation, a shielding factor can only be calculated if the spectral photon flux is exactly known. Hence the spectral distribution of the emitted laser-X-ray radiation is critical for evaluating a protection approach [9]. In addition, the dose rates measured is a combination of bremsstrahlung and characteristic line emission for all the materials.

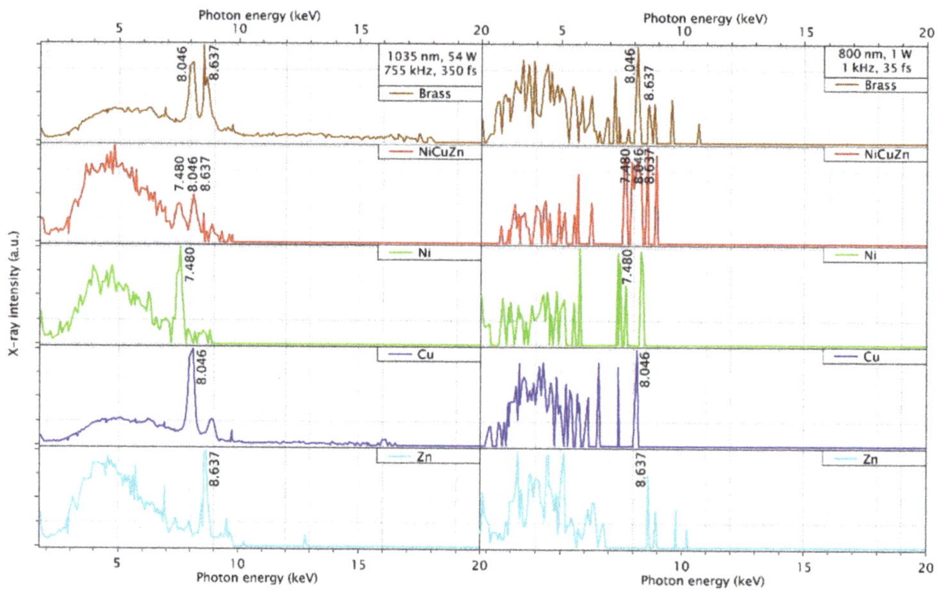

Figure 4. X-ray spectra measured for the different target material and the incident laser peak intensity listed as brass and NiCuZn alloy and its composition metals Ni, Cu, and Zn are investigated using a Silix lambda detector at a distance of 150 mm from interaction zone in air at an intensity 4.2×10^{14} W/cm^2 (**left**) and 2.3×10^{16} W/cm^2 (**right**) respectively for the above mentioned two lasers.

3.3. Discrepency in Dose Rates

This section will take a closer look at the dose rate over time since the laser spot is moving on the material in a spiral format during the material processing. Here, even small changes in laser intensity as well as the position of the focus undergo large effects on the generation of X-rays.

In Figure 7, we see the time-resolved measurement of the dose rate for stainless-steel with Coherent Monaco laser. The process takes about 49 s and consists of 20 spirals. The durations of the spirals are plotted at the top of the plot. The highest dose rate is observed when the laser focus is displaced by ~0.4 mm above the material surface (solid lines in Figure 7). In this situation, the X-ray emission stays at an almost constant level during the entire process duration. When the focus is set at the material surface (dashed lines) the X-ray emission drops after an initial high peak. Additionally, an oscillation is visible which correlates well with the time evolution of the spirals. The strong discrepancy induced by a small shift in focus position is only present at high laser irradiance. In the lower irradiance regime ($<10^{14}$ W/cm^2) the X-ray emission is strongest when the laser focus is set at the material surface, at an overall lower emission level.

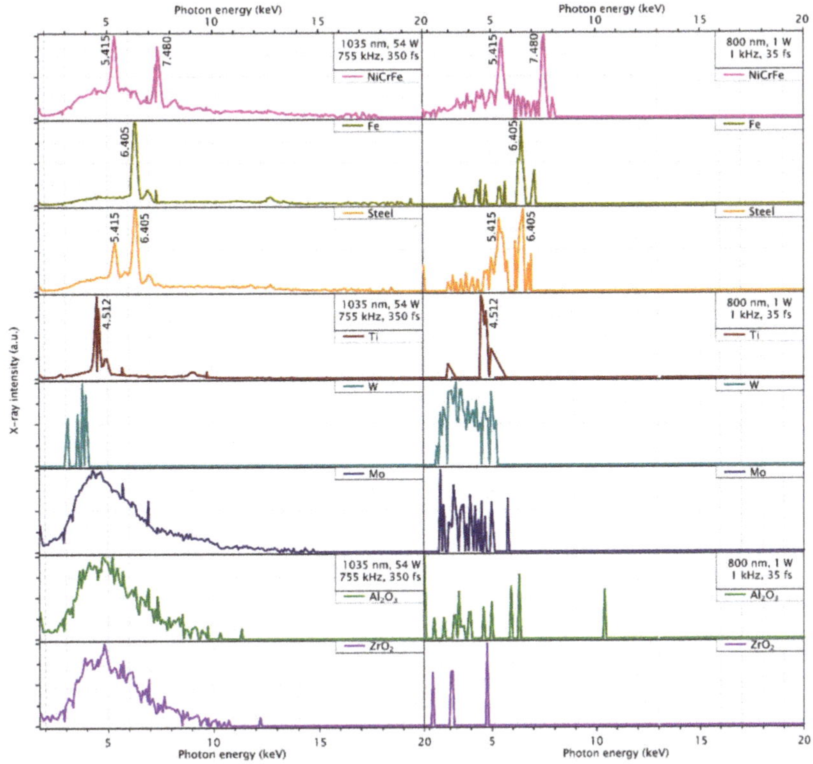

Figure 5. X-ray spectra measured for on the different target material and the incident laser peak intensity listed as NiCrFe and stainless-steel alloys and iron, titanium, tungsten, and molybdenum are investigated using the Silix lambda detector at a distance of 150 mm from the interaction zone in air at an intensity 4.2×10^{14} W/cm^2 (**left**), 2.3×10^{16} W/cm^2 (**right**) respectively for the above mentioned two lasers. The measured spectra of ceramics Al_2O_3 and ZrO_2 are plotted in the same experimental conditions.

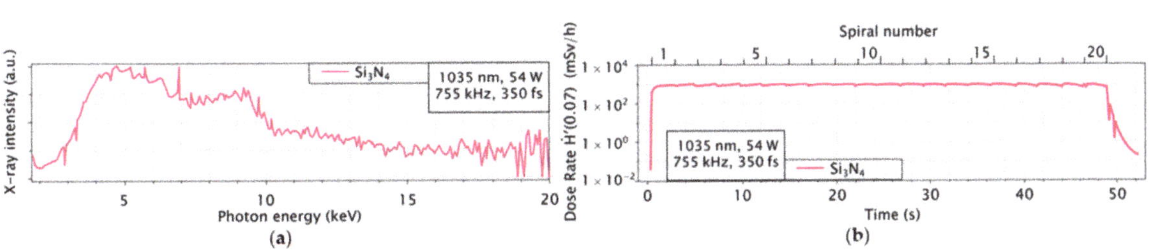

Figure 6. Shown in (**a**) is the spectrum of Si_3N_4 measured with the Silix lambda and in (**b**) is the corresponding dose rate over time measured with the OD-02.

This observation supports the idea that particle and/or plasma shielding strongly affects the X-ray generation for high repetition rate processes at high laser intensities. In this scenario, a slight shift of the focus above the material surface may increase coupling efficiency of laser energy into the ablation plume of previous ablation events, and thus increases the amount of X-ray emission from the re-heated ablation plume. This effect is for high laser intensities most dominant as a large and long living plume can be present.

At lower laser intensities the ablation plume is weaker and the effect disappears to a point where the ablation rate of a defocused laser beam is lower resulting in lower X-ray emission compared to the focused beam.

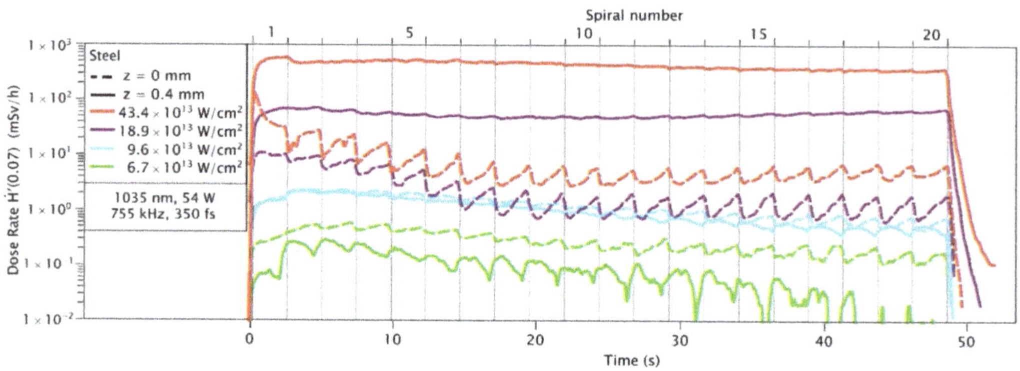

Figure 7. Dose rate $\dot{H}'(0.07)$ recorded during different laser processing steps as function of the processing time. The OD-02 dosimeter was placed at a distance of 150 mm from the interaction zone. Each of the individual processing steps is marked by a number on the top of the graph and separated by vertical lines. The laser intensity is 4.2×10^{14} W/cm^2 at a repetition rate 755 kHz and the focal spot diameter 22 µm.

3.4. Comparison Silix and OD-02

The X-ray radiation during the micromachining is measured with two detection systems. For the dose rate measurements, the Silix lamda spectrodosimeter is used in addition to a highly sensitive ionisation chamber (OD-02). In addition to the dose rate, the Silix lambda simultaneously measures the spectrum in the X-ray energy range 2–20 keV. The measurement time for the dose rate of the Silix lambda spectrodosimeter is set to 6 s. For the dose rate measurements of the OD-02, the measurement time is 0.078 s. In order to compare both measurements, the measured dose rates shown in Figure 8 were averaged over the whole scanning time.

From the Figure 8, all the materials follow a similar trend. For a comparison of the two detectors, the maximum and average X-ray dose rates from the OD-02 detector are reported in Table 3, together with the X-ray dose rates from the Silix lambda spectrodosimeter for the two laser systems at the respective maximum intensity. The measurements of the two devices are in good agreement. The strong deviation of more than 70% in the case of Si_3N_4 can be explained by the spectrum, as the measured X-ray radiation exceeds the measurement range of the Silix lambda spectrodosimeter. However, the X-ray energy regime should be considered while comparing these two detectors. OD-02 is specified 6–100 keV and Silix lambda X-ray spectrometer is specified 2–20 keV. The deviations in the measurements can be explained by the different measuring ranges as well as the spectral radiation depending on laser parameters and the material.

Table 3. Comparison of the measured dose rates from the Silix and the OD-02.

Dose Rate $H'(0.07)$ mSv/h	KMLabs Dragon 2.26×10^{16} W/cm^2			Coherent Monaco 4.22×10^{14} W/cm^2		
	OD-02	**OD-02 (Mean)**	**Silix Lambda**	**OD-02**	**OD-02 (Mean)**	**Silix Lambda**
Brass	0.10	0.05	0.09	748	305	171
NiCuZn	0.13	0.05	0.09	248	33	33
Cu	0.15	0.11	0.12	678	229	212
Ni	0.13	0.06	0.08	70	0.77	5.46
Zn	0.06	0.04	0.04	53	10	14
NiCrFe	0.40	0.13	0.30	822	351	215
Steel	0.29	0.09	0.15	432	295	169
Fe	0.08	0.05	0.05	1220	453	237
Mo	0.07	0.06	0.04	745	610	231
Ti	0.05	0.04	0.05	793	166	159
W	0.13	0.12	0.10	72	0.16	2.98
Al_2O_3	0.0024	0.0011	-	21	20	10
ZrO_2	0.0031	0.0007	-	25	18	12
Si_3N_4		-	-	988	889	268

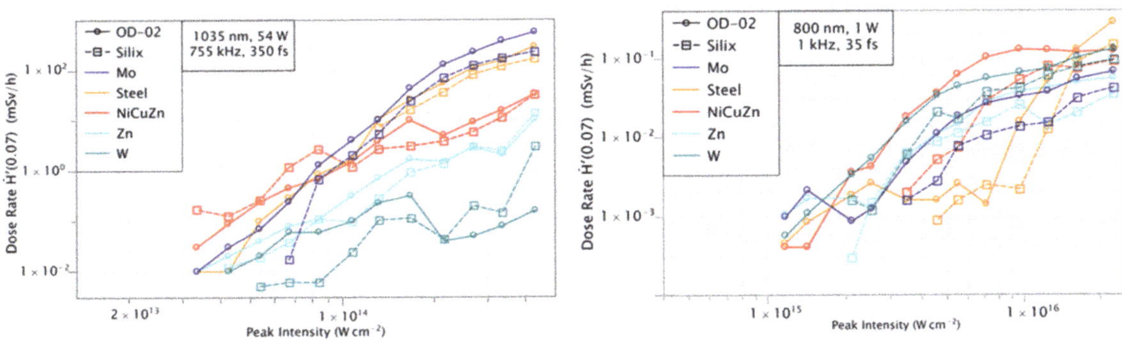

Figure 8. Comparison of the accumulated dose rates using Silix lambda and OD-02 detectors for an intensity range 5×10^{14} and 5×10^{16} W/cm^2 by tuning the laser pulse energy for Coherent Monaco (**a**) and KMLabs Dragon laser (**b**). The dotted line represents the dose measurement with the Silix and the solid line the dose measurement with the OD-02.

4. Conclusions

In conclusion, we have presented a comparison of the emitted X-ray dose rate from laser-driven plasma of several target materials, including pure metals, different alloys, and ceramics using two different ultrafast laser systems.

The X-ray dose rate strongly depends on different laser parameters, e.g., wavelength, pulse duration, repetition rate, and the pulse energy. For a laser intensity above 10^{13} W/cm^2, all target materials investigated, show a potential hazardous X-ray dose rate which increases with laser intensity. The use of mid-infrared laser wavelengths and multi-kHz repetition rates leads to an additional increase in dose rate compared to standard near-infrared kHz laser systems, even for lower pulse energies. A strong dependency of the dose rate on the laser focus position with respect to the target surface indicates that an additional factor, such as heat accumulation or particle/plasma shielding, may contribute to the X-ray emission during material processing. Such effects are especially relevant in case of multi-pulse irradiation with high repetition rate lasers.

A proper prediction of the X-ray emission remains as a challenge because of many parameters concerning both the laser system and the target, which affect the generation process during laser–material interaction. In order to relate the X-ray dose rate estimation with the spectral information from the laser produced plasma, we have used of a calibrated Silix lambda spectrodosimeter. This detector provides a photon energy spectrum of the X-ray radiation with a dose rate, offering more information about the origin of the X-ray emission below 20 keV. The dose rates from the Silix lambda spectrodosimeter compared with a commonly used OD-02 dosimeter for all the measurements, showing a good agreement between the two detectors.

Author Contributions: Conceptualization, T.P., P.J., J.-W.V., U.M. and M.K.; Investigation, P.M. and J.F.D.; Original draft preparation, P.M., P.S., J.F.D., G.D. and M.K.; writing—review and editing, P.M., P.S., J.F.D., G.D. and M.K.; Supervision, T.P., P.J., J.-W.V., U.M. and M.K. All authors have read and agreed to the published version of the manuscript.

Funding: German Research Foundation under Germany's Excellence Strategy within the Cluster of Excellence Quantum Frontiers EXC-2123 and Germany's Excellence Strategy within the Cluster of Excellence PhoenixD (EXC 2122, Project ID 390833453).

Institutional Review Board Statement: Not applicable.

Informed Consent Statement: Not applicable.

Data Availability Statement: Data sharing is not applicable to this article.

Acknowledgments: The publication of this article was funded by the Open Access Fund of the Leibniz Universität Hannover.

Conflicts of Interest: The authors declare no conflict of interest.

References

1. Gower, M.C. Industrial applications of laser micromachining. *Opt. Express* **2000**, *7*, 56–67. [CrossRef] [PubMed]
2. Cheng, J.; Liu, C.-S.; Shang, S.; Liu, D.; Perrie, W.; Dearden, G.; Watkins, K. A review of ultrafast laser materials micromachining. *Opt. Laser Technol.* **2013**, *46*, 88–102. [CrossRef]
3. Thogersen, J.; Borowiec, A.; Haugen, H.K.; McNeill, F.E.; Stronach, I.M. X-ray emission from femtosecond laser micromachining. *Appl. Phys. A* **2001**, *73*, 361–363. [CrossRef]
4. Weber, R.; Giedl-Wagner, R.; Förster, D.J.; Pauli, A.; Graf, T.; Balmer, J.E. Expected x-ray dose rates resulting from industrial ultrafast laser applications. *Appl. Phys. A* **2019**, *125*, 1–12. [CrossRef]
5. Legall, H.; Bonse, J.; Krüger, J. Review of x-ray exposure and safety issues arising from ultra-short pulse laser material processing. *J. Radiol. Prot.* **2021**, *41*, R28. [CrossRef] [PubMed]
6. Bunte, J.; Barcikowski, S.; Püster, T.; Burmester, T.; Brose, M.; Ludwig, T. Secondary Hazards: Particle and X-Ray Emission. In *Femtosecond Technology for Technical and Medical Applications*; Dausinger, F., Lubatschowski, H., Lichtner, F., Eds.; Springer: Berlin, Germany, 2004; Volume 96, pp. 309–321.
7. Kephart, J.F.; Godwin, R.P.; McCall, G.H. Bremsstrahlung emission from laser—Produced plasmas. *Appl. Phys. Lett.* **1974**, *25*, 108–109. [CrossRef]
8. Legall, H.; Schwanke, C.; Pentzien, S.; Dittmar, G.; Bonse, J.; Krüger, J. X-ray emission as a potential hazard during ultrashort pulse laser material processing. *Appl. Phys. A* **2018**, *124*, 1–8. [CrossRef]
9. Legall, H.; Schwanke, C.; Bonse, J.; Krüger, J. X-ray radiation protection aspects during ultrashort laser processing. *J. Laser Appl.* **2020**, *32*, 022004. [CrossRef]
10. Behrens, R.; Pullner, B.; Reginatto, M. X-ray emission from materials processing lasers. *Radiat. Prot. Dosim.* **2019**, *183*, 361–374. [CrossRef]
11. Kruer, W.L. *The Physics of Laser Plasma Interactions*, 1st ed.; CRC Press: Boca Raton, FL, USA, 2019.
12. Weisshaupt, J.; Juvé, V.; Holtz, M.; Ku, S.; Woerner, M.; Elsaesser, T.; Ališauskas, S.; Pugžlys, A.; Baltuška, A. High-brightness table-top hard X-ray source driven by sub-100-femtosecond mid-infrared pulses. *Nat. Photonics* **2014**, *8*, 927–930. [CrossRef]
13. Schroeder, W.A.; Omenetto, F.G.; Borisov, A.B.; Longworth, J.W.; McPherson, A.; Jordan, C.; Boyer, K.; Kondo, K.; Rhodes, C.K. Pump laser wavelength-dependent control of the efficiency of kilovolt x-ray emission from atomic clusters. *J. Phys. B At. Mol. Opt. Phys.* **1998**, *31*, 5031–5051. [CrossRef]
14. Di Niso, F.; Gaudiuso, C.; Sibillano, T.; Mezzapesa, F.P.; Ancona, A.; Lugarà, P.M. Role of heat accumulation on the incubation effect in multi-shot laser ablation of stainless steel at high repetition rates. *Opt. Express* **2014**, *22*, 12200–12210. [CrossRef]
15. Vorobyev, A.Y.; Guo, C. Direct observation of enhanced residual thermal energy coupling to solids in femtosecond laser ablation. *Appl. Phys. Lett.* **2005**, *86*, 011916. [CrossRef]
16. König, J.; Nolte, S.; Tünnermann, A. Plasma evolution during metal ablation with ultrashort laser pulses. *Opt. Express* **2005**, *13*, 10597–10607. [CrossRef] [PubMed]

17. Chen, F.F. *Introduction to Plasma Physics*; Plenum Press: New York, NY, USA, 1974.
18. Attwood, D. *Soft X-rays and Extreme Ultraviolet Radiation: Principles and Applications*; Cambridge University Press: Cambridge, UK, 2000.
19. Eliezer, S. *The Interaction of High-Power Lasers with Plasmas*; CRC Press: Boca Raton, FL, USA, 2002.
20. Forslund, D.W.; Kindel, J.M.; Lee, K. Theory of hot-electron spectra at high laser intensity. *Phys. Rev. Lett.* **1977**, *39*, 284–288. [CrossRef]
21. German Federal Office for Radiation Protection. Limit Values in Radiation Protection. Available online: https://www.bfs.de/EN/topics/ion/radiation-protection/limit-values/limit-values_node.html (accessed on 7 July 2021).
22. Sankar, P.; Thomas, J.; Shashikala, H.D.; Philip, R. Enhanced bremsstrahlung X-ray emission from Ag nanoparticles irradiated by ultrashort laser pulses. *Opt. Mater.* **2019**, *92*, 30–35. [CrossRef]

materials

MDPI

Communication

Micromachining of Invar with 784 Beams Using 1.3 ps Laser Source at 515 nm

Petr Hauschwitz [1,2,*], Bohumil Stoklasa [3], Jiří Kuchařík [3], Hana Turčičová [1], Michael Písařík [1], Jan Brajer [1], Danijela Rostohar [1], Tomáš Mocek [1], Martin Duda [1,2] and Antonio Lucianetti [1]

1 HiLASE Centre, Institute of Physics, Czech Academy of Sciences, Za Radnici 828, 25241 Dolni Brezany, Czech Republic; hana.turcicova@hilase.cz (H.T.); Michael.Pisarik@Hilase.cz (M.P.); jan.brajer@Hilase.cz (J.B.); danijela.rostohar@hilase.cz (D.R.); tomas.mocek@hilase.cz (T.M.); martin.duda@hilase.cz (M.D.); antonio.lucianetti@hilase.cz (A.L.)

2 Faculty of Nuclear Sciences and Physical Engineering, Czech Technical University in Prague, Brehova 7, 115 19 Prague, Czech Republic

3 Meopta-optika, s.r.o., Kabelikova 1, 750 02 Prerov, Czech Republic; bohumil.stoklasa@meopta.com (B.S.); Jiri.Kucharik@meopta.com (J.K.)

* Correspondence: petr.hauschwitz@hilase.cz

Received: 17 June 2020; Accepted: 1 July 2020; Published: 2 July 2020

Abstract: To fulfil the requirements for high-resolution organic light-emitting diode (OLED) displays, precise and high-quality micrometer-scale patterns have to be fabricated inside metal shadow masks. Invar has been selected for this application due to its unique properties, especially a low coefficient of thermal expansion. In this study, a novel cost-efficient method of multi-beam micromachining of invar will be introduced. The combination of a Meopta beam splitting, focusing and monitoring module with a galvanometer scanner and HiLASE high-energy pulse laser system emitting ultrashort pulses at 515 nm allows drilling and cutting of invar foil with 784 beams at once with high precision and almost no thermal effects and heat-affected zone, thus significantly improving the throughput and efficiency.

Keywords: multi-beam micromachining; beam splitting; invar; shadow masks; OLED

1. Introduction

Invar is a Fe–Ni class alloy with unique properties such as excellent strength, impact toughness, processability and a low coefficient of thermal expansion [1]. Those properties are making invar very attractive for various industrial applications including bi-metal applications, storage tanks of liquified natural gas, and shadow masks for production of organic light-emitting diodes (OLED) [2]. High-resolution shadow masks are crucial in red, green and blue evaporation process of organic luminous materials during the production of OLED displays [3]. The geometry, size and overall quality of holes in shadow mask are directly connected with OLED pixel quality [4]. Chemical etching is nowadays a common microfabrication method for production of OLED shadow mask [2]. However, it is a complicated multi-step process generally composed of coating, cleaning, exposure and an etching process with no control over the taper angle. Moreover, it is difficult to fabricate a pattern smaller than the material thickness due to isotropic manner of chemical etching and thus reach the high resolution required for future virtual reality displays [5,6].

As an alternative, laser micromachining provides high-quality, single-step and environmentally friendly approach without the use of chemicals. Laser microfabrication of shadow masks was investigated with several laser systems demonstrating 85 μm channels fabricated in polymethyl methacrylate with a CO_2 laser [7], 250 μm wide channels in wax using a CO_2 laser [8], 250 μm wide lines in plastics and glass with the use of a Nd:YAG laser at the fundamental wavelength of 1064 nm [9], or 140 μm lines fabricated in a steel shadow mask using the third harmonics of a Nd:YAG laser [10]. However, to produce high-resolution shadow masks with small features in a range of a few tens of microns, ultrashort pulsed lasers have to be deployed [8,11–13]. Invar drilling with ultrashort laser systems was investigated, demonstrating 200 μm diameter in invar utilizing a 785 nm Ti:shappire laser [4] and hole dimensions below 30 μm with excellent quality and minimal heat-affected zone [6].

However, the main drawback of ultrashort pulse laser micromachining is the processing speed which limits the widespread use in industry, especially in the case of a common single-beam direct laser writing approach. Moreover, with the emerging high-power ultrashort laser systems [14], high-quality invar micromachining becomes very inefficient as most of the laser power cannot be used. This is due to the necessity of processing close to the damage threshold to maintain high quality and minimal heat affected zone. Therefore, new techniques for rapid large-scale processing are required. The most promising rapid large-scale techniques include polygonal scanning systems [15,16], direct laser interference patterning [17,18] and multi-beam scanning approaches [19].

Beam splitting using a diffractive optical element (DOE) in a combination with galvanometer scanner and high-power ultrashort laser systems is a promising way to meet industry standards in high speed processing of large areas. DOE beam-splitter distributes the incident laser beam intensity into the desired far-field pattern which is usually an 1D or 2D array of beams. Each beam has the same characteristics as the original beam, except for pulse energy and angle of propagation [20]. Multibeam systems providing high throughputs due to beam splitting into 10–100 beamlets have recently become commercially available on the market able to drill holes in the range of 20 μm in diameter into 20 μm thick metal foils [21,22].

Consequently, this study aims to demonstrate a technology capable of producing microstructures in a cost-efficient way by introducing a prototype of a Meopta beam splitting, focusing and monitoring module. The module divides an initial high-quality beam into more than 700 beamlets for parallel processing of a thin invar foil. By utilizing the module in a combination with HiLASE high-energy pulse ultrashort laser system and a galvanometer scanner, it was possible to freely adjust the dimensions and geometry of produced microholes suitable for the production of OLED displays.

2. Materials and Methods

Invar (FeNi36) foils provided by Goodfellow GmbH (Friedberg, Germany) with a thickness of 20 μm and dimensions of 50 × 50 mm were used as received (Ra~0.07 μm). The foils were treated by Perla laser system from HiLASE (Dolni Brezany, Czech Republic), equipped with second harmonic generation module emitting at wavelength of 515 nm, with pulse duration of 1.3 ps, beam quality factor M2 better than 1.5, repetition rate of 1 kHz and pulse energy up to 10 mJ [14,23]. The generated beam (Figure 1c) was guided through the galvanometer scanner without F-theta lens into the optical module developed by Meopta-optika, s.r.o., consisting of a DOE beamsplitter, 100 mm focusing lens and a polarizing beamsplitter for pattern observation on the sample surface. The module is responsible for focusing and splitting the initial beam by means of diffractive optics into a matrix of 28 × 28 beamlets with homogeneous distribution across the whole pattern and suppression of zero order diffraction. The module allows the separation distance between beamlets to be adjusted by changing the distance between the DOE and focusing lens. Beam splitter and camera allows to monitor the intensity, shape and focal position of each beamlet. The beamsplitter passes linearly polarized beam on to the sample surface. The reflected light from the sample with random polarization is then able to reach the camera. The separation distance between each beamlet on the sample plane was 150 μm. The sample was placed vertically on to the vacuum holder with an optional connection to the cooling water circuit. The whole setup is depicted in Figure 1.

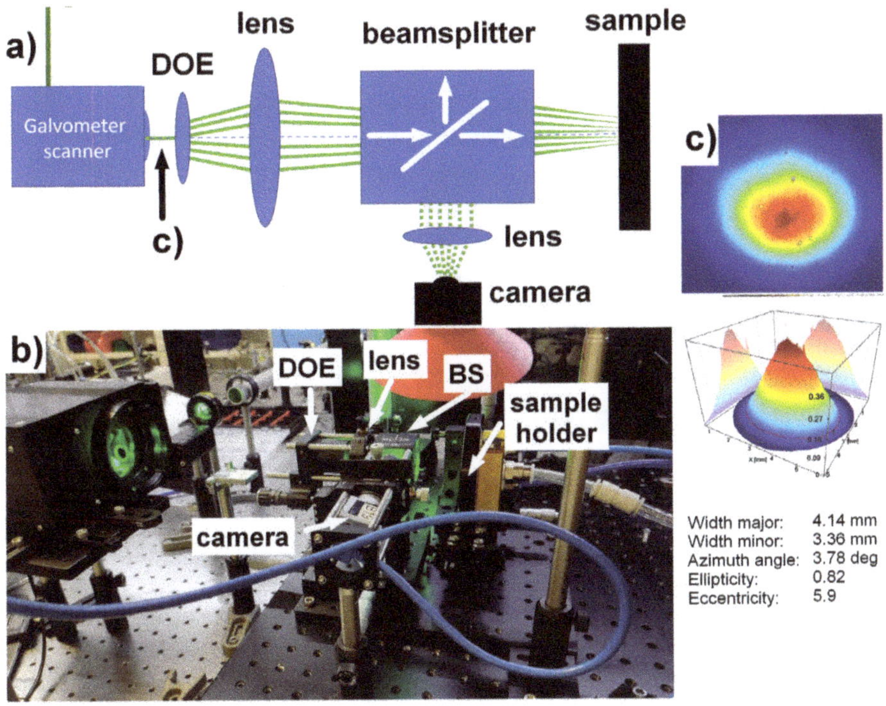

Figure 1. Schematics (**a**) and photo (**b**) of the experimental setup with a detail of input beam (**c**).

Topography of selected surfaces was analyzed with a laser scanning confocal microscope Olympus OLS 5000. The pattern shape and beamlets intensity distribution were captured by a Basler ace acA4024-29um camera with pixel size of 1.85 µm.

3. Results and Discussion

The impact of the experimental setup misalignments on the resulting multi-spot pattern homogeneity, the tolerance of deviation angles during beam deflections affecting the pattern shape, as well as the laser and processing parameters for high-quality cutting and drilling have been studied in a set of experiments.

First, the pattern homogeneity had to be adjusted to reach the same intensity in each beamlet by tilting the beam-splitting element. The pattern shape was observed in real-time on a camera inside the Meopta beam-splitting module during the alignment, as depicted in Figure 2.

As shown in Figure 2, the pattern shape reflected from the sample surface exhibits undesired speckles, which can be further improved by mirror polishing of the sample. In addition to pattern homogeneity, the working plane was easily found by observing the pattern on camera as the sharp beam profile of each beamlet (inset of Figure 2b) can be observed only when the sample is located exactly in the focal plane.

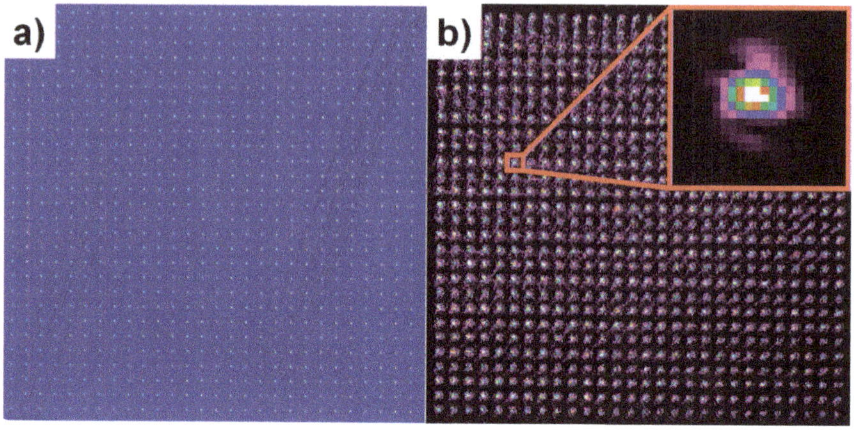

Figure 2. Final pattern shape on camera in a sample plane (**a**) and the same pattern reflected from the sample surface (**b**).

In the next step, the sample was irradiated with 100,000 consecutive laser pulses with energy of 0.6 mJ which corresponds to the fluence of 0.28 J/cm^2 for each beamlet. The first experiments revealed extensive heat accumulation connected with a large heat-affected zone and interconnection of microholes into one hole in the center of the pattern due to extensive heating and melting (Figure 3a). Consequently, the samples were placed on a water-cooled holder to minimize the effect of heat accumulation, as depicted in Figure 3b.

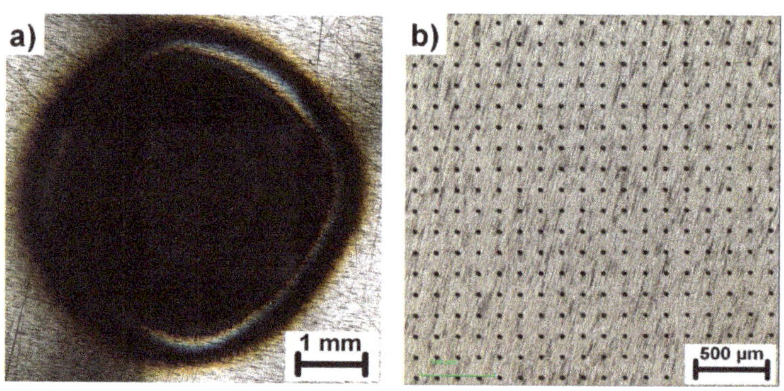

Figure 3. Overview of the heat affected zone on the sample processed without water-cooled holder (**a**) compared to the sample processed with the water-cooled holder (**b**). Both samples were processed with the same fluence of 0.28 J/cm^2 and 100,000 pulses.

To determine an optimal processing window for high-quality multi-beam drilling, different combinations of laser parameters were analyzed. First, the ablation threshold for the simultaneous drilling of 784 holes was estimated. Figure 4a presents a microhole ablated close to the ablation threshold with 100,000 pulses and pulse energy of 0.3 mJ in the initial beam (beamlet fluence of 0.15 J/cm^2). No ablation was observed for pulse energies below 0.3 mJ, hence it is considered as the ablation threshold.

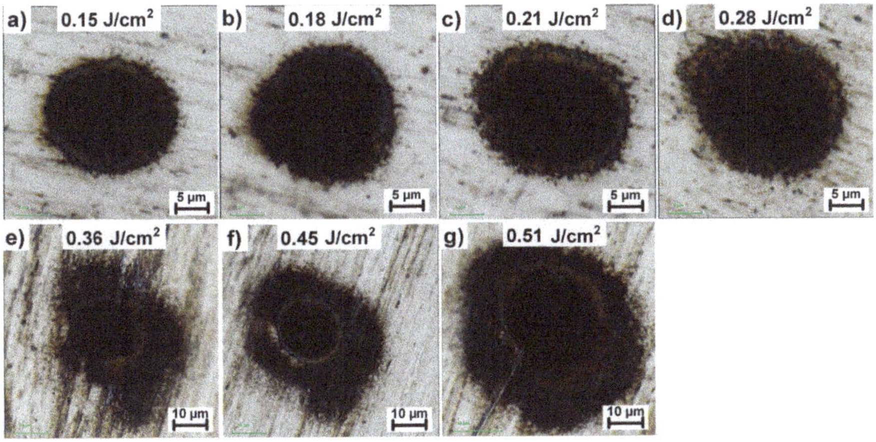

Figure 4. Evolution of microhole quality and heat affected zone with the increase in fluence. Sample is irradiated with 100,000 consecutive laser pulses. (**a**–**d**) gentle ablation regime, (**e**–**g**) high fluence regime.

The extension of the heat-affected zone and overall hole quality have been examined using different pulse energies in the range of 0.3 mJ to 1.2 mJ which correspond to the beamlet fluence of 0.15 J/cm^2 to 0.51 J/cm^2, as shown in Figure 4.

In line with the results presented in Figure 4, two ablation regimes have been identified. The highest quality microholes have been reached in a gentle ablation regime for fluences up to two-times the ablation threshold, i.e., up to 0.28 J/cm^2. In this case, the extension of the heat-affected zone was found to be less than 3 µm. By increasing the fluence over this value, the quality of microholes significantly deteriorated due to the extensive heat-affected zone. Moreover, as shown in Figure 5a, the removal rate (ablated volume per time and power) for microholes drilled in a higher fluence regime over 0.28 J/cm^2 is much smaller compared to lower fluences.

This phenomenon may be explained by the decrease in beam quality connected with high pulse energies which may overcome the tolerances of a diffractive beamsplitter and thus affect the intensity distribution within the beamlet. This issue will be further addressed in the following research.

On the other hand, the removal rate is sharply increasing with the fluence in the gentle ablation regime reaching the peak around 0.28 J/cm^2, which was identified as the optimal fluence for effective drilling.

Furthermore, the number of pulses required for piercing the sample have been determined (Figure 5b). With the threshold fluence of 0.15 J/cm^2 at least 2.5 million pulses were required to pierce through the 20 µm thick invar foil, thus removing less than 0.01 nm per pulse. By increasing the fluence above the ablation threshold, the sample was pierced with less than 700,000 pulses for fluences between 0.18 J/cm^2 and 0.28 J/cm^2. The lowest number of pulses required for piercing the foil was in the case of 0.28 J/cm^2 with only 500,000 pulses, which is in accordance with the optimal removal rate value. For the higher fluence regime, the sample was pierced only in the case of 0.36 J/cm^2 after exposition with 1 million pulses. Higher fluences did not lead to cutting through the invar foil even after 3 million pulses. Therefore, the optimal processing window for effective micromachining of invar foil has been identified as 0.18 J/cm^2 to 0.28 J/cm^2.

Additionally, the effect of laser parameters on the microhole diameter input/output aspect ratio have been studied. As demonstrated in Figure 5c, the aspect ratio decreases with higher fluences as well as with increasing number of pulses. Similarly, the shape of the exit diameter also improves with a higher number of applied pulses (Figure 6).

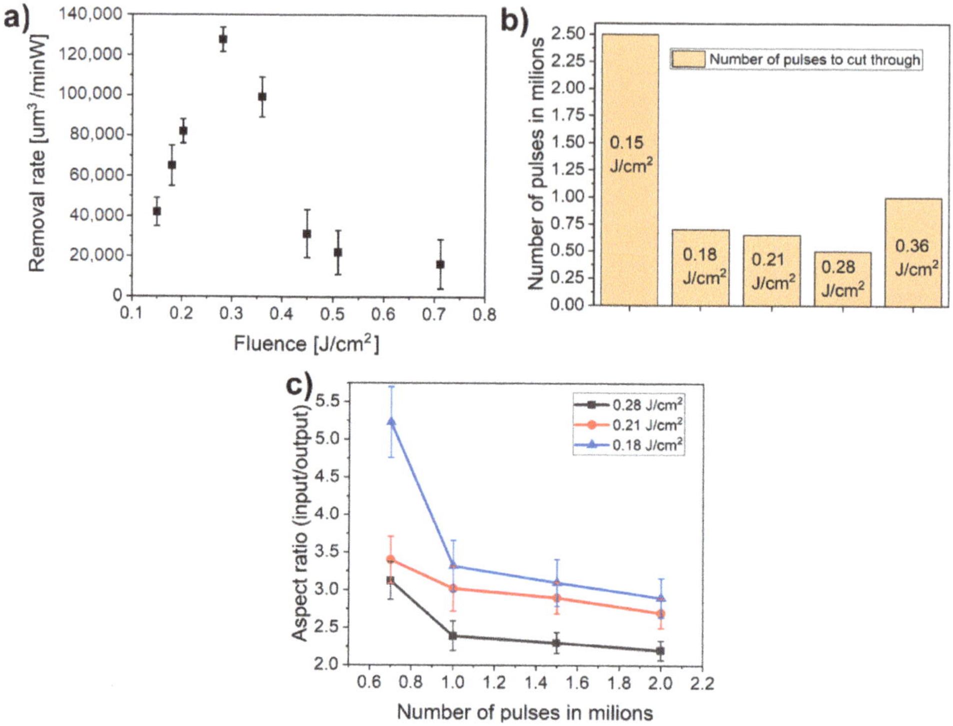

Figure 5. (**a**) Removal rate as a function of fluence; (**b**) Number of pulses necessary to cut through the whole sample; (**c**) Evolution of the aspect ratio as a function of number of pulses.

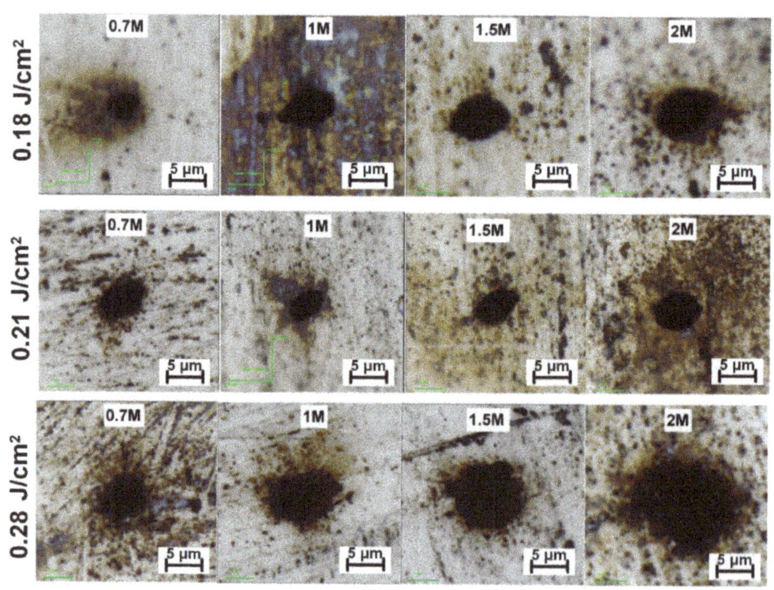

Figure 6. Geometry evolution of exit hole diameters with increasing number of pulses from 0.7 million to 2 million pulses.

Generally, the exit microhole diameter is larger and less elliptical for higher fluences and pulse counts, as demonstrated in Figure 6. The best aspect ratio and circularity were reached for the sample irradiated with 2 million pulses and 0.28 J/cm^2 per beamlet.

Following up on the optimal parameters, a galvanometer scanner was deployed to deflect the beam in a small area between microholes to fabricate different geometries on the invar foil. Since the separation distance between produced microholes is 150 μm, the square with a side width of 100 μm was chosen for the cutting experiment. To improve cutting efficiency, the input cut width was increased by cutting 15 squares with the same center position and decreasing diameter per 3 μm for each square. The cutting speed was adjusted to 1 mm/s to ensure high enough overlapping of ~95% with the laser repetition rate of 1 kHz. The cutting results are depicted in Figure 7.

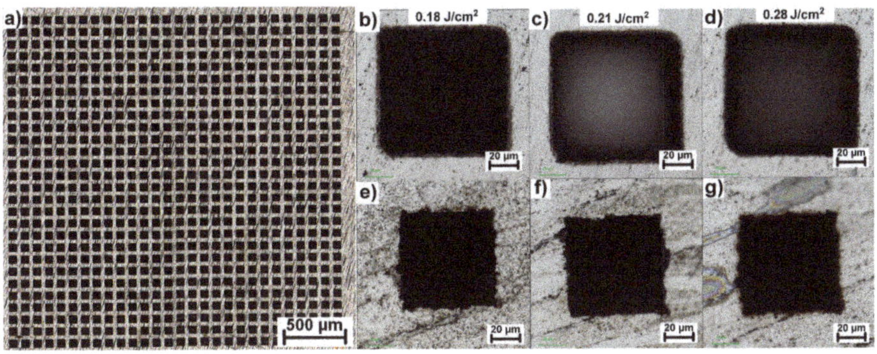

Figure 7. (**a**) Overview of a pattern cut with a combination of 28 × 28 beamsplitter and galvanometer scanner; (**b–d**) details of a square cuts fabricated with different fluences inside the optimal processing window and 400 overscans and their corresponding exit sides (**e–g**).

As demonstrated in Figure 7, it was possible to fabricate square geometries and cut through the invar foil with all 784 beams at once. The complete penetration was reached for 700, 440 and 250 overscans for the fluences of 0.18 J/cm^2, 0.21 J/cm^2, and 0.28 J/cm^2, respectively. In addition, the consistency of square shape and their separation distance was measured on 20 randomly selected squares across the pattern confirming the exact same parameters across the pattern with the standard deviation smaller than 3 μm in all cases.

4. Conclusions

Utilization of a Meopta beam-splitting, focusing and monitoring module in a combination with HiLASE high-energy pulse laser system emitting ultrashort pulses at 515 nm resulted in efficient cutting and drilling of invar foil simultaneously by 784 beamlets, arranged in a matrix of 28 × 28 beamlets. The features of optical module allow the setup to be aligned quickly to reach homogeneous intensity distribution across the whole pattern, as well as focus adjustment. By determining the ablation threshold, optimal fluence levels and pulse counts, the optimal processing window for effective high-quality drilling and cutting with heat affected zone below 3 μm has been identified as 0.18 J/cm^2 to 0.28 J/cm^2. The combination of galvanometer scanning head and beam-splitting module enabled multi-beam fabrication of square-shaped microholes with adjustable dimensions. With the use of this solution, the throughput can be increased 7 times compared to the state of the art commercial multi-beam systems and more than 700 times compared to the single beam approach, thus showing high potential for significant improvement in the fabrication speed and efficiency during the production of invar shadow masks.

Author Contributions: Conceptualization, B.S., M.P.; Methodology, B.S., M.P., P.H.; Validation, B.S., M.P., P.H., J.B.; Formal analysis, B.S., J.K.; Investigation, P.H., B.S., H.T., J.K.; Resources, B.S., H.T., M.D.; Writing-Original

Draft, P.H.; Writing, Review and Editing, P.H., J.K., D.R., A.L., M.D.; Visualization, P.H.; Supervision, B.S., J.B., M.P., T.M.; Project administration, J.B., B.S.; Funding acquisition, B.S., M.P., J.B., T.M. All authors have read and agreed to the published version of the manuscript.

Funding: This work is a result of project TN01000008 NCK CEPO—New methods for laser micromachining. This work was co-financed by the European Regional Development Fund and the state budget of the Czech Republic (project HiLASE CoE: Grant No. CZ.02.1.01/0.0/0.0/15_006/0000674) and from the European Union's Horizon 2020 research and innovation programme (Grant agreement NO 739573) and by the Ministry of Education, Youth and Sports of the Czech Republic (Programme NPU I Project No. LO1602).

Conflicts of Interest: The authors declare no conflict of interest. The funders had no role in the design of the study; in the collection, analyses, or interpretation of data; in the writing of the manuscript, or in the decision to publish the results.

References

1. Ono, F.; Hamatani, Y.; Mukumoto, Y.; Komatsu, S.; Ishikawa, N.; Chimi, Y.; Iwase, A.; Kambara, T.; Mueller, C.; Neumann, R. Modification of Fe–Ni Invar alloys by high-energy ion beams. *Nucl. Instrum. Methods Phys. Res. Sect. B Beam Interac. Mater. At.* **2003**, *206*, 295–298. [CrossRef]
2. Kim, C. Production of shadow-mask-improved technology. *J. Mater. Process. Technol.* **2002**, *127*, 409–418. [CrossRef]
3. Shin, H.Y.; Suh, M.C. A study on full color organic light emitting diodes with blue common layer under the patterned emission layer. *Org. Electron.* **2014**, *15*, 2932–2941. [CrossRef]
4. Chung, I.-Y.; Kim, J.-D.; Kang, K.-H. Ablation drilling of invar alloy using ultrashort pulsed laser. *Int. J. Precis. Eng. Manuf.* **2009**, *10*, 11–16. [CrossRef]
5. Kim, S.H.; Choi, S.G.; Choi, W.K.; Yang, B.Y.; Lee, E.S. Pulse electrochemical machining on Invar alloy: Optical microscopic/SEM and non-contact 3D measurement study of surface analyses. *Appl. Surf. Sci.* **2014**, *314*, 822–831. [CrossRef]
6. Choi, W.; Kim, H.Y.; Jeon, J.W.; Chang, W.S.; Cho, S.H. Vibration-assisted femtosecond Laser drilling with controllable taper angles for AMOLED fine metal mask fabrication. *Materials* **2017**, *10*, 212. [CrossRef]
7. Klank, H.; Kutter, J.P.; Geschke, O. CO_2-laser micromachining and back-end processing for rapid production of PMMA-based microfluidic systems. *Lab Chip* **2002**, *2*, 242–246. [CrossRef]
8. Fan, Y.; Li, H.; Yi, Y.; Foulds, I.G. Laser micromachined wax-covered plastic paper as both sputter deposition shadow masks and deep-ultraviolet patterning masks for polymethylmethacrylate-based microfluidic systems. *J. Micro/Nanolithogr. MEMS MOEMS* **2013**, *12*, 049701. [CrossRef]
9. Tahir, B.A.; Ahmed, R.; Ashiq, M.G.; Ahmed, A.; Saeed, M.A. Cutting of nonmetallic materials using Nd: YAG laser beam. *Chin. Phys. B* **2012**, *21*, 044201. [CrossRef]
10. Shiu, P.; Knopf, G.; Ostojic, M.; Nikumb, S. Rapid fabrication of tooling for microfluidic devices via laser micromachining and hot embossing. *J. Micromech. Microeng.* **2008**, *18*, 025012. [CrossRef]
11. Rizvi, N.H.; Apte, P. Developments in laser micro-machining techniques. *J. Mater. Process. Technol.* **2002**, *127*, 206–210. [CrossRef]
12. Kumar, A.; Gupta, A.; Kant, R.; Akhtar, S.N.; Tiwari, N.; Ramkumar, J.; Bhattacharya, S. Optimization of laser machining process for the preparation of photomasks, and its application to microsystems fabrication. *J. Micro/Nanolithogr. MEMS MOEMS* **2013**, *12*, 041203. [CrossRef]
13. Heo, J.; Min, H.; Lee, M. Laser micromachining of permalloy for fine metal mask. *Int. J. Precis. Eng. Manuf. Green Technol.* **2015**, *2*, 225–230. [CrossRef]
14. Smrž, M.; Novák, O.; Mužík, J.; Turčičová, H.; Chyla, M.; Nagisetty, S.S.; Vyvlečka, M.; Roškot, L.; Miura, T.; Černohorská, J.; et al. Advances in high-power, ultrashort pulse DPSSL technologies at HiLASE. *Appl. Sci.* **2017**, *7*, 1016. [CrossRef]
15. Mincuzzi, G.; Gemini, L.; Faucon, M.; Kling, R. Extending ultra-short pulse laser texturing over large area. *Appl. Surf. Sci.* **2016**, *386*, 65–71. [CrossRef]
16. De Loor, R. Polygon scanner system for ultra short pulsed laser micro-machining applications. *Phys. Proced.* **2013**, *41*, 544–551. [CrossRef]
17. Voisiat, B.; Gedvilas, M.; Indrišiūnas, S.; Račiukaitis, G. Picosecond-laser 4-beam-interference ablation as a flexible tool for thin film microstructuring. *Phys. Proced.* **2011**, *12*, 116–124. [CrossRef]

18. Hauschwitz, P.; Jagdheesh, R.; Alamri, S.; Rostohar, D.; Kunze, T.; Brajer, J.; Kopeček, J.; Mocek, T. Fabrication of functional superhydrophobic surfaces on carbon fibre reinforced plastics by IR and UV direct laser interference patterning. *Appl. Surf. Sci.* **2019**, *508*, 144817. [CrossRef]
19. Gillner, A.; Finger, J.; Gretzki, P.; Niessen, M.; Bartels, T.; Reininghaus, M. High power laser processing with ultrafast and multi-parallel beams. *J. Laser Micro Nanoeng.* **2019**, *14*, 129–137.
20. Katz, S.; Kaplan, N.; Grossinger, I. Using Diffractive Optical Elements: DOEs for beam shaping–fundamentals and applications. *Opt. Photonik* **2018**, *13*, 83–86. [CrossRef]
21. Holtkamp, J.; Eifel, S.; Ryll, J. Material Processing with Ultrashort-pulsed Lasers: Potentials—Requirements—Approaches. *Laser Tech. J.* **2014**, *11*, 36–39. [CrossRef]
22. Holtkamp, J. Pulsar Photonics: Innovative Beam Forming Concepts, Swissphotonics. Available online: https://swissphotonics.net/libraries.files/holtkamp (accessed on 1 July 2020).
23. Duda, M.; Novák, O.; Chyla, M.; Smrž, M.; Mocek, T. Balancing the conversion efficiency and beam quality of second harmonic generation of a two-picosecond Yb: YAG thin-disk laser. *Laser Phys.* **2020**, *30*, 025405. [CrossRef]

materials

MDPI

Article

Dual Laser Beam Processing of Semiconducting Thin Films by Excited State Absorption

Christoph Wenisch, Sebastian Engel, Stephan Gräf * and Frank A. Müller

Otto Schott Institute of Materials Research (OSIM), Friedrich Schiller University Jena, Löbdergraben 32, 07743 Jena, Germany; christoph.wenisch@uni-jena.de (C.W.); sebastian.engel@uni-jena.de (S.E.); frank.mueller@uni-jena.de (F.A.M.)

* Correspondence: stephan.graef@uni-jena.de

Abstract: We present a unique dual laser beam processing approach based on excited state absorption by structuring 200 nm thin zinc oxide films sputtered on fused silica substrates. The combination of two pulsed nanosecond-laser beams with different photon energies—one below and one above the zinc oxide band gap energy—allows for a precise, efficient, and homogeneous ablation of the films without substrate damage. Based on structuring experiments in dependence on laser wavelength, pulse fluence, and pulse delay of both laser beams, a detailed concept of energy transfer and excitation processes during irradiation was developed. It provides a comprehensive understanding of the thermal and electronic processes during ablation. To quantify the efficiency improvements of the dual-beam process compared to single-beam ablation, a simple efficiency model was developed.

Keywords: dual laser beam processing; excited state absorption; semiconducting thin films; multi-beam micromachining; nanosecond laser; stimulated emission depletion

Citation: Wenisch, C.; Engel, S.; Gräf, S.; Müller, F.A. Dual Laser Beam Processing of Semiconducting Thin Films by Excited State Absorption. *Materials* **2021**, *14*, 1256. https://doi.org/10.3390/ma14051256

Academic Editors: Jörg Krüger and Jörn Bonse

Received: 5 February 2021
Accepted: 1 March 2021
Published: 6 March 2021

1. Introduction

In 1994, Hell et al. theoretically described the stimulated emission depletion (STED) microscopy, which was experimentally demonstrated a few years later and today enables to resolve structures smaller than 10 nm [1–3]. Here, a Gaussian laser beam excites carriers, which are subsequently depleted back to their ground state by a second donut-shaped STED beam with a specific material-dependent wavelength. Although the focusability of both laser beams is still limited by diffraction, the resulting fluorescent volume is significantly decreased to the zero-intensity center of the STED beam [4].

This approach is now also used for structuring different photopolymers with feature sizes in the low double-digit nm range [5]. In this case, polymerization in the outer, high-intensive region of the donut-shaped beam is suppressed by stimulated depletion of the electrons required for polymerization or by activation of inhibitors. Unfortunately, the technique is limited to certain photopolymers and specific light sources. As an alternative, the structures can be transferred to other classes of materials by replica casting. However, direct sub-diffraction structuring of semiconductors and dielectrics using the STED-technique would improve flexibility, reduce process complexity, and lower overall manufacturing costs [6,7].

In this context, an approach proposed by Engel et al. [8] is very promising for optically active materials like direct semiconductors. Briefly, comparable to STED microscopy, a diffraction limited Gaussian laser beam with sufficient photon energy E_P is used to excite electrons into the conduction band (CB). A second temporally and spatially aligned donut-shaped beam with suitable E_P in the range of the optical band gap energy E_{BG} depletes these excited states and transfers the electrons back to the valence band (VB) by stimulated emission. The depletion only occurs in the high-intensive ring-shaped region of the beam, whereas the excited electrons in the zero-intensity center keep unaffected. This excited central region can subsequently absorb a third Gaussian laser beam by excited state absorption (ESA) at a wavelength otherwise transmitted in non-excited regions. Based on several processes such as intra-band absorption, avalanche effects, or coulomb explosion, the excess energy provided by this ESA-based process step is potentially suitable for sub-diffraction structuring, although the single beams are subject to diffraction limited focusing.

Based on previous studies [9], the focus of the present work is on the ESA-based ablation as an important element of the proposed sub diffraction direct laser writing technique (Figure 1a) [8]. Several studies already implemented an ESA-based microfabrication by a hybrid laser process of wide bandgap semiconductors such as fused silica, sapphire, or quartz [7,10–13]. The non-thermal ablation by the excitation of electrons above the vacuum energy improves ablation quality and decreases debris formation on the surface. For these dual-beam processes, Excimer and Raman lasers with wavelengths in the UV-range and (ultra-)short pulse lasers are most commonly used to increase absorption through photodissociation and changes in transient absorption [7]. This process is also applicable to lower bandgap semiconductors like gallium nitride, lithium niobate, and silicon carbide [13–17]. In this case, the single laser beams already exceed E_{BG}, but the excitation beyond vacuum energy for improved non-thermal ablation is only achieved by the dual-beam setup. Similarly, an increased absorption of a second, otherwise transmitted laser beam with $E_P < E_{BG}$, without exceeding the vacuum energy enables energy and cost efficient processing as already demonstrated for silicon and silicon carbide [18,19]. The key factor here is that commercially available, compact, and less expansive lasers in the visible and infrared spectrum can be used [18].

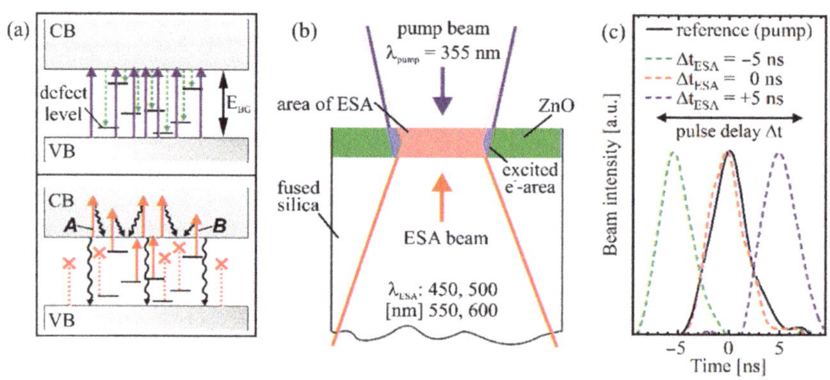

Figure 1. (**a**) Schematic illustration of the theoretical excited state absorption (ESA)-based ablation process with excitation (top) and a subsequent ESA (bottom), indicated by solid arrows. The electrons, excited prior by the pump beam with $E_P > E_{BG}$, rapidly relax radiative or non-radiative (dashed arrows) and partially migrate to defect levels located within the band gap. The subsequent ESA beams with $E_P < E_{BG}$ are absorbed by either intra-band ***A*** or defect level → conduction band (CB) ***B*** transitions, both enabled only by the prior pump excitation. Waved and dashed arrows indicate non-radiative and forbidden transitions, respectively. (**b**) Sample cross section of 1 mm thick fused silica substrate coated with a 200 nm thin ZnO layer. The beam directions are indicated by arrows. (**c**) Illustration of selected pulse delays $\Delta t = -5, 0, +5$ ns (dashed lines) and their temporal overlap with the pump pulse (solid line).

Based on this dual-beam ablation technique, Zinc(II) oxide (ZnO) as a direct bandgap semiconductor was used. Especially as thin films on an low absorbing substrate like fused silica, ZnO is commonly used in state-of-the-art applications like optoelectronics, metamaterials, or photonics, and is therefore a promising candidate for the ESA- and potential STED (in combination with ESA)-based ablation [20,21]. Thus, we focused on the selective, high quality thin film ablation at optimized processing parameters and cost efficiency. To analyze the suitability of the dual-beam setup for thin film structuring, the ablation process is studied with respect to the laser peak fluences, temporal delay, and wavelengths of the respective beams.

2. Materials and Methods

2.1. Sample Preparation and Characterization

Fused silica substrates (Infrasil 301, Heraeus, Hanau, Germany) with a thickness of 1 mm were coated by RF-magnetron sputtering of 200 nm thin ZnO layers using a sputtering time of 37 min at a pressure of 0.295 Pa, a gas flow (argon with 2% oxygen) of 6 cm^3/min, and a power of 150 W. The coated and uncoated samples were optically characterized by UV/VIS transmittance spectroscopy (MCS/100-3, J&M Analytik, Essingen, Germany).

The photoluminescence emission spectra of the coated samples were measured at room temperature with a HeCd laser (IK3202R-D, Kimmon Koha, Tokyo, Japan) at a laser wavelength λ = 325 nm and a continuous wave power of 17 mW. The fluorescence was detected at an angle of 45° by an optical spectrometer (Maya2000 Pro, Ocean Insight, Rostock, Germany). A 350 nm longpass filter (XUL0350, Asahi Spectra Co., Tokyo, Japan) was utilized in front of the detector to restrict the detection range above E_{BG}, where only weak emission is expected [22].

2.2. Laser Processing Setup

The dual-beam setup consists of two Nd:YAG lasers (SLI-10, Amplitude Systems) with a fundamental wavelength λ = 1064 nm. The third harmonic of one of them was used as pump beam with λ_{pump} = 355 nm and a pulse duration of τ_{pump} = 4.7 ns. The second Nd:YAG laser equipped with an additional optical parametric oscillator provides selected ESA beam wavelengths λ_{ESA} = 450, 500, 550, and 600 nm with τ_{ESA} = 4.8 ns. The beams were collinearly focused on the sample surface from opposite sides. Consequently, the ESA beams must pass the fused silica substrate (Figure 1b). For synchronization and temporal peak-to-peak delay, adjustments of both beams at the sample surface, a digital delay generator (DG535, Stanford Research Systems) and a silicon photodetector (ET-2000, EOT) were used. A digital oscilloscope (XDS3302 Plus, OWON Technology Inc., Zhangzhou, China) with a rise time < 1.2 ns monitored the temporal pulse shape (Figure 1c).

The ablation process was investigated using single laser pulses of the respective pump and ESA beams in order to exclude accumulation and incubation effects that would lead to an altered absorption. These include steady sample heating, contamination of the surface by resolidified ZnO, or the formation of deep level defects and color centers [11,23,24]. To ensure optimum laser operation with highest output stability, the laser was operated at its standard repetition rate of 10 Hz during the measurements. The separate pulses were then selected by mechanical shutters, synchronized with the delay generator already used for laser operations. Furthermore, the lasers were operated at their optimum output energy E_{pump} = 160 mJ and E_{ESA} = 27–29 mJ and attenuated by neutral density filters (FW2AND and NDC-100C-4M, Thorlabs Inc., Newton, MA, USA). To further reduce the impact of pulse energy fluctuations and sample inhomogeneities, the results of 5 independent ablation spots fabricated with identical processing parameters were averaged for all performed single- and dual-beam ablation measurements.

2.3. Generation and Analysis of Ablation Spots

The ablation behavior of the ZnO layer for the single laser beams was characterized by optical microscopy (VH-Z100, Keyence, Osaka, Japan) and white light interferometry (CCI HD, Ametek Inc., Berwyn, IL, USA) as a function of their respective pump-pulse energy $E_{pump} \leq 13$ µJ and ESA-pulse energy E_{ESA}. The latter was labeled according to the utilized ESA-wavelengths λ_{ESA} as $E_{450} \leq 19$ µJ, $E_{500} \leq 12$ µJ, $E_{550} \leq 25$ µJ, $E_{600} \leq 31$ µJ. The single-beam ablation threshold energy E_{th} and the beam diameter $2\omega_f$ ($1/e^2$-diameter) were determined using the method proposed by Liu [25]. For this purpose, the squared ablation diameters D^2 were plotted in semilog plot versus the pulse energy E. According to

$$D^2 = 2\omega_f \cdot \ln\left(\frac{E}{E_{th}}\right), \tag{1}$$

the intersection of the linear fit at $D^2 = 0$ and its slope determines E_{th} and $2\omega_f$, respectively. Using these parameters, the laser peak fluence at the ablation threshold was calculated by $F_{th} = 2E_{th}/\pi\omega_f^2$. Hereinafter, all fluence values refer to laser peak fluences.

For fluences below F_{th} in order to prevent single-beam ablation, ESA-based laser processing with a combination of pump and ESA beam was analyzed. The impact of the different parameters for optimal ablation quality and efficiency was characterized by varying the ESA beam fluence F_{ESA} ($F_{450} \leq 1.6$ J/cm^2, $F_{500} \leq 4.5$ J/cm^2, $F_{550} \leq 5.7$ J/cm^2, $F_{600} \leq 5.3$ J/cm^2) below their individual F_{th} at a constant pulse delay of $\Delta t = 5$ ns and several pump beam fluences at $F_{pump} = 0.2$ J/cm^2, 0.1 J/cm^2, and 0.02 J/cm^2. Using the highest pump beam fluence $F_{pump} = 0.2$ J/cm^2 and the same values of F_{ESA}, Δt was varied from −10 to 500 ns to investigate the influence of the pulse delay. Here, a negative temporal delay ($\Delta t < 0$) implies that the ESA beam precedes the pump pulse (Figure 1c).

3. Results and Discussion

3.1. Optical Characterization of the ZnO Thin Film

The UV/VIS transmittance spectrum of the uncoated fused silica substrate T_S (Figure 2a) shows no absorption for the applied λ and thus no interaction with the radiation. The deviation to $T = 1$ is caused by reflectance losses at the interfaces [26]. The transmittance of the 200 nm thin ZnO layer on the substrate T_{ZnO} shows a single steep absorption edge at $\lambda \approx 380$ nm with a direct optical band gap at $E_{BG} = 3.26$ eV [20,27], determined by a Tauc-plot [28]:

$$\alpha E_P = G \cdot (E_P - E_{BG})^R, \quad (2)$$

where G is a constant that depends on the transition probability. The parameter R is determined by the optical transmittance type and is $R = 0.5$ for directly allowed optical transmissions [29,30]. Plotting αE_P over E_P and using a linear fit of the straight portion of the absorption edge, the intersection at $\alpha E_P = 0$ determines E_{BG} (Figure 2b). The results demonstrate optimal conditions for a strong fundamental single photon absorption of the pump beam ($\lambda_{pump} = 355$ nm). The optical penetration depth is determined by $d_p = 1/\alpha$ with the absorption coefficient $\alpha = \ln(T^{-1})/d_L$. $d_p = 62$ nm and corresponds by definition to the depth at which the beam intensity has dropped to 1/e. This value is smaller than the layer thickness d_L and thus almost all of the pulse energy is used to promote electrons to the CB, which are available for the subsequent ESA-based ablation process.

By analyzing the sinusoidal interference fringes in the weak and medium absorbing region of the T_{ZnO}-spectrum by the envelope method of Swanepoel [26], the interference free transmittance T_E was derived. Here, the T_{ZnO}-maxima and minima were used to fit an upper T_M and lower T_m envelope function, respectively. Both envelopes were computer-generated using the program OriginPro 2020b (Origin-Lab Corp.) [30]. At shorter wavelengths in the strong absorbing region above E_{BG}, the envelope functions converge to a single curve, merging with the measured values of T_{ZnO}. The interference free absorption coefficient was calculated from the determined T_E values (Table 1) [31].

Table 1. Optical parameters (T_E, n, α, d_p) at the utilized λ calculated from the transmittance data by the method of Swanepoel (Figure 2a) [26], as well as ablation parameters for single-beam ablation (E_{th}, $2\omega_f$, F_{th}) determined by the method of Liu (Figure 3a) [25].

λ [nm]	355	450	500	550	600
T_E	0.04	0.82	0.82	0.83	0.83
n	-	2.07	2.05	2.04	2.03
α [1/cm]	1.6×10^5	9.7×10^3	9.5×10^3	9.4×10^3	9.2×10^3
d_p [nm]	62	1027	1047	1065	1088
$2\omega_f$ [µm]	28.4	28.5	20.2	23.6	19.8
E_{th} [µJ]	1.6	6.2	7.8	12.9	8.5
F_{th} [J/cm^2]	0.49	1.96	4.86	5.90	5.51

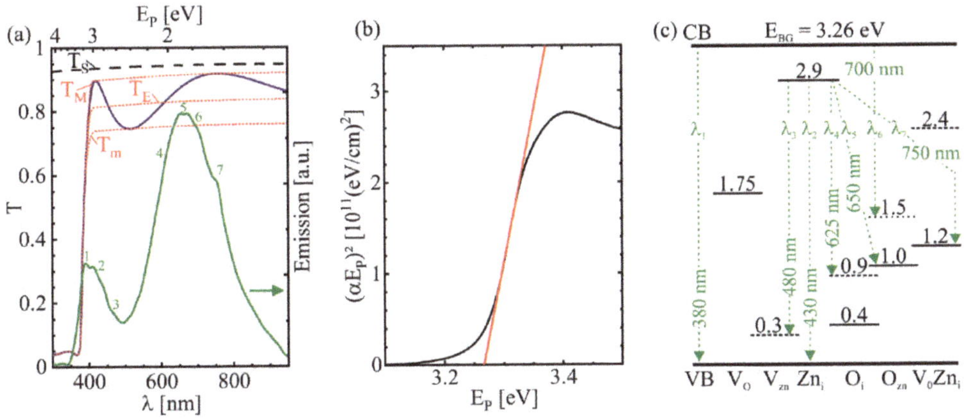

Figure 2. (**a**) UV/VIS transmittance spectra of 1 mm thin uncoated fused silica substrate (- - -) and fused silica coated with a 200 nm thin ZnO-layer (—). The dotted lines labeled T_M, T_m, and T_E are the fits of the upper and lower envelope function as well as their geometric mean, respectively [26]. In the emission spectrum of the ZnO film (—), λ = 325 nm was used for excitation. Selected emission peaks assigned to specific transitions are numbered. (**b**) Tauc plot [28] of T_{ZnO} (—). The linear fit (—) at the straight portion of the band edge allows to determine E_{BG} by the intersection at $\alpha E_P = 0$. (**c**) Schematic of the location of intrinsic point defect levels within the band gap by full-potential linear Muffin-tin orbital method calculations according to Xu et al. [32]. The numbers on the lines indicate ΔE_P of the defect states compared to the energy of the valence band (VB)-maximum with filled (—), partially filled (---), and empty (- - -) states. The positions of the energy levels are true to scale with respect to E_{BG} = 3.26 eV. Selected transitions are labelled with dashed arrows and a number corresponding to the emission wavelengths in (**a**).

Furthermore, the amplitude and oscillation of the interference fringes contain information about the ZnO-layer thickness d_L and the refraction index n, respectively. The refraction index of the substrate was derived from the transmittance of the uncoated substrate. The interference free refraction index in the weak absorbing region was calculated using the envelope functions as demonstrated by Swanepoel [26]. By using λ and n of adjacent fringe maxima or minima and the order number, d_L was calculated to be 203 nm. The measured and calculated parameters for the utilized λ are listed in Table 1 [26,31].

Below the band gap energy E_{BG}, n and α steadily increase and the small variation of λ below E_{BG} indicates the comparably weak absorption of the ESA wavelengths without additional pump excitation. The difference between T_E and T_S is caused primarily by the deviating n, as the upper envelope function that intersects the fringe maxima almost coincides with T_S [26]. With increasing absorption at E_{BG}, α increases rapidly.

The sinusoidal interference fringes in the spectrum are caused by reflection losses due to interference effects of the radiation between the air–film and film–substrate interfaces [33]. This indicates homogeneous, smooth, and low scattering surfaces [34]. Thus, only at sufficiently high beam fluences, an independent ESA beam ablation is expected by either a multi-photon absorption or processes including various intrinsic point defects. The latter include deep level defects inside the ZnO layer or shallow donors that are located typically at the surface [20,22,35,36]. As illustrated in Figure 2c, the location of the intrinsic defect levels were calculated by Xu et al. with a full-potential linear Muffin-tin orbital method [32]. These include vacant zinc (V_{Zn}), vacant oxygen (V_O), interstitial zinc (Zn_i), interstitial oxygen (O_i), substituted oxygen at zinc positions (O_{Zn}), and complexes of V_0 and Zn_i (V_0Zn_i).

The emission spectrum in Figure 2a shows a weaker emission in the UV-range from 360–500 nm (close to E_{BG}), compared to λ = 550–800 nm. The sharp band emission at λ_1 = 380–390 nm overlaps with the band edge and is caused by recombination of photo-induced charge carriers through exciton–exciton collision processes (Figure 2c) [21,22,37]. The specific emissions at λ_2 = 430 nm and λ_3 = 480 nm are attributed to $Zn_i \rightarrow$ VB and

$Zn_i \rightarrow V_{Zn}$ transitions, respectively [22]. Their weak emission indicates low roughness and homogeneous surface quality, in line with the findings in the T_{ZnO} spectrum as these transitions occur primarily at the surface [22]. The strongest emission in the visible region corresponds to deep level defects in the bulk of the layer [22,32,36]. Here, the broad emission is comprised of several transitions at λ_4 = 625 nm, λ_5 = 650 nm, λ_6 = 700 nm, and λ_7 = 750 nm, induced by $Zn_i \rightarrow O_i$, $Zn_i \rightarrow O_{Zn}$, CB $\rightarrow O_{Zn}$, and $Zn_i \rightarrow V_0Zn_i$ [22].

3.2. Single-Beam Ablation

It becomes evident from Table 1 that F_{th} of the ESA beams is about one order of magnitude larger than the pump beam. The pump beam with λ_{pump} = 355 nm is absorbed fundamentally by single photon absorption, indicated by the linear increase in D^2 (at the semilog scale in Figure 3a) and the transmittance in Figure 2a ($E_{pump} > E_{BG}$) [38,39]. In contrast, the ESA beams require either populated defect levels that absorb the laser wavelengths and promote electrons to CB [35], or a multi photon process ($E_{ESA} < E_{BG}$) [7]. However, such nonlinear processes would cause an exponential deviation from the linear trend [38] and is therefore unlikely. Thus, the ESA at defect levels is expected as the primary absorption mechanism. The steeper slope angle of the pump beam indicates a larger beam diameter $2\omega_f$ = 28 μm [40]. It is comparable or larger than the ESA beams (Table 1) and therefore it provides ideal conditions for optimal utilization of the pulse energy for the ESA process.

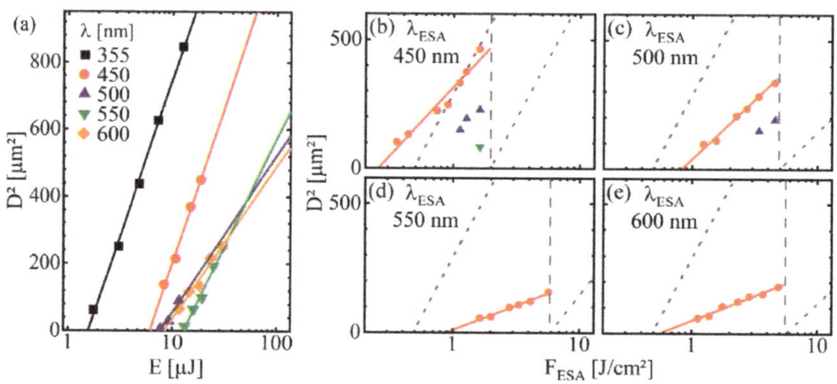

Figure 3. (**a**) Semilog plots of D^2 over E with the corresponding linear fits, to determine the ablation parameters E_{th}, $2\omega_f$, and F_{th} of single-beam absorption by the method of Liu [25]. The exact values at the utilized λ are listed in Table 1. (**b–e**) Semilog plots of D^2 over F_{ESA} for ESA based ablation at different λ_{ESA} with (**b**) λ = 450 nm, (**c**) λ = 500 nm, (**d**) λ = 550 nm, and (**e**) λ = 600 nm. For excitation, different F_{pump} values of 0.2 J/cm^2 (-•-), 0.1 J/cm^2 (▲), and 0.02 J/cm^2 (▼) were used. F_{ESA} was varied below their respective F_{th} (Table 1), indicated by the vertical dashed line. The values for F_{pump} = 0.2 J/cm^2 were linearly fit to D^2 = 0. The diagonal dotted lines highlight the F_{th} fits of λ = 355 nm (---) and the respective λ_{ESA} (---) plotted in (**a**).

The behavior at λ_{ESA} = 450 nm deviates slightly from the other wavelengths, where F_{th} is smaller and $2\omega_f$ is larger. This suggests a partially different excitation process due to the high E_P closest to E_{BG}. This might be explained by the excitation of VB-electrons directly to defect levels close to CB. Moreover, defect levels could be able to absorb the beam and excite electrons directly to CB (Figure 2c), which would lower F_{th} [32,35]. As the defect concentration is expected to be highest at the ZnO–fused silica interface, most of the energy would be absorbed here. At sufficient F_{ESA}, the abrupt absorption at this interface can cause an explosion-like ablation of the whole layer without the necessity to heat the entire ZnO inside the laser spot. For single-beam ablation of the ESA-beams, the resulting spots are mostly inhomogeneous at low F_{ESA} (Figure 4b,g) and the further increase of F_{ESA} leads to substrate damage (Figure 4a,f). Here, an inhomogeneous ablation with ablation depths d_a of several microns were observed in the dark areas of the ablation spot. The intense absorption at the fused silica interface exceeds the substrate ablation threshold and limits the F_{ESA}-range significantly. Thus, for the F_{th} calculations, F_{ESA} was decreased and the spots at higher F_{ESA} exceeding the damage threshold of the fused silica substrate were excluded from analysis, as the measured D^2 are highly inconsistent and do not represent the ablation characteristic of the ZnO-layer.

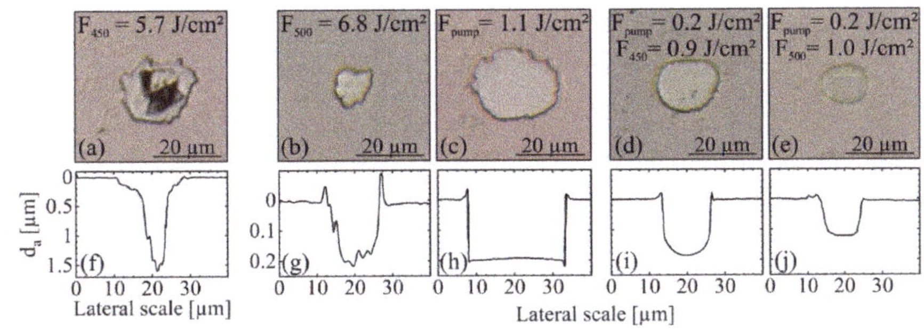

Figure 4. Microscopic images of single-beam ablation spots with (**a**) $F_{450} = 5.7\ J/cm^2$, (**b**) $F_{500} = 6.8\ J/cm^2$, and (**c**) $F_{pump} = 1.1\ J/cm^2$, as well as ESA-based dual-beam ablation spots at (**d**) $\Delta t = 5$ ns with $F_{pump} = 0.2\ J/cm^2 + F_{450} = 0.9\ J/cm^2$ and (**e**) $\Delta t = 10$ ns with $F_{pump} = 0.2\ J/cm^2 + F_{500} = 1.0\ J/cm^2$. (**f–j**) White light interferometric depth profiles of spots (**a–e**).

3.3. Dual-Beam Ablation

3.3.1. Influence of the ESA Beam Fluence

At first, F_{ESA} was varied (Figure 3b–e) and the values for optimum ablation conditions were set to a small positive temporal delay of $\Delta t = 5$ ns and $F_{pump} = 0.2\ J/cm^2$. In the case of an ablation process solely based on ESA, the pump beam induces the transient absorption of the spatially and temporally superimposed ESA beam (Figure 1). This requires to prevent surface modification of the individual beams by ablation [8]. Therefore, all measurements were performed using laser peak fluences below their respective F_{th} (Table 1). This is indicated in Figure 3b–e where all values are below the vertical dashed lines, originating at F_{th} of the respective ESA-beams. Additionally, to compare the dual-beam process with single-beam ablation, the diagonal dashed lines show the linear fits of the F_{th} calculations determined by the fits of E_{th} in Figure 3a.

Decreasing F_{ESA} results in a decreased D^2 as less additional energy is available to further excite the already excited electrons. This limits the ablation to an area closer to the beam center, where the intensity of the Gaussian beam profile is still sufficient for ablation. Here, the utilizable fluence range for ESA-based ablation extends about one order of magnitude down to $F_{ESA} \approx 0.3\ J/cm^2$ for $\lambda = 450$ nm. Slightly below these values, the ablation spots are characterized by their non-circular shape. By further decreasing F_{ESA}, inhomogeneously distributed substructures were observed within the irradiated area. These surface modifications at low laser fluences are caused by locally enhanced carrier densities that are generated by either an inhomogeneous laser beam profile or locally enhanced ablation at dust, scratches, or crystal defects [41]. It has to be noted that the analysis only includes ablated structures that resulted in distinct and well pronounced ablation spots, excluding the aforementioned value-ranges.

The comparison of the different ESA wavelengths reveals a similar behavior of the beams with the highest photon energy at $\lambda = 450$ and 500 nm showing highly increased D^2 when compared to $\lambda = 550$ and 600 nm at similar fluences (Figure 3b–e). Higher E_P allow an increased number of populated defect levels to absorb these ESA beams and to populate the CB by an ESA (Figure 2c). It has to be noted that a single photon absorption of VB-electrons directly to the CB is not possible at λ_{ESA} with $E_P < E_{BG}$. In addition, a multiphoton absorption is negligible at the low applied fluences. Furthermore, a transition to another defect level is unlikely due to the specific required wavelength. Thus, besides the intra-band transition of CB-electrons, a transition from defect levels close to the VB into the CB is the most likely absorption mechanism. The existence of a considerable amount of these defect levels is confirmed by the characteristic fluorescence (Figure 2a), where the highest number of emitted photons is attributed to these defect level transitions [42–44].

Thus, with the highest E_P, using λ_{ESA} = 450 nm is optimal to generate the biggest ablation spots at the lowest F_{ESA} (Figure 3b). Here, at F_{pump} = 0.2 J/cm^2 (red markers), even less additional F_{ESA} was necessary than the single pump beam requires for ablation. This is indicated by values above the purple line (linear F_{th}-fit of Figure 3a).

To analyze the effect of F_{pump} on the ESA-based ablation, Δt = 5 ns at the identical values of F_{ESA} for each wavelength were used. As seen in Figure 3d,e, below F_{pump} = 0.2 J/cm^2 no distinct ablation spots can be observed for λ = 550 and 600 nm. The utilizable F_{ESA} range reduces drastically with decreasing F_{pump}. Without a sufficient excited electron concentration, the ESA-based ablation process stops abruptly. Only for λ = 450 nm at F_{pump} = 0.02 J/cm^2 distinct ablation spots can be observed (Figure 3b,c).

3.3.2. Ablation Efficiency

When compared to single-beam ablation, the ESA-based process allows to decrease the amount of laser energy required for ablation (Table 1). This improvement was evaluated based on the method of Liu [25]. For this purpose, D^2 of the ESA-based ablation spots in Figure 3b–e (for F_{pump} = 0.2 J/cm^2 at Δt = 5 ns) was plotted in a semilog plot as a function of F_{ESA}. The linear extrapolation allows to calculate the effective ESA-beam diameter $2\omega_f{}^{eff}$ (slope of the fit) and the effective ESA-beam threshold peak fluence $F_{th}{}^{eff}$ (fit intersect at D^2 = 0) (Table 2).

Table 2. Calculation of dual-beam ablation parameters ($2\omega_f{}^{eff}$, $F_{th}{}^{eff}$) based on the method of Liu [25] and dual-beam efficiency parameters (F_E, F_{ET}) determined from Equations (3) and (4).

λ [nm]	450	500	550	600
$2\omega_f{}^{eff}$ [μm]	21.4	20.1	12.8	13
$F_{th}{}^{eff}$ [J/cm^2]	0.26	0.83	0.90	0.55
F_E	0.86	2.03	2.16	1.46
F_{ET}	0.39	0.50	0.48	0.43

Here, the values of $2\omega_f{}^{eff}$ for λ = 450 and 500 nm are close to their respective $2\omega_f$ of single-beam ablation. Consequently, almost the entire area of the fluence profile exceeds the ablation threshold and contributes to the ESA-based ablation. This suggests an effective utilization of the pulse energy. For λ = 550 and 600 nm, the values deviate significantly by a factor of two, which becomes evident by the decreased slope of the fits in Figure 3d,e.

Similarly to F_{th} that defines the minimum required fluence for single-beam ablation, $F_{th}{}^{eff}$ defines the minimum F_{ESA} at given F_{pump} that is required for ESA-based dual-beam ablation. These values decreased by a factor of 5–10, but are still proportional to F_{th}. With the highest E_P, λ_{ESA} = 450 nm can utilize the energy, induced by the pump, most optimally. Here, $F_{th}{}^{eff}$ = 0.26 J/cm is even below F_{th} = 0.49 J/cm^2 of the single pump beam, indicated by values above the purple line, as described earlier (Figure 3b).

To evaluate the improvements of the ESA-based process, compared to single-beam ablation, fluence efficiency

$$F_E = \frac{F_{th}^{eff} + F_{pump}}{F_{th}^{pump}} \quad (3)$$

and total fluence efficiency as the sum of the normalized single-beam fluences

$$F_{ET} = \frac{F_{th}^{eff}}{F_{th}^{ESA}} + \frac{F_{pump}}{F_{th}^{pump}} \quad (4)$$

were defined (Table 2). For F_E-values below one, the combined fluences of the ESA- and the pump-beam are still below F_{th}^{pump} for single-beam ablation ($F_E = 1$, if $F_{th}^{eff} + F_{pump} = F_{th}^{pump}$). As already mentioned, only $\lambda = 450$ nm at $\Delta t = 5$ ns and $F_{pump} = 0.2$ J/cm^2 reached $F_E = 0.86$. Similarly, replacing the single-beam threshold fluence in Equation (3) to F_{th} of the ESA-beams, allows the comparison of the efficiency improvement with the ESA-beams. In order to exclude an ordinary accumulation effect of the pump and ESA beam, F_{ET} was defined. For $F_{ET} < 1$, an additional induced transient absorption must be considered as part of the ablation process (Table 2).

3.3.3. Ablation Quality

Figure 4a,b show selected single-beam ablation spots for the utilized ESA wavelengths. At high F_{ESA}, the absorption of defect levels at the fused silica–ZnO interface leads to substrate damage (Figure 4a,f). At F_{ESA} close to F_{th}, the ablation spots become increasingly inhomogeneous (Figure 4b). As described earlier, the further decrease of F_{ESA} results in only partially interconnected spots inside the beam. In comparison, the pump beam hits the ZnO–air interface first (Figure 1b) and the fundamental absorption leads to an almost circular and homogeneous single-beam ablation of the entire ZnO layer (Figure 4c). When reaching the ZnO–substrate interface, the pump beam is already highly attenuated preventing abrupt heating and damaging of the substrate (Figure 4h). The maximum d_a observed in the depth profiles (Figure 4g–j) are in good agreement with the calculated layer thickness $d_L = 203$ nm.

Compared to single-beam ablation, the spot diameters are decreased by the ESA-based ablation process, indicated by decreased values of $2\omega_f^{eff}$ when compared to $2\omega_f$ (Tables 1 and 2). The ablation area is restricted by the superposition of both pulses. This limits the ablation to the mostly uniform high-intensive center of the pulses and results in an enhanced ablation quality with circular ablation spots. In comparison to single pump beam ablation, the absorbed energy and induced heat at the ZnO–air interface is reduced and homogeneously distributed throughout the entire ZnO-layer. This results in a reduced melt formation at the edges protruding above the layer surface (Figure 4g–j), as well as decreasing the surface contamination by resolidified ZnO-droplets around the ablation spots (Figure 4d,e). By increasing Δt, these effects are reduced even further, as the heat dissipates and an ESA at defect levels dominates the ablation process (Figure 4i,j).

The optimization of the parameters allows the complete removal of the ZnO layer without damaging the fused silica substrate (Figure 4d,i) and a precise control of d_a (Figure 4e,j). The reduced F_{ESA} prevents the fused silica–ZnO interface from abruptly heating to the point of substrate damage (Figure 4a,f). As the fundamentally absorbed pump beam is focused on the ZnO–air surface, the initial abrupt heating together with a high concentration of excited carriers diffuse gradually and homogeneously through the ZnO-layer ($d_p = 62$ nm). Optimal ablation conditions were found at $\Delta t \approx 5$ ns. The ZnO layer is already excited by the pump beam, in particular at the ZnO–substrate interface, where the defects are located primarily. It thus requires only a low excess of additionally absorbed ESA photons and energy to ablate the ZnO layer from the fused silica substrate.

3.3.4. Influence of Temporal Pulse Delay

To determine the importance of defect levels compared to absorption solely based on intra-band transition, the temporal delay between the pulses was varied for different F_{ESA} at the fixed optimum of $F_{pump} = 0.2$ J/cm (Figure 5). At the highest F_{ESA}, for $\lambda = 450$ and 500 nm (Figure 5a,b), delays above 300 ns still resulted in a measurable ablation. Compared to $\lambda = 550$ and 600 nm (Figure 5c,d), this delay is much larger with Δt mostly below 50 ns. As the fluorescent lifetime of ZnO band gap electrons is well below 10 ns [42,44], an ablation at these high Δt cannot be explained solely by intra-band transition-based absorption. Thus, the defect levels with their increased fluorescent lifetime serve as the main driving force [35]. First, the pump beam promotes electrons into CB (Figure 1a). From there, besides relaxation back to the VB, electrons transfer rapidly to deep defect levels, which are suitable as absorption centers for the subsequent ESA beam (Figure 2c). The decrease of D^2 and the Δt-range is almost proportional to F_{ESA}. Only F_{ESA}-values close to their respective F_{th} deviate from this trend. Especially for λ = 550 and 600 nm, these values increase overproportional at the highest F_{ESA}, where the ESA-beams can almost ablate the ZnO solely by single-beam ablation.

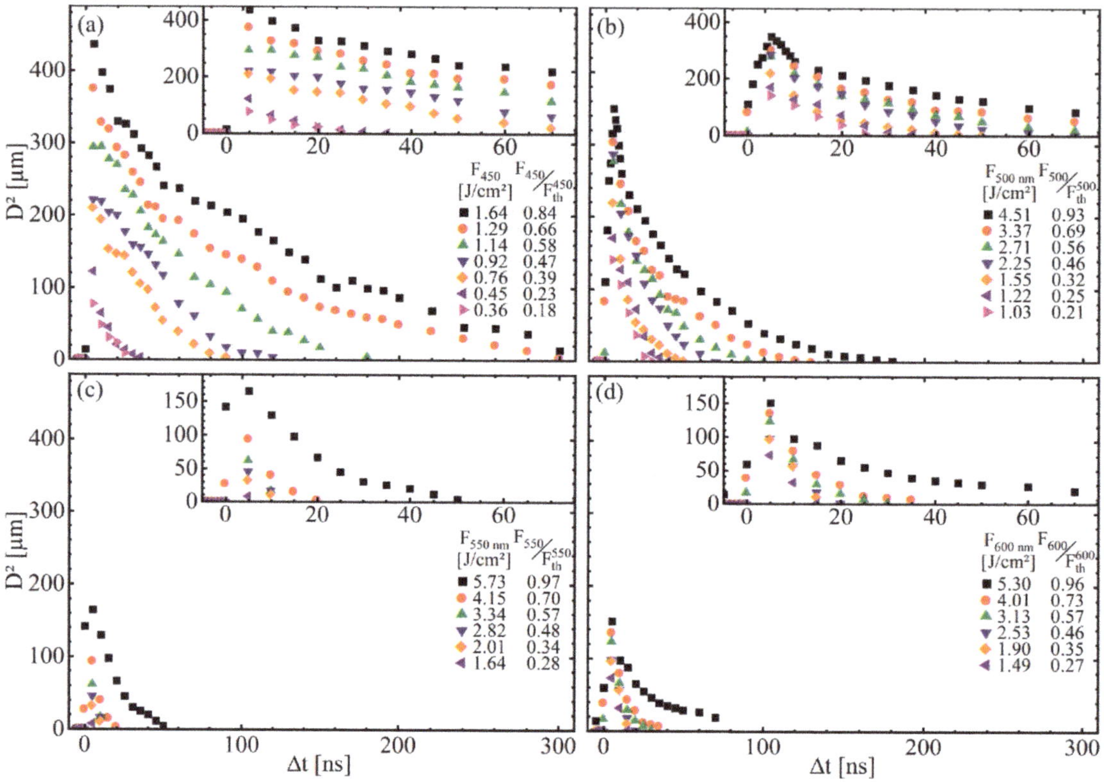

Figure 5. D^2 plotted versus Δt to determine the optimal delay between the pulses. For excitation, F_{pump} = 0.2 J/cm^2 was used at (**a**) λ_{ESA} = 450 nm, (**b**) λ_{ESA} = 500 nm, (**c**) λ_{ESA} = 550 nm, (**d**) λ_{ESA} = 600 nm. F_{ESA} was varied in the identical increments as for Figure 3b (color coded with F_{ESA} and the F_{ESA}/F_{th}-ratio). In the top-right corners, the section of short Δt is extended.

Figure 5c,d reveals deviations from this trend, especially for λ = 550 and 600 nm, where the values increase overproportionately at the highest values of F_{ESA}. These fluence values are close the respective ablation thresholds, which almost allow ablation of the ZnO layer solely by the ESA beam.

At low temporal delays (Δt < 10 ns), the impact of λ_{ESA} is less pronounced (Figure 5). Here, the effect of an intra-band transition and sample heating dominates as the beams still overlap. For λ = 550 and 600 nm, an increasing Δt leads to a rapidly decreasing D^2 because the defect level absorption emerging as the dominant process is only utilized effectively at λ = 450 and 500 nm. As shown in Figure 1c, at Δt = +5 and −5 ns, the temporal overlap is similar, but the resulting D^2 differ significantly, as prior excitation of electrons by the pump beam is required for ESA.

Exemplary, for λ = 500 nm at F_{ESA} = 4.51 J/cm^2, Δt was varied in one ns-steps between Δt = −5 to +10 ns to analyze the area of temporal beam overlap in more detail (Figure 5b). At the optimum conditions around $\Delta t \approx$ 5 ns, the highest number of prior excited electrons is available for an ESA (Figure 1c). At Δt = 0 ns, where both beams overlap optimally, the excited electrons are only partially used for the ESA, as parts of the radiation excite carriers after the highest intensity of the ESA beam reaches the sample. At negative temporal delays and further decreasing beam overlap, only minor ablation is observed for F_{ESA} close to F_{th}. Here, the number of excited electrons is insufficient to reach the required ablation threshold. Increasing Δt above the optimum also leads to a decreasing D^2-values. However, the rate is much lower than for negative delays.

At $\Delta t < 50$ ns, the heat generated by the pump excitation must be considered, as it effects the ablation process considerably, particularly close to the temporal beam overlap (Figure 1c). Here, increased sample temperatures act as an offset for the ESA, as less additionally absorbed energy is required for ablation. Thus, a wider area of the ESA beam surpasses F_{th}, resulting in increased D^2. $F_{pump} = 0.2$ J/cm^2, well below $F_{th} = 0.49$ J/cm^2 was used to reduce sample heating.

For polycrystalline ZnO-layers, thermal conductivities $k_{th} < 10$ W/m·K are found in literature, which is well below $k_{th} \sim 30$–100 W/m·K for epitaxially grown or bulk ZnO [45–49]. The thermal diffusion length is determined by $\mu = 2(\alpha_{th} \cdot \Delta t)^{0.5}$ with $\alpha_{th} = k_{th}/c_V$ where c_V is the volumetric heat capacity with about 2.4–2.8·10^6 J/m^3·K [47,49]. With $d_p = 62$ nm, most of the heat is created by the pump beam at the ZnO–air interface. It takes about 5 ns to reach the ZnO–fused silica interface, where the highest defect concentration and thus, the strongest ESA is expected. This is in good agreement with the ablation maximum measured at a delay of about 5 ns.

Furthermore, the rapid D^2-decrease in the delay range 20–50 ns (Figure 5) can be attributed to heat dissipation and correlates with literature values [45,50]. As $2\omega_f$ is about 100 times larger than d_L and μ for the time scale in consideration, one-dimensional heat conduction can be assumed [47,51,52]. Here, the heat should be mostly dissipated. Consequently, the defect level absorption is now the dominant factor for ESA, and it is no longer superimposed by pump beam heating. At higher Δt, the ablation slowly decreases due to the finite fluorescent lifetime of the defect level electrons that slowly lowers the available excited electron density for the ESA [43,53].

4. Conclusions

In the present study, we investigated a dual-beam laser process based on ESA by applying several wavelengths ($\lambda_{pump} = 355$ nm, $\lambda_{ESA} = 450, 500, 550, 600$ nm) at various F_{pump} and F_{ESA}. The ESA-beams with the highest photon energies produced the largest ablation spots at the lowest beam fluences. A small temporal delay of +5 ns is optimal for the dual-beam ablation process, as it utilizes a combination of heat and excited carriers for increased absorption. Longer temporal delays result in heat dissipation and quickly lower the ablation diameters. Now, the ESA beam absorption is determined solely by the excited carrier concentration. The quality of the ablation spots was improved by reducing the debris and melt formation and the required laser energy was decreased. Furthermore, a model for the evaluation of the ESA-based efficiency improvement was developed. Based on these findings, future investigations on a combination of STED and ESA with regards to STED direct writing processes were advanced.

Author Contributions: Conceptualization, C.W. and S.E.; data curation, C.W.; formal analysis, S.G. and F.A.M.; funding acquisition, S.E., S.G., and F.A.M.; investigation, C.W. and S.E.; methodology, C.W. and S.E.; project administration, S.G. and F.A.M.; resources, F.A.M.; software, C.W.; supervision, S.G. and F.A.M.; validation, C.W., S.E., and F.A.M.; visualization, C.W.; writing—original draft, C.W.; writing—review and editing, S.E., S.G., and F.A.M. All authors have read and agreed to the published version of the manuscript.

Funding: This research was funded by the German Research Foundation (DFG), grant number GR4710/4-1.

Conflicts of Interest: The authors declare no conflict of interest.

References

1. Hell, S.W.; Wichmann, J. Breaking the diffraction resolution limit by stimulated emission: Stimulated-emission-depletion fluorescence microscopy. *Opt. Lett.* **1994**, *19*, 780–782. [CrossRef] [PubMed]
2. Klar, T.A.; Hell, S.W. Subdiffraction resolution in far-field fluorescence microscopy. *Opt. Lett.* **1999**, *24*, 954–956. [CrossRef]
3. Rittweger, E.; Han, K.Y.; Irvine, S.E.; Eggeling, C.; Hell, S.W. STED microscopy reveals crystal colour centres with nanometric resolution. *Nat. Photon.* **2009**, *3*, 144–147. [CrossRef]
4. Gottfert, F.; Wurm, C.A.; Mueller, V.; Berning, S.; Cordes, V.C.; Honigmann, A.; Hell, S.W. Coaligned dual-channel STED nanoscopy and molecular diffusion analysis at 20 nm resolution. *Biophys. J.* **2013**, *105*, L01–L03. [CrossRef]
5. Malinauskas, M.; Farsari, M.; Piskarskas, A.; Juodkazis, S. Ultrafast laser nanostructuring of photopolymers: A decade of advances. *Phys. Rep.* **2013**, *533*, 1–31. [CrossRef]
6. Frolich, A.; Fischer, J.; Zebrowski, T.; Busch, K.; Wegener, M. Titania woodpiles with complete three-dimensional photonic bandgaps in the visible. *Adv. Mater.* **2013**, *25*, 3588–3592. [CrossRef] [PubMed]
7. Sugioka, K.; Meunier, M.; Piqué, A. *Laser Precision Microfabrication*; Springer: Berlin, Germany, 2010; Volume 135.
8. Engel, S.; Wenisch, C.; Gräf, S.; Müller, F. Sub-diffraction direct laser writing by a combination of STED and ESA. In *Laser-Based Micro-and Nanoprocessing XIV*; International Society for Optics and Photonics, SPIE LASE: San Francisco, CA, USA, 2020; p. 112680D.
9. Wenisch, C.; Engel, S.; Gräf, S.; Müller, F.A. Fundamentals of a new sub-diffraction direct laser writing method by a combination of stimulated emission depletion and excited state absorption. *J. Laser Micro Nanoeng.* **2020**, *15*, 169–173.
10. Théberge, F.; Chin, S. Enhanced ablation of silica by the superposition of femtosecond and nanosecond laser pulses. *Appl. Phys. A* **2005**, *80*, 1505–1510. [CrossRef]
11. Zhang, J.; Sugioka, K.; Takahashi, T.; Toyoda, K.; Midorikawa, K. Dual-beam ablation of fused silica by multiwavelength excitation process using KrF excimer and F2 lasers. *Appl. Phys. A* **2000**, *71*, 23–26.
12. Obata, K.; Sugioka, K.; Akane, T.; Midorikawa, K.; Aoki, N.; Toyoda, K. Efficient refractive-index modification of fused silica by a resonance-photoionization-like process using F 2 and KrF excimer lasers. *Opt. Lett.* **2002**, *27*, 330–332. [CrossRef]
13. Sugioka, K.; Wada, S.; Tashiro, H.; Toyoda, K. Ablation of wide band-gap materials by multi-wavelength irradiation using a VUV Raman laser. *Appl. Surf. Sci.* **1997**, *109*, 179–183. [CrossRef]
14. Zhang, J.; Sugioka, K.; Wada, S.; Tashiro, H.; Toyoda, K. Direct photoetching of single crystal SiC by VUV-266 nm multiwavelength laser ablation. *Appl. Phys. A* **1997**, *64*, 367–371. [CrossRef]
15. Zhang, J.; Sugioka, K.; Wada, S.; Tashiro, H.; Toyoda, K.; Midorikawa, K. Precise microfabrication of wide band gap semiconductors (SiC and GaN) by VUV–UV multiwavelength laser ablation. *Appl. Surf. Sci.* **1998**, *127*, 793–799. [CrossRef]
16. Akane, T.; Sugioka, K.; Hammura, K.; Aoyagi, Y.; Midorikawa, K.; Obata, K.; Toyoda, K.; Nomura, S. GaN ablation etching by simultaneous irradiation with F 2 laser and KrF excimer laser. *J. Vac. Sci. Tech. B Microelectron. Nanometer Struct. Proces. Meas. Phenom.* **2001**, *19*, 1388–1391. [CrossRef]
17. Obata, K.; Sugioka, K.; Midorikawa, K.; Inamura, T.; Takai, H. Deep etching of epitaxial gallium nitride film by multiwavelength excitation process using F 2 and KrF excimer lasers. *Appl. Phys. A* **2006**, *82*, 479–483. [CrossRef]
18. Zoppel, S.; Zehetner, J.; Reider, G.A. Two color laser ablation: Enhanced yield, improved machining. *Appl. Surf. Sci.* **2007**, *253*, 7692–7695. [CrossRef]
19. Zoppel, S.; Merz, R.; Zehetner, J.; Reider, G.A. Enhancement of laser ablation yield by two color excitation. *Appl. Phys. A* **2005**, *81*, 847–850. [CrossRef]
20. Djurišić, A.; Ng, A.M.C.; Chen, X. ZnO nanostructures for optoelectronics: Material properties and device applications. *Prog. Quantum Electron.* **2010**, *34*, 191–259. [CrossRef]
21. Ogata, K.; Sakurai, K.; Fujita, S.; Fujita, S.; Matsushige, K. Effects of thermal annealing of ZnO layers grown by MBE. *J. Cryst. Growth* **2000**, *214*, 312–315. [CrossRef]
22. Marković, S.; Simatović, I.S.; Ahmetović, S.; Veselinović, L.; Stojadinović, S.; Rac, V.; Škapin, S.D.; Bogdanović, D.B.; Častvan, I.J.; Uskoković, D. Surfactant-assisted microwave processing of ZnO particles: A simple way for designing the surface-to-bulk defect ratio and improving photo (electro) catalytic properties. *RSC Adv.* **2019**, *9*, 17165–17178. [CrossRef]
23. Wang, X.; Lim, G.; Zheng, H.; Ng, F.; Liu, W.; Chua, S. Femtosecond pulse laser ablation of sapphire in ambient air. *Appl. Surf. Sci.* **2004**, *228*, 221–226. [CrossRef]
24. Rudolph, P.; Bonse, J.; Krüger, J.; Kautek, W. Femtosecond-and nanosecond-pulse laser ablation of bariumalumoborosilicate glass. *Appl. Phys. A* **1999**, *69*, S763–S766. [CrossRef]
25. Liu, J. Simple technique for measurements of pulsed Gaussian-beam spot sizes. *Opt. Lett.* **1982**, *7*, 196–198. [CrossRef]
26. Swanepoel, R. Determination of the thickness and optical constants of amorphous silicon. *J. Phys. E Sci. Instrum.* **1983**, *16*, 1214. [CrossRef]
27. Sernelius, B.E.; Berggren, K.-F.; Jin, Z.-C.; Hamberg, I.; Granqvist, C.G. Band-gap tailoring of ZnO by means of heavy Al doping. *Phys. Rev. B* **1988**, *37*, 10244. [CrossRef]
28. Tauc, J.; Grigorovici, R.; Vancu, A. Optical properties and electronic structure of amorphous germanium. *Phys. Stat. Solidi B* **1966**, *15*, 627–637. [CrossRef]
29. Farrag, A.A.-G.; Balboul, M.R. Nano ZnO thin films synthesis by sol–gel spin coating method as a transparent layer for solar cell applications. *J. Sol. Gel Sci. Technol.* **2017**, *82*, 269–279. [CrossRef]

30. Shaaban, E.; Yahia, I.; El-Metwally, E. Validity of Swanepoel's method for calculating the optical constants of thick films. *Acta Phys. Pol. Ser. A Gen. Phys.* **2012**, *121*, 628. [CrossRef]
31. Xue, S.; Zu, X.; Zhou, W.; Deng, H.; Xiang, X.; Zhang, L.; Deng, H. Effects of post-thermal annealing on the optical constants of ZnO thin film. *J. Alloys Compd.* **2008**, *448*, 21–26. [CrossRef]
32. Xu, P.; Sun, Y.; Shi, C.; Xu, F.; Pan, H. The electronic structure and spectral properties of ZnO and its defects. *Nucl. Instrum. Methods Phys. Res. Sec. B Beam Interact. Mater. Atoms* **2003**, *199*, 286–290. [CrossRef]
33. Wang, T.; Zheng, S.; Hao, W.; Wang, C. Studies on photocatalytic activity and transmittance spectra of TiO2 thin films prepared by rf magnetron sputtering method. *Surf. Coat. Technol.* **2002**, *155*, 141–145. [CrossRef]
34. Caglar, M.; Caglar, Y.; Ilican, S. The determination of the thickness and optical constants of the ZnO crystalline thin film by using envelope method. *J. Optoelectron. Adv. Mater.* **2006**, *8*, 1410.
35. Han, N.S.; Shim, H.S.; Seo, J.H.; Kim, S.Y.; Park, S.M.; Song, J.K. Defect states of ZnO nanoparticles: Discrimination by time-resolved photoluminescence spectroscopy. *J. Appl. Phys.* **2010**, *107*, 084306. [CrossRef]
36. Lin, B.; Fu, Z.; Jia, Y. Green luminescent center in undoped zinc oxide films deposited on silicon substrates. *Appl. Phys. Lett.* **2001**, *79*, 943–945. [CrossRef]
37. Johnson, J.C.; Knutsen, K.P.; Yan, H.; Law, M.; Zhang, Y.; Yang, P.; Saykally, R.J. Ultrafast carrier dynamics in single ZnO nanowire and nanoribbon lasers. *Nano Lett.* **2004**, *4*, 197–204. [CrossRef]
38. Sugioka, K.; Midorikawa, K. VUV-UV multiwavelength excitation process for high-quality ablation of fused silica. In *Damage to VUV, EUV, and X-Ray Optics IV; and EUV and X-Ray Optics: Synergy between Laboratory and Space III*; International Society for Optics and Photonics, SPIE OPTICS + OPTOELECTRONICS: Prague, Czech Republic, 2013; p. 877704.
39. Mardare, D.; Tasca, M.; Delibas, M.; Rusu, G. On the structural properties and optical transmittance of TiO2 rf sputtered thin films. *Appl. Surf. Sci.* **2000**, *156*, 200–206. [CrossRef]
40. Martin, S.; Hertwig, A.; Lenzner, M.; Krüger, J.; Kautek, W. Spot-size dependence of the ablation threshold in dielectrics for femtosecond laser pulses. *Appl. Phys. A* **2003**, *77*, 883–884. [CrossRef]
41. Bonse, J.; Baudach, S.; Krüger, J.; Kautek, W.; Lenzner, M. Femtosecond laser ablation of silicon–modification thresholds and morphology. *Appl. Phys. A* **2002**, *74*, 19–25. [CrossRef]
42. Layek, A.; Manna, B.; Chowdhury, A. Carrier recombination dynamics through defect states of ZnO nanocrystals: From nanoparticles to nanorods. *Chem. Phys. Lett.* **2012**, *539*, 133–138. [CrossRef]
43. Tang, A.-H.; Mei, Z.-X.; Hou, Y.-N.; Du, X.-L. Photodynamics of GaZn–VZn complex defect in Ga-doped ZnO. *Chin. Phys. B* **2018**, *27*, 117802. [CrossRef]
44. Özgür, Ü.; Alivov, Y.I.; Liu, C.; Teke, A.; Reshchikov, M.; Doğan, S.; Avrutin, V.; Cho, S.-J.; Morkoç, A.H. A comprehensive review of ZnO materials and devices. *J. Appl. Phys.* **2005**, *98*, 11. [CrossRef]
45. Huang, Z.X.; Tang, Z.A.; Yu, J.; Bai, S. Thermal conductivity of nanoscale polycrystalline ZnO thin films. *Phys. B Condens. Matter* **2011**, *406*, 818–823. [CrossRef]
46. Akhir, R.M.; Abd Wahab, Z. Thermal diffusivity studies of ZnO-CuO at high temperatures. *J. Teknologi* **2015**, *76*, 19–23.
47. Yamashita, Y.; Honda, K.; Yagi, T.; Jia, J.; Taketoshi, N.; Shigesato, Y. Thermal conductivity of hetero-epitaxial ZnO thin films on c and r-plane sapphire substrates: Thickness and grain size effect. *J. Appl. Phys.* **2019**, *125*, 035101. [CrossRef]
48. Alvarez-Quintana, J.; Martínez, E.; Pérez-Tijerina, E.; Pérez-García, S.A.; Rodríguez-Viejo, J. Temperature dependent thermal conductivity of polycrystalline ZnO films. *J. Appl. Phys.* **2010**, *107*, 063713. [CrossRef]
49. Xu, Y.; Goto, M.; Kato, R.; Tanaka, Y.; Kagawa, Y. Thermal conductivity of ZnO thin film produced by reactive sputtering. *J. Appl. Phys.* **2012**, *111*, 084320. [CrossRef]
50. Nedyalkov, N.; Koleva, M.; Nikov, R.; Atanasov, P.; Nakajima, Y.; Takami, A.; Shibata, A.; Terakawa, M. Laser nanostructuring of ZnO thin films. *Appl. Surf. Sci.* **2016**, *374*, 172–176. [CrossRef]
51. Diez, M.; Ametowobla, M.; Graf, T. Time-resolved reflectivity and temperature measurements during laser irradiation of crystalline silicon. *J. Laser Micro Nanoeng.* **2017**, *12*, 230–234.
52. Jiang, P.; Qian, X.; Yang, R. Time-domain thermoreflectance (TDTR) measurements of anisotropic thermal conductivity using a variable spot size approach. *Rev. Sci. Instrum.* **2017**, *88*, 074901. [CrossRef] [PubMed]
53. Zhong, Y.; Djurisic, A.B.; Hsu, Y.F.; Wong, K.S.; Brauer, G.; Ling, C.C.; Chan, W.K. Exceptionally long exciton photoluminescence lifetime in ZnO tetrapods. *J. Phys. Chem. C* **2008**, *112*, 16286–16295. [CrossRef]

materials MDPI

Article

Backward Flux Re-Deposition Patterns during Multi-Spot Laser Ablation of Stainless Steel with Picosecond and Femtosecond Pulses in Air

Tong Zhou [1], Sebastian Kraft [2], Walter Perrie [1,*], Jörg Schille [2], Udo Löschner [2], Stuart Edwardson [1] and Geoff Dearden [1]

[1] Laser Group, School of Engineering, University of Liverpool, Brownlow Street, Liverpool L69 3GH, UK; pstzhou4@liverpool.ac.uk (T.Z.); me0u5040@liverpool.ac.uk (S.E.); gdearden@liverpool.ac.uk (G.D.)
[2] Laserinstitut Hochschule Mittweida, Hochschule Mittweida University of Applied Sciences, Technikumplatz 17, 09648 Mittweida, Germany; kraft@hs-mittweida.de (S.K.); schille@hs-mittweida.de (J.S.); loeschne@hs-mittweida.de (U.L.)
* Correspondence: wpfemto1@liverpool.ac.uk

Abstract: We report on novel observations of directed re-deposition of ablation debris during the ultrafast laser micro-structuring of stainless steel in the air with multi-beams in close proximity on the surface. This interesting phenomenon is observed with both 10 ps and 600 fs NIR laser pulses at 5 kHz repetition rate. Ablation spot geometries could be altered with the use of beam splitting optics or a phase-only Spatial Light modulator. At low fluence (F ~ 1.0 J cm^{-2}) and pulse exposure of a few hundred pulses, the debris appears as concentrated narrow "filaments" connecting the ablation spots, while at higher fluence, (F ~ 5.0 J cm^{-2}) energetic jets of material emanated symmetrically along the axes of symmetry, depositing debris well beyond the typical re-deposition radius with a single spot. Patterns of backward re-deposition of debris to the surface are likely connected with the colliding shock waves and plasma plumes with the ambient air causing stagnation when the spots are in close proximity. The 2D surface debris patterns are indicative of the complex 3D interactions involved over wide timescales during ablation from picoseconds to microseconds.

Keywords: laser ablation; ultrafast; re-deposition

Citation: Zhou, T.; Kraft, S.; Perrie, W.; Schille, J.; Löschner, U.; Edwardson, S.; Dearden, G. Backward Flux Re-Deposition Patterns during Multi-Spot Laser Ablation of Stainless Steel with Picosecond and Femtosecond Pulses in Air. *Materials* **2021**, *14*, 2243. https://doi.org/10.3390/ma14092243

Academic Editors: Jörg Krüger and Jörn Bonse

Received: 20 March 2021
Accepted: 23 April 2021
Published: 27 April 2021

Publisher's Note: MDPI stays neutral with regard to jurisdictional claims in published maps and institutional affiliations.

1. Introduction

The interaction of intense ultrafast laser radiation with atoms, gases and solid materials has led to remarkable scientific advances such as High Harmonic Generation for attosecond spectroscopy [1,2], the use of filamentation for atmospheric probing [3,4], two-photon microscopy [5,6] and intraocular fs-LASIK in eye surgery [7]. In particular, laser ablation (LA) of materials with ps and sub-ps temporal pulse length has advanced materials analysis in areas such as Laser Ablation Inductively Coupled Mass Spectrometry (LA-ICP-MS) [8–10] and Laser-Induced Breakdown Spectroscopy (LIBS) [11,12]. With temporal pulse lengths <10 ps in ultrafast laser ablation, the instantaneous energy deposition reduces plasma absorption while minimizing melt and thermal diffusion during the pulse and yield high precision material removal [13,14]. This allows for easy generation of plasmonic, interferometric and hierarchical microstructures on, for example, stainless steel [15–17]. In metals, which have absorption coefficients typically $\alpha \sim 10^6$ cm^{-1}, a thin layer with thickness d ~ 10–30 nm is converted to a plasma at a solid density which expands well after the pulse is absorbed [18,19].

In vacuo, laser ablation can be described as a free expansion [20–23] while the laser plume which develops in the presence of an environmental gas is physically much more complex involving timescales from picosecond to nanosecond and microsecond. After electron heating during the pulse, the lattice heats typically over a few picoseconds due to e-phonon coupling, raising the surface temperature well above the evaporation point.

This results in fast surface electron emission due to thermionic [24] or multi-photon absorption [25,26] and a remarkable early stage "air plasma" can develop during the first 150 ps [27,28], with electron density $n_e \sim 10^{20}$ cm^{-3} and a transient electric field developing above the surface [29].

On the nanosecond timescale in air, the plasma plume expands rapidly and initially longitudinally (at speed $v \sim 10^6$ cm s^{-1}), colliding with the high density of surrounding gas molecules, ($N_{1atm} \sim 2.6 \times 10^{19}$ cm^{-3}), confining the plasma to the surface region while creating a blast (shock) wave which moves ahead of the plume [30–34]. As the longitudinal expansion decelerates rapidly, the plasma expands laterally after a few $\times$100 ns ($v_{lat} \sim 10^5$ cm s^{-1}) and can form a vortex structure with plasma plume concentrated at the ablation spot edge [35]. Transient electron temperatures in the plasma can reach $T_e >> 10^4$ K [24], then plasma cooling (over a few hundreds of ns to μs) occurs due to plasma expansion, electron-ion recombination and collisions with the background gas molecules. When thermal equilibrium is achieved in the plasma (~100 ns), this is the regime for LIBS and material analysis with fluorescence from highly excited atoms/ions [33,34]. As the plasma cools further, molecular species are formed at later times (~2–50 μs) due to atomic collisions, recombination and oxidation occur after the shock wave collapses [36]. Aerosols and nanoclusters are generated during a nucleation-condensation process with nanoparticle agglomerates re-deposited symmetrically by backward flux around a single spot [35,37]. While time-resolved spectral information using gated ICCDs can help elucidate the plasma dynamics, time-resolved scattering can detect nanoparticle formation and re-deposition on the microsecond timescale [35].

Debris re-deposition was first investigated during UV, excimer micro-structuring of polymers (e.g., Polyimide, PI), responsible for the developing cone structure with debris field dependent on spot shape, inferring strong horizontal forces close to the substrate surface [38]. Apparent field rotations with non-spherical spots were numerically modelled as a purely gas dynamic effect [39]. The debris radius was also shown to follow blast wave theory during excimer ablation of polyimide in air and inert gases [40]. Time-delayed (20–80 μs delay) weak emission detected at the plume periphery consisted mainly of continuum radiation consistent with thermal radiation from solid particles [20]. The difference in ablation geometries observed with a linear array of closely spaced ablation spots inferred stronger plume interactions in the middle [41]. Monte Carlo simulation of the expansion of a copper plasma in the presence of a background gas (Ar) shows compression of the ambient gas atoms by the plume (snowplough effect) for pressures >50 Pa and narrowing of the plume with increasing pressure while predicting backward plume motion and vortical flow at the plume periphery [42]. In the case of excimer ablation of stainless steel in air, (F = 10 J cm^{-2}/308 nm/25 ns) time-resolved ICCD images of the ablation plume up to 10 μs delay show this developing vortical structure after 1 μs and fully developed at 10 μs delay with a high density of nanoparticles deposited at the periphery [35]. Time-resolved light scattering during ablation also demonstrated that debris re-deposition occurred over a time delay of 1–60 μs after the pulse.

Polymers (such as PI, a photoresist) have strong absorption coefficients $\alpha > 10^4$ cm^{-1} in the UV leading to electronic excitation and "cold" ablation via direct bond breaking [43]. In the air, a plasma plume, carbonization (thermal component) and re-deposition around the ablation spot occurs but can be minimized using, for example, H_2 as a reactive, ambient gas [44]. Low ablation thresholds $F_{th} < 50$ m J cm^{-2} and precise etch rates from 25 nm/pulse are observed [45]. On steel, UV (248 nm/25 ns) ablation re-deposition generates iron oxide nanoparticles with a wide distribution φ = 2–20 nm while at 500 fs/248 nm, this narrows to $\varphi = 3 \pm 2$ nm [46]. The use of NIR, ns pulses result in the incorporation of nitrogen, as well into the re-deposited layer [47].

More recently, there has been an emphasis on temporal plume expansion with bursts of ultrashort pulses [48], and with a very high repetition rate USP Lasers [49,50] driven by the requirement to increase material ablation rates through a better understanding of the plume expansion and plasma absorption by the following pulses.

The interaction dynamics of shock waves during fs laser multi-spot ablation at a water/air interface were recently observed using transient reflection creating colliding supersonic airflows [51,52]. The authors point to the potential for producing focussed ablation plumes relevant to pulsed laser thin film deposition [53,54]. This idea has been investigated here using the observed backward re-deposition patterns from multi-spot ultrafast laser ablation on stainless steel as a novel approach highlighting the resulting plasma plume and shock wave interactions. Symmetric jets, with debris ejected at right angles to the spot axis are reported for the first time, and we present a tentative explanation of the physics behind these observations. The results may well impact the crucial area of Laser-Induced Forward Transfer of nanoparticle thin films at ambient pressure [55,56].

2. Materials and Methods

Experiments were carried out with two separate laser and optical systems based at the Universities of Liverpool and Mittweida where the temporal pulse lengths available were 10 ps and 600 fs, respectively. Figure 1 shows a schematic of the optical system in Liverpool. The output from a Nd:VAN seeded Regenerative amplifier (High-Q IC-355-800 ps, 10 ps/1064 nm Photonic Solutions Ltd., Edinburgh, UK) was attenuated, expanded (×3), then directed at low AOI to a phase-only Spatial Light Modulator (SLM, Hamamatsu-10468-03, Hamamatsu Photonics, Hamamatsu, Japan) for generating multi-spot patterns and focussed to a sample mounted on a three-axis stage able to bring the substrate surface to the focal plane. Computer Generated Holograms (CGHs) controlling spot numbers and separation on the substrate were generated using Inverse Fourier Transforms in the Hamamatsu software, while a pick-off optic (not shown) could direct spot patterns to a CCD camera prior to multi-spot ablation. This allows precise electronic control of spot separation with no mechanical movements. A 4f optical system ($f_1 = f_2 = 400$ mm) relayed the modulated beam from the SLM (addressed with CGHs) to the input aperture of a galvo system which directed the beams to the target surface, focussed by an f-theta lens (f = 100 mm). A fast-mechanical shutter (Thorlabs SH05, Thorlabs Ltd., Ely, UK) allowed the pulse number on target to be varied, synchronised to the scanning software (SCAPS GmbH). The expanding plumes were imaged to a time-resolved spectrometer (Andor Shamrock, model SR303i with intensified CCD, iStar 734, 2 ns gate width, Andor Technology Ltd., Belfast, UK) and synchronised from the 5 kHz Regenerative amplifier.

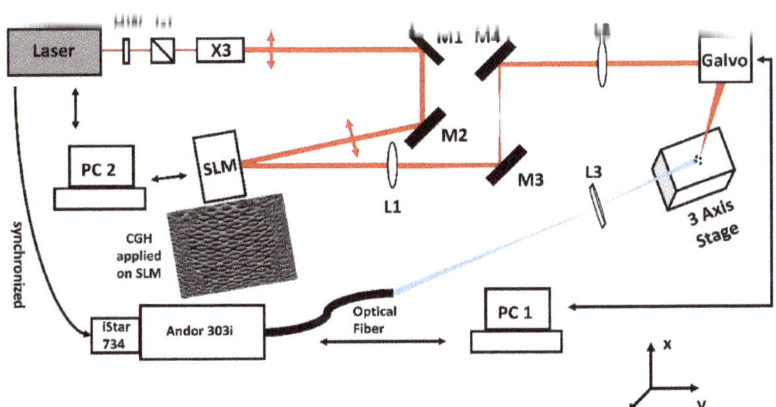

Figure 1. Optical set-up for 10 ps/5 kHz multi-spot ablation of stainless steel in the air. An attenuated and expanded beam from a Nd:Van Regen amplifier is directed to the phase-only SLM at low AOI then imaged via a 4f optical system (f = 400 mm) to the galvo input aperture. Appropriate phase-only CGH's could create arbitrary spot geometries and separations at the steel surface. A time-resolved spectrometer with triggered ICCD (synchronised to Regen amplifier) allowed measurement of the spectral plasma dynamics by focusing the plasma emission on a fibre coupler.

Figure 2 shows a schematic of the optical system for 600 fs/5 kHz double spot ablation (Mittweida). The pump laser (FX-Series, edgewave GmbH, 1030 nm/600 fs, Würselen, Germany) output was attenuated by HWP/polarising beam splitter BS. Afterwards, a second HWP/PBS combination produce two optical lines (1,2) with adjustable power distribution. Line 1 path length was altered by translating mirrors M (1.1) and M (1.2) to synchronise the ablation spots temporally. This synchronisation is proven by the ablation interference patterns with Line 2 at the sample surface. The ablation spot separation was adjusted by slightly tilting mirror M (1.4). Both lines were focussed onto the sample surface by an f = 100 mm optic L2. At the focal plane, the laser spot radii are w_{86} = 15 µm. A spot monitor (CCD) on the level of the material surface to enable a precise temporal and geometrical adjustment. A probe laser (Cavilux, Fa. Cavitar Ltd., 688 nm/13 ns, Tampere, Finland) electronically synchronised to the pump laser allowed pump-probe shadowgraphy of expanding plasma plumes. The shadowgraphs were recorded with a 14-bit cooled CCD camera (pco.1600, PCO AG, Kelheim, Germany).

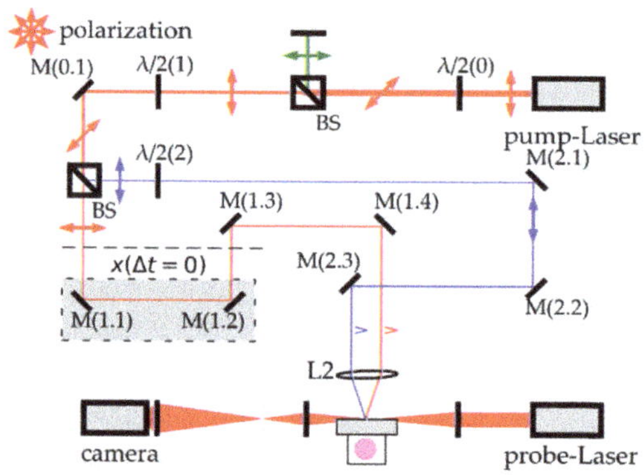

Figure 2. Scheme of the optical set-up for double spot ablation with simultaneous shadowgraphy of stainless steel in the air. The pump laser, probe laser and axis and shadowgraph capture were electrically synchronised. The attenuated and split pump beams are focussed and temporally overlapped at the sample surface by one optic lens L2. The temporal (by moving M (1.1) and M (1.2)) and geometrical adjustment (by tilting M (1.4)) can be monitored with a spot monitor in the focal plane.

3. Results

3.1. 2-Spot Ablation with 10 ps Pulses at 1064 nm/5 kHz Repetition Rate

The substrate used was ANSI 304 stainless steel and optically polished to a roughness Ra ~50 nm. The focussed single beam diameter was measured from the observed ablation crater diameters with increasing pulse energy [57] and found to be $\varphi = 22.2 \pm 0.2$ µm. No significant variation with multi-spot geometry was found. Single-pulse ablation threshold (N = 1) was measured to be $F_{th} = 0.29 \pm 0.01$ J cm^{-2} decreasing with pulse number, and incubation coefficient measured to be $S = 0.85 \pm 0.01$ in excellent agreement with the literature [58]. Figure 3 shows the re-deposition patterns observed during two spot ablation with 10 ps laser ablation of stainless steel in air while varying separation and pulse number at fluence F = 0.90 J cm^{-2}, (a) 200 pulses, (b) 400 pulses (c), 800 pulses, all 75 µm separation, (d)–(f) 95 µm separation, (g)–(i) and 145 µm separation, respectively. It required multi-hundred pulse exposure to observe debris for good optical contrast. The ablation debris is concentrated between the spots at d = 75 µm separation with a width comparable to the ablation spot diameter, while at 95 µm separation this narrows to around a 10 µm wide "filament". The concentration of this directed re-deposition, observed at low fluence, is an interesting phenomenon, indicating transient forces during the plume expansion and collisions with the air, resulting in some ablation debris acquiring momentum components preferentially directed along the axis between the spots. There is evidence also that at the midplane, some debris is expanding normal to the axis. As spot separation increased to 145 μm at this fluence, there was negligible interaction between the plumes. The debris radius near spots R_d ~ 30 μm.

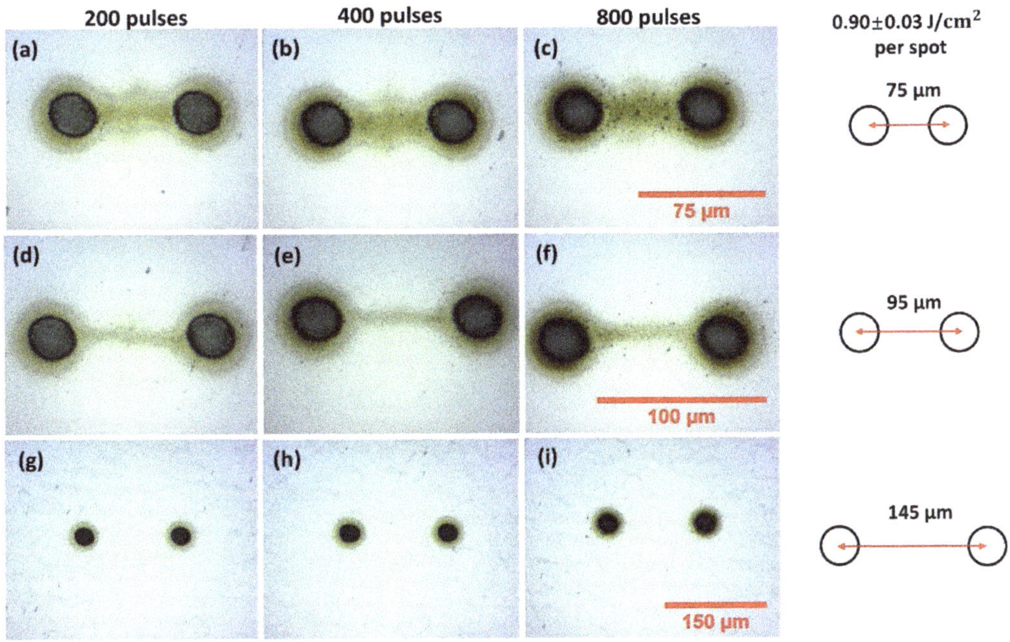

Figure 3. Optical images of observed two spot re-deposition during 10 ps laser ablation of stainless steel in air while varying spot separation and pulse number at F = 0.90 J cm^{-2}, (**a**) 200 pulses, (**b**) 400 pulses, (**c**) 800 pulses, all 75 μm separation, (**d–f**) 95 μm separation, (**g–i**) 145 μm separation respectively. Debris is concentrated in a filament between the spots at 75 μm, thinning to a line about 10 μm wide at 95 μm spot separation. No interaction between the spots is observed at 145 μm separation at this low fluence.

The effect on debris re-deposition of increasing fluence to F = 4.51 J cm^{-2} on stainless steel is shown in the optical images of Figure 4a–i. At this higher fluence in Figure 4a–c, we observe diverging debris jets ejected normal to the spot axis. This extends to a radial distance of R_{jet} ~200 μm, well beyond that around each spot R_d ~ 30 μm, inferring that an energetic process may be involved. In Figure 4b,c, with increased exposure, removal of debris from the surface between the spots (in the form of two slightly curved lines) supports the view that strong shock wave interactions between the colliding plumes during ablation may be responsible, clear in Figure 4c,f. These effects essentially disappear at the highest, 145 μm separation with a return to the concentration of material between the spots Figure 4g–i, similar to the patterns at low fluence (Figure 3). The tiny ablation spots along the axis are due to low energy ghost beams appearing during multi-pulse exposure, while the top spot is the remaining zero order. Their presence here helps detect local physical effects of shock wave and air movements affecting the debris motion.

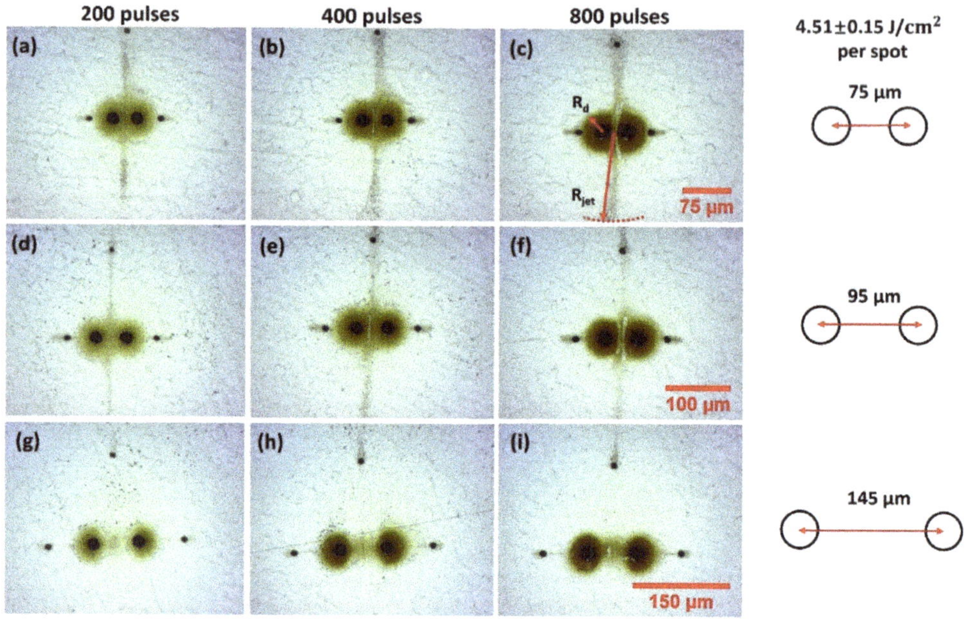

Figure 4. Optical images of observed two spot re-deposition during 10 ps laser ablation of stainless steel in air while varying spot separation and pulse number at fluence F = 4.51 J cm^{-2}, (**a**) 200 pulses, (**b**) 400 pulses (**c**) 800 pulses, all 75 µm spot separation, (**d–f**) 95 µm separation, (**g–i**) 145 µm separation. At this higher fluence in (**a–c**), we observe diverging debris jets ejected normal to the spot axis while in (**c**,**f**), removal of surface debris by shock waves is apparent. These effects essentially disappear at the highest separation with a return to the concentration of material between the spots (**g–i**). The tiny ablation spots along the axis are due to low energy ghost beams while the top spot remains zero order.

3.2. Ablation Rates and Debris Radii (10 ps Pulses)

The measured ablation volume/pulse of single and two spot geometries with pulse number N is shown in Figure 5a for a fluence F = 2.9 J cm^{-2} (E_p = 6 µJ/pulse). These results confirm that ablation rates are essentially independent of spot geometry and spot separation when $N \geq 200$, whether single or double spot, within experimental error. Hence, the proximity of the spots does not affect ablation rates significantly. The ablation volume/pulse V ~ 5.7 μm^3/pulse corresponding to a mass ablation M ~ 0.05 ng/pulse. Crater volumes and geometries were measured with a white light interferometer, Wyko NT3300. The single spot debris radius and jet radius with pulse energy and exposure are shown in Figure 5b on an Ln-Ln plot. This confirms that the debris radii follow a power-law $R \propto E^{0.47}$ for a single spot while the much higher Jet debris radii, $R_{jet} \propto E^{0.41}$. This relationship approximates that predicted by blast wave theory [59], however, higher than the expected $R \propto E^{1/3}$ which has also been observed by other authors [60].

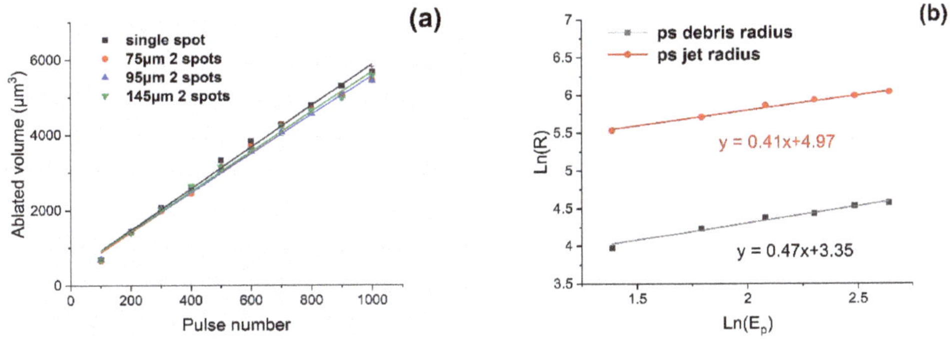

Figure 5. (**a**) Measured ablation volume versus pulse number for single and double spot ablation at d = 75 µm, 95 µm and 145 µm separation with fluence F = 2.9 J cm^{-2}/spot (Ep = 6 µJ/spot). Spot geometry does not affect ablation volume for $N \geq 200$, within experimental error, (**b**) Observed single spot debris radius and jet radius with pulse energy and exposure on an Ln-Ln plot. The radii follow a power-law $R \propto E^{0.47}$ for debris and $R_{jet} \propto E^{0.41}$ respectively.

3.3. SEM Imaging of the Debris Fields, Two Spot Patterns

Figure 6a–d shows a series of SEM images of ablation debris from two spot ablation of stainless steel in the air with 10 ps pulses at low fluence F = 0.9 J cm^{-2}, N = 800 pulses and spot separation d = 75 µm. The concentration of debris between spots is clear in Figure 6a, with evidence of some material ejected normal to the spot axis in the centre. At low fluence, there are two main components to the debris—particle agglomerates appear on the collision plane (and around the spots), while solid spherical nanoparticles with diameters 50–150 nm appear at the spot edge, Figure 6b. These are likely formed during collisions of the expanding plumes and condensed from the stagnation region at the midplane. Figure 6c (2000×) shows the particle agglomerates near the centre at higher magnification while Figure 6d (35,000×) confirms that the particle agglomerate consists of both solid np's and agglomerated chains of fine np's. There is a significant change in the nature of the debris generated at higher fluence, F = 4.8 J cm^{-2}, as shown in the SEM images of Figure 6e–h. Deposition now produces a thick deposit near the ablation spots while the shock waves lift material from the surface between the spots Figure 6e and deposit well away from the spots, Figure 6f. Figure 6g,h, with increasing magnification show that thin jet debris consists of np chain agglomerates and is almost devoid of solid nanoparticles. This is consistent with higher surface temperature achieved during ablation, well above the evaporation temperature, T_{ev} = 2861 K. The high concentration of the np chain agglomerate debris supports the assertion that this material is formed during strong stagnation of the plume collisions in the midplane.

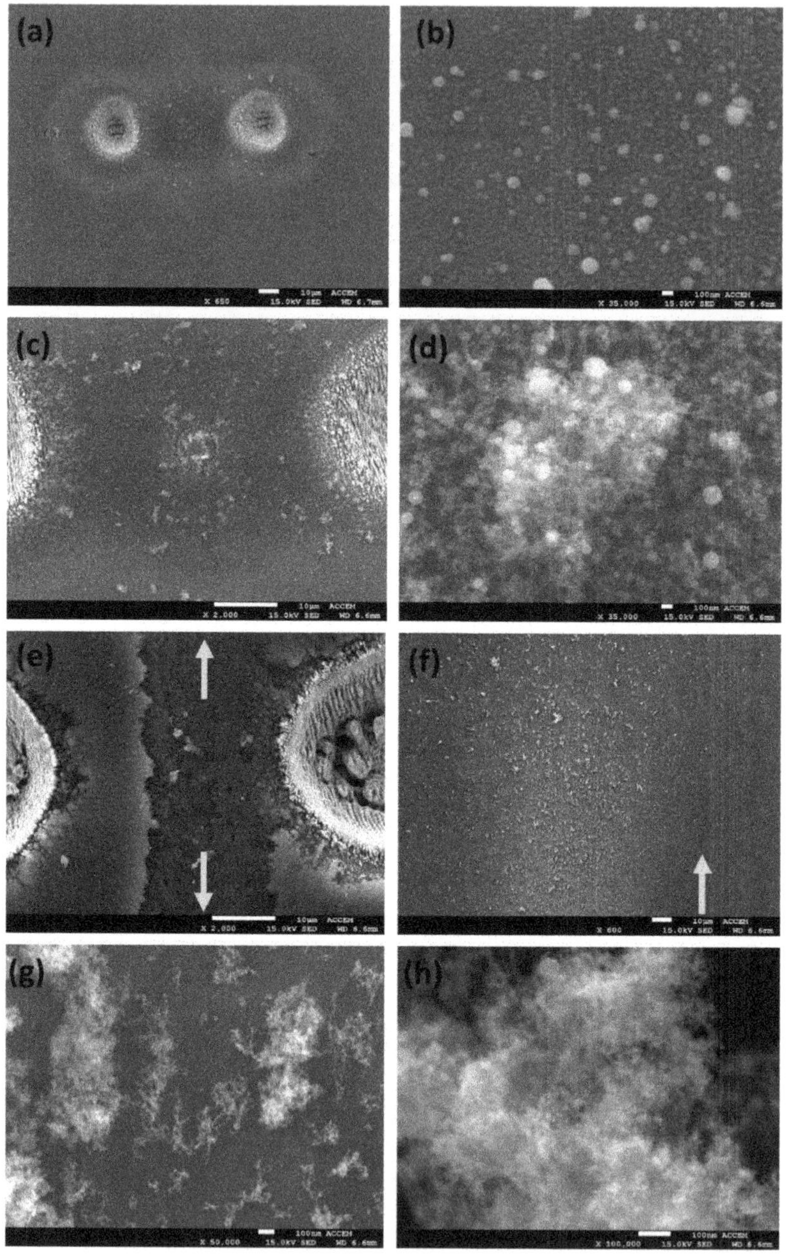

Figure 6. SEM images of the ablation debris from two spot ablation of stainless steel at low fluence (F = 0.9 J cm^{-2} (**a**–**d**) and high fluence F = 4.8 J cm^{-2} (**e**–**h**), N = 800 pulses, spot separation d = 75 μm. (**a**) image of the whole debris field, (**b**) 50–150 nm diameter np's observed at spot periphery in (**a**) red ring, (**c**) particle agglomerate at the centre, (**d**) high magnification image of (**c**) showing round np's and np agglomerate, (**e**) High fluence re-deposition pattern showing material lifted directly from the surface by the energetic colliding plumes and shock waves, (**f**) jet debris ejected normal to spots, (**g**) high magnification image of jet np chain agglomerate, (**h**) highest, 100,000× magnification of jet np chain agglomerate which still shows little structure.

3.4. Time-Resolved Plasma Emission Spectra

Figure 7 shows the two spots (E = 20 μJ/spot, d = 75 μm) time-resolved (0–95 ns) plasma emission spectrum of stainless steel in air over Δλ = 395 nm–415 nm. Gate width was set at 5 ns, gate delay interval 2 ns and data accumulated over 50 spectra. The substrate was scanned at 2 mm/s while an f = 125 mm bi-convex lens imaged the whole plasma emission to a fibre coupler (NA ~0.2, Figure 1) then to the spectrometer (Andor Shamrock 303i, 50 μm slit, 1800 L/mm grating) and cooled ICCD camera. The ICCD was triggered externally from the Laser Regenerative amplifier. Continuum dominated the spectra at early times, likely black body radiation from the hot plasma near the surface [21], while spectral line intensities rise sharply, then decrease along with the background continuum as the ablation plasma cools. Spectral line widths also decrease with time as electron density decreases, reducing Stark broadening [61]. The spectral lines in this region have been identified as due mainly to excited neutral atoms of Fe I, Cr I and Mn I: Fe I: 395.667 nm, Cr I: 396.368 nm, Cr I: 396.974 nm, Mn I: 397.708 nm, Fe I: 398.396 nm, Mn I: 399.161 nm, Fe I/Fe II blended line: 403.130 nm, Mn I: 403.307 nm, Fe I: 404.581 nm, Fe I: 406.359 nm, Fe I: 407.581 nm (centre), Fe I: 411.854 nm, Fe I: 413.290 nm, Fe I/Fe II/Fe III blended line: 414.26 nm. Single spot (20 μJ/pulse) spectra were very similar with lower intensities [62].

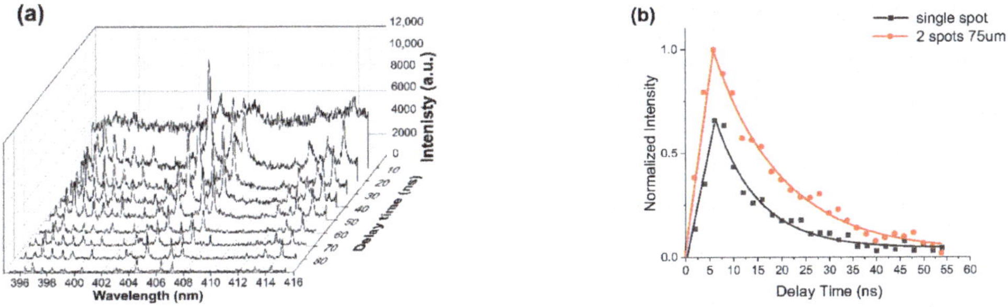

Figure 7. (**a**) Two spots (E = 20 μJ/spot, d = 75 μm,) time-resolved plasma emission spectrum (Δλ = 395–415 nm) of stainless steel over time delay 0–95 ns. Continuum dominates at early times while atomic lines appear as the plasma cools. The three intense lines near the centre are due to Fe I: 404.581 nm, Fe I: 406.359 nm, Fe I: 407.581 nm, (**b**) Integrated intensity (Δλ = 395 nm–415 nm) with time for single and double spot (d = 75 μm) showing exponential decrease with plasma lifetimes τ1/e ~ 9.2 ± 0.5 ns (single) and 13.9 ± 0.7 ns (double) respectively. The fits are exponential.

Figure 7b shows the time-integrated plasma emission (Δλ = 395–415 nm) for single and double spot (d = 75 μm) confirming that the plasma lifetimes $\tau_{1/e}$ ~ 9.2 ± 1.0 ns and 13.9 ± 0.7 ns, respectively, hence double spot plasma lifetime increasing over the single spot. These lifetimes are similar to those observed with 20 μJ, 150 fs laser ablation of Al in the air [21]. The short plasma lifetimes are a consequence of both the low pulse energies and rapid collisional cooling of the dense ambient air.

Plasma excitation temperature for single spot ablation (E = 20 μJ) has been estimated by the well-known Boltzmann method [11] from the Fe I line intensities I_{mn}, transition probabilities (gA_{mn}, g degeneracy) and upper energy levels, E_m. A plot of $Ln(\lambda I_{mn}/gA_{mn})$ versus E_m yielded a linear plot inferring T_e ~7500 K for single spot near 40 ns delay time. We also estimated the electron density from the Stark broadening of the Fe I line at λ = 404.58 nm yielding N_e ~ 10^{18} cm^{-3}.

By removing the ICCD from the spectrometer and placing this at the image plane of the focus lens, (f = 75 mm, M ~ 4), the time-resolved plasma plumes were observed, Figure 8. Gate width here is 5 ns, energy/spot = 20 μJ and spot separation d = 75 μm. With spots normal to the optic axis, we can observe plasma expansion, collision and stagnation after 15 ns. When the plumes are imaged parallel to the optic axis and 10–15 ns delay, we see some interesting structure at right angles to the spot axis which may be connected to the jets. The lateral plume expansion velocity can be estimated to be $v_\perp$ ~3.5 × 10^3 ms^{-1}, decelerating after 15 ns, while the elliptical plume shape which develops supports lateral plasma expansion [35,63].

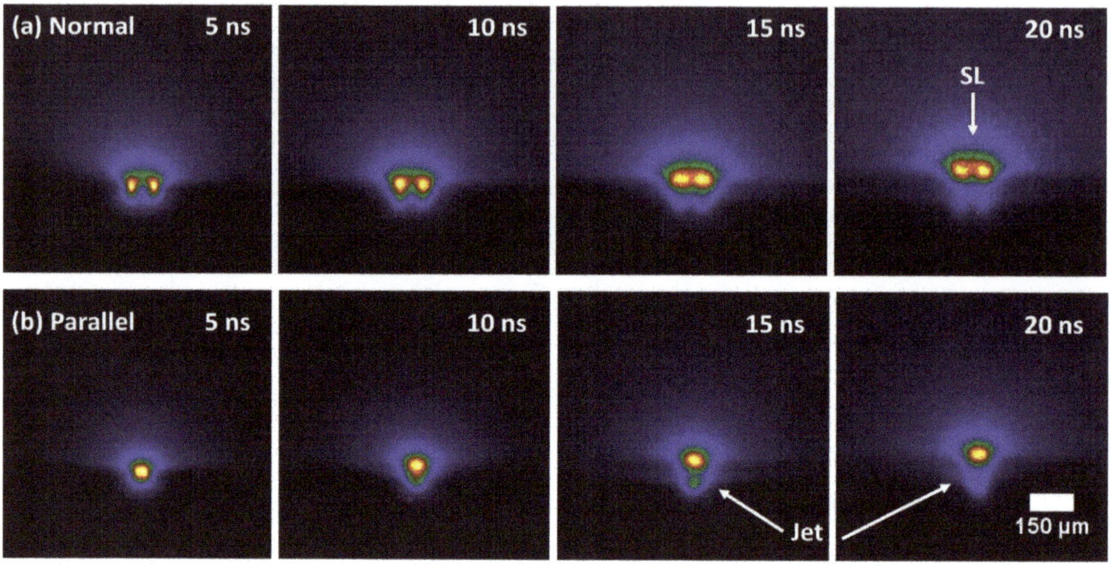

Figure 8. Time-resolved imaging of single and double spot ablation plume emission (20 μJ/spot, d = 75 μm) of stainless steel with time delays 5–20 ns. ICCD gate width was 5 ns (**a**) 2-spot normal to optic axis showing plume collisions and stagnation at 20 ns delay (**b**) two spots parallel to optic axis with an indication of jet structure 15–20 ns.

3.5. Two Spot Ablation with 600 fs/5 kHz Temporal Pulses at 1030 nm

The effect of increasing peak intensity by over 1 order of magnitude was investigated with the experimental system of Figure 2, while maintaining the same repetition rate of 5 kHz. Results are shown in Figure 9 for pulse numbers 200, 500 and 1000 at fluence F = 1.41 J cm^{-2} (peak intensity I = 2.4 × 10^{12} W cm^{-2}). Again, we observe symmetric debris ejection or jets at right angles out to a radius of R_{jet} ~ 150 μm with spot separation d = 75 μm. As spot separation increases, we return to the directed, filamentary re-deposition (d = 100 μm) between the spots, and just apparent at d = 150 μm, N = 1000), similar to patterns observed with 10 ps pulses, Figure 3a–f.

The results of high fluence two spot ablation with fluence F = 5.7 J cm^{-2} (20 μJ/spot, I = 9.6 × 10^{12} W cm^{-2}) are shown in Figure 10. where plume interactions create strongly diverging jets at spot separation d = 75 μm. At d = 100 μm separation, jets are more collimated with re-deposition jet radius R_{jet} > 300 μm. There is a slight tilt in the spot axis here relative to the horizontal. With N = 500 and 1000 at d = 100 μm, shock wave and plume interactions also remove debris from the surface (compare Figure 4c,f), evidence of the quasi-stationary shock waves [51,52]. At d = 150 μm material is again concentrated between the spots as interactions weaken. Peak intensity therefore appears to play a minor role in the debris re-deposition during the plume interactions from 600 fs to 10 ps pulse length on stainless steel in the air.

Figure 11a,b show SEM images of the diverging symmetric jet debris from 600 fs double spot (d = 100 μm) ablation of stainless steel in air (20 μJ/spot, F = 4.5 J cm^{-2}, N = 1000). This material likely consists of np chain and is concentrated at the jet ends, almost 400 μm from the spots.

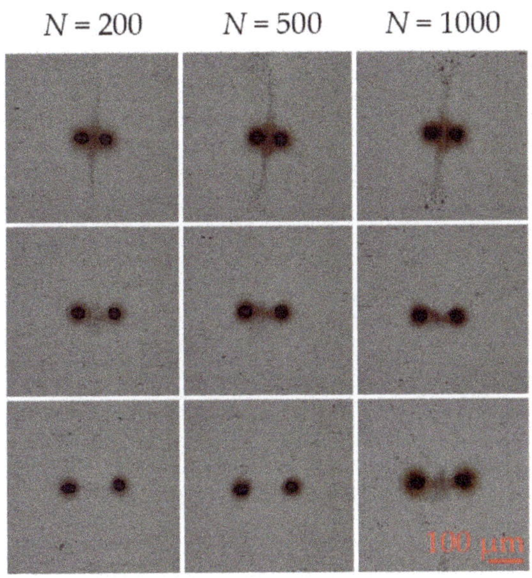

Figure 9. Resulting debris re-deposition and jet formation after 600 fs laser double pulse ablation with fluence F_0 = 1.41 J cm^{-2} (E_P = 5 μJ/pulse). Optical images of stainless steel surfaces after applying for various pulse numbers (200, 500, 1000) at different spot separations (50 μm, 100 μm and 150 μm). Debris jets are visible at 75 μm at the investigated *N*. At larger separations, the debris is concentrated in a filament between the spots (*d* = 100 μm) and becomes apparent at *d* = 150 μm separation, *N* = 1000. Fluence here is 1.5 times higher than with 10 ps pulses (Figure 3).

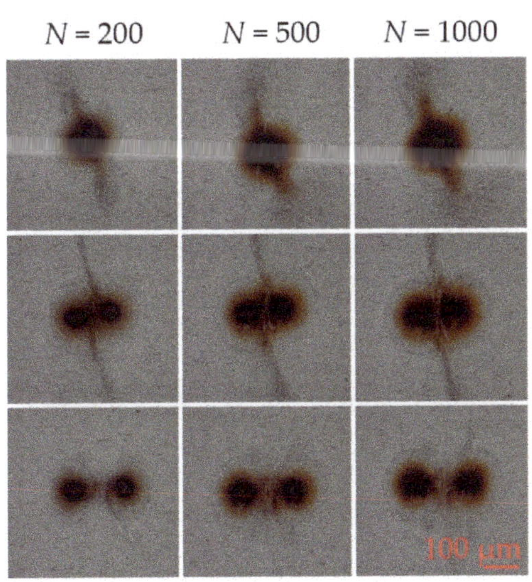

Figure 10. Resulting debris re-deposition and jet formation after 600 fs laser double spot ablation with fluence F_0 = 5.7 J cm^{-2} (E_P = 20 μJ/pulse). Within the investigated pulse numbers *N* (200, 500, 1000) and pulse separations *d* of 50 μm, 100 μm and 150 μm, the optical images reveal an interaction between the two spots. Strongly diverging debris jets at 75 μm and collimated jets at *d* = 100 μm are visible. At the largest separation *d* = 150 μm, where the interactions are weaker, the material is again concentrated between spots.

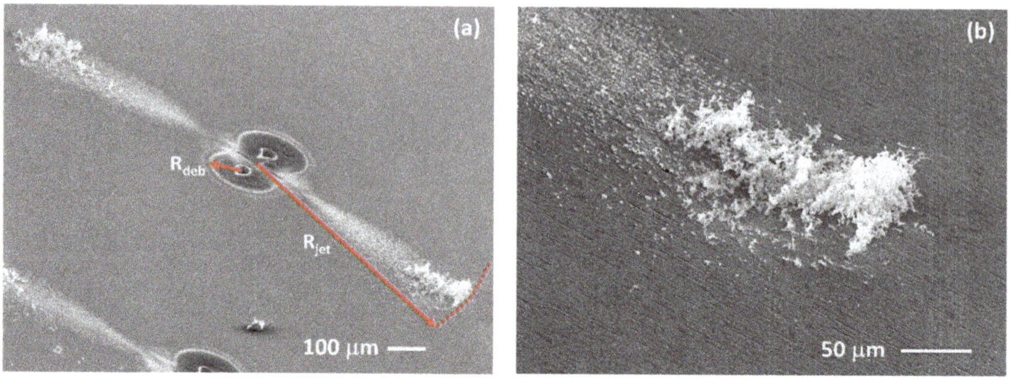

Figure 11. Tilted SEM images of the jets after double spot femtosecond ablation of s. steel in the air (E_P = 20 µJ/pulse, N = 1000, d = 100 µm). (**a**) shows the symmetric diverging debris jets (np chain agglomerates) with an accretion of material at the jet ends, almost 400 µm from the double spot centre. (**b**) higher magnification of concentrated jet debris near the jet end. The debris radii near the spots and jet radii are indicated (R_{deb} and R_{jet} respectively).

The debris and jet radii generated with 600 fs pulses are shown in Figure 12. For comparison, the data from 10 ps two spot ablation. Logarithmic fits are included, and the exponents vary from n = 0.33 to 0.47. The fs and ps debris radii are close exponent while the fs jet radii appear to have the lowest, n = 0.33. The higher radii for given energy with 10 ps pulses is due to the smaller spot separation of 75 µm, while this was 100 µm with 600 fs pulses. There may also be differences due to uncertainties in the estimation of the radii.

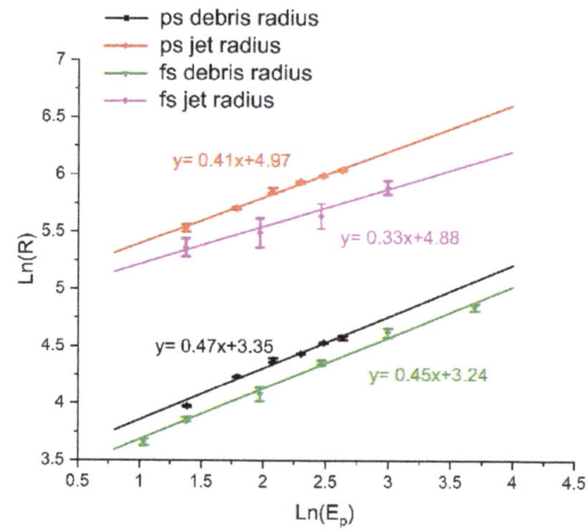

Figure 12. Ln-Ln plots of the two spots debris and jet radii ([R] = µm) measured for 600 fs and 10 ps ablation. The logarithmic fits ([E_P] = µJ) are shown to be reasonably close in exponent except for femtosecond ablation which is lower. The spot separations were 100 µm (600 fs) and 75 µm (10 ps), respectively. Error bars represent 1 σ.

The reproducibility of the results reported is supported by the excellent observed fits to the Ln-Ln plots with indicated errors. Ultrafast laser ablation minimises thermal diffusion and melt leading to a deterministic evaporation process [19]. The observed nanoparticle agglomerated jets can be deflected with a significant airflow over the substrate. However, when the surrounding ambient air is stable, the jets emanate at right angles and have the same length, Figure 11a.

3.6. Time-Resolved Shadowgraphy (600 fs/5 kHz).

Ablation plumes and their development after ablation were imaged with the pump-probe experimental set-up shown in Figure 2. The probe beam (λ = 688 nm, τ_H = 13 ns) was electronically synchronised to the pump beam (λ = 1030 nm). Time-resolved measurements are often carried out with a single pulse exposure–but here, after simultaneous multi-pulse, multi-spot exposure, we can see the developing plumes and their interactions. The connection axis of two spots is aligned perpendicular to the imaging plane. The total delay time regarding the arrival of the first pulse pair with 5 kHz repetition rate is τ = 1002 μs, hence a delay time of 2 μs after the last, N = 6th pulse, Figure 13. There is a strong plasma plume overlap confined to the surface at d = 100 μm separation with diverging plume above the spots containing solid (dark) micron size particles, strongly absorbing/scattering. The previous pulses have formed these. These also appear at 150 μm spot separation but disappear entirely at d = 200 μm, where the plasma plumes near the surface are distinct and plume absorption much more uniform. This particle is likely the np chain agglomerate observed on the surface, shown in the SEM images of Figure 11. which appear in the jets due to the strong plume interactions. Note in the shadowgraphs a visible expanding spherical shock wave from the last pulse pair overlaps the material previously ejected. The shock wave speed, from the time delay, v_s ~375 m/s just above the speed of sound while the lateral plasma expansion has slowed significantly to around $v \leq 50$ m/s after 2 μs delay.

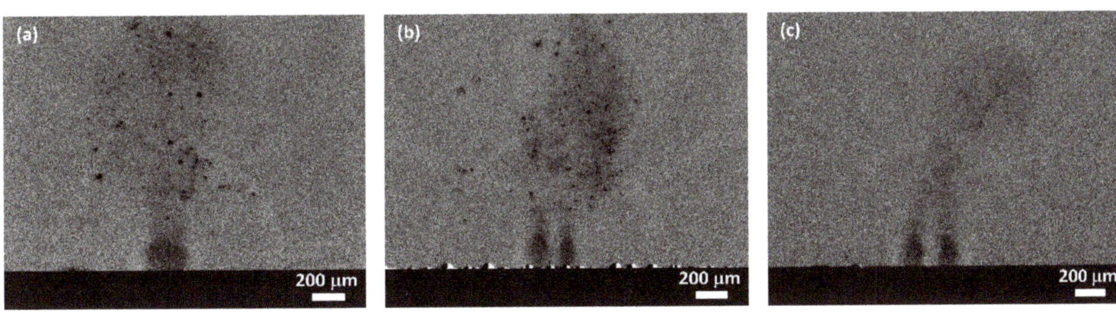

Figure 13. Time-resolved shadowgraphs of the interacting plumes with two spot ablation in the air after N = 6 and delay time of τ = 2 μs after ablation and τ (total) = 1002 μs. These images demonstrate that large condensed absorbing particles are apparent in the debris above the spots when the separation is smallest and where the plume collisions are strongest, (**a**) d = 100 μm, (**b**) d = 150 μm, (**c**) d = 200 μm where these particles have all but disappeared. Note that the spherical shock waves from the last pulse overlap the material ejected beforehand.

4. Discussion

Laser ablation on metal in the ambient atmosphere can be likened to a mechanical detonation, creating an ablation plume expanding supersonically against the background gas, causing a shock wave. As the plume does work by expanding against atmospheric pressure, the expansion velocity decreases with time, and the shock wave radius is given by Taylor's blast wave theory [59],

$$R = S(\gamma)(E/\rho_0)^{1/5} t^{2/5} \tag{1}$$

where $S(\gamma)$ ~1 is a function only of the air specific heat γ (~1.4), E is the energy released, ρ_0 is the undisturbed background gas density and t is the time after ablation. The effect is to force most of the air within the shock front into a thin shell just inside the front, compressing and heating the air. The initial pressure driving the front $p_{max} \gg p_0$, (1 atm).

When $p_{max} \sim p_0$, the self-similar solution of Equation (1) is no longer valid. In this case, the radius for this upper limit is given by [20],

$$R = (E/p_0)^{1/3} \tag{2}$$

The ablation plasma plume follows behind the shock front and a contact discontinuity can be observed inside the shock front [33]. For the range 2 μJ $\leq E \leq$ 20 μJ, single spot debris radii range from 40–120 μm while R calculated from Equation (2) yields 270 μm $\leq R \leq$ 580 μm. The debris radius can be related to the shock radius through $R_D \sim fR$ where f < 1 and here, f ~ 0.15–0.2, similar to that observed by other authors [60]. From the time-resolved plasma emission (10 ps), backward re-deposition with single spot ablation likely starts about ~100 ns after ablation and from the pump-probe observations, (600 fs) continues over 10 μs and longer. The debris power laws yield $R_{deb} \propto E^{0.3-0.5}$ for both single spot and jets but the much larger jet radii if applied to $R_D \sim fR$ yields f ~ 0.7–0.8 using Equation (2) inferring that an additional energetic process is involved during the plasma plume interactions.

Multi-spot ablation in vacuum between two independent and closely spaced seed plasmas collide due to the lateral plasma expansion. With a low density and high relative velocity, plasmas tend to interpenetrate, relevant in collisionless astrophysical plasmas, leading to ion reflection and particle acceleration [64]. However, with higher density and a low relative velocity, the plasmas rapidly decelerate at the collision plane, forming a stagnation layer (SL). Accretion and compression of the material within the SL leads to a local increase in density and temperature. The degree of stagnation can be described by a collisionality parameter $\xi = d/\lambda_{ii}$, where d is the distance between the two plasmas and λ_{ii} is the ion-other ion mean free path, given by, [65,66]

$$\lambda_{ii\ (1-2)} = \frac{4\pi\varepsilon_0^2 m_i^2 v_{12}^4}{q^4 Z^4 n_i \ln(\Lambda_{1-2})} \tag{3}$$

where ε_0 is the permittivity of free space, m_i is the ion mass, v_{12} is the relative ion flow velocity (prior to impact), q is the elementary charge, Z is the average ionisation state, n_i is the plasma density at the collision plane and ln $(\Lambda_{1\text{-}2})$ is the Coulomb Logarithm, a slowly varying function, with a value O (10–20) [67]. The parameter ξ is very sensitive to the relative plasma velocity term $v_{12}{}^4$ while only linearly dependent on separation d. If used in ambient air, this description is more complex than in vacuum due to the presence of shock waves and rapid plasma deceleration due to collisions with the air. From time-resolved plasma emission at 15 ns, Figure 8. We estimated that $v_\perp \sim 3.5 \times 10^3$ m s^{-1} so that $v_{12} = 2v_\perp \sim 7 \times 10^3$ m s^{-1}. Inserting this value into Equation (3), we find $\lambda_{ii} \sim 3.1$ μm so that the plasma collision region is limited to the micron scale with collisionality parameter $\xi = d/\lambda_{ii}$= 75 μm/3.1 μm ~ 24.

In a plasma, the Debye length is the characteristic length over which electrons and ions can be separated, and in an ideal plasma (e.g., astrophysical) has many particles per Debye sphere N_D given by

$$N_D = N_e\left(\frac{4\pi}{3}\right)\lambda_D^3 \gg 1 \tag{4}$$

The classical plasma parameter g = $1/N_e\lambda_D{}^3 << 1$ so that collective effects dominate the plasma. In laser ablation, we can calculate g for each plasma plume knowing N_e and λ_D which is given by [67] $\lambda_D = 743\ (T_e)^{1/2}\ (N_e)^{-1/2}$ where the electron temperature T_e is in eV while N_e is in cm^{-3}. At delay time τ = 50 ns, we measured T_e (10 ps, E_p = 20 μJ) from a Boltzmann plot to be ~7500 K (1 eV = 11,600 K) hence plasma temperature $T_e \sim 0.65$ eV while $N_e \sim N_i \sim 10^{18}$ cm^{-3} from measured Stark broadening of the Fe I line at λ = 404.58 nm. The Debye length in each plasma plume is then $\lambda_D \sim 6.0 \times 10^{-7}$ cm (6 nm) while the particle number in a Debye sphere is, from Equation (4), N_D = 0.92. The collision parameter g = $1/N_e\lambda_D{}^3$ = 4.6 hence the plasma plumes are each highly collisional as expected. We can also estimate the Coulomb Logarithm [67], $Ln\Lambda = 9N_D/Z = 8.3$ assuming $Z \sim 1$ is the average ionisation state, supported by the time-resolved spectroscopy, Figure 7a.

Recently, the interaction of two colliding Al plasmas (in the air) and their shock waves were observed in two spot nanosecond laser ablation using shadowgraphy, schlieren images and interferometry [68]. From refractive index profiles, expanding shock fronts and their reflections were observed after collision along with compression and stagnation and of the air behind the shock fronts. With pulse fluence F ~ 27 J cm^{-2}, focus intensity I ~ 1.6 $GWcm^{-2}$ and 1 mm spot separation, compressed air density reached $n_0 \sim 5 \times 10^{20}$ cm^{-3} behind the interacting shocks while plasma density $n_i \sim 5.10^{18}$ cm^{-3}. The stagnation was described as "soft" [69] with a plasma hill developing over times scales from 0.7–3 µs.

More recently, stationary transient straight shockwaves (on a 10 ns timescale) were detected during multi-spot fs ablation of water in the air creating supersonic air flows which collided [51,52]. Fluence per spot F ~ 18 J cm^{-2} with peak intensities I ~ 10^{14} W cm^{-2} and spot separations from d ~ 14–20 µm. The length of the shock waves was related to the local flow velocity at a given radial position from the spots and observed when the relative speed of shock wave propagation exceeded the velocity of sound in the air. The symmetric geometry of the observed two spot transient shock waves is highly reminiscent of the observed patterns of debris removed between double spot ablation in this work at higher fluence (Figures 4, 6 and 11) with ps and fs pulse lengths. This indicates that material removal between spots during ablation at high fluence may be evidence of shock wave interactions.

5. Conclusions

The jets appearing at higher fluence (and small spot separation) could be created as follows using a simplified 2D approach. When the high-pressure shock waves meet at the collision plane, the pressure due to each shock wave $p_{max} = 0.155\ E/R^3$ ($\gamma = 1.4$) [59]. If we set $E \sim E_p = 20$ µJ and R = 50 µm, $p_{max} = 2.48 \times 10^7$ Pa ~248 atm. The air between these shocks will be highly compressed by this "piston" as they meet and the curved expanding shocks could compress, accelerate and expel the air symmetrically in a diverging jet in both directions normal to the axis, Figure 14a. The plasmas following then stagnate and ion Coulomb repulsion off-axis at low impact parameters converts their axial momentum to transverse momentum assuming elastic collisions. The observed material lifted from the surface leaves patterns very similar to the transient stationary shock waves observed during multi-spot induced supersonic air flows at a water/air interface [51,52].

At low fluence and larger separations, shock wave pressures are much reduced, plasma density decreases, reducing stagnation to "soft", hence allowing plasma interpenetration between the spots. Weak shock waves pass through each other and likely reflect back along the axis from the plasmas. Multiple collisions can decelerate ions and a degree of ion reflection may occur [64] so that particles acquire momentum directed along the spot axis then arrive at the surface through backward flux, Figure 14b.

Two colliding air breakdown plasmas created with high energy, nanosecond laser pulses demonstrated reflection and transmission of expanding shock waves depending on pulse energy and plasma seed separations [70]. One might ask if oxidation during ultrafast laser ablation is significant here, but we have also observed the Jets in pure Nitrogen at 1 atm (10 ps, not reported here) with the aid of a gas cell. We estimate that oxidation of Fe atoms to Fe_3O_4 could at most add 10% additional energy, not nearly enough to explain the phenomena here.

Time-resolved plasma emission yielded important plasma parameters such as lifetime and temperatures, and plasma collisions between spots show plume stagnation, resulting in bi-directional jets. The effects of quasi-stationary shock waves are very clear, compressing the air and lifting debris from the surface between the spots. Time-resolved shadowgraphy with 600 fs pulses showed micron size particles (which constitute the jets) only when the ablation spots were in close proximity. In fact, the re-deposited jet debris consists of agglomerated nano-particle chains.

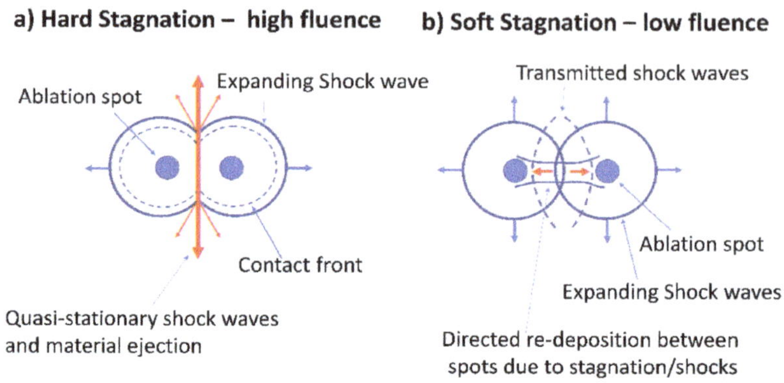

Figure 14. Schematic diagrams summarising current view of two spot ablation at high and low ablation (**a**) at high fluence, the air between the shocks is compressed by a "piston" as they meet and the curved shocks will accelerate and expel the air symmetrically in a diverging jet in both directions normal to the axis. The plasmas then stagnate and Coulomb interactions off-axis at low impact parameters convert their axial momentum to transverse momentum, (**b**) at low fluence and larger separations, shock wave pressures are much reduced, plasma density decreases, reducing stagnation to "soft", hence allowing plasma interpenetration and directed deposition between the spots.

Our observations of the directed deposition at low fluence and jets during high-fluence, multi-spot ultrafast laser ablation of stainless steel in air constitute a potentially interesting new area of research, providing a basis for further investigations to build a thorough understanding of these complex phenomena. Our study and its findings are considered important for a deeper understanding of the interaction of multi-spot arrays in laser patterning [71,72] and enhanced laser deposition of thin films [53,55]. The phenomena of plasma collisions and shocks observed and explored here should also be relevant to astrophysics and physics research, such as in magnetic re-connection [73] and phenomena such as bi-directional jet formation and particle acceleration [74,75] observed at ultrahigh laser intensities (10^{14}–10^{15} W cm^{-2}) in two spot ablation with high transient B fields.

Author Contributions: Conceptualization, G.D., U.L. and W.P., methodology, W.P., J.S. and S.E.; validation, T.Z. and S.K.; formal analysis, W.P., T.Z. and S.K.; investigation, T.Z. and S.K.; resources, G.D. and U.L.; data curation, T.Z. and S.K.; writing—original draft preparation, W.P.; writing—review and editing, all authors; visualisation, J.S., S.E.; supervision, G.D. and U.L.; project administration, G.D., S.E., J.S. and U.L. All authors have read and agreed to the published version of the manuscript.

Funding: This research received no external funding.

Institutional Review Board Statement: Not applicable.

Informed Consent Statement: Not applicable.

Data Availability Statement: The data presented in this study are available on request from the corresponding author.

Acknowledgments: The authors would like to express their thanks to Andy Snaylam (Laser group, Liverpool University) and the SEM SRF Albert Crewe Centre for Electron Microscopy (Liverpool) for their support & assistance in this research.

Conflicts of Interest: The authors declare no conflict of interest.

References

1. Krausz, F.; Stockman, M.I. Attosecond metrology: From electron capture to future signal processing. *Nat. Photonics* **2014**, *8*, 205–213. [CrossRef]
2. Austin, D.R.; Johnson, A.S.; McGrath, F.; Wood, D.; Miseikis, L.; Siegel, T.; Hawkins, P.; Harvey, A.; Mašín, Z.; Patchkovskii, S. Extracting sub-cycle electronic and nuclear dynamics from high harmonic spectra. *Sci. Rep.* **2021**, *11*, 1–8. [CrossRef] [PubMed]

3. Wille, H.; Rodríguez, M.; Kasparian, J.; Mondelain, D.; Yu, J.; Mysyrowicz, A.; Sauerbrey, R.; Wolf, J.-P.; Woeste, L. Teramobile: A mobile femtosecond-terawatt laser and detection system. *EPJ Appl. Phys.* **2002**, *20*, 183–190. [CrossRef]
4. Tochitsky, S.; Welch, E.; Panagiotopoulos, P.; Polyanskiy, M.; Pogorelsky, I.; Kolesik, M.; Koch, S.W.; Moloney, J.V.; Joshi, C. Filamentation of long-wave infrared pulses in the atmosphere. *JOSA B* **2019**, *36*, G40–G51. [CrossRef]
5. So, P.T.; Dong, C.Y.; Masters, B.R.; Berland, K.M. Two-photon excitation fluorescence microscopy. *Annu. Rev. Biomed. Eng.* **2000**, *2*, 399–429. [CrossRef]
6. Varnavski, O.; Goodson, T., III. Two-photon fluorescence microscopy at extremely low excitation intensity: The power of quantum correlations. *J. Am. Chem. Soc.* **2020**, *142*, 12966–12975. [CrossRef]
7. Abouzeid, H.; Ferrini, W. Femtosecond-laser assisted cataract surgery: A review. *Acta Ophthalmol.* **2014**, *92*, 597–603. [CrossRef]
8. Russo, R.E.; Mao, X.; Gonzalez, J.J.; Mao, S.S. Femtosecond laser ablation ICP-MS. *J. Anal. At. Spectrom.* **2002**, *17*, 1072–1075. [CrossRef]
9. Diwakar, P.K.; Harilal, S.S.; LaHaye, N.L.; Hassanein, A.; Kulkarni, P. The influence of laser pulse duration and energy on ICP-MS signal intensity, elemental fractionation, and particle size distribution in NIR fs-LA-ICP-MS. *J. Anal. At. Spectrom.* **2013**, *28*, 1420–1429. [CrossRef] [PubMed]
10. Pozebon, D.; Scheffler, G.; Dressler, V. Recent applications of laser ablation inductively coupled plasma mass spectrometry (LA-ICP-MS) for biological sample analysis: A follow-up review. *J. Anal. At. Spectrom.* **2017**, *32*, 890–919. [CrossRef]
11. Le Drogoff, B.; Margot, J.; Chaker, M.; Sabsabi, M.; Barthelemy, O.; Johnston, T.; Laville, S.; Vidal, F.; Von Kaenel, Y. Temporal characterization of femtosecond laser pulses induced plasma for spectrochemical analysis of aluminum alloys. *Spectrochim. Acta B* **2001**, *56*, 987–1002. [CrossRef]
12. Zhu, Y.; Zhou, P.-W.; Zhong, S.-C.; Peng, Q.-X.; Zhu, L.-G. A multi-spot laser induced breakdown spectroscopy system based on diffraction beam splitter. *Rev. Sci. Instrum.* **2019**, *90*, 123105. [CrossRef] [PubMed]
13. Ihlemann, J.; Wolff, B.; Simon, P. Nanosecond and femtosecond excimer laser ablation of fused silica. *Appl. Phys. A* **1992**, *54*, 363–368. [CrossRef]
14. Allahyari, E.; Nivas, J.J.; Avallone, G.; Valadan, M.; Singh, M.; Granata, V.; Cirillo, C.; Vecchione, A.; Bruzzese, R.; Altucci, C. Femtosecond laser surface irradiation of silicon in air: Pulse repetition rate influence on crater features and surface texture. *Opt. Laser Technol.* **2020**, *126*, 106073. [CrossRef]
15. Rajab, F.H.; Liauw, C.M.; Benson, P.S.; Li, L.; Whitehead, K.A. Picosecond laser treatment production of hierarchical structured stainless steel to reduce bacterial fouling. *Food Bioprod. Process.* **2018**, *109*, 29–40. [CrossRef]
16. Xu, S.; Ding, R.; Yao, C.; Liu, H.; Wan, Y.; Wang, J.; Ye, Y.; Yuan, X. Effects of pulse durations and environments on femtosecond laser ablation of stainless steel. *Appl. Phys. A* **2018**, *124*, 1–8. [CrossRef]
17. Hauschwitz, P.; Jochcová, D.; Jagdheesh, R.; Cimrman, M.; Brajer, J.; Rostohar, D.; Mocek, T.; Kopeček, J.; Lucianetti, A.; Smrž, M. Large-beam picosecond interference patterning of metallic substrates. *Materials* **2020**, *13*, 4676. [CrossRef] [PubMed]
18. Kautek, W.; Krüger, J. Femtosecond Pulse Laser Ablation of Metallic, Semiconducting, Ceramic, and Biological Materials. In *Laser Materials Processing: Industrial and Microelectronics Applications*; Springer: Berlin/Heidelberg, Germany, 1994; pp. 600–611.
19. Schille, J.; Schneider, L.; Kraft, S.; Hartwig, L.; Loeschner, U. Experimental study on double-pulse laser ablation of steel upon multiple parallel polarized ultrashort-pulse irradiations. *Appl. Phys. A* **2016**, *122*, 1–11. [CrossRef]
20. Dyer, P.; Sidhu, J. Spectroscopic and fast photographic studies of excimer laser polymer ablation. *Int. J. Appl. Phys.* **1988**, *64*, 4657–4663. [CrossRef]
21. Yalçın, Ş.; Tsui, Y.Y.; Fedosejevs, R. Pressure dependence of emission intensity in femtosecond laser-induced breakdown spectroscopy. *J. Anal. At. Spectrom.* **2004**, *19*, 1295–1301. [CrossRef]
22. Yalçin, S.; Tsui, Y.Y.; Fedosejevs, R. Images of femtosecond laser plasma plume expansion into background air. *IEEE Trans. Plasma Sci.* **2005**, *33*, 482–483. [CrossRef]
23. Farid, N.; Harilal, S.; Ding, H.; Hassanein, A. Dynamics of ultrafast laser plasma expansion in the presence of an ambient. *Appl. Phys. Lett.* **2013**, *103*, 191112. [CrossRef]
24. Lichtman, D.; Ready, J. Laser beam induced electron emission. *Phys. Rev. Lett.* **1963**, *10*, 342. [CrossRef]
25. Bechtel, J.; Smith, W.L.; Bloembergen, N. Two-photon photoemission from metals induced by picosecond laser pulses. *Phys. Rev. B* **1977**, *15*, 4557. [CrossRef]
26. Mao, S.S.; Mao, X.-L.; Greif, R.; Russo, R.E. Simulation of infrared picosecond laser-induced electron emission from semiconductors. *Appl. Surf. Sci.* **1998**, *127*, 206–211. [CrossRef]
27. Russo, R.; Mao, X.; Liu, H.; Yoo, J.; Mao, S. Time-resolved plasma diagnostics and mass removal during single-pulse laser ablation. *Appl. Phys. A* **1999**, *69*, S887–S894. [CrossRef]
28. Mao, S.S.; Mao, X.; Greif, R.; Russo, R.E. Initiation of an early-stage plasma during picosecond laser ablation of solids. *Appl. Phys. Lett.* **2000**, *77*, 2464–2466. [CrossRef]
29. Mao, S.S.; Mao, X.; Greif, R.; Russo, R.E. Simulation of a picosecond laser ablation plasma. *Appl. Phys. Lett.* **2000**, *76*, 3370–3372. [CrossRef]
30. Zeng, X.; Mao, X.; Greif, R.; Russo, R. Experimental investigation of ablation efficiency and plasma expansion during femtosecond and nanosecond laser ablation of silicon. *Appl. Phys. A* **2005**, *80*, 237–241. [CrossRef]
31. Nica, P.; Gurlui, S.; Osiac, M.; Agop, M.; Ziskind, M.; Focsa, C. Investigation of femtosecond laser-produced plasma from various metallic targets using the Langmuir probe characteristic. *Phys. Plasmas* **2017**, *24*, 103119. [CrossRef]

32. Wen, S.-B.; Mao, X.; Greif, R.; Russo, R.E. Expansion of the laser ablation vapor plume into a background gas. I. analysis. *Int. J. Appl. Phys.* **2007**, *101*, 023114. [CrossRef]
33. Wu, J.; Wei, W.; Li, X.; Jia, S.; Qiu, A. Infrared nanosecond laser-metal ablation in atmosphere: Initial plasma during laser pulse and further expansion. *Appl. Phys. Lett.* **2013**, *102*, 164104. [CrossRef]
34. Harilal, S.; Farid, N.; Freeman, J.; Diwakar, P.; LaHaye, N.; Hassanein, A. Background gas collisional effects on expanding fs and ns laser ablation plumes. *Appl. Phys. A* **2014**, *117*, 319–326. [CrossRef]
35. Pereira, A.; Delaporte, P.; Sentis, M.; Marine, W.; Thomann, A.L.; Boulmer-Leborgne, C. Optical and morphological investigation of backward-deposited layer induced by laser ablation of steel in ambient air. *Int. J. Appl. Phys.* **2005**, *98*, 064902. [CrossRef]
36. Harilal, S.S.; Brumfield, B.E.; Cannon, B.D.; Phillips, M.C. Shock wave mediated plume chemistry for molecular formation in laser ablation plasmas. *Anal. Chem.* **2016**, *88*, 2296–2302. [CrossRef]
37. Bulgakova, N.M.; Panchenko, A.N.; Zhukov, V.P.; Kudryashov, S.I.; Pereira, A.; Marine, W.; Mocek, T.; Bulgakov, A.V. Impacts of ambient and ablation plasmas on short-and ultrashort-pulse laser processing of surfaces. *Micromachines* **2014**, *5*, 1344–1372. [CrossRef]
38. Taylor, R.; Leopold, K.; Singleton, D.; Paraskevopoulos, G.; Irwin, R. The effect of debris formation on the morphology of excimer laser ablated polymers. *Int. J. Appl. Phys.* **1988**, *64*, 2815–2818. [CrossRef]
39. Miotello, A.; Kelly, R.; Braren, B.; Otis, C.E. Novel geometrical effects observed in debris when polymers are laser sputtered. *Appl. Phys. Lett.* **1992**, *61*, 2784–2786. [CrossRef]
40. Küper, S.; Brannon, J. Ambient gas effects on debris formed during KrF laser ablation of polyimide. *Appl. Phys. Lett.* **1992**, *60*, 1633–1635. [CrossRef]
41. Burghardt, B.; Scheede, S.; Senczuk, R.; Kahlert, H.-J. Ablation plume effects on high precision excimer laser-based micromachining. *Appl. Phys. A* **1999**, *69*, S137–S140. [CrossRef]
42. Garrelie, F.; Champeaux, C.; Catherinot, A. Study by a Monte Carlo simulation of the influence of a background gas on the expansion dynamics of a laser-induced plasma plume. *Appl. Phys. A* **1999**, *69*, 45–50. [CrossRef]
43. Ravi-Kumar, S.; Lies, B.; Zhang, X.; Lyu, H.; Qin, H. Laser ablation of polymers: A review. *Polym. Int.* **2019**, *68*, 1391–1401. [CrossRef]
44. Jacob, J.; Shanmugavelu, P.; Balasubramaniam, R. Investigation of the performance of 248 nm excimer laser assisted photoresist removal process in gaseous media by response surface methodology and artificial neural network. *J. Manuf. Process.* **2019**, *38*, 516–529. [CrossRef]
45. Elaboudi, I.; Lazare, S.; Belin, C.; Talaga, D.; Labrugère, C. Underwater excimer laser ablation of polymers. *Appl. Phys. A* **2008**, *92*, 743–748. [CrossRef]
46. Péreira, A.; Cros, A.; Delaporte, P.; Itina, T.; Sentis, M.; Marine, W.; Thomann, A.; Boulmer-Leborgne, C. Formation of Iron Oxide Nanoparticles by Pulsed Laser Ablation. In *Proceedings of Atomic and Molecular Pulsed Lasers VI*; SPIE: Bellingham, WA, USA, 2006; p. 62630Q.
47. Pereira, A.; Delaporte, P.; Sentis, M.; Cros, A.; Marine, W.; Basillais, A.; Thomann, A.; Leborgne, C.; Semmar, N.; Andreazza, P. Laser treatment of a steel surface in ambient air. *Thin Solid Films* **2004**, *453*, 16–21. [CrossRef]
48. Förster, D.J.; Faas, S.; Gröninger, S.; Bauer, F.; Michalowski, A.; Weber, R.; Graf, T. Shielding effects and re-deposition of material during processing of metals with bursts of ultra-short laser pulses. *Appl. Surf. Sci.* **2018**, *440*, 926–931. [CrossRef]
49. Kraft, S.; Schille, J.; Mauersberger, S.; Schneider, L.; Loeschner, U. Time-resolved visualization of high-repetition ultrashort pulse laser ablation. *Appl. Opt.* **2020**, *59*, 452–458. [CrossRef]
50. Kraft, S.; Schille, J.; Mauersberger, S.; Schneider, L.; Loeschner, U. Pump-Probe Imaging for Process Control and Optimization in High-Speed Laser Micro Machining. In *Laser-Based Micro-and Nanoprocessing XIV*; SPIE: Bellingham, WA, USA, 2020; p. 112681H.
51. Vreugdenhil, M.; Van Oosten, D.; Hernandez-Rueda, J. Dynamics of femtosecond laser-induced shockwaves at a water/air interface using multiple excitation beams. *Opt. Lett.* **2018**, *43*, 4899–4902. [CrossRef]
52. Baasanjav, D.; Hernandez-Rueda, J.; Mosk, A.P.; Van Oosten, D. Optical method for micrometer-scale tracerless visualization of ultrafast laser induced gas flow at a water/air interface. *Appl. Opt.* **2020**, *59*, 5205–5209. [CrossRef]
53. Gupta, S.L.; Thareja, R.K. ZnO thin film deposition using colliding plasma plumes and single plasma plume: Structural and optical properties. *Int. J. Appl. Phys.* **2013**, *114*, 224903. [CrossRef]
54. Pandey, P.K.; Thareja, R.K.; Singh, R.P.; Costello, J.T. Deposition of nanocomposite Cu–TiO_2 using heterogeneous colliding plasmas. *Appl. Phys. B* **2018**, *124*, 1–8. [CrossRef]
55. Donnelly, T.; O'Connell, G.; Lunney, J.G. Metal nanoparticle film deposition by femtosecond laser ablation at atmospheric pressure. *Nanomaterials* **2020**, *10*, 2118. [CrossRef]
56. Serra, P.; Piqué, A. Laser-induced forward transfer: Fundamentals and applications. *Adv. Mater. Technol.* **2019**, *4*, 1800099. [CrossRef]
57. Liu, J. Simple technique for measurements of pulsed Gaussian-beam spot sizes. *Opt. Lett.* **1982**, *7*, 196–198. [CrossRef]
58. Zhao, W.; Wang, W.; Jiang, G.; Li, B.Q.; Mei, X. Ablation and morphological evolution of micro-holes in stainless steel with picosecond laser pulses. *Int. J. Adv. Manuf. Technol.* **2015**, *80*, 1713–1720. [CrossRef]
59. Taylor, G.I. The formation of a blast wave by a very intense explosion I. Theoretical discussion. *Proc. R. Soc. Lond.* **1950**, *201*, 159–174.

60. Singh, S.; Argument, M.; Tsui, Y.; Fedosejevs, R. Effect of ambient air pressure on debris redeposition during laser ablation of glass. *Int. J. Appl. Phys.* **2005**, *98*, 113520. [CrossRef]
61. Liu, H.; Mao, X.; Yoo, J.; Russo, R. Early phase laser induced plasma diagnostics and mass removal during single-pulse laser ablation of silicon. *Spectrochim. Acta B* **1999**, *54*, 1607–1624. [CrossRef]
62. Kramida, A.; Ralchenko, Y.; Reader, J. *NIST Atomic Spectra Database (ver. 5.3)*; NIST: Gaithersburg, MA, USA, 2015.
63. Harilal, S.; Bindhu, C.; Tillack, M.; Najmabadi, F.; Gaeris, A. Internal structure and expansion dynamics of laser ablation plumes into ambient gases. *Int. J. Appl. Phys.* **2003**, *93*, 2380–2388. [CrossRef]
64. Cargill, P.; Goodrich, C.; Papadopoulos, K. Interaction of two collisionless shocks. *Phys. Rev. Lett.* **1986**, *56*, 1988. [CrossRef] [PubMed]
65. Fallon, C.; Hayden, P.; Walsh, N.; Kennedy, E.; Costello, J. The effect of wedge angle on the evolution of a stagnation layer in a colliding plasma experiment. *J. Phys. Conf. Ser.* **2014**, *548*, 12036. [CrossRef]
66. Fallon, C.; Hayden, P.; Walsh, N.; Kennedy, E.; Costello, J. Target geometrical effects on the stagnation layer formed by colliding a pair of laser produced copper plasmas. *Phys. Plasmas* **2015**, *22*, 93506. [CrossRef]
67. Gibbon, P. Introduction to plasma physics. *arXiv* **2020**, arXiv:2007.04783.
68. Yang, Z.; Wei, W.; Han, J.; Wu, J.; Li, X.; Jia, S. Experimental study of the behavior of two laser produced plasmas in air. *Phys. Plasmas* **2015**, *22*, 073511. [CrossRef]
69. Rambo, P.; Denavit, J. Interpenetration and ion separation in colliding plasmas. *Phys. Plasmas* **1994**, *1*, 4050–4060. [CrossRef]
70. Guthikonda, N.; Manikanta, E.; Chelikani, L.; Sai Shiva, S.; Sree Harsha, S.; Ikkurthi, V.; Prem Kiran, P. Interaction of two counterpropagating laser induced plasmas and shock waves in air. *Phys. Plasmas* **2020**, *27*, 23107. [CrossRef]
71. Jin, Y.; Perrie, W.; Harris, P.; Allegre, O.; Abrams, K.; Dearden, G. Patterning of Aluminium thin film on polyethylene terephthalate by multi-beam picosecond laser. *Opt. Lasers Eng. Opt. Laser Eng.* **2015**, *74*, 67–74. [CrossRef]
72. Tang, Y.; Perrie, W.; Rico Sierra, D.; Li, Q.; Liu, D.; Edwardson, S.P.; Dearden, G. Laser–material interactions of high-quality ultrashort pulsed vector vortex beams. *Micromachines* **2021**, *12*, 376. [CrossRef]
73. Taylor, J. Relaxation and magnetic reconnection in plasmas. *Rev. Mod. Phys.* **1986**, *58*, 741. [CrossRef]
74. Totorica, S.; Abel, T.; Fiuza, F. Particle acceleration in laser-driven magnetic reconnection. *Phys. Plasmas* **2017**, *24*, 41408. [CrossRef]
75. Nilson, P.; Willingale, L.; Kaluza, M.; Kamperidis, C.; Minardi, S.; Wei, M.; Fernandes, P.; Notley, M.; Bandyopadhyay, S.; Sherlock, M. Bidirectional jet formation during driven magnetic reconnection in two-beam laser–plasma interactions. *Phys. Plasmas* **2008**, *15*, 92701. [CrossRef]

materials

MDPI

Article

Squared Focal Intensity Distributions for Applications in Laser Material Processing

Henrike Schlutow [1], Ulrike Fuchs [1], Frank A. Müller [2] and Stephan Gräf [2,*]

[1] Asphericon GmbH, Stockholmer Str. 9, 07747 Jena, Germany; h.wilms@asphericon.com (H.S.); u.fuchs@asphericon.com (U.F.)

[2] Otto Schott Institute of Materials Research (OSIM), Friedrich Schiller University, Löbdergraben 32, 07743 Jena, Germany; frank.mueller@uni-jena.de

* Correspondence: stephan.graef@uni-jena.de; Tel.: +49-3641-947754

Abstract: Tailored intensity profiles within the focal spot of the laser beam offer great potential for a well-defined control of the interaction process between laser radiation and material, and thus for improving the processing results. The present paper discusses a novel refractive beam-shaping element that provides different squared intensity distributions converted from the Gaussian output beam of the utilized femtosecond (fs) laser. Using the examples of surface structuring of stainless-steel on the micro- and nano-scale, the suitability of the beam-shaping element for fs-laser material processing with a conventional f-Theta lens is demonstrated. In this context, it was shown that the experimental structuring results are in good agreement with beam profile measurements and numerical simulations of the beam-shaping unit. In addition, the experimental results reveal the improvement of laser processing in terms of a significantly reduced processing time during surface nano-structuring and the possibility to control the ablation geometry during the fabrication of micro-channels.

Keywords: beam shaping; squared top-hat; fs-laser; laser surface structuring; laser-induced periodic surface structures; micro-channels

Citation: Schlutow, H.; Fuchs, U.; Müller, F.A.; Gräf, S. Squared Focal Intensity Distributions for Applications in Laser Material Processing. *Materials* **2021**, *14*, 4981. https://doi.org/10.3390/ma14174981

Academic Editors: Jörg Krüger and Jörn Bonse

Received: 14 July 2021
Accepted: 27 August 2021
Published: 31 August 2021

1. Introduction

In modern laser material processing, beam shaping is gaining growing attention, as it allows the focal intensity distribution to be adjusted to the interaction process between the laser radiation and the material [1–3]. This makes laser processing even more flexible, precise and effective. Moreover, the range of achievable types of structures is extended [4–6] and surface properties can be adjusted in a targeted manner [7–9]. Top-hat profiles are characterized by a uniform intensity distribution over the beam cross-section in a specific working plane. They can be generated by a large variety of available beam-shaping techniques, including apertures [10], refractive [11–13] and diffractive optical elements [10,14], as well as beam integrators or homogenizers [10,15]. Finally, a spatial light modulator provides a flexible optical device that allows to create various intensity profiles based on the dynamical modification of the amplitude, phase and polarization of the incoming laser beam [16–18].

The advantage of refractive beam shapers is provided by their simple structure and a very high conversion efficiency. They are less sensitive to wavelength changes, easier to manufacture and can withstand higher laser powers when compared to diffractive elements. Therefore, the present work aims at the introduction of a highly flexible and compact refractive, freeform beam-shaping element that is suitable for laser material processing applications.

Large-area structuring of surfaces on the micro- and nano-meter scale usually requires scanning of the focused laser beam across the material surface. In the case of the commonly used Gaussian intensity distribution, a certain inhomogeneity of the deposited energy occurs, which in turn has an influence on the processing result. A first improvement was demonstrated in this context by using a beam shaper that allows to generate a rotationally symmetric top-hat profile [19]. However, due to the rectangular symmetry of the (unidirectional) scan procedure with a specific overlap of the adjacent scan lines, the use of a squared top-hat seems to be even more advantageous with respect to homogeneous energy coupling. This squared top-hat is derived from the collimated Gaussian intensity profile of the input beam by combining the investigated refractive beam shaper with a focusing optics. The latter can be a simple focusing lens as well as a complex f-Theta objective, as is very often used for laser-based surface structuring. Therefore, a main objective of this study was to evaluate whether the x-y-symmetry of the focal distribution can further improve material processing when working with a scanner and an f-Theta lens. This aspect plays an essential role with regard to modern laser systems and their high repetition rates, whose maximum utilization ensures high processing efficiency. For this purpose, the beam-shaping element was practically tested in different applications on stainless-steel as a substrate material. This includes surface nano-structuring in the form of laser-induced periodic surface structures (LIPSS), which allow to engineer surfaces with versatile functional properties [7,20]. Furthermore, the ablation-based micro-structuring of the sample surface using femtosecond lasers (fs-lasers) was demonstrated as a conventional processing technique [21].

2. Materials and Methods

2.1. Focal Beam-Shaping and Characterization

The most common approach for shaping focal intensity distributions is based on Fourier optics, where the focusing optics transforms the incoming beam profile into the desired shape. This is well-explained for rotational symmetry in [19,22]. However, for non-rotationally symmetric focal intensity distributions, the symmetry of the beam-shaping element needs to be broken, while the focusing optics remains the same. Therefore, the beam-shaping element becomes a freeform surface. As a phase plate, it imprints a phase modulation on the incoming plan wave of the collimated beam, which stays collimated as this modulation is in the order of λ (PV) and thus very small. The focusing optics performs the Fourier transformation of this modified wave front and therefore determines the width of the generated profiles inverse proportional to the numerical aperture (NA). Consequently, this approach is modular with regards to the focusing optics. The phase plate (a | SqAiryShape) itself is a freeform distribution based on a super Gaussian profile:

$$z(h) = \mathrm{He}{-}^{2}\left(\frac{4h^2}{D^2}\right)^{\frac{M}{2}} \quad (1)$$

of order M = 8, diameter D and plateau height H in x-y-symmetry. The element is made of fused silica via CNC-based grinding and polishing. It can therefore withstand high-power laser intensities as well as ultrashort laser pulses, as employed in the experimental studies of the present work.

As a measure of how much the beam shaping will be affected by diffraction effects, the β-factor:

$$\beta = \frac{2\pi RD}{f_L \lambda} \quad (2)$$

can be used [23], with R being the half diameter of the entrance beam, D being the half diameter of the focal distribution, f_L being the focal length and λ being the wavelength. Using the specific parameters of the present study (R = 10 mm, D = 25 µm, f_L = 100 mm and λ = 1030 nm) leads to β = 15.25. Having such a large value ensures stable beam-shaping profiles, which are essential for well-controlled material processing.

The squared focal intensity distribution was characterized in order to compare the experimental results with simulations. For this purpose, a supercontinuum laser (SC-400-4, Fianium, Southampton, UK) was used as a light source, from which λ = 1064 nm was selected via a spectrometer (LLTF Contrast, Fianium, Southampton, UK), coupled to a fiber, collimated (ACM25-20-L-C-1064, asphericon, Jena, Germany) and expanded (BAM25-175-D-C-1064, asphericon, Jena, Germany) to a collimated beam with 10 mm diameter. This beam fulfilled the input conditions for the freeform beam-shaping element. All following optical components used for characterization of the beam shaping are depicted in Figure 1. The beam-shaping element (a | SqAiryShape) was placed in the collimated beam, which was subsequently focused by a plano-convex lens with 300 mm focal length (#38-631, Edmund Optics, Mainz, Germany). The focal region was then imaged onto a camera (SP928, Ophir, Germany) by using a microscope objective (Aspheric Lens Kit 5720-B, Newport, Irvine, CA, USA). The setup was calibrated to obtain the real physical size of the focal distribution.

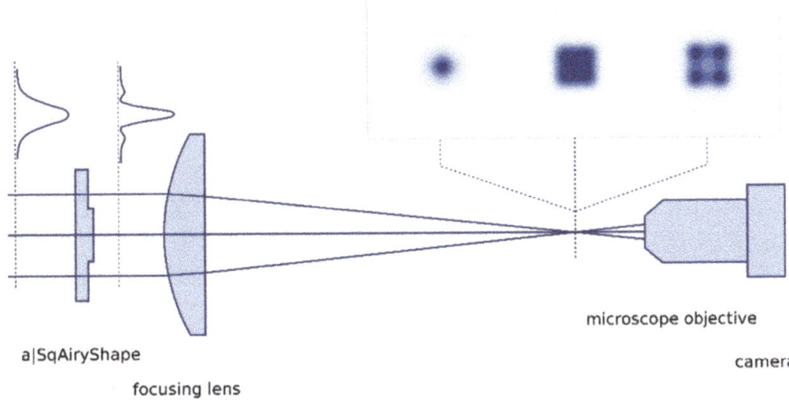

Figure 1. Experimental setup for characterization of the freeform beam-shaping element.

In the simulation, only the freeform beam-shaping element and the plano-convex focusing lens were considered. The focal intensity distribution was calculated via the point spread function with CodeV (Synopsis). This calculation is based on the squared Fourier transform of the pupil function [24]. The latter includes all aberrations and thus the phase manipulation introduced by the beam-shaping element.

Close to the focal point, various intensity distributions, such as a squared top-hat or squared donut, emerge. The following laser processing experiments were carried out with the squared top-hat, which occurs closest to the focal point. This is the top-hat shown in Figure 2. Comparison with the simulation, especially through the cross-sections in the bottom of Figure 2, reveals close agreement between measurement and simulation in terms of shape and size of the focus spot.

A sequence of those cross-sections taken along the optical axis is plotted in Figure 3. The upper panel (Figure 3a) shows the beam waist of the Gaussian input beam without the freeform beam-shaping element. With the beam-shaping element (panel b), the Gaussian distribution is notably flattened to a top-hat. Note that the beam shaping only occurs close to the focal point (z = 0 mm), whereas the profile remains almost Gaussian for larger distances. The blue-shaded distribution corresponds to the one shown in Figure 2.

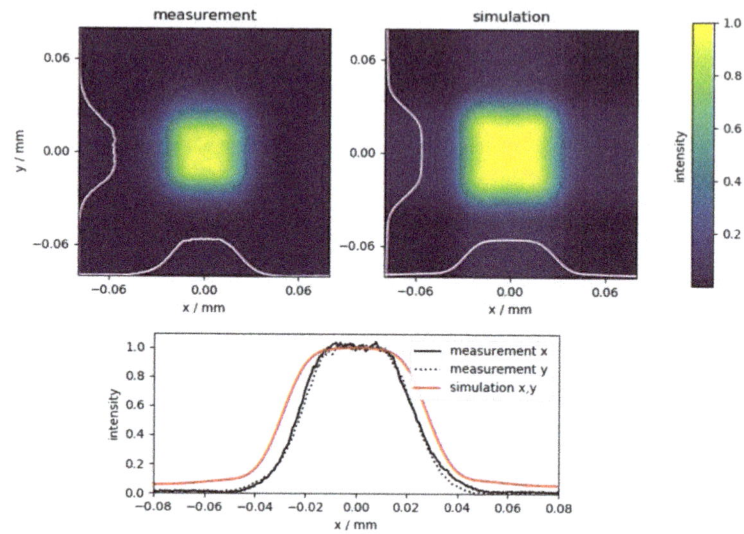

Figure 2. Color maps and cross-sections of the squared focal intensity distribution of the top-hat closest to the focal plane (λ = 1064 nm, f = 300 mm) normalized to the maximum intensity for comparison between measurement and simulation.

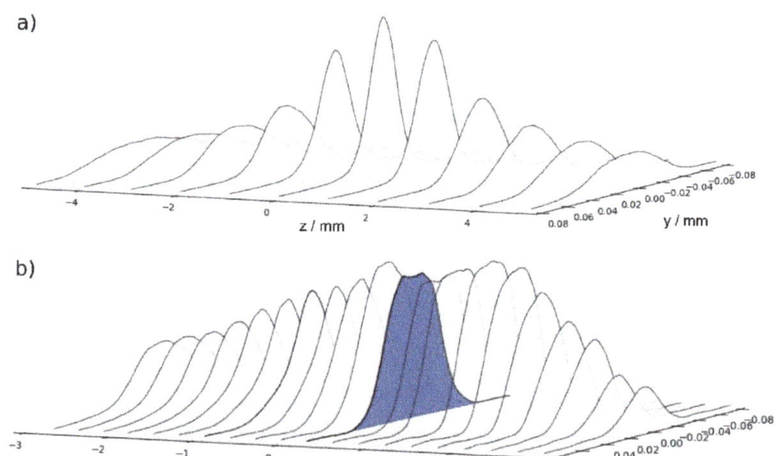

Figure 3. Profile cross-sections measured along the optical axis (z) in the focal region (**a**) without and (**b**) with freeform beam-shaping element.

2.2. Material Processing Setup and Sample Preparation

The operation of the beam-shaping element was investigated by means of surface structuring experiments using the experimental setup illustrated in Figure 4. The linearly polarized Gaussian output beam ($M^2 \sim 1.08$) of the diode-pumped Yb:KYW thin-disc fs-laser system (JenLas D2.fs, Jenoptik, Germany) with a central wavelength λ = 1025 nm is characterized by a pulse duration τ = 300 fs (FWHM) and pulse energies $E_{imp} \leq 40$ μJ at a repetition frequency $f_{rep} = 100$ kHz. Before passing the beam shaper, the output beam was widened by a beam expander (5×). The shaped beam was then focused onto the sample surface by a galvanometer scanner (IntelliScan14, Scanlab, Puchheim, Germany). The focal length of the associated f-Theta objective (JENar, Jenoptik, Jena, Germany) was f_L = 100 mm.

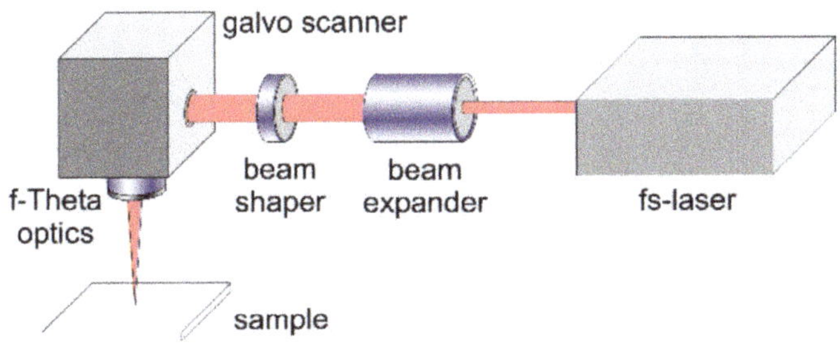

Figure 4. Experimental setup used for surface structuring experiments.

The structuring experiments were carried out on commercially available austenitic stainless-steel (X2CrNiMo17-12-2, Outokumpu, Krefeld, Germany) at normal incidence and under air atmosphere. Prior to laser irradiation, the sample surface was manually grounded and polished to a mirror finish, with an average surface roughness R_a ~4 nm. This procedure involves the use of SiC abrasive paper of 800, 1200 and 2400 grit and 6, 3 and 1 μm polycrystalline diamond suspension, respectively. Besides, the sample surfaces were ultrasonically cleaned in acetone and isopropanol both before and after laser structuring. The morphology of the samples was characterized by scanning electron microscopy (SEM) (SigmaVP, Carl Zeiss, Oberkochen, Germany) at an accelerating voltage of 5 kV using a secondary electron detector. The spatial periods and the orientation of the LIPSS were quantified by 2D-Fourier transform analysis (2D-FT) of the SEM micrographs. White light interference microscopy (WLIM) (CCI HD, Taylor Hobson, Weiterstadt, Germany) was utilized to evaluate the surface topography. The microscope was equipped with a 50× objective.

3. Results and Discussion

3.1. Single Spot Experiments

The first part of the experiments was to investigate whether the theoretical calculations for the focal intensity distribution correlate with the geometry of the ablated region within the focal spot on the material surface. For this purpose, the surface was irradiated with 10 single fs-laser pulses with a temporal pulse spacing of 10 μs (f_{rep} = 100 kHz) and a single-pulse energy of E_{imp} = 6.5 μJ. Without the beam-shaping element in the beam path, the utilized f-Theta objective results in a focal spot diameter of $2w_f$ = (24 ± 0.5) μm, determined using the method of Liu [25]. This corresponds to a fs-laser peak fluence of $F = 2E_{imp}/(\pi w_f^2) = 2.9$ J/cm² at the pulse energy used.

Figure 5 shows SEM micrographs of the ablation spots obtained at different distances (z-positions) of the stainless-steel surface from the focusing objective using the freeform beam-shaping element. At the reference position (z = 0 mm) and at z = −0.6 mm, squared top-hat intensity profiles are available that result in square material ablation of size (30 × 30) μm² and (40 × 40) μm², respectively. As described later, these intensity profiles are predestined for numerous laser material processes that are based on scanning procedures with x-y-symmetry (Figure 6). Assuming a perfectly rectangular fluence distribution of both top-hat profiles, the larger focal dimensions together with the pulse energy E_{imp} = 6.5 μJ result in a lower fs-laser peak fluence of F = 0.72 and F = 0.41 J/cm² respectively, when compared to the initial Gaussian focal spot. It should be noted that the peak fluence, F, is identical to the average fluence, F_{av}, of the fluence distribution. The larger fluence at z = 0 compared to z = −0.6 mm is indicated by the stronger melt formation in the ablation spot fabricated with the smaller top-hat profile.

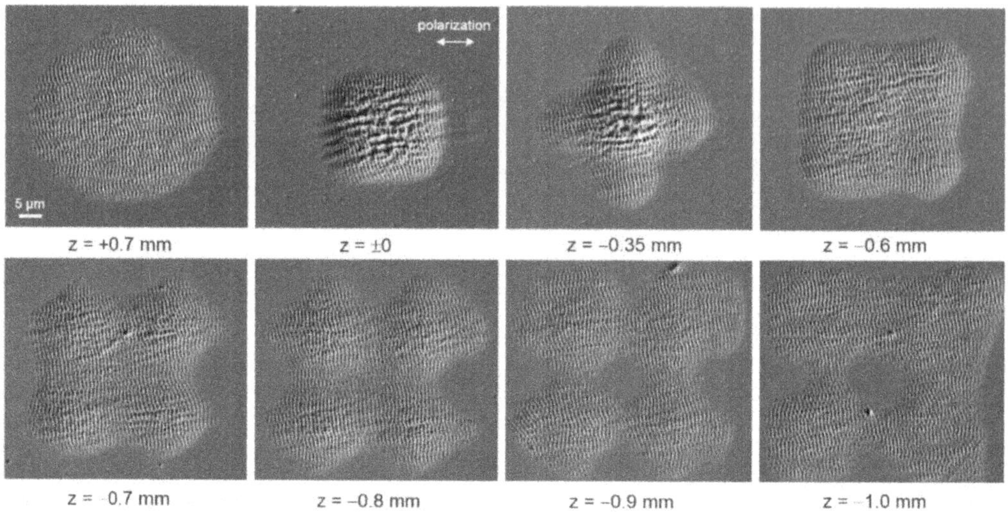

Figure 5. SEM micrographs of the stainless-steel surface after irradiation of 10 linearly polarized single fs-laser pulses at different z-positions of the sample surface within the focal intensity distribution. For comparability, the single-pulse energy was kept constant at E_{imp} = 6.5 µJ.

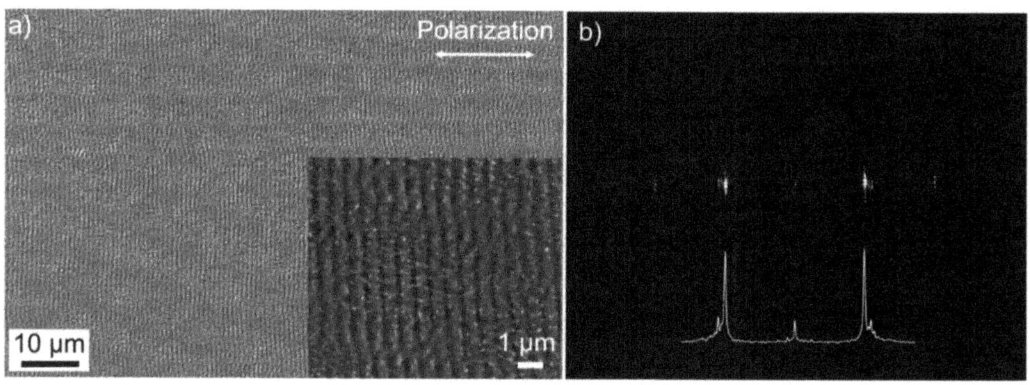

Figure 6. LIPSS structuring of stainless-steel surfaces using the squared top-hat profile (z = 0 mm) of the linearly polarized fs-laser beam ($2w_f$ ~30 µm, E_{imp} = 3.5 µJ, v = 1 m/s, Δx = 10 µm): (**a**) SEM micrograph and (**b**) 2D-FT spectrum and its corresponding cross-section calculated from the SEM micrograph quantifying the homogeneity and orientation of the LIPSS.

In addition to the top-hat profiles, the beam-shaping element provides other intermediate stages, which are characterized by more exotic intensity distributions. At z = −1.0 mm, a donut-shaped focal intensity distribution with square beam cross-section can be observed, characterized by the zero-intensity center on the beam axis. In contrast, at z = −0.35 mm, the intensity distribution is almost completely reversed, which is why a stronger intensity can be observed at the center. Both examples are intensity distributions suitable for the generation of novel surface structures (e.g., bio-inspired surfaces) [5].

The SEM micrographs of the single-spot experiments reveal a well-defined modulated surface topography within the ablation crater, whose periodicity is in the sub-µm range and therefore much smaller when compared to the diffraction-limited focal spot diameter of a few tens of μm. These periodic patterns are termed laser-induced periodic surface structures (LIPSS), which for metals are typically oriented perpendicular to the linear beam polarization [26]. The most widely accepted theory describes the formation of LIPSS as a result of interference of the incident laser radiation with surface electromagnetic waves generated by scattering at the nano-rough surface [27,28]. These scattering processes are possible despite the polished initial surface, since the LIPSS formation process is generally a multi-pulse process.

As Figure 5 shows, the exact morphology of the LIPSS pattern within the focal spot depends on the fluence distribution in the beam cross-section, i.e., on the intensity profile. A particular contribution is provided by melt formation in the intensive regions of the beam cross-section. However, it becomes evident that a particularly homogeneous LIPSS distribution can be realized by the appropriate choice of the z-position, which suggests here a constant fluence in the beam profile. This is a key aspect for homogeneous large-area structuring with LIPSS [29]. In addition, the possibility to control the LIPSS distribution within the focal spot by choosing a certain beam profile leads to an extension of the current state-of-the-art and, thus, to a higher flexibility of the direct-writing structuring method. The fluence values calculated above for the top-hat profile are comparable with the fluence required for ablation-based LIPSS formation on stainless-steel at comparable irradiation parameters [30,31].

3.2. Laser Surface Structuring on the Nanoscale

Based on the demonstrated LIPSS formation within the focal spot, the nanostructures can be scaled to large surface areas by a relative movement between the focused fs-laser beam and the sample surface. This is particularly achievable with metals due to the linear absorption of the fs-laser radiation. In this context, the specific optical properties make stainless-steel a well-suited candidate for the production of highly regular LIPSS [31]. This concerns in particular the exact alignment and a small dispersion of the spatial frequencies of the LIPSS, which are coherently linked to each other despite the unidirectional scanning procedure [30,31].

The SEM micrograph in Figure 6a shows the stainless-steel surface obtained from scanning the squared top-hat profile (z = 0 mm) with a scan speed of v = 1 m/s and a line spacing of Δx = 10 μm across the sample surface. The single-pulse energy was reduced to E_{imp} = 3.5 μJ, i.e., to F = 0.39 J/cm^2, in order to avoid the extensive melt formation observed in Figure 5. The calculated 2D-FT spectrum (Figure 6b) confirms the high regularity of the LIPSS aligned perpendicular to the linear beam polarization by the very narrow characteristic peaks. The spatial periods of the LIPSS were determined to be around (950 ± 20) nm.

The obtained regularity is comparable with our previous work on rotationally symmetric beam shaping [19], although the following main differences should be discussed:

(1) As already demonstrated in [30,31], highly regular LIPSS can also be generated with conventional Gaussian beam profiles. However, the radial intensity dependence and the circular spot area require a larger overlap of the laser pulses in both x- and y-directions to realize an almost homogeneous energy deposition. The optimal process parameters for Gaussian beam processing were derived in [19] to be v = 0.67 m/s, Δx = 6 μm, E_{imp} = 2.6 μJ, F = 1.15 J/cm^2 at f_{rep} = 100 kHz and $2w_f$ = 24 μm. These values result in a processing rate of about 32 s/cm^2 and in a laser pulse number $N_{eff\_2D} = (\pi w_f^2 \cdot f_{rep})/(v \cdot \Delta x)$ ~11.3, that effectively hit the focal spot area [28].

(2) The main difference between the ideal squared top-hat and the Gaussian profile results from the relative movement during scanning. Figure 7a illustrates that for the Gaussian profile at a certain position y at the surface, every single pulse of the total required number (N_{eff_2D}) contributes to structuring with different fluence values. Consequently, the specific fluence of some of the individual pulses can be significantly smaller than the ablation and LIPSS formation threshold of the material.

(3) In the case of the top-hat profile (z = 0) with its square shape, the slightly larger beam diameter (here given by the beam width in x- and y-directions) and steeper flanks, LIPSS structures with almost equal properties can be achieved. Nevertheless, the structuring can be performed with larger scanning speed (v = 1 m/s) and line separation (Δx = 10 μm). As described above, the pulse energy must be increased slightly for this to exceed the required LIPSS formation threshold. The optimum parameters, however, result in $N_{eff\_2D} = 9$ and a processing rate of about 14 s/cm^2, which is more than a factor of 2 faster than structuring with the conventional Gaussian beam.

(4) The accumulated fluence of the ideal top-hat profile with $F_{tot} = N_{eff\_2D} \cdot F = 3.51$ J/cm^2 is smaller than for the Gaussian intensity distribution (F_{tot} = 6.47 J/cm^2), since during structuring with the top-hat, each single pulse contributes equally to F_{tot} (Figure 7b).

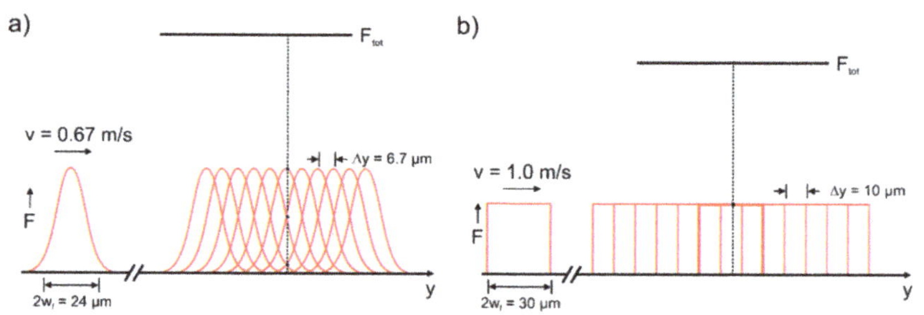

Figure 7. Overlap and contribution of individual pulses during scanning of a single line using (**a**) the Gaussian focal intensity distribution and (**b**) an ideal top-hat beam.

3.3. Surface Micro-Structuring

In order to investigate the influence of the intensity distribution on the micro-structuring of surfaces, channels were created using the top-hat profile (z = 0 mm) and 10 over-scans with v = 0.1 m/s. Earlier studies with rotationally symmetrical top-hat and donut-shaped beam profiles already showed that steeper channel walls and a better surface quality (especially at the bottom) can be achieved in comparison to the Gaussian profile [19].

These findings can also be observed in Figure 8, which shows 3D-WLIM micrographs of channels produced with the top-hat profile using different pulse energies, E_{imp}. It becomes evident for moderate pulse energies that the homogeneous fluence distribution across the beam profile leads to a very high quality of both the walls and the bottom of the channel (Figure 8a,b). The corresponding arithmetical roughness values of the channel surface were measured via WLIM to be S_a = 0.1072 μm for E_{imp} = 2.5 μJ and S_a = 0.1844 μm for E_{imp} = 4.6 μJ. As indicated by the cross-sections in Figure 8d, the corresponding depth of the channels increases with increasing pulse energy, from about 6.2 μm at E_{imp} = 2.5 μJ (Figure 8a) to about 12.5 μm at E_{imp} = 7 μJ (Figure 8c). In addition, a slight increase in the channel width can be observed. However, the WLIM micrographs indicate that at very high pulse energies and thus large laser peak fluences, an inhomogeneous and rough channel bottom results from extensive ablation and the melt formation already detected in the single-spot experiments. The irregularity is expressed in particular in hole-like depressions that are not adequately displayed by the perspective of the 3D micrograph in Figure 8c. However, a qualitative measure is given by the grey-shaded area in the cross-section of Figure 8d that illustrates the remarkably larger variation, especially at the channel bottom, when compared to smaller E_{imp}. This is also confirmed by the larger surface roughness that was measured to be S_a = 0.5174 μm for E_{imp} = 7 μJ.

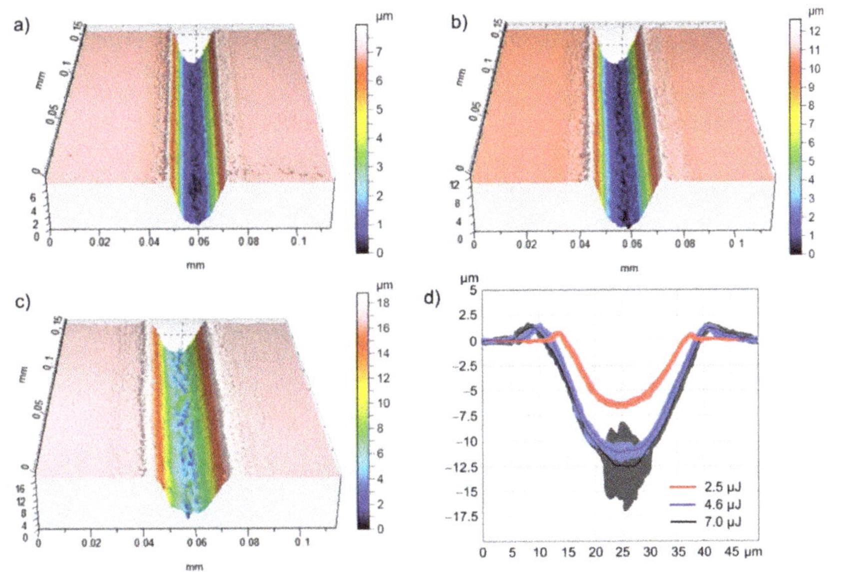

Figure 8. WLIM micrographs of the stainless-steel surface illustrating the 3D geometry of channel-like structures obtained from 10 over-scans with v = 0.1 m/s using the squared top-hat profile at z = 0 mm and different single-pulse energies: (**a**) E_{imp} = 2.5 µJ, (**b**) E_{imp} = 4.6 µJ and (**c**) E_{imp} = 7 µJ. A comparison between the cross-sections of the channels is illustrated in (**d**). Here, the solid line corresponds to the mean profile and the shadow illustrates the variation of the profile series measured along the channel.

Structuring with the donut-shaped intensity profile at z = −0.9 mm allows to create channels with steep walls and a w-shaped cross-sectional geometry that is determined by the specific intensity distribution (see Figure 5). According to the cross-sectional height profile of the channel (Figure 9c), 10 over-scans with v = 0.1 m/s and E_{imp} = 4.6 µJ result in a width of about 40 µm and a maximum ablation depth of about 10 µm. The channel walls are characterized by their very homogeneous and regular surfaces in the form of superimposed nanoscale LIPSS (Figure 9a). The high quality is confirmed by the fact that the modulation depth of LIPSS is typically in the order of 200 nm [30]. Contrary to a rotationally symmetrical donut, the used squared intensity profile provides the zero-intensity center and two axes in x- and y-directions with almost zero intensity. Consequently, the areas with lower (zero) intensity are not passed over by highly intensive beam parts during scanning in these directions, resulting in a channel with a less ablated central area (Figure 9b). This could be used, for example, to periodically propagate these w-shaped structures to large surface areas based on a suitable scan line distance. In dependence on the focal length of the focusing optics, this would result in a microscale periodic grating with periods in the range of 10–20 µm. Similar surface structures with comparable structural sizes can be obtained, e.g., from Direct Interference Laser Patterning, which is used among others to generate surfaces with functional properties (optics, tribology, biology, wetting) [32].

Generally, the results show that the donut and top-hat profiles provided by the beam-shaping element are advantageous for realizing micro-channels with specific wall inclination angles as well as tailor-made cross-sectional geometry. This option is also available (in situ) during the structuring process, since the individual intensity profiles can be addressed in a relatively simple way by changing the z-position of the sample surface.

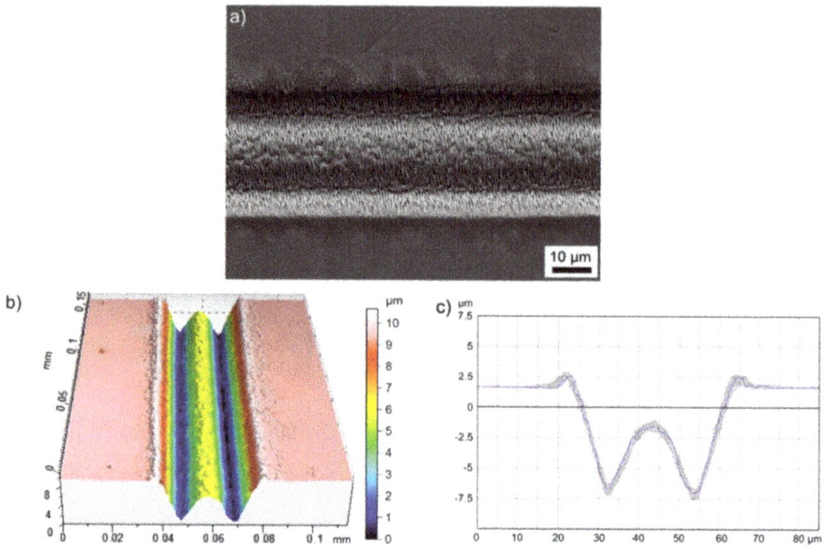

Figure 9. Micro-channel fabricated on stainless-steel using the squared donut-like intensity distribution at z = −0.9 mm, 10 over-scans with v = 0.1 m/s and a single-pulse energy of 4.6 µJ: (**a**) SEM micrograph, (**b**) WLIM micrograph and (**c**) cross-sectional height profile. The blue line in (**c**) corresponds to the mean profile and the grey shadow illustrates the profile series measured along the channel in (**b**).

4. Conclusions

The present study deals with a versatile refractive beam shaper that allows to convert the initial Gaussian intensity distribution of the fs-laser beam into different squared beam profiles at different z-positions. Numerical simulations for the beam-shaping unit were verified experimentally by spatial beam profile measurements and by surface structuring on the micro- and nano-scale. It was demonstrated that the squared top-hat profiles available in the focal region are advantageous to significantly reduce the processing time during large-area LIPSS structuring, while preserving their high regularity. Using the beam shaper for the generation of channel-like structures via multiple line scans, it was shown that the different focal intensity distributions resulted in precise channels with a controllable cross-sectional geometry.

Author Contributions: All authors contributed equally to conceptualization, methodology, validation, writing—original draft preparation, and visualization. All authors have read and agreed to the published version of the manuscript.

Funding: This research received no external funding.

Institutional Review Board Statement: Not applicable.

Informed Consent Statement: Not applicable.

Data Availability Statement: The data underlying this article will be shared on reasonable request from the corresponding author.

Conflicts of Interest: The authors declare no conflict of interest.

References

1. Malinauskas, M.; Zukauskas, A.; Hasegawa, S.; Hayasaki, Y.; Mizeikis, V.; Buividas, R.; Juodkazis, S. Ultrafast laser processing of materials: From science to industry. *Light-Sci. Appl.* **2016**, *5*, e16133. [CrossRef]
2. Raciukaitis, G.; Stankevicius, E.; Gecys, P.; Gedvilas, M.; Bischoff, C.; Jager, E.; Umhofer, U.; Volklein, F. Laser processing by using diffractive optical laser beam shaping technique. *J. Laser Micro Nanoen.* **2011**, *6*, 37–43. [CrossRef]
3. Sugioka, K.; Cheng, Y. A tutorial on optics for ultrafast laser materials processing: Basic microprocessing system to beam shaping and advanced focusing methods. *Adv. Opt. Technol.* **2012**, *1*, 353. [CrossRef]
4. Allegre, O.J.; Jin, Y.; Perrie, W.; Ouyang, J.; Fearon, E.; Edwardson, S.P.; Dearden, G. Complete wavefront and polarization control for ultrashort-pulse laser microprocessing. *Opt. Express* **2013**, *21*, 21198–21207. [CrossRef]
5. Skoulas, E.; Manousaki, A.; Fotakis, C.; Stratakis, E. Biomimetic surface structuring using cylindrical vector femtosecond laser beams. *Sci. Rep.* **2017**, *7*, 45114. [CrossRef]
6. Ouyang, J.; Perrie, W.; Allegre, O.J.; Heil, T.; Jin, Y.; Fearon, E.; Eckford, D.; Edwardson, S.P.; Dearden, G. Tailored optical vector fields for ultrashort-pulse laser induced complex surface plasmon structuring. *Opt. Express* **2015**, *23*, 12562–12572. [CrossRef] [PubMed]
7. Müller, F.A.; Kunz, C.; Gräf, S. Bio-inspired functional surfaces based on laser-induced periodic surface structures. *Materials* **2016**, *9*, 476. [CrossRef]
8. Gräf, S. Formation of laser-induced periodic surface structures on different materials: Fundamentals, properties and applications. *Adv. Opt. Technol.* **2020**, *9*, 11–39. [CrossRef]
9. Stratakis, E.; Bonse, J.; Heitz, J.; Siegel, J.; Tsibidis, G.; Skoulas, E.; Papadopoulos, A.; Mimidis, A.; Joel, A.-C.; Comanns, P. Laser engineering of biomimetic surfaces. *Mater. Sci. Eng. R Rep.* **2020**, *141*, 100562. [CrossRef]
10. Dickey, F.M. Theory and techniques for laser beam shaping. *Int. Congr. Appl. Lasers Electro.-Opt.* **2001**, *2001*, 1393–1402.
11. Frieden, B.R. Lossless conversion of a plane laser wave to a plane wave of uniform irradiance. *Appl. Opt.* **1965**, *4*, 1400–1403. [CrossRef]
12. Rhodes, P.W.; Shealy, D.L. Refractive optical systems for irradiance redistribution of collimated radiation—Their design and analysis. *Appl. Opt.* **1980**, *19*, 3545–3553. [CrossRef] [PubMed]
13. Hoffnagle, J.A.; Jefferson, C.M. Design and performance of a refractive optical system that converts a gaussian to a flattop beam. *Appl. Opt.* **2000**, *39*, 5488–5499. [CrossRef] [PubMed]
14. Veldkamp, W.B.; Kastner, C.J. Beam profile shaping for laser radars that use detector arrays. *Appl. Opt.* **1982**, *21*, 345–356. [CrossRef]
15. Bollanti, S.; Di Lazzaro, P.; Murra, D. More about the light beam shaping by the integration method. *Eur. Phys. J.-Appl. Phys.* **2004**, *28*, 179–186. [CrossRef]
16. Häfner, T.; Strauss, J.; Roider, C.; Heberle, J.; Schmidt, M. Tailored laser beam shaping for efficient and accurate microstructuring. *Appl. Phys. A Mater. Sci. Process.* **2018**, *124*, 111. [CrossRef]
17. Li, J.; Kuanga, Z.; Vilara, J.G.; Deardena, G.; Perriea, W.; Edwardson, S. Dynamic ultrafast laser beam shaping for material processing at the imaging plane using a spatial light modulator. In Proceedings of the 9th International Conference on Photonic Technologies LANE, Gurth, Germany, 19–22 September 2016.
18. Jin, Y.; Allegre, O.J.; Perrie, W.; Abrams, K.; Ouyang, J.; Fearon, E.; Edwardson, S.P.; Dearden, G. Dynamic modulation of spatially structured polarization fields for real-time control of ultrafast laser-material interactions. *Opt. Express* **2013**, *21*, 25333–25343. [CrossRef]
19. Möhl, A.; Kaldun, S.; Kunz, C.; Müller, F.A.; Fuchs, U.; Gräf, S. Tailored focal beam shaping and its application in laser material processing. *J. Laser Appl.* **2019**, *31*, 042019. [CrossRef]
20. Bonse, J.; Kirner, S.V.; Höhm, S.; Epperlein, N.; Spaltmann, D.; Rosenfeld, A.; Krüger, J. Applications of laser-induced periodic surface structures (lipss). *Proc. SPIE* **2017**, *10092*, 100920N.
21. Sugioka, K.; Meunier, M.; Piqué, A. *Laser Precision Microfabrication*; Springer: Berlin, Germany, 2010.
22. Cordingley, J.J. Method for Severing Integrated-Circuit Connection Paths by a Phase-Plate-Adjusted Laser Beam. U.S. Patent 5,300,756, 22 October 1991.
23. Dickey, F.M. *Laser Beam Shaping: Theory and Techniques*, 2nd ed.; CRC Press, Taylor & Francis Group: Boca Raton, FL, USA, 2014.
24. Hopkins, H.H.; Yzuel, M.J. The computation of diffraction patterns in the presence of aberrations. *Opt. Acta Int. J. Opt.* **1970**, *17*, 157–182. [CrossRef]
25. Liu, J.M. Simple technique for measurements of pulsed gaussian beam spot sizes. *Opt. Lett.* **1982**, *7*, 196–198. [CrossRef] [PubMed]
26. Bonse, J.; Krüger, J.; Höhm, S.; Rosenfeld, A. Femtosecond laser-induced periodic surface structures. *J. Laser Appl.* **2012**, *24*, 042006. [CrossRef]
27. Sipe, J.E.; Young, J.F.; Preston, J.S.; van Driel, H.M. Laser-induced periodic surface structure. I. Theory. *Phys. Rev. B* **1983**, *27*, 1141–1154. [CrossRef]
28. Bonse, J.; Gräf, S. Maxwell meets marangoni-a review of theories on laser-induced periodic surface structures. *Laser Photon. Rev.* **2020**, *14*, 2000215. [CrossRef]
29. Kunz, C.; Engel, S.; Müller, F.A.; Gräf, S. Large-area fabrication of laser-induced periodic surface structures on fused silica using thin gold layers. *Nanomaterials* **2020**, *10*, 1187. [CrossRef]

30. Gräf, S.; Kunz, C.; Undisz, A.; Wonneberger, R.; Rettenmayr, M.; Müller, F.A. Mechano-responsive colour change of laser-induced periodic surface structures. *Appl. Surf. Sci.* **2019**, *471*, 645–651. [CrossRef]
31. Gnilitskyi, I.; Derrien, T.J.Y.; Levy, Y.; Bulgakova, N.M.; Mocek, T.; Orazi, L. High-speed manufacturing of highly regular femtosecond laser-induced periodic surface structures: Physical origin of regularity. *Sci. Rep.* **2017**, *7*, 8485. [CrossRef]
32. Müller, D.W.; Fox, T.; Grützmacher, P.G.; Suarez, S.; Mücklich, F. Applying ultrashort pulsed direct laser interference patterning for functional surfaces. *Sci. Rep.* **2020**, *10*, 3647. [CrossRef] [PubMed]

materials

MDPI

Article

High Aspect Ratio Structuring of Glass with Ultrafast Bessel Beams

Christian Vetter, Remo Giust, Luca Furfaro, Cyril Billet, Luc Froehly and Francois Courvoisier *

FEMTO-ST Institute, University Bourgogne Franche-Comté, CNRS, 15B Avenue des Montboucons, CEDEX, 25030 Besançon, France; christian.vetter@iof.fraunhofer.de (C.V.); remo.giust@univ-fcomte.fr (R.G.); luca.furfaro@univ-fcomte.fr (L.F.); cyril.billet@univ-fcomte.fr (C.B.); luc.froehly@univ-fcomte.fr (L.F.)

* Correspondence: francois.courvoisier@femto-st.fr

Abstract: Controlling the formation of high aspect ratio void channels inside glass is important for applications like the high-speed dicing of glass. Here, we investigate void formation using ultrafast Bessel beams in the single shot illumination regime. We characterize the morphology of the damages as a function of pulse energy, pulse duration, and position of the beam inside fused silica, Corning Eagle XG, and Corning Gorilla glass. While a large set of parameters allow for void formation inside fused silica, the operating window is much more restricted for Eagle XG and Gorilla glass. The transient formation of a molten layer around voids enables us interpreting the evolution of the morphology with pulse energy and duration.

Keywords: glass; ultrafast laser processing; Bessel beam

Citation: Vetter, C.; Giust, R.; Furfaro, L.; Billet, C.; Froehly, L.; Courvoisier, F. High Aspect Ratio Structuring of Glass with Ultrafast Bessel Beams. *Materials* **2021**, *14*, 6749. https://doi.org/10.3390/ma14226749

Academic Editors: Jörg Krüger and Jörn Bonse

Received: 15 October 2021
Accepted: 4 November 2021
Published: 9 November 2021

1. Introduction

Cutting and drilling glass is an important technological problem, particularly when the width over which the material has to be modified is much smaller than the length of the modification. This is high aspect ratio structuring. In this context, ultrafast laser processing is very attractive because the infrared wavelength and the very high intensity of the pulses enable energy deposition in three dimensions, including inside the bulk of glass [1]. The laser-induced micro/nano-structures can be index modifications, nanogratings or even voids [2]. These modifications can be combined with chemical etching, which led to a number of advances in the field of photonics, microfluidics chips, mechanics [3,4].

Because point-by-point scanning is relatively slow, a number of techniques were developed to improve the overall speed for the micro-structuring. In addition, elongated voids cannot be formed by scanning, since a nano-void produced by a first pulse would be erased by the microexplosion produced by the second pulse next to it [5]. Bessel beams were revealed to be excellent candidates to control the formation of high aspect ratio elongated structures inside transparent materials [6,7]. Bessel beams are formed by a conical superposition of plane waves, where the central hotspot maintains its diameter over the whole length of the interference region [8,9]. Importantly, when the focusing angle of the Bessel beam is sufficiently high, the conical flow of energy crosses the high-intensity region only in the central hotspot. This drastically reduces the influence of the Kerr effect, so that longitudinally-invariant structures can be processed within dielectrics [10–12].

Laser structuring with high aspect ratio is particularly useful in the context of stealth dicing, a concept in which a series of pulses under high-speed translation of the sample is used to create an entire modification plane [13]. A mechanical, chemical, or thermal stress is then used to cleave the glass along the modified plane. The main benefit of this approach is that cutting is possible at very high speed (typically 10 cm to 1 m per second). Filamentation, i.e., ultrafast pulse self-channeling in glass, was first used for stealth dicing purposes [14,15]. Bessel beams offer in addition the possibility to control very easily the onset of the material damage by simple geometrical considerations since nonlinear effects are reduced. They were used to cut glass and sapphire [16–20]. Since beam length and focusing angle can be independently adjusted, it is also possible to produce very long Bessel beams with the same angle that allows for cutting thick glass. This however requires high pulse energies since the energy is spread over the entire focal line of the beam [21]. With millijoule energy, Bessel beams were used to cleave glass up to 1 cm thick [22,23]. Recently, breaking the symmetry of the Bessel beam was used to improve the precision and ability of guiding fractures [24–27]. Controlling the formation of voids with ultrafast laser pulses is key to improve the stealth dicing of glass.

Here, we show that, depending on the material, voids do not form for the same parameters. We compare three glass types: fused silica, Corning® Eagle XG®, and Corning® Gorilla® glass. We investigate the regimes in which various structures are produced using single shot Bessel beams depending on pulse energy, pulse duration, and position in the sample. We observed that these three parameters control the formation of various types of structures inside glass. Future development of applications such as laser cutting should therefore operate in the right parameter window.

2. Materials and Methods

Our experimental setup (see Figure 1) is composed of a chirped pulse amplified (CPA) Ti-Sapphire laser source, at 800 nm central wavelength and of a reflective axicon (Cailabs) associated to a telescope arrangement to magnify the cone angle [28]. The laser pulses can be stretched from 100 fs to 3 ps using the grating compressor of the amplifier. The experimental characterization of the beam is shown in Figure 2. The Bessel beam has a cone angle of 19.5° in air, which corresponds to a central spot diameter of 0.9 µm Full Width at Half Maximum (FWHM). The Bessel beam length is ~220 µm FWHM. One can notice the high degree of circular symmetry of the Bessel beam. All samples were 700 µm thick.

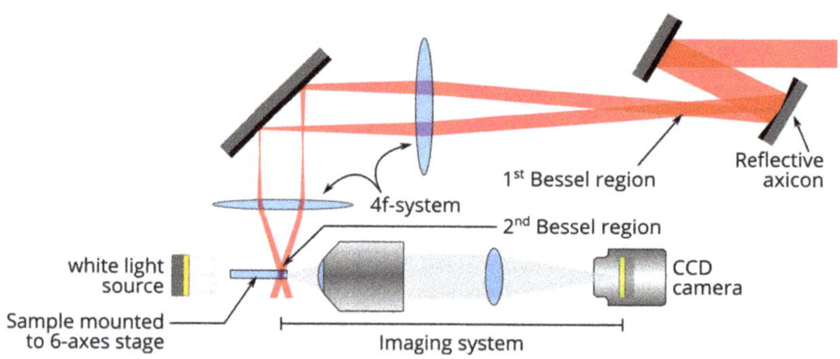

Figure 1. Experimental setup. Ultrafast laser beam is shaped by a reflective axicon (Cailabs). It is then demagnified by a telescopic arrangement in a 2f-2f configuration. Laser-written structures are observed using an incoherent white light source.

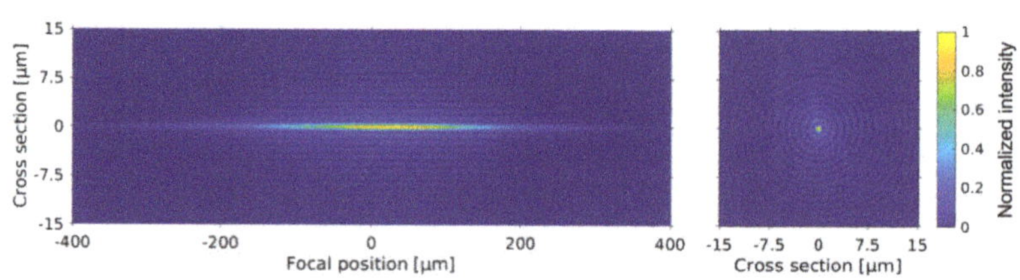

Figure 2. Characterization of experimental Bessel beam. **(left)** Longitudinal cross-cut of fluence distribution as a function of relative propagation distance in air. Please note aspect ratio of axes. **(right)** Cross-section of fluence distribution at center of beam.

After processing, the laser-modified regions were characterized by scanning the sample with white light, brightfield illumination, in an optical microscope arrangement with a numerical aperture of 0.8 and aberration-correction. Stitching the microscope images provided high resolution images of the whole high aspect ratio structure. Figure 3 shows the result of single shot illumination in fused silica at a pulse energy of 52 μJ, for increasing pulse durations. A periodic background pattern can be observed and simply arises from the illumination inhomogeneity associated to the stitching operation.

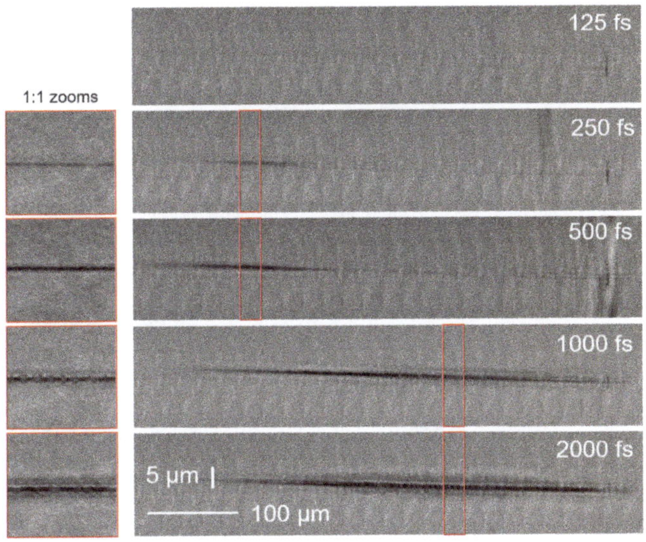

Figure 3. Microscope images of damages produced in fused silica glass for several pulse durations, for same beam position inside sample and for a constant single shot energy of 52 μJ. Please note image aspect ratios (left insets show 1:1 zooms of panels to their right). Beam propagates from left to right.

3. Results

3.1. Microstructure Types

In Figure 3, at a pulse duration of 125 fs, only a line of faint index change is observable. In the cases of 250 and 500 fs, high- aspect ratio voids are observed, they are characterized by black marks. We readily see that the void structure is shorter than the Bessel beam length. The void is present only in the moderate intensity region while in the highest intensity region, the void structure has almost vanished. From 1 ps, the black mark is split around its center into small dots: these are void bubbles (see scanning electron microscopy image in Fig. 4 of reference [29]). This process is called bubbling hereafter. Faint bubbling appears here in the central region of the Bessel beam and is slightly stronger for the case of 2 ps.

Importantly, the morphology of the material transformation can vary along the beam. An example is shown in Figure 4 where we report the results for the interaction of a 3 ps Bessel beam in Gorilla glass for different focusing positions inside the sample. In this example, the material modification undergoes minor variations with the position. We can observe three sections with different morphologies from left to right: (i) a void with faint bubbling in the relatively low intensity region of the Bessel beam (onset), (ii) a wide index modification in the highest intensity segment of the Bessel beam, and (iii) a void. The central panel allows us to understand the ordering of the material modification type with increasing intensity: index modification on a small diameter (central lobe), void formation, structure with more or less randomly distributed bubbles, wide index index modification on a diameter much larger than the beam central lobe. The wide modification is developed longitudinally step-wise, suggesting a threshold-based mechanism. It erased all structures like void or bubbles. Note that the bubbles appear elliptical because we compressed the horizontal axis scale by a factor 5.

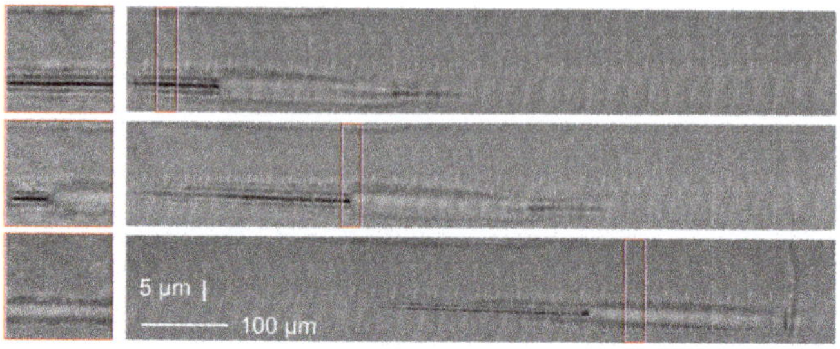

Figure 4. Brightfield microscopy images of damages produced in Gorilla glass with 3 ps pulse duration at a constant energy of 52 μJ as in Figure 4. Position of beam in sample was varied from top to bottom. Please note image aspect ratios (left insets show 1:1 zooms of panels to their right).

We further explored, in a parametric study, the evolution of the laser-induced structures as a function of pulse energy, pulse duration, and beam position. We summarized our results in Figure 5 for three positions of the Bessel beam inside the fused silica sample. In Figure 5a, the beam is positioned at the center of the sample such that none of the entrance and exit surfaces are damaged. We classified the modifications in 5 groups, ranging from no damage to strong bubbling. We note that we did not make a separate class for the wide index modification, such as the one shown in Figure 4, because those modifications are conventionally useless for applications. Also, they often occur alongside voids, which we are more interested in. For the drilling and cutting of glass applications, the narrow index modifications and nice voids, shown respectively as gray and green markers, are the most interesting features. When bubbling occurred on a substantial section of the beam, the structure was classified as bubbling.

In Figure 5a, we see that the relatively large range of parameters allow for inducing nice voids in fused silica, similarly as in reference [30]. Higher energies and longer pulse durations tend to create bubbling. When the pulse duration is increased, the energy required to open a void is reduced, but bubbling also arises earlier. The energy range over which nice voids can be opened is reduced at longer pulse durations. In Figure 5b, the beam crosses the entrance side. In this case, the shortest pulse durations provide conditions where voids can be opened on a larger range of parameters. The presence of the interface increases the ability of void opening after energy deposition, as was already noticed in a former reference [6]. In Figure 5c, the beam crosses the exit interface. In this case, the short pulse durations induce voids with very small diameters. A much larger range of energies and pulse durations enable void formation. In almost all the cases tested here, nice voids could be produced. We hypothesize that our results can be understood by the following: the presence of the interface allows the phenomenon of ablation cooling [31] where a fraction of the energy deposited inside the material can be evacuated via the open channel at the surface. This allows for a fast quenching of the material relaxation which increases the capability of "freezing" a void before the compressed melt part surrounding the void can close it. In the case where the beam crosses the entrance surface (Figure 5b), the dynamics of plasma formation is slightly different from the two other cases because a dense plasma can form on the surface which can then shield light preventing void formation in the very first micrometres from the surface. This could prevent the effect of the ablation cooling described above.

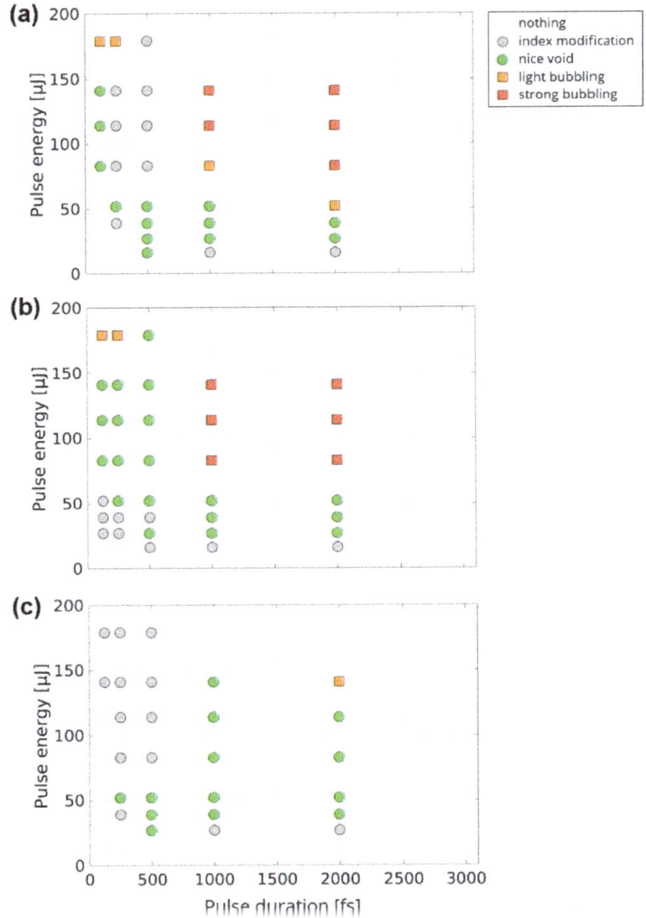

Figure 5. Morphology of single shot-induced damage in fused silica as a function of pulse energy and pulse duration. This is performed for a Bessel beam position: (**a**) at center of sample, (**b**) crossing the entrance surface, (**c**) crossing exit surface.

3.2. Other Glasses

In Figure 6, we show the results for Eagle XG glass (Figure 6a) and Gorilla glass (Figure 6b) when the beam is enclosed within the sample, as in Figure 5a. For these two materials, the situation highly differs from the case of fused silica. Overall, it is much more difficult to create voids, particularly for short pulses, where no modification is apparent below a threshold pulse duration of 1 ps.

The operating window for void formation is restricted to a small energy range before bubbling sets in. This window is even smaller in the case of Gorilla glass. For most of the pulse durations in Gorilla glass, above the energy for the bubbling regime, only faint structures are found, whereas this phenomenon occurs in Eagle XG only for 1.5 ps and never in fused silica. It could be attributed to a slower relaxation in Gorilla glass than in that of the other media.

We attribute the differences between the different glasses in terms of void opening to the difference in softening point. Indeed, it exceeds 1500 °C for fused silica, while it is only of 971 °C for Eagle XG, and 853 °C for Gorilla glass. Therefore, assuming a similar profile of laser-deposited energy, the molten region is wider in the case of Eagle XG and

Gorilla glass than in the case of fused silica. This would lead to a faster quenching of the relaxation in fused silica, with stronger gradients, in contrast with the other two glasses.

In Eagle XG and Gorilla glass, beam positioning close to the entrance and exit surfaces yield to similar tendencies as in the case of fused silica. While no major differences could be observed with Figure 6 when the beam crosses the entrance surface, we observed a much larger operating window for void opening when the beam crosses the exit surface for both glass types.

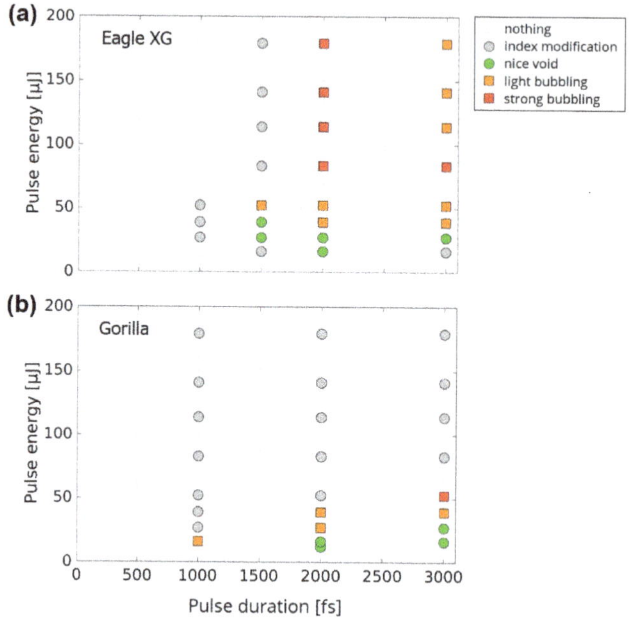

Figure 6. Morphology of single shot-induced damage in (**a**) Eagle XG and (**b**) Gorilla glass as a function of pulse energy and pulse duration. Beam is centered inside sample.

3.3. *Large Heat-Affected Zone for Picosecond Pulses*

Figure 7 shows the result of a 3 ps laser shot in Eagle XG. One can notice that the heat affected zone is very wide, typically above 8 µm in diameter. Importantly, in this regime, the bubbles are not aligned: it seems that they have randomly moved from the optical axis during the relaxation stage. This well supports the interpretation of a large molten layer around the void at large pulse energies and duration.

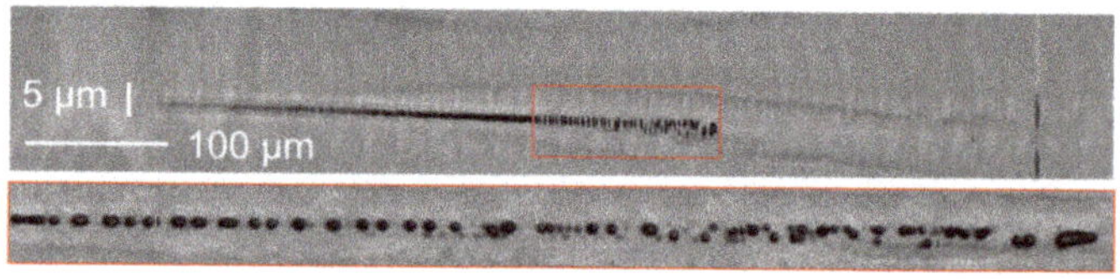

Figure 7. Strong bubbling in Eagle XG glass. Pulse duration is 3 ps, pulse energy 141 µJ. Please note image aspect ratio. Bottom inset shows a 1:1 zoom of marked area in panel above.

4. Conclusions

We observed that void formation in transparent glasses strongly depends on energy and pulse duration. In fused silica, voids can be formed for a relatively large set of parameters. By increasing pulse energy and pulse duration, the high aspect ratio void channel splits into bubbles with a diameter of approximately 1 μm. This structure can even vanish for higher energies. In Eagle XG and Gorilla glass, only very long pulse durations could yield void formation, but for a very limited energy range. For a pulse duration of 2 ps and 16 μJ pulse energy, a void can be formed in all three materials, with a length of 150 ± 10 μm in Eagle XG, of 170 ± 10 μm in fused silica and the highest length is for Gorilla glass with 230 ± 10 μm. For all materials, we remark that void formation is possible over a larger range of energies when the beam crosses the exit surface.

We interpret the evolution of the morphology of the damages induced by ultrashort Bessel beams in these glasses in the following way. For sufficiently high energies, a void can form inside glass, either after a micro-explosion [32,33] or by cavitation inside a molten zone [34]. We infer that this void can be transiently surrounded by a molten layer, whose thickness depends on the glass type and pulse duration. The longest pulse durations and the highest energies tend to increase the thickness of the molten layer. A low softening point, such as in the case of Eagle XG and Gorilla also increase the molten layer. Thicker molten layers increase the occurrence of bubbling or are even closing the void. We understand the formation of bubbles as a redistribution of the material during the cooling stage by splitting or even fully closing the void transiently formed. We interpret the role of the exit surface as a cooling agent. The evacuation of a fraction of the hot material via the void channel produced at the center of the Bessel beam, allows for quenching the relaxation and maintains the void structure even for parameters where the void would be partially or totally reclosed by the molten material around it. Recent results on double pulse illumination let us anticipate that double pulse could partially reduce the amount of the molten layer, and increase the temperature contrast between the optical axis and the surrounding lobes [35].

These results shed light on the formation of high aspect ratio void channels inside different glasses. We believe they will impact on future technologies for ultrafast laser material processing of glass.

Author Contributions: Conceptualization, F.C., R.G., L.F. (Luc Froehly) and C.V.; methodology, C.V., L.F. (Luc Froehly), F.C.; software, C.V.; formal analysis, F.C.; investigation, C.V.; resources, L.F. (Luca Furfaro) and C.B.; data curation, C.V.; writing, F.C.; writing—review and editing, all; visualization, C.V.; supervision, F.C. and R.G. All authors have read and agreed to the published version of the manuscript.

Funding: This research was funded by Corning Incorporated, Region Franche-Comte council and Agence Nationale de la Recherche (EQUIPEX + SMARTLIGHT platform ANR-21-ESRE-0040), I-SITE BFC project (contract ANR-15-IDEX-0003), and the EIPHI Graduate School ANR-17-EURE-0002.

Institutional Review Board Statement: Not applicable.

Informed Consent Statement: Not applicable.

Data Availability Statement: The data presented in this study are available upon reasonable request from the corresponding author.

Acknowledgments: We gratefully acknowledge the technical support of E. Dordor.

Conflicts of Interest: The authors declare no conflict of interest. The funders had no role in the design of the study; in the collection, analyses, or interpretation of data, or in the writing of the manuscript.

References

1. Sugioka, K.; Cheng, Y. Ultrafast lasers—Reliable tools for advanced materials processing. *Light Sci. Appl.* **2014**, *3*, e149. [CrossRef]
2. Gattass, R.R.; Mazur, E. Femtosecond laser micromachining in transparent materials. *Nat. Photonics* **2008**, *2*, 219–225. [CrossRef]
3. Malinauskas, M.; Žukauskas, A.; Hasegawa, S.; Hayasaki, Y.; Mizeikis, V.; Buividas, R.; Juodkazis, S. Ultrafast laser processing of materials: from science to industry. *Light Sci. Appl.* **2016**, *5*, e16133. [CrossRef] [PubMed]

4. Sugioka, K. Progress in ultrafast laser processing and future prospects. *Nanophotonics* **2017**, *6*, 393–413. [CrossRef]
5. Watanabe, W.; Itoh, K. Motion of bubble in solid by femtosecond laser pulses. *Opt. Express* **2002**, *10*, 603. [CrossRef]
6. Bhuyan, M.K.; Courvoisier, F.; Lacourt, P.A.; Jacquot, M.; Salut, R.; Furfaro, L.; Dudley, J.M. High aspect ratio nanochannel machining using single shot femtosecond Bessel beams. *Appl. Phys. Lett.* **2010**, *97*, 081102. [CrossRef]
7. Courvoisier, F. Ultrafast Laser Micro-Nano Structuring of Transparent Materials with High Aspect Ratio. In *Handbook of Laser Micro- and Nano-Engineering*; Sugioka, K., Ed.; Springer International Publishing: Cham, Switzerland, 2020; pp. 1–37. [CrossRef]
8. Durnin, J.; Miceli, J.J.; Eberly, J.H. Diffraction-free beams. *Phys. Rev. Lett.* **1987**, *58*, 1499–1501. [CrossRef]
9. Duocastella, M.; Arnold, C. Bessel and annular beams for materials processing. *Laser Photon. Rev.* **2012**, *6*, 607–621. [CrossRef]
10. Polesana, P.; Franco, M.; Couairon, A.; Faccio, D.; Trapani, P.D. Filamentation in Kerr media from pulsed Bessel beams. *Phys. Rev. A* **2008**, *77*, 043814. [CrossRef]
11. Garzillo, V.; Jukna, V.; Couairon, A.; Grigutis, R.; Trapani, P.D.; Jedrkiewicz, O. Optimization of laser energy deposition for single-shot high aspect-ratio microstructuring of thick BK7 glass. *J. Appl. Phys.* **2016**, *120*, 013102. [CrossRef]
12. Lamperti, M.; Jukna, V.; Jedrkiewicz, O.; Trapani, P.D.; Stoian, R.; Itina, T.E.; Xie, C.; Courvoisier, F.; Couairon, A. Invited Article: Filamentary deposition of laser energy in glasses with Bessel beams. *APL Photonics* **2018**, *3*, 120805. [CrossRef]
13. Kumagai, M.; Uchiyama, N.; Ohmura, E.; Sugiura, R.; Atsumi, K.; Fukumitsu, K. Advanced dicing technology for semiconductor wafer—Stealth dicing. *IEEE Trans. Semicond* **2007**, *20*, 259–265. [CrossRef]
14. Hosseini, S.A.; Herman, P. Method of Material Processing by Laser Filamentation. U.S. Patent 20130126573 A1, 23 May 2013.
15. Butkus, S. Rapid Cutting and Drilling of Transparent Materials via Femtosecond Laser Filamentation. *J. Laser Micro Nanoeng.* **2014**, *9*, 213–220. [CrossRef]
16. Bhuyan, M.K.; Jedrkiewicz, O.; Sabonis, V.; Mikutis, M.; Recchia, S.; Aprea, A.; Bollani, M.; Trapani, P.D. High-speed laser-assisted cutting of strong transparent materials using picosecond Bessel beams. *Appl. Phys. A* **2015**, *120*, 443–446. [CrossRef]
17. Mishchik, K.; Beuton, R.; Caulier, O.D.; Skupin, S.; Chimier, B.; Duchateau, G.; Chassagne, B.; Kling, R.; Hönninger, C.; Mottay, E.; et al. Improved laser glass cutting by spatio-temporal control of energy deposition using bursts of femtosecond pulses. *Opt. Express* **2017**, *25*, 33271. [CrossRef]
18. Jenne, M.; Flamm, D.; Ouaj, T.; Hellstern, J.; Kleiner, J.; Grossmann, D.; Koschig, M.; Kaiser, M.; Kumkar, M.; Nolte, S. High-quality tailored-edge cleaving using aberration-corrected Bessel-like beams. *Opt. Lett.* **2018**, *43*, 3164. [CrossRef]
19. Dudutis, J.; Pipiras, J.; Stonys, R.; Daknys, E.; Kilikevičius, A.; Kasparaitis, A.; Račiukaitis, G.; Gečys, P. In-depth comparison of conventional glass cutting technologies with laser-based methods by volumetric scribing using Bessel beam and rear-side machining. *Opt. Express* **2020**, *28*, 32133. [CrossRef] [PubMed]
20. Li, Z.; Wang, X.; Wang, J.; Allegre, O.; Guo, W.; Gao, W.; Jia, N.; Li, L. Stealth dicing of sapphire sheets with low surface roughness, zero kerf width, debris/crack-free and zero taper using a femtosecond Bessel beam. *Opt. Laser Technol.* **2021**, *135*, 106713. [CrossRef]
21. Mitra, S.; Chanal, M.; Clady, R.; Mouskeftaras, A.; Grojo, D. Millijoule femtosecond micro-Bessel beams for ultra-high aspect ratio machining. *Appl. Opt.* **2015**, *54*, 7358. [CrossRef]
22. Meyer, R.; Froehly, L.; Giust, R.; Hoyo, J.D.; Furfaro, L.; Billet, C.; Courvoisier, F. Extremely high-aspect-ratio ultrafast Bessel beam generation and stealth dicing of multi-millimeter thick glass. *Appl. Phys. Lett.* **2019**, *114*, 201105. [CrossRef]
23. Feuer, A.; Thomas, J.U.; Freitag, C.; Weber, R.; Graf, T. Single-pass laser separation of 8 mm thick glass with a millijoule picosecond pulsed Gaussian–Bessel beam. *Appl. Phys. A* **2019**, *125*, 332. [CrossRef]
24. Meyer, R.; Jacquot, M.; Giust, R.; Safioui, J.; Rapp, L.; Furfaro, L.; Lacourt, P.A.; Dudley, J.M.; Courvoisier, F. Single-shot ultrafast laser processing of high-aspect-ratio nanochannels using elliptical Bessel beams. *Opt. Lett.* **2017**, *42*, 4307. [CrossRef]
25. Meyer, R.; Giust, R.; Jacquot, M.; Dudley, J.M.; Courvoisier, F. Submicron-quality cleaving of glass with elliptical ultrafast Bessel beams. *Appl. Phys. Lett.* **2017**, *111*, 231108. [CrossRef]
26. Jenne, M.; Flamm, D.; Chen, K.; Schäfer, M.; Kumkar, M.; Nolte, S. Facilitated glass separation by asymmetric Bessel-like beams. *Opt. Express* **2020**, *28*, 6552. [CrossRef] [PubMed]
27. Flamm, D.; Grossmann, D.G.; Sailer, M.; Kaiser, M.; Zimmermann, F.; Chen, K.; Jenne, M.; Kleiner, J.; Hellstern, J.; Tillkorn, C.; et al. Structured light for ultrafast laser micro- and nanoprocessing. *Opt. Eng.* **2021**, *60*, 025105. [CrossRef]
28. Boucher, P.; Hoyo, J.D.; Billet, C.; Pinel, O.; Labroille, G.; Courvoisier, F. Generation of high conical angle Bessel–Gauss beams with reflective axicons. *Appl. Opt.* **2018**, *57*, 6725. [CrossRef] [PubMed]
29. Velpula, P.K.; Bhuyan, M.K.; Courvoisier, F.; Zhang, H.; Colombier, J.P.; Stoian, R. Spatio-temporal dynamics in nondiffractive Bessel ultrafast laser nanoscale volume structuring. *Laser Photon. Rev.* **2016**, *10*, 230–244. [CrossRef]
30. Bhuyan, M.K.; Velpula, P.K.; Colombier, J.P.; Olivier, T.; Faure, N.; Stoian, R. Single-shot high aspect ratio bulk nanostructuring of fused silica using chirp-controlled ultrafast laser Bessel beams. *Appl. Phys. Lett.* **2014**, *104*, 021107. [CrossRef]
31. Kerse, C.; Kalaycıoğlu, H.; Elahi, P.; Çetin, B.; Kesim, D.K.; Önder, A.; Yavaş, S.; Aşık, M.D.; Öktem, B.; Hoogland, H.; et al. Ablation-cooled material removal with ultrafast bursts of pulses. *Nature* **2016**, *537*, 84–88. [CrossRef]
32. Juodkazis, S.; Nishimura, K.; Tanaka, S.; Misawa, H.; Gamaly, E.G.; Luther-Davies, B.; Hallo, L.; Nicolai, P.; Tikhonchuk, V.T. Laser-Induced Microexplosion Confined in the Bulk of a Sapphire Crystal: Evidence of Multimegabar Pressures. *Phys. Rev. Lett.* **2006**, *96*, 166101. [CrossRef]
33. Beuton, R.; Chimier, B.; Quinoman, P.; de Martínez, P.G.A.; Nuter, R.; Duchateau, G. Numerical studies of dielectric material modifications by a femtosecond Bessel–Gauss laser beam. *Appl. Phys. A* **2021**, *127*, 334. [CrossRef]

34. Bhuyan, M.K.; Somayaji, M.; Mermillod-Blondin, A.; Bourquard, F.; Colombier, J.P.; Stoian, R. Ultrafast laser nanostructuring in bulk silica, a "slow" microexplosion. *Optica* **2017**, *4*, 951. [CrossRef]
35. del Hoyo, J.; Meyer, R.; Furfaro, L.; Courvoisier, F. Nanoscale confinement of energy deposition in glass by double ultrafast Bessel pulses. *Nanophotonics* **2020**, *10*, 1089–1097. [CrossRef]

materials

MDPI

Article

Prediction of Optimum Process Parameters Fabricated by Direct Laser Interference Patterning Based on Central Composite Design

Mikhael El-Khoury [1,*], Bogdan Voisiat [1], Tim Kunze [2] and Andrés Fabián Lasagni [1,2]

1 Institut für Fertigungstechnik, Technische Universität Dresden, George-Bähr-Str. 3c, 01069 Dresden, Germany; bogdan.voisiat@tu-dresden.de (B.V.); andres_fabian.lasagni@tu-dresden.de (A.F.L.)

2 Fraunhofer-Institut für Werkstoff- und Strahltechnik IWS, Winterbergstr. 28, 01277 Dresden, Germany; tim.kunze@iws.fraunhofer.de

* Correspondence: mikhael.el-khoury@tu-dresden.de

Received: 30 June 2020; Accepted: 5 September 2020; Published: 15 September 2020

Abstract: In this study, we report on the optimization of the direct laser interference patterning process by applying the design of experiments approach. The periodic line-like microstructures of a 8.50 μm spatial period were fabricated by a two-beam interference setup with nanosecond laser pulses, varying laser fluence, pulse overlap, and hatch distance. Central composite design with three factors and five levels was implemented to optimize the required number of experiments. The experimental and numerical results show the impact of various structuring process parameters on surface uniformity. The responses measured are the structure height, height error, and waviness of the pattern. An analysis of the microstructures on the patterned surface was conducted by confocal microscopy and scanning electron microscopy. A 3D-characterization method based on morphological filtering, which allows a holistic view of the surface properties, was applied, and a new qualification scheme for surface microstructures was introduced. Empirical models were also developed and validated for establishing relationships between process parameters and performance criteria. Multi-objective optimization was performed to achieve a minimal value of structure height errors and waviness.

Keywords: nanosecond laser; direct laser interference patterning; design of experiments; central composite design; morphological filtering; surface texture homogeneity; micro structuring; bearing steel

1. Introduction

The functionalization of technical surfaces by producing deterministic topographies today represents an innovation carrier of modern materials engineering. Nature has shown to be the best surface engineer, and the design of these textured surfaces often follows a biomimetic approach motivated by natural designs [1,2]. Therefore, mimicking natural designs helps in understanding the role of surface microstructures and to correlate topographies to macroscopic surface properties. For instance, these well-defined and highly-oriented structures fabricated at the micron and sub-micron scale on surfaces of modern industrial products enable a clear innovation potential to improve products performance significantly [3]. This upgrade concerns a wide range of applications, such as antifouling [4], wetting control, [5,6], tribology [7–10], electrical conductivity improvement [11], cell adhesion [12], as well as surface optical appearance alteration [13,14]. However, the reproduction of these versatile surface structures represents one of the most significant technical challenges today due to their complexity.

In this frame, non-contact manufacturing processes, such as laser-based microprocessing, arose as an extremely viable approach for mimicking natural surfaces because it cannot only provide both the required technological and economic aspects but also ensures the capability to produce high-resolution features [15]. Nowadays, the most prominent laser patterning approaches are direct laser writing, laser-induced periodic surface structures, and direct laser interference patterning [15].

In direct laser writing, the focused laser beam is scanned over the material surface employing pulse-to-pulse strategies, and the resolution is limited by optical diffraction at the focal position. In the case of laser-induced periodic surface structures, repetitive patterns are obtained based on self-organization processes with feature sizes even below the diffraction limit and in the range of the wavelength, or even much smaller [16]. On the other hand, direct laser interference patterning (DLIP) takes advantage of the physical principle of interference of coherent light waves to produce periodic structures on a surface by transferring the pattern shape directly to the material when sufficient laser energy per unit of area (fluence) is applied [17–20]. The interference patterns are formed by splitting a coherent laser beam into multiple beams and hereafter overlapping them on the samples' surface (see Figure 1a,b). Therefore, due to constructive and destructive interference, a specific intensity pattern is obtained, and the size of the periodic structures can be controlled by varying the angle between the interfering beams and the laser wavelength, according to Equation (1):

$$\Lambda_2 = \frac{\lambda}{2\sin(\theta)} \tag{1}$$

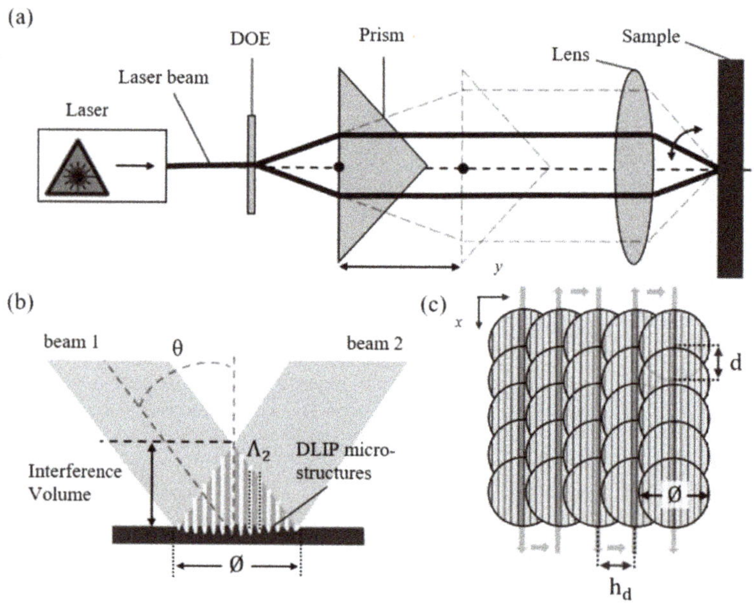

Figure 1. (**a**) Schematic representation of DLIP optical setup; (**b**) schematic view of the interaction zone (with a diameter *Ø*) of two beams intercepting at angle 2θ and forming an interference pattern with a particular period of Λ_2; (**c**) distribution of pulses during the DLIP process: Ø, d, and h_d denote the laser beam diameter (at level $1/e^2$), pulse overlap, and hatch distance, respectively.

Despite the simple optical arrangement required for DLIP for fabricating periodic structures, it is also important to assure in several cases a uniform distribution of these structures to guarantee, overall, a specific surface functionality.

As reported in several studies, the quality of the final surface morphology strongly depends on laser-material interaction and, thus, on the used laser beam profile and the structuring strategy [21,22]. During the DLIP process, laser-material interaction occurs predominantly at the positions corresponding to the interference maxima, inducing various metallurgical processes, such as melting, ablation, and recrystallization [20]. During nanosecond-pulsed laser processing of metals, structuring mechanisms are mainly based on recoil vapor pressure as well as on Marangoni convection, which have an effect on the overall picture of melt flow [22–24]. In most of the commercial laser systems, the laser beam profile has a Gaussian distribution (TEM_{00} profile), which necessitates the use of advanced processing strategies, such as consecutively overlapped irradiation of interfering laser pulses in order to form homogeneous structures on large surface areas. For example, Aguilera et al. [22] used this technology and varied different processing parameters in order to produce homogeneous structures on a large surface area. Experiments were carried out in such a way that one process parameter (factor) was applied and varied through different values (levels), then the response was analyzed, whereas the other factors remain unaffected. This procedure is called one variable at a time [25]. For instance, in the mentioned study, discrete values of overlap distance, hatch distance, and fluence were chosen for specific special periods, and it was found that for fluence F = 1.42 J/cm^2, 98.5% overlap and hatch distance of 20 µm, for 120 µm beam diameter spot, the structured surface was uniform and, thus, obtaining a homogeneous periodic pattern [22]. However, this approach is time-consuming since several variables have to be to screened independently, resulting in a large number of experiments. Furthermore, the number of experiments increases exponentially with the increase of the number of the factors and their levels.

Additionally, in one variable at a time method, it is impossible to single out the effects of factors interaction that can only be observed when varying multiple factors at the same time. Furthermore, by applying one variable at a time approach, it is possible to miss a process window with optimal settings of factors that will give the desired response. Therefore, these factors should not be examined independently. They should be taken into account simultaneously and must be investigated together since one factor might depend on the level of the other factor. In this case, a more effective approach is a statistical design of the experiment, which aims to decrease the number of experiments and to study the effect of interactions between different factors. For this purpose, many experimental design methods, namely, Plackett and Burman, factorial, Box–Behnken, and central composite design (CCD), have been developed [26–28]. Among these experimental methods, CCD developed by Box and Wilson is a very efficient experimental design method to reduce the number of experiments in the studies with a large number of factors and levels [28]. CCD has more advantages compared to other experimental design methods. For instance, it provides high-quality predictions in studying linear and quadratic interaction effects of factors influencing a system. Whereas interactions, unobserved in Plackett and Burman's experimental methods and Box–Behnken has less coverage than in the case of CCD [28,29]. Therefore, CCD has been widely used in the fields of engineering and science [29–34]. The CCD consists of three main parts and of $2^k + 2k + m$ runs.

The factorial part of CCD is a two-level design with 2^k factorial points at the corners of a cube denoting its design in space as shown in Figure 2. For a cube design, the number 2 in the last expression results from the amount of levels, and k is set to 3, representing the number of factors. The other part of CCD is fixed at the center of the design space and consists of m center points (see Figure 2), which represent the middle levels of all the factors investigated. The replication of these points allows estimation of experimental error, detection of curvature in the fitted data, and checking the adequacy of the model. Consequently, the replication of the entire experimental design is not required [28].

The last part comprising CCD is to define the axial points. There are $2k$ axial points in a CCD, and they establish new extreme levels (the lowest and the highest level) for each factor. The distance between the axial and center points is denoted by $\pm\,\alpha$ value, where $\alpha = 2^{k/4} \cong 1{,}68179$ for $k = 3$. This value gives rotatability to the design, which ensures that the variance of the model prediction is constant at all points equidistant from the design center [35]. It makes the CCD method able to explore the wide process space and to capture a strong curvature for studying the effects of the interactions between the design factors on the model [36–38].

In this contribution, we present the optimization and fabrication of homogeneous periodic surface microstructures on bearing steel (100Cr6) using the design of experiments approach and employing a two-beam-DLIP setup with an infrared (IR) nanosecond laser. Since it has been shown that the improvement of the structure homogeneity is more dependent on the strategy used during the experiments than on the pulse duration of the laser source, the aim is to optimize the DLIP process parameters such as laser peak-fluence, pulse overlap, and hatch distance (see Figure 1c) with respect to the structures' height and surface texture homogeneity by performing the CCD method. The surface topography is characterized using confocal microscopy and scanning electron microcopy analysis. Furthermore, a 3D-characterization method for measuring the pattern homogeneity was applied based on morphological filtering [39–42], which allows a holistic view of the surface properties, and a new qualification approach of DLIP surface structures was introduced. The method presented here is of significant relevance to assure, in the future, a certain performance over the whole treated area as well as to permit in relevant industrial processes to quantitatively describe the produced topography in terms of homogeneity. It is required, for instance, for quality management.

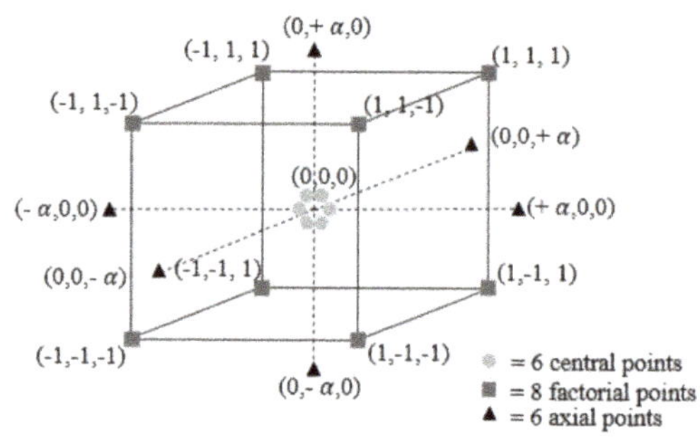

Figure 2. Central composite design with three factors and five levels each.

2. Materials and Methods

2.1. Materials

The laser texturing experiments were performed on a hardened bearing steel surface (100Cr6), commonly used for the manufacturing of automotive components. The test samples were cut into round shaped substrates with a diameter of 40 mm and 10 mm thickness. Each test surface was ground, resulting in surface roughness S_a of 0.74 µm (DIN-ISO 25178). Before the laser treatment, all samples were cleaned using isopropanol.

2.2. Nanosecond Two-Beam-DLIP Setup and Process Strategy

The laser experiments were carried out using a two-beam DLIP-µFab system (developed by Fraunhofer IWS, Dresden, Germany), which produces the interference spot that contains a line-like intensity pattern. The system is equipped with a pulsed Q-switched Nd:YLF laser (Laser-export Tech-1053 Basic, Moscow, Russia), operating at 1053 nm wavelength and providing 12 ns pulses with pulse energy up to 290 µJ at 1 kHz. The laser emits the fundamental transverse mode (TEM_{00}) with a laser beam quality factor of $M^2 < 1.2$. This system also includes a compact DLIP optical head, where the main beam is split into two beams using a diffractive optical element (DOE), then the beams are parallelized by a prism and finally overlapped using a lens with a focal distance of 40 mm (see Figure 1a). Such an optical configuration provides the fully-automatic control of the spatial period of the interference profile between 1.45 µm and 8.50 µm by varying the incidence angle of the beams (θ) on the sample, which, in turn, is realized by moving the prism with respect to the DOE [43].

In this study, different pulse peak-fluences F_p (ranging from 4.97 J/cm^2 up to 7.07 J/cm^2) were used to determine the energy range needed for uniform structuring of bearing steel surface. The peak-fluence on the interference spot was calculated according to Equation (2):

$$F_p = \frac{2n \cdot P}{f \cdot \pi \cdot w^2}, \tag{2}$$

where n is a number of interfering beams, P and f is power and repetition rate of the laser, respectively, and w denotes a beam radius (at level 1/e^2). In this work, the beam radius w was determined using the D-squared method and was equal to 52.5 µm [44,45].

To structure larger areas, the sample was moved by XY-stages (PRO Series, Aerotech Ltd., Tadley, UK) with linear speeds ranging from 0.22 cm/s to 1.60 cm/s. The arrangement of the pulse position in the structuring process is illustrated schematically in Figure 1c. This process occurs consecutively such that first overlap in the x-direction (feed direction) occurs then substrate is moved in the y-direction by hatch distance, making an overlap also in y-direction. Notable that x-direction was chosen as feed direction since it is parallel to the orientation of the line-like pattern, and thus guarantees a well-defined periodic structure. The pulse-to-pulse overlap in x-direction is denoted as P_O (%) and represented as a function of pulse-to-pulse separation distance d ($d = v_{scan} \cdot f$, where v_{scan} is the scanning speed of x-axis and f is the used laser pulse repetition rate) and the laser beam diameter Ø using Equation (3):

$$P_O\,[\%] = \left(1 - \frac{d}{\text{Ø}}\right) \cdot 100\% \tag{3}$$

In the experiments, the pulse-to-pulse overlap was varied between 82.56% and 98.52%. On the other hand, the hatch distance h_d (distance between the vertical lines) was controlled by shifting the sample with the y-axis in such a way that h_d was always kept multiple of the spatial period. In addition, hatch distance h_d was varied from 25.5 µm up to 68 µm. The laser pulses overlap in y-direction is also introduced, and it can be represented as a function of hatch distance h_d and the laser beam diameter Ø (at level 1/e^2) using Equation (4):

$$H_D\,[\%] = \left(1 - \frac{h_d}{\text{Ø}}\right) \cdot 100\% \tag{4}$$

2.3. Central Composite Design Method

In the present study, the experimental plan with the variation of parameters and statistical analyses of the experimental data was carried out using MINITAB 18 statistical package. The experiments were designed based on the CCD method. In Figure 2, each axis corresponds to a factor while each point on the cube represents certain levels. The three selected factors are fluence (X_1), pulse overlap (X_2), and hatch distance overlap (X_3). It is recommended that six center points are taken in a CCD with three factors [35].

As was stated before, the center point is replicated to find the experimental error, and so the replication of the entire experimental design is usually not required. However, during pretests model variability (i.e., how well the regression model fits the experimental data) determined by the R^2 factor was <80%, which is less than the acceptable value according to [38]. Therefore, it was decided to make a replication of the entire experimental design in order to increase the statistical significance of the measurements and improve the models' regression fit. As a result, the factorial, center and axial points in a CCD method build up an experimental design with five levels for each factor and three replicates, making 60 runs in total ($3(2^k + 2k + m) = 3(8 + 6 + 6) = 60$). The designed 60 experiments of the DLIP process were conducted in random order to exclude any bias in the response variables and to avoid a systematic error associated with the specific factor combinations as it was suggested in [28,37].

The experimental plan with the coded and uncoded levels of design factors is presented in Table 1. The low, middle, and high levels of each factor are coded as −1, 0, and +1, respectively, while the lowest and the highest levels are coded as −1.5 and +1.5.

The mathematical relationship of Y response on the corresponding factors is expressed by the following second-order polynomial equation [36,37]:

$$Y = \beta_0 + \sum_{i=1}^{k} \beta_i X_i + \sum_{i=1}^{k} \beta_{ii} X_i^2 + \sum_{i=1}^{k} \sum_{j>i}^{k} \beta_{ij} X_i X_j + \varepsilon\ ;\ i = 1,\ 2,\ \ldots,\ k;\ j = 2,\ \ldots,\ k;\ i \neq j, \quad (5)$$

where Y is the observed response value (structures height, structure-height-error, and waviness percentage); X_i and X_j are the coded values of factors, β_0 is the constant, β_i, β_j, and β_{ij} are the linear, quadratic, and interaction coefficients respectively, k is the number of the factors, and ε is the error term. MINITAB was also used to generate the Pareto charts, response surface, contour plots of factors, as well as the optimization plots. Excluding the control factors, each test was carried out under the same experimental conditions in the ambient environment without post-treatment.

Table 1. Factors and their adopted (uncoded) values at different coded levels.

Factors (Y)	Symbol	Coded: −1.5	−1	0	+1	+1.5
		Uncoded Values of Coded Levels:				
Peak-Fluence: F (J/cm^2)	X_1	4.97	5.32	6.02	6.72	7.07
Pulse Overlap: P_O (%)	X_2	82.56	85.22	90.54	95.86	98.52
Hatch Distance: H_D (%)	X_3	40	46	58	70	76

2.4. *Surface Characterization*

The 3D surface topography of structured samples was characterized using confocal and coherence scanning interferometry microscopy (Sensofar, S Neox non-contact 3D Surface Profiler, Barcelona, Spain) employing a 50× magnification objective, with a lateral and vertical resolution of 340 nm and 4 nm, respectively. Using this objective, a total area of 351 µm × 264 µm could be recorded in each measurement. Afterward, using the software MountainsMap® 7.4 (Digital Surf, Besançon, France), the surface profiles of the recorded topographies are extracted applying morphological filters (ISO16610-14), and the topographical 3D roughness parameters are calculated by the recognized measurement (ISO 25178-2). In addition, topographical measurements have been carried out using a scanning electron microscopy at an operating voltage of 15 kV (JEOL, JSM 6610LV, Tokyo, Japan).

To describe the homogeneity of the fabricated structures, two topographical parameters were used, namely, structure height error and waviness. Waviness shows how the structure height is changing at distances larger than the structure period. This kind of structure inhomogeneity is caused by too large a hatch distance between the laser pulses [22]. However, when the structure hatch distance is small enough, the waviness of the structure becomes close to zero. At this point, the homogeneity of the structure is described better by the structure height error parameter.

2.5. *Development of a Topographical Analysis Method*

To perform a homogeneity analysis of the structured surface, an analysis algorithm, based on the extraction of surface envelopes from the measured surface (S) using morphological filters (MF), was developed. A morphological filter is based on two morphological operations, dilation, and erosion, that work using a structuring element (SE) of a given size [41,42]. In this case, the SE was set to the size of the structure period Λ. By applying the dilation (dMF) and erosion (eMF) morphological filtering the upper (U) and lower (L) structure envelopes were achieved, respectively (profile inset Figure 3a). The U and L envelopes represent the distribution of heights and depths of structure hills and valleys, respectively. Accordingly, $H = |U - L|$ represent the fabricated structure height distribution. Then, the average structure height (h) and its error (h_{err}) can be calculated by finding an average and root mean square of H, respectively. Equations (6) and (7) represents the mathematical procedures described in this paragraph:

$$U = eMF_{SE=\Lambda}(S);\ L = dMF_{SE=\Lambda}(S);\ H = |U - L|; \tag{6}$$

$$h_{err} = \frac{RMS(H)}{H} \cdot 100\%. \tag{7}$$

In order to separate structure height error from the waviness calculations, special filtering is applied to the measured surface S. Spatial filtering is performed by calculating the fast Fourier transform of the S, then applying spatial filter and finally performing the inverse Fourier transform on the filtered Fourier space data:

$$\text{(i)} : FS\ =\ iFFT(S\_Filter\ (FFT(S))) \tag{8}$$

As it was mentioned in Section 2.4, the waviness is proportional to the hatch distance between the laser pulses. Therefore, the waviness is measured by using similar technique described in previous paragraph, but with structuring element of the MF filter equal to the hatch distance that was used to form the structure. Altogether, the calculation of the waviness consist of few steps. First, the upper (U_{FS}) and lower (L_{FS}) envelops of the filtered surface (FS) are calculated:

$$\text{(ii)} : U_{FS} = eMF_{SE=\Lambda}(FS);\ \text{(iii)} : L_{FS} = dMF_{SE=\Lambda}(FS). \tag{9}$$

Then the upper and lower envelopes of U_{FS} and U_{FS} are calculated with $SE = h_d$:

$$\begin{aligned} \text{(iv)} : U_{U_{FS}} &= eMF_{SE=h_d}(U_{Fs});\ (v) : U_{U_{FS}} = dMF_{SE=h_d}(U_{Fs}); \\ \text{(vi)} : U_{L_{FS}} &= eMF_{SE=h_d}(L_{Fs});\ \text{(vii)} :\ L_{L_{FS}} = dMF_{SE=h_d}(L_{Fs}). \end{aligned} \tag{10}$$

Finally, the waviness of the function is expressed by Equation (11):

$$\begin{aligned} H_U = \left(U_{U_{FS}} - U_{U_{FS}}\right);\ H_L = \left(U_{L_{FS}} - L_{L_{FS}}\right);\ H_{Wav} = H_U + H_L;\ H_{total} = U_{U_{FS}} - L_{L_{FS}}; \\ W[\%] = \frac{H_{wav}}{H_{total}} 100 \end{aligned} \tag{11}$$

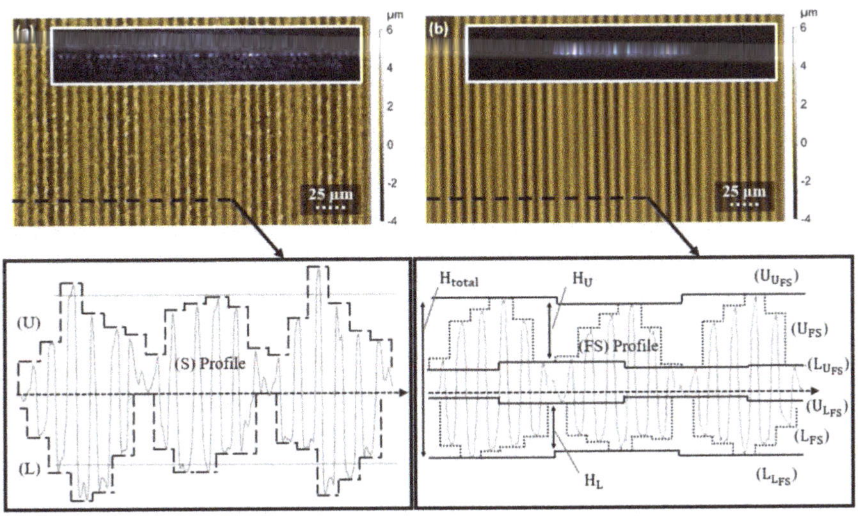

Figure 3. Topography images of (**a**) measured DLIP surface and (**b**) filtered surface with corresponding roughness profiles. The insets show Fourier transform of each of the surfaces.

An example of this procedure is shown in Figure 3, in which explanation is done on 2D profiles instead of 3D for simplicity. It shows the topography image of a DLIP structured surface measured by confocal microscope in Figure 3a,b represents its filtered Fourier space. The inserts in both images show the fast Fourier transforms of the corresponding topographies and visualizes how the smallest scale elements from surface (a) that form the noise (unreal measured peaks, solidified debris, dirt particles, etc.) are filtered by using the special filtering method (ISO25178), leaving only the surface waviness and the smaller line-like pattern. Additionally, the extracted profile pictures of selected areas are shown for both cases, showing the different topography feature indicators described in the previous section.

3. Results and Discussions

3.1. Statistical Analysis of Results

The surface of the steel sample was patterned using the two-beam DLIP configuration. The μsec processing strategy was already described in Section 2.2. Areas with a size of 3 × 3 mm were structured with different processing parameters. The varied process parameters were (i) hatch distance, (ii) pulse overlap, and (iii) peak-laser-fluence (see Table 1).

The scanning electron micrographs of three exemplary patterned surfaces are shown in Figure 4b,d. The surfaces were processes with the following process parameters: F = 6.02 J/cm^2, P_O = 90.54%, H_D = 58% (Figure 4b), F = 6.02 J/cm2, P_O = 98.52%, H_D = 58% (Figure 4c) and F = 6.72 J/cm^2, P_O = 98.52%, H_D = 70% (Figure 4d). The reference topography with initial surface roughness is presented in Figure 4a. Due to the high roughness of the initial samples' surface, the grinding stripes are still be visible after the laser process (see features perpendicular to the line-like structure in Figure 4b). In this case, low laser fluence and pulse overlap were used, which leads to the formation of shallow structures with height in the range of surface roughness. Differently, at higher fluence values and/or increased pulse overlap, the initial surface roughness is flattened as it can be seen from Figure 4c,d. Furthermore, the high magnification images depicted in the insets of Figure 4c,d clearly show that during nanosecond-pulsed laser treatment besides ablation phenomena, redeposition of the molten material driven by Marangoni convection and recoil vapor pressure [22,24] takes part in the structuring mechanism, creating structures with higher aspect ratios (height to spatial period ratio) [46].

In addition, to the periodic microstructures produced by the interference pattern, also waviness of the structured topography is very pronounced for the used hatch distances 42.5 μm, which corresponds to H_D = 58% in Figure 4b,c. This structure topography can be explained since the interference patterns are obtained using two overlapped beams with a Gaussian intensity distribution (TEM_{00}), which results in an interference pattern also with a Gaussian distribution [47,48]. Therefore, due to the Gaussian beam profile, the fluence in the center of the spot is higher, which lead to high cumulative energy and, thus, strong ablation and a significant quantity of molten material occur. Furthermore, since the sample is moved in the x direction (parallel to the orientation of the interference lines) and the pulses are overlapped, which leads to deeper structures at the central area as well as shallow structures at the periphery, producing the larger repetitive structure. Moreover, the repetitive length of waviness modulation is equivalent to the hatch distance used as reported in [22].

For determining the general surface texture homogeneity, the experimental results obtained by using the topographical analysis method described in Section 2.5 were analyzed statistically. Analysis of variance (ANOVA) was performed to identify the significance of the factors and their interactions as well as for estimating the adequacy of the model. Pareto charts of the ANOVA standardized effect estimates are presented in Figure 5. A Pareto chart is very useful for reviewing a large number of factors and for presenting the magnitude and the importance of the effects. In the plotted diagrams, a vertical reference line indicates the minimum magnitude of statistically significant effects, which depends on the significance level denoted by α and set in our model to 0.05 (5% of risk) by convention described in [49]. In addition, the bars that cross the reference line are statistically significant.

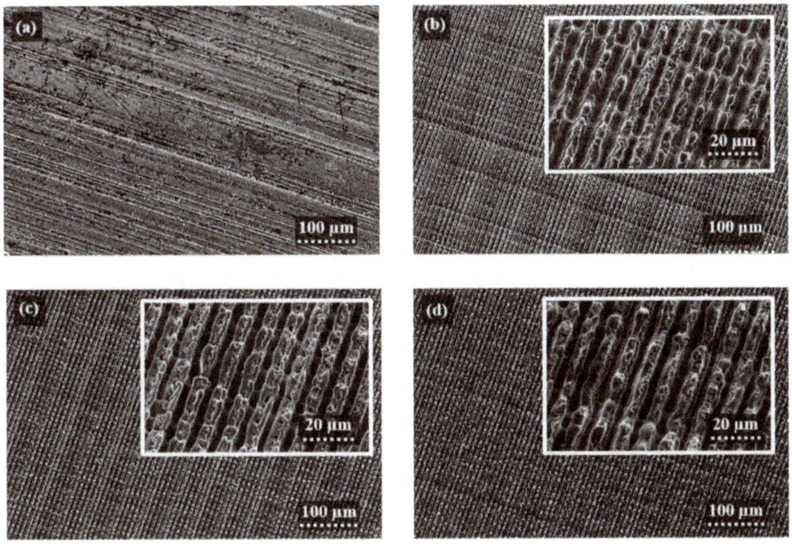

Figure 4. Scanning electron micrographs of initial surface topography (**a**), and the nanosecond DLIP structures produced on 100Cr6 steel using spatial period $\Lambda = 8.50$ μm, and the corresponding processing parameters: $F = 6.02$ J/cm^2, $P_O = 90.54\%$, $H_D = 58\%$ (**b**), $F = 6.02$ J/cm^2, $P_O = 98.52\%$, $H_D = 58\%$ (**c**), and $F = 6.72$ J/cm^2, $P_O = 98.52\%$, $H_D = 70\%$ (**d**). The insets show the corresponding magnification of the topographies.

For instance, in Figure 5a where different standardized effects in the structure height response are shown, it is worth to point out that pulse overlap (X_2) as well as laser-fluence (X_1) have the highest effect on the formation of structure height. Other significant effects according to the developed model are square interaction of each of pulse overlap ($X_{2\times2}$) and laser-fluence (X_1X_1) as well as their two-way interaction (X_1X_2). Other relevant single effect which is worth to mention is the hatch distance (X_3), whereas the square interaction of hatch distance (X_3X_3) as well as the two-way interactions between hatch distance with each of fluence (X_1X_3) and pulse overlap (X_2X_3) are not significant at the 0.05 level with the current model terms.

In the same manner, the Pareto chart of Figure 5b, shows the standardized effects for structure height error. In this case, almost all factors have significant effects at the 0.05 level on the model, except those of single, square and two-way interactions of pulse overlap (X_2, X_2X_2, X_2X_3, and X_1X_2). Finally, in the Pareto chart shows in Figure 5c, it is possible to see that for the standardized effects for waviness, almost all factors have significant effects at the 0.05 level, except the effect of single interaction of pulse overlap (X_2) as well as the effects of each of the two-way interactions between pulse overlap with each of fluence (X_1X_2) and hatch distance (X_2X_3).

Moreover, from the Pareto charts, it is possible to determine the most influencing factors among all the relevant candidates. This is visible when calculating the contribution in percentages of each factor for the different developed models, which is shown in Table 2. The results show that pulse overlap (X_2), followed by fluence (X_1), have the highest contribution to the structure height, whereas in the case of height error and waviness, the hatch distance (X_3) followed by fluence (X_1) have the highest contributions.

The regression equations obtained by removing insignificant terms from the model for each of the responses are given as follows:

$$\begin{gathered}\text{Model \#1}: \; S = 0.883 \; and \; R^2 = 84.82\%; \\ h\;(m) = 275.50 + 2.26X_1 + 6.41X_2 + 0.06X_3 - 0.79X_1X_1 \\ -0.03X_2X_2 + 0.15X_1X_2\end{gathered} \tag{12}$$

$$\begin{gathered}\text{Model \#2}: \; S = 7.740 \; and \; R^2 = 87.54\%; \\ h_{error}\;(\%) = 1368 - 328.60X_1 + 0.11X_2 - 9.22X_3 + 22.90X_1X_1 + 0.04X_3X_3 + 0.55X_1X_3\end{gathered} \tag{13}$$

$$\begin{gathered}\text{Model \#3}: \; S = 8.954 \; and \; R^2 = 84.22\% \\ W\;(\%) = 1943 - 167.40X_1 - 27.30X_2 - 1.92X_3 + 15.13X_1X_1 \\ +0.15X_2X_2 + \; 0.03X_3X_3 - 0.53X_1X_3\end{gathered} \tag{14}$$

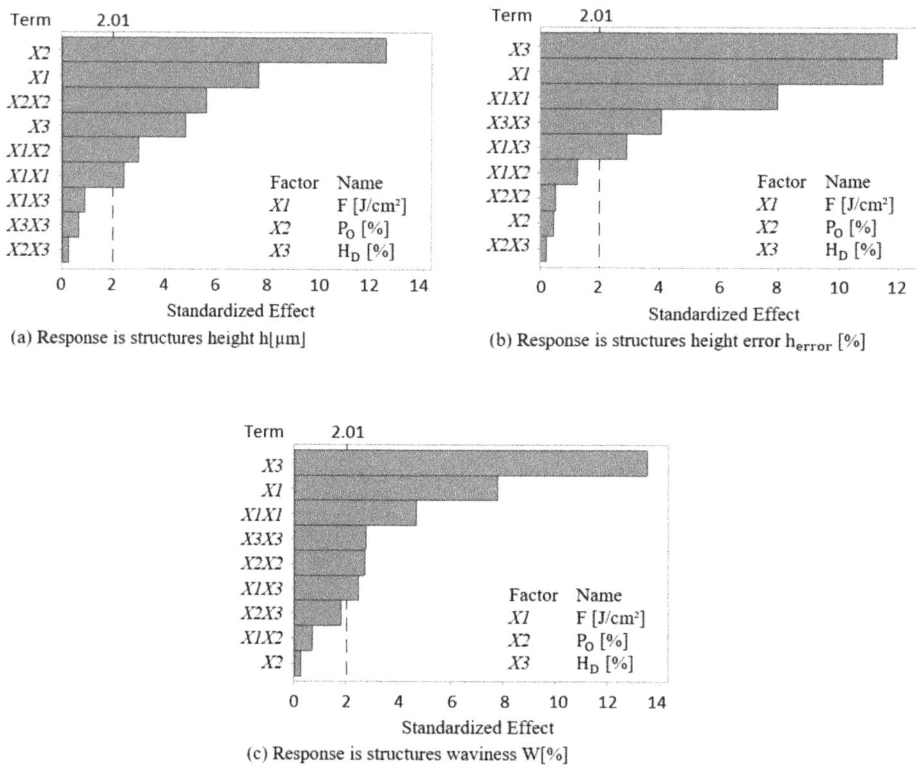

Figure 5. Pareto charts of the standardized effect of (**a**) structures height, (**b**) structures height error, and (**c**) surface waviness.

The positive and the negative sign in Equations (12)–(14) represent the synergistic and antagonistic effects of the factor on the response for each of the models, respectively. Furthermore, the determination coefficient (R^2) of model #1 is 84.82%, showing a acceptable agreement with the experimental data. Moreover, the standard error of the regression (S) of model #1 is 0.883. This means that this statistical model can explain 84.82% variability in the response and that the average distance of the structure height data points from the fitted line is about 0.883 μm. It is worth mentioning that S is represented in the units of the dependent variable. Likewise, in model #2 the determination coefficient (R^2) and the standard error of the regression (S) are equal to 87.54% (>80%) and 7.74%, respectively. Finally, for model #3 the corresponding determination coefficient and the standard error of the regression are as following R^2 = 84.22% (>80%) and S = 8.954%. It can be concluded from both values that each of the models is statistically significant.

In order to compare the results from the models with experimental data, the correlation graphs were analyzed showing a good correlation, as shown in Figure 6. In the plots, the upper and lower limits of the confidence and prediction intervals are displayed as dashed lines. The confidence interval displays the range of 95% of possible values for the mean response, whereas the prediction interval displays the range of 95% of possible values for a single new observation. The R^2 value in each of the correlation graphs, shows that the developed model can explain >80% variability in the response.

Table 2. Contribution of significant main factors (in %), their interactions and quadratic effects of factors from the model for each of the responses, with X_1 = Fluence, X_2 = Pulse overlap and X_3 = Hatch Distance.

Response	X_1	X_2	X_3	$X_1 X_1$	$X_2 X_2$	$X_3 X_3$	$X_1 X_2$	$X_1 X_3$	$X_2 X_3$	Error
Factors										
h (µm)	17.5	46.56	6.96	1.74	9.49	0.13	2.69	0.25	0.02	14.78
h_{error} (%)	31.64	0.05	34.24	15.25	0.06	3.99	0.37	2.02	0.01	12.02
W (%)	17.75	0.03	53.5	6.43	2.15	2.2	0.15	1.8	0.96	14.67

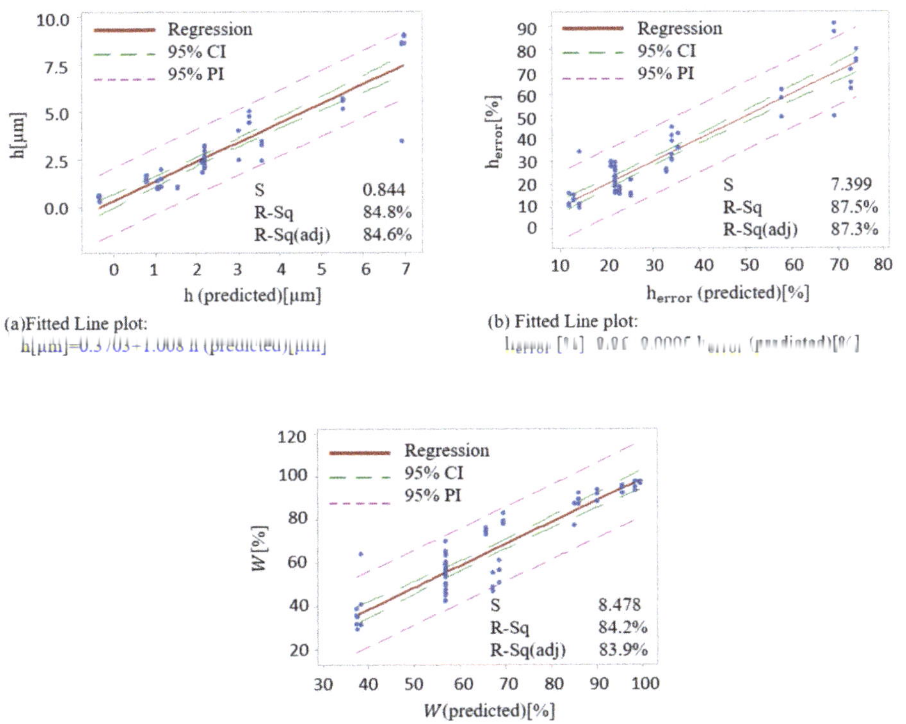

(a)Fitted Line plot: h[µm]=0.3703+1.008 h (predicted)[µm]

(b) Fitted Line plot: [illegible]

(c) Fitted Line plot: W[%]=-1.234+0.9994 W(predicted)[%]

Figure 6. Correlation fitted line plots between experimental and predicted values for each of (**a**) structures height, (**b**) structures height error, and (**c**) surface waviness.

After checking the statistical significance of the model, important interactions of the factors that mostly affect the response were analyzed by using a graphical tool called interaction plots. These interaction plots are shown in Figure 7 and they are plotted from fitted values of predicted responses from the region of interest that consist of central and factorial points, excluding axial ones due to higher magnitude of prediction error. Figure 7a shows that the change in the mean response (height), from a low to a high level of laser fluence factor, depend on the level of the other factor which is pulse overlap. Additionally, the effect of laser fluence on the mean height of the structure is stronger for higher values of pulse overlap (Po), which is visible by the increasing slope of the curves with increasing Po level. The maximum height of the structures is reached when both fluence and pulse overlap are kept at a relatively high-level of 7.07 J/cm^2 and 95.86%, respectively. Moreover, Figure 7b,c shows the presence of interaction between the fluence and the hatch distance, which significantly affect the structure height error as well as surface waviness. It is worth mentioning that an increase of both the fluence and the hatch distance tends to decrease the structures height error as well as the surface waviness and thus to improve homogeneity. However, the increase of fluence is effective only until the negative vertex displayed in Figure 7b,c. After this critical point, the curve changes its slope, which means that a further increase of the laser fluence may have an opposite effect in the structure height and will decrease homogeneity. Indeed, a very high value of fluence can negatively affect the quality and the height of the fabricated structures, as the accumulated energy may increase, and the possibility of uncontrolled overmelt occurs, which was already shown in previous investigations [50].

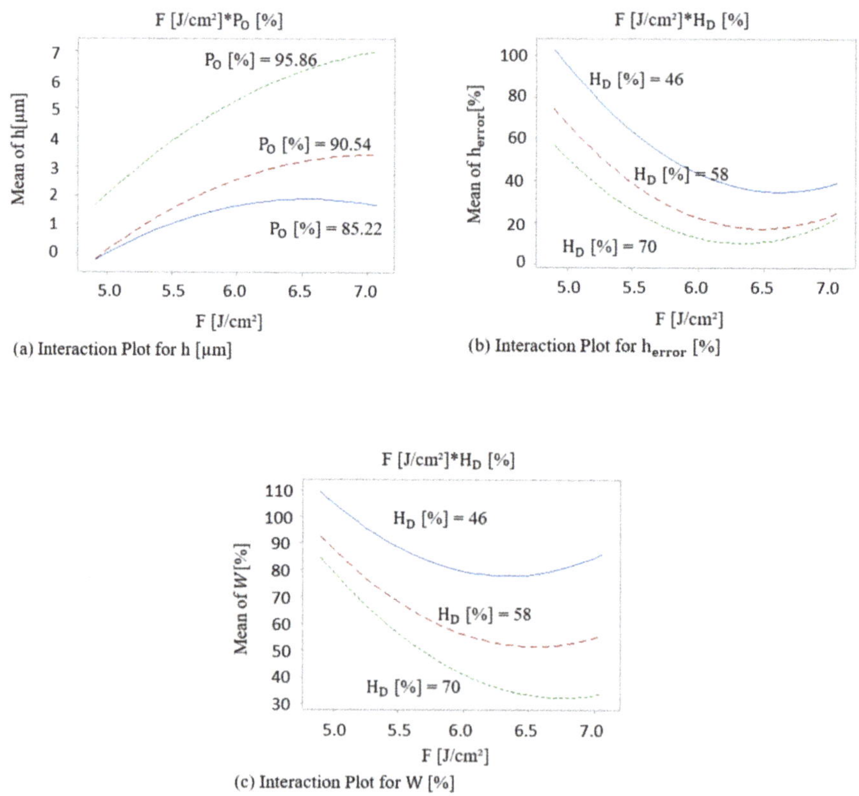

Figure 7. Interaction plots of F (J/cm^2)·P$_O$ (%) for the (**a**) structures height, and of F (J/cm^2)·H$_D$ (%) for (**b**) structure height error, and (**c**) surface waviness.

Finally, all the effects of the individual main effect of each factor, their quadratic terms, as well as their interactions can be summarized with the help of 2D contour plots, which are generally the graphical representation of the regression equation. Therefore, the accuracy of the contour plot depends on how well the model represents the true relationships between the variables. Each response surface presents the effect of laser fluence and hatch distance on structure height, height error, and surface waviness, while pulse overlap is held at a fixed specific level of 85.22%, 90.54%, and 95.86%. Each contour plot in Figure 8 has the dominant characteristic of the non-linear surface (fan-shaped, in this case). Such non-linearity implies a strong $X_1 \times X_3$ (fluence with hatch distance) interaction effect, whereas it can be concluded from Figure 8b,c that the pulse overlap does not have a significant effect on the interaction between laser fluence and hatch distance, which indicates that interactions $X_2 \times X_3$ and $X_1 \times X_2$ are negligible. Moreover, the response surface plots exhibit a saddle shape, which means that any increase or decrease of fluence from the saddle peak results in a decrease of each of the measured response factors. For instance, in the case of Po = 85.22%, H_D = 60%, and for fluences from 6.5 J/cm^2 and higher, the structure height saturates and even slightly reduces, because of material overmelting, as previously reported in [50].

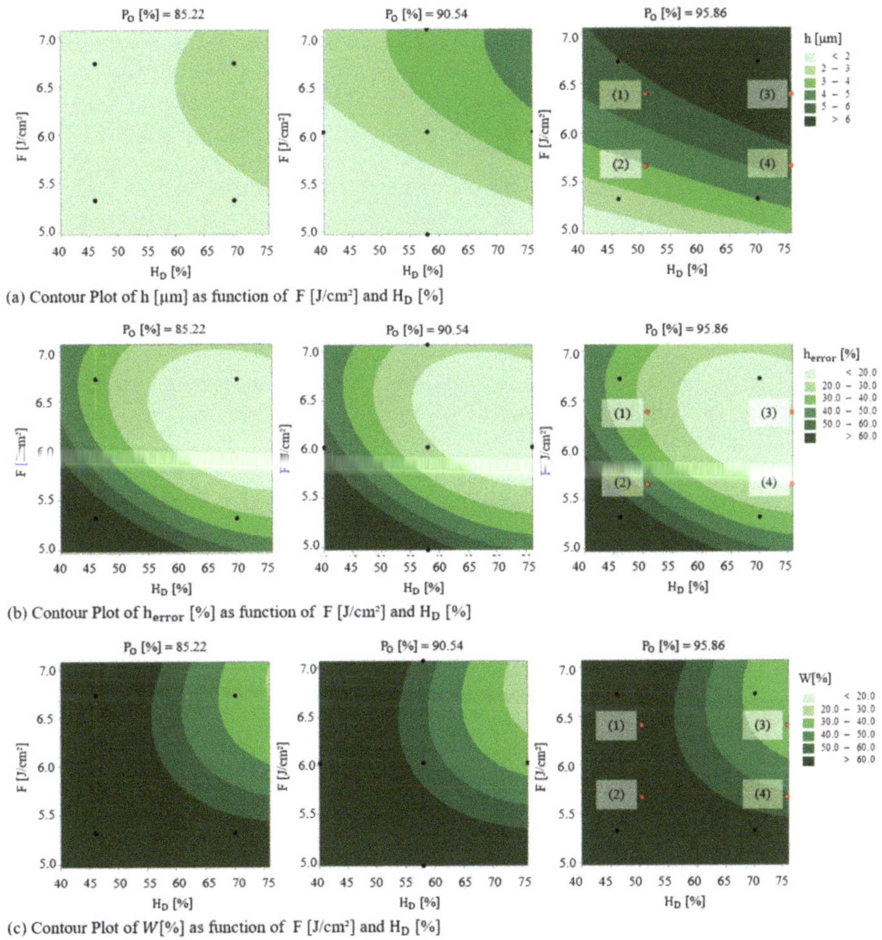

Figure 8. Contour plots of (**a**) height, (**b**) height error, and (**c**) surface waviness.

Similarly, for Po = 90.54%, H_D = 55%, and for fluences from 6.5 J/cm^2 and higher, the structure height error reaches its minimum and then again increases. The same behavior is observed for surface waviness by increasing laser fluence more than 6.5 J/cm^2 at Po = 90.54% and H_D = 72%. It is attributed to the negative effect of the quadratic term ($X_1 \times X_1$) of the fluence. On the other hand, the quadratic term ($X_3 \times X_3$) of the hatch distance has a positive effect on the response. The best values of response for each of the structure height (>6 μm), height error (<20%), and surface waviness (~24%) are in the upper right corner of the plot, which corresponds with high values of both laser fluence (X_1) and hatch distance (X_3). The lowest values of the structures height (<2 μm), height error (>60%), and surface waviness (>60%) are in the lower-left corner of the plot, which corresponds to low values of both X_1 and X_3.

The tendency that the increase of levels of varied factors of DLIP process improves the response in the form of patterned surface homogeneity can be explained by redistribution of cumulative laser intensity that controls the quantity of molten and ablated material during the movement of the substrate in the x and y directions. Nevertheless, the factors involved in the DLIP process have an optimal level after which a further increase will lead to worse response values, which means that the homogeneity will be damaged and the height of the structure will collapse. This is in agreement with a generally accepted theory for near-surface melt dynamics during laser processes, where the melt flow (based on Marangoni convection) is considered as the main driving force in the microstructure formation besides recoil and plasma pressure [22,24]. In this case, the excess of deposited intensity on the processed surface that leads to uncontrolled melt of the material that is further explained in [50].

Since both error contour plots (Figure 8b,c) showed that the low error zones can be found for high laser-fluence and hatch distance (upper right corner), a correlation graph between the structure height error and surface waviness was realized, permitting to estimate the strength of this relationship. The correlation graph presented in Figure 9 shows that a high correlation exists between the structure height error and surface waviness. The fitted equation for the quadratic model that describes the relationship between h_{error} (%) and W (%) is:

$$W(\%) = 37.16 - 1.185\, h_{error}(\%) + 0.01539\, h_{error}(\%)^2 \quad (15)$$

The R^2 in each of the correlation graphs shows that the developed model can explain >80% variability in the response. However, this statistically significant relationship does not imply that the height error (h_{error}) causes surface waviness (W (%)). Nevertheless, since the model fits the data well, this equation can be used to predict h_{error} (%) for a value of W (%), or find the settings for W (%) that correspond to a desired value or range of values for h_{error} (%).

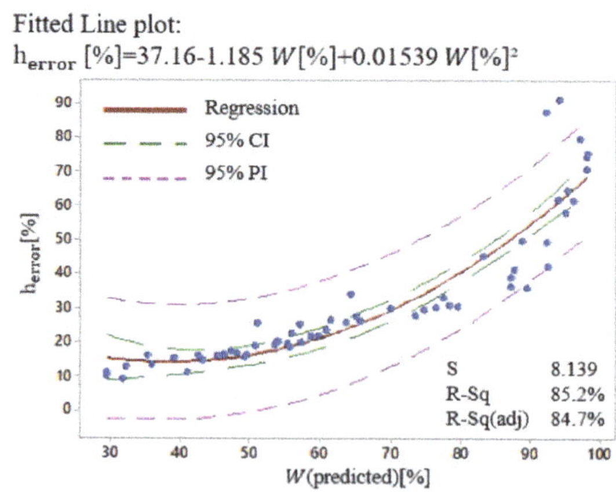

Figure 9. Correlation fitted line plots between height error (h_{error} (%)) and surface waviness (W (%)).

3.2. Model Validation

To confirm the validity and accuracy of the developed model, additional experiments were done in triplicates according to manually chosen parameters (marked by red dots in Figure 8). The DLIP structuring runs were conducted in the same conditions as in the previous described experiment. The corresponding topographies with extracted profiles are presented in Figure 10.

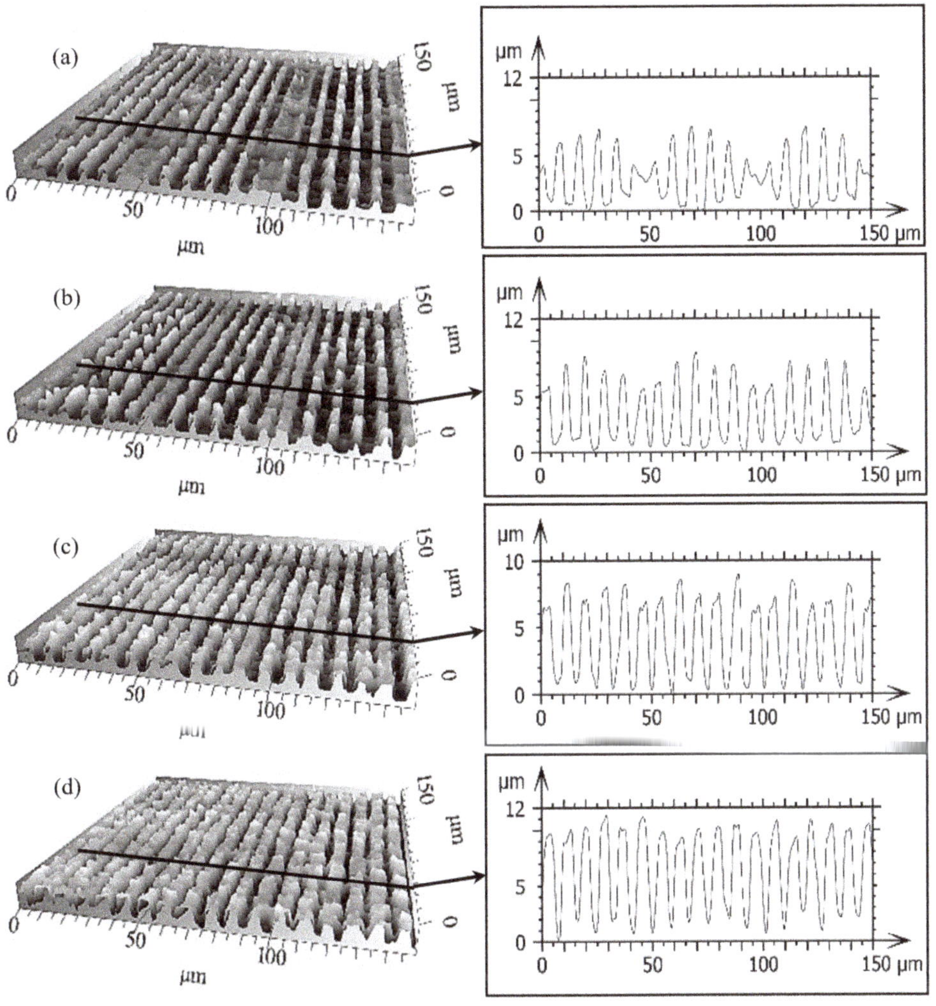

Figure 10. Confocal microscopy pictures of the nanosecond DLIP structures produced on 100Cr6 steel using spatial period $\Lambda = 8.50\mu m$, and the corresponding processing parameters: $F = 5.69$ J/cm^2, $P_O = 95.86\%$, $H_D = 52\%$ (**a**), $F = 6.4$ J/cm^2, $P_O = 95.86\%$, $H_D = 52\%$ (**b**), $F = 5.69$ J/cm^2, $P_O = 95.86\%$, $H_D = 76\%$ (**c**), and $F = 6.4$ J/cm^2, $P_O = 95.86\%$, $H_D = 76\%$ (**d**). The insets show the cross-section profiles of the corresponding topographies.

After the analysis, the relative error between the calculated surface quality parameters and the experimental values was calculated for the structures height, height error, and surface waviness (Figure 11). The results show that the predicted value of the structure height was very close to the experimental results with a relative error varying between 8.5% and 11% for different parameter sets. Additionally, the relative error for surface structures error varied between 10% and 20%. In consequence, the results indicate that the prediction model achieved in the present study is reliable.

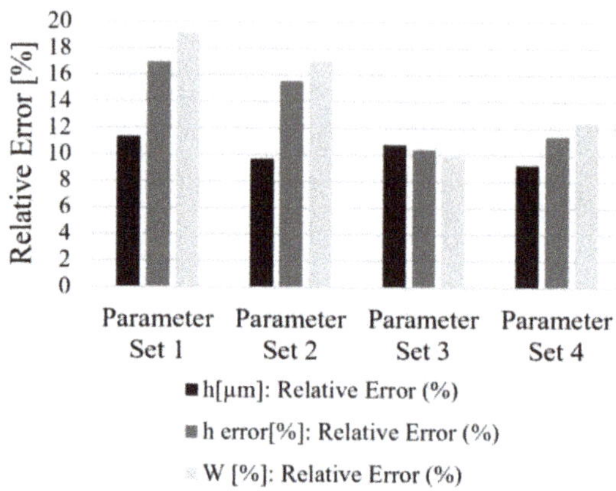

Figure 11. Bar charts summarizing relative error between model-predicted and verification experiments with parameter sets: (**1**) F = 5.69 J/cm^2, P_O = 95.86%, H_D = 52%, (**2**) F = 6.4 J/cm^2, P_O = 95.86%, H_D = 52%, (**3**) F = 5.69 J/cm^2, P_O = 95.86%, H_D = 76%, and (**4**) F = 6.4 J/cm^2, P_O = 95.86%, H_D = 76%.

3.3. Multi-Objective Optimization

Finally, a multi-objective optimization was performed employing the response optimizer of Minitab, in order to identify the optimum process parameters that minimize the error in structures height and waviness. The optimization plot shows the effect of each process parameter (the model factors; see columns in Figure 12a) on the surface texture characteristics (the responses or composite desirability; see rows in Figure 12a). The vertical red lines on the graph represent the current factor settings, and the numbers displayed in red at the top of a column show those current factor level settings. In the same manner, the horizontal blue lines and the corresponding blue numbers represent the response values for the current factor level. Moreover, the composite desirability value denoted by D shows how the response from the predicted factor levels met the initial requirements. Furthermore, the optimization plot also allows us interactively change and adjust the input variable settings to perform sensitivity analysis and to search for more desirable or improved solutions.

The predictive nature of the optimization plot is tested against an experimental example, where the aim was to structure the surface with minimal waviness and line-like microstructures with 5 μm in height which should have minimal height error. In order to reach a desired surface quality, the developed model suggests to use the process parameters of F = 6.58 J/cm^2, P_O = 92.23%, and H_D = 73.45% with the composite desirability value equal to 98.7%. Afterwards, the predicted and optimized parameters were used in the structuring process. The resulting surface topography is visualized in the scanning electron micrograph presented in Figure 12b. This surface topography is characterized by a 5.43 μm structure height, ~13.78% height error, and ~25.83% waviness, thus, similar well enough to the predicted values of 4.99 μm, 12.23%, and 29.63%, respectively. Consequently, this demonstrates that the developed model is statistically reliable and can be used for prediction and optimization of the processing parameters.

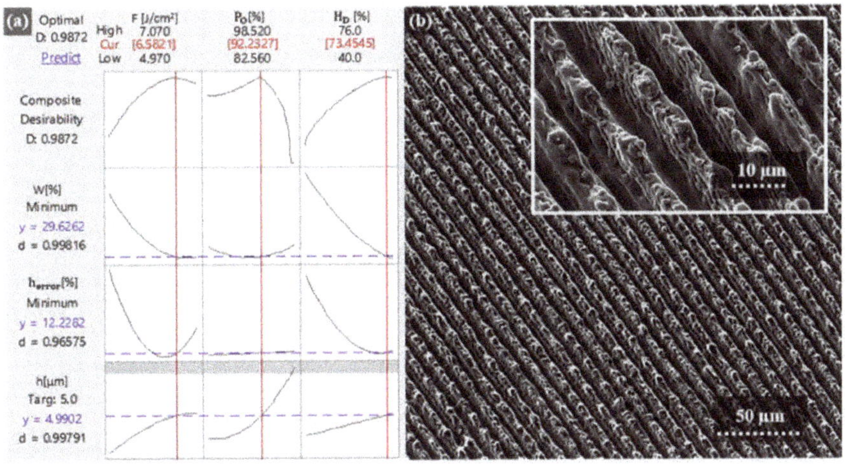

Figure 12. Summary of the multi-objective optimization process where in (**a**) Minitab Response optimizer is presented and in (**b**) the Scanning electron micrograph visualizes line-like DLIP microstructures produced on 100Cr6 steel using the processing parameters predicted by the Response optimizer.

4. Conclusions

The present work deals with the experimental investigation and analysis of DLIP processes on bearing steel material (100Cr6) using a laser texturing strategy by a pulsed nanosecond infrared laser. The main goal was to investigate the fundamental relationship between the process parameters and resulting surface texture quality measures by means of a central composite design (CCD) method. This includes the development of an empirical model which is expressed by second-order polynomial equations providing linear and quadratic interaction effects of laser processing parameters influencing measured topographical properties. The developed model was able to accurately describe (with an accuracy of more than 80%) the correlation of varied factors and the measured response. The data analysis using the Pareto charts showed that both laser fluence and pulse overlap process parameters have the highest influence on the resulting structure depth. Furthermore, it was found that the laser fluence and hatch distance affect predominantly the structure height error and surface waviness of the fabricated structure. Moreover, the model allowed to identify cross-correlation between laser fluence and pulse overlap in the case of the structures' height response as well as between laser fluence and hatch distance in each of surface waviness and structure height error. This implies that the change in the mean response from low to high level of a factor depend on the level of the other factor. Furthermore, the model allows to predict optimal process parameters for fabricating target surface textures with specific quality features. Finally, the model helped to understand how the certain undesired topographical values, such as structure height error and waviness, can be reduced in order to improve the homogeneity of the periodic surface structures.

Author Contributions: Conceptualization, M.E.-K. and T.K.; methodology, M.E.-K., T.K. and A.F.L.; data curation, M.E.-K.; fformal analysis, M.E.-K.; investigation, M.E.-K.; resources, T.K.; software, M.E.-K.; visualization, M.E.-K.; writing—original draft, M.E.-K.; writing—review & editing, B.V., T.K. and A.F.L.; supervision, B.V., T.K. and A.F.L.; project administration, T.K. and A.F.L.; funding acquisition, T.K. and A.F.L. All authors have read and agreed to the published version of the manuscript.

Funding: This work was carried out in the framework of the SHARK project (http://www.sharkproject.eu) which has received funding from the European Union's Horizon 2020 Framework Program for research and innovation under grant agreement No. 768701. The work of M.E. and A. F. L. was also performed in the framework of the Reinhart–Koselleck project [323477257], which has received funding from the German Research Foundation (German: Deutsche Forschungsgemeinschaft DFG).

Conflicts of Interest: The authors declare that there is no conflict of interest.

References

1. Favret, E.A.; Fuentes Néstor, O. *Functional Properties of Bio-Inspired Surfaces: Characterization and Technological Applications*; World Scientific: Hackensack, NJ, USA, 2009.
2. Han, Z.; Mu, Z.; Yin, W.; Li, W.; Niu, S.; Zhang, J.; Ren, L. Biomimetic multifunctional surfaces inspired from animals. *Adv. Colloid Interface Sci.* **2016**, *234*, 27–50. [CrossRef] [PubMed]
3. Müller, F.; Kunz, C.; Gräf, S. Bio-Inspired Functional Surfaces Based on Laser-Induced Periodic Surface Structures. *Materials* **2016**, *9*, 476. [CrossRef] [PubMed]
4. Rosenkranz, A.; Hans, M.; Gachot, C.; Thome, A.; Bonk, S.; Mücklich, F. Direct Laser Interference Patterning: Tailoring of Contact Area for Frictional and Antibacterial Properties. *Lubricants* **2016**, *4*, 2. [CrossRef]
5. Alamri, S.; Aguilar-Morales, A.I.; Lasagni, A.F. Controlling the wettability of polycarbonate substrates by producing hierarchical structures using Direct Laser Interference Patterning. *Eur. Polym. J.* **2018**, *99*, 27–37. [CrossRef]
6. Cardoso, J.; Aguilar-Morales, A.; Alamri, S.; Huerta-Murillo, D.; Cordovilla, F.; Lasagni, A.; Ocaña, J. Superhydrophobicity on hierarchical periodic surface structures fabricated via direct laser writing and direct laser interference patterning on an aluminium alloy. *Opt. Lasers Eng.* **2018**, *111*, 193–200. [CrossRef]
7. Rosenkranz, A.; Stratmann, A.; Gachot, C.; Burghardt, G.; Jacobs, G.; Mücklich, F. Improved Wear Behavior of Cylindrical Roller Thrust Bearings by Three-Beam Laser Interference. *Adv. Eng. Mater.* **2015**, *18*, 854–862. [CrossRef]
8. Costa, H.; Hutchings, I. Some innovative surface texturing techniques for tribological purposes. *Proc. Inst. Mech. Eng. Part J J. Eng. Tribol.* **2014**, *229*, 429–448. [CrossRef]
9. Guo, L.; Wong, P.; Gachot, C. Facilitating the Study of the Texturing Effect on Hydrodynamic Lubrication. *Lubricants* **2018**, *6*, 18. [CrossRef]
10. Kasem, H.; Stav, O.; Grützmacher, P.; Gachot, C. Effect of Low Depth Surface Texturing on Friction Reduction in Lubricated Sliding Contact. *Lubricants* **2018**, *6*, 62. [CrossRef]
11. Heilmann, S.; Zwahr, C.; Knape, A.; Zschetzsche, J.; Lasagni, A.F.; Füssel, U. Improvement of the Electrical Conductivity between Electrode and Sheet in Spot Welding Process by Direct Laser Interference Patterning. *Adv. Eng. Mater.* **2018**, *20*, 1700755. [CrossRef]
12. Zwahr, C.; Günther, D.; Brinkmann, T.; Gulow, N.; Oswald, S.; Holthaus, M.G.; Lasagni, A.F. Laser Surface Pattering of Titanium for Improving the Biological Performance of Dental Implants. *Adv. Healthc. Mater.* **2016**, *6*, 1600858. [CrossRef] [PubMed]
13. Voisiat, B.; Teutoburg-Weiss, S.; Rank, A.; Lasagni, A.F. DLIP holographic structuring: From basic concept to advanced monitoring methods and industrial scale production. In Proceedings of the Laser-Based Micro- and Nanoprocessing XIII, San Francisco, CA, USA, 4 March 2019.
14. Teutoburg-Weiss, S.; Sonntag, F.; Günther, K.; Lasagni, A.F. Multiple method micromachining laser platform for fabricating anti-counterfeit elements with multiple-scaled features. *Opt. Laser Technol.* **2019**, *115*, 465–476. [CrossRef]
15. Waugh, D.G.; Lawrence, J. *Laser Surface Engineering: Processes and Applications*; Woodhead: Cambridge, UK, 2016.
16. Bonse, J.; Krüger, J.; Höhm, S.; Rosenfeld, A. Femtosecond laser-induced periodic surface structures. *J. Laser Appl.* **2012**, *24*, 042006. [CrossRef]
17. Nakata, Y. Interference laser processing. *Adv. Opt. Technol.* **2016**, *5*, 29–38. [CrossRef]
18. Indrišiūnas, S.; Voisiat, B.; Gedvilas, M.; Račiukaitis, G. New opportunities for custom-shape patterning using polarization control in confocal laser beam interference setup. *J. Laser Appl.* **2017**, *29*, 011501. [CrossRef]
19. Lasagni, A.F.; Gachot, C.; Trinh, K.E.; Hans, M.; Rosenkranz, A.; Roch, T.; Eckhardt, S.; Kunze, T.; Bieda, M.; Günther, D.; et al. Direct laser interference patterning, 20 years of development: From the basics to industrial applications. In Proceedings of the Laser-Based Micro- and Nanoprocessing XI, San Francisco, CA, USA, 7 March 2017.
20. Lasagni, A.F. Advanced Design of Periodical Structures by Laser Interference Metallurgy in the Micro, Nano Scale on Macroscopic Areas. Ph.D. Thesis, Shaker Verlag GmbH, Aachen, Germany, 2007.
21. He, C.; Steger, M.; Gillner, A. High-Efficiency Nanostructuring using Multi-Beam Interference by Con-secutively Deposited Ultrashort Laser Pulses on Tool Steel. *J. Laser Micro/Nanoeng.* **2018**, *13*, 1–5.

22. Aguilar-Morales, A.I.; Alamri, S.; Kunze, T.; Lasagni, A.F. Influence of processing parameters on surface texture homogeneity using Direct Laser Interference Patterning. *Opt. Laser Technol.* **2018**, *107*, 216–227. [CrossRef]
23. Chichkov, B.N.; Momma, C.; Nolte, S.; Alvensleben, F.; Tünnermann, A. Femtosecond, picosecond and nanosecond laser ablation of solids. *Appl. Phys. A Mater. Sci. Process.* **1996**, *63*, 109–115. [CrossRef]
24. Volkov, A.N.; Zhigilei, L.V. Melt dynamics and melt-through time in continuous wave laser heating of metal films: Contributions of the recoil vapor pressure and Marangoni effects. *Int. J. Heat Mass Transf.* **2017**, *112*, 300–317. [CrossRef]
25. Czitrom, V. One-Factor-at-a-Time versus Designed Experiments. *Am. Stat.* **1999**, *53*, 126.
26. Siebertz, K.; Bebber, D.V.; Hochkirchen, T. Statistische. In *Versuchsplanung Design of Experiments (DoE)*; Springer: Berlin, Germany, 2017.
27. Dean, A.M.; Voss, D.; Danel, D. *Design and Analysis of Experiments*; Springer: Cham, Switzerland, 2017.
28. Montgomery, D.C. *Design and Analysis of Experiments*; Wiley: Hoboken, NJ, USA, 2020.
29. Tanco, M.; Viles, E.; Pozueta, L. Comparing Different Approaches for Design of Experiments (DoE). In *Lecture Notes in Electrical Engineering Advances in Electrical Engineering and Computational Science*; Springer: Dordrecht, The Netherlands, 2009; pp. 611–621.
30. Genna, S.; Tagliaferri, F.; Papa, I.; Leone, C.; Palumbo, B. Multi-response optimization of CFRP laser milling process based on response surface methodology. *Polym. Eng. Sci.* **2017**, *57*, 595–605. [CrossRef]
31. Kibria, G.; Sen, A.; Aziz, H.M.T.; Doloi, B.; Bhattacharyya, B. Pulsed Nd:YAG Laser Surface Texturing of Pure Titanium Material. In *Lecture Notes on Multidisciplinary Industrial Engineering Precision Product-Process Design and Optimization*; Springer: Singapore, 2018; pp. 361–390.
32. Moradi, M.; Karamimoghadam, M. High power diode laser surface hardening of AISI 4130; statistical modelling and optimization. *Opt. Laser Technol.* **2019**, *111*, 554–570. [CrossRef]
33. Witek-Krowiak, A.; Chojnacka, K.; Podstawczyk, D.; Dawiec, A.; Pokomeda, K. Application of response surface methodology and artificial neural network methods in modelling and optimization of biosorption process. *Bioresour. Technol.* **2014**, *160*, 150–160. [CrossRef]
34. Diler, E.A.; Ipek, R. An experimental and statistical study of interaction effects of matrix particle size, reinforcement particle size and volume fraction on the flexural strength of Al–SiCp composites by P/M using central composite design. *Mater. Sci. Eng. A* **2012**, *548*, 43–55. [CrossRef]
35. Box, G.E.P.; Hunter, J.S. Multi-Factor Experimental Designs for Exploring Response Surfaces. *Ann. Math. Stat.* **1957**, *28*, 195–241. [CrossRef]
36. Mathews, P.G. *Design of Experiments with MINITAB*; New Age: New Dehli, India, 2010.
37. Khan, R.M. *Problem Solving and Data Analysis Using Minitab: A Clear and Easy Guide to Six Sigma Methodology*; Wiley: Chichester, UK, 2013.
38. Wu, C.F.J.; Hamada, M. *Experiments: Planning, Analysis, and Parameter Design Optimization*; Wiley: New York, NY, USA, 2000.
39. Dietzsch, M.; Gerlach, M.; Gröger, S. Back to the envelope system with morphological operations for the evaluation of surfaces. *Wear* **2008**, *264*, 411–415. [CrossRef]
40. Kumar, J.; Shunmugam, M. A new approach for filtering of surface profiles using morphological operations. *Int. J. Mach. Tools Manuf.* **2006**, *46*, 260–270. [CrossRef]
41. Raja, J.; Muralikrishnan, B.; Fu, S. Recent advances in separation of roughness, waviness and form. *Precis. Eng.* **2002**, *26*, 222–235. [CrossRef]
42. *International standard: Geometrical Product Specifications (GPS)—Filtration—Part 41: Morphological Profile Filters: Disc and Horizontal Line-Segment Filters*; ISO 16610-41:2015; ISO: Geneva, Switzerland, 2015.
43. Roch, T.; Benke, D.; Lasagni, A.F. Method and Arrangement for Forming a Structuring on Surfaces of Components by Means of a Laser Beam 2014. US 9,764,424 B2, 19 September 2017.
44. Liu, J.M. Simple technique for measurements of pulsed Gaussian-beam spot sizes. *Opt. Lett.* **1982**, *7*, 196. [CrossRef] [PubMed]
45. Hecht, E. *Optics*; Pearson: Harlow, UK, 2017.
46. Indrisiunas, S.; Voisiat, B.; Žukauskas, A.; Račiukaitis, G. Direct laser beam interference patterning technique for fast high aspect ratio surface structuring. In Proceedings of the Laser Applications in Microelectronic and Optoelectronic Manufacturing (LAMOM) XX, San Francisco, CA, USA, 4 March 2015.

47. Alamri, S.; Lasagni, A.F. Development of a general model for direct laser interference patterning of polymers. *Opt. Express* **2017**, *25*, 9603. [CrossRef]
48. Furlan, V.; Biondi, M.; Demir, A.G.; Pariani, G.; Previtali, B.; Bianco, A. Sub-micrometric surface texturing of AZ31 Mg-alloy through two-beam direct laser interference patterning with a ns-pulsed green fiber laser. *Appl. Surf. Sci.* **2017**, *423*, 619–629.
49. Moore, D.S.; McCabe, G.P.; Craig, B.A. *Introduction to the Practice of Statistics*; W.H. Freeman, Macmillan Learning: New York, NY, USA, 2017.
50. El-Khoury, M.; Alamri, S.; Voisiat, B.; Kunze, T.; Lasagni, A.F. Fabrication of hierarchical surface textures using multi-pulse direct laser interference patterning with nanosecond pulses. *Mater. Lett.* **2020**, *258*, 126743.

materials

MDPI

Article

Competition Effects during Femtosecond Laser Induced Element Redistribution in Ba- and La-Migration Based Laser Written Waveguides

Manuel Macias-Montero [1,†], Pedro Moreno-Zárate [2,†], Francisco Muñoz [3], Belén Sotillo [4], Marina Garcia-Pardo [1], Rosalía Serna [1], Paloma Fernandez [4] and Javier Solis [1,*]

1 Laser Processing Group, Institute of Optics (IO, CSIC), Serrano 121, 28006 Madrid, Spain; manuel.macias@csic.es (M.M.-M.); mgpardo9@gmail.com (M.G.-P.); r.serna@io.cfmac.csic.es (R.S.)
2 Electronic Engineering Department, National Technological Institute of Mexico, Campus Acatlan de Osorio, Carretera Acatlan—San Juan Ixcaquistla k.m. 5.5, Acatlan de Osorio 74949, Mexico; pemzamx@gmail.com
3 Institute of Ceramics and Glass (ICV, CSIC), Kelsen 5, 28049 Madrid, Spain; fmunoz@icv.csic.es
4 Department of Materials Physics, Faculty of Physics, Complutense University of Madrid, 28040 Madrid, Spain; bsotillo@fis.ucm.es (B.S.); arana@fis.ucm.es (P.F.)
* Correspondence: j.solis@io.cfmac.csic.es; Tel.: +34-(56)-16800
† Both authors equally contributed to the manuscript.

Abstract: Fs-laser induced element redistribution (FLIER) has been a subject of intensive research in recent years. Its application to various types of glasses has already resulted in the production of efficient optical waveguides, tappers, amplifiers and lasers. Most of the work reported on FLIER-based waveguides refers to structures produced by the cross-migration of alkali (Na, K) and lanthanides (mostly La). The latter elements act as refractive index carrying elements. Herein, we report the production of Ba-based, FLIER-waveguides in phosphate glass with an index contrast > 10^{-2}. Phosphate glasses modified with the same amount of Na_2O and K_2O, and variable amounts of BaO and/or La_2O_3 were used to produce the FLIER-waveguides with Ba and or La acting as index carriers. Ba-only modified glasses show a waveguide writing threshold and light guiding performance comparable to that of La-based structures. However, mixed Ba-La glasses show a much higher element migration threshold, and much smaller compositionally modified regions. This behavior is consistent with a competition effect in the cross-migration of both elements (Ba and La) against the alkalis. Such an effect can be applied to inhibit undesired element redistribution effects in fs-laser processing applications in multicomponent glasses.

Keywords: fs-laser writing; waveguides; element redistribution; Soret effect; diffusion competition effects

Citation: Macias-Montero, M.; Moreno-Zárate, P.; Muñoz, F.; Sotillo, B.; Garcia-Pardo, M.; Serna, R.; Fernandez, P.; Solis, J. Competition Effects during Femtosecond Laser Induced Element Redistribution in Ba- and La-Migration Based Laser Written Waveguides. *Materials* **2021**, *14*, 3185. https://doi.org/10.3390/ma14123185

Academic Editors: Jörg Krüger and Jörn Bonse

Received: 21 April 2021
Accepted: 4 June 2021
Published: 9 June 2021

1. Introduction

The modification of the local composition of glasses irradiated underneath the surface with focused femtosecond laser beams has been studied for a long time [1,2]. This effect has recently gained considerable attention [3] due to its successful use for the production of several different high-performance photonic devices [4–6]. Femtosecond-induced element redistribution (FLIER) can be considered as a universal phenomenon in multicomponent glasses subjected to subsurface, high repetition rate, fs-laser excitation. This phenomenon can be understood in terms of the thermo-diffusion processes (i.e., the Ludwig–Soret effect [7]) associated with the chemical potential imbalance induced in the heated glass volume. The glass compositional modification upon FLIER mimics the elemental thermal diffusion occurring in basaltic liquids (silicates) in the Earth's mantle, but on a much shorter time scale (10^8 times faster) and over a well-defined micrometric volume [8]. The focal volume shape, local thermal gradients and heating-cooling cycles thus strongly condition the final result of the FLIER process [3,8]. Its effects can be particularly relevant when both relatively heavy (e.g., lanthanides) and light elements (e.g., alkali) are present in the glass composition. In spite of this, FLIER effects have apparently been overlooked in the past, in many occasions, in the discussion of the origin of the refractive index contrast [9,10] in fs-laser-written waveguides [11].

Thermo-diffusion involves several parameters including thermal and stress gradients, viscosity and its temperature dependence, multiple diffusion coefficients [3], etc. At the end of the day, these parameters condition the local chemical potential of the different glass constituents [12]. Indeed, the prediction of the sign and magnitude of the Soret coefficient of a given component in a multicomponent mixture is still an open problem that requires to consider microscopic parameters and numerical modeling [13]. Still, FLIER can certainly be controlled in practice [14,15] and exploited for producing high-performance photonic devices, as indicated above. Even more, one of the key features of FLIER-based fs-laser writing for photonic applications arises from the potential of ad hoc glass compositional design [4,16]. A given glass composition can be slightly modified by adding small amounts of a modifier made of a relatively heavy ion-oxide (that will act as refractive index carrier) and fast diffusing and lighter (typically alkali) ion-oxide modifier that counter-migrates the index carrier. This gives rise to the formation of regions with increased refractive index and light guiding capabilities. As a matter of fact, by using the electronic polarizabilities [17,18] of the ions involved, it is possible to predict quite accurately the index contrast achievable upon laser writing via FLIER [19]. This principle has been successfully applied to several glass families including phosphates and borates where lanthanides have been used as index carriers [4,5] and, more recently, to silicates [8] using Ba as index carrier.

Apparently, at least in the case of phosphate-based glasses, heavier ions belonging to the same group (i.e., lanthanides (La, Er and Yb)) migrate in the same direction and experience approximately the same amount of enrichment in the higher refractive index region [5]. This apparently applies to the counter-migrating lighter ions (Na, K) too in the low index zone. For the case of Ba, counter-migration of the lighter elements (Na and Si) away from the refractive index increased region has been observed [4,8]. These observations are consistent with what can be called "positive Soret effect" for the heavier constituents of the glass and "negative" for the lighter counter-migrating species, a common observation for thermo-diffusion in glasses or sols. However, not all of the glass constituents necessarily move upon laser excitation. This depends on the material composition [13], the excitation conditions and type of ions involved [20], the shape of the focal volume and the correlated thermal gradients involved [8,21].

In the refractive index structures produced by FLIER, ion cross-diffusion occurs in a hot and viscous high-temperature glass matrix. Therefore, one can expect the presence of either cooperative or competition effects when different types of index carriers (belonging to different groups) are present in the glass composition. However, to the best of our knowledge, there are no studies regarding the simultaneous use of several types of index carriers in the production of waveguides by fs-laser writing via FLIER. This aspect is a very relevant for potential applications of fs-laser processing beyond the production of waveguides. As below indicated, FLIER processes can be detrimental for certain properties of multicomponent glasses and, therefore, a deeper knowledge of the migration behavior of different types of ions upon fs-laser excitation is very desirable. In this work, we aim at analyzing the presence of such cooperative or competition ion migration effects upon FLIER in compositionally pre-designed glasses.

For such a purpose, phosphate glasses modified with the same amount of Na_2O and K_2O, and different amounts of BaO and/or La_2O_3 were used to produce FLIER-based waveguides. The general behavior and performance of the Ba-only and La-only modified glasses is rather similar in terms of migration threshold, laser energy dependence of the size of the modified index structures and index contrast. However, the samples modified with both Ba and La oxides show a strong increase in the migration threshold, and a clear reduction of the size and index contrast of the structures for comparable writing laser energies. These features indicate that strong migration competition effects occur when index carriers of different types (valence) are introduced in the glass composition. This competition effect can be exploited to inhibit undesired cross-thermo-diffusion effects in fs-laser writing applications in multicomponent glasses where preserving the glass composition may be a requirement. The preservation of the local composition of the glass upon fs-laser irradiation is a key issue for instance in fs-laser-induced crystallization processes for data storage applications [22], the congruent synthesis of non-linear crystals inside precursor glasses by fs-laser writing [23,24] or the fabrication of hybrid micro- and nano-structures in semiconductor-doped glasses by ultrafast lasers [25].

2. Materials and Methods

The phosphate-based glass samples were obtained through melting and quenching of batches made by mixing $(NH_4)_2HPO_4$, Na_2CO_3, K_2CO_3, BaO, and La_2O_3 (Sigma-Aldrich Spain, Madrid) reagent grade powders. The compositions of the produced samples are shown in Table 1.

Table 1. Composition of the designed samples.

Sample	Alkali Oxide Modifiers		Refractive Index Carrier Modifier		Glass Former	Other Modifiers
	Oxides Composition in mol %					
	K_2O	Na_2O	BaO	La_2O_3	P_2O_5	Al_2O_3
Ba-glass	15	15	10	0	55	5
La-glass	15	15	0	10	60	0
Ba-La-glass	15	15	5	5	60	0

Three different sample compositions (namely Ba-, La- and Ba-La-glass) were produced. In order to facilitate the alignment procedure during the characterization of the guiding performance of the laser-written structures in the infrared (~1600 nm), all the samples were doped with a very small amount of Er_2O_3, 0.25 wt.%, and Yb_2O_3, 0.5 wt.%, to use the green color up-conversion emission of Er^{3+} when a weak pump laser at 976 nm is coupled in the waveguide [4]. In the Ba-glass sample, a 5 mol% of Al_2O_3 was added to the composition in order to improve its toughness and thus being comparable to the one in the La_2O_3-containing samples. All glasses were formulated for them to have an O/P ratio close to 3, which in phosphate glasses stands for metaphosphate compositions. The batches were slowly calcined up to 400 °C overnight in alumina crucibles; then, melted at 1000 °C (Ba and Ba-La glasses) or 1200 °C (La-glass) for 1 h. The melts were poured onto brass plates and then crashed into small pieces and put into a graphite boat where they were submitted to a homogenization and fining treatment following the procedure applied for phosphate glasses in [26]. For this case, the glasses were remelted at 800 °C (Ba and Ba-La glasses) and 900 °C (La-glass) for 9 h under a constant flow of N_2. The final glass samples were completely dehydroxylated and homogenized without any bubbles or stria and no weight loss was detected that could have originated from volatilization losses. The glass transition temperature (T_g) of the samples was determined from thermal expansion curves recorded in a Netzsch 402 EP dilatometer (Netzsch-Gerätebau GmbH, Selb, Germany) at a heating rate of 5 $K{\cdot}min^{-1}$. The T_g of the three glass samples ranged between 510 °C and 550 °C. The observed differences in T_g are consistent with the relatively small compositional differences among the samples.

The samples were then cut (typically in the shape of $10 \times 20 \times 6$ mm^3 plates) and polished to optical quality before optical characterization and fs-laser writing. Ellipsometric spectra were measured at several spatial locations in each sample in order to achieve statistically significant values in the near IR region (800–1700 nm). The acquired Ψ-spectra were fitted using the Cauchy equation ($n(\lambda) = A + (B/\lambda^2)$) for the refractive index n as a function of the wavelength (λ). This dispersion equation describes very well the behavior of the refractive index of the samples in the studied spectral region, where they are transparent (absorption coefficient $k = 0$). Further details regarding the ellipsometry measurement procedure can be found elsewhere [27].

Waveguide-writing via FLIER was performed using a high-repetition-rate, Yb-doped fiber fs-laser (Satsuma HP^2 laser from Amplitude, Pessac, France). The laser generates laser pulses of tunable duration (350 fs–10 ps) at 1030 nm. The laser has a repetition rate that can be varied in the 1 kHz-2 MHz interval with energies up 10 µJ/pulse. In all the experiments described, we used 350 fs-laser pulses at a repetition rate of 500 kHz. The writing beam was slit-shaped (1.2 mm slit width) before being focused with a 0.68 Numerical Aperture (NA) aspheric lens 100 µm underneath the surface. Its polarization was circular in order to minimize the propagation losses of the waveguides. During writing, the sample was translated at a linear speed of 60 µm/s in all cases. A detailed description of the laser writing setup can be found elsewhere [15,28].

Processed samples were grinded and polished to bring the end facets of the laser-written structures to the surface. Optical microscopy observation (in transmission) along the guiding axis of the structures was performed with a Nikon Eclipse system.

After processing, the near field guided modes of the laser-written structures were also imaged by coupling-in light at several different wavelengths in the 980 nm–1640 nm interval with a SMF-28 single mode fiber and using a 50× objective and an infrared camera (Goodrich SUI). The evaluation of the total losses of each structure was made by measuring the output power of the waveguide at 1640 nm with a power meter (Ophir PD300). Propagation losses were calculated as total minus coupling and Fresnel losses, as described elsewhere [6]. The local elemental composition changes were quantified by using Energy-dispersive X-ray Microanalysis (EDX) in a Scanning Electron Microscope (SEM, Leica Cambridge Ltd., Cambridge, UK).

3. Results and Discussion

3.1. Optical Properties of the Pre-Designed Glass Samples and Index Change Estimates upon FLIER

Table 2 shows the Cauchy coefficients of the refractive index of the samples obtained from the fit of the ellipsometric parameter Ψ measured at three different spatial locations in each sample. The error in the determination of the refractive index values (absolute) has been estimated to be smaller than $\pm 5 \times 10^{-3}$ [27].

Table 2. Cauchy coefficients of the samples before laser processing and index values at 1590 nm.

Sample	Cauchy Coefficients		Refractive Index (1590 nm)
	A	B	
Ba-glass	1.114	0.0141	1.500
La-glass	1.133	0.0144	1.515
Ba-La-glass	1.125	0.0133	1.510

The spectral dependence of the index (n) in the 800–1700 nm range has been plotted in Figure 1a for the three glass samples. The measured refractive index values show a very similar dispersion for the three glasses, but the absolute n values are distinctly different. The glasses are essentially formed by the same constituents and proportions (~60 mol.% P_2O_5 (glass former) and 30 mol.% of Na_2O and K_2O (modifiers)). The larger electronic polarizability of La_2O_3 compared to BaO provides a larger index to the La-glass over the whole spectral interval, while the Ba-La-glass shows intermediate values also conditioned by the substitution of 5 mol.% of P_2O_5 by Al_2O_3. The electronic polarizabilities of the constituents of the three glass samples are shown in Table 3.

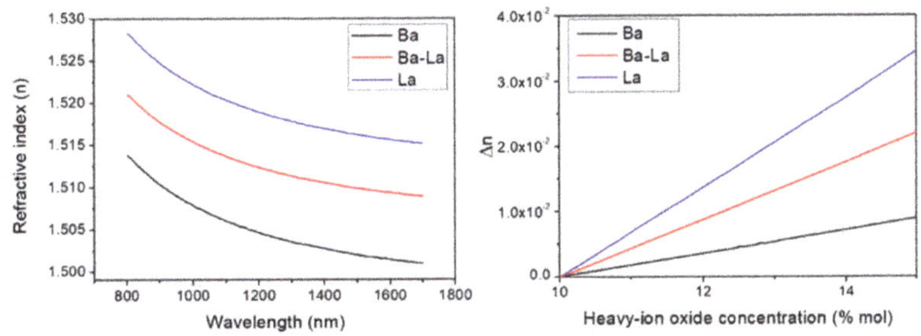

Figure 1. Spectral dependence of the refractive index of the glass samples measured by spectroscopic ellipsometry (**a**). Index change as a function of the heavy-ion concentration estimated by the electronic polarizability method (**b**).

Table 3. Polarizabilities of ions used for local index calculations in the samples upon FLIER.

Polarizability (Å^3)	P_2O_5	Na_2O	K_2O	BaO	La_2O_3	Al_2O_3
α_{cation}	0.021	0.175	0.841	1.595	1.048	0.054
α_O^{2-}	1.350	3.221	1.858	3.652	2.780	1.365
α_{Total}	6.792	3.571	3.540	5.247	10.436	4.203

By using the electronic polarizability method [14,15,29] and the determined refractive index values for wavelengths much longer than the glass matrix resonances, it is possible to accurately estimate the changes in the refractive index of the glass associated to small changes in its local composition caused by FLIER [16]. This approach has been shown to work particularly well in the case of phosphate-based glasses [19,30]. We have used this approach, using the glass constituent's polarizabilities shown in Table 3, to estimate the index changes that take place when the local concentration of the index carrier oxide increases [19]. For the calculation, it is assumed that the local concentration of the index carrier oxide (BaO or La_2O_3) increases by the same amount as the concentration of the fast-diffusing ion oxides (Na_2O and K_2O) decreases (e.g., an increase of 2 mol.% of La_2O_3 is accompanied by a corresponding decrease of the Na_2O and K_2O concentrations of 1 mol.% each). For the two heavy ions considered, the Ba and La glass index increases nearly linearly with the local concentration increase of the carrier oxide, due to the relatively minor contribution of the counter-migration of K and Na, with a much smaller polarizability. It is found that the Ba-La glass shows again an intermediate behavior. For a local concentration increase of the index carrier of 20% (relative), index changes above or close to 10^{-2} are expected in the La- and La-Ba-glasses which for the Ba-glass are reduced down to 3.6×10^{-3}.

3.2. Characterization and Performance of the Produced Structures

3.2.1. Morphology of the Laser Written Structures

Figure 2 shows several optical micrographs in transmission corresponding to the cross section of the laser-written structures transverse to the sample movement axis (X) for three representative values of the writing pulse energy. As indicated above, after processing, the samples were polished to bring the end facets of the laser-written structures to the surface and, therefore, the cross sections shown correspond to the buried waveguides produced upon laser writing underneath the surface. A top view of the structures (not shown) indicates that the structures (in the form of a continuous line) homogenously spread along the sample movement axis.

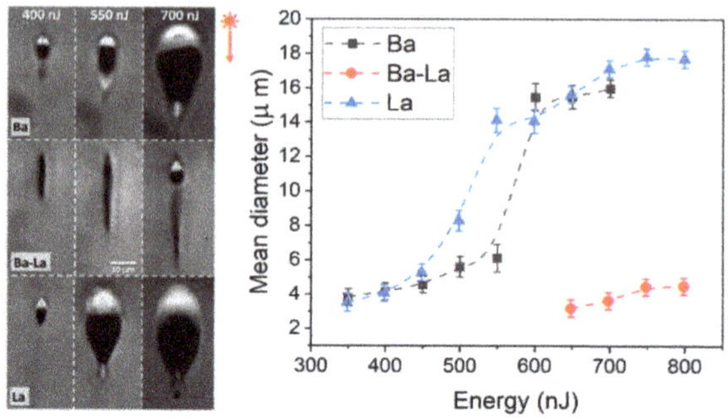

Figure 2. (**Left** panel) Transmission optical microscopy images of the cross section of structures produced in Ba-, Ba-La-and La-samples at the indicated writing pulse energies. (**Right** plot) Mean diameter of the structures produced in the three different composition samples as a function of the writing pulse energy.

To facilitate their comparison, the images are shown at the same magnification. In all cases, the structures show an elongated shape along the beam propagation axis due to the combined effect of spherical aberration (SA) and non-linear propagation [21,31]. As a matter of fact, the length of the structures along the beam propagation axis is nearly independent of the sample composition for a given pulse energy. This behavior is related to the relatively small compositional differences among the samples, generating relatively small differences in their linear and non-linear refractive indices, that condition, respectively, the extent of SA and non-linear self-focusing experienced by the laser beam. However, the size and shape of the structures in the transverse dimension (perpendicular to both the laser propagation and sample moving axis) show a strong difference between the samples incorporating a single index carrier element (Ba- and La-glass) or two (Ba-La-glass). In the former case, a bright contrasted region with increased refractive index is clearly visible for writing energies above ~350 nJ/pulse. As confirmed by EDX measurements (see below), the high index region is caused by the migration of Ba or La to the top of the structure while the region underneath, depleted in the carrier element, shows a depressed index and shows a dark contrast [4,8,15,27,28]. It is worth noting that Ba or La enrichment can also be observed (to a much lesser extent) at the bottom of the structures produced at the higher energies. This effect has previously been observed both in La- and Ba-modified glasses [4,8,19] and is related, as discussed in Ref. [8], to the actual shape of the generated thermal gradient. The plot in Figure 2 shows the mean diameter of the bright contrasted region at the top of the structures as a function of the writing pulse energy. The mean diameter of the structures was computed as the square root of the product of the dimensions of the bright region along the laser propagation axis (Z) and transversally to it (Y) in the images shown in Figure 2.

For the Ba- and La-glasses, above ~450 nJ, the size of the structure shows a sudden and strong increase caused by an excessive heat accumulation [32] not compensated by heat diffusion [15]. The earlier increase of the structure size in the La-glass as a function of the laser energy seems thus related to its expectable lower thermal diffusivity compared with that of the Ba-glass. In contrast, in the Ba-La glass the refractive index increased region is observed only for the higher pulse energies studied (above 650 nJ). For lower values, the laser modified zone adopts the appearance of a dark, non-linear self-focusing filament. Such a difference in the material response is also illustrated quantitatively in the plot of Figure 2. While for the Ba- and La- samples, the bright regions are observed for energies as low as 350 nJ, its formation requires ~650 nJ in the Ba-La sample. At this energy and above, its average diameter is ~3–4 μm while the Ba- and La-samples show an average size for the high index zone about four times bigger at a comparable energy. Such morphological differences cannot be attributed to differences in the optical or thermal properties of the Ba-La-glass compared to those of the Ba- and La-glasses, since both optical and thermal properties belong to the group of additive properties of glasses [33] and should therefore show (as seen in the optical case, Figure 1) intermediate values with respect to those observed in the glasses with a "single index carrier".

The comparison of the morphology of the structures in the three glass compositions analyzed strongly suggests that the laser energy threshold required for generating the cross-migration of the index carrier ions and the alkali species is substantially higher in the Ba-La-sample when compared to the case of the Ba- and La- samples, and that the presence of two heavy index carriers of different valence seems to be hindering their thermo-diffusion against alkali, due to a possible competition effect. In this respect, it is worth noting that a somewhat similar effect of migration inhibition effect has been observed before in the form of two different energy thresholds for inducing the cross-migration of light or heavy ions against alkali in a phosphate glass modified with lanthanides, potassium, silicon and aluminum oxides [20]. The general trend observed there, and later on quantitatively confirmed in [5], was that all the lanthanides showed a similar migration threshold and moved by the same extent and in the same direction. Above such a threshold, the migration of the lighter non-alkali elements was apparently inhibited or minimized below the EDX measurements resolution [20].

3.2.2. Guiding Performance of the Structures

The performance as optical waveguides of the compositional structures generated via FLIER in the different glass samples was assessed for laser wavelengths in the 980 nm–1640 nm interval. Figure 3 shows the near field image of the propagated modes at 1590 nm for two representative laser pulse energies in the three glass samples. As anticipated from the morphology data, the structures produced in the Ba-La-glass do not support any guided modes for energies below 700 nJ. On the contrary, the structures produced in Ba- and La-glasses show single mode propagation and a relatively small mode field diameter (MFD) for energies between ~400 nJ up to approximately 600 nJ where they start to show multimodal propagation.

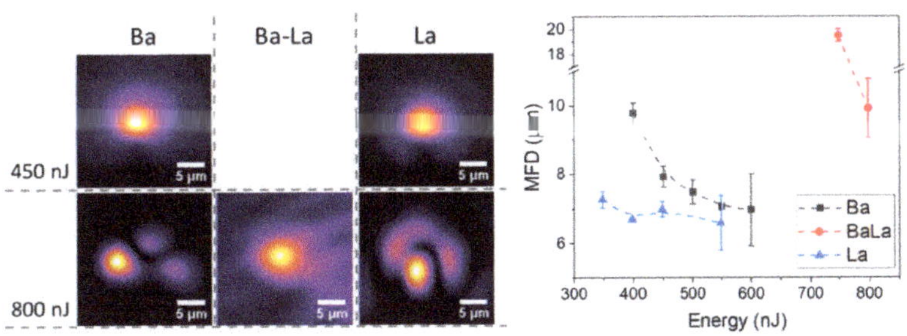

Figure 3. (**Left** panel) Near field images and (**right** plot) corresponding mode field diameters (MFD) at 1590 nm for the single-mode structures produced in the different glass compositions.

The plot in Figure 3 shows the evolution of the MFD (for the single mode waveguides) as a function of the laser pulse energy. The plot indicates that the waveguide formation threshold is slightly smaller for the La-glass (350 nJ) while the MFD remains nearly constant (~7 μm) for pulse energies up to ~550 nJ. At this energy, the transmission of the waveguides turns multimodal, generating a large uncertainty in the MFD estimation. For the Ba-glass, at its waveguide formation threshold (400 nJ), the MFD (~10 μm) is substantially larger than for the La-glass and decreases with the pulse energy down to values close to 7 μm. As for the La-glass, above a certain value (600 nJ), the structures behave as multimodal.

The differences observed as a function of laser pulse energy in the behavior of the waveguides written in the Ba- and La-glasses are consistent with the expected differences in their thermal diffusivity and in the polarizabilities of the index carriers involved. The lower diffusivity of the La-glass and the higher polarizability of La_2O_3 facilitates the formation of a structure capable of supporting a single guide mode for energies slightly lower than those required for the he Ba-glass. However, in the latter case, at the waveguide formation threshold, the index increase in the guiding region is clearly smaller than in the La-glass (larger MFD for the same structure size, Figure 2) due to the lower index change expected upon Ba-enrichment. For the same amount of local enrichment of the index carrier (Ba or La), the local index increase should be about three times larger for the La-glass. This can be more clearly seen in Figure 4, where we have plotted the index contrast of the single mode structures as a function of the writing pulse energy, as derived from the size of the high index region and its mode field diameter for several wavelengths [19,34]. The figure shows that, already at the waveguide formation threshold, an index contrast above 10^{-2} is induced in the La-glass. This parameter shows a nearly constant behavior in the single mode region (350–550 nJ/pulse). According to the plot in Figure 2, for energies in this interval, the index contrast observed is consistent with a local enrichment in La in the guiding region around and above 20% relative to the initial material composition. This might suggest that the transition to a multimodal behavior in the La-glass sample above 550 nJ might be rather conditioned by the size of the structure than by the index contrast achieved, at least in the vicinity of the multimodal transition energy at ~550 nJ.

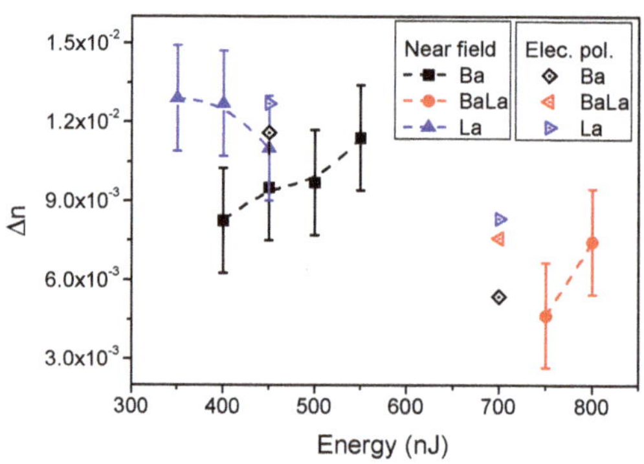

Figure 4. Refractive index contrast at the guiding region estimated from the measured MFD of the single mode waveguides produced in the three glass compositions indicated (Ba-, La- and Ba-La-glass) (solid symbols). The open symbols correspond to the index contrast estimated using experimental EDX local compositional measurements and the electronic polarizability method, as described in the text.

The index contrast of the Ba-glass sample shows nevertheless an increasing behavior with the laser pulse energy. Given the slower increase of the structure size with energy in this case, and the clear diminution of the MFD with the same parameter, the observed behavior suggests a progressive increase in the local content of Ba in the guiding region, that can lead to index contrast values above 10^{-2}. By using the values in Figure 2, a local Ba relative enrichment above 40% is foreseen.

Once again, the behavior of the laser-written structures in the Ba-La-glass strongly differs and is not "in between" that observed for the Ba- and La-glass samples. Along with a waveguide formation threshold about twice as big (750 nJ), the index contrast achieved in the guiding region is much smaller, about a factor of two smaller than the one in La-glass. This comparatively poor contrast would be consistent (see Figure 2) with a local enrichment around 10% in the index carriers, much smaller than that observed in the Ba- and La-samples at a much higher laser writing energy. This aspect points again to the presence of strong migration competition effects that are even more evident in the measured local compositional changes described below.

Regarding the propagation losses, although the optimization of this parameter is beyond the scope of this work, it must be emphasized that the propagation losses achieved in the structures compare well with previous results of FLIER waveguides based on phosphate- and silicate-based glasses for the Ba- and La-glass samples [4–6,8]. In the La-glass sample, the losses in the single mode structures are typically in the 0.5–1.0 dB/cm range, while, in the Ba-glass samples, they are somewhat higher, in the 0.7–1.3 dB/cm interval. Much higher losses (2–3 dB/cm) are observed in the structures produced in the Ba-La glass samples. This can be related to both the lower index contrast and much higher writing energies, causing energy coupling fluctuations.

3.2.3. Local Compositional Changes and Migration Competition Effects

As indicated in Section 2, the local composition of the laser-induced structures was measured in an SEM by means of EDX. Figure 5 shows several representative SEM images and compositional maps of structures produced at the same energy in the three samples (700 nJ). Since the images have been recorded on the cross sections of the structures normal to the sample scan axis, they can be easily compared with those shown in Figure 2. For all of them, the enrichment in the heavier elements in the guiding region is evidenced by the increased Z-contrast (bright zones) in the backscattered electron SEM images. The correspondence between optical and Z-contrast in FLIER-based optical waveguides has been widely reported (see for instance [4,6,15]). The opposite contrast (dark contrasted zones) is consistent with a local depletion of heavy elements, leading to depressed index zone adjacent to the guiding region.

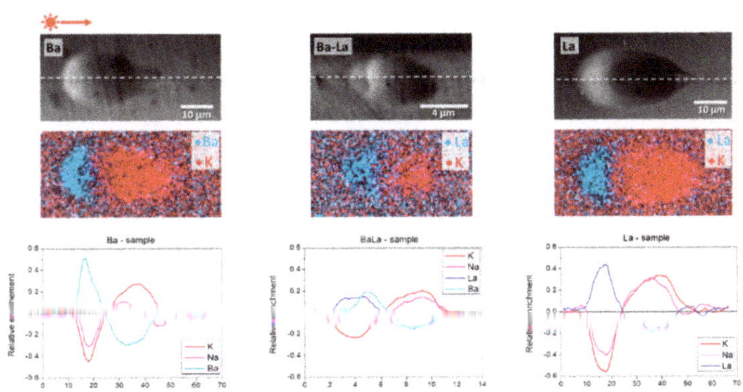

Figure 5. (**Top** row) SEM backscattered electron images and EDX compositional maps corresponding to Ba, La, and K for structures produced at 700 nJ in the Ba-, La- and Ba-La-glass samples. (**Bottom** row) Corresponding composition line scans along the dashed line shown in the SEM images.

This can be more clearly appreciated in the compositional maps included, corresponding to the spatial distribution of La, Ba and K in each of the samples (for clarity, the spatial distribution of Na is not included in the maps but is shown in the compositional cross sections in the same figure). For the selected energy (700 nJ), the structures in the Ba- and La-glass show very similar appearance including the similarities in the size and element distribution maps (obviously replacing Ba by La in the corresponding sample). As above indicated, both structures are multimode while for the Ba-La glass the structure shown, just above the FLIER threshold (650 nJ in this sample) does not support a guided mode.

Several additional features are worth noting in the element distribution over the FLIER region. The first one is that the relative enrichment in Ba and La, respectively, in the guiding region of the Ba- and La-glass structures reaches a very similar value, close to 50%, slightly higher in the Ba-glass case. This implies that the guiding region reaches a peak concentration in the index carrier oxide close to 15 mol% in the guiding region. Such an enrichment is accompanied by a more or less similar relative depletion in K and Na, although the K depletion is always bigger than the Na one. The same applies to the longer region depleted in Ba or La, located below the guiding zone, with a depletion around 20–30%, slightly higher in the Ba case. Interestingly, the extent of the region over which compositional changes are observed is also in both glass samples somewhat longer for the K than for the Na case.

The index contrast estimates derived from the structure size (see Figure 2) and MFD measurements (see Figure 3) have been compared to the values derived from the local composition of the structures obtained by the EDX and the electronic polarizability approach, as described in [19]. The index contrast was computed by using an averaged composition over the index carrier enrichment region by integrating the compositional cross sections of each individual element except oxygen (see Figure 5) and assuming oxide stoichiometry. The so-calculated averaged composition was input in the electronic polarizabilities model to compute the averaged local index for two energies (450 and 700 nJ). The obtained values have been plotted in Figure 4. It can be seen that there is an excellent correlation between the measured compositional changes and the experimentally determined index contrast in the single mode region where Δn values close to 1.2×10^{-2} are reached for both the Ba- and La-glass samples. At energies above 600 nJ, the index contrast estimated from compositional measurements decreases to values ~7.0×10^{-3}, something expectable from the much bigger size of the structure over which the index carrier is redistributed, also causing the observed multimodal behavior.

In contrast, in the Ba-La-glass sample the relative enrichment in Ba- and La- at the top of the structure at 700 nJ is much smaller, around 15–20% (less than half of what is observed in the Ba- and La-glass samples, compare the linescans shown in Figure 5). Since the initial content of the sample in La_2O_3 and BaO is just 5 mol%, the peak concentration of index carrier oxides barely reaches 12 mol%, much lower than in the Ba- or La-glass samples at the same energy. The same applies to the Na and K depletion, that is lower than 20% in average. It is also worth noting that the amount of enrichment and depletion in the Ba- and La- content is similar in the two regions of the structure (bright and dark-contrasted in the SEM image), generating a nearly symmetric compositional structure along the laser beam propagation axis. Indeed, the overall length of the compositionally modified FLIER region in the Ba-La glass (~10 μm) is much smaller than the one in the Ba- and La-glass samples at the same energy (~60 μm). Notice that the length of the laser-affected zone along the laser beam propagation axis is very similar for the three glass compositions, at the same laser pulse energy, as shown in Figure 2, and longer than the extension of the FLIER region. The index contrast estimate based on EDX compositional measurements at 700 nJ leads to a value around 5×10^{-3} which is consistent with the fact that the structure, less than ~4 μm in diameter, does not support a guided mode in the near IR.

All these features of the structures produced in the Ba-La-glass, compared to the behavior of the Ba- and La-glass samples, show that the cross-migration of Ba and La against alkalis is hindered by the simultaneous presence of the two index carriers. Whatever the origin of this behavior is, the presence of both (Ba and La) oxide modifiers clearly inhibits their cross-migration against the alkalis over a very broad interval of laser pulse energies (more than 700 nJ) while, above the cross-migration threshold, it reduces the extent of the migration process both in magnitude (smaller compositional changes) and spatial spread (shorter compositionally modified regions).

This kind of blocking effect somewhat resembles the so-called mixed alkali effect (MAE) in glasses [35–37], although in a very different situation. Please note that in what follows in the comparison with the MAE, we refer not to the presence of Na_2O and K_2O as fast diffusing modifiers in the glass compositions. In this case, we refer to the concurrent effect associated with the presence of both index carriers (Ba and La) that hinders their cross-thermo-diffusion against the alkalis in the FLIER process.

In general, the MAE refers to several phenomena peculiar to mixed-cation glasses, including the huge rise in electrical resistivity occurring on mixing of two mobile ions [35].

Indeed, although the MAE, evidenced as a non-additivity of many glass properties, was initially observed as a thermomechanical effect, it has been more thoroughly described in terms of the decrease of several orders of magnitude in the electrical conductivity and ionic diffusivity when one alkali oxide is gradually replaced by another in a series of glasses [36,37]. Such a decrease is accompanied by a strong increase of the activation energy of the ionic conductivity [35]. It is also worth noting that the MAE has been observed in a wide variety of glass families, including silicate, borate and phosphate-based glasses, something that can be related to the fact that alkalis are usually considered to simply fill the interstitial space between structural rigid polyhedra and convert bridging oxygens to nonbridging oxygens [37].

The origin of the MAE has been correlated with the interaction between the alkali cations via structural defects such as non-bridging oxygens [38], "memory effects" [39,40] or, more recently, to topological effects caused by the network strain associated to different cation radii [37]. An important common feature of these "memory" or topological effects is that alkali ions have individualized sites that relax to suit their inhabitants below T_g. According to the thorough literature summary given in [37], "when the alkali leaves the site, the site retains "memory" of that ion, making it difficult for ions of the other type to hop into it". The recent use of detailed molecular dynamics (MD) simulations and comparison to MAE experiments enables to confirm that interstices containing mismatched alkali species relax toward different ultimate structures and the competition between these interstices results in stress on the network [38].

When comparing our results regarding the cross-migration of Ba and La ions against alkali by thermo-diffusion in the Ba-, La-, and Ba-La-glass samples, there are two features that strongly resemble the MAE. The first is the existence of an energy threshold for the cross-diffusion of species in the FLIER process that resembles the existence of an activation energy for the ionic conductivity in fast ionic conductors [41], directly related to the diffusion of cations in the presence of a DC electric field. The second is the strong increase in the cross thermo-diffusion threshold in terms of laser pulse energy when both Ba- and La- oxides are present in the composition, as similarly observed with the ionic diffusion activation energy in the MAE. The atomic number, mass, valence, and ionic radii of the ions involved in the FLIER process are shown in Table 4.

Table 4. Atomic number, mass valence and ionic radius (crystalline and effective, assuming a coordination number of six [36]) of the cations involved in the FLIER process.

Element	Na	K	Ba	La
Atomic number	11	19	56	57
Mass (a.m.u.)	22.99	39.10	137.3	138.9
Valence	+1	+1	+2	+3
Cation radius (pm) Crystalline (Effective)	116 (102)	152 (138)	140 (135)	117.2 (103.2)

The table shows that, in spite of their very close atomic number and mass, there is a relatively large difference between the cationic effective radii of Ba^{+2} and La^{+3} (~20%). We might speculate that, even at high temperature, for a low-viscosity glass material that is generated upon high repetition (500 kHz) pulsed laser irradiation, there is still a "memory effect" associated with the type of ion that occupied a given site in the glass. In such a case, we may think of a "memory effect" like the one described in the frame of the dynamic structure model [39,40] or like the one associated with the network strain model [37]. Whatsoever the origin of the "memory effect" is, this would imply that pathways for ion thermo-diffusion are limited to sites of that ion type, and are dependent on relaxation of those sites in order to form new diffusion pathways. The presence of a cation in an unlike site would be increasingly less likely to form with an increasing size ratio [37]. The consequence would be that in the Ba-La glass sample, the sites left by the jump of a given heavy cation would most probably be used by an index carrier of the same type, hindering the overall cross-migration process.

However, when several lanthanides are present in the composition of a phosphate-based glass, they experience similar levels of thermo-diffusion in the same direction, as experimentally shown in references [5,20] for La, Er and Yb with the same valence (+3), and ionic radii differing around 10%. Therefore, despite the cation size may play a certain role in limiting the simultaneous diffusion of index carrier elements, it seems that it would not be sufficient by itself to account for the high differences here observed between the Ba- or La-glass samples and the Ba-La-glass. Additionally, it must be considered that the MAE is strongly reduced when the temperature of the glass increases, as it has been observed for the thermal conductivity or the viscosity of phosphate and aluminosilicate glasses [42–44], which makes it difficult to justify the existence of a similar effect in a very high temperature melt, such as the one induced upon fs-laser irradiation.

Besides the size (ionic radius) of the element, there is an additional factor that may turn out decisive and that has not been considered before, which is the valence of the index carrier elements. When having single valence index carrier elements, e.g., lanthanides as indicated above, their cross-diffusion with the alkalis takes place all at once without mutual interference, even for those with relatively dissimilar size. At the temperatures involved in the process, the relaxation of the network will be sufficiently fast so that cations with different size but equal valence migrate without constraints. However, the cross-migration of index carrier cations would also be regulated through the electrostatic interaction with the electronic density of the oxygens that belong to the PO_4 network building units. Same valence elements can cross-diffuse with alkalis in order to easily keep the charge neutrality. This makes that Ba^{2+} ions only migrate through positions of nearby Ba^{2+} and that La^{3+} do so via La^{3+} positions to not produce local decompensated charges, resulting in a largely reduced cross-migration. Similarly, to the mixed modifier effect that accounts for non-linear property changes in the presence of different size cations, it is proposed that here applies what could be called a "mixed valence effect" and that would be worth validating in other glass composition systems. Whatsoever the origin of the migration competition effects is, they could potentially be used to inhibit thermo-migration effects in fs-laser writing applications where the preservation of the composition of the glass can be needed as a requirement [13,20,22–25].

4. Conclusions

We have analyzed the formation of refractive index micro-structures by FLIER in ad hoc compositionally designed phosphate glasses. The glasses were modified by the addition of small amounts of Na_2O and K_2O and heavier ion (Ba and La) oxides. The latter ions act as index carriers. As a consequence of the laser excitation, cross-thermo-diffusion of the alkalis and index carrier cations occurs in the excited volume. Regions enriched in BaO and La_2O_3 and depleted in N_2O and K_2O are formed in the laser-excited volume. These regions show an increased refractive index sufficient to support guided modes in the near IR. The glass samples modified with a single index carrier ion oxide (either Ba- or La-oxide) show a relatively low waveguide writing threshold (350–400 nJ) and a light guiding performance comparable to each other. In both cases, index contrast values above 10^{-2}, and low propagation losses are achieved. In contrast, when both types of index carriers (Ba and La cations) are present in the glass composition, a much higher element migration threshold is observed, and the size of the compositionally modified regions is substantially smaller. Indeed, the cross-thermo-diffusion of Ba and La against Na and K is inhibited for laser pulse energies below 750 nJ. The morphological, optical and compositional analysis of the produced structures is consistent with a competition effect in the thermo-diffusion of Ba^{2+} and La^{3+} cations that strongly resembles the mixed alkali effect (MAE). Such a diffusion competition effect, apparently related to different valence of the index carrier ions involved, provides a feasible compositional strategy to suppress FLIER effects. This compositional design approach can be crucial to enable the use of fs-laser processing in multicomponent glasses where the preservation of the local composition of the glass is a necessary requirement to preserve some specific properties of the glass.

Author Contributions: Conceptualization, F.M. and J.S.; data curation, M.G.-P.; formal analysis M.G.-P., M.M.-M., P.M.-Z. and R.S.; funding acquisition, F.M., P.F., R.S. and J.S.; investigation P.M.-Z., B.S. and M.M.-M.; methodology, M.M.-M., P.M.-Z., F.M. and J.S.; project administration, F.M., P.F., R.S. and J.S.; resources, F.M., P.F., R.S., and J.S.; supervision, F.M. and J.S.; visualization, M.M.-M. and P.M.-Z.; writing—original draft, M.M.-M., P.M.-Z., F.M. and J.S.; writing—review editing, M.M.-M., P.M.-Z., F.M., B.S., M.M.-M., M.G.-P., P.F., R.S. and J.S. All authors have read and agreed to the published version of the manuscript.

Funding: This research was funded through grant numbers TEC2017-82464-R, MAT2017-87035-C2-1-P, RTI2018-096498-B-I00 (MCIU/AEI/FEDER, EU), and CSIC PIE-201850E057 and PIE-202050E195 projects.

Institutional Review Board Statement: Not applicable.

Informed Consent Statement: Not applicable.

Data Availability Statement: The data presented in this study are available on request from the corresponding authors.

Acknowledgments: M.M.-M. acknowledges the Juan de la Cierva Incorporación grant (IJCI-2017-33317)) of the Spanish Ministry of Research and Innovation. P.M.-Z. acknowledges the postdoctoral scholarship #235346 awarded by the National Council of Science and Technology from Mexico (CONACYT). B.S. acknowledges the postdoctoral grant from the "Atracción de Talento" Program funded by the Comunidad de Madrid (2017-T2/IND-5465). MGP acknowledges funding from PTA2019-016763-I (AEI/MICINN), P.F. acknowledges Complutense University of Madrid and Banco Santander for support via the project UCM-Santander 2019 (PR87/19-22613).

Conflicts of Interest: The authors declare no conflict of interest.

References

1. Yonesaki, Y.; Miura, K.; Araki, R.; Fujita, K.; Hirao, K. Space-selective precipitation of non-linear optical crystals inside silicate glasses using near-infrared femtosecond laser. *J. Non-Cryst. Solids* **2005**, *351*, 885–892. [CrossRef]
2. Liu, Y.; Shimizu, M.; Zhu, B.; Dai, Y.; Qian, B.; Qiu, J.; Shimotsuma, Y.; Miura, K.; Hirao, K. Micromodification of element distribution in glass using femtosecond laser irradiation. *Opt. Lett.* **2009**, *34*, 136–138. [CrossRef]
3. Fernandez, T.T.; Sakakura, M.; Eaton, S.M.; Sotillo, B.; Siegel, J.; Solis, J.; Shimotsuma, Y.; Miura, K. Bespoke photonic devices using ultrafast laser driven ion migration in glasses. *Prog. Mater. Sci.* **2018**, *94*, 68–113. [CrossRef]
4. Dias, A.; Muñoz, F.; Alvarez, A.; Moreno-Zárate, P.; Atienzar, J.; Urbieta, A.; Fernandez, P.; Pardo, M.; Serna, R.; Solis, J. Femtosecond laser writing of photonic devices in borate glasses compositionally designed to be laser writable. *Opt. Lett.* **2018**, *43*, 2523. [CrossRef] [PubMed]
5. del Hoyo, J.; Moreno-Zarate, P.; Escalante, G.; Valles, J.A.; Fernandez, P.; Solis, J. High-Efficiency Waveguide Optical Amplifiers and Lasers via FS-Laser Induced Local Modification of the Glass Composition. *J. Light. Technol.* **2017**, *35*, 2955–2959. [CrossRef]
6. Macias-Montero, M.; Dias, A.; Sotillo, B.; Moreno-Zarate, P.; Ariza, R.; Fernandez, P.; Solis, J. Waveguide tapers fabrication by femtosecond laser induced element redistribution in glass. *J. Light. Technol.* **2020**, *38*, 6578–6583. [CrossRef]
7. Rahman, M.A.; Saghir, M.Z. Thermodiffusion or Soret effect: Historical review. *Int. J. Heat Mass Transf.* **2014**, *73*, 693–705. [CrossRef]
8. Montero, M.M.; Muñoz, F.; Sotillo, B.; Hoyo, J.; Ariza, R.; Fernandez, P.; Siegel, J.; Solis, J. Femtosecond laser induced thermophoretic writing of waveguides in silicate glass. *Sci. Rep.* **2021**, *11*, 1–12. [CrossRef]
9. Osellame, R.; Chiodo, N.; Della Valle, G.; Cerullo, G.; Ramponi, R.; Laporta, P.; Killi, A.; Morgner, U.; Svelto, O. Waveguide lasers in the C-band fabricated by laser inscription with a compact femtosecond oscillator. *IEEE J. Sel. Top. Quantum Electron.* **2006**, *12*, 277–285. [CrossRef]
10. Fernandez, T.; Gross, S.; Arriola, A.; Withford, M.; Privat, K. Revisiting ultrafast laser inscribed waveguide formation in commercial alkali-free borosilicate glasses. *Opt. Express* **2020**, *28*, 10153–10164. [CrossRef]
11. Davis, K.M.; Miura, K.; Sugimoto, N.; Hirao, K. Writing waveguides in glass with a femtosecond laser. *Opt. Lett.* **1996**, *21*, 1729–1731. [CrossRef]
12. Kempers, L.J.T.M. A comprehensive thermodynamic theory of the Soret effect in a multicomponent gas, liquid, or solid. *J. Chem. Phys.* **2001**, *115*, 6330–6341. [CrossRef]

13. Shimizu, M.; Fukuyo, T.; Matsuoka, J.; Nakashima, K.; Sato, K.; Kiyosawa, T.; Nishi, M.; Shimotsuma, Y.; Miura, K. Determination of thermodynamic and microscopic origins of the Soret effect in sodium silicate melts: Prediction of sign change of the Soret coefficient. *J. Chem. Phys.* **2021**, *154*, 074501. [CrossRef]
14. Sakakura, M.; Kurita, T.; Shimizu, M.; Yoshimura, K.; Shimotsuma, Y.; Fukuda, N.; Hirao, K.; Miura, K. Shape control of elemental distributions inside a glass by simultaneous femtosecond laser irradiation at multiple spots. *Opt. Lett.* **2013**, *38*, 4939–4942. [CrossRef] [PubMed]
15. Del Hoyo, J.; Vazquez, R.M.; Sotillo, B.; Fernandez, T.T.; Siegel, J.; Fernández, P.; Osellame, R.; Solis, J. Control of waveguide properties by tuning femtosecond laser induced compositional changes. *Appl. Phys. Lett.* **2014**, *105*, 131101. [CrossRef]
16. Tan, D.; Wang, Z.; Xu, B.; Qiu, J. Photonic circuits written by femtosecond laser in glass: Improved fabrication and recent progress in photonic devices. *Adv. Photonics* **2021**, *3*, 024002. [CrossRef]
17. Duffy, J.A. The electronic polarisability of oxygen in glass and the effect of composition. *J. Non-Cryst. Solids* **2002**, *297*, 275–284. [CrossRef]
18. Dimitrov, V.; Komatsu, T. An Interpretation of Optical Properties of Oxides and Oxide Glasses in Terms of the Electronic Ion Polarizability and Average Single Bond Strength. *J. Univ. Chem. Technol. Metall.* **2010**, *45*, 219–250.
19. Moreno-Zarate, P.; Muñoz, F.; Sotillo, B.; Macias-Montero, M.; Atienzar, J.; Garcia-Pardo, M.; Fernandez, P.; Serna, R.; Solis, J. Role of the La/K compositional ratio in the properties of waveguides written by fs-laser induced element redistribution in phosphate-based glasses. *Materials* **2020**, *13*, 1275. [CrossRef]
20. Fernandez, T.T.; Sotillo, B.; del Hoyo, J.; Valles, J.-A.; Vazquez, R.M.; Fernandez, P.; Solis, J. Dual Regimes of Ion Migration in High Repetition Rate Femtosecond Laser Inscribed Waveguides. *IEEE Photonics Technol. Lett.* **2015**, *27*, 1068–1071. [CrossRef]
21. Fernandez, T.T.; Siegel, J.; Hoyo, J.; Sotillo, B.; Fernandez, P.; Solis, J. Controlling plasma distributions as driving forces for ion migration during fs laser writing. *J. Phys. D Appl. Phys.* **2015**, *48*, 155101. [CrossRef]
22. Jin, M.; Zhou, W.; Ma, W.; Wang, Q.; Liang, X.; Zhang, P.; Xiang, W. The inhibition of CsPbBr3 nanocrystals glass from self-crystallization with the assistance of ZnO modulation for rewritable data storage. *Chem. Eng. J.* **2021**, 129812. [CrossRef]
23. Zhang, X.; He, X.; Liu, Q.; Poumellec, B.; Lancry, M.; Brisset, F. Abnormal elemental redistribution in silicate glasses irradiated by ultrafast laser. *J. Alloys Compd.* **2017**, *727*, 444–448. [CrossRef]
24. Stone, A.; Sakakura, M.; Shimotsuma, Y.; Miura, K.; Hirao, K.; Dierolf, V.; Jain, H. Femtosecond laser-writing of 3D crystal architecture in glass: Growth dynamics and morphological control. *Mater. Des.* **2018**, *146*, 228–238. [CrossRef]
25. Mardilovich, P.; Fletcher, L.B.; Troy, N.W.; Yang, L.; Huang, H.; Risbud, S.H.; Krol, D.M. Ultrafast Laser Fabrication of Hybrid Micro- and Nano-Structures in Semiconductor-doped Borosilicate Glasses. *Int. J. Appl. Glas. Sci.* **2013**, *4*, 87–99. [CrossRef]
26. Muñoz, F.; Balda, R. A highly efficient method of dihydroxylation and fining of Nd phosphate laser galsses. *Int. J. App. Glass Sci.* **2019**, *10*, 157–161. [CrossRef]
27. Moreno-Zarate, P.; Gonzalez, A.; Funke, S.; Días, A.; Sotillo, B.; del Hoyo, J.; Garcia-Pardo, M.; Serna, R.; Fernandez, P.; Solis, J. Imaging Ellipsometry Determination of the Refractive Index Contrast and Dispersion of Channel Waveguides Inscribed by fs-Laser Induced Ion-Migration. *Phys. Status Solidi* **2018**, *215*, 1800258. [CrossRef]
28. Toney Fernandez, T.; Haro-González, P.; Sotillo, B.; Hernandez, M.; Jaque, D.; Fernandez, P.; Domingo, C.; Siegel, J.; Solis, J. Ion migration assisted inscription of high refractive index contrast waveguides by femtosecond laser pulses in phosphate glass. *Opt. Lett.* **2013**, *38*, 5248–5251. [CrossRef] [PubMed]
29. Duffy, J.A. Electronic polarizability and related properties of the oxide ion. *Phys. Chem. Glasses* **1989**, *30*, 1–4.
30. Tomihara, Y.; Tricot, G.; Revel, B.; Kishimoto, K.; Okamoto, T.; Saitoh, A. The Relationship among Electronic Polarizability, Photoelasticity, and Refractivity in Ternary Phosphate Glasses. *Phys. Status Solidi Basic Res.* **2020**, *257*, 1–8. [CrossRef]
31. del Hoyo, J.; de la Cruz, A.R.; Grace, E.; Ferrer, A.; Siegel, J.; Pasquazi, A.; Assanto, G.; Solis, J. Rapid assessment of nonlinear optical propagation effects in dielectrics. *Sci. Rep.* **2015**, *5*, 07650. [CrossRef] [PubMed]
32. Eaton, S.M.; Zhang, H.; Herman, P.R.; Yoshino, F.; Shah, L.; Bovatsek, J.; Arai, A. Heat accumulation effects in femtosecond laser-written waveguides with variable repetition rate. *Opt. Express* **2005**, *13*, 4708–4716. [CrossRef]
33. Dragic, P.D.; Ballato, J. 120 Years of Optical Glass Science: From the law of mixtures to mixing the unmixable. *Opt. Photonics News* **2014**, 44–51. [CrossRef]
34. Hussey, C.D.; Martinez, F. Approximate Analytic Forms For The Propagation Characteristics Of Single-Mode Optical Fibres. *Electron. Lett.* **1985**, *21*, 1103–1104. [CrossRef]
35. Ingram, M.D. Amorphous Materials: Mixed Alkali Effect. In *Encyclopedia of Materials: Science and Technology*; Elsevier: Amsterdam, The Netherlands, 2001; pp. 220–223. ISBN 978-0-08-043152-9.
36. Isard, J.O. The mixed alkali effect in glass. *J. Non-Cryst. Solids* **1969**, *1*, 235–261. [CrossRef]
37. Wilkinson, C.J.; Potter, A.R.; Welch, R.S.; Bragatto, C.; Zheng, Q.; Bauchy, M.; Affatigato, M.; Feller, S.A.; Mauro, J.C. Topological Origins of the Mixed Alkali Effect in Glass. *J. Phys. Chem. B* **2019**, *123*, 7482–7489. [CrossRef] [PubMed]
38. Greaves, G.N.; Ngai, K.L. Ionic transport properties in oxide glasses derived from atomic structure. *J. Non-Cryst. Solids* **1994**, *172–174*, 1378–1388. [CrossRef]
39. LaCourse, W.C. A defect model for the mixed alkali effect. *J. Non-Cryst. Solids* **1987**, *95–96*, 905–912. [CrossRef]
40. Bunde, A.; Ingram, M.D.; Maass, P.; Ngai, K.L. Mixed alkali effects in ionic conductors: A new model and computer simulations. *J. Non-Cryst. Solids* **1991**, *131–133*, 1109–1112. [CrossRef]
41. Tuller, H.L.; Button, D.P.; Uhlmann, D.R. Fast ion transport in oxide glasses. *J. Non-Cryst. Solids* **1980**, *40*, 93–118. [CrossRef]

42. Shannon, R.D. Revised effective ionic radii and systematic studies of interatomic distances in halides and chalcogenides. *Acta Crystallogr. A* **1976**, *32*, 751–767. [CrossRef]
43. Tsuchida, J.E.; Ferri, F.A.; Pizani, P.S.; Martins Rodrigues, A.C.; Kundu, S.; Schneider, J.F.; Zanotto, E.D. Ionic conductivity and mixed-ion effect in mixed alkali metaphosphate glasses. *Phys. Chem. Chem. Phys.* **2017**, *19*, 6594–6600. [CrossRef] [PubMed]
44. Kim, K.D.; Lee, S.H. Viscosity behavior and mixed alkali effect of alkali aluminosilicate glass melts. *J. Ceram. Soc. Jpn.* **1997**, *105*, 827–832. [CrossRef]

materials

MDPI

Article

Single Femtosecond Laser-Pulse-Induced Superficial Amorphization and Re-Crystallization of Silicon

Camilo Florian [1,2], Daniel Fischer [1], Katharina Freiberg [3], Matthias Duwe [4], Mario Sahre [1], Stefan Schneider [4], Andreas Hertwig [1], Jörg Krüger [1], Markus Rettenmayr [3], Uwe Beck [1], Andreas Undisz [5] and Jörn Bonse [1,*]

1 Bundesanstalt für Materialforschung und -prüfung (BAM), Unter den Eichen 87, D-12205 Berlin, Germany; camilo.florian@princeton.edu (C.F.); daniel.fischer@rfischergmbh.de (D.F.); mario.sahre@bam.de (M.S.); andreas.hertwig@bam.de (A.H.); joerg.krueger@bam.de (J.K.); uwe.beck@bam.de (U.B.)
2 Princeton Institute for the Science and Technology of Materials (PRISM), Princeton University, 70 Prospect Avenue, Princeton, NJ 08540, USA
3 Otto-Schott-Institut für Materialforschung (OSIM), Lehrstuhl für Metallische Werkstoffe, Friedrich-Schiller-Universität Jena, D-07743 Jena, Germany; katharina.freiberg@uni-jena.de (K.F.); m.rettenmayr@uni-jena.de (M.R.)
4 Accurion GmbH, Stresemannstraße 30, D-37079 Göttingen, Germany; mdu@accurion.com (M.D.); st@accurion.com (S.S.)
5 Institut für Werkstoffwissenschaft und Werkstofftechnik (IWW), Technische Universität Chemnitz, Erfenschlager Straße 73, D-09125 Chemnitz, Germany; andreas.undisz@mb.tu-chemnitz.de
* Correspondence: joern.bonse@bam.de; Tel.: +49-30-8104-3562

Abstract: Superficial amorphization and re-crystallization of silicon in <111> and <100> orientation after irradiation by femtosecond laser pulses (790 nm, 30 fs) are studied using optical imaging and transmission electron microscopy. Spectroscopic imaging ellipsometry (SIE) allows fast data acquisition at multiple wavelengths and provides experimental data for calculating nanometric amorphous layer thickness profiles with micrometric lateral resolution based on a thin-film layer model. For a radially Gaussian laser beam and at moderate peak fluences above the melting and below the ablation thresholds, laterally parabolic amorphous layer profiles with maximum thicknesses of several tens of nanometers were quantitatively attained. The accuracy of the calculations is verified experimentally by high-resolution transmission electron microscopy (HRTEM) and energy dispersive X-ray spectroscopy (STEM-EDX). Along with topographic information obtained by atomic force microscopy (AFM), a comprehensive picture of the superficial re-solidification of silicon after local melting by femtosecond laser pulses is drawn.

Keywords: femtosecond laser; silicon; amorphization; crystallization; spectroscopic imaging ellipsometry; transmission electron microscopy; atomic force microscopy

Citation: Florian, C.; Fischer, D.; Freiberg, K.; Duwe, M.; Sahre, M.; Schneider, S.; Hertwig, A.; Krüger, J.; Rettenmayr, M.; Beck, U.; et al. Single Femtosecond Laser-Pulse-Induced Superficial Amorphization and Re-Crystallization of Silicon. *Materials* **2021**, *14*, 1651. https://doi.org/10.3390/ma14071651

Academic Editor: Joe Sakai

Received: 25 February 2021
Accepted: 23 March 2021
Published: 27 March 2021

1. Introduction

Through the rapid recent developments in laser technology in combination with advanced optical beam management strategies, laser processing has nowadays entered many industrial production processes [1,2]. In most cases, the processing relies on the laser-induced removal of material, i.e., on laser ablation [3]—a process that exhibits a sharply defined threshold of the fluence (areal energy density) of the incident laser radiation. However, below the ablation threshold fluence, other material specific phenomena may occur that also exhibit a distinct threshold fluence, e.g., structural or chemical changes triggered by effects such as melting [3], oxidation [4], re-crystallization [5,6], etc. Some of these non-ablative phenomena are widely explored and already used in applications, e.g., in optical data storage [7–10].

Given its technological relevance, silicon is the material that is studied best with regard to the interaction with intense laser radiation. Experimentally, it can be manufactured in a well-controlled manner and theoretically it is already well understood [11]. Observed effects are usually interpreted as laser-induced phase transitions and have very actively been investigated over the last five decades while exploring the possibility of removing defects from crystalline semiconductor surfaces through laser irradiation (a process referred to as laser annealing) [3,12–14].

Studying interactions of intense ultrashort (fs-ps) laser pulses with semiconductors gave rise to exploring the intriguing effect of non-thermal melting, where a strong optical excitation of the electronic system of the solid may lead to a destabilization of the bonding lattice structure on an ultrafast (sub-ps) timescale [15–24]. For silicon, this effect typically manifests at conduction band carrier densities >10^{22} cm^{-3} (corresponding to ~10% of the total valence band population) [16,25] at laser fluences exceeding the ablation threshold [26]. In contrast, at lower degrees of optical excitation, thermal melting relies on the process of electron–phonon scattering and, thus, occurs on longer timescales of picoseconds after the impact of the laser pulse. Laser-induced thermal melting of bulk semiconductors usually manifests via heterogeneous nucleation as an interfacial melt-in, followed by interfacial re-solidification processes [27–29], while locally converting (releasing) the latent heat of fusion. Driven by the gradual increase of undercooling of the superficial melt pool via heat conduction into the bulk material, the velocity of the solid/liquid interface may accelerate toward the end of the re-solidification process [27]. Depending on the velocity of the re-solidification front, the quenched material can re-solidify either epitaxially as a single-crystal, or it can turn into a less ordered poly-crystalline or even into an amorphous state since the atoms have not enough time to form an ordered lattice [14]. For semiconductors, the critical interfacial velocity (v_{crit}) for solidification as amorphous material typically lies between a few m/s and some tens of m/s, and crucially depends on the interfacial lattice orientation of the crystalline substrate [14,30] and the type of the semiconductor [14,23,31–34]. Note that the energy deposition depth of ultrashort laser pulse irradiation may significantly differ for semiconductors and metals and will lead to different outcomes regarding local melting and solidification. Therefore, kinetic aspects are linked to the specific laser irradiation conditions. Here, the reader is referred to pertinent literature, including thermodynamic and atomistic numerical studies [27,29,32,34–36].

Upon irradiation of semiconductors with ultrashort (fs-ps) laser pulses, amorphous surface layers with a thickness of some tens of nanometers were reported, as determined by analytical techniques such as transmission electron microscopy (TEM), electron backscatter diffraction (EBSD) analyses, micro-Raman spectroscopy (µ-RS), confocal scanning laser microscopy (CSLM), real-time reflectivity measurements (RTR), and fs-time-resolved microscopy (fs-TRM) [33,34,36–47]. The specific interest of such a contact-less surface modification technology is based on the remarkably different structural, electrical and optical properties of the amorphous and the crystalline silicon phases that enable applications in electronics and photonics and manifest through alterations of the local chemical etching rate, electric conductivity, or the high refractive indices at telecom wavelengths [48,49].

In a previous publication [42], a non-destructive all-optical method to reconstruct the radial depth profile of the amorphous layer was proposed that is inferred upon single-pulse irradiation of single-crystalline <111> silicon with a spatially Gaussian fs-laser beam. It relies on CSLM measurements of the surface reflectivity across a laser-amorphized spot along with a thin-film optical model considering all Fresnel reflections of a system consisting of an amorphous silicon layer (a-Si) of varying thickness, covered by a native oxide (~3 nm) and sitting on a substrate of single-crystalline silicon (c-Si) [40,42]. A laterally parabolic a-Si layer thickness distribution with a maximum vertical extent of ~60 nm was retrieved from the reflectivity measurements for a surface spot amorphized by a single 130 fs Ti:Sapphire laser pulse at a peak fluence of ϕ_0 = 0.42 J/cm^2. A direct measurement of the amorphous layer thickness by chemical etching was proposed but could not be performed at that time.

In this work, we extend the previous study [42] by employing spectroscopic imaging ellipsometry (SIE) for a fast non-destructive quantitative determination of the lateral thickness gradient of the superficial amorphous layer induced by single spatially Gaussian-shaped 30 fs laser pulses of varying energies (peak fluences) on two different silicon wafers with varying crystal lattice orientation. Taking advantage of the spectroscopic ellipsometric approach along with the well-known radial beam profile, a model of the fluence dependence of the laser-induced amorphization is determined with unprecedented precision and experimentally verified by cross-sectional high-resolution transmission electron microscopy (HRTEM) and energy dispersive X-ray spectroscopy (STEM-EDX).

2. Materials and Methods

Two single-crystalline silicon (c-Si) wafers with different orientation (Werk für Fernsehelektronik, Berlin, Germany) were chosen as target materials, specifically Czochralsky-grown n-type Si<111> (electrical resistivity 1.3×10^{-2}–1.9×10^{-2} Ω.cm) and p-type Si<100> (electrical resistivity 1.2×10^{-1}–2×10^{-1} Ω.cm) wafers, both with a thickness of ~0.4 mm and a diameter of two inches. On the polished silicon samples, typically a native oxide layer of about 1 nm to 3 nm thickness is present due to the exposure to ambient air.

The silicon wafers were irradiated at ambient conditions by near-infrared fs-laser pulses generated by a commercial Ti:Sapphire multi-pass amplifier system (Compact Pro, Femtolasers, Vienna, Austria). The laser system emitted linearly polarized laser pulses of τ~30 fs duration at a center wavelength of λ~790 nm. The laser pulse energy was measured by a pyroelectric detector. The wafers were mounted on a motorized *x*-*y*-*z*-translation stage and positioned perpendicular to the direction of the laser beam (*z*). The fs-laser beam was focused by a spherical dielectric mirror (focal length f = 500 mm) to the front side of the samples, resulting in a Gaussian ($1/e^2$) radial spot diameter of $2w_0$ = 112.6 µm, as determined by the method of Liu [50]. By means of a half-wave plate in front of the compressor unit of the laser amplifier, the laser pulse energy E_p of the focused laser beam was varied between 10 µJ and 40 µJ, corresponding to incident peak fluences $\phi_0 = 2E_p/(\pi {w_0}^2)$ in front of the samples between 0.20 J/cm² and 0.80 J/cm². For a given laser pulse energy, the radial fluence profile $\phi(r)$ incident to a surface spot can then be calculated via

$$\phi(r) = \frac{2E_p}{\pi w_0^2} e^{-2\left(\frac{r}{w_0}\right)^2} \tag{1}$$

As an example, such a radial Gaussian fluence profile is quantitatively visualized as a red curve in the lower part of Figure 1 for a laser pulse of E_p = 12 µJ, resulting in a peak fluence value of (ϕ_0 = 0.24 J/cm²).

During laser processing, the sample translation stages were simultaneously moved at constant speeds in both the *x*- and the *y*-directions, while continuously irradiating the wafers at 1 kHz pulse repetition rate. In this way, for each selected laser pulse energy (peak fluence) a set of several almost identical laser irradiation spots were generated, laterally separated at the sample surfaces, and were available for further post-irradiation characterizations.

The irradiated wafer surface regions were inspected by an optical microscope in brightfield imaging mode (Eclipse L200, Nikon, Tokyo, Japan) using a white light halogen lamp for illumination along with a 10× microscope objective.

Surface topographies of all laser-irradiated spots were acquired by atomic force microscopy (AFM, Dimension 3100, Digital Instruments, Santa Barbara, CA, USA) in tapping mode using silicon cantilever probes with a nominal tip radius of 10 nm under ambient laboratory conditions. The corresponding images of 100 × 100 µm² size contain 512 data points in *x*-, and 256 lines in *y*-direction, with a nominal resolution in *z* of 70 pm (4.6 µm/16 bit in the full *z*-scale range). The data are displayed as two-dimensional color maps of the surface topography, using a common color scale for encoding topographic height (*z*-) variations ranging between −30 nm and +60 nm, with the original surface plane located at $z = 0$.

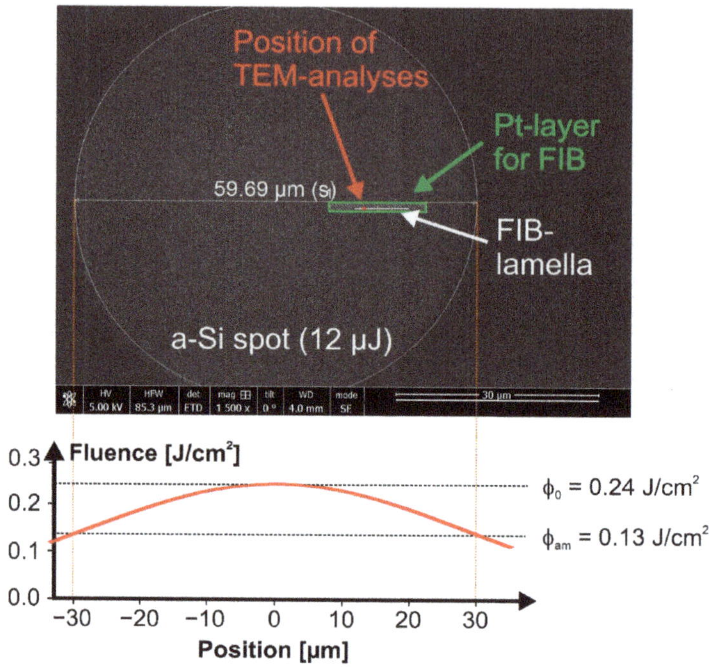

Figure 1. Top-view SEM image of an amorphous (a-Si) spot created by a single fs-laser pulse [λ~790 nm, τ = 30 fs, E_p = 12 µJ/ϕ_0 = 0.24 J/cm^2] on the surface of a Si<111> wafer. Its diameter of 59.69 µm is indicated as an additional marking in white. The plot in the lower part visualizes the corresponding radially Gaussian laser beam profile through the center of the laser beam along with the peak fluence (ϕ_0) and amorphization threshold fluence (ϕ_{am}). The rectangular green box indicates the region of the post-irradiation deposition of a Pt-layer prior to the focused ion beam (FIB) preparation process. The horizontal white line within that box marks the orientation of the FIB lamella, while the red square indicates the position of transmission electron microscopy (TEM)/scanning transmission electron microscopy (STEM) imaging.

Further optical characterization of all laser-irradiated spots on Si<100> and Si<111> was performed using a Nanofilm_EP3 imaging ellipsometer (Accurion GmbH, Göttingen, Germany) equipped with a Nikon 10× achromatic long working-distance microscope objective (NA 0.21), operated at an angle of incidence (AOI) of 45° with a continuous wave (cw) diode laser emitting at 637 nm wavelength as illumination source. The measurement applied a polarizer–analyzer nulling scheme and directly yielded two-dimensional micrographs of the ellipsometric quantities Ψ and Δ (called Ψ-Δ-maps hereafter). By definition, the value of tan(Ψ) denotes the amplitude ratio of the complex reflection coefficients for p- and s-polarized light waves. Δ equals the sample-induced phase-shift between p- and s-polarized waves and is very sensitive to variations of the (optical) layer thickness of thin surface layers.

For quantification of the lateral amorphous layer profiles of selected fs-laser-irradiated spots in the form of thickness maps, a Nanofilm_EP4 spectroscopic imaging ellipsometer (Accurion GmbH, Göttingen, Germany) was applied to acquire hyperspectral Ψ-Δ-maps (wavelength of illumination ranging from 370 to 950 nm in 10 nm steps) using a laser-stabilized Xenon broadband light source and a grating monochromator for the sample illumination (bandwidths 4.6 nm to 5.2 nm). The measurements were performed using the instrument's rotating compensator mode in combination with achromatic long working-distance microscope objectives (Nikon 20× NA 0.35 and Nikon 10× NA 0.21) at AOIs of 45° (20×) and 55° (10×) for the Si<100> and Si<111> samples, respectively. The corresponding field of view (FOV) sizes were approximately 500 × 500 μm^2 (10×) and 250 × 250 μm^2 (20×) with effective image pixel sizes of 0.586 × 0.586 μm^2 and 0.362 × 0.362 μm^2, respectively. At the given conditions, the imaging resolution is better than 2 μm. Details on the ellipsometry instrumentation, the setup and the modes of operation may be found elsewhere [51–54].

Top-view scanning electron microscopy (SEM) allowed to locate the laser-irradiated spots at the surface due to the altered morphology or electrical conductivity of the smooth superficially amorphized material. Cross-sections perpendicular to the surface were characterized by HRTEM and STEM-EDX combined with an energy dispersive X-ray spectroscopy system at a spot on the Si<111> wafer irradiated at E_p = 12 μJ (ϕ_0 = 0.24 J/cm^2). Surface-preserving sample preparation for TEM was carried out using focused ion beam (FIB) milling and an in-situ lift-out technique [55]. The preparation of the TEM lamella started by the deposition of a protective Pt capping layer at the region of interest (ROI). Figure 1 shows a schematic of a top-view scanning electron microscopy (SEM) image of the selected laser-amorphized spot along with the off-centered ROI marked by a green hatched box. The lamella was investigated using a NEOARM 200F (JEOL, Freising, Germany) analytical transmission electron microscope operating at 200 kV electron acceleration voltage. The device was equipped with a cold field emission gun, 4k × 4k CCD-camera (OneView, Gatan Inc., Pleasanton, CA, USA) and a windowless double solid-state detector with a total detector area of 200 mm^2 (Centurio, JEOL, Freising, Germany) for EDX. The orientation of the lamella and the location for high-resolution imaging are additionally indicated by the horizontal white line and the red square symbol in the green box in Figure 1.

3. Results

Figure 2 shows a compilation of images of a series of nine laser-irradiated spots at the Si<111> wafer generated by single fs-laser pulses of different laser pulse energies/peak fluences (as indicated at the top). The upper image row provides optical micrographs, the second row the corresponding atomic force micrographs. The two lower rows display maps of the ellipsometric quantities Ψ and Δ obtained from imaging ellipsometry (IE, Nanofilm_EP3, Accurion GmbH, Göttingen, Germany) for the visualization of changes of the polarization state of the probing 637 nm radiation through the laser-induced surface modifications. For the most sensitive visualization of laser-induced alterations, the ellipsometry maps are displayed in a multi-color scheme with individually optimized color ranges. Several characteristic annular structures can be recognized in the series of laser-irradiated surface spots displayed in Figure 2. In a previous work [40] employing single Ti:sapphire fs-laser pulses (800 nm, 130 fs) these annuli were already associated with physical processes of laser-induced melting of silicon with subsequent amorphization (outermost modification; line set #1), the local destruction of the native oxide layer (line set #2), ablation of silicon (line set #3), and the onset of (poly-crystalline) re-crystallization in the center of the spot exposed to the highest laser pulse energies (line set #4). The latter can be explained as follows: the interfacial velocities and lifetimes of the melt pool are strongly affected by the temperature gradients and the amount of latent heat stored in the liquid layer of transiently varying thickness (with a maximum extent initially imposed by the peak laser fluence). The release of latent heat of crystallization (enthalpy of fusion) can retard the re-solidification, particularly in the central region of the irradiated spot, where the lifetime of the melt layer is the longest. Hence, at large laser pulse energies (peak fluences), re-crystallization is possible [5]. For a scheme visualizing the different processes, the reader is referred to the graphical abstract of this article. The origin of the modification of line set #5 in an intermediate range of local fluences is not fully clear yet; supposedly, it is associated with a local non-ablative modification of the native oxide layer, e.g., via melting and effects of further oxidation. The assignments of the origin of the features associated with the line sets #2 and #5 to the native oxide layer are supported by some thermodynamic arguments, i.e., that silicon melts at a lower temperature than amorphous silicon dioxide (T_m(c-Si)~1685 K < T_m(a-SiO_2)~1983 K, [56]), while the evaporation temperature [T_{ev}(a-SiO_2)~2503 K] of amorphous silicon dioxide lies between the melting temperature and the evaporation temperature T_{ev}(c-Si)~3510 K of crystalline silicon [3].

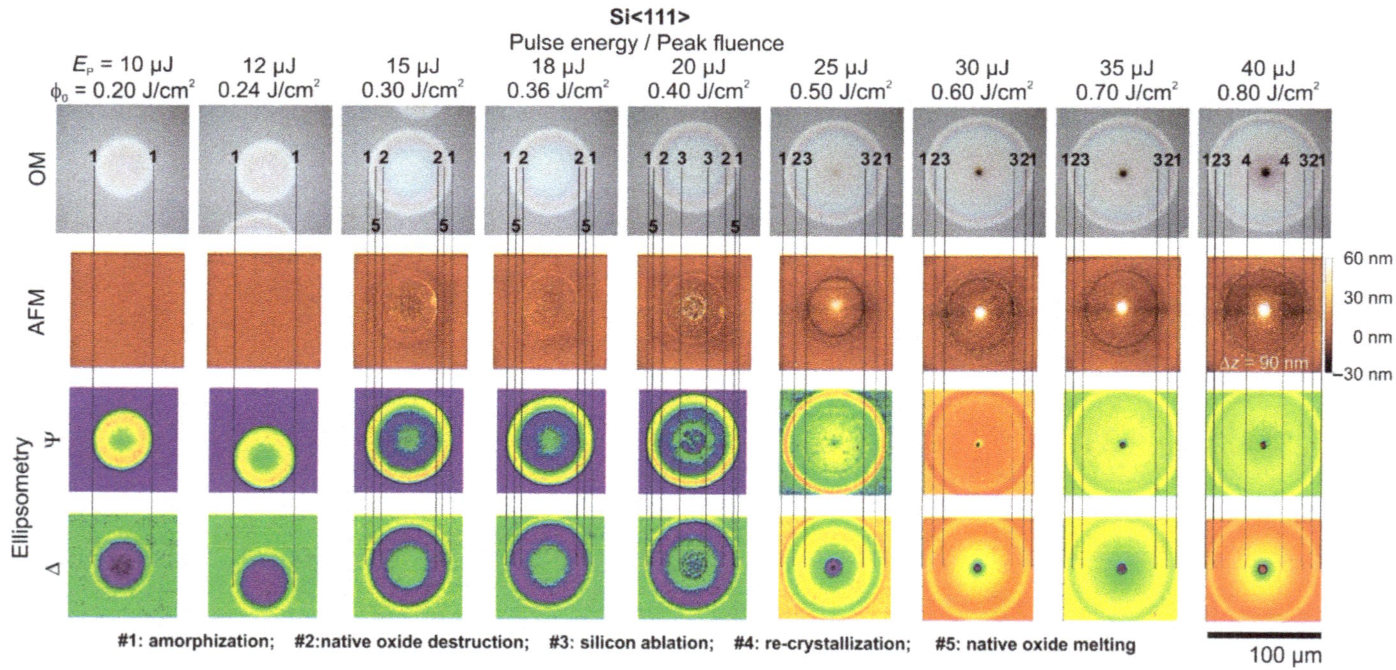

Figure 2. Comparison of brightfield optical microscopy (OM) images, atomic force microscopy (AFM) images, and corresponding spatial maps of the ellipsometric quantities Ψ and Δ (taken at 637 nm wavelength) for a series of nine single fs-laser [λ~790 nm, τ = 30 fs] pulse-irradiated spots on a Si<111> wafer. The fs-laser pulse energy E_p varies between 10 µJ and 40 µJ among the spots from left to right, corresponding to peak laser fluences between ϕ_0 = 0.20 and 0.80 J/cm^2. The AFM images are provided in a common color scale, encoding height variations Δz of −30 to +60 nm. The vertical (numbered) line sets mark the extent of characteristic surface features (for details see the text at the bottom of the figure). A common lateral scale bar is provided in the lower right corner.

The laser pulse energy/peak fluence dependence of the diameters of the distinct features marked by the different line sets was analyzed in detail by means of the method proposed by Liu [50], providing characteristic single-pulse threshold fluences of ϕ_{am}(Si<111>) = 0.13 J/cm^2 for melting with subsequent amorphization (from line set #1), ϕ_{annu}(Si<111>) = 0.26 J/cm^2 for the destruction of the native oxide layer (from line set #2), ϕ_{abl}(Si<111>) = 0.39 J/cm^2 for ablation (from line set #3). Additionally, a value of ϕ_{cr}(Si<111>) = 0.68 J/cm^2 was estimated from the diameter of the re-crystallization feature of the laser spot irradiated at 40 μJ (ϕ_0 = 0.80 J/cm^2) along with its known radial fluence profile (Equation (1)). These threshold values of melting and ablation are somewhat smaller than the values previously reported in [40] since a 4 to 5 times shorter pulse duration is employed here. For the amorphization threshold fluence, this is well supported by the theoretical work of Rämer et al. [57] providing a melting threshold of 0.125 J/cm^2 for silicon irradiated by single 50 fs laser pulses at 800 nm wavelength. In contrast, the threshold of re-crystallization is particularly increased since the Gaussian beam diameter is larger by a factor of ~2 here, resulting in a larger melt pool that increases the total amount of latent heat stored and released during the re-crystallization.

The most striking observation in the OM images is a significant increase of the surface reflectivity within the laser-modified spots on Si<111> (line set #1 in Figure 2). Previous micro-Raman spectroscopy results already revealed the presence of amorphous material in these regions [40]. The significant changes of the refractive index (n) and the extinction coefficient (k) of amorphous silicon can then explain the increase of the surface reflectivity. The color changes within the amorphous regions point toward interference effects through a wavelength dependence of the optical constants (n, k) along with a laterally varying thickness of the superficial semi-transparent amorphous layer upon the white light illumination employed in brightfield optical microscopy. As expected, in regions outside of the destruction of the native oxide layer (line set #2) no surface topographic changes were observed by AFM (see the spots irradiated at E_p = 10 μJ (ϕ_0 = 0.20 J/cm^2) and E_p = 12 μJ (ϕ_0 = 0.24 J/cm^2)). The effect manifests for all pulse energies larger than E_p = 15 μJ (ϕ_0 = 0.30 J/cm^2) as a very shallow and fine annular rim (height ~15 nm ± 5 nm, width < 2 μm) in the AFM images that was not resolved by OM here. Inside those regions, a small increase of the surface roughness can be observed in the AFM images, resulting from residuals of the laser-induced decomposition of the native oxide layer. For laser pulse energies exceeding E_p = 20 μJ (ϕ_0 = 0.40 J/cm^2), additionally the ablative removal of silicon from the surface can be seen (bordered by line set #3), resulting in some few tens of nanometers deep ablation craters along with a further increased surface roughness. Interestingly, at laser pulse energies above E_p = 25 μJ (ϕ_0 = 0.50 J/cm^2) a characteristic protrusion even exceeding the original surface plane by heights of up to ~60 nm manifests in the center of the ablation craters. For the highest laser pulse energies, this central hillock becomes visible as dark spot in the center of the optical micrographs. Supposedly, this central protrusion is caused by radial transport of molten silicon toward the center of the spots caused by the volume expansion of liquid silicon by up to ~9% during the re-solidification [40,58]. Note that at room temperature the mass density/specific volume of amorphous silicon is ~1.8% smaller/larger than that of single-crystalline silicon [59]. In such a scenario, the laser-induced melt pool solidifies from its bottom toward the surface and simultaneously from its outer border toward the center of the irradiated spot. The material expansion of silicon upon re-solidification then "squeezes" the still molten silicon to the center, where the solidification process finally terminates. Here, surface oxidation effects may be strongest and additionally affect the surface reflectivity. Melt flow caused by the thermocapillary (Marangoni) effect can be ruled out here as, for a spatially Gaussian laser beam, it would result in a radially outward directed displacement of the silicon [60,61].

The ellipsometric maps of Ψ and Δ visualize most of the mentioned annular features and are able to expose even the subtle surface features detected by AFM that are not resolved in OM here. Both ellipsometric quantities are very sensitive to changes of the optical properties of the silicon material, manifesting either via structural material changes such as amorphization or due to thickness variations of the surface layers. Even the regions associated with the destruction of the native oxide layer (bordered by line set #2) can be distinguished as a step-like local jump in Ψ for laser pulse energies between 15 μJ (ϕ_0 = 0.30 J/cm^2) and 18 μJ (ϕ_0 = 0.36 J/cm^2), before stronger changes caused by ablation and re-solidification dominate the ellipsometry maps.

Figure 3 displays an analogous collage of identical experimental data for the single fs-laser pulse irradiation of the Si<100> wafer material. The most striking differences to the data previously shown in Figure 2 are the somewhat smaller diameters of the laser-modified spots and, for $E_p \geq 15$ μJ ($\phi_0 \geq 0.30$ J/cm^2), the occurrence of a central disc-shaped area having the same optical properties as the non-irradiated wafer material in the surrounding of the spots (see the OM and ellipsometric images). This central disc is associated with the process of re-solidification that can occur either in a single- or in a poly-crystalline state [40,47]. It has a reduced threshold value of ϕ_{cr} (Si<100>) = 0.25 J/cm^2 here for the Si<100> compared to Si<111>, fully in line with the results reported by Cullis et al. [14] for the ns-laser irradiation and by Merkle et al. [38] for the ps-laser irradiation of silicon wafers with different interfacial crystal orientations; depending on the orientation of the crystalline lattice, values of v_{crit}(Si<111>) ~11 m/s and v_{crit}(Si<100>) ~15 m/s were determined for the critical interfacial velocity upon ns-laser irradiation [14]. Bucksbaum et al. [32] reported for UV ps-laser irradiation a saturation value of the interfacial velocity of ~25 m/s being widely independent of the peak laser fluences. For pulse energies of E_p = 15 μJ (ϕ_0 = 0.30 J/cm^2) and E_p = 18 μJ (ϕ_0 = 0.60 J/cm^2) the AFM images indicate the local decomposition of the native silicon oxide layer in the center of the irradiated spots, resulting in an increased surface roughness that manifests also as a slightly elevated (averaged) surface topography. Since OM and SIE mainly image the electronic configuration of the inspected material and both do not have the necessary spatial resolution, these nanometric topography changes are not visible in the corresponding OM and SIE micrographs here. At laser pulse energies exceeding E_p = 20 μJ (ϕ_0 = 0.40 J/cm^2) the ablation of silicon becomes visible as a fine rim bordering the ablation craters in the OM, AFM, and ellipsometry micrographs of Figure 3.

3.1. *Layer Thickness Analysis by Spectroscopic Imaging Ellipsometry (SIE)*

For a quantification of the thickness of the amorphous layer profiles, additional multi-wavelength measurements were performed by SIE (Nanofilm_EP4). In order to avoid the complexity imposed by melt displacement, ablation, or the laser-induced modification/destruction of the native oxide layer, this set of SIE measurements was restricted to surface spots on both silicon wafer materials generated at the lowest two laser pulse energies (peak fluences) of E_p = 10 μJ (ϕ_0 = 0.20 J/cm^2) and 12 μJ (ϕ_0 = 0.24 J/cm^2), respectively. These laser irradiation conditions cause laser-induced amorphization on both samples. Each pixel of the acquired hyperspectral Ψ–Δ maps contains an ellipsometric spectrum, i.e., the measured values of Ψ and Δ for 59 different wavelengths of the probing beam, equidistantly spaced in the range from 370 to 950 nm. Pixel by pixel, each of these spectra was then fitted by a computational thin-film multi-layer model using the 2 × 2 transfer matrix calculus for stratified isotropic media (see, for example, [62]) and a least-squares non-linear regression algorithm (Levenberg–Marquardt) as provided by the *Accurion EP4Model* software (Vers. 19.8.3, Accurion GmbH, Göttingen, Germany). The approach assumed a two-layer model (substrate/layer 1/layer 2/ambient) consisting of c-Si (bulk)/a-Si(d_{am})/a-SiO_2(d_{ox})/air. The thickness of the amorphous silicon layer (d_{am}) and that of the covering amorphous silica layer (d_{ox}) were taken as fit parameters, while the wavelength-dependent optical constants of all different materials were taken from a material database originally provided by the former company Sopra S.A. (France) [63]. Additionally, an offset of the local angle of incidence (AOI) was used as fit parameter to consider changes in the direction of the probing light by the buried a-Si/c-Si interface. Interfacial roughness effects were neglected in the ellipsometric modeling as inferred from the previous AFM measurements. As a result of the fit procedure, the single-pixel values of the fit parameters were converted into parameter maps, i.e., maps of the thickness for the amorphous silicon and silica layers.

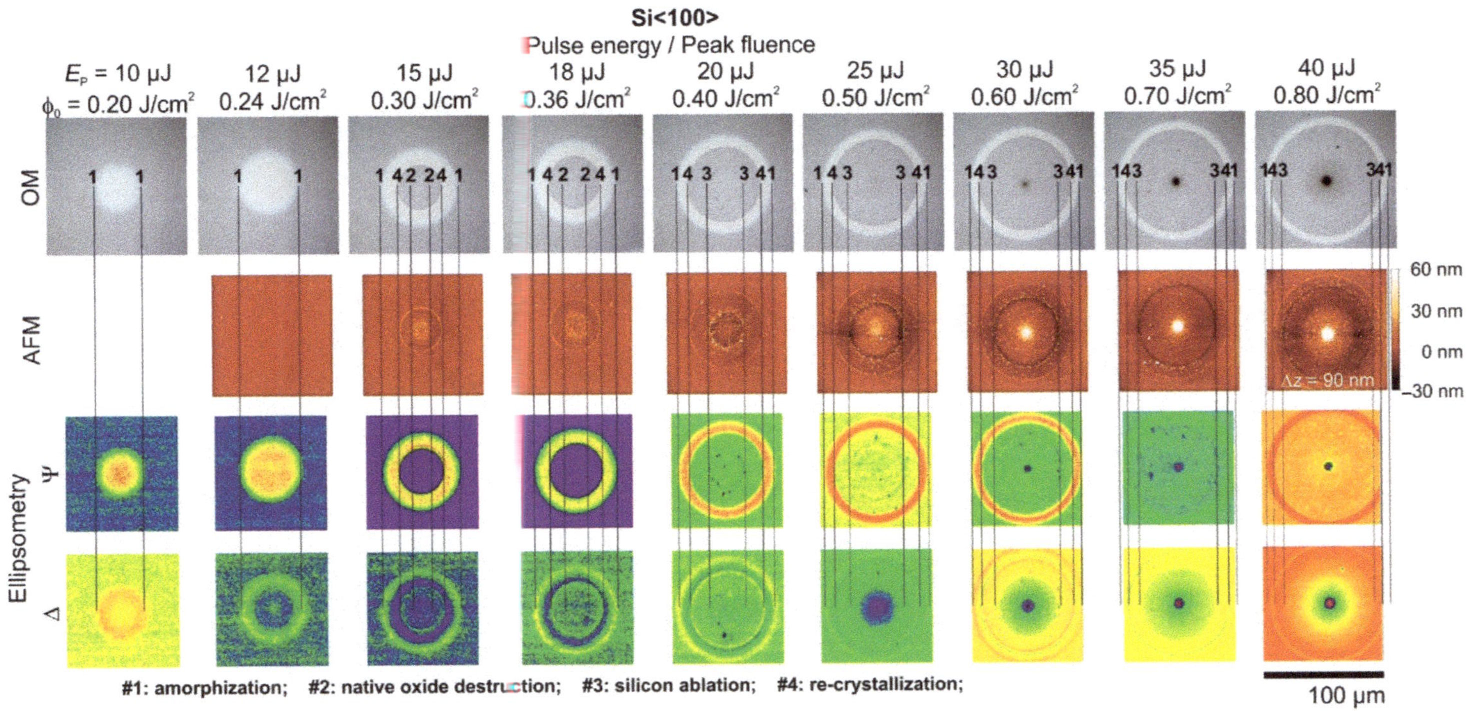

Figure 3. Comparison of brightfield optical microscopy (OM) images, atomic force microscopy (AFM) images, and corresponding spatial maps of the ellipsometric quantities Ψ and Δ (taken at 637 nm wavelength) for a series of nine single fs-laser (λ~790 nm, τ = 30 fs) pulse-irradiated spots on a Si<100> wafer. The fs-laser pulse energy E_p varies between 10 µJ and 40 µJ among the spots from left to right, corresponding to peak laser fluences between ϕ_0 = 0.20 and 0.80 J/cm^2. The AFM images are provided in a common color scale, encoding height variations Δz of −30 to +60 nm. The vertical (numbered) line sets mark the extent of characteristic surface features (for details see the text at the bottom of the figure). A common lateral scale bar is provided in the lower right corner.

Figure 4 compares the results of the SIE-based evaluation of the amorphous silicon layer thickness $d_{am}(x,y)$ for the four selected fs-laser-irradiated spots at the two laser pulse energies and for the two different wafer materials. The images share common lateral scale bars. The amorphous silicon layer thickness d_{am} is encoded in a joint linear grayscale with brighter values representing larger thickness values up to 60 nm. The enhanced tendency for laser-induced amorphization for the <111> crystal orientation manifests in larger amorphized spot areas and significantly larger amorphous layer thicknesses when compared to the <100> crystal orientation (compare Figure 4a,b with Figure 4c,d). Moreover, for the spot irradiated at E_p = 12 µJ (ϕ_0 = 0.24 J/cm^2) at the Si<100> wafer even a local minimum of d_{am} can be seen in the center (Figure 4d) as a precursor to the re-crystallization occurring at somewhat larger peak fluences exceeding ϕ_{cr}(Si<100>) = 0.25 J/cm^2.

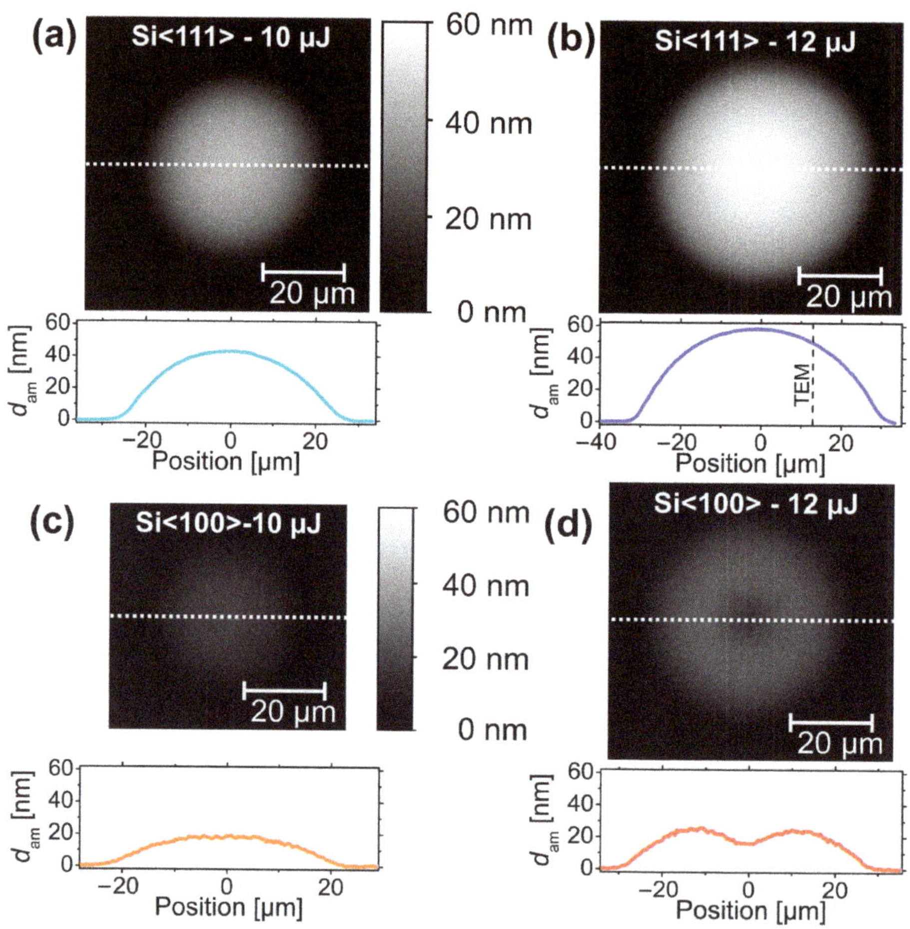

Figure 4. Maps of the amorphous silicon layer thickness (d_{am}) as determined by spectroscopic imaging ellipsometry (SIE) at four different fs-laser-irradiated spots on Si<111> (**a**,**b**) and Si<100> (**c**,**d**) at two laser pulse energies of 10 µJ (ϕ_0 = 0.20 J/cm^2; (**a**,**c**)) or 12 µJ (ϕ_0 = 0.24 J/cm^2; (**b**,**d**)). The maps have a common scale bar provided in (**a**,**c**) and are encoded by a joint linear grayscale that indicates the thickness. Below each map, a corresponding horizontal cross-section (location indicated by a white dashed line) of the a-Si layer thickness is drawn. The vertical black dashed line in (**b**) indicates the position of the TEM/STEM measurements as marked by the red square in Figure 1.

The simultaneous fit of the amorphous silica (SiO_2) cover layer yielded an almost constant thickness of d_{ox}~3 nm to 5 nm inside and ~2 nm to 3 nm outside the laser-amorphized regions for each of the examined SIE maps. This is exemplified in Figure 5 visualizing the modeled spatial variation of the silicon oxide layer thickness for spots on Si<111> irradiated by single pulses of E_p = 12 μJ/ϕ_0 = 0.24 J/cm^2 (a, left) and E_p = 15 μJ/ϕ_0 = 0.30 J/cm^2 (b, right).

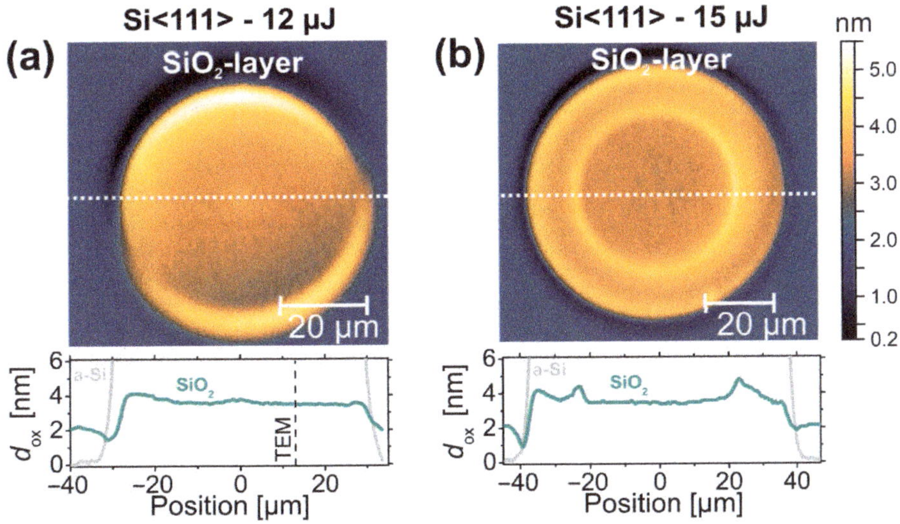

Figure 5. Top: maps of the silicon oxide layer thickness (d_{ox}) as determined by SIE at the surface spots irradiated on Si<111> by a single laser pulse of (**a**) 12 μJ (ϕ_0 = 0.24 J/cm^2) and (**b**) 15 μJ (ϕ_0 = 0.30 J/cm^2); bottom: horizontal cross-sections (location indicated by a white dashed line) of the oxide (SiO_2) layer thickness (dark cyan curves) along with the data of the a-Si layer thickness (gray curves) for comparison. The vertical black dashed line in (**a**) indicates the position of the TEM/STEM measurements as marked by the red square in Figure 1. The thickness maps share a common color scale provided in (b). Note the different image sizes.

The ring-shaped local maxima/minima in the upper and lower parts of the two maps arise from the ellipsometric imaging geometry performed at non-normal incidence here (AOI = 55°). In view of a typical native oxide layer thickness, the fitted values of d_{ox}~2 nm outside the laser spot appear reasonable. Comparing the cross-sections visualized by the dark cyan (SiO_2) and gray (a-Si) curves assembled in the bottom parts of Figure 5a,b indicates that the fs-laser-induced amorphization is additionally accompanied by a local increase of the thickness of the covering oxide layer of ~2 nm here. At the peak fluence ϕ_0 = 0.24 J/cm^2 below the threshold of the laser-induced destruction of the native oxide layer (ϕ_{annu} = 0.26 J/cm^2), a step-like oxide layer profile can be seen in Figure 5a. Particularly at the location of the TEM/STEM analyses (marked by the black dashed vertical line), the SIE-based modeling predicts a thickness of ~3.5 nm. At the increased peak fluence ϕ_0 = 0.30 J/cm^2, i.e., above ϕ_{annu}, a central disc of slightly reduced oxide layer thickness is additionally visible in Figure 5b.

These observations of the oxide layer profiles further support the scenario of the local destruction of the native oxide layer at peak fluences $\phi_0 \geq \phi_{annu}$. Since the wafer surface is left at high temperatures $T > T_{ev}$(a-SiO_2) ~2503 K in ambient air after the laser irradiation, the laser-ablated silicon oxide re-grows in the center of the irradiated spot ($\phi_{abl} > \phi \geq \phi_{annu}$) at a transiently increased rate compared to the native oxide of the non-irradiated wafer. In contrast, in the outer annular region, where $\phi_{am} \leq \phi < \phi_{annu}$, the laser-induced heating of the silicon increased the thickness of the covering oxide layer by ~2 nm to 3 nm here. Note that the local maxima of d_{ox} observed in the bottom part of Figure 5b at the positions where ϕ_{annu} is locally reached (±22 µm in Figure 5b) are additionally affected by optical scattering effects imposed by the fine topographic rim previously seen in the AFM/OM data of Figure 2.

3.2. Layer Analysis by Transmission Electron Microscopy (TEM)

In order to verify assumptions made in the SIE data modeling and to verify the corresponding amorphous layer thickness results experimentally, cross-sectional TEM/STEM analyses were performed on the spot with the largest a-Si thickness, i.e., for Si<111> irradiated at E_p = 12 µJ (ϕ_0 = 0.24 J/cm^2). Figure 6a presents a TEM cross-section through the lamella prepared by FIB at the position marked by the red square in Figure 1. Below the poly-crystalline Pt protection layer, an amorphous a-Si layer of almost constant thickness (d_{am}~42 nm to 44 nm) was measured at this specific position on top of the crystalline silicon material of the substrate (c-Si), where the laser fluence in the Gaussian beam dropped to a local value of ϕ_0~0.22 J/cm^2 (estimated by Equation (1)). Higher magnifications of the a-Si/c-Si interface are presented in Figure 6c,d, revealing a transition zone with an extent of ~3.9 nm (see Figure 6c) and no indications of crystal defects formed upon re-solidification, e.g., twins or stacking faults (see Figure 6d). Such a low roughness of the a-Si/c-Si interface justifies the previously made assumption of flat interfaces in the ellipsometry layer model discussed in Section 3.1. The different structural order is demonstrated by the two fast Fourier transforms shown as insets in Figure 6c. The two-dimensional Fourier transforms (2D-FTs) were attained from high-resolution TEM images of the a-Si and c-Si regions.

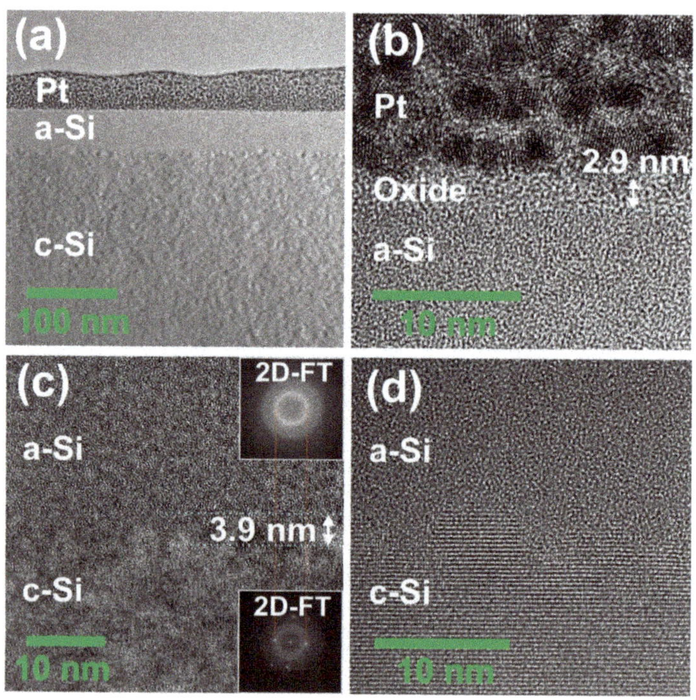

Figure 6. TEM images of an fs-laser-amorphized spot in cross-section (E_p = 12 µJ/ϕ_0 = 0.24 J/cm^2) on c-Si<111> taken at the position marked by the red square in Figure 1. (**a**) Overview; (**b**) high-resolution image of native oxide layer between the Pt capping layer and the a-Si layer; (**c**,**d**) high-resolution images of the a-Si/c-Si interface. Note the different magnifications. The insets in (**c**) are two-dimensional fast Fourier transforms (2D-FTs) of high-resolution transmission electron microscopy (HRTEM) images of the a-Si and c-Si regions, respectively.

Additionally, the lamella was investigated by STEM and EDX mapping for recording cross-sectional elemental maps of the chemical elements platinum (Pt), silicon (Si), and oxygen (O). Dopant elements were not detected due to their low concentration. In Figure 7, these elemental maps (512 × 512 pixels, Figure 7b–d) are compared to the corresponding STEM image as separate reference (Figure 7a).

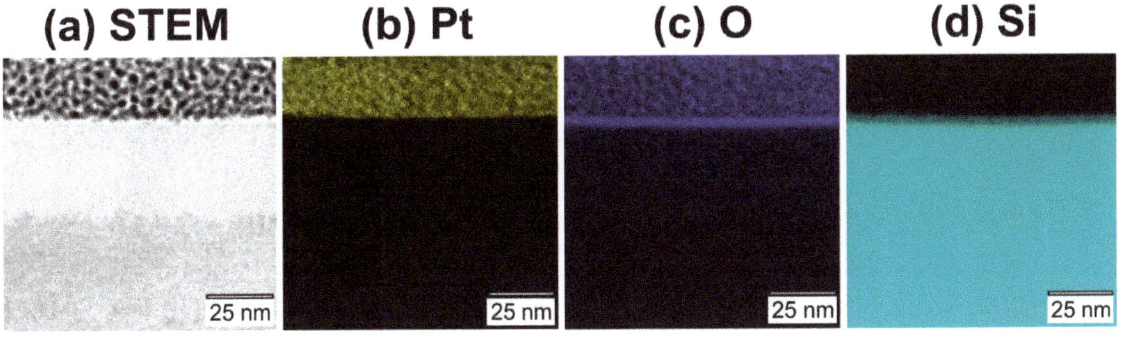

Figure 7. STEM image (**a**) and elemental energy dispersive X-ray spectroscopy (STEM-EDX) maps of platinum (Pt, yellow, (**b**)), oxygen (O, blue, (**c**)), silicon (Si, cyan, (**d**)).

The elemental maps confirm the previously made assignment of the cross-sectional layer structure and demonstrate homogeneous distributions of the elements Pt (see Figure 7b), O (see Figure 7c), and Si (see Figure 7d) within their respective regions. For a complementary quantification of the layer thicknesses of the silicon oxide and the a-Si layers with an improved signal-to-noise ratio, the EDX mapping data were binned across a width of ~53 nm in the direction parallel to the layer interfaces (see Figure 8a). The corresponding accumulated EDX counts of Pt, O, and Si are plotted in Figure 8b versus the position in the z-direction (depth), with the origin ($z = 0$) located at the Pt–sample interface.

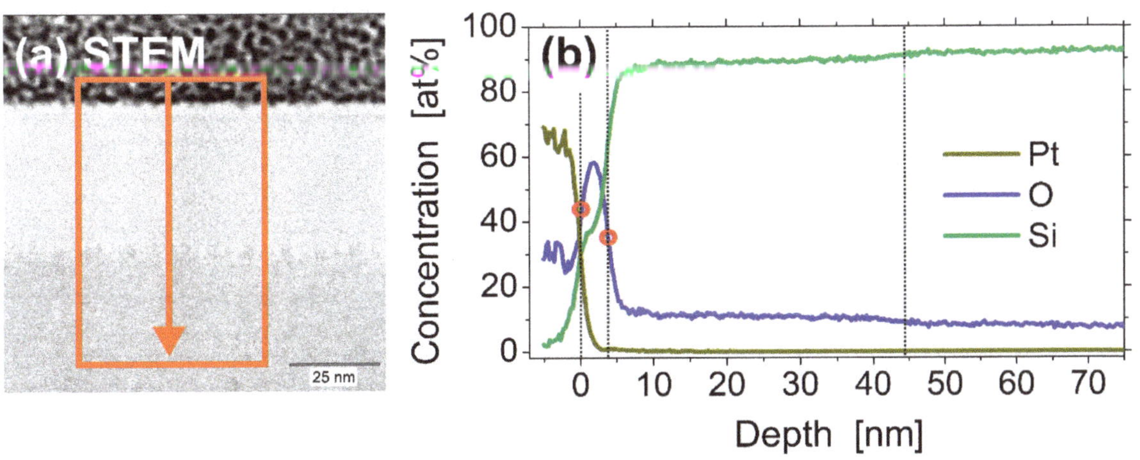

Figure 8. STEM image (**a**) and EDX-based depth profiles (**b**) of the relative atomic concentrations of platinum (Pt, olive green), oxygen (O, blue), silicon (Si, bright green). The data are obtained by binning over the region of interest (ROI) indicated in (**a**) as an orange rectangle. The red circles in (**b**) mark the half-maximum positions of the oxide layer interfaces. The vertical dotted lines indicate the nominal positions of the layer interfaces.

The Pt-signal of the capping layer exhibits a sharp transition to the underlying native oxide silicon layer. No significant mixing of Pt with the silicon oxide can be detected here. The concentration curve of the oxygen exhibits a peak at a depth of ~1.8 nm and further confirms the information obtained by the TEM imaging. For calculation of the thickness of the oxide layer, a 50% criterion was applied. Evaluating the difference of the half-maximum positions (marked by red circles) of the two interfaces of the oxide layer results in an averaged thickness of ~3.8 nm here (Figure 8b, blue curve). This value well agrees with the silicon oxide layer thickness of 3.5 nm obtained from Figure 5 in the SIE-based approach discussed in Section 3.1.

Interestingly, the oxygen signal does not completely vanish in regions associated with the silicon: within the amorphous silicon layer, a concentration around ~11 at% of O was detected over a depth of d_{am} ~44 nm, before saturating at a level of ~8 at% in the region of single-crystalline silicon (Figure 8b, blue curve). Different effects may contribute to this finding. First, during the period of time in the liquid state (melt duration) of the silicon (a few nanoseconds only for the given laser irradiation conditions [34]), some oxygen may dissolve in the liquid silicon and remain in the material after re-solidification. Second, after the preparation of the FIB lamella and during its storage and transfer to the TEM device, a thin native oxide layer will have formed at the two surfaces of the lamella, before being investigated in TEM/STEM. Local difference between the a-Si and c-Si regions may then be caused by the slightly different surface oxidation conditions at the altered silicon lattice structure. In view of the short melt duration and the rather homogeneous distribution of O across the entire depth of the a-Si layer, the second scenario appears to be more likely here.

4. Discussion

In order to elucidate more details of the fs-laser-induced amorphization and particularly to study its fluence dependence, the data of the amorphous silicon layer obtained by SIE (Section 3.1) were further analyzed. On basis of Equation (1), for all four laser-irradiated spots displayed in Figure 4, each image pixel location (x,y) was associated with a local fluence value $\phi(r = \sqrt{(x^2 + y^2)})$. Figure 9 semi-logarithmically re-plots the resulting amorphous silicon layer thickness profiles d_{am} as a function of the local laser fluence ϕ for horizontal cross-sections through the center of the spots displayed in a local fluence range between 0.08 and 0.3 J/cm^2. For quantitative comparison, the thickness of the amorphous layer measured by TEM on Si<111> was added as an experimental data point (black full square) at its local fluence value calculated by Equation (1) from the position indicated in Figure 1. At that local fluence of ϕ_0 ~0.22 J/cm^2, the a-Si thickness value of ~50 nm predicted by the SIE curve deviates by ~10% to 15% from that quantified by TEM—a reasonably good agreement in view of the assumptions made in the SIE modeling and the complexity of the experiments involved. Supposedly, the deviation mainly arises from minor differences of the optical constants of the fs-laser-amorphized silicon and the covering silicon oxide to the literature values applied here for the SIE modeling [63] and from the small surface roughness that was not considered by the optical model.

Obvious differences can be seen between the data sets of the Si<111> and Si<100> wafer materials. Most strikingly, the amorphous layer thickness (slope) is significantly larger for Si<111>, and two different thresholds of ϕ_{am}<111> = 0.13 J/cm^2 and ϕ_{am}<100> = 0.15 J/cm^2 can be seen for the onset of superficial amorphization (compare the set of blue/cyan data points with the red/orange ones in Figure 9). Both findings (slopes, thresholds) reflect the reduced amorphization tendency of Si<100> arising from its larger critical interfacial velocity value (see the discussion in Section 3). Importantly, close to the amorphization threshold fluence, all curves exhibit a linear scaling in this data representation. This finding confirms a functional dependence in the form of d_{am}~$\ln(\phi/\phi_{am})$ that was previously assumed already in [42]. Moreover, using that relation together with the radial fluence profile $\phi = \phi(x,y)$ presented in Equation (1), it becomes clear that the amorphous layer thickness profiles shown in Figure 4a,c exhibit in a good approximation a parabolic thickness profile in the form $d_{am}(x,y)$~$[\ln(\phi_0/\phi_{am}) - 2(x^2+y^2)/w_0{}^2]$ [42]. For local laser fluences exceeding ~0.2 J/cm^2, some deviations from this simple scaling law of d_{am}~ln(ϕ/ϕ_{am}) are notable in Figure 9. While for the Si<111> a moderate thickness saturation occurs, for the Si<100> a thickness reduction can be seen in the fluence range between 0.22 and 0.24 J/cm^2. At even larger fluences ($\phi > \phi_{cr}$) re-crystallization sets in for the Si<100> (see Figure 3), resulting in d_{am}~0 nm.

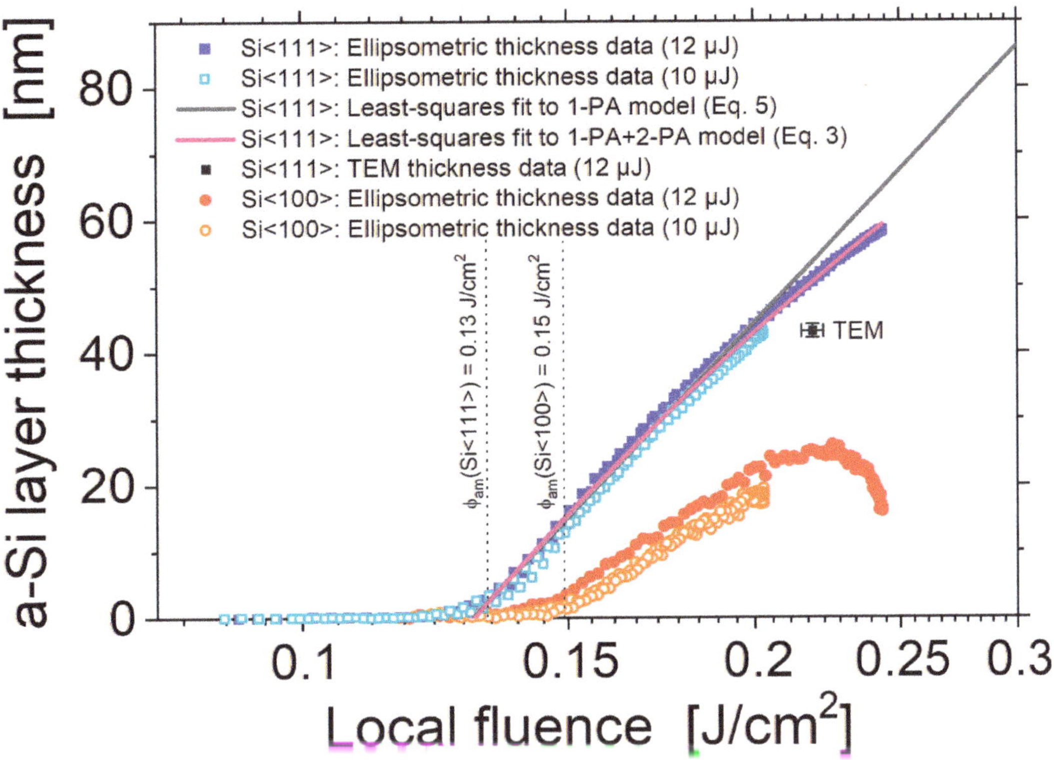

Figure 9. Amorphous layer thickness d_{am} versus local laser fluence ϕ. The data points are obtained from SIE measurements at the four different fs-laser-irradiated spots analyzed previously in Figure 4 for Si<111> (blue full squares (12 μJ) and cyan open squares (10 μJ)) and for Si<100> (red full circles (12 μJ) and open orange circles (10 μJ)). A quantitative measurement by TEM is indicated as a single black square with its respective uncertainties. The two vertical dashed lines indicate the corresponding amorphization thresholds of both silicon materials as previously deduced by OM. The solid pink and solid gray lines are least-squares fits to Equations (3) and (5), respectively.

Some further conclusions can be drawn from a mathematical analysis of the absorption processes of the laser radiation occurring in the silicon upon ultrashort-pulse irradiation. For simplicity, the analysis is performed at the center of the laser spot, neglecting the Gaussian beam profile here. The absorption of the optical radiation at ~800 nm wavelength in crystalline silicon is promoted either via linear absorption (1-PA) processes (via indirect interband transitions or via free-carrier absorption (FCA) through already existent carriers in the conduction band) or via direct two-photon absorption (2-PA). Neglecting diffusion and recombination processes during the optical excitation, the intensity distribution $I(z)$ of the laser beam propagating inside the silicon along the z-direction perpendicular to the surface can be described by a one-dimensional ordinary differential equation [25,57]:

$$\frac{dI(z,t)}{dz} = -[\alpha_0 + \alpha_{fca}(z,t) + \beta \cdot I(z,t)] \cdot I(z,t) \tag{2}$$

α_0 and β denote the linear and two-photon interband absorption coefficients, respectively. The (linear) intraband free-carrier absorption is included via coefficient $\alpha_{fca}(z,t)$. Since the FCA depends linearly on the number of available (laser-induced) carriers in the conduction band, the spatial attenuation of the laser intensity with z is strongly affected by the transient electron density and can strongly change during the fs-laser pulse and with depth [35].

Given the depth- and time-dependence of α_{fca}, in general, the differential equation must be solved numerically, which is beyond the scope of this work. However, it is instructive to analyze the limiting solutions of Equation (2); upon neglecting the FCA and assuming solely 1-PA and 2-PA, it can be solved analytically via separation of the variables along with the boundary condition that the intensity at the surface $I(z = 0) = I_0$ is reduced to a level of $I(d_m) = I_{th,m}$ at the depth d_m where the melting threshold $I_{th,m}$ is reached. The solution can then be re-written as the following equation for the melt depth when relating the intensity in the solid to the incident peak fluence ($I_0 = (1-R)\phi_0/\tau$) [64].

$$d_m = \frac{1}{\alpha_0} \cdot \ln\left(\frac{\left[\frac{\alpha_0}{\phi_{th,m}} + \frac{\beta(1-R)}{\tau} \right] \cdot \phi}{\alpha_0 + \frac{\beta(1-R)}{\tau} \cdot \phi} \right) \tag{3}$$

with R being the surface reflectivity at the laser wavelength, τ the laser pulse duration, and $\phi_{th,m}$ the melting threshold (not to be confused with the amorphization threshold ϕ_{am} here). For dominating 2-PA ($\alpha_0 = 0$), the melt depth reads [65]

$$d_m = \frac{\tau}{\beta(1-R)} \cdot \left(\frac{1}{\phi_{th,m}} - \frac{1}{\phi} \right) \tag{4}$$

while for dominating 1-PA ($\beta = 0$), the melt depth simplifies to

$$d_m = \frac{1}{\alpha_0} \cdot \ln\left(\frac{\phi}{\phi_{th,m}} \right) \tag{5}$$

Note that for pure 2-PA at large fluences d_m saturates at a constant value (see Equation (4)). Least-squares fits were performed using the analytical solutions of Equations (3) and (5) to the experimental data for the irradiation of Si<111> at $E_p = 12$ μJ ($\phi_0 = 0.24$ J/cm^2) presented in Figure 9. The surface reflectivity of crystalline silicon was assumed to be constant during the laser pulse duration of $\tau = 30$ fs and accounts to $R = 0.33$ for 790 nm radiation at normal incidence [40]. α_0 and β were chosen as free fit parameters, while the melting threshold was assumed to coincide with the amorphization threshold ($\phi_{th,m} = \phi_{am}$). The values of $\alpha_{0,fit} = 4.38 \times 10^4$ cm^{-1} and $\beta_{fit} = 15.7$ cm/GW obtained from the least-squares fits to Equation (3) strongly deviate from the literature values (α_0~1.1×10^3 cm^{-1} [40] and β~6.8 cm/GW [66]), indicating that the FCA makes a significant contribution to a reduction of the fs-laser-induced melt depth in our experiments and that Equation (3) cannot be applied here. This becomes also obvious when comparing the (small signal) optical penetration depth $1/\alpha_0(790\text{ nm}) = 9.95$ μm with the value $1/\alpha_{0,fit} = 0.10$ μm deduced from the least-squares fit to Equation (5) that is deviating by two orders of magnitude here. Note that the latter value is consistent with the melt depths reported for silicon when solving the full Equation (2) numerically in combination with a carrier density rate equation, a two-temperature model (TTM) and molecular dynamics (MD) simulations for somewhat longer Ti:Sapphire pulses of $\tau = 130$ fs [35] and the maximum melt depth values obtained in time-resolved experiments [67].

Nevertheless, another important conclusion can be drawn from the remarkably different slopes of the experimental data in Figure 9 observed for Si<111> and Si<100> at local fluences close to the amorphization thresholds. For Si<100> the slope value is reduced by a factor of ~2 compared to the Si<111>. Since the coupling of the optical pulse energy into the silicon is not expected to depend significantly on the lattice orientation (resulting in the same melt depth d_m), it is inferred here that the approximately two-times-smaller amorphization layer thicknesses dam must arise from differences in the re-solidification process, caused by the fact that the (larger) critical velocity of amorphization is reached later for Si<100> compared to Si<111>. In other words, at least for the Si<100> the melt depth is significantly larger than the amorphous layer thickness $[d_{\mathrm{m}}(\mathrm{Si}<100>) >> d_{\mathrm{am}}(\mathrm{Si}<100>)]$. Nevertheless, as proven by the experimental data in Figure 9, a scaling law $d_{\mathrm{am}} = d_0 \times \ln(\phi/\phi_{\mathrm{am}})$ remains valid under these conditions, indicating that a constant fraction of the maximum melt depth solidifies as amorphous top-layer. In contrast, for the Si<111> no indications were found by TEM/STEM that the melt depth may be different from the amorphous layer thickness—although it cannot completely be ruled out here if a perfectly epitaxial re-growth occurs.

Table 1 compiles the different threshold fluences (ϕ_{am}, ϕ_{annu}, ϕ_{abl}, ϕ_{cr}) analyzed in this work along with a comparison to other relevant literature values.

Table 1. Characteristic threshold fluence for the irradiation of single-crystalline silicon in air or vacuum by single Ti:Sapphire fs-laser pulses (τ = 30 fs to 150 fs, λ = 780 nm to 800 nm, normal incidence); specific experimental conditions are indicated as footnotes. Abbreviations: AFM: atomic force microscopy, CSLM: confocal scanning laser microscopy, OM: optical microscopy, OES: optical emission spectroscopy, μ-RS: micro-Raman spectroscopy, SEM: scanning electron microscopy, SIE: spectroscopic imaging ellipsometry, TEM: transmission electron microscopy.

Threshold	J/cm^2	Effect	Detection Methods	Reference
ϕ_{am} Si<111>	0.13 ^{1} 0.27 ^{2}	Melting and amorphization	AFM, OM, SIE, TEM AFM, CSLM, OM, μ-RS	This work [40]
Si<100>	0.15 ^{1} ~0.15 ^{2}		AFM, OM, SIE OM	This work [68]
ϕ_{annu} Si<111>	0.26 ^{1} 0.41 ^{2}	Destruction of the native oxide layer	AFM, OM AFM, CSLM, OM, μ-RS	This work [40]
Si<100>	0.29 ^{1}		AFM, OM	This work
ϕ_{abl} Si<111>	0.39 ^{1} 0.52 ^{2}	Ablation	OM, AFM AFM, CSLM, OM, μ-RS	This work [40]
Si<100>	0.37 ^{1} ~0.3–0.4 ^{2} ~0.3 ^{3}		AFM, OM AFM, OES AFM, SEM, TEM	This work [69,70] [68]
ϕ_{cr} Si<111>	0.68 ^{1} 0.58 ^{2}	Re-crystallization	AFM, OM, SIE AFM, CSLM, OM, μ-RS	This work [40]
Si<100>	0.25 ^{1}		AFM, OM, SIE	This work

Pulse durations: ^{1} 30 fs. ^{2} 150 fs. ^{3} 130 fs.

5. Conclusions

Single near-infrared fs-pulse laser-induced amorphization and re-crystallization of single-crystalline silicon (<111> and <100>) were studied with unprecedented resolution in a multi-method approach involving top-view optical microscopy (OM), spectroscopic imaging ellipsometry (SIE), atomic force microscopy (AFM), cross-sectional-view high-resolution transmission electron microscopy (HRTEM), and imaging energy dispersive X-ray spectroscopy (EDX). For laser fluences below the ablation threshold in the melting regime, significant differences of the thickness of the final amorphous surface layer were found among the two wafer materials. A multi-spectral all-optical approach based on SIE was developed allowing to retrieve spatially resolved thickness profiles with nanometric precision in a non-destructive manner. While for a radially Gaussian laser beam irradiating Si<111> at fluences up to 0.2 J/cm^2 some parabolic amorphous layer profiles with maximum thicknesses of ~50 nm were determined, the corresponding maximum layer thickness for Si<100> was about half of this value at the same local fluence. The fs-laser generated amorphous silicon layer exhibited a very low interfacial roughness amplitude (~4 nm) to the underlying single-crystalline <111> substrate material. Neither stacking faults nor any traces of twinning were found by high-resolution TEM. The superficial oxide layer was analyzed by high-resolution EDX chemical mapping and depth profiling and indicated a thickness of ~3.5 nm, in agreement with the SIE-based thickness analysis. Moreover, the spectroscopic imaging ellipsometry was capable of visualizing a subtle laser-induced oxide thickness increase of ~2 nm in the laser-amorphized regions here. Mathematical modeling of the melt layer thickness on the basis of several different absorption processes (1-PA, 2-PA, FCA) underlined the relevance of free-carrier absorption processes in the fs-laser-induced melting of silicon. Our results support a scenario that for Si<111> the fs-laser-induced melt layer transfers completely into amorphous material, while for Si<100> only an upper part of the melt pool finally turns amorphous at the end of the solidification process when a critical interfacial velocity is exceeded. Moreover, laser-fluence-dependent re-crystallization effects can manifest in the center of the irradiated spots, i.e., for peak fluences exceeding ~0.25 J/cm^2 for Si<100> and 0.68 J/cm^2 for Si<111>, respectively. Our results provide evidence that spectroscopic imaging ellipsometry is capable of a fast and precise characterization of nanometer-thick laser-induced structural and chemical surface modifications.

Author Contributions: Conceptualization, C.F., D.F., A.U. and J.B.; methodology, C.F., D.F., K.F., M.D., M.S., S.S., A.H., J.K., M.R., U.B., A.U. and J.B.; software, C.F., D.F. and M.D.; validation, C.F., D.F., K.F., M.D., M.S., S.S., A.H., J.K., M.R., U.B., A.U. and J.B.; formal analysis, C.F., D.F., M.D., M.S., A.U. and J.B.; investigation, C.F., D.F., K.F., M.D., M.S., A.U. and J.B.; resources, M.D., S.S., M.R., U.B., J.K., A.U. and J.B.; data curation, C.F., D.F., M.D., A.U. and J.B.; writing—original draft preparation, J.B.; writing—review and editing, C.F., D.F., K.F., M.D., M.S., S.S., A.H., J.K., M.R., U.B., A.U. and J.B.; visualization, C.F., D.F., K.F., A.U. and J.B.; supervision, J.B.; project administration, S.S., A.H., U.B., J.K., A.U. and J.B.; funding acquisition, C.F., M.D., S.S., U.B., M.R., A.U. and J.B. All authors have read and agreed to the published version of the manuscript.

Funding: C.F. acknowledges the support from the European Commission through the Marie Curie Individual Fellowship—Global grant No. 844977 and funding from the Horizon 2020 CellFreeImplant European project. D.F., M.D., S.S., A.H. and U.B. gratefully acknowledge the funding from the German Central Innovation Program (AiF-ZIM) under grants No. ZF4044219AB7 and ZF4460401AB7. K.F., M.R. and A.U. acknowledge support by the German Research Foundation (grant Nos. UN 341/3-1 and Inst 275/391-1). J.B. acknowledges the projects CellFreeImplant and LaserImplant. These two projects have received funding from the European Union's Horizon 2020 research and innovation programme under grant agreements No. 800832 (CellFreeImplant) and No. 951730 (LaserImplant).

Institutional Review Board Statement: Not applicable.

Informed Consent Statement: Not applicable.

Data Availability Statement: The data presented in this study are available on request from the corresponding author.

Conflicts of Interest: The authors declare no conflict of interest. The funders had no role in the design of the study; in the collection, analyses, or interpretation of data; in the writing of the manuscript, or in the decision to publish the results.

References

1. Belaforte, D.A. The global market for industrial laser processing. *Photonics Views* **2020**, *17*, 35–37. [CrossRef]
2. Bonse, J.; Lasagni, A.F. Laser micro- and nano-material processing—part 1. *Adv. Opt. Technol.* **2020**, *9*, 7–9. [CrossRef]
3. Bäuerle, D. *Laser Processing and Chemistry*, 4th ed.; Springer: Berlin, Germany, 2011. [CrossRef]
4. Bonse, J.; Sturm, H.; Schmidt, D.; Kautek, W. Chemical, morphological and accumulation phenomena in ultrashort-pulse laser ablation of TiN in air. *Appl. Phys. A* **2000**, *71*, 657–665. [CrossRef]

5. Yen, R.; Liu, J.M.; Kurz, H.; Bloembergen, N. Space-time resolved reflectivity measurements of picosecond laser-pulse induced phase transitions in (111) silicon surface layers. *Appl. Phys. A* **1982**, *27*, 153–160. [CrossRef]
6. Bonse, J.; Baudach, S.; Krüger, J.; Kautek, W.; Lenzner, M. Femtosecond laser ablation of silicon—Modification thresholds and morphology. *Appl. Phys. A* **2000**, *71*, 19–25. [CrossRef]
7. van Houten, H.; Leibbrandt, W. Optical phase change recording. *Commun. Acm* **2000**, *43*, 64–71. [CrossRef]
8. Siegel, J.; Schropp, A.; Solis, J.; Afonso, C.N.; Wuttig, M. Rewritable phase-change optical recording in films induced by picosecond laser pulses. *Appl. Phys. Lett.* **2004**, *84*, 2250–2252. [CrossRef]
9. Wiggins, S.M.; Bonse, J.; Solis, J.; Afonso, C.N.; Sokolowski-Tinten, K.; Temnov, V.V.; Zhou, P.; von der Linde, D. The influence of wavelength on phase transformations induced by picosecond and femtosecond laser pulses in GeSb thin films. *J. Appl. Phys.* **2005**, *98*, 113518. [CrossRef]
10. Wuttig, M.; Yamada, N. Phase-change materials for rewriteable data storage. *Nat. Mat.* **2007**, *6*, 824–832. [CrossRef] [PubMed]
11. Chelikowsky, J. Silicon in all its forms. *MRS Bull.* **2002**, *27*, 951–960. [CrossRef]
12. Shtyrkov, E.I.; Khaibullin, I.B.; Zharipov, M.M.; Galyatudinov, M.F.; Bayatzitov, R.M. Local laser annealing of implantation doped semiconductor layers. *Sov. Phys. Semicond.* **1976**, *9*, 1309–1310.
13. Robinson, A.L. Femtosecond laser annealing of silicon. *Science* **1984**, *226*, 329–330. [CrossRef]
14. Cullis, A.G.; Chew, N.G.; Webber, H.C.; Smith, D.J. Orientation dependence of high speed silicon crystal growth from the melt. *J. Cryst. Growth* **1984**, *68*, 624–638. [CrossRef]
15. Shank, C.V.; Yen, R.; Hirlimann, C. Time-resolved reflectivity measurements of femtosecond-optical-pulse-induced phase transition in silicon. *Phys. Rev. Lett.* **1983**, *50*, 454–457. [CrossRef]
16. Stampfli, P.; Bennemann, K.H. Theory for the instability of the diamond structure of Si, Ge, and C induced by a dense electron-hole plasma. *Phys. Rev. B* **1990**, *42*, 7163–7173. [CrossRef] [PubMed]
17. Siegal, Y.; Glezer, E.M.; Huang, L.; Mazur, E. Laser-induced phase transitions in semiconductors. *Ann. Rev. Mater. Sci.* **1995**, *25*, 223–247. [CrossRef]
18. von der Linde, D.; Sokolowski-Tinten, K. The physical mechanisms of short-pulse laser ablation. *Appl. Surf. Sci.* **2000**, *154–155*, 1–10. [CrossRef]
19. Rousse, A.; Rischel, C.; Fourmaux, S.; Uschmann, I.; Sebban, S.; Grillon, G.; Balcou, P.; Förster, E.; Geindre, J.P.; Audebert, P.; et al. Non-thermal melting in semiconductors measured at femtosecond resolution. *Nature* **2001**, *410*, 65–68. [CrossRef]
20. Jeschke, H.O.; Garcia, M.E.; Lenzner, M.; Bonse, J.; Krüger, J.; Kautek, W. Laser ablation thresholds of silicon for different pulse durations: Theory and experiment. *Appl. Surf. Sci.* **2002**, *197–198*, 839–844. [CrossRef]
21. Lindenberg, A.M.; Larsson, J.; Sokolowski-Tinten, K.; Gaffney, K.J.; Blome, C.; Synnergren, O.; Sheppard, J.; Caleman, C.; MacPhee, A.G.; Weinstein, D.; et al. Atomic-scale visualization of inertial dynamics. *Science* **2005**, *308*, 392–395. [CrossRef]
22. Bonse, J.; Wiggins, S.M.; Solis, J. Dynamics of phase transitions induced by femtosecond laser pulse irradiation of indium phosphide. *Appl. Phys. A* **2005**, *80*, 243–248. [CrossRef]
23. Bonse, J.; Bachelier, G.; Siegel, J.; Solis, J. Time- and space-resolved dynamics of melting, ablation, and solidification phenomena induced by femtosecond laser pulses in germanium. *Phys. Rev. B* **2006**, *74*, 134106. [CrossRef]
24. Zier, T.; Zijlstra, E.S.; Garcia, M.E. Silicon before the bonds break. *Appl. Phys. A* **2014**, *117*, 1–5. [CrossRef]
25. Sokolowski-Tinten, K.; von der Linde, D. Generation of dense electron-hole plasmas in silicon. *Phys. Rev. B* **2000**, *61*, 2643–2650. [CrossRef]
26. Bonse, J.; Rosenfeld, A.; Krüger, J. Implications of transient changes of optical and surface properties of solids during femtosecond laser pulse irradiation to the formation of laser-induced periodic surface structures. *Appl. Surf. Sci.* **2011**, *257*, 5420–5423. [CrossRef]
27. von Allmen, M.; Blatter, A. *Laser-Beam Interactions with Materials*, 2nd ed.; Springer: Berlin/Heidelberg, Germany, 1995.
28. Lorazo, P.; Lewis, L.J.; Meunier, M. Thermodynamic pathways to melting, ablation, and solidification in absorbing solids under pulsed laser irradiation. *Phys. Rev. B* **2006**, *73*, 134108. [CrossRef]
29. Shugaev, M.V.; He, M.; Levy, Y.; Mazzi, A.; Miotello, A.; Bulgakova, N.M.; Zhigilei, L.V. Laser-Induced Thermal Processes: Heat Transfer, Generation of Stresses, Melting and Solidification, Vaporization, and Phase Explosion. In *Handbook of Laser Micro- and Nano-Engineering*; Sugioka, K., Ed.; Springer: Cham, Switzerland, 2020. [CrossRef]
30. Yater, J.A.; Thompson, M.O. Orientation dependence of laser amorphization of crystal Si. *Phys. Rev. Lett.* **1989**, *63*, 2088–2091. [CrossRef]
31. Thompson, M.O.; Mayer, J.W.; Cullis, A.G.; Webber, H.C.; Chew, N.G.; Poate, J.M.; Jacobson, D.C. Silicon melt, regrowth, and amorphization velocities during pulsed laser irradiation. *Phys. Rev. Lett.* **1983**, *50*, 896–899. [CrossRef]
32. Bucksbaum, P.H.; Bokor, J. Rapid melting and regrowth velocities in silicon heated by ultraviolet picosecond laser pulses. *Phys. Rev. Lett.* **1984**, *53*, 182–185. [CrossRef]
33. Bonse, J.; Wiggins, S.M.; Solis, J. Dynamics of femtosecond laser-induced melting and amorphization of indium phosphide. *J. Appl. Phys.* **2004**, *96*, 2352–2358. [CrossRef]
34. Garcia-Lechuga, M.; Puerto, D.; Fuentes-Edfuf, Y.; Solis, J.; Siegel, J. Ultrafast moving-spot microscopy: Birth and growth of laser-induced periodic surface structures. *ACS Photonics* **2016**, *3*, 1961–1967. [CrossRef]
35. Lipp, V.P.; Rethfeld, B.; Garcia, M.E.; Ivanov, D.S. Atomistic-continuum modeling of short laser pulse melting of Si targets. *Phys. Rev. B* **2014**, *90*, 134106. [CrossRef]

36. Gupta, M.C.; Zhigilei, L.V.; He, M.; Sun, Z. Generation and Annealing of Crystalline Disorder in Laser Processing of Silicon. In *Handbook of Laser Micro- and Nano-Engineering*; Sugioka, K., Ed.; Springer: Cham, Switzerland, 2020. [CrossRef]
37. Liu, P.L.; Yen, R.; Bloembergen, N.; Hodgson, R.T. Picosecond laser-induced melting and resolidification morphology on Si. *Appl. Phys. Lett.* **1979**, *34*, 864–866. [CrossRef]
38. Merkle, K.L.; Baumgart, H.; Uebbing, R.H.; Phillipp, F. Picosecond laser pulse irradiation of crystalline silicon. *Appl. Phys. Lett.* **1982**, *40*, 729–731. [CrossRef]
39. Smirl, A.L.; Boyd, I.W.; Boggess, T.F.; Moss, S.C.; van Driel, H.M. Structural changes produced in silicon by intense 1-μm ps pulses. *J. Appl. Phys.* **1986**, *60*, 1169–1182. [CrossRef]
40. Bonse, J.; Brzezinka, K.W.; Meixner, A.J. Modifying single-crystalline silicon by femtosecond laser pulses: An analysis by micro Raman spectroscopy, scanning laser microscopy and atomic force microscopy. *Appl. Surf. Sci.* **2004**, *221*, 215–230. [CrossRef]
41. Höche, T.; Ruthe, D.; Petsch, T. Low-fluence femtosecond-laser interaction with a Mo/Si multilayer stack. *Appl. Phys. A* **2004**, *79*, 961–963. [CrossRef]
42. Bonse, J. All-optical characterization of single femtosecond laser-pulse-induced amorphization in silicon. *Appl. Phys. A* **2006**, *84*, 63–66. [CrossRef]
43. Izawa, Y.; Izawa, Y.; Setsuhara, Y.; Hashida, M.; Fujita, M.; Sasaki, R.; Nagai, H.; Yoshida, M. Ultrathin amorphous Si layer formation by femtosecond laser pulse irradiation. *Appl. Phys. Lett.* **2007**, *90*, 044107. [CrossRef]
44. Crawford, T.H.R.; Yamanaka, J.; Botton, G.A.; Haugen, H.K. High-resolution observations of an amorphous layer and subsurface damage formed by femtosecond laser irradiation of silicon. *J. Appl. Phys.* **2008**, *103*, 053104. [CrossRef]
45. Bonse, J.; Rosenfeld, A.; Grebing, C.; Steinmeyer, G.; Mailman, N.; Botton, G.A.; Haugen, H.K. Ablation and structural changes induced in InP surfaces by single 10 fs laser pulses in air. *J. Appl. Phys.* **2009**, *106*, 074907. [CrossRef]
46. Werner, K.; Gruzdev, V.; Talisa, N.; Kafka, K.; Austin, D.; Liebig, C.M.; Chowdhury, E. Single-shot multi-stage damage and ablation of silicon by femtosecond mid-infrared laser pulses. *Sci. Rep.* **2019**, *9*, 19993. [CrossRef]
47. Zhang, X.; Zhang, L.; Mironov, S.; Xiao, R.; Guo, L.; Huang, T. Effect of crystallographic orientation on structural response of silicon to femtosecond laser irradiation. *Appl. Phys. A* **2021**, *127*, 196. [CrossRef]
48. Elliott, S.R. The structure of amorphous hydrogenated silicon and its alloys: A review. *Adv. Phys.* **1989**, *38*, 1–88. [CrossRef]
49. Agrawal, A.M.; Michel, J. Amorphous Silicon Microphotonics. In *Springer Handbook of Glass*; Musgraves, J.D., Hu, J., Calvez, L., Eds.; Springer-International Publishing: Cham, Switzerland, 2019. [CrossRef]
50. Liu, J.M. Simple technique for measurements of pulsed Gaussian-beam spot sizes. *Opt. Lett.* **1982**, *7*, 196–198. [CrossRef]
51. Funke, S.; Miller, B.; Parzinger, E.; Thiesen, P.; Holleitner, A.W.; Wurstbauer, U. Imaging spectroscopic ellipsometry of MoS_2. *J. Phys. Condens. Mat.* **2016**, *28*, 385301. [CrossRef]
52. Funke, S.; Wurstbauer, U.; Miller, B.; Matković, A.; Green, A.; Diebold, A.; Röling, C.; Thiesen, P.H. Spectroscopic imaging ellipsometry for automated search of flakes of mono- and n-Layers of 2D-materials. *Appl. Surf. Sci.* **2017**, *421*, 435–439. [CrossRef]
53. Braeuninger-Weimer, P.; Funke, S.; Wang, R.; Thiesen, P.; Tasche, D.; Viöl, W.; Hofmann, S. Fast, noncontact, wafer-scale, atomic layer resolved imaging of two-dimensional materials by ellipsometric contrast micrography. *ACS Nano* **2018**, *12*, 8555–8563. [CrossRef] [PubMed]
54. Duwe, M.; Quast, J.-H.; Schneider, S.; Fischer, D.; Beck, U. Thin-film metrology of tilted and curved surfaces by imaging Mueller-matrix ellipsometry. *J. Vac. Sci. Technol. B* **2019**, *37*, 062908. [CrossRef]
55. Freiberg, K.E.; Hanke, R.; Rettenmayr, M.; Undisz, A. Surface preserving targeted preparation using focused ion beam demonstrated by the example of oxide layers on Ni-Ti alloys. *Pract. Metallogr.* **2016**, *53*, 193–205. [CrossRef]
56. Liu, J.M.; Lopre, L.A.; Kurz, H.; Bloembergen, N. Phenomenology of picosecond heating and evaporation of silicon surfaces coated with SiO_2 layers. *Appl. Phys. A* **1984**, *34*, 25–29. [CrossRef]
57. Rämer, A.R.; Osmani, O.; Rethfeld, B. Laser damage in silicon: Energy absorption, relaxation, and transport. *J. Appl. Phys.* **2014**, *116*, 03508. [CrossRef]
58. Chiba, T.; Komura, R.; Mori, A. Formation of micropeak array on a silicon wafer. *Jpn. J. Appl. Phys.* **2000**, *39*, 4803–4810. [CrossRef]
59. Custer, J.S.; Thompson, M.O.; Jacobson, D.C.; Poate, J.M.; Roorda, S.; Sinke, W.C.; Spaepen, F. Density of amorphous silicon. *Appl. Phys. Lett.* **1994**, *64*, 437–439. [CrossRef]
60. Schwarz-Selinger, T.; Cahill, D.G.; Chen, S.-C.; Moon, S.-J.; Grigoropoulos, C.P. Micron-scale modifications of Si surface morphology by pulsed-laser texturing. *Phys. Rev. B* **2001**, *64*, 155323. [CrossRef]
61. Acosta-Zepeda, C.; Saavedra, P.; Bonse, J.; Haro-Poniatowski, E. Modeling of silicon surface topographies induced by single nanosecond laser pulse induced melt-flows. *J. Phys. D* **2019**, *125*, 175101. [CrossRef]
62. Tompkins, H.G.; Irene, E.A. *Handbook of Ellipsometry*; William Andrew Publishing, Springer: Norwich, UK, 2005.
63. Database of Optical Constants, Sopra, S.A. France. Available online: http://www.sspectra.com/sopra.html (accessed on 13 February 2021).
64. Krüger, J.; Kautek, W. The femtosecond pulse laser: A new tool for micromachining. *Las. Phys.* **1999**, *9*, 30–40.
65. Preuss, S.; Späth, M.; Zhang, Y.; Stuke, M. Time resolved dynamics of subpicosecond laser ablation. *Appl. Phys. Lett.* **1993**, *62*, 3049–3051. [CrossRef]
66. Sabbah, A.J.; Riffe, D.M. Femtosecond pump-probe reflectivity study of silicon carrier dynamics. *Phys. Rev. B* **2002**, *66*, 165217. [CrossRef]

67. Ionin, A.A.; Kudryashov, S.I.; Seleznev, L.V.; Sinitsyn, D.V.; Bunkin, A.F.; Lednev, V.N.; Pershin, S.M. Thermal melting and ablation of silicon by femtosecond laser radiation. *J. Exp. Theor. Phys.* **2013**, *116*, 347–362. [CrossRef]
68. Borowiec, A.; Mackenzie, M.; Weatherly, G.C.; Haugen, H.K. Transmission and scanning electron microscopy studies of single femtosecond-laser-pulse ablation of silicon. *Appl. Phys. A* **2003**, *76*, 201–207. [CrossRef]
69. Pronko, P.P.; VanRompay, P.A.; Singh, R.K.; Qian, F.; Du, D.; Liu, X. Laser-induced avalanche ionization and electron-lattice heating of silicon with near IR femtosecond pulses. *Mat. Res. Soc. Symp. Proc.* **1996**, *397*, 45–51. [CrossRef]
70. Pronko, P.P.; VanRompay, P.A.; Horvath, C.; Loesel, F.; Juhasz, T.; Liu, X.; Mourou, G. Avalanche ionization and dielectric breakdown in silicon with ultrafast laser pulses. *Phys. Rev. B* **1998**, *58*, 2387–2390. [CrossRef]

materials

MDPI

Article

A Practical Comparison of Beam Shuttering Technologies for Pulsed Laser Micromachining Applications

Damon G. K. Aboud, Michael J. Wood, Gianluca Zeppetelli, Nithin Joy and Anne-Marie Kietzig *

Department of Chemical Engineering, McGill University, Montreal, QC H3A 0C5, Canada; damon.aboud@mcgill.ca (D.G.K.A.); michael.wood3@mail.mcgill.ca (M.J.W.); gianluca.zeppetelli@mail.mcgill.ca (G.Z.); nithin.joy@mail.mcgill.ca (N.J.)
* Correspondence: anne.kietzig@mcgill.ca

Abstract: In this report we investigate the performance of various beam shutter technologies when applied to femtosecond laser micromachining. Three different shutter options are considered: a mechanical blade shutter, a bistable rotary solenoid shutter, and an electro-optic modulator (EOM) shutter. We analyzed the behavior of each shutter type during repeated open/close commands (period of $10 \leq T \leq 200$ ms) using both high-speed videography and practical micromachining experiments. To quantify the performance at varying cycle periods, we introduce a new variable called the compliance that characterizes the average state of the shutter with respect to its intended position. We found that the solenoid shutter responds poorly to sequential commands. The mechanical shutter provides reliable performance for cycled commands as short as $T = 40$ ms, but begins to lag significantly behind the control signal for $T \leq 20$ ms. The EOM shutter provides the most precise and reliable performance, with an opening time of only 0.6 ms and a high compliance with the signal commands, even when cycled very quickly ($T = 10$ ms). Overall, this study acts as an extensive practical guide for other laser users when considering different shutter options for their laser system and desired application.

Keywords: pulsed laser; laser micromachining; mechanical shutter; solenoid shutter; electro-optic modulator shutter; opening time; lifetime

Citation: Aboud, D.G.K.; Wood, M.J.; Zeppetelli, G.; Joy, N.; Kietzig, A.-M. A Practical Comparison of Beam Shuttering Technologies for Pulsed Laser Micromachining Applications. *Materials* **2022**, *15*, 897. https://doi.org/10.3390/ma15030897

Academic Editors: Jörg Krüger and Jörn Bonse

Received: 11 January 2022
Accepted: 21 January 2022
Published: 25 January 2022

1. Introduction

The beam shutter is a crucial component of a laser micromachining system. However, it is often rarely or only roughly mentioned in research studies. The ability to accurately control when a surface is exposed to the laser beam allows for the fabrication of intricate microstructures and geometrically well-defined surface textures. Having control over the exact number of pulses irradiating the surface ensures uniformity of the surface textures or structures being ablated.

Over the past twenty years, researchers have used several different shuttering technologies such as electromechanical shutters, electromagnetic shutters, and electro-optical shutters. For example, electromechanical shutters have been applied in various applications, such as the development of superamphiphobic patterns on PTFE [1], the fabrication of conical spike arrays on silicon [2], and a fundamental study of the threshold fluences and incubation coefficients of different metals [3]. Electromagnetic shutters have been applied in the biomimetic surface texturing of metals [4] and the formation of periodic surface structures on dielectric materials [5]. An electro-optical shutter was employed to study the ablation threshold and damage morphology of common metals [6]. Further, characterization studies have also been conducted on electro-optical shutters such as optical Kerr gates [7]. Some examples of recent advances in shutter technology include the reduction in vibrations of electromechanical shutters [8,9], integration of photodiodes into mechanical shutters [10], and the fabrication and characterization of an optical shutter based on a piezoelectric cantilever [11].

Without an effective shuttering system, laser texturing applications are severely limited. For example, as shown in Figure 1a, it is possible to micromachine an array of square pillars without a shutter, whereas long, overlapping lines can be intersected in the x- and y-directions, producing a grid. However, as demonstrated by the topographical heat map and corresponding cross-sectional profile line, this method of generating surface textures causes some portions of the surface to receive twice the amount of laser pulses. The unavoidable side effect of this approach is the creation of some areas which are deeper than others along with differing local surface chemistries. This problem of overlapping fluence profiles with uncontrolled depth has been witnessed in numerous applications, e.g., wettability studies on ablated gridlike structures [12,13] and dynamic studies concerning the influence of micromachining on droplet mobility and splashing [14,15].

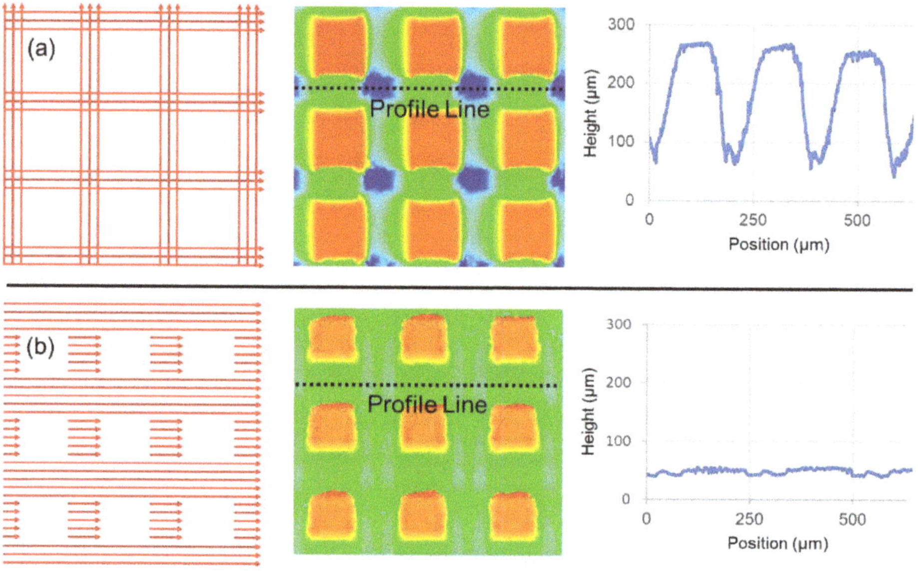

Figure 1. Comparison of square pillar microstructures fabricated using a simple grid pattern without a shutter (**a**) and the same structures fabricated using a sophisticated shutter system, allowing for greater control of the accumulated ablation depth (**b**).

In contrast, Figure 1b shows an example of the same intended, inscribed microstructure now realized using a beam shuttering device to allow for dead zones in the raster scan while only machining in the x-direction. This added component makes it possible to micromachine structures with a far greater level of control—in this case, the fabrication of square pillars arrayed within flat valleys of even depth.

In this report, we investigate the performance of three different shuttering options: a mechanical blade shutter, a bistable rotary solenoid shutter, and an electro-optic modulator (EOM). The mechanical and solenoid shutters function by blocking the light using a physical blade which is moved mechanically into or out of the beam path. In contrast, EOM shutters function using electro-optical devices such as Pockels cells, which shutter the laser beam electromagnetically. Having a deeper understanding of what shutter systems are available for various applications can assist the user in making informed decisions on what technology to use. Hence, the goal of this report is to provide a practical comparison for laser system users of three different beam shutter technologies.

2. Materials and Methods

2.1. Micromachining Setup

The micromachining setup used in this work consists of a Libra Ti:Sapphire laser system (Coherent, Inc., Santa Clara, CA, USA) with a central wavelength of 800 nm, pulse duration <100 fs, and a 1 kHz repetition rate. For this work, the pulse energy was set at 100 μJ and a spot size of 8 μm was used, corresponding to a pulse peak fluence of 398 J/cm^2. This irradiation source is complemented with a sample positioning system consisting of XY linear translation stages which are actuated by an XPS universal high-performance motion/driver controller (Newport Corp. Irvine, CA, USA). This same motion/driver controller outputs a transistor–transistor logic (TTL) signal to signify the open/close position of a beam-blocking shutter in conjunction with the stage movements. All axis movements, including stages and beam shuttering, are user-defined by position–velocity–time trajectory tables, where each axis adheres to a list of positions specified in said table at defined times with a defined running velocity for each position point.

2.2. Shuttering Methods

2.2.1. Mechanical Shutter

We included in our tests a widely used, commercially available shutter—the unistable Uniblitz VS25 optical shutter (Vincent Associates, Inc., Rochester, NY, USA). This unit has an aperture of 25 mm and two shutter blades which have a specified opening time of 6 ms. This shutter interfaces with the *XPS* through a VCM-D1 shutter driver (Vincent Associates). Figure 2a presents a box chart visualization of the signal pathway for this shutter.

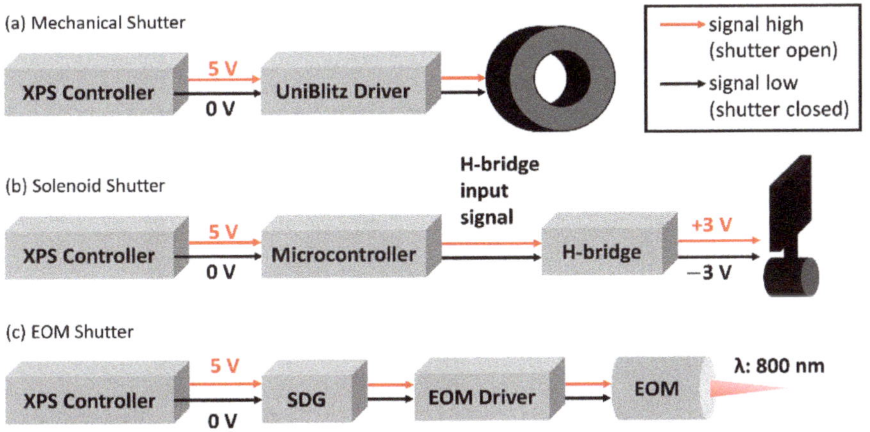

Figure 2. Box chart visualizing the signal pathway for each shutter. (**a**) Mechanical shutter. (**b**) Solenoid Shutter. (**c**) EOM shutter.

2.2.2. Solenoid Shutter

We next included a simple solenoid shutter in our tests—the bistable *BOS7/10* rotary optical shutter (Takano Co., Ltd., Chiyoda City, Tokyo, Japan). This unit has a 12.3 mm × 10.3 mm shutter blade which rotates over an operating angle of 50° and has a quoted response time of <17 ms. A permanent magnet ensures that the shutter remains stationary at either extreme of this rotating path when the solenoid is de-energized. The shutter is actuated to rotate to either its open or closed position by the application of positive or negative 3 V. As shown in Figure 2b, we programmed an Arduino microcontroller to read the TTL signal from the *XPS* and activate a H-bridge to handle this voltage switching (See Supporting Note S1 for further details).

2.2.3. Electro-Optic Modulator Shutter

Finally, we included an electro-optic beam shuttering method in our tests. Ultrafast laser systems achieve useful power through Chirped Pulse Amplification, whereas a stretched seed beam is passed multiple times through a solid-state laser gain medium to gain the power of a pump beam. In our case, a *QX-1020* KD*P electro-optic shutter (Gooch & Housego, PLC, Ilminster, UK) with a rise-fall time of 800 ps controls entry of the seed beam to the regenerative amplifier cavity containing the gain medium. This electro-optic shutter is actuated by an SDG Elite synchronization and delay generator (Coherent, Inc., Santa Clara, CA, USA) which can in turn be gated using an external TTL signal. As shown in Figure 2c, the TTL signal from the XPS is used to shutter the laser seed beam, resulting in controlled laser beam output from the Libra (see Supporting Note S2 for further details).

2.2.4. Measurement of Shutter Action

To accurately measure the position of each shutter tested in this report, we used a *FastCam SA5* high-speed camera (Photron USA, Inc., San Diego, CA, USA) equipped with a *Zoom 7000* 18–108 mm macro zoom lens (Navitar, Inc., Ottawa, ON, Canada) to observe the shuttering action in real time at 2000 to 5000 frames per second. Figure 3 displays representative snapshots of each shutter in the closed, halfway open, and fully open states. Note that for the EOM shutter, there is no observable physical component. Therefore, we recorded the intensity of light on a surface at which the laser beam was aimed. Since the pulse duration of the laser is on the order of femtoseconds, the pulses occur on a timescale approximately 10^{12} times faster than the camera frame rate and hence no intermediate intensities are recordable. As a result, our experimental setup does not allow for the recording of a frame in which this shutter is halfway open. Supporting Videos S1–S3 show the original videos from which the snapshots in Figure 3 were obtained.

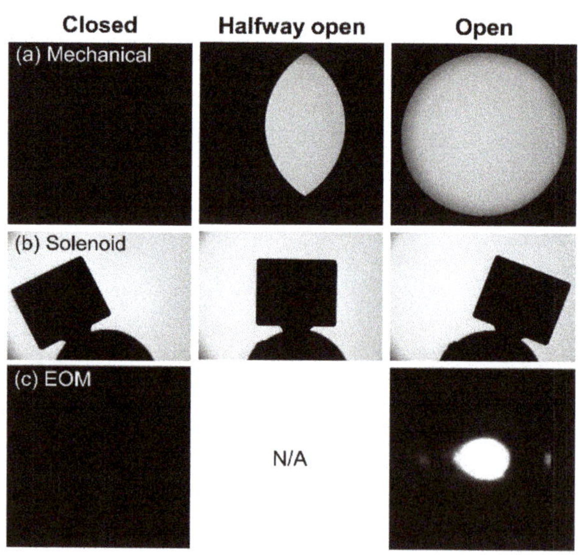

Figure 3. Frames of high-speed video footage used to measure the position of each shutter over time. (**a**) Mechanical shutter. (**b**) Solenoid Shutter. (**c**) EOM shutter.

2.3. *Substrate Material*

All micromachining experiments were performed on a single, polished coupon of P20 tooling steel purchased from McMaster Carr (Elmhurst, IL, USA). This material has a chemical composition of: Fe (94.82%), C (0.38%), Si (0.30%), Mn (1.37%), S (0.002%), Cr (1.95%), Ni (1.00%), Mo (0.18%).

3. Results

We began our work with tests of possible delays introduced by the electronic control equipment in the signal pathway. That is, we took simultaneous oscilloscope readings of the *XPS* controller TTL signal and the signal sent forth by the UniBlitz driver or Arduino microcontroller, with a temporal resolution of 0.04 ms. As shown in Figure 4, neither the commercial mechanical shutter driver nor the microcontroller we programmed ourselves to activate the H-bridge introduce any measurable delay in the electrical signaling of their respective shutters. There is no offset in the square high/low TTL signal and the respective square high/low shutter driver signals. These findings tell us that any deviation from ideal shutter behavior will be the result of mechanical—not electrical—limitations of the systems.

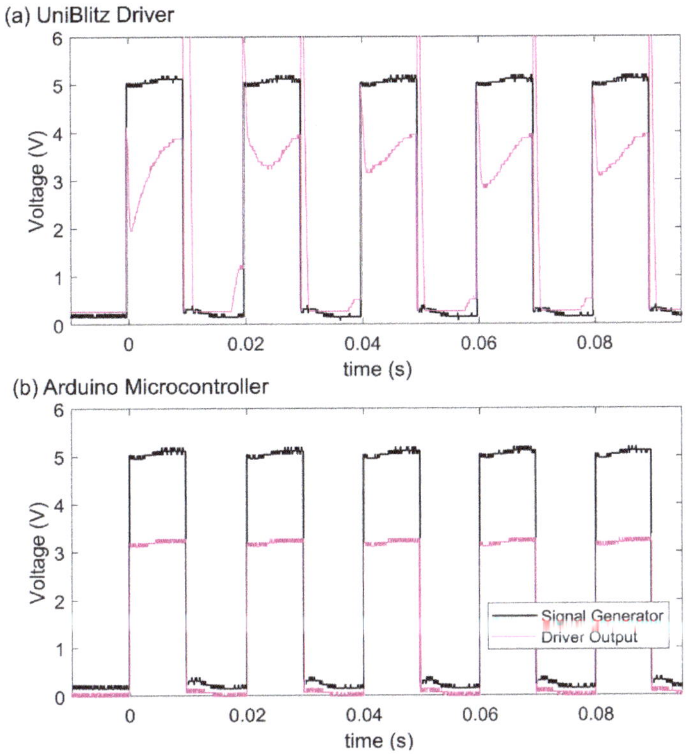

Figure 4. Simultaneous oscilloscope readings of the XPS controller signal and the: (**a**) Uniblitz driver output signal to the mechanical shutter, and (**b**) Arduino microcontroller output signal to the EOM and solenoid shutters.

The practical opening time of each different shutter type was next tested using a laser micromachining experiment. As shown by the illustration at the top of Figure 5, a hole was first drilled on the left side of the sample. Next, the shutter was closed, and the beam position began shifting with a translational velocity of 20 mm/s towards the right. Finally, after 5 ms (at a distance of exactly 100 μm), the shutter was signaled to open while the beam continued to shift across the surface. This test was repeated eight times for each shutter. Based on this simple experiment, the practical opening time can be elucidated in Figure 5 from the distance between the large hole on the left and the first discernible ablated spot to the right. For example, in the case of the mechanical shutter we observe an average distance of 170.5 ± 4.4 μm, corresponding to a practical opening time of 3.03 ± 0.22 ms. For the solenoid shutter, we find that t_{open} = 12.20 ± 0.29 ms, and for the EOM shutter we find that t_{open} = 0.62 ± 0.22 ms.

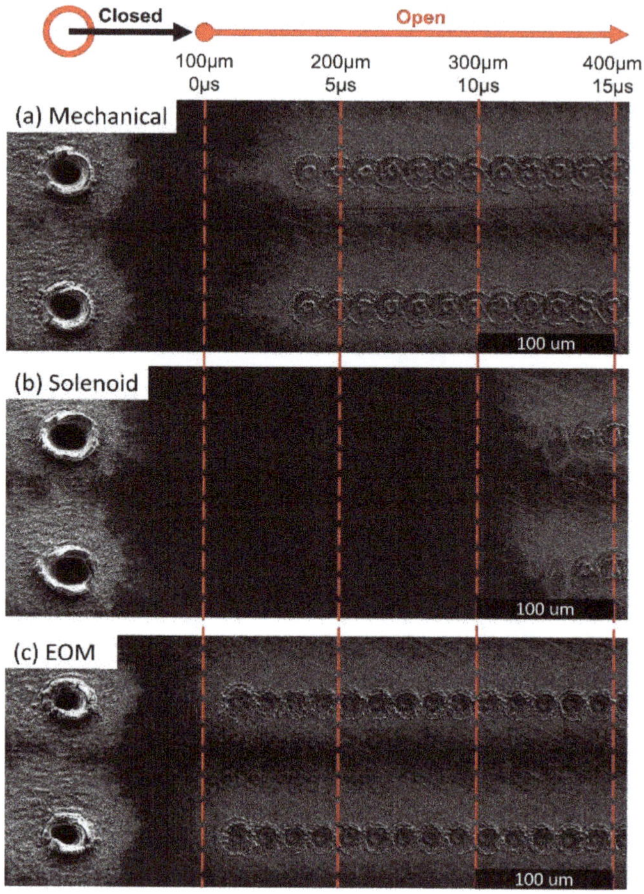

Figure 5. SEM micrographs demonstrating how the opening time of each shutter was measured. The opening time can be discerned based on the distance of the first ablating pulse from the deep hole on the left. (**a**) Mechanical shutter. (**b**) Solenoid Shutter. (**c**) EOM shutter.

Next, we consider the performance of each shutter while responding to a long sequence of open/close commands. Figure 6a graphs the measured position of each shutter for a period of T = 200 ms (i.e., 100 ms open, 100 ms closed, repeating). In this figure, the grey shaded blocks represent times where the shutter is commanded to be closed, and the white shaded blocks represent open segments. Meanwhile, the actual shutter position is represented by a number ranging from zero (completely closed) to one (completely open). It is clear that both the mechanical and the EOM shutter respond nearly perfectly to the signal commands at this frequency, while the solenoid shutter has a noticeable time lag. In addition, the position of the solenoid shutter oscillates several times while switching to a different state. This occurs due to the physical momentum of the solenoid shutter's blade, which bounces back slightly towards the center position after reaching the intended open/closed position. Hence, it takes approximately 50 ms for this shutter type to come to rest in the intended position after it first arrives there. This problem can be easily visualized in Supporting Video S2, which shows a high-speed video of the solenoid shutter in action.

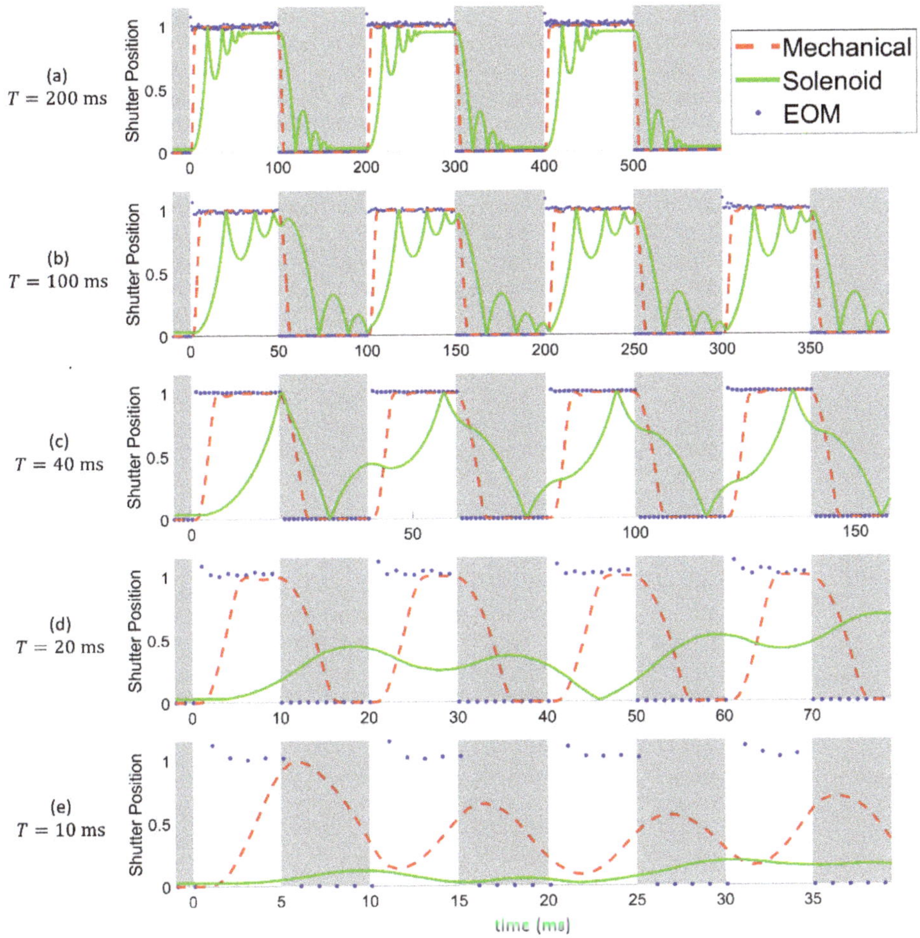

Figure 6. Measured position of each shutter over time for different cycling periods. (**a**) $T = 200$ ms. (**b**) $T = 100$ ms. (**c**) $T = 40$ ms. (**d**) $T = 20$ ms. (**e**) $T = 10$ ms.

Figure 6c graphs the measured positions of the shutters for $T = 40$ ms. Here, we see that the opening time of the mechanical shutter is clearly visible, since the dashed red line representing the mechanical shutter appears to rise and fall much later than the change in the command signal. However, at this cycling period, the solenoid shutter is no longer able to keep up with the speed of the commands. As explained above, the solenoid shutter requires approximately 50 ms to come to rest once it reaches the intended position, during which time it continues to bounce at the end of its movement path. Hence, when a new command signal is received before this oscillation period is complete, the shutter blade begins to act quite uncontrollably, bouncing back and forth rapidly between the extremes of its movement path. This oscillating behavior of the solenoid shutter's blade illuminates another important consideration when selecting a shutter for laser processes: for shutters that rely on the movement of physical components, the opening time of the shutter is not sufficient to characterize its performance. For example, based on the solenoid shutter's measured opening time of $t_{open} = 12.20 \pm 0.29$ ms, some users might assume that this shutter would perform adequately at a cycling period of $T = 40$ ms. However, Figure 6c clearly shows that at this cycling period, the momentum of the shutter blade causes serious performance problems. Therefore, when considering different shutter options for laser micromachining applications, the influence of the momentum of the shutter's blades should be accounted for. In this specific case, the slow response of the solenoid shutter can be attributed to its operating voltage. The BOS7/10 solenoid used in this study can operate at a voltage ranging from 3–12 V. At higher voltages, the shutter actuates more quickly, but the duty cycle of the device is decreased. Hence, if the solenoid is used at a 100% duty cycle with a higher operating voltage it will overheat, causing the internal resin bobbin to melt, which can lead to a short circuit in the coil. Therefore, for this type of shutter, there is an inherent tradeoff between the performance of the device and its lifetime. We operated the solenoid shutter at a voltage of 3 V, at which the response time is relatively slow, but the shutter can be operated at any duty cycle.

Figure 6d,e presents our observations for T = 20 and 10 ms. At these very fast cycling times, the solenoid shutter no longer functions at all, reaching shutter positions no greater than 0.22 in the graph. At such low shutter positions, the edge of the shutter's blade does not move far enough for even the periphery of the laser beam to pass. From a practical perspective, the solenoid shutter remains closed throughout the entire experiment. The mechanical shutter still performs relatively well at T = 20 ms, faithfully following the command signal with only a short lag time of 3 ms. However, at P = 10 ms (Figure 6e), this shutter finally fails. This failure was expected at this cycling period since the manufacturer states that the shutter has an opening time of 3–6 ms, and hence a cycling time of 6–12 ms, which matches the duration of the signal tested. In contrast, the EOM shutter continues to perform nearly perfectly throughout every cycling period tested. Even at a cycling period of only T = 10 ms, the EOM shutter is almost always in the correct open/closed position. Only a few datapoints represent positional errors wherein the shutter is open during a close command or closed during an open command.

To quantify the performance of the different shutters at various cycling periods, we introduce a new parameter that we call the compliance, C, which is calculated based on the shutter's position during the *open* signals sent by the controller. So if the total duration of *open* signals sent by the controller is given by $t_{open,signal}$, and the measured time that the shutter is actually open (during the *open* signal) is $t_{open,meas}$, then $C = t_{open,meas}/t_{open,signal}$. Using this definition, the compliance is graphed versus the cycling period in Figure 7. Clearly, each shutter performs best at longer cycling times. For example, at T = 200 ms, the values are C_{EOM} = 1, C_{mech} = 0.95, and C_{sol} = 0.71, whereas for T = 10 ms, the values are as low as C_{EOM} = 0.96, C_{mech} = 0.02, and C_{sol} = 0. This graph also serves as a clear visualization that in general, the EOM shutter is the highest performing option, and the solenoid shutter has the worst performance.

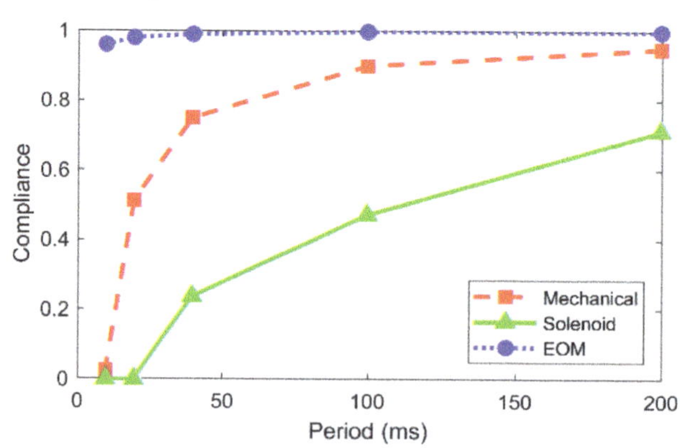

Figure 7. Compliance versus cycling period for each shutter.

Figure 8 provides a physical demonstration of the conclusions drawn from Figures 6 and 7. For each shutter, a series of horizontal dashes are micromachined at various cycling times. The translation speed used for each line is adjusted such that the length of each dash, and the spaces between them, are intended to be 100 μm (as shown by the yellow lines). Accordingly, dashes at shorter cycling periods are machined at a faster translation speed. The red and black boxes at the top of the figure indicate the horizontal sections in which the shutters should be open (O) and closed (C). These images confirm the trends observed in Figure 7. That is, for long cycling times all three shutter options successfully execute the signal instructions. Additionally, as the cycling period is reduced, the dashes begin to lag behind the signal instructions. The mechanical shutter exhibits noticeable lag times at T = 20 ms and fails completely at T = 10 ms. The solenoid shutter exhibits noticeable lag times throughout the entirety of the experiment and fails completely at T = 20 ms. The EOM shutter performs extremely well at each cycling period tested, only showing noticeable lag behind the command signal when T = 10 ms.

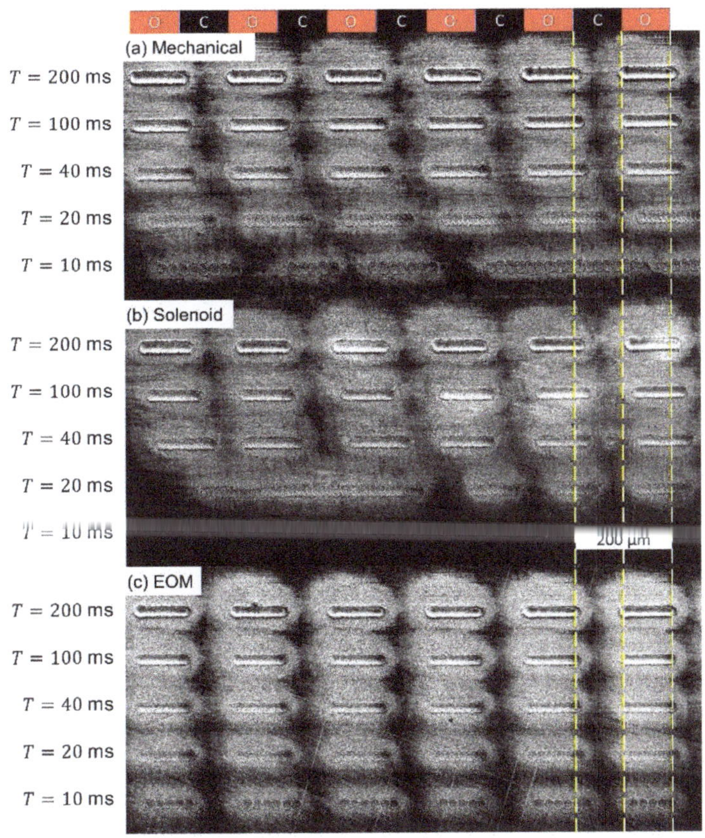

Figure 8. SEM micrographs demonstrating the performance of different shutters when subjected to a cycling open/closed signal with varying period. Ideally, each ablated line should be 100 μm long, and remain aligned with those above it. (**a**) Mechanical shutter. (**b**) Solenoid Shutter. (**c**) EOM shutter.

As a final test of each shutter technology considered in this report, we attempted to micromachine an array of 100 × 100 μm^2 square holes, spaced 100 μm apart. The beam was raster scanned across the surface with a translation speed of 5 mm/s, corresponding to an open/close time of 20 ms, and hence a cycling period of 40 ms when considering a wide array of inscribed features. Figure 9 displays topographical heat map images of the results, so that the depth of the features can be visualized. Figure 9a shows the features inscribed by the mechanical shutter, which are clearly affected by the lag time of this device. On the right feature, a dashed square box illustrates the intended shape of the square, and the arrows indicate the direction of the raster scanning beam. It is clear that the lag time of the shutter causes each pass of the beam to be displaced slightly from the previous, resulting in misaligned edges of the microstructure. This effect is even more clearly demonstrated by the solenoid shutter (Figure 9b), where subsequent passes of the beam do not overlap at all. The magnitude of this problem can actually be predicted by the solenoid shutter's measured opening time of 12.20 ms. Considering the translation velocity of 5 mm/s, the opening time of the shutter leads to a displacement of 61 µm in each direction, such that subsequent lines, when the beam is raster scanned left and right, become misaligned by a total of 122 µm—greater than the width of the intended microstructures. Therefore, it is not possible for this shutter to inscribe overlapping lines to develop features smaller than 122 µm.

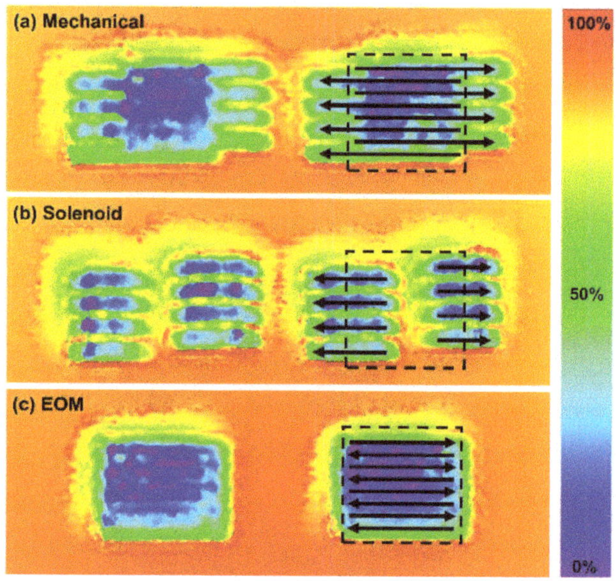

Figure 9. Heatmaps visualizing the topography of ablated microstructures on steel. As shown in the bar on the right side of the image, red colors correspond to high sections of material, and blue sections correspond to low sections. (**a**) Mechanical blade shutter. (**b**) Bistable rotary solenoid shutter. (**c**) EOM shutter.

Figure 9c represents the EOM shutter, which has a clear square shape resulting from the low lag times and high compliance of this shutter technology. In this case, misalignment of consecutive raster scan passes is only noticeable from the wavy edges on the left and right sides of the square holes.

The misalignment issue demonstrated in Figure 9 stemming from the back-and-forth relative motion of the beam can indeed be avoided if a raster scanning trajectory is not used. Rather, the laser trajectory can be designed to exclusively open the shutter during rightwards passes. In this scenario, the delay caused by the shutter leads to a relative horizontal displacement of the beam (and hence micromachined features) in a single direction. However, this possibly increases the processing time required to ablate the surface, since half of the beam's trajectory is not being utilized for machining—a consideration of importance especially for slow translation systems. Therefore, perfect alignment of the beam during a conventional back-and-forth raster scan is desirable whenever possible.

All of the figures above prove that the EOM shutter considered in this report demonstrates the highest performance in every metric tested: the opening time, consistency during cycling, overall compliance, and practical laser machining of microstructures. These comparisons are summarized in Table 1. For the sake of comparison, Table 1 also provides technical details about several other shutter options not tested in this report. The information in Table 1 was gathered both from publicly available datasheets on the manufacturers' websites, and from personal communications with the manufacturers. Supporting Note S3 provides screenshots and website links to the datasheets. Comparing the data in Table 1, it is noticeable that the solenoid shutters are the most cost-effective, but they have very long opening times. Hence, solenoid shutters are appropriate only for applications where a short opening time is irrelevant. Unfortunately, since EOMs are not generally marketed as shutters, we were unable to obtain the same comparative information (such as lifetime and cost) for that shutter type. However, in Supporting Note S2 we have listed the names and specifications of some Pockels cells (and drivers) available on the market today, which could be used as shutters.

Table 1. Comparison of cost and performance characteristics of shutters. In the left column, the shutter models in bold font are the ones that were empirically tested in this report. Values marked with an asterisk (*) were measured experimentally. All other values are obtained from the manufacturers.

Shutter Name	Type	Opening Time [ms]	Lifetime [Cycles]	Compliance (T = 40 ms)	Compliance (T = 200 ms)	Cost [USD]
Vincent Associates—CS45	Electromechanical	3.03 ± 0.22 *	1.0×10^6	0.75 *	0.95 *	705–1570
ThorLabs—SHB025	Electromechanical	3	1.5×10^7			962
NM Laser Products—LST200SLP	Electromechanical	1	$>10^9$			495
Takano—BOS 7/10	Solenoid	12.20 ± 0.29 *	5×10^6	0.24 *	0.71 *	145
Brandstrom Instruments (Custom)	Solenoid	25–35	2.5×10^6			250–350
Ellis/Kuhnke Controls—CDR030	Solenoid	30	2×10^7			370
Gooch & Housego Model QX Pockels Cell	EOM	0.62 ± 0.22 *	Not Available	0.99 *	1.00 *	Not Available

Considering the application of our findings to the laser micromachining field today, it should be noted that in general, most industrial-grade, high-frequency, ultrashort pulsed laser systems already utilize an EOM for beam shuttering [6,7]. This is necessary to accommodate the high scanning speeds and high repetition rates required to machine products in a time-efficient manner. However, in more fundamental academic research, many facilities rely on low-frequency pulsed lasers which are often shuttered using conventional electromechanical devices. Yet, in many cases, the purchase of an electromechanical shutter is unnecessary, since an EOM is already integrated into the laser's regenerative amplifier cavity but is simply not being used to its full potential as a shutter for micromachining applications [12]. Therefore, integrating EOM shuttering into many laser micromachining setups would have no associated cost.

4. Conclusions

In this report, we compared the performance characteristics of three different shutter options: a mechanical blade shutter, a bistable rotary solenoid shutter, and an electro-optic modulator.

When each shutter was tested with a cycled on/off signal at various frequencies, we observed that the momentum of the shutter's physical components can influence the shutter's response to subsequent signal pulses, leading to unreliable actuation and reduced compliance. Therefore, the opening time of a shutter is doubly important when responding to a long series of on/off commands, in which a slow response to one command leaves the shutter's physical barrier still in motion when the next command is received. This effect was most prominent for the solenoid shutter, which was observed oscillating its position at the end of its movement path.

Comparing the prices and performance of each shutter, the solenoid shutter is the most affordable option, but has very poor performance in terms of the opening time and overall compliance. Therefore, solenoid shutters should only be considered in applications with cycling times greater than 100 ms and where a slow opening time is not detrimental.

In contrast, the EOM demonstrated the best performance in every category tested: the opening time, consistency during cycling, overall compliance, and practical laser machining of microstructures. Therefore, for laser systems which rely on chirped pulse amplification within a regenerative amplifier cavity, the EOM should be applied as the beam shuttering method, since the optical components are already present. Furthermore, for other types of laser systems that are not based on a regenerative amplifier cavity, an EOM could still be considered as an effective, albeit pricier, shuttering system by installing it outside of the laser system itself.

Supplementary Materials: The following are available online at https://www.mdpi.com/article/10.3390/ma15030897/s1, Note S1: Solenoid Shutter, Note S2: Signal Delay Generator, Table S1: List of some Pockels cells available on the market, Table S2: List of some Pockels cell drivers available in the market, Note S3: Screenshots and Links for Information on Shutter Specifications and Cost, Video S1: high-speed video of mechanical shutter responding to open/close commands with a cycling period of 100 ms, Video S2: high-speed video of solenoid shutter responding to open/close commands with a cycling period of 100 ms, Video S3: high-speed video of EOM shutter responding to open/close commands with a cycling period of 100 ms.

Author Contributions: Formal analysis, investigation, visualization, D.G.K.A.; Conceptualization, D.G.K.A., M.J.W. and A.-M.K.; software, D.G.K.A., M.J.W. and G.Z.; writing—original draft preparation, methodology, D.G.K.A., M.J.W., N.J. and G.Z.; project administration, writing—review and editing, A.-M.K. All authors have read and agreed to the published version of the manuscript.

Funding: This research was funded by the Natural Sciences and Engineering Research Council of Canada (NSERC); grant number RGPIN-2016-04641.

Institutional Review Board Statement: Not applicable.

Informed Consent Statement: Not applicable.

Data Availability Statement: The data presented in this study are available on request from the corresponding author.

Conflicts of Interest: The authors declare no conflict of interest.

References

1. Chu, D.; Singh, S.C.; Yong, J.; Zhan, Z.; Sun, X.; Duan, J.A.; Guo, C. Superamphiphobic Surfaces with Controllable Adhesion Fabricated by Femtosecond Laser Bessel Beam on Ptfe. *Adv. Mater. Interfaces* **2019**, *6*, 1900550. [CrossRef]
2. Zhu, J.; Yin, G.; Zhao, M.; Chen, D.; Zhao, L. Evolution of Silicon Surface Microstructures by Picosecond and Femtosecond Laser Irradiations. *Appl. Surf. Sci.* **2005**, *245*, 102–108. [CrossRef]
3. Byskov-Nielsen, J.; Savolainen, J.-M.; Christensen, M.S.; Balling, P. Ultra-Short Pulse Laser Ablation of Metals: Threshold Fluence, Incubation Coefficient and Ablation Rates. *J. Appl. Phys.* **2010**, *101*, 97–101. [CrossRef]
4. Skoulas, E.; Manousaki, A.; Fotakis, C.; Stratakis, E. Biomimetic Surface Structuring Using Cylindrical Vector Femtosecond Laser Beams. *Sci. Rep.* **2017**, *7*, 45114. [CrossRef]
5. Papadopoulos, A.; Skoulas, E.; Tsibidis, G.D.; Stratakis, E. Formation of Periodic Surface Structures on Dielectrics after Irradiation with Laser Beams of Spatially Variant Polarisation: A Comparative Study. *J. Appl. Phys.* **2018**, *124*, 146. [CrossRef]
6. Mannion, P.; Magee, J.; Coyne, E.; O'connor, G.; Glynn, T. The Effect of Damage Accumulation Behaviour on Ablation Thresholds and Damage Morphology in Ultrafast Laser Micro-Machining of Common Metals in Air. *Appl. Surf. Sci.* **2004**, *233*, 275–287. [CrossRef]
7. Yu, B.; Bykov, A.; Qiu, T.; Ho, P.; Alfano, R.; Borrelli, N. Femtosecond Optical Kerr Shutter Using Lead–Bismuth–Gallium Oxide Glass. *Opt. Commun.* **2003**, *215*, 407–411. [CrossRef]
8. Martínez, S.; Hernández, L.; Reyes, D.; Gomez, E.; Ivory, M.; Davison, C.; Aubin, S. Note: Fast, Small, and Low Vibration Mechanical Laser Shutters. *Rev. Sci. Instrum.* **2011**, *82*, 046102. [CrossRef] [PubMed]

9. Zhang, G.H.; Braverman, B.; Kawasaki, A.; Vuletić, V. Note: Fast Compact Laser Shutter Using a Direct Current Motor and Three-Dimensional Printing. *Rev. Sci. Instrum.* **2015**, *86*, 126105. [CrossRef] [PubMed]
10. Huang, P.-W.; Tang, B.; Xiong, Z.-Y.; Zhong, J.-Q.; Wang, J.; Zhan, M.-S. Note: A Compact Low-Vibration High-Performance Optical Shutter for Precision Measurement Experiments. *Rev. Sci. Instrum.* **2018**, *89*, 096111. [CrossRef] [PubMed]
11. Bowden, W.; Hill, I.; Baird, P.; Gill, P. Note: A High-Performance, Low-Cost Laser Shutter Using a Piezoelectric Cantilever Actuator. *Rev. Sci. Instrum.* **2017**, *88*, 016102. [CrossRef] [PubMed]
12. Cardoso, J.; Garcia-Girón, A.; Romano, J.-M.; Huerta-Murillo, D.; Jagdheesh, R.; Walker, M.; Dimov, S.; Ocaña, J.L. Influence of Ambient Conditions on the Evolution of Wettability Properties of an Ir-, Ns-Laser Textured Aluminium Alloy. *RSC Adv.* **2017**, *7*, 39617–39627. [CrossRef]
13. Ngo, C.-V.; Chun, D.-M. Fast Wettability Transition from Hydrophilic to Superhydrophobic Laser-Textured Stainless Steel Surfaces under Low-Temperature Annealing. *J. Appl. Surf. Sci.* **2017**, *409*, 232–240. [CrossRef]
14. Yang, H.; Sun, K.; Xue, Y.; Xu, C.; Fan, D.; Cao, Y.; Xue, W. Controllable Drop Splashing on Picosecond Laser Patterned Hybrid Superhydrophobic/-Philic Surfaces. *Appl. Surf. Sci.* **2019**, *481*, 184–191. [CrossRef]
15. Roemer, G.-W.; Jorritsma, M.; Del Cerro, D.A.; Chang, B.; Liimatainen, V.; Zhou, Q.; In't Veld, B.H. Laser Micro-Machining of Hydrophobic-Hydrophilic Patterns for Fluid Driven Self-Alignment in Micro-Assembly. In Proceedings of the 12th International Symposium on Laser Precision Microfabrication, Takamatsu, Japan, 7–10 June 2011.

MDPI
St. Alban-Anlage 66
4052 Basel
Switzerland
Tel. +41 61 683 77 34
Fax +41 61 302 89 18
www.mdpi.com

Materials Editorial Office
E-mail: materials@mdpi.com
www.mdpi.com/journal/materials

www.ingramcontent.com/pod-product-compliance
Lightning Source LLC
Chambersburg PA
CBHW061821210926
51850CB00006B/774
9783036566320